TEXTBOOK OF ORAL AND MAXILLOFACIAL SURGERY

Second Edition

TEXTBOOK OF ORAL AND MAXILLOFACIAL SURGERY

Second Edition

B SRINIVASAN, B.Sc, MDS
Formerly Professor of Oral and Maxillofacial Surgery & Dean Annamalai University;
Vice-Chancellor, Sri Chandrasekharendra Saraswati Viswa Mahavidyalaya,
Kanchipuram, India

ELSEVIER
A division of
Reed Elsevier India Private Limited

Textbook of Oral and Maxillofacial Surgery, 2/e
Srinivasan

ELSEVIER
A division of
Reed Elsevier India Private Limited

Mosby, Saunders, Churchill Livingstone, Butterworth Heinemann and Hanley & Belfus are the Health Science imprints of Elsevier.

First Edition 1994
Reprinted 1996, 1998, 2000, 2001
Second Edition 2004 © Elsevier
Reprinted 2005

ISBN 81-8147-018-4

Published by Elsevier, a division of Reed Elsevier India Private Limited,
17A/1, Main Ring Road, Lajpat Nagar-IV, New Delhi-110024, INDIA.

Printed and bound at Gopsons Papers Ltd., NOIDA.

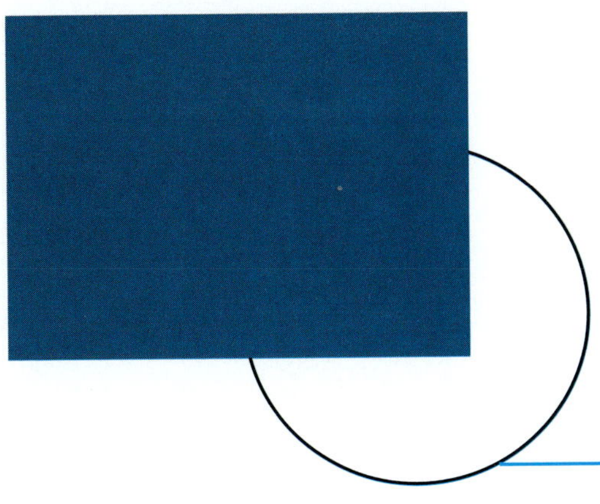

Preface to the Second Edition

The need for a consolidated textbook on Oral and Maxillofacial Surgery for undergraduates and dental practitioners motivated me to publish this book in 1994. Since then, the book has been reprinted many times. This bears ample testimony that the first edition has served its purpose usefully.

There has been literally a knowledge explosion in the past decade. In keeping with the objective of the publication, the need for the second edition was keenly felt. In response to the overwhelming feedback from academics and other users of this book, I ventured to revise and bring out the second edition. In the process, a few chapters have been added, many have been updated and new illustrations and photographs have been added.

I was very fortunate to have a clear direction provided by the review of the first edition by the *British Journal of Oral and Maxillofacial Surgery* in the year 1995. While complimenting me on a few chapters, the review offered many constructive criticism for improvement. This has resulted in the addition of new chapters on Clefts and Recent Advances, updating of chapters like Scope and Objectives, Evaluation of Health Status, Orofacial infections, Cysts, Oral Tumors, Implant Dentistry and Salivary Glands. Many new photographs have also been added.

It is my earnest hope and desire that the users find this book useful and they continue to offer their feedback for the improvement of the presentation.

B. Srinivasan

Preface to the First Edition

The specialty of oral surgery has never been exclusive to any one branch of health sciences. During the second world war, oral surgery emerged as one of the major dental specialties. Tremendous advancement in knowledge, application of new concepts and evolvement of new techniques have considerably widened the scope of oral surgery. Today, it occupies an enviable position as connecting link between dentistry and medicine.

Traditionally, dental education has remained vocational in nature, designed to train "safe" general dental practitioner. Dynamics of research activities, resultant technological advances and information transfer however alert us that this clinical subject is no more static. With increasing stress on principles of general medicine and general surgery in the present undergraduates dental curriculum, more and more of dental practitioners are making attempts to perform oral surgery procedures in their daily practice. Ideally,the undergraduate education should aim to provide the student an adequate knowledge and ability to ensure an acceptable standard of proficiency, with professional competence to do the routine minor oral surgery procedures. But during the period of training, students develop inhibition and fear complex towards oral surgery. Our dental students depend mainly upon voluminous textbooks published in the west, furnishing information on the incidence, disease pattern and techniques as applicable to those societies.

It is in this background that the author undertook the uphill task of writing a concise, yet com prehensive textbook on this subject, aimed at our undergraduate dental students. An attempt has been made to provide fundamental knowledge, with a stress on the value and importance of technology and philosophy of oral surgery rather than on the technicalities alone. The emphasis is on those facts that every student "must" learn, while others which are desirable to be known are included briefly by way of additional information. To facilitate understanding, the book has been profusely illustrated with simple line drawings, radiographs and clinical photographs. The text is written in the simple and easy-to-understand language.

I sincerely hope that the book will achieve the objectives for which it has been written. Suggestions for its improvement will be welcome.

B. Srinivasan

October, 1994

Acknowledgements

It has been a very pleasant task for me to bring out the second edition of this book with the support provided by computer technology. Yet the main source of motivation was provided by the wide and remarkable acceptance of the first edition by the large student community of the country, appreciation of my professional colleagues and well-wishers and their constructive suggestions.

Therefore, firstly, my sincere thanks are due to the student community. Their overwhelming response and their suggestions for the improvement of the first edition were very useful in fulfilling my task.

Secondly, I am extremely thankful to *The British Journal of Oral and Maxillofacial Surgery* for publishing the review of the first edition by Mr. Ilankovan, Consultant Maxillofacial Surgeon (UK). The review was so extensive and thoughtful, it formed the nucleus for the revision of the book. I profusely thank him.

My task in updating the book became relatively easier as a result of my browsing through many Internet resources. The list is too large to individually acknowledge. However, I thank the authors of all those Internet resources.

I express my profound gratitude to M/s Elsevier, for undertaking to publish the second edition. I was delighted to receive the whole-hearted and excellent support and cooperation from everybody associated with this organization. It is my pleasure to acknowledge the excellent editorial support from Ms. Ritu Sharma, Editor of this book and my sincere thanks to Ms. Nalini and Ms. Sangeetha of the Chennai office for coordinating with the Delhi office.

I sincerely hope that this second edition fulfills the expectations of the dental community of the country.

Contents

CHAPTER 1

Scope and Objectives

GENERAL CONSIDERATIONS

"Let each person exercise the art that he knows"

Oral and maxillofacial surgery is defined as that part of dental practice which deals with diagnosis, surgical and adjunctive treatment of diseases, injuries and defects of human jaws, oral cavity and associated structures. In practice, the scope of the specialty varies from country to country and also with training and skill of the individual practitioner. The success seems to depend on the broad educational background and experience of the practioner. Hence, the undergraduate course in oral surgery should direct the student towards precise understanding of the common problems that would be encountered in everyday practice. In other words, a student has to be trained to differentiate between the procedures that one is expected to undertake and the ones which need expert consultation.

There is an increasing concern regarding the new diagnostic tests and technologies that have been made available to the specialty, particularly, musculoskeletal and joint imaging and to identify the high-risk patients in early disease states. Basic diagnostic parameters of any such tests include sensitivity, specificity, positive and negative predictive values. Practitioners can then use them on the patients to find out the possibilities of further course of the disease process and to distinguish the possibilities of true-positive, true-negative, false-positive and false-negative results. The challenge is to provide the scientific base for tomorrow's biomedically oriented diagnostic services.

MOTIVATION

"The direction in which education starts will determine one's future life"

One wonders, whether it is a conscious decision or is it because of pleasure of job satisfaction that one may choose to specialize in oral surgery. It is a matter of conjecture as to what prompts anybody to concentrate on one particular field. Perhaps, during the formative period of the professional studies, it is the motivation that might play a major role in taking such a decision.

SIMPLE VS DIFFICULT PROCEDURES

"Courage well seasoned with prudence widens the boundaries of success"

Unfortunately, the time spent to study oral surgery in the present-day overcrowded undergraduate curriculum is relatively short. Hence, the student trainee graduates with inadequate knowledge. Probably, there is no other period in one's life more frustrating when one realizes that he/she is not trained to apply the basic scientific knowledge to a clinical situation. During the student's life, one has to learn to amalgamate the knowledge and correlate it to the patient's needs. It is the knowledge of basic principles and techniques that provide sound foundation on which the student builds confidence to the clinical practice. The basic philosophy of training should be directed to learn, as to *"how to distinguish between the difficult case that looks simple and the simple case that looks difficult."* As a general rule, it is better to undertake any procedure that can be completed within 30 to 45 minutes under local anesthesia leaving other cases to the concerned specialist.

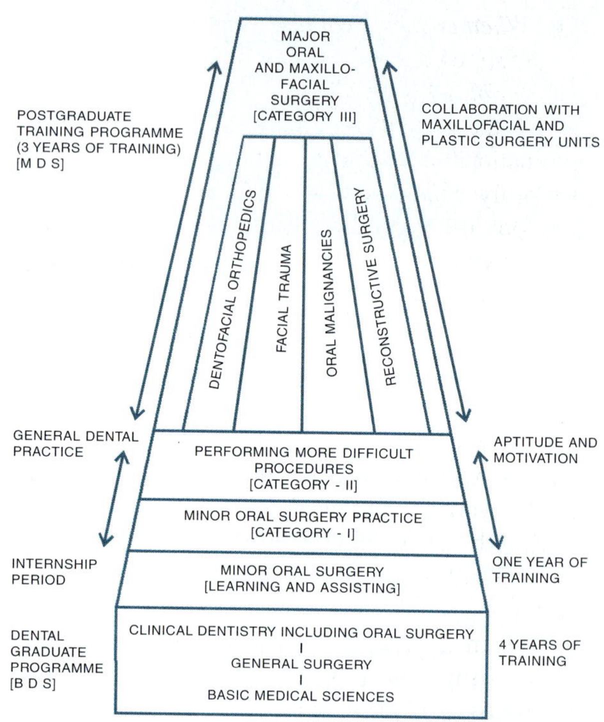

Fig. 1.1 Scope of oral and maxillofacial surgery.

SCOPE (Fig. 1.1)

"There is only one good-knowledge and one evil-ignorance"

The scope of oral surgery ranges from dental extraction to major oral and maxillofacial surgery. Eventually, there may be two types of oral surgeons, practicing minor and major oral surgery respectively, each acceptable in one's own national and regional situation by virtue of the training or personal relationship with the surgical colleagues. Thus, professionals with additional qualifications, training and skill are likely to extend their areas of interest. If so, which is the most suitable profile of education and training in oral surgery? Mere development of the specialty of maxillofacial surgery will not change the traditional practice or scope of oral surgery. More often, separation between oral surgery and maxillofacial surgery proves to be more illusory than it is often assumed to be so. There is enough scope for both these aspects of the specialty. With bilateral development of separate but overlapping aspects of the specialty, it is most likely that both will complement each other. Clear thinking on the basis of competence rather than competition will have a beneficial effect on the quality of professional practice.

Due to the changing phase of the specialty from time to time, there has been great concern among many regarding the present and the possible future pattern of practice. They are often curious to learn about

"Where they come from?
How they come to be?
Where they appear to be going?

Whether they wish to be there?
If so, why?
If not, why not?"

At the global level, there are national and even international differences on the scope of practice. In a rapidly changing environment, one should not overlook the lessons of history since, history often lays down a series of stepping stones. To overlook such trends is not a welcome proposition.

HISTORICAL REVIEW

Formerly, dentistry was confined to the mechanical aspects of teeth while surgical aspects of the oral cavity were taken care by the general surgeons. During the early 20th century, dentists who limited to exodontia and minor dentoalveolar surgery gained recognition for their surgical skills. In 1918, they formed the society of exodontists. Later, the terminology was expanded to a society of exodontists and oral surgeons. In 1946, the term "exodontist" was eliminated. In 1975, the name of the specialty was changed to "society of oral and maxillofacial surgeons".

To understand the scope of oral /oral and maxillofacial surgery, there is a need to evaluate its relationship with the other specialties of dentistry and medicine. Relationship of oral surgery with orthodontics necessitates the management of malocclusion and jaw deformities. It may be either to prevent or to correct the orthognathic problems. Prosthodontics requires very close cooperation with oral surgery for the surgical preparation of the oral cavity for better functioning of the prosthesis. Practice of periodontics and conservative dentistry may need the application of oral surgery as an useful aid in the management of periapical pathology. Oral surgery and general medicine have become increasingly important and interdependent. Unfortunately, many patients may not even be aware of the significant relationship between oral surgery and the medical conditions like anticoagulant and antihypertensive therapy. There seems to be no substitute for understanding and experience when, oral surgery is performed on otherwise medically compromised patients.

Relationship between oral surgery and plastic surgery is historically close. It has made slow but steady progress. Many of the medical specialties like general surgery, ENT and orthopedic surgery come under the purview of oral and plastic surgery due to the constant urge for new and better approach. However, many of them necessarily impinge upon and compete with each other. Careful analysis of the situation reveals that both the specialties need extensive knowledge of fundamental biological sciences. It can be comparable to a triangle with biological sciences as the base, plastic surgery as the stem from general surgery on one side of the triangle and oral surgery from dental surgery on the other side of the triangle. Cosmetic surgery is at the apex. As the respective specialties approach towards the respective basic skill, the common ground diminishes but the potential cooperation with each other increases. Each specialty justifies its continued existence but the boundaries between the areas of the respective professional interests are not well defined. This seems to be an excellent example of fruitful coexistence (Fig. 1.1).

OBJECTIVES

The nature of dental practice is changing rapidly. The general dental practitioner is very rarely involved in life-saving pursuits. Hence an average dental student takes more interest in mechanically oriented dental specialties to practice *safe* dentistry. Although the scope is wide, practice of oral surgery is not what it ought to be. There is a need to consider it as a "healing science" if one were to practice oral surgery within its scope. Hence, the undergraduate curriculum needs to be oriented to achieve the following set of objectives so that the trainee is aware of the procedures under three categories:

(1) *Procedures that a graduate can perform independently and confidently:* (a) Administration of local anesthesia and to perform dentoalveolar surgery, (b) to recognize and manage the complications arising out of minor oral surgery, (c) to manage the uncomplicated infections of the oro-facial region, (d) to perform preprosthetic and endodontic surgery, as an office procedure, (e) to do biopsy of the suspected lesions, (f) to manage uncomplicated fractures of mandible and small cysts of the oral cavity, (g) to prescribe analgesics, sedatives, antibiotics and other essential drugs judiciously, (h) to recognize and guide the medically compromised patients. In other words, the dental graduate should be trained in such a way, so that he is trained to assume legal, ethical and moral responsibilities of the patients for minor oral surgery.

(2) *One can become familiar with hospital dental practice for treating the patients with:* (a) difficult impactions, (b) space infections, (c) preprosthetic surgery and more complicated maxillofacial injuries which may not require the services of the specialist.

(3) *Procedures that should be attempted only by the qualified specialist oral surgeon:* (a) Very difficult impactions, (b) roots displaced into the maxillary sinus, (c) complicated maxillofacial injuries and space infections, (d) orthognathic surgery, (d) reconstructive preprosthetic surgery, (e) dental implants, (f) transplantation of tissues, (g) temporomandibular joint problems, (h) oral oncology, (i) congenital malformations of orofacial region—all of them are undoubtedly within the domain of the specialist-oral and maxillofacial surgeon.

Complicated hospital management of medically compromised patients form the joint responsibility with the physicians. This would mean that the training in oral surgery should identify clearly the procedures that one can easily undertake, in contrast to the conditions that can be attempted with guidance and additional training only.

EDUCATIONAL AND TRAINING AVENUES

Stolinga has outlined four possible educational and training avenues. Oral and maxillofacial surgery can be considered as a postgraduate dental specialty requiring 3-4 years of training including additional medical training for one year, e.g. U.S., Canada, India, Japan, Northern Europe and most of South America. In some of these countries, additional medical degree has been made mandatory.

The trainee is trained to acquire qualification in medicine and dentistry followed by training in oral surgery. The time required varies from 6 to 11 years. The scope of surgery for such trainees is unlimited, e.g. in German-speaking countries, a composite 6-years training, including 2-3 years of medical training, is followed by 3-4 years of stomatology. Subsequently, one has to undergo additional training for a period of two years in oral and maxillofacial surgery.

In China and Eastern Europe, as a specialty of medicine called stomatology, the trainee begins the training in oral surgery after acquiring the medical qualification including broad outline of dentistry. It extends for a period of 4-5 years. This pattern of education exists in Southern Europe.

STRENGTH OF THE SPECIALTY

(a) This is an anatomically based specialty for the surgical management of the orofacial region. Adequate dental training is essential for the successful practice of the specialty.

(b) Growth of this specialty, in terms of scope and quality of training has been phenomenal during the 20th century.

WEAKNESS OF THE SPECIALTY

Ideal requirements of the specialty training are:

(a) Training in dentistry at the undergraduate level.

(b) Additional basic general surgery training (if not qualification) at the PG level and specialized training at the advanced PG level.

Unfortunately, there is no universally acceptable formula to achieve these objectives. Too long a period of training will make it too expensive. The specialty overlaps with other regional specialties like ENT, ophthalmology, etc. Likewise, we are unable to claim any sort of generalization which plastic surgery has so ably succeeded in maintaining their fields of activity.

It is most unfortunate that some members of the dental profession believe that basic dentoalveolar surgery could be done by the qualified oral dental surgeons while other surgical problems of the maxillofacial region are best done by a medically qualified oral surgeons. Laskin (1973) calls this phenomenon as "White Hat Syndrome". This is definitely a major threat to the growth of our specialty.

With recognition of oral surgery as a dental specialty and improved training, hopefully, the student trainee will consider the training phase as a formative period, preparing one's own self with basic principles and philosophy of oral surgery. By adhering to the basic principles and accumulating experience, confidence will increase along with the grasp of the variety and complexity of oral surgery procedures.

CHAPTER 2 Evaluation of Health Status

GENERAL CONSIDERATIONS

In spite of advances in the training of recent dental graduates, one area of neglect during the dental training is the concept of medical management of the dental patient. Therefore, one of the major problems confronting any dental practitioner has been to evaluate the general health status of the prospective patient. This is significant because of the possible difficulties that one may encounter during the management of medically compromised dental patients. With advancement in medicine and the consequent increase in the life expectancy of the population, more and more of geriatric patients seek dental treatment. If such patients are hospitalized, experts from medical specialties take the responsibility of the patients. There is a wide variation in the evaluation of health status of a patient requiring ambulatory dentoalveolar surgery and major oral and maxillofacial surgery. This only proves that biological and physiological considerations are as important as mechanical and surgical aspects of dentistry. If the situation warrants, the dental practitioner must be capable of communicating with the medical colleagues on this aspect. In other words, it is mandatory on the part of the dental practitioner to possess comprehensive data, relevant to safe oral surgery practice. It is in this direction, evaluation of health status of the patient is essential.

The evaluation of the health status of the patients who require surgery helps the surgeon to provide safe and comprehensive care. The clinician must be capable of recognizing the preexistence of such a condition, so that, management of such patients including emergency care will be possible. With advances in medicine, the management of emergencies has made tremendous progress. Unfortunately, the basic understanding of the disease-state has remained neglected in the training programmes of the dental graduate. Prevention through preoperative recognition and evaluation of patients at-risk is preferable, so that, emergencies can be prevented or at least minimized.

COMPREHENSIVE MEDICAL HISTORY

Most of the patients who are already under health care will possess the relevant data. But they may not volunteer any "relevant" information unless questioned about them. Hence, a comprehensive questionnaire can be provided to such patients, so that, the necessary data could be elicited. If further informations are required, the family physician could be requested to provide them, as the situation demands. For the benefit of the clinician, a sample questionnaire is provided.

SIGNIFICANCE OF ELICITING MEDICAL HISTORY

A physician usually reviews the various systems of the body in a sequential manner. But, the objective of the dental surgeon is to elicit the relevant details of the general health of the patient which is likely to affect the dental treatment adversely. This necessitates a quick review of the patient before examining the oral cavity. Priority must be given to evaluate the diabetic and hypertensive states and review of cardiovascular and respiratory systems. Enlisting the patient's cooperation is an important aspect of an accurate and comprehensive examination so that the dental surgeon will be able to utilize the data for the comprehensive evaluation of the health status of the patient. The significance of the medical history is as follows:

COMPREHENSIVE HEALTH STATUS QUESTIONNAIRE

1. Biographic data

- Name................Age.................Sex..........
- Address............Tel No...........................
- Name of the family physician:.................

2. History of the health Database

- Details of the past serious illness and hospitalization, if any

(a) *Cardiovascular diseases*
Anginal attacks, myocardial infarction (heart attack, if any). Any other relevant data including history of rheumatic fever, hypertension, implantation of pacemakers, etc

(b) *Metabolic disorders*
Diabetes

(c) *Bleeding disorders*
Hemophilia, liver disorders, leukemia, details of bleeding episodes, if any

(d) *Details of allergic manifestations*
Skin rashes, drug allergy, H/O allergy to local anesthetics

(e) *Respiratory problems*
Persistent cough, tuberculosis, asthma

(f) *Past medications, if any*
Anticoagulants, steroids, tranquilizers, antihistamines, oral contraceptives, antihypertensive drugs, antidiabetic drugs, any drug, for cardiac problems

(g) *Kidney disorders*

(h) *Neurological problems, e.g., epileptic fits*

(i) *Past obstetric and gynecological problems, if any*

(j) *Details of any relevant past laboratory investigations*

(k) *Past details of hospitalizations, if any*

(l) *Any problems during the earlier dental treatment*

(m) *Health-related habits (addiction) like abuse of alcohol, tobacco, illicit drugs, etc.*

3. History of present illness

(a) Chief complaints with reference to general health
(b) History of the present health problems
(c) Current medications
(d) Details of obstetric data
(e) Peptic and gastric ulcers
(f) Chronic diseases like liver, kidney disorders, tuberculosis, etc.

(a) To identify the systemic diseases of the patient (detected already or undetected) so that surgery may not lead to serious threat to the health or life of the patient.

(b) To identify the patients who are already under medication so that the possibility of any drug interaction is prevented. This may serve as a clue to the underlying systemic disease that the patient might have inadvertently omitted to mention while recording the history.

(c) To enable the dental surgeon to communicate with the appropriate medical consultant so that necessary instructions may be obtained to render safe dental treatment including any precautions to be taken, necessity of any change in the medication schedule or any other information relevant to the concerned patient.

To establish a good patient/doctor relationship, patient's evaluation must assure the dental practitioner that treatment could be carried out with relative safety without any avoidable complications. The basic methods for obtaining medical history could be through a questionnaire and a dialogue interview. This includes *Verbal exchange* (personal therapeutic interview) and a *Non-verbal exchange* through which feelings (like acceptance of the patient, support and involvement to help the patient) are communicated to the patient. This component is helpful to reduce or eliminate the incidence of *fear, anxiety and phobia.*

Fear is a defensive "*Fight or Flight*" response to an actual threat. The common dental related fear may be for pain, needle, extraction or surgery. The four common elements of all types of fear are fear for physical harm, fear of loss of control, fear of helplessness and fear of unknown.

Anxiety is a subjective state of mind with unpleasant feeling of apprehension. The response of the patient will be out of proportions. This state of mind will exist even before the onset of the feared situation. The main aim is to escape out of the situation.

Phobia is an irrational fear of an object or a situation. The reaction of the patient is usually exaggerated. It may be so severe so as to interfere with day-to-day functioning.

Stress is the physiological response to fear and anxiety. In maladaptive response, parasympathetic responses dominate resulting in syncope.

Therefore, it is the responsibility of the clinician to identify the patients who are prone to anxiety, fear and stress. All efforts must be directed to develop a good interpersonal relationship between the patient and doctor even at the stage of eliciting history itself.

ASSESSMENT OF RISK IN ORAL SURGERY PATIENTS

The systemic diseases that may have oral manifestations and that may influence the provision of dental care are of great importance to the practice of oral surgery. Many systemic conditions may develop oral manifestations as the earliest indicators. Due to this reason, the patients may seek the help of the dental surgeon. It is desirable that the condition is diagnosed early so that appropriate treatment could be instituted before producing serious morbidity. For example, blood dyscrasia like leukemia or thrombocytopenia present themselves as gingival enlargements with episodes of bleeding. Since early diagnosis will depend on the dental surgeon, he/she should be familiar to the oral and systemic manifestations of such diseases.

In the recent past, Acquired Immune Deficiency Syndrome (AIDS) has been found to manifest itself with changes like candidosis, hairy leukoplakia and advanced periodontal disease. The dental practitioner must be aware of such conditions so that those patients could be confidently referred to the appropriate specialists for necessary treatment.

A few conditions are not only important to be diagnosed early, but they also influence the practice of oral surgery. On such occasions, the dental surgeon must be able to recognize and evaluate such patients "at-risk" to avoid any possible complications.

RISK IN THE ELDERLY

The elderly are defined as those over 65 years of age. They constitute nearly 15 to 20% of the population. With advancement of health sciences, it is likely that elders will live longer. Elders are no longer considered as poor surgical risks on the basis of the age alone. Since more and more elderly persons are seeking treatment, oral surgeons need to be comfortable with assessing the risk from the surgical procedures. *Surgical risk* is the probability of mortality or morbidity during the operative or postoperative phase. It may be grouped as follows:

Patient-related: due to patient's systemic conditions

Anesthesia-related: due to problems of anesthesia

Procedure-related: due to the surgical procedure

Provider-related: depends on the skill of the surgeon.

An elderly patient's overall perioperative risk is the cumulative risk due to physiological (chronological aging), pathological (due to diseases) and psychological changes.

Age related physiological changes: After the 4th decade, aging process occurs gradually throughout the remaining part of life. Marked variations have been observed in the physiological parameters. Although a general functional decline is expected as the age advances, some elderly have been observed to show minimal decline in the physiological functions. They are identified as *successful agers*, in contrast to those who exhibit decline in most of the functions as *usual agers*. Even though aging is considered to be physiological, it may predispose to pathological changes. In general, aged persons retain their ability to adapt to stress but this ability is decreased with age. It has been estimated that 4 out of 5 elderly have at least one chronic disease. The most common conditions are—arthritis, hypertension, hearing problems, cardiac ailments, diabetes mellitus, visual disturbances and cerebrovascular disease. More often, elders present themselves with clinical features, less typical than those of younger counterparts. The presence of multiple diseases may additionally make the typical presentation less common. Thus, risk assessment aims to identify all those factors that can affect the successful outcome of the surgical procedure including factors that may affect the treatment planning preoperatively, success intraoperatively and successful recovery postoperatively.

The following are some important systemic conditions of dental importance. They are broadly classified into two main groups:

(a) Diseases that may influence the provision of dental surgery.
(b) Systemic diseases that may develop oral manifestations.

Conditions that may influence the dental care

The dental practitioner must be aware and periodically update the knowledge with special reference to new developments in the concept, nature and diagnosis of "dentally relevant" systemic diseases. If risks are to be avoided in clinical practice, the dental or oral and maxillofacial surgeon must possess the medical background on the following aspects of the patient before undertaking any treatment:

(a) Medical status of the patient (to be updated periodically).
(b) To anticipate the potential systemic effects of the therapeutic procedures on the medically compromised patient.
(c) Ability to prevent such interaction by instituting appropriate measures by way of precaution.
(d) To manage such interaction, if any.

Although one is expected to retain the knowledge of applied general medicine, attention will now be focussed on some important systemic conditions for the benefit of the oral surgery trainee.

MEDICALLY COMPROMISED PATIENTS

A. Cardiovascular disorders

The chief complaints of this group of patients are: (a) chest pain, (b) dyspnea and (c) edema. Most of them suffer from either hypertensive, congenital, valvular, myocardial or coronary diseases. Many of the physiological abnormalities and therapeutic approach are similar. The factors that regulate the systemic circulation in health have important roles in compensating for cardiac disease. Failure of these compensatory mechanisms to return the circulatory system to normal functioning results in the production of the symptoms. It is generally believed that progressive and gradual increase of mortality or morbidity is directly proportional to increase in age. More than the chronological age, it is the biological age that should be considered important. *Biological age* is determined by the combination of physiological changes (due to aging), pathological changes (which are not related to aging) and psychosocial changes. The risk of surgical mortality or morbidity is defined as having a cardiac problem following non-cardiac surgery. Therefore, any patient over 40 years of age must be fully evaluated if the following features of cardiovascular problems are clinically present:

- History of ischemic heart disease
- Dyspnea
- Discomfort and chest pain on exertion
- Ankle edema
- Palpitation
- Postural hypotension.

The overall postoperative risk is the summation of all risks due to physiological, pathological and psychosocial changes. Risk from physiological changes are due to chronological changes but, pathological changes are due to diseases and psychosocial changes. The cardiovascular system of aged persons will normally adapt less to stress since elderly patients are predisposed to decompensation.

(a) Risk factors in cardiovascular disease

First order risk factors: Smoking of tobacco has caused a significant shift in the age vs incidence curve.

Hyperlipidemia: It means increase in the fat content in the blood serum. In diabetes and alcoholism, hyperlipidemia adds greatly to the risk of cardiovascular disorders. The most dangerous situation is when cholesterol reaches 200 mg %. Arterial hypertonicity has effect on the entire cardiovascular system.

Second order risk factor: Diabetes mellitus and obesity are considered to be important risk factors. Combination of the risk factors serves as a springboard to heart diseases. Psychological risk factors, in combination with stress of modern life, fear and anxiety are some of the main contributing factors.

(b) Hypertension

This is a common cardiovascular disease, affecting at least 80% of the adults, as a major public health problem. Hypertension is critically important in the pathogenesis of many cardiovascular diseases. The genetic factor is perhaps more important. Early development of hypertension is attributed to high habitual dietary salt intake. Likewise, salt restriction has proved to be an effective method of lowering the elevated blood pressure. Primary hypertension has been attributed to an association with factors like heredity, weight, salt intake, and nonspecific stresses and strains of life. The greater the weight gain, the greater the rise in blood pressure. Factors, known to be responsible for secondary hypertension, are kidney problems (nephritis), tumors of adrenal gland and narrowing of the blood vessels.

Physiology. "Closed system" of circulation is present where blood circulates in the vessels. It has been proved that the closed system is a prerequisite for the regulation of blood pressure. Systolic blood pressure represents the force of contraction of the heart and the degree of blood pressure that the blood vessels have to withstand. Diastolic pressure represents the peripheral resistance. It is the function of (a) velocity and viscosity of blood and (b) elasticity and lumen of the blood vessels. Systolic and diastolic blood pressures show lots of variations. Age, sex, pregnancy, emotions, exercise, posture, sleep, etc., lead to changes in the blood pressure. Heredity, diet, obesity, climate, psychological make up, type of work, habits like smoking tobacco and alcohol consumption predispose to hypertension. There is no precise dividing line between normal and elevated blood pressure. World Health Organization defines hypertension as B.P. higher than 160/90 mm Hg. The systolic pressure depends mainly on cardiac output. Factors affecting the systolic pressure include aortic compliance, extracellular fluid volume, neural and harmonal activity. Diastolic pressure depends on systemic vascular resistance.

Classification (based on etiology).

Primary hypertension: If the cause is unknown.

Secondary hypertension: If the cause is known.

Renal parenchymal disease.

Renal artery disease.

Endocrine and metabolic disease.

Neurological, vascular and other abnormalities.

Examination of the optic fundus is a reliable index to the severity and prognosis of the condition. Pupils must be dilated (unless contraindicated) to observe the retinal changes. The changes are graded in the following manner:

Grade I

Minimal narrowing or irregularity of the arterioles.

Grade II

Narrowing or irregularity is marked with tortuosity or spasm.

Grade III

Narrowing or irregularity is marked with tortuosity, flame-shaped hemorrhages and cotton-wool exudates.

Grade IV

Changes as in Grade III with papilledema.

Note: Grades III and IV indicate very severe hypertension.

Management. Major emphasis is on early detection, adequate treatment and appropriate preventive measures like elimination of stress, adequate rest and use of anxiety-reduction protocol.

The aim of antihypertensive therapy is to maintain BP within physiological limits. The risk factors that may favor to initiate the drug therapy are the familial history of diabetes and hypertension. Physicians mainly use diuretics, adrenergic inhibitors (sympatholytics) and vasodilators. If any patient gives history of any of these drugs, that must arouse suspicion in the minds of the clinicians. A graduated treatment schedule is usually advocated.

Step I: Diuretic to start with
Step II: Adrenergic blocker is added
Step III: Vasodilator is then added
Step IV: Treatment of hypertensive emergencies
Step V: Treatment of secondary hypertension and complications of established or uncontrollable hypertension.

The following major complications can arise if BP is left uncontrolled or poorly controlled.

Heart has to work more if the diastolic pressure is constantly high. In due course of time, heart muscles are no longer able to cope up with increased work load. The patient becomes breathless. Fluid accumulates in the lungs and limbs. Kidney is unable to excrete the waste products adequately. The patient becomes critically ill. Excess workload of the heart also leads to hardening of the coronary vessels that nourish the heart. Uncontrolled hypertension predisposes to stroke. Since the brain tissue has no capacity to regenerate, stroke must be prevented. When submitted to hypertensive state, kidney fails and starts to accumulate toxic waste products. The patient therefore becomes critically ill.

Thus, prevention is the key to success. Sometimes, persons over 40 years imagine that unless any problem arises, hypertension need to be treated sporadically with drugs. Once hypertension is diagnosed, constant monitoring is mandatory. It must be remembered that hypertension is a silent killer and hence constant vigilance is the only way to successful management of this condition.

(c) Angina pectoris

The word "angina" refers to choking or strangling sensation and "pectoris" refers to chest. Although chest pain may be due to many causes, this term denotes chest pain, characteristic of "ischemic heart disease". This is a progressive narrowing of coronary arteries. On exertion, myocardial demand for oxygen increases. This demand is primarily met by coronary vasodilation resulting in increased blood flow 4 or 5 fold. But, whenever an imbalance develops between myocardial oxygen demand and coronary blood flow, it results in myocardial ischemia. Depending on the severity, angina or infarction develops. This leads to the development of chest pain, reduced myocardial contractility and cardiac arrhythmias. Prolonged ischemia may lead to necrosis of myocardial cells (infarction). The biochemical events and nerve pathways are not completely understood. Any episode persisting for more than 20 minutes suggests unstable angina or myocardial infarction. Severe discomfort may be associated with nausea, generalized weakness, increased salivation and altered pulse rate and blood pressure.

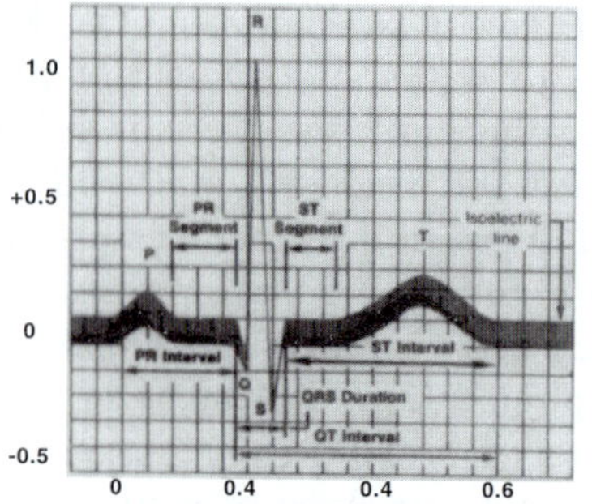

Seconds

The Normal Electrocardiogram

ECG Intervals

	Normal Duration (sec)	
	Average	Range
PR interval	0.18	0.12-0.20
QRS duration	0.08	0.07-0.10
QT interval	0.40	0.33-0.43
ST interval (QT minus QRS)	0.32	

(a)

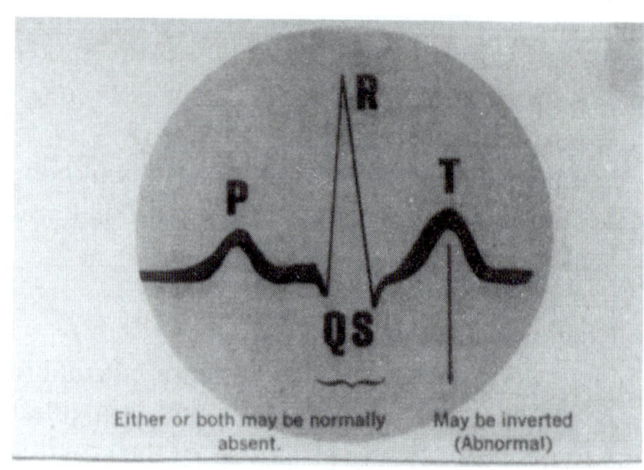

(b)

Fig. 2.1 Electrocardiogram.

Electrocardiogram (ECG) (Fig. 2.1a, b). It is a record of electric changes during depolari-zation and repolarization of the heart. It provides data on the performance of the heart. Evaluation of this data reveals the existence of any cardiac problem. Heart functions as a muscle pump with auricles and ventricles alternatively contract to pump the blood. This cardiac contraction spreads the electric current through the heart.

The ECG recording starts with SA (sinoatrial) node. Depolarization of cells in the atrial wall causes contraction of the auricle. The contraction moves like a wave towards AV (atrioventricular) node. Blood is squeezed through the valves into the ventricles. This compression of the auricle is seen in the ECG as P wave.

The elecrical changes reach the AV node. The AV nodc and AV bundle act as a delay circuit providing 1/10th of a second delay (pause in the ECG) when blood fills the ventricles. Then AV node fires its charge causing a simultaneous ventricular contraction (representing QRS in the ECG) that forces blood into pulmonary and systemic circulation. Finally, walls of the ventricles repolarize (T in the ECG) and return back to normal, waiting to restart the cycle. Thus, the basic ECG waves are labelled as P wave, representing atrial depolarization (stimulation), QRS complex representing ventricular depolarization and S-T segment, T and U waves representing ventricular stimulation and repolarization (or the recovery phase) respectively.

The most reliable ECG recordings are made with the subject reclining and completely relaxed to minimize any contributions by the skeletal muscles. A properly recorded ECG provides a picture of the amount of time required for the depolarization wave to pass through the cardiac conduction system and the additional time needed for the ventricular process. Each PQRST complex can be separated into various components for detailed analysis.

Select an ECG wave from lead I and II in which P, Q, R, S and T components are readily visible. In the normal ECG, all heart beats are displayed in an evenly spaced pattern consisting of three major components- P wave, QRS complex and T wave. The P wave represents the electric impulse as it moves through the atria and QRS reflects impulse conduction through the ventricles. T wave represents the repolarization of the ventricles during which time, entire heart is in a state of relaxation (diastole). The duration of P wave, P-R interval, width of QRS complex, T wave, length of S-T segment and Q-T interval are to be noted.

Two pieces of information can be gathered at a glance from the ECG. They are: rate (pulse) and rhythm. If these are normal, then rule out any ailments. It is possible to determine the axis of depolarization, size of the heart and the possibility of any damage of the heart muscle. Rate and rhythm are decided from the wave forms. The rest can be realized from the shape of the waves. Rate represents the number of heart beats per minute while rhythm represents the regularity with which these beats occur. If the rate is high, it is called *tachycardia* and if it is low, it is called *bradycardia*. Rhythm is related to the natural pacemakers of the heart muscle known as SA and AV nodes. Pacing by these two nodes control the entire synchronization of the heart functions. Irregular pacing can result from SA or AV nodes malfunction referred to as blocks. Irregular pacing means breakdown of the synchronization of the pumping activity of the heart. This results in the contraction of the heart chambers with very little or no blood in them.

Presence of an infarct causes changes in the actual shape of the wave. P-QRS-T complex changes with an infarct. In atrial hypertrophy, P wave is affected and in ventricular hypertrophy QRS is affected.

(d) Cardiac arrhythmias

Preoperative, intraoperative and postoperative monitoring of the heart rate and rhythm have become standard procedures in oral and maxillofacial surgery practice. Recognition of various cardiac arrhythmias are of great importance. The competence of the cardiovascular system can be estimated from (a) patient's history, (b) data about the heart beat and blood pressure, (c) observation of color, texture of skin and color of the finger nails. Tissue perfusion is maintained by the intact cardiovascular system. Abnormalities of cardiac rate and rhythm can compromise the efficiency and effect of tissue perfusion. By recognizing the prefatal arrhythmias, fatal arrhythmias can be prevented by appropriate measures.

Cardiac evaluation:

(1) Cardiac history must include irregularities of the heart rate, rhythm and conduction.

(2) Hypertensive heart disease is characterized by breathlessness, orthopnea, ankle edema and paraxysmal and nocturnal dyspnea. Coronary artery disease is characterized by pain in the substernal area on exertion, relieved by nitroglycerine.

(3) Atrial arrhythmias are not immediate threat to life. They only affect ventricular function.

(4) Ventricular arrhythmias:

(a) Insignificant, isolated premature ventricular contraction.

(b) Fatal - serious ventricular fibrillation. Hence they are not suitable for surgery.

When irregular pulse is felt or irregular heart beat is heard on auscultation, it will be difficult to differentiate clinically between atrial and ventricular disturbances. Therefore, oral surgeon will be able to detect, preoperatively or postoperatively from ECG and intraoperatively from the ECG monitor, all the needed informations on rate, rhythm, origin of beats and myocardial ischemia.

(5) Cardiac asystole, bradycardia and other arrhythmias cause hemodynamic disturbances. If ventricular rate is normal, arrhythmia is seldom accompanied by hemodynamic disturbances. If it is rapid, disturbances of varying intensity will usually occur. If it is more than 180 per minute, then, it will be too fast for ventricular filling. Consequently, there is a drop in cardiac output and rise in peripheral resistance that may prevent blood from reaching the vital organs. Prognosis is poor when prefatal arrhythmias occur in a patient with diseased heart, especially with coronary heart disease. In such cases, the question to be answered is—what is the significance of ventricular arrhythmias when the patient's condition is further compromised by anesthesia and surgery.

(6) Negative T wave following oral and maxillofacial surgery must alert the oral surgeon. The inversion of T wave could have been caused by surgical trauma to the sympathetic nerve supply to the heart or by the occurrence of myocardial infarction. Exact cause is not known.

(7) It has been confirmed with studies that there is an increase of heartbeat of the maxillofacial surgeons-an occupational hazard-during the preinduction phase of general anesthesia. There appears to be more stress associated with administration of general anesthesia than with local anesthesia. During the administration of local anesthesia, vasopressor agents contained in local anesthetics initiate cardiac changes which can be demonstrated by the ECG changes.

Assessment of the risk for angina. To minimize the complications, it is necessary to assess the degree of risk while treating the patients. The patient's history of anginal attack must alert the practitioner so that necessary precautions can be taken prior to the treatment. For the benefit of the practitioner, angina have been classified in the following manner:

Class I: Angina occurring with unusual effort

Class II: Angina occurring with usual effort

Class III: Angina occurring with minimal effort

Class IV: Angina occurring at rest (without effort).

After categorization of the patient, the practitioner must take a decision concerning the level of treatment that can be provided to the concerned patient. Before commencing the treatment, it is better to get the clearance from the physician who has been taking care of the cardiac problems. It is preferable to follow the anxiety-reduction protocol. It is safer to avoid vasoconstrictors with local anesthetics. Nitroglycerine must be readily available in case of emergency. Patients with unstable angina are at increased risk. A number of conditions can mimic angina. The discomfort of esophageal spasm or mucosal inflammation, pain due to peptic ulcer and gall bladder diseases (chronic calculus cholecystitis) may simulate anginal attack. The left-sided referred pain to the arm, neck, jaw must alarm a watchful dental surgeon. ECG is an important tool in evaluating patients with history of angina pectoris.

(e) Myocardial infarction

Acute myocardial infarction results from severe and extensive ischemia of the cardiac muscle so as to create irreversible necrosis of the myocardial cells. Chest discomfort of varying intensity is the main complaint. It is felt by the patient at the retrosternal region with radiating pain and discomfort along the left side of the jaw and arm. Other symptoms include nausea, vomiting, weakness, dizziness, perspiration and severe dyspnea. This condition may simulate conditions like pericarditis, pulmonary embolism, costochondritis, pancreatitis, gastritis, cholecystitis and peptic ulcer. ECG is generally abnormal in these patients. Without the clearance from the attending physician, no form of invasive treatment should be undertaken. It is safe to avoid any elective treatment at least for a period of 6 months after the last episode. Usually, such patients will be on anticoagulant therapy. Therefore, such patients may be hospitalized so that anxiety-reduction protocol, antibiotic prophylaxis, monitoring of the vital signs and rest under medical care will be possible.

(f) Congestive cardiac failure

This is a common outcome of many cardiovascular lesions and form a major cause for the physical disability. This condition must be viewed as a complex clinical process (syndrome) resulting from inability of the heart to adequately perfuse the peripheral tissues with blood. The severity of the clinical features depends on the degree of myocardial impairment and the demands of the individual. With mild impairment of cardiac function, symptoms may be evident with strenuous exertion. With severe impairment, symptoms will appear even with minimal activity. Diagnosis is usually established from history and symptoms like dyspnea, easy fatiguability, anorexia, abdominal pain and non-productive cough. This condition must be distinguished from other causes of dyspnea and fatigue. Precipitating factors of this condition are hypertension, myocardial infarction, myocarditis, anemia, thyrotoxicosis, pulmonary infection and emotional stress. The treatment includes (a) general measures like bed rest, restricted sodium intake, control of the associated disorders like hypertension and obesity and control of the risk factors like smoking, (b) appropriate therapy and (c) supportive therapy.

(g) Infective endocarditis

Infective endocarditis is a microbial infection of the endocardium, affecting the heart valves and endocardium. Damage to the myocardial endothelium allows for the deposition of platelets and fibrin to form the non bacterial thrombotic vegetation. A persistent bacteremia results from the microorganisms reentering the blood from the infected cardiac lesion. Prior to antibiotic era, this condition has been considered to be fatal. Rheumatic heart disease may predispose to this condition. The major causative organism is *Streptococcus viridans*. Invasive procedures undoubtedly induce bacteremia but it is impossible to predict as to which patient will develop this infection. Therefore, antibiotic prophylaxis is recommended for the patients at risk for developing infective endocarditis. Prophylaxis has been found to be the most effective mechanism when used preoperatively in optimum doses. Poor oral hygiene, periodontal and periapical infections may produce bacteremia even during chewing. Therefore, persons at risk should maintain the best possible oral hygiene to minimize the risk of infective endocarditis. There is evidence that the use of prophylactic antibiotics reduces the potential infections prior to any procedures in the oral cavity. But, frequent applications of antimicrobial agents to bacterial populations carry the risk of developing drug-resistant microorganisms. Therefore, the clinician has to take appropriate decisions based on risk-benefit ratios for the antibiotic prophylaxis.

RECOMMENDED STANDARD REGIMEN

Note : Any of the following schedule

DRUG	DOSE REGIMEN
Amoxycillin	3.0 g orally 1 hour before the procedure, followed by 1.5 g, 6 hours after the initial dose. For patients allergic to amoxycillin/penicillin, the following drugs may be recommended.
Erythromycin	Erythromycin ethylsuccinate 800 mg or Erythromycin stearate 1 g orally, 2 hours before the procedure, then half the dosage 6 hours after the initial dose.

Clindamycin	300 mg orally, 1 hour before the procedure and 150 mg 6 hours after the initial dose.

ALTERNATE REGIMEN RECOMMENDED

DRUG	DOSE
(a) For patients unable to take oral medications	
Ampicillin	2 gm, I.V. or I.M. administration 30 minutes before the procedure followed by ampicillin 1 gm I.V. or I.M.
(b) For patients allergic to ampicillin/amoxycillin/ penicillin and who are unable to take oral medications	
Clindamycin	I.V. administration of 300 mg, 30 minutes before the procedure and I.V. administration of 150 mg 6 hours after the initial dose.
(c) For the patients considered as high-risk and who are not candidates for the standard regimen	
Ampicillin	I.V. or I.M. 2 gm plus gentamicin
Gentamicin	1.5 mg per kg but not to exceed 80 mg
Amoxycillin	30 minutes before the procedure, followed by amoxycillin 1.5 gm parentally 8 hours after the initial dosage.
(d) For high-risk patients allergic to penicillin/amoxycillin/ ampicillin	
Vancomycin	I.V. administration of 1 gm 1 hour before starting the procedure. No repeat dose required after the procedure.

Note: (1) I.M. injections for endocarditis prophylaxis should be avoided in patients receiving heparin or warfarin. I.V or oral regimen advised.
(2) Patients who have compromised renal function need modification or even omit the second dose of gentamycin or vancomycin.

Ultrasonic scaler and cardiac pacemakers. Magnetic, electrical, or electromagnetic fields of sufficient strength can interfere with the action of the pacemaker. For example, ultrasonic scaler gives rise to electromagnetic fields and hence is a potential hazard for patients fitted with cardiac pacemakers.

B. Metabolic disorders

Diabetes

Diabetes is a serious, life-long metabolic disorder. Many of the patients with diabetes may not be aware that they have diabetes. This condition has several components that have different etiology and pathogenesis but share glucose intolerance as the common factor. This condition may develop either because of lack of insulin or because of the presence of factors that oppose the action of insulin. This results in the increase of the blood glucose level (hyperglycemia) and increase in ketone bodies in the blood. The long term prognosis depends on the maintenance of optimum blood glucose level. Uncontrolled diabetic patients run the risk of complications during the postoperative period. But, controlled diabetic withstands the anesthesia and surgery well.

Three main types of diabetes have been identified:

(a) Type I: Insulin Dependent Diabetes Mellitus. (IDDM)
(b) Type II: Non-Insulin Dependent Diabetes Mellitus. (NIDDM)
(c) Gestational diabetes.

Type I diabetes (IDDM) is considered as an autoimmune disease. It results when the immune system turns against and acts on beta cells of Islets of Langerhans so that little or no insulin is produced. But, what causes this action is not known, although genetic factors, chemicals from the environment and viruses are believed to be involved in the process.

Type II diabetes (NIDDM) is the most common form. It usually develops in adults who are over 40 and are mostly overweight. In this group of persons, beta cells produce insulin but for some reasons, body cannot utilize insulin effectively. This results in unhealthy build-up of blood sugar level. One cause of prereceptor insulin resistance is the presence of antiinsulin antibodies. Another cause is the secretion of an abnormal insulin molecule that has defective binding to insulin receptors. Obesity is the most common cause with insulin resistance.

Gestational diabetes develops or discovered during pregnancy. Usually it disappears after the termination of pregnancy but these women have greater risk of developing Type II diabetes later in their life. If uncontrolled, it can complicate pregnancy including the possibility of developing birth defects. Glucose intolerence during pregnancy increases neonatal morbidity. The diabetogenicity of pregnancy may become evident early in gestation but does not necessarily need the administration of insulin.

Blood glucose estimation is absolutely essential for the diagnosis of this condition. This continues to be one of the leading causes of death and disability. Associated long term effects are observed in every major part of the body. The symptoms of Type I are abrupt onset of polyuria, polydypsia and rapid weight loss with partial or total absence of insulin secretion. Massive renal glucose and ketone body wastage due to induced osmotic diuresis is accompanied by large loss of sodium, potassium, calcium, phosphate and other ions in urine. Severe loss of water and electrolytes along with severe acidemia produce cardiovascular collapse. In Type II, serum insulin concentration is normal or elevated.

Oral Glucose-Tolerance Test (OGTT) remains to be the best method for the diagnosis of diabetes. It helps in the detection of early stages of carbohydrate intolerance. The concentration of blood glucose truly reflects a balance between absorption, production and utilization of glucose. The familiar symptoms are tiredness, pruritus, increased urine volume(polyuria), weight loss, increased thirst (polydypsia) and increased appetite (polyphagia). Usually, any person over the age of 40 must be evaluated for diabetes. If the patient is already on antidiabetic drugs, they do not present any problem provided they strictly adhere to the treatment schedule. In case of patients who regularly receive insulin, a few precautions should be taken.

(a) As far as possible, minor oral surgery should be performed under local anesthesia, without altering the usual dose of insulin.

(b) It is better to perform surgery early in the morning instead of late in the evening.

(c) The patient is likely to develop hypoglycemia if starved for a long period, after the usual dose of insulin. But, if insulin requirement is increased due to infection or nonspecific stress, it predisposes to diabetic ketosis. Diabetes with hypoglycemia and ketosis may be responsible for the loss of consciousness.

(d) Most of the diabetics will furnish details regarding their medication. If so, this data must be carefully recorded. Patients who have been treated with oral antidiabetic agents or controlled with diet alone usually do not present any serious problems, if their treatment schedule is not altered. Timing of surgery in such patients may not be a critical factor.

(e) All surgery must be performed under the umbrella of suitable antibiotics. The need for the surgical intervention in patients with diabetes mellitus should have a clear understanding of this metabolic disorder including the general guidelines of its management.

Risk of developing diabetes

People, who give family history of diabetes and those who are obese, are the population-at-risk for diabetes.

Insulin therapy

The object of diabetic management is to keep the patient symptom-free and prevent complications when he pursues a normal life style. Appropriate diet is the most important part of diabetic management, while insulin is the important medication. In stabilizing a new adult diabetic patient, one may begin with 10 to 20 units of intermediate acting insulin with blood sugar level as a guide. Usually, two-thirds of total dose is given before breakfast and one-third in the afternoon. With minor procedure under local anesthesia, there is no change in the anti-diabetic treatment. With major procedures, the regimen changes.

(1) An I.V. drip of 1000 ml of 5 % glucose in water is started preoperatively. One-third to one-half of the usual morning dose is administrated preoperatively and the remainder postoperatively.

(2) Insulin requirement in pregnancy decreases in the first trimester, levels off during the early part of second trimester and increases in the second half of pregnancy. By third trimester, the patient requires a morning and late afternoon dose.

Recent advances

(1) Newer forms of purified insulin of human insulin are being produced through genetic engineering.

(2) External and implantable insulin pumps are being developed to deliver appropriate amounts of insulin. Similarly, administration of insulin through nasal spray or in the form of tablets are being attempted. This will eliminate the need for the daily injection of insulin. Laser treatment for diabetic eye diseases are helpful for better healing and to prevent blindness.

(3) Constant searches are on for identifying the causes of diabetes. Scientists are looking for the genes involved in diabetes so that some gene markers can help to identify the population-at-risk.

(4) Attempts have been made to develop vaccination for Type I diabetes. Devices are being developed that can "read" blood glucose level without a needle prick.

Chronic complications of diabetes

With increased longevity of life, chronic complications in the diabetic individuals become inevitable. The worse the complication, the earlier it can be identified in the course of diabetes. The following are some of them:

Arteriosclerotic complications are common and occur twice as frequently as in non-diabetic persons. It also differs in the degree and severity. It occurs at an early age and progresses rapidly with poorer prognosis. Major vessels involved are cerebral, coronary and peripheral arteries.

Cerebrovascular disease: Cerebrovascular accidents are common. There seems to be higher involvement of vertebrobasillar system of the brain.

Coronary artery disease: This is due to the accumulation of fat and cholesterol resulting in atheroma. The lumen becomes narrow down. This predisposes to thrombus formation leading to partial or complete obstruction of the vessels. Partial obstruction leads to angina while complete occlusion results in myocardial infarction. Incidence is greater in diabetic patients.

Peripheral vascular disease: Accelerated arteriosclerosis leads to decreased blood flow to the extremities.

Ophthalmic complications: Uncontrolled diabetic state leads to reversible blurred vision. This is caused by the accumulation of fructose and sorbitol that increases the osmolarity within the lens leading to swelling of the lens. If this process continues, cataract develops. The second major eye problem is *diabetic retinopathy*. This condition is due to retinal ischemia. The ischemic areas of the retina release a blood vessel stimulating factor resulting in the formation of new blood vessels in the retina, anterior chamber of the eye and iris. Repeated hemorrhage into the anterior chamber can lead to *glaucoma*.

Diabetic nephropathy: This is a clinical syndrome with progressive renal dysfunction, hypertension, varying degrees of nephrotic syndrome and finally renal failure. Almost all patients with nephropathy develop retinopathy also.

Neuropathy: This develops in many ways. This refers to the abnormalities of the function of peripheral nerves. This mostly develops around 10 years after the onset of diabetes.

Dermopathy: The patients may develop pigmented atrophic lesions over the shins, more common in young diabetic women.

C. Hematologic disorders

A wide variety of diseases includes disturbances of hemopoietic organs and cellular elements of blood, abnormalities of lymphoreticular and hemostatic mechanisms. Conditions resulting from underproduction to over production of (a) red blood cells (anemia or erythrocytosis), (b) leukocytes (leukopenia or leukocytosis), (c) platelets (thrombocytopenia or thrombocytosis), (d) defective hemostasis and (e) neoplasias of lymphoreticular system. These disturbances may represent a primary disorder (primary) or may be due to an underlying disorder (secondary). Proper laboratory investigations should follow a logical sequence:

(a) Disorders of RBC

Anemia. This condition is usually discovered accidentally since it presents vague non-specific symptoms. There is no correlation between the degree of anemia and its severity. There is significant decrease in RBCs and hemoglobin.

In megaloblastic anemia, the large erythroid precursors have morphologically immature nuclei associated with normally hemoglobinized cytoplasm. It may be due to foliate or Vit. B 12 deficiency.

In aplastic anemia, RBCs, neutrophils and platelets are abnormally low. Bone marrow aspiration will reveal overall hypocellularity. Pancytopenia is the characteristic finding.

Iron deficiency anemia is the most common type. The important cause of iron deficiency is blood loss, characterized by hypochromic microcytic anemia.

Hemolytic anemia is the clinical condition in which the life span of the RBC is reduced with failure of bone marrow to restore the quantity of erythrocytes. Normally, life span of an erythrocyte is 120 days and RBC production balances with the rate of destruction. In anemia, wound healing may be prolonged. Therefore, elective dental and oral surgical procedures should not be undertaken unless hemoglobin level is above 10 gm/100ml of blood.

(b) Disorders of WBC

Leukemia. This denotes neoplasm of the hemopoietic tissues. WBCs may appear immature. Acute lymphoblastic leukemia occurs in 80% of childhood leukemias. Acute myelogenous leukemias is the usual type of adult acute leukemia. Most common feature is cervical lymphadenopathy. Severe gingival bleeding may be due to thrombocytopenia. The common cause of morbidity and mortality is uncontrollable infection. Increased susceptibility to infection may be due to decrease in normal WBCs. Therefore, it is better to postpone all except emergency care until the patient is in remission.

(c) Disorders of platelets

Platelets are disc-shaped blood cells. They adhere to a variety of substances, particularly with collagen (when blood vessel is damaged), at the site of vessel injury. This is followed by the aggregation of a large number of platelets (thrombocytes) to form a platelet plug. Interaction of these activated platelets with the coagulation system leads to the sequence of events resulting in the formation of fibrin clot. Bleeding tendency can be the result of an abnormality at any stage of these events. When the platelet count falls below 150,000/ml then it is clinically significant (thrombocytopenia). This is most commonly drug-induced, although bone marrow disorders, infections, immunological and inherited disorders have been associated with this condition. Drugs commonly implicated are as follows:

Marrow suppressive agents: e.g., chemotherapeutic agents, chloramphenicol, phenylbutazone, alcohol, thiazide diuretics.

Immunological agents: e.g., Quinine, aspirin, sulfonamides, rifampicin, methyldopa, aminosalicylic acid, indomethacin.

Unknown mechanism: e.g. Heparin.

Vascular purpura can be seen in conditions like Cushing's syndrome, amyloidosis, Vitamin C deficiency. *Thrombocytopenic purpura* refers to escape of blood into subcutaneous tissues called *petechia*. Spontaneous gingival bleeding can be managed with oxidizing mouthwashes but platelet transfusions will be required to arrest the bleeding. Purpura is clinically identified by the extravasation of blood under the skin or mucous membrane resulting from rupture of the capillary walls. It appears as distinct macules varying from bright red to brownish, rust colored petechiae. Purpura caused by thrombocytopenia may be the result of decreased platelet production or increased destruction.

Spontaneous gingival bleeding can be arrested with oxidizing mouth washes, platelet transfusions, withdrawal of the drug responsible for this condition and promotion of clot integrity by giving 100 mg/kg of e-aminocaproic acid (EACA) as a loading dose orally or intravenously followed by 50 mg/kg every 6th hourly for 8 days. It inhibits fibrinolysis after the clot formation. Block injections should be avoided in this group of patients. Intraligamentary anesthesia will be helpful. If patients are already on steroid therapy, it may further complicate the management.

(d) Hemostatic disorders

The normal sequence of events that leads to hemostasis occur in two phases:

Phase I involves immediate control mechanism related to the vasculature and formation of the platelet plug at the site of vessel injury.

Phase II involves long-term control mechanism related to the biochemical events, humoral coagulation factors, platelet factors and calcium resulting in the formation of a fibrin clot.

Abnormalities of the coagulation factors can result in many hemostatic disorders. During the process of coagulation, two pathways - intrinsic and extrinsic - converge in a common pathway in the formation of fibrin. In the intrinsic pathway plasma procoagulants are activated following the vessel damage. More rapid extrinsic pathway involves the interaction of the tissue factor with factor VII. When vascular integrity is disturbed, interaction with fibrinolytic system, thrombocytes and blood vessels ensure hemostasis. Comprehensive history is the important component for screening the coagulation factors. This should include history of previous and family history of abnormal bleeding. Laboratory investigations must be directed towards the various components of the coagulation process. Prothrombin time detects the abnormalities of extrinsic and common pathways. Partial prothrombin time screens the abnormalities of intrinsic and common pathways. Both the investigations are affected by the abnormalities of common pathway. Thrombin time and fibrinogen level assess the qualitative and quantitative aspects of conversion of fibrinogen to fibrin.

All the four investigations along with platelet count and bleeding time constitute the comprehensive assessment of the hemostatic process.

Inherited disorders. Persons with inherited coagulation disorders give life-long history of abnormal bleeding. Minor forms may escape early detection but may be detected following stress of the hemostatic mechanism like dental extraction. The common inherited disorders include deficiency of Factors VIII and IX known as Hemophilia A and Hemophilia B (Christmas disease). Both are sex-linked recessive traits with affected males and carrier females. von Willebrand's disease is an autosomal dominant trait with variable penetration. Bleeding is proportional to the severity of the deficiency. Major therapy for them consists of plasma or Factor VIII (for hemophilia A and von Willebrand's disease) and Factor IX (for hemophilia B) concentrates. The most important advance has been the comprehensive care approach.

Acquired disorders.

(a) Vitamin K deficiency: Vitamin K is necessary for the synthesis of Factors I (prothrombin), VII, IX and X. It is responsible for the final activation of the already formed coagulation proteins produced by liver. Since normal diet contains excess of Vit K, dietary lack is not common. But, it being fat soluble, malabsorption syndrome can be associated with Vit K deficiency in addition to the deficiencies of Vit A, D and E. Many drugs can interact with Vit K. For example, antibiotics can interfere with Vit K production by the intestinal bacteria. Similarly, coumarin anticoagulants, salicylates and propylthiouracil can have Vit K antagonists.

(b) Liver disorders: Hepatic diseases can cause a number of coagulation abnormalities. Obstructive jaundice results in malabsorption of Vit K but can be reversed by parenteral administration of Vit K. But in the hepatocellular liver disorders, deficiency of Vit K dependent factors, Factor V and fibrinogen are common. It is also associated with thrombocytopenia.

(c) Anticoagulant therapy: Heparin acts at several stages of coagulation process by serving as a cofactor to antithrombin III. This complex heparin-antithrombin inhibits thrombin and active forms of Factors IX, X and XI. If bleeding occurs during heparin therapy, simple discontinuation may be adequate, since the therapeutic levels of heparin clear-up from the circulation quickly in 6 hours time. In case of life-threatening bleeding episodes, intravenous infusion of protamine sulfate will immediately reverse the process.

Coumarin-type of anticoagulants are Vit K antagonists. They lower the levels of Factors II (prothrombin), VII, IX and X. Barbiturates accelerate the coumarin metabolism and lessen its effect. Salicylates can interfere with Vit K metabolism and potentiates its effects. Phenylbutazone tends to displace coumarin from its protein binding sites and potentiates its effect. When bleeding results during coumarin therapy, stopping the drug results in the gradual return to normal level in 7 days time. Administration of Vit K can correct the defects within 24 hours.

D. Endocrine disorders

They are often slow in onset and subtle in presentation. They decrease the longevity of life and erode the quality of life. Hence, their identification and management offer great benefit to the patient and professional gratification to the clinician. In spite of great advances in the imaging techniques, many endocrine disorders remain undiagnosed for a long time after their onset.

Pituitary dysfunction

Pituitary gland is concerned with many vital processes. There is a reciprocal relationship between pituitary gland and other endocrine glands and central nervous system. The hypothalamic-pituitary relationship is most important in Neuro-endocrinology. Adenohypophysis produces the following hormones: thyrotropic hormone, adrenocorticotropic hormone, gonadotropic hormone and growth hormones. Pituitary-adrenal axis is important in all kinds of nonspecific stress. When the body is subjected to such non specific stress, anterior pituitary produces ACTH, which stimulates the adrenal cortex to produce corticosteroids. The adrenal mechanism regulates the following:

Mobilization of proteins, glucose level of the blood, resorption of water and electrolytes in the renal tubules of the kidney, process of inflammation, integrity of the connective tissue and immune responses are some of them. Diabetes and hypertension are the significant complications associated with hypopituitarism. Thyroid function may be increased or decreased called hyper- and hypothyroidism respectively. Hypothyroidism can be classified by age of onset and by etiology. In practice, dental surgeon may be the first person to recognize the condition from the orofacial changes. Myxedematous coma can be precipitated by infection, surgery and CNS depressants. These persons will be hypersensitive to drugs due to lowered metabolic rate and CNS depression.

Extreme care should be exercised when administering analgesics, anesthetics, barbiturates, hypnotics and tranquilizers. In hyperthyroidism, emotional stress, infection, trauma and surgery can precipitate crisis, which may prove fatal. Therefore, all types of dental treatment must be postponed until the patient is brought to euthyroid state. Dental therapy must be provided under controlled environment hospital. Local anesthetics without epinephrine should be used since, myocardium in these persons is highly sensitive to epinephrine. The dental surgeon must be capable of recognizing the symptoms of thyroid crisis and managing the crisis.

Adrenal dysfunction

Disorders of adrenal gland may be hyper-adrenocorticism (Cushing's syndrome) or hypoadrenocorticism (Addison's disease). In hypoactivity, overall growth and development of heart failure, diabetes, hearing loss and emotional depression occur. In case of persons with Addison's disease, administration of corticosteroids may lead to suppression of the individual's immune response and consequently, he is prone to infections and there is a possibility of adrenal crisis. Adrenal medulla functions as a sympathetic ganglion and secretes mainly epinephrine. The mineralocorticoids influence cell permeability where excretion of potassium and retention of salts are retarded. Osteoporosis may occur in the jaws. The dental surgeon must be aware of the fact that the loss of sodium and the retention of potassium affect the cardiovascular and nervous systems. Glucocorticoids, which are concerned with intermediate carbohydrate metabolism, include hydrocortisone and cortisone.

The relationship of the adrenal gland to stress has been studied extensively. Under continuous stress, pituitary - adrenal associated serious conditions may develop.

Thyroid dysfunction

The function of thyroid gland is to elaborate, store and secrete thyroxin, which is concerned with the regulation of metabolic rate. Thyroid disorders are of great concern to the dental surgeon in several ways. Thyroid gland secretes thyroxine [T4] and calcitonin. The most common thyroid disorders are iodine deficiency-related goiter and hyper-thyroidism (thyrotoxicosis). The term "Thyro-toxicosis" refers to excess of T3 and T4 in the blood stream. Patients with this condition who are untreated or incompletely treated may develop thyroid crisis. Precipitating factors for the crisis are infection, trauma and surgery. Early symptoms include extreme restlessness, nausea, vomiting, abdominal pain, profuse sweating, tachycardia, and pulmonary edema. Later, the patient may develop congestive cardiac failure, coma, severe hypotension and eventually death. Treatment includes large dose of antithyroid drugs, propranolol to antagonize the adrenergic component, hydrocortisone, I.V. glucose solution with cardio-pulmonary resuscitation.

Hypothyroidism is called Myxedema in adults and cretinism in children. CNS depressants, sedatives or narcotic analgesics may cause exaggerated response. Once hypothyroidic patient is under optimal medical care, no special problems will develop in terms of dental management. Therefore, no treatment planning modifications are required.

E. Pregnancy and breastfeeding

Although the pregnant patient is not a **"medically compromised"** person, in its strict sense, pregnancy is an altered physiological state that has an impact on treatment planning and patient care. Maternal well-being is ensured by being aware of this fact while, fetal well-being is protected by observing the recommended precautions by the clinician. A survey will reveal that significant changes can be observed in endocrine, cardiovascular, respiratory, urinary, hematological and gastrointestinal systems. Endocrine changes like increase in the maternal and placental hormones, resulting in many systemic alterations, are most significant.

Cardiovascular system: Cardiac output increases by nearly 40%, reaching the peak during early part of second semester. Supine position causes marked decrease in cardiac output from 28th week as a result of compression of the inferior vena cava by the uterus causing decreased venous return. By turning the patient towards left side (15 degrees tilt) in the sitting posture, uterine compression is eliminated. There is a slight decrease in the diastolic pressure. A systolic murmur develops in 90% of pregnant women which is considered to be physiological or functional. If it persists after pregnancy, then further investigation is necessary. Sometimes dyspnea may develop at rest, aggravated by supine position. During late pregnancy, *supine hypotensive syndrome* may occur in supine position, manifested by bradycardia, abrupt fall in BP, sweating, nausea, vomiting, weakness, air hunger and mild depression. Rolling over to the left side will relieve the problem at rest while it is aggravated by supine position. The blood changes include anemia, increase in blood volume with iron deficiency and increased WBC count. Several coagulation factors are increased like Factors VII, VIII, IX, X and fibrinogen. Fibrinolytic activity combined with decreased velocity of venous flow in the lower extremities may lead to risk of thromboembolism.

Respiratory system: Alterations begin early in pregnancy. Arterial oxygen tension rises slightly while arterial carbon dioxide tension decreases. Maternal oxygen reserve is significantly decreased. This puts the mother and fetus at risk for hypoxia.

Genitourinary system: Renal system changes are due to increased plasma flow and glomerular filtration rate. Antibiotics and other drugs that depend on the renal clearance may require increased dosage to maintain effective serum level. Urine stasis may be due to uterine compression on the ureters. Frequent urinalysis for bacteriuria will be appropriate.

Gastrointestinal system: The changes are enzymatic, anatomic and physiologic. Hepatic changes are elevation of serum levels of alkaline phosphatase and decrease of total protein and albumin-globulin ratio. Gastric acid production increases with decreased gastric motility. Presence of morning sickness must also be kept in mind. During the first trimester, formation of systems and organs takes place. Thus the fetus is most susceptible to malformations during this period. Therefore, one must be careful to avoid medications and stressful events.

Pregnant women may spontaneously abort during the treatment period and may present with an undiagnosed stillborn fetus. The clinician should be aware that after fetal death, pregnancy tests may remain positive because of the persistence of viable chorionic tissue. Dynamic ultrasound imaging that fails to demonstrate fetal movements or heart contractions will provide a clue to fetal death. The importance lies in the fact that the possibility of maternal coagulopathy exists.

General guidelines for the management of pregnant patients

Establish the contact with the patient's obstetrician and/or the physician regarding the patient's medical status. This also decreases stress and anxiety for both the clinician and the patient.

Dental radiography: It is advisable to avoid this, particularly during the first trimester. If necessary, appropriate shielding methods must be adopted by using protective lead apron, apart from high speed films and filtration. Posture should be such that the patient is in a comfortable position by turning towards the left side to avoid compression on the inferior vena cava. In general, it is better to avoid treatment during the first semester and long treatment session during the third semester. It is safe to carry out the treatment during the second trimester. Monitor prolonged elevation of body temperature. Always follow anxiety reduction protocol.

Therapeutics during pregnancy: "Food and Drug Administration" of US and National Health and Medical Research Council of Australia have categorized the drugs prescribed for pregnant patients based on the risk of fetal injury.

Cat. A (Safe to mother and fetus). Drugs taken by many pregnant women and women of childbearing age without any adverse effects to the mother and fetus.

Cat. B (Safe but restrict the use). Drugs taken by a limited number of pregnant women without any harmful effects on fetus although animal studies have shown risk.

Cat. C (Safe with risk). Drugs with known toxic effects can be harmful without causing malformations. The effects of these drugs may be reversible.

Cat. D Drugs with positive evidence of human fetal risk but in certain situations, the drug may be used inspite of its toxicity.

Cat. X High risk drugs which are known to cause permanent damage to the fetus and therefore should never be used.

Note: Drugs classified under Cat. A or B can be prescribed without risk. Likewise, drugs under Cat. X should never be prescribed. Drugs falling under the Cat. C and D will present difficulties for the clinician, if the necessity arises in terms of therapeutic decisions and medicolegal consequences.

Category A

Analgesics:	Codeine, paracetamol.
General anesthetics:	Nitrous oxide, enflurane, halothane, ketamine, thiopentone.
Local anesthetics:	Lignocaine, bupivacaine, prilicaine, mepivacaine.
Antihistamines:	Meclozine, cyclizine, chlorcyclizine, hydroxyzine, chlorpheniramine, pheniramine.
Antiinfectives:	Cephalosporins [cephalexin, cephalothin] Erythromycin. Penicillins [amoxycillin, ampicillin, benzylpenicillin, cloxacillin] Antimycotics - nystatin[topical], miconazole[topical] Miscellaneous - Clindamycin, lincomycin.
Drugs acting on autonomous nervous system :	Anticholinergic agents - atropine, papaverine, hyoscine, methobromide. Adrenergic stimulants adrenaline[epinephrine], ephedrine, Isoprenaline, salbutamol. Topical steroids - betamethasone, halcinonide, triamcinolone.
Hypnotics and sedatives:	Chloral hydrate, chlormethiazole, Valerian.
Vaccines:	Tetanus.

Category B

General anesthetics:	Isoflurane.
Local anesthetics:	Editocaine.
Antiinfectives:	Cephalosporins except cephalexon and cephalothin.
Penicillins:	Amoxycillin with clavulanic acid.
Antimycotic:	Amphotericin
Antiviral:	Acyclovir
Miscellaneous:	Metronidazole, trimethoprim
Drugs on autonomic system:	Belladona, phenylpropanolamine.
Vaccine:	Hepatitis-B.

Category C

Analgesics:	Pethidine, morphine, pentazocine, Non-steroid antiinflammatory - diclofenac, ibuprofen, Indomethacin, mefenamic acid, phenylbutazone, piroxicum, salicylamide, sodium salicylate
General anesthetics:	Isoflurane.
Antihistamines and antiemetics:	Phenothiazines.
Antiinfectives	Sulphonamides.
Miscellaneous:	Chloramphenicol. (enters the fetal circulation and if given just before parturation, may cause *"grey baby syndrome"* with cyanosis and hypothermia).
Systemic steroids:	Betamethasone, cortisone, hydrocortisone, prednisone, prednisolone, triamcinolone.

Hypnotics and sedatives:	Barbiturates, benzodiazepines.
Neuroleptics and antipsychotics:	Phenothiazines, butyrophenones.

Category D

Anticonvulsives:	Carbamazepines, clonazepam
Antiinfectives:	Aminoglycosides - gentamycin, kanamycin, neomycin, amikacin. Tetracyclines.

Drugs and lactation

During lactation, the drugs consumed by the mother can be excreted in the milk and in some cases it can affect the infant in any of the following ways:

(a) May have direct adverse effect on the infant.
(b) Sucking reflex may be inhibited.
(c) Taste of the milk may be altered.
(d) Even small amount of the drug may cause allergy or drug hypersensitivity.

As in the case of classification of drugs in pregnancy, drugs which can affect the breast milk are classified into three categories.

Category I: Very low concentration of the drug in milk is excreted and no adverse effects on the infants have been noticed.

Local anesthetics:	Lignocaine, bupivacaine, prilocaine, procaine, mepivacaine
Analgesics:	Codeine, pethedine
Nonsteroid anti-Inflammatory drugs:	Ibuprofen, mefenamic acid
Anticholinergic drugs:	Hyoscine
Anticonvulsants:	Benzodiazepine
Vasoconstrictors:	Adrenaline, felypressin
Antiinfectives:	Aminoglycosides - gentamycin, kanamycin, neomycin, amikacin cephalosporins, erythromycin
Antimycotics:	Nystatin
Antipsychotics:	Chlorpromazines, phenothiazines
Hypnotics and sedatives:	Benzodiazepines, chlormethiazole

Category II: Adverse effects may occur

Analgesics:	Opiates, aspirin, paracetamol, salicylates
Anticonvulsants:	Carbamazepine, phenobarbitone
Antiinfectives:	Penicillins, cephalosporins, amphotericin, tetracyclines, lincomycin, clindomycin, metronidazole
Antimycotics:	Miconazole
Antiviral:	Idoxuridine
Antipsychotics:	Chlorprothixene
Antihistamines:	Promethazine, bronchodilator, theophylline
Hypnotics and sedatives:	Barbiturates, chloral hydrate.

Category III: Adverse effects have been reported in the infants.

Nonsteroid anti-Inflammatory drugs:	Indomethacin, phenylbutazone
Anticholinergics:	Atropine
Antiinfectives:	Chloramphenicol, sulphonamide, tetracyclines, sulphonamides, trimethoprim sulphamethoxazole
Steroids (topical):	Cortisone, triamcinolone.
Sedatives:	Diazepam, meprobromate

F. Pulmonary disorders

(a) Chronic bronchitis

This is a condition associated with excessive tracheobronchial mucous production to produce cough with expectoration. This is characterized by the obstruction of air flow during respiration. *Emphysema* is defined as the distension of air spaces distal to the terminal bronchioles. They may even coexist with overlapping symptoms. The most important etiology is smoking with environmental pollution. Since these patients have compromised respiratory function, the patient should be placed in an upright position instead of supine position. This is to avoid orthopnea and respiratory discomfort. Local anesthesia is not contraindicated. During the dental procedure, rubber dam should be avoided. Narcotics and barbiturates are respiratory depressants and therefore should be avoided. Anticholinergics and antihistamines are also contraindicated. Persons who are on steroids need supplementation. Patients who receive theophyllin should not be given erythromycin since it can interfere with metabolism of theophyllin. Outpatient general anesthesia is not preferable.

(b) Asthma

This is a syndrome with cough, wheezing and dyspnea caused by bronchospasm. Etiology is multifactorial. It may be allergic or idiosyncratic type. Bronchi and bronchioles occlude by thick mucus plug. Status asthmaticus is the most serious manifestation of this condition. The patient should be advised to keep the bronchodilator (inhaler) during the dental appointment. It is preferable to avoid aspirin or NSAID. Antihistamines should be used cautiously. Barbiturates and narcotics should also be avoided. Provision of stress free environment is essential. Local anesthetics can be used but preparations containing epinephrine or levonordefrin which contain sulfite as a preservative should be avoided.

(c) Tuberculosis

This is important to be considered for several reasons. Since it is an infectious condition, the clinician must take all precautions so that neither the patient nor the clinician contract the disease. The dental surgeon may be the first to identify and establish the diagnosis. If so, the patient must be referred to the concerned specialist for appropriate treatment. Effective chemotherapy depends on multiple drug utilization and patient compliance for drug therapy for sufficient period. The primary drugs used are: isoniazid, rifampicin, streptomycin, ethambutol and pyrazinamide.

For the purpose of management of these patients in the dental clinic, they can be broadly classified into four groups:

(a) Patients with past history of tuberculosis.
(b) Patients with active sputum-positive tuberculosis.
(c) Patients with clinical features suggestive of tuberculosis.
(d) Patients with positive tuberculin test.

Get the history of past treatment. Appropriate review is mandatory. Always obtain the clearance from the physician before proceeding with the treatment. In cases of relapse or during the active phase, treatment should be deferred.

G. Immunological and allergic disorders

The reasons for understanding these conditions are to identify the patients with history of allergy and immunological reactions, to recognize the oral soft-tissue reactions due to allergy, to plan the treatment for those who have severe alterations in immune system due to drugs and immune deficiency and to identify and manage acute allergic reactions in case of emergency.

Coombs and Gell classification of immunologic hypersensitivity reactions:

Type I — Anaphylactic
Type II — Cytotoxic
Type III— Immune complex-mediated
Type IV — Cell-mediated or delayed

Allergic reactions occur due to immunological reactions to a non-infectious foreign substance (antigen). The reactions involve different types of immunological reactions of immunological hypersensitivity. Functions of the immune system are processing and cellular recognition of antigen, response to presentation of antigen, cellular action against antigen and eradication of antigen.

Type I: These hypersensitivity reactions relate to the humoral system. Anaphylaxis refers to the involvement of the smooth muscles of bronchi in which antigen-antibody reactions result in the release of histamine from the mast cells. Soon, smooth muscles contract leading to acute respiratory distress. Urticaria develops as a superficial lesion of the skin while angioneurotic edema develops in the deeper layers of the skin or tissues like tongue or larynx.

Type II: These reactions take place following mismatched blood transfusions.

Type III: These reactions are known as immune-complex-mediated hypersensitivity with vasculitis as its main feature. The clinical examples are Lupus Erythematoses and streptococcal glomerulonephritis.

Type IV: This involves cellular immune system. The clinical examples are dermatitis, and transplant rejections. The infectious type of allergic reactions are noticed in Tuberculin test.

These hypersensitive reactions are of very great clinical significance. For example, if any patient gives history of allergy, then history must specifically be directed to all the aspects of allergy. The clinical features of an allergic reaction include urticaria, skin rashes, edema, dyspnea and strained breath, stomatitis, rhinorrhea or conjunctivitis. The adverse reactions may be predictable or unpredictable. Reactions to local anesthetics, vasoconstrictors, penicillin, analgesics, rubber products and dental products are well known examples.

Management of severe type I reactions. In spite of ample precautions taken by the clinicians, sometimes, these reactions develop. Fortunately, many of them are mild and of non-emergency nature. When they are severe and become life-threatening, the clinician must be ready to deal with such emergency situations. Since they occur soon after the event like injection or medication not much of time is left for the clinician to react. The following are some of the important procedures to be adopted immediately:

(1) Patient must be placed immediately in a head down or supine position.
(2) Ensure the patency of the airway.
(3) Continuous administration of oxygen.
(4) Provide support to circulation and respiration. If facilities are not available, arrange for help.
(5) Monitor all the vital signs. Even though many may develop fainting, one should not assume that it is only fainting and fail to carry out all the emergency measures.
(6) In the event of the patient developing angioneurotic edema, the clinician must inject 0.5 ml of 1:1000 epinephrine into the tongue. Support the respiration with artificial aids, if necessary. If pulse cannot be detected, cardiac massage should be started without wasting any time. Otherwise it will turn out to be fatal.

H. Neurological disorders

Epilepsy

This term refers to a group of disorders consisting of chronic, recurrent and paroxysmal neurological changes caused by abnormal electrical activities of the brain. These fits or seizures may be (a) convulsive in nature accompanied by motor manifestations or (b) changes in neurological functions in the form of sensory or emotional changes. Etiology may be intracranial trauma or neoplasm, drug withdrawal, hypoglycemia , febrile illness or may be idiopathic. Even though etiology may be unknown, epileptic seizures may be precipitated by a few specific stimuli like loud noise, flickering lights, undesirable or monotonous sounds. The basic events that take place have been identified as excessive neuronal discharges that spread to thalamic and brain stem nuclei. These changes include altered synaptic transmissions or membrane potentials, decreased elecrical threshold or increased neuronal excitability. But so far, not even one type of brain lesion has been correlated with epilepsy. Just like the management of conditions like hypotension, one has to make sure that patients take their medications as per the directions of the clinician. Problems associated with the medications of this condition are phenytoin-induced ataxia and gingival hyperplasia, phenobarbital-induced drowsiness, altered mental function, confusion and argumentativeness. Very serious emergency, associated with this clinical entity is the occurrence of repeated seizures over a very short period, emitting sudden cry followed by loss of consciousness without a recovery period, called *status epilepticus*. The patient may become hypoxic and may suffer from brain damage and may even prove to be fatal if not managed properly. The initial tonic phase of epilepsy consists of muscle rigidity. It may be followed by clonic activity consisting of uncoordinated movements of the head and limbs, incontinence of urine or feces. When these movements cease, the person becomes comatose. With the gradual return of consciousness the patient develops stupor, headache and confusion. Jaw relaxation occurs after the termination of seizure. EEG findings are not very conclusive.

Use of anticonvulsive therapy constitutes first line of management. The most common drug used is Phenytoin sodium (Dilantin). Carbamazepine, phenobarbitol and valproic acid have also been tried with varying results.

If the person gives history of medication, then there is no problem. But if the patient exhibits the clinical features of epilepsy for the first time during the dental clinical appointment, then the responsibility of the dental surgeon is to make a provisional diagnosis and arrange for further management. Once the epileptic patient is identified, proper history must be elicited from the patient including type of seizure, age of onset, etiology if identifiable, details of current medications, degree of control of the condition, precipitating factor if known, date of the previous attack and history of any injuries with the seizure. These details will be very helpful to the dental surgeon in many ways.

(1) Non-compliance or non-responsiveness of drug therapy must alert the clinician that the patient must be referred to the physician for management.

(2) The clinician must be aware of the possible toxic effects of the drugs like drowsiness, dizziness, G.I. tract upset, allergic manifestations in the form of rashes or erythema multiforme-like reactions.

(3) Phenytoin sodium, valproic acid and carbamazepine can induce leukopenia, or thrombocytopenia. This will result in delayed healing or gingival bleeding or increased microbial infections. In cases of patients on valproic acid medications, the possibility of platelet aggregation resulting in petechial hemorrhage must be remembered. Administration of Aspirin and non-steroidal antiinflammatory drugs may aggravate bleeding episodes. All these patients should not be prescribed erythrocin and propoxyphene for the fear of drug interaction.

Management of epileptic seizure. The dental clinic staff must be fully prepared to manage these patients in the event of these patients developing epileptic fits. Appropriate preventive measures must be taken by the dental surgeon. If the patient develops fits, all efforts must be directed to prevent any injury to the patient. As far as possible, the patient must not be shifted. The chair must be adjusted to supine position with the patient turned to one side so that aspiration of secretions is avoided or minimized. Seizures last for a few seconds to a few minutes. Soon after, the patient falls into deep sleep from which the patient cannot be aroused. If the patient develops status epileptics, Diazepam 10 mg can be given intravenously.

Stroke

This clinical condition is known as cerebrovascular accident. It is a serious and even fatal condition developing as the end result of cerebrovascular disorder. This term refers to the events resulting from the focal necrosis of the brain due to disturbance of the cerebral blood supply. The most common type of disturbances that are responsible are hypertensive vascular disease, atherosclerosis and myocardial infarction in which the patient develops thrombosis in any of the cerebral vessels. The predisposing (risk) factors include cardiac abnormalities, diabetes mellitus, physical inactivity, stress, elevated blood lipid level and smoking. The associated pathological changes are infarction, intracerebral and subarachnoid bleeding. The development of infarction depends on factors like site and duration of occlusion, size of the occluded vessel and the possibility of establishment of collateral circulation. The effect depends on the involved area and the artery. Mortality following stroke depends on the type of stroke. Majority of the cases are involved in cerebral hemorrhage. If the patient survives, only 10% completely develop without any neurological deficit, 40% develop with minor deficit, 40% may need special services while 10% will need hospitalization for efficient management. The common neurological deficits are unilateral paralysis, numbness, dysphasia, diplopia, blindness and dysarthria. The rate and type of recovery and the severity of residual deformities are invariably unpredictable.

The clinical features of stroke are:

(1) Temporary impairment of speech.
(2) Transient or temporary dimness of vision (which is likely to be confused with migraine).
(3) Weakness of the face or limbs on one side of sudden onset.
(4) Unexplained dizziness or unsteadiness.

If any patient develops the above mentioned clinical features, the clinician must evaluate the patient to arrive at the correct diagnosis. Differential diagnosis are diabetes, acute alcoholism, uremia, intracranial tumor, drug poisoning and extradural hemorrhage. Laboratory investigations which will be useful are blood sugar level, urinalysis, blood count, ESR, blood cholesterol and lipid level, ECG and chest radiograph. Lumbar puncture will be helpful to detect blood or protein in CSF and altered CSF pressure. In specialized centres, CT scan, nuclear magnetic resonance and arteriography are done.

Management.

(1) Prevention.
(2) Identification of the risk factors.
(3) Attempt to reduce these factors.
(4) If the patient develops stroke:
    (a) to provide life-supporting measures immediately.
    (b) to prevent further development of hemorrhage or thrombosis.
    (c) providing anticoagulant therapy, corticosteroids and in some cases surgical intervention.
    (d) if the patient survives, adoption of rehabilitation measures.
(5) Physician to be consulted before instituting dental treatment to elicit history of the treatment of stroke.
(6) Stress-free environment and short morning appointments.
(7) Monitoring of BP and effective pain control methods.

I. Multiple medications and drug interaction

Many drugs are prescribed for symptoms rather than the disease. Elderly persons receive multiple medications and therefore, whenever any geriatric person attends the dental clinic, history must be elicited carefully so that the drugs prescribed by the dental surgeon should not interact and produce any effects. Unfortunately, these drug responses are unpredictable. Such variable responses may be due to the different rate of degeneration in body tissues. As a general rule, the greater the number of drugs taken together, the greater the risk of damage to the patient. Sometimes, this is aggravated by the self-medication by the patient. In general, drugs that may cause problems when taken together are antibiotics, anesthetics, analgesics, non-steroid anti-inflammatory drugs, anticoagulants, diuretics, antidiabetics and antihypertensives. So, the dental surgeon must be aware of the possible drug interactions and the art of managing the geriatric group of patients.

J. Liver disorders

Jaundice (Icterus)

Jaundice refers to yellow discoloration of the skin or sclera caused by an excessive level of bilirubin. It can be confirmed when the serum level of bilirubin exceeds 2 to 3 mg. It may be due to the following reasons.

(1) Excessive bilirubin production: Increased red cell destruction (hemolysis) and ineffective erythropoiesis may lead to excessive bilirubin production. In acute or chronic liver disorder, reduction of hepatic excretion of conjugated bilirubin results in increased bilirubin load. Thus, serum level of conjugated bilirubin results.

(2) Reduced hepatic uptake of bilirubin: In case of reduced plasma, clearance of unconjugated bilirubin results in impaired uptake at the liver cell membrane or from an altered transport within the cell. Hemolysis increases the severity of jaundice.

(3) Impaired hepatic conjugation of bilirubin: e.g., premature infants.

(4) Impaired excretion of conjugated bilirubin: Patients with liver cell injury develop jaundice due to the impaired excretion of conjugated bilirubin.

E.g., Toxic (carbon tetrachloride or ethanol toxicity)
Viral (hepatitis type A or B)
Metabolic (hypoxia)
Miscellaneous (bacterial endotoxin).

Damage to bile ductules within the portal triads can also lead to intrahepatic cholestasis.

Extrahepatic ductal obstruction may result from gallstones, strictures or neoplasm.

Liver enlargement usually indicates liver disease. It may be due to

(a) Changes in the parenchymal cells, e.g. infiltration of fat or glycogen.
(b) Intra or extrahepatic cholestasis.
(c) Venous congestion, e.g., heart failure, constrictive pericarditis, occlusion of hepatic vein.
(d) Diffuse inflammation, e.g., toxic or viral hepatitis.
(e) Fibrosis with regeneration nodules, e.g., Cirrhosis.
(f) Miscellaneous : pyogenic or amoebic abscess, cyst, granuloma and neoplasm.

Hepatic tenderness suggests inflammation, acute stretching of the liver capsule.

Hepatic coma is a metabolic encephalopathy manifested by fluctuating changes in the level of consciousness, impaired motor coordination with increased reflexes, tremor, varying rigidity and hyperventilation with respiratory alkalosis. This is due to the failure to detoxify exogenous substances like ammonia and other products of bacterial metabolism. These products accumulate and modify the brain functions.

Assessment of liver functions: The biochemical tests commonly done for the evaluation of patients with liver disorders do not provide a quantitative measure of liver functions. But they are useful to establish the differential diagnosis and to determine the prognosis. Serum bilirubin test is insensitive to liver disease. Patients known to have a high risk of requiring liver disease may benefit from an early recognition of the liver involvement even before the onset of the clinical entity.

In patients with jaundice, diagnosis can be confirmed from history, physical examination and biochemical studies done in the following four groups of patients:

(1) Patients with unconjugated hyperbilirubinemia.
(2) Patients with acute liver damage (hepatitis).
(3) Patients with chronic parenchymal liver disorder (cirrhosis).
(4) Patients with intrahepatic or extrahepatic cholestasis.

Viral hepatitis is an infectious disease caused by hepatotropic virus..

– Type A - Acute viral hepatitis, (infectious hepatitis - short incubation).

– Type B - Serum hepatitis (homologous serum jaundice, posttransfusion hepatitis, long incubation).

Type A occurs as a sporadic illness or epidemic outbreaks. It results in lasting immunity.

Type B hepatitis is usually related to higher titer of the virus that may be present in the blood of the patients with the illness or as carriers. Transmission may be through parenteral route (most common route, e.g., needle pricks, blood transfusions) or vertical transmission e.g., from mother to infant or through insect vectors as in bed bugs and mosquitoes. Rarely, transmission has also been reported in case of surgeons, dental surgeons and other hospital personnel who have direct exposure to blood. The potential risk of Hepatitis B transmission may be reduced by the routine use of operating gloves. Prophylaxis is recommended as a routine procedure by active immunization against hepatitis A and B.

Warning: Professionals should be very careful while covering the needle, to avoid accidental needleprick. Instead of holding the cover, it can safely be left on the table while inserting the needle into the sleeve.

K. Renal disorders

Renal, electrolyte or acid-base disorders may manifest themselves as any of the clinical features like hematuria, oliguria, dysuria, anuria, polyuria, hypertension, edema, uremia, proteinuria, crystalluria and alteration in the serum concentrations of sodium, potassium, bicarbonate, phosphate, calcium or magnesium. *Hypertension* is usually present in patients with vascular or glomerular disease, *edema* in tubular or glomerular disease, *hematuria* in a variety of conditions involving ureter, urethra, prostate, bladder, and glomerulus through infections, neoplasms, trauma, renal infarct and coagulation defects. During the early phase of the disease, mild, asymptomatic condition is known as *renal insufficiency*. As the disease progresses, more damage occurs progressively resulting in decreased ability to perform its excretory, endocrine and metabolic functions beyond its compensatory capacity. At this stage, it is called *renal failure*. Retention of the excretory products and disturbance of endocrine and metabolic functions lead to the waste products in blood called *uremia*. This reflects the cardiovascular, hematologic, neuromuscular systems of the body. Once the condition is established, the aim and objective are to slow down the progress of the disease and to preserve the quality of life.

Assessment of renal function

(a) Glomerular filtration. Normally, renal blood flow is approximately 25 to 30 % of cardiac output. Glomerular filtration is a physical process determined by the interplay between the forces involved in filtration and those opposing it. The outcome of net filtration is protein-free filtrate of plasma.

(b) Acid-base homeostasis. The pH is maintained around 7.3 to 7.5. The overall excretory function can best be assessed by the determination of Glomerular Filtration Rate (GFR) from the plasma concentration of creatinin. The *urinalysis* is the simplest, most reliable and economical screening test for the detection of the renal disorders. Urine should be collected from midstream as a fresh specimen. The routine analysis include pH, presence of protein, sugar (glucose) and blood. Radiological examination of the kidneys provides the anatomic details of the kidneys and the collecting system. Computed tomographic scanning provides transverse images of kidneys, adrenal glands and perirenal region. Ultrasonography is very popular since it is noninvasive and economical. It is useful to study the renal anatomy.

Acute renal failure is an abrupt reduction in glomerular and renal tubular function. It may be a life-threatening syndrome associated with retention of blood urea and several other excretory substances. It can be identified as oliguric phase, diuretic phase and recovery phase.

Chronic renal failure is a progressive loss of renal function that may be irreversible developing uremia (urine in the blood). Clinical manifestations may involve the following systems:

(a) *Cardiovascular* (hypertension, edema, congestive cardiac failure, pericarditis and cardiomyopathy)
(b) *Endocrine* (sexual dysfunction, thyroid dysfunction, growth harmone)
(c) *Dermatological* (pruritis, pigmentation, ecchymosis, purpura)
(d) *Gastrointestinal* (anorexia, nausea, vomiting, diarrhea, G.I.tract bleeding, gastritis, colitis, pancreatitis, peptic ulcer)
(e) *Hematologic* (bleeding diathesis, anemia)
(f) *Neurologic* (insomnia, headache, irritability, drowsiness, neuropathy, coma, seizures)
(g) *Pulmonary* (edema, bleeding).

The dental aspects and management of renal disease as a single systemic disorder rather than discussing individual renal problems. Hemodialysis is by far the most prevalent therapy for the end-stage renal disorder. Soon after dialysis, it is better to carry out the treatment since bleeding problems will be negligible. It will also be the optimal metabolic condition of the patient. Since renal transplant recipients are potential carriers of Hepatitis B, appropriate asceptic measures may be used. Many of these patients are on anti-inflammatory and immunosuppressive medications, and they may mask the early symptoms and signs of inflammation and infections. Prophylactic use of antibiotics are advocated. All precautions must be taken as for patients on steroid therapy. While prescribing any drug, compromised renal function must be borne in mind. There is no contraindication for using local anesthetics with vasoconstrictors. As far as possible, it is better to undertake hospital dental care in this group of patients.

L. Delayed healing

In some cases, diabetic patients may go undiagnosed. This possibility should be considered in case of patients with recurrent infection and delayed healing. In poorly controlled cases, there is need to assess the stability of the condition. The current type of antidiabetic treatment is a useful guide to the possible risk of adverse interaction with oral surgery. Patients on corticosteroid therapy may become a problem due to reduced responses to stress following adrenal suppression and immunosuppression. In addition, decreased healing potential results in delayed healing.

PATIENTS WITH POOR PROGNOSIS

Even if the procedure in the oral cavity to be performed is a simple one, it is the general condition of the patient which ultimately guides the decision-whether to do the treatment or not. Whenever, patients with serious complications need any treatment, it is wise to defer or at least to limit the procedure to the minimum extent possible. For example, patients with congestive cardiac failure, terminal stage of malignancy, uremia, liver cirrhosis, or leukemia should not be taken up for any prolonged treatment, which by itself may aggravate the existing condition. At the most, the comprehensive treatment should be limited to relief from pain. If the circumstances warrant, local anesthesia should be preferred. In case of any emergency situation, - where the basic life support is used for the Airway maintenance, Breathing, and maintenance of Circulation. The cardiovascular problems are described by the patient as a "squeezing" sensation, heaviness in the chest, pain radiating along the left shoulder and the mandibular region. Gastrointestinal problems like dyspepsia with hypermotility of the gastrointestinal tract and intercostal muscular spasm occasionally can mimic pain of cardiac origin. Hyperventilation can also be of psychic origin. Most of the indices of pulmonary function decline due to physiological aging. The vital capacity decreases as the age progresses. Hence, an elderly person, who has developed pulmonary pathological changes, will be at increased risk.

AGE RELATED PROBLEMS

Persons older than 65 years are usually identified as elderly. Aging is one of the natural, inevitable biological phenomena. The onset and progress of the process vary due to many factors. The biological aging is not identifiable with chronological aging. With increase in the life expectancy, aging population will increase. As the age advances, physiological functions of the body get compromised. It is characterized by gradual constriction of homeostatic reserve of every organ of the body. These changes include loss of flexibility, alterations in the body composition and loss of cells that are not replaced. Water content gradually falls from 70 to 50% in old age. Loss of flexibility with loss of elastic tissue leaves small airway poorly supported. After the age of 40 years, there is a gradual decrease in renal blood flow and glomerular filtration rate. Deteriorating mental function may lead to dementia.

The goal of dentistry has always been to restore oral health in a predictable manner and in this context, the aging population can be grouped in the following manner:

(a) Functionally independent elderly patients.
(b) Functionally dependent elderly patients.
(c) Physiologically weak elderly patients.

In conclusion, it may be said that the updated knowledge about the altered physiology is mandatory to safely treat the elderly patients. They can be summarized as follows:

(1) Distinct loss of physiological reserve.
(2) Nutritional deficiencies are common.
(3) There is an increased susceptibility to pressure ulcers and abrasions from minor trauma.
(4) Changes in the lens and iris lead to presbyopia with loss of visual acuity and functional vision impairment.
(5) Hearing impairment is common.
(6) There is high prevalence of coronary artery and hypertensive heart disease.
(7) Pulmonary reserve declines with age.
(8) Specific age related effects on esophageal phase of swallowing, and development of numerous disease states that can cause dysphagia are common.
(9) There is an overall decline in the metabolic activity of the liver.
(10) Anatomic renal changes may be correlated with functional changes. Therefore, non-steroidal antiinflammatory drugs (NSAIDs) should be used with caution.
(11) Muscle size and mass are reduced with age resulting in decreasing strength.
(12) Age related boneloss is extremely common.
(13) Age related neuronal loss affects certain areas of the brain. This may result in difficulty with word finding (tip-of-the-tongue phenomenon). Complex tasks that require quick responses can be hard to perform.
(14) Physiological aging of the body systems (as described above) along with local factors may interact with oral structures and functions (mastication, swallowing, hydration, taste and smell). Hydration of the oral cavity - through saliva - is disturbed.

An appreciation of the intricacies of the physiological changes restored alone can enhance the oral care of the elderly.

Appendix

DENTAL MANAGEMENT OF MEDICALLY COMPROMISED PATIENTS

1. HYPERTENSION

(i) Anxiety - reduction protocol.
(ii) Brief morning appointments.
(iii) Use less of vasoconstrictors.
(iv) No elective procedures in uncontrolled diabetes and hypertension.
(v) Hypertensive patient is a potential bleeder.
(vi) Monitor patient's medications.
(vii) Patients on diuretics develop dry mouth.
(viii) Terminate the appointment if the patient is overstressed.
(ix) Patients on medication without any renal or cardiac problem can be treated.

2. ANGINA

(a) Patient with H/O angina

(i) Always get the clearance from the physician.
(ii) Anxiety-reduction protocol.
(iii) Monitor all vital signs.
(iv) Keep nitroglycerine sublingual tablets ready (instruct the patient to keep it handy).
(v) Brief morning appointments preferable.
(vi) Avoid vasopressors for hemostasis.
(vii) Inject local anesthetics slowly. Ensure profound anesthesia.
(viii) With signs of fatigue and stress, terminate the appointment.

(b) Management of angina (?)
(during the dental appointment)

(i) Stop the procedure immediately.
(ii) Place nitroglycerine tablet sublingually and wait for 2-3 minutes.
(iii) If pain is not relieved, monitor the vital signs. Repeat the second dose-even third if necessary.
(iv) In the mean time, arrange for physician's help.
(v) Must continue to attend to the patient's needs until the physician takes over the responsibility of the patient.

3. ANXIETY REDUCTION PROTOCOL

Preoperative

(a) Sedation on the previous night, to promote undisturbed sleep.
(b) Tranquilizer-one hour before the appointment.
(c) Brief morning appointment.

Intraoperative

(a) Minimal noise.
(b) Instruments to be kept out of sight of the patient.
(c) Provide verbal assurance and maintain the communication with the patient throughout the appointment to monitor the level of consciousness.
(d) Local anesthesia of sufficient intensity.
(e) Provide conscious sedation, if necessary.

Postoperative

(a) Proper postoperative instructions.
(b) Effective analgesics (ensure to avoid drug interaction).
(c) Reassurance.

4. PATIENT WITH H/O MYOCARDIAL INFARCTION

(i) Mandatory to get physician's clearance before commencing treatment.
(ii) No elective procedure at least for 6 months after the episode.
(iii) Anxiety reduction protocol.
(iv) Monitor vital signs.
(v) Antibiotic prophylaxis.
(vi) Brief morning appointment.
(vii) Advice the patient to always carry nitroglycerine tablets.
(viii) Inject the anesthetic drug slowly. Ensure profound anesthesia.
(ix) With signs of fatigue, terminate the appointment.
(x) Since they are on anticoagulant therapy, this group of patients are potential bleeders. Sometimes, the drug schedule may have to be restructured by the physician.

5. ABNORMAL BLEEDING

The systemic conditions to be ruled out:

(a) Hemophilia.
(b) Purpura.
(c) Vitamin C deficiency.
(d) Leukemia.
(e) Anticoagulopathy.
(f) Liver disorders.
(g) Infection.
(h) Anemia.

6. CONGESTIVE CARDIAC FAILURE

(a) Physician's advice mandatory.
(b) Evaluate all the medications and the nature of the condition.
(c) DEFER ALL ELECTIVE PROCEDURES.
(It is an absolute contraindication.)

7. DIABETES

(a) Monitor blood sugar level.
(b) Use anxiety reduction protocol.
(c) Morning brief appointments after meals.
(d) Medications to be continued as advised by the physician.
(e) To carry out under cover of antibiotics.
Treat the infections aggressively.
(f) Maintain verbal contact during the procedure - to monitor the level of consciousness.

8. STROKE
(Cerebrovascular accident)

(a) Identification of stroke prone patient
H/O hypertension, diabetes, smoking, coronary atherosclerosis.

(b) Patient with H/O stroke
(i) High risk for another episode.
(ii) Physician's opinion is mandatory before starting the treatment.
(iii) Short morning appointments.
(iv) Monitor vital signs.
(v) Attention to bleeding tendency because of anticoagulant therapy.
(vi) Use minimum of vasoconstrictor with local anesthetics as per the opinion of the physician.

9. PATIENTS ON STEROID THERAPY
(Adrenal insufficiency)

1. No precautions required if:

(a) Dosage is low - less than 20 mg/day.
(b) On larger dosage for less than 1 month.
(c) Patient is on topical steroids.
(d) H/O steroid therapy stopped atleast one year earlier.

2. For others:

(a) Double the dosage one day prior to the treatment.
(b) Continue the higher dosage one day after the treatment.
(c) Taper the dosage.

10. THYROID PROBLEMS

A. Hyperthyroidism

Possibilities

(a) Adverse reaction to epinephrine.
(b) Thyrotoxic crisis with stress and infection.
(c) Congestive cardiac failure.
(d) Life-threatening cardiac arrhythmias.

Guidelines

1. Detection of the undiagnosed disease.
2. Diagnosed patients:
   (i) Monitor the present medications.
   (ii) Clinical assessment and referral to the physician for reevaluation, if necessary.
   (iii) No treatment if the patient is not under control.
   (iv) Restrict vasoconstrictors, if local anesthesia is used.
3. Management of the thyroid crisis:
   (i) Seek medical aid immediately.
   (ii) Parenteral hydrocortisone 100 mg to 200 mg.
   (iii) I.V. Glucose.
   (iv) Cardiopulmonary resuscitation, if necessary.

B. Hypothyroidism

Possibilities

(i) Exaggerated response to CNS depressants.
Eg., sedatives, narcotics.
(ii) Myxedema with CNS depressants.
Stress, infections.

Guidelines

(a) Detection of the undiagnosed disease.
(b) Diagnosed patients can be treated, only after consultation with the physician.
(c) As far as possible, avoid surgery until the physician clears the patient for fitness.
(d) Avoid infections and CNS depressants like narcotics and barbiturates.
(e) In case of Myxedema - coma,
Hydrocortisone 100 to 300 mg.
Artificial respiration, if necessary.
Seek medical aid immediately.

11. PATIENTS ON ANTICOAGULANT THERAPY

(a) Consult the physician regarding therapy.
(b) Hospitalization is mandatory.
(c) Rescheduling the medication (only in consultation with the physician for stopping of platelet-inhibiting drugs)
Aspirin - 5 days prior to treatment.
Coumarin - 2 days prior to treatment.
Heparin - 6 hours prior to treatment.
(d) During elective surgery:
Use the measures to promote clot formation and its retention.
(e) Medications to be started once stable clots form.
(f) Patient to be instructed not to dislodge the clot.
(g) Avoid non-steroidal antiinflammatory drugs.

12. HEPATITIS

(Emergency measures)

(a) Consult the physician.
(b) Avoid any elective procedures.
(c) Minimize or avoid medications and treatment.
(d) During the treatment:
Strictly adhere to asceptic techniques like gloves, mask, disposables and adequate sterilization.
(e) Use rubber dam to minimize the contact with saliva and blood.

13. PREGNANCY

(a) Dental radiography
  (i) Avoid during first trimester.
  (safe during second semester)
  (ii) Appropriate shielding aprons.
(b) Always consult obstetrician.
(c) Since pregnancy is emotionally and physically stressful condition, anxiety reduction protocol should be followed.
(d) During advanced pregnancy:
  (i) Avoid prolonged elevation of body temperature.
  (ii) To avoid fetal pressure on inferior vena cava, the patient is placed in an upright position in the dental chair with trunk tilted 15 degrees towards left side during treatment.

14. THERAPEUTICS DURING PREGNANCY

Category I (Safe to mother and fetus)

Analgesics -	Codeine, paracetamol
Antibiotics -	Penicillin, erythromycin, cephalosporin, Topical antimycotics
Anesthetics-	Thiopentone, halothane, ketamine, Lignocaine
Others -	Adrenaline, atropine, tetanus vaccine

Category II (Safe but restrict the use)

Antiinfectives -	Amoxycillin, antimycotics, Antiviral agents, metronidazole, trimithoprim
Others -	Hepatitis B

Category III (Relatively unsafe)

Analgesics -	Aspirin, opoid analgesics (pethidine)
Antiinfectives -	Tetracycline, gentamycin, neomycin, sulphonamides, chloramphenicol
Others -	Steroids, barbiturates, diazepam, carbamazepine.

Aids to Diagnosis

INTRODUCTION

Oral diagnosis is the art of utilizing the scientific knowledge to identify the oral diseases and also to distinguish one disease from another. This forms the fundamental basis to oral surgical practice. Diagnosis of the clinical condition can be made on the basis of comprehensive history, clinical examination and the appropriate investigations. A clinician may take advantage of one's own clinical experience to arrive at a "spot diagnosis". Unfortunately, the underlying cause of error in diagnosis lies itself in such quick decisions. Hence, every clinician must use this method sparingly. On the contrary, it is preferable to employ a standard methodical system of diagnosis.

SEQUENTIAL STEPS OF THE DIAGNOSTIC PROCESS

The key to successful treatment is in definitive diagnosis. The diagnostic process involves the following sequential steps:

(a) Historical database

This is to obtain a comprehensive overview of the patient's past and present health status, including the complaints.

(b) Clinical examination (extra and intraoral)

(i) Inspection
(ii) Palpation
(iii) Percussion
(iv) Auscultation

(c) Provisional diagnosis

All the clinical findings and the historical database are correlated to arrive at the provisional diagnosis.

(d) Investigations

There are many specific methods of investigations available to the clinician. Such common methods are:

(i) Hematological
(ii) Radiological
(iii) Biochemical
(iv) Histopathological

(v) Microbiological
(vi) Special methods.

(e) Definitive (final) diagnosis

On the basis of investigations performed with the background of historical database and clinical examination, the clinician will be able to arrive at the differential diagnosis. Once, the definitive disease process is identified, the final diagnosis is confirmed by a process of elimination through differential diagnosis. Only when the diagnosis is confirmed, the practitioner can generate the treatment plan and establish the follow-up programme.

GENERAL GUIDELINES

Thus, a thorough, open communication between the patient and the clinician becomes a prerequisite for the correct diagnostic process. The communication skill is as important as the clinical knowledge. For example, when pain and discomfort are the concern, the patient is often disturbed. Non-verbal communications like kind approach, willingness to help and development of mutual trust are helpful to explore the chief complaints of the patient. During the process, the clinician elicits the symptoms, as expressed by the patient and hence, they are purely subjective. But, the clinical findings of the practitioner on the basis of certain parameters are objective called signs. The main aim of the (objective) signs is to confirm the (subjective) symptoms. Hence, guidelines have been provided here for the development of a protocol to clinically evaluate the responses of the patient and the clinical features. The clinical methods cannot be learnt by merely attending lectures or from textbooks. Success depends on careful examination and developing one's own clinical acumen. It should be the main aim of the clinician to acquire the following qualities for a successful oral surgical practice:

(1) Acquisition of mastery in the theoretical knowledge of surgery.
(2) Development of mastery in the practical knowledge of the diagnostic process.
(3) Gentle handling of the patient with "Lady's fingers".
(4) Watchful eyes, to enhance the power of observation with "Eagle's eyes".
(5) Boldness in decision-making and in action during the surgical practice with "Lion's heart".

Dexterity and speed are the two wings of the diagnostic process. The clinician should not sacrifice one for the other. One should realize that both are complementary and not as a replacement to each other. It is equally a good practice to explain to the patient what the clinician proposes to do. But, one should carefully avoid discussions in the presence of the patient using the terms which are likely to induce psychic trauma or likely to hurt the patient's self-respect and ego.

In oral surgery practice, clinician is often confronted with the diagnosis of the following conditions:

(1) Dental and facial pain
(2) Swelling
(3) Ulcer
(4) Maxillofacial injuries
(5) Temporomandibular joint disorders
(6) Medically compromised patient
(7) Facial deformity.

All these aspects of the diagnostic processes are dealt with in the concerned chapters. Hence, an account of general principles involved in the diagnosis and formulation of treatment plan are given.

ART OF HISTORY TAKING

This must be acquired by every prospective clinician. The aim is mainly to highlight the important clinical features so that the clinician can identify the etiological factors and the tissue of origin. In other words, this will enable the clinician to explore the "Soil and the Seed" effect of the disease so that a provisional diagnosis could be made. Therefore, intelligent history taking is the first step for proper diagnosis. Likewise, inadequate and inaccurate history is responsible for the wrong diagnosis. One must always bear in mind that leading questions must be avoided when history is elicited from the patient. In children and unconscious patients, history can be obtained from the relatives. The data must be recorded with patient's own words. The following are some of the variable factors, which may modify the symptom pattern:

(1) Individual and nocturnal variations in the threshold of pain.
(2) Intellectual variations, responsible for the incorrect sequence of the complaints.
(3) Language barrier.
(4) Deliberate variations in the narration of the history, e.g., exaggeration, concealing of facts, description of wrong complaints to elicit sympathy or due to loss of memory.
(5) Inefficient history taking by the clinician.

To reduce these variables to the minimum, it is preferable to use a questionnaire routinely in clinical practice. For the convenience of the patient and the oral surgeon the questionnaire is divided under a few well defined categories.

Procurement of database

General particulars

(a) *Name, sex, age,* and *address* of the patient are important for the identification and recording of the data. In a way, this gives confidence and mutual trust among the patient and doctor. Age is important for confirming the diagnosis of age related conditions in different age groups. Sex is equally important to diagnose the sex-related lesions.

(b) *Occupation:* It is useful to record the past or present occupation of the patient to confirm the diagnosis, since the occupation may predispose to certain conditions.

(c) *Chief complaints and history of past treatment (if any).* The chief complaint is considered to be the heart of the history database and hence careful attention must be paid. The symptoms provide valuable clue to the system that is affected. If the patient has more than one complaint, they must be recorded in a chronological order. Every complaint must be carefully recorded along with the mode of onset, its origin, duration and progress. Brief history of the treatment, if any, and the response of the patient to the treatment must also be recorded. The description must be precise and specific.

Personal history

Enquiry about the personal habits of the patient like abuse of tobacco and alcohol, drug-addictions, food habits, marital status and important relevant family history are useful in the diagnostic process.

Symptomatology: The study and recording of symptoms include awareness, history, knowledge and pattern of symptoms of the patient. Symptoms should always be recorded in the patient's own descriptive language. The commonly used terms are grouped under the following categories:

(a) *Discomfort:* Pain, numbness, itching, burning, breathlessness, heaviness, pressure, tingling sensation, rawness, rise in body temperature (pyrexia), and sweating.

(b) *Functional changes:* Loss of smell (anosmia), difficulty to open the mouth (trismus), difficulty to swallow (dysphagia), loss of taste, loss of speech (dysarthria), grinding of teeth (bruxism), double vision (diplopia), loss of vision, bleeding gums, loss of hearing, bleeding from the nose (epistaxis), clicking of the joint, hole (sinus or fistula), loss of facial expression (facial paralysis).

(c) *Textural changes:* Dryness of the mouth (xerostomia), swelling (tumor), ulcer and roughness. While recording these complaints, interrogation of the patient regarding the chief complaint must explore the nature of the problem, periodicity, duration, exact location, and precise description of the problem.

Signs: Systemic features involving the entire body.

(1) *Pyrexia* indicates rise in the body temperature, which represents reaction of the body to proteins. The normal oral temperature is 98.4 degrees F (36.8 degree C). The rectal temperature is 1 degree F (0.6 degree C) higher. The basal metabolic rate (BMR) is increased by about 12% to the rise of each degree centigrade. The causes of pyrexia are:

(a) Tissue breakdown
(b) Impaired heat loss
(c) Disturbance in thermoregulatory mechanism
(d) Increased heat production.

Pyrexia may be continuous or intermittent. Mode of onset may be acute or gradual. Duration may be short in acute pyrexia while, prolonged in chronic pyrexia. It may be associated with symptoms like cough, pain, etc.

(2) *Pulse* is said to be the mirror of the heart. The data to be recorded are rate, rhythm, force, tension, volume, symmetry with the opposite side and condition of the vessel wall like thickening etc. The general guidelines to record the pulse are as follows:

(a) Pulse is to be recorded, when the patient is calm and quiet.

(b) Variations of pulse rate in different age groups and at different parts of the day should be borne in mind. Increase in pulse rate is directly proportional to the increase in body temperature.

(3) *Respiration rate* is 16-18/min. Rate, rhythm, and type of respiration must be recorded.

(4) *Blood pressure.* It is preferable to record the blood pressure of all the patients who are awaiting surgery and the patients who give history of cardiovascular disorders. The signs are objective in nature.

(5) *The soft-tissue changes* are recorded by the clinician with the following terms: erythematous, pigmented, ulceration, tumors, vesicles, nodules, swellings, etc. But the underlying hard tissue changes are to be examined with radiograph.

DIAGNOSIS

The skillful assembling of the symptoms in a chronological sequence and correlation with the signs will enable the clinician to analyze the clinical findings and to diagnose the condition. If the diagnosis cannot be confirmed, sophisticated and specific investigations may be required. One of the specific diagnostic tests for the confirmative diagnosis is histopathological examination (biopsy).

Oral surgery patients, in general, can be categorized under four groups:

Group I: New patient with specific oral surgical problem

Group II: New patient for routine review

Group III: Regular follow-up

Group IV: Patient from a hospital, primarily for the dental treatment.

Every patient for oral surgery must be completely examined before undertaking treatment.

EXAMINATION OF A SWELLING

Routine examination of any swelling must proceed chronologically in the following sequence.

History

(1) How long, since it was first noticed?
(2) Associated symptoms like pain, etc.
(3) Mode of its onset
(4) Is it getting larger?
(5) Slow or fast growth (progress of the swelling)
(6) Any possible etiological factor or any relevant data like recurrence.

Clinical examination

(1) Inspection.

(a) Number, exact anatomical location
(b) Color, size, shape, surface, and mobility
(c) Margin
(d) Pulsatile or not

(e) Skin or mucous membrane over the swelling
(f) Any pressure effects?

(2) Palpation.
(a) Tenderness
(b) Consistency, mobility, and measurements
(c) Reducible or not
(d) Fluctuation, surface, margins, and compressibility
(e) Temperature
(f) Transillumination
(g) Relationship to the surrounding structures
(h) Regional lymphadenopathy
(i) Examination of the pressure effect.

(3) General examination for the patient.

Provisional (clinical) diagnosis is made on the basis of clinical examination.

Routine investigations

(1) Blood - total and differential leucocyte counts (TC, DC), ESR, blood sugar, Hb%
(2) Urine - sugar and albumin
(3) Aspiration
(4) Radiological examination
(5) Histopathological examination.

Definitive (final) diagnosis is confirmed, based on differential diagnosis by a process of elimination, as to whether swelling is congenital, traumatic, inflammatory, neoplastic (benign or malignant) or miscellaneous.

Follow-up review of the swelling: After treatment, the patient must be periodically examined for recurrence, if any.

EXAMINATION OF AN ULCER

Ulcer is defined as a break in continuity of the overlying epithelium (skin or mucous membrane).

History

(1) Number (single or multiple)
(2) Location, size, shape, mode of its onset
(3) Duration
(4) Associated features like pain, systemic features and discharge
(5) Increase in size - fast or slow.

Clinical examination

(1) General examination of the patient
(2) Margin, floor, discharge and surrounding region
(3) Palpation
 (a) Confirmation of inspection findings.
 (b) Lymphadenopathy.

Provisional (clinical) diagnosis is made on the basis of clinical examination.

Investigations

(1) Routine blood investigations
(2) Routine urine investigations
(3) Microbiological examination of the discharge
(4) Histopathological examination
(5) Exfoliative cytology.

Definitive (final) diagnosis is made on the basis of these investigations.

PATHOLOGICAL CONSIDERATIONS

Biopsy

Biopsy is relatively a minor surgical procedure carried out on tissues removed from the living organism to confirm the diagnosis histopathologically. Autopsy denotes the histopathological study on tissues removed after death.

The size, location and characteristics of the lesion determine the type of the biopsy procedure to be undertaken. The various procedures in use are as follows:

(1) Incision biopsy
(2) Excision biopsy
(3) Aspiration biopsy
(4) Punch biopsy
(5) Exfoliative cytology

(6) Fine needle aspiration cytology (FNAC).

It is imperative that a dental surgeon should have the knowledge of basic oral pathology. The increasing awareness of the clinicians and the general public makes it morally and legally mandatory to examine every suspicious lesion available. Based on the capacity of the dental surgeon and the nature of the lesion, appropriate method can be selected. The diagnosis is the responsibility of the clinician and histopathological diagnosis becomes an important link in confirming the diagnosis and treatment planning. The accuracy of histopathological diagnosis depends on how the possible errors in the biopsy procedure are eliminated or minimized.

Indications

(1) If any clinician is unable to diagnose the true nature of the lesion, biopsy is useful.

(2) Excision biopsy is indicated in lesions less than 2 cm diameter. Care must be taken to include adequate margin of the surrounding normal tissue. Then, it becomes diagnostic as well as therapeutic.

(3) If the lesion is too large, incision biopsy is indicated. A representative area of the lesion is chosen including the surrounding normal zone. Care must be taken to avoid the central zone of necrosis.

(4) Clinically, if the lesion does not correlate or confirm the histopathological diagnosis, biopsy must be repeated from a more representative area. This is particularly true with doubtful malignant lesions.

(5) Punch biopsy has very restricted role in oral surgery practice.

(6) Aspiration biopsy is always indicated in all the "cystic" lesions. It is done with 18- gauge needle to identify the true nature of the content of the lesion. Fine needle aspiration biopsy can be very useful in suspected malignancies to differentiate from benign lesions.

(7) Cysts of the jaws are notorious for the varied presentations in the same lesion. For example, in one area, it may be cystic while in certain other areas, the specimen will reveal ameloblastic transformation. Since the prognosis depends on the correct diagnosis, serial biopsy is done by multiple histopathological sections of the same lesion.

(8) Although exfoliative cytology is an useful procedure, it seems to be less reliable. This technically difficult procedure lies exclusively under the domain of an oral pathologist. This requires special skill and armamentarium.

(9) Positive diagnosis is of value, while negative response must be viewed with caution.

(10) Biopsy should not be performed on vascular and pigmented lesions.

If the dental surgeon is ignorant of the various technical details concerning biopsy, the operator is likely to have frustrating and eventful experience. Mere absence of formaldehyde need not be an excuse for not performing biopsy.

Requirements of the transport media

(1) Ideally, the solution for the storage of a biopsy specimen should preserve the tissue in its original state, until it reaches the pathologist. Once the tissue is removed from the patient, the process of autolysis sets in. The enzymes that once converted amino acid to protein, reverses this process so that, proteins of the cells breakdown into aminoacid. It diffuses out of the cell, so that no protein remains inside the cell for the coagulation by fixation process. Hence, as soon as the tissue is removed, it must be immersed into a fixative.

(2) Fixative has the advantage of first changing the tissue protein framework, thus facilitating sectioning and strengthening of the protein linkages against breakdown during the staining process.

(3) It is desirable that a fixative enhances the affinity of the dye by combining with the dye and the tissue to be dyed.

Ideal medium. 10% formalin solution is the widely used media, fulfilling these ideal requirements. It is prepared by mixing 10 parts of commercial 40% solution of formalin with 90 parts of water. If the specimen is allowed to remain for adequate period, formalin penetrates into the tissue at a moderate rate, producing optimum fixation. If the specimen is too bulky or if it is kept for inadequate period, shrinkage occurs during staining. The tissue should be rinsed in normal saline to remove excess blood because hematin of hemoglobin reacts with formalin thereby reducing its effective concentration.

Alternative media. If formalin is not available, substitution can be made by using a local anesthetic solution that is readily available in any dental surgeon's clinic. It is an acceptable solution since it is isotonic with a preservative in it. Among the local anesthetics, 2% mepracaine hydrochloride with levonordefrin 1 in 20,000 as vasoconstrictor appear similar to formaldehyde microscopically, and therefore can be an alternate media.

Local anesthetic contains sodium bisulfate used as an antioxidant for the vasoconstrictor. It is also used as a preservative, to extend the shelf life. This is the ingredient responsible to fix the tissues.

Pathologist must always be informed, if the fixative is other than formaldehyde, so that, possible tissue effects can be anticipated. Whatever be the medium used, there should be no delay in fixation or transportation of the specimen for histopathological examination.

Common problems in biopsy procedure

During handling of tissues.

(1) A brief history with proper label should always be ready, before commencing the procedure. This is to avoid the change in the identity of the specimen with dangerous consequence.

(2) During preoperative preparation of the operating field, colored solution like tincture iodine, mercurochrome or gentian violet should be avoided, since cells take up the coloration. Application of dehydrating agents like alcohol distorts the cells through water loss.

(3) If local anesthetic solution is injected into the lesion, cells may be distorted. Moreover, injection stream may spread the tumor cells to the adjacent area, thereby spreading the lesion and infection. Hence, it should be injected only around the lesion and not intralesionally.

(4) Excision of the specimen should be from a representative area. It should be of proper dimension and not too small.

(5) As far as possible, sharp blades should be used. If blunt or crushing instruments like scissors are used, cells will be damaged.

(6) Electrosurgery should not be used for the purpose.

(7) Sharp toothed forceps should not be used for grasping the tissue, since artifacts may be produced in the specimen. If artery forceps is used, the specimen will be crushed.

During fixation of the specimen.

(1) Immediate fixation of the specimen is very important. It should be rinsed gently in normal saline to remove excess blood pigments on the surface. Immediately, it should be put into a properly labeled container containing 10% formaldehyde solution.

(2) The removed specimen may curl and assume unnatural shape. If it is fixed at this stage, tangential sectioning of the specimen may occur.

(3) If the container is not sealed properly, water will evaporate, leaving behind $CaCO_3$ residue. If the tissue is placed in such a situation, improper fixation results. It may even result in an artifact of acantholysis that may even mimic pemphigus. Hence, such evaporation should be avoided. For the same reason, leakage of formalin during transportation should be avoided. Apart from dehydration, leakage may smudge the label, thereby confusing the identity of the specimen.

Exfoliative cytology

This deals with microscopic examination of the characteristics of the individuals with special stains. Although, the technique is widely used in the field of oral pathology, it is only considered as an adjunct to biopsy procedures because of certain inherent limitations of this technique. However, this procedure is indicated where, surgical removal of the specimen is not feasible or contraindicated. It is particularly useful to examine a diffuse lesion of multicentric origin, which has to be kept under observation for longer duration. Similar to biopsy procedure, accuracy entirely depends on the cells, representative of the lesion removed during the procedure.

This technique is advantageous since it is simple, quick, painless, and noninvasive. It can be repeated as often as needed without causing any discomfort to the patient. But it cannot be performed by everybody as a routine office procedure, unless, the operator is specially trained to do so. The result is more often unreliable to diagnose the oral lesions.

Cells to be examined can be obtained by scrapping the surface of the lesion with a moistened wooden spatula in one direction. The central necrosed area should be avoided. If necessary, topical anesthetic can be applied before scrapping the surface. The material obtained is then spread on a clean glass slide. Then, the slide is kept in a jar containing equal parts of 95% ethyl alcohol and ether for 15 minutes. To avoid distortion of the cells, specimen must be fixed immediately. Many studies have been undertaken to determine the efficacy of exfoliative cytology. It has revealed that false negative reports are a major cause of concern of this technique. Regarding the diagnosis of a neoplasm, there seems to be no correlation between histological grading and cytological smear. So it is considered to be an adjunct and not a replacement for biopsy.

Intraoral mucosal punch biopsy

Usually, intraoral mucosal biopsies are done with blade, which necessitates suturing. Punch biopsy offers a fast, simple, inexpensive and safe method for most of the areas of the oral cavity providing excellent diagnostic material. But, this method is limited to 2-6 mm of material. However, this is used for diagnostic purpose only. Hence, it can be an alternative for incisional biopsy but cannot replace the excision biopsy procedure. This procedure is useful in mass screening.

Technique. An appropriate site for doing the punch biopsy is chosen. The biopsy punch is held at the end of the handle and the cutting edge of the blade is placed at right angle to the oral mucosal surface. The punch is slowly rotated clockwise and anticlockwise alternatively a few times. Moderate pressure on the punch is maintained throughout, depending on the desired depth of the cut. Once the external bevel disappears into the tissue, the blade is considered to have penetrated into the connective tissue but not deeper than superficial lamina propria. To ascertain whether the depth of the incision is adequate, the punch can be withdrawn and the tissue that has been cut can be gently lifted to assess the need for further punch of the tissue. If further depth is required, punch is repositioned and the procedure is further continued. Once the desired depth of the cut is achieved, the base of the tissue is released with B.P. blade no. 15 or with a pair of scissors. Bleeding is usually minimal. Very rarely, suture is required to arrest the hemorrhage. The specimen is placed with the epithelial surface on a piece of cardboard before immersing it in the fixative.

It is found that labial and buccal mucosa are the convenient areas to perform punch biopsy, since external support can be adequately provided during the procedure. Fixed mucosa can easily be incised up to the periosteal level. If tongue is the site for biopsy, then, care is taken to support the adjacent area of the tongue to be biopsied. It is not feasible to perform this procedure in the floor of the mouth.

Postoperative instructions. Immediate postsurgical care is minimal. Pressure with gauze is usually enough to achieve hemostasis. The patient should be cautioned that saliva may be blood-tinged during the first postoperative day. If suture is placed, then the patient is recalled for the suture removal. Prescription of antibiotics, analgesics and anti-inflammatory drugs are left to the operator and the need of the patient.

Advantages.

(1) Easy to perform.

(2) Postsurgical morbidity is minimal.

(3) Since wound heals by secondary intention, suturing is not required usually and another visit for suture removal is not necessary.
(4) This procedure is useful to any accessible mucosal surface.

Disadvantages.

(1) It is difficult to use the punch for getting adequate representative tissue deeper than superficial lamina propria. It is designed to remove epithelial mesenchymal lesion.
(2) It cannot be used in the inaccessible areas like posterior maxillary buccal alveolar ridge or lingual aspect of the anterior region of the mandible.
(3) It is equally difficult to use this technique on the freely mobile mucosa that cannot be properly supported, e.g. floor of the mouth and the soft palate.
(4) It will be difficult to arrest the hemorrhage, if it is used around the mental foramen or nasopalatine foramen.

DIAGNOSTIC RADIOGRAPHY

A. General principles

The principle of radiography is mainly to demonstrate the normal and altered anatomy of various structures in two or three planes. Information obtained from the two-dimensional radiographs depends on the ability to add the third dimension in the reader's mind. For example, in the maxillary sinus view, the reader should imagine the skull as rotating about an axis through the external auditory meatus. Similarly, in the lateral view skull, the axis of rotation is around the sphenoid bone. The two-dimensional image of a three-dimensional object is visible in varying degrees of radiolucency and radioopacity depending on the relative density of the object. Since it is two-dimensional, ideal method would be to have two different projections, one at right angle to the other. Unfortunately, (a) the complexity of the faciomaxillary region, (b) density of cranial base and (c) superimposition of various structures contribute to limitations in the interpretation of these photographs. In order to avoid superimposition, various techniques have been advocated. It is necessary to understand the different radiographic techniques, their variations and the relationship to anatomical landmarks. If the radiographic techniques are correctly applied, most of the mandibular radiographs can be interpreted accurately. Radiography becomes more complicated for the middle third of the face.

B. Intraoral radiographs

Periapical radiographs (Fig. 3.1 a, b)

The intraoral radiographs provide a well-defined trabecular pattern of the dentoalveolar regions of maxilla and mandible. They include periapical and occlusal radiographs. The periapical views are the best radiographs for evaluating the dental and periapical pathology.

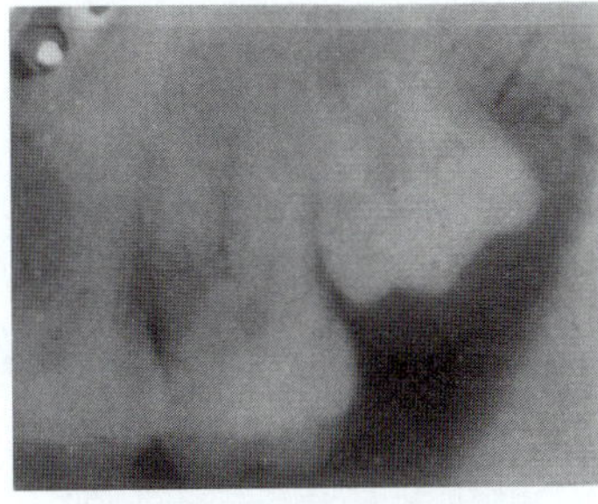

Fig. 3.1 (a) I.O. Periapical view - Maxilla.

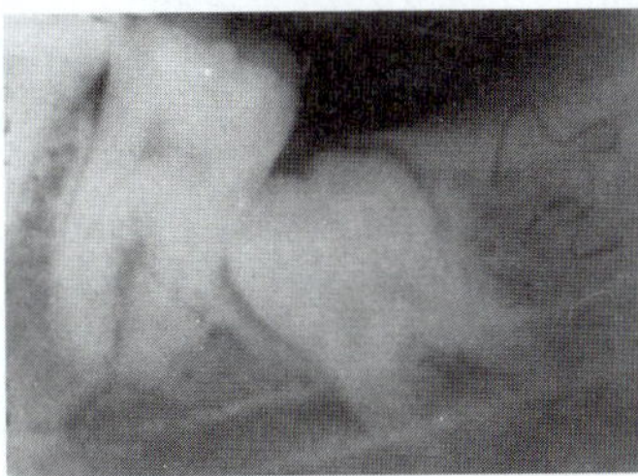

Fig. 3.1 (b) I.O. Periapical view - Mandible.

Occlusal view (Fig. 3.2)

For the maxilla, the occlusal film is placed between upper and lower teeth as far posterior as possible with the lead shield portion of the film facing the mandibular teeth. Then, the X-ray cone is placed over the nasal bridge with an angle of 75 degrees and the film is exposed. The target is the centre of the palate. For the mandible, the film is placed occlusally with the lead portion of the film facing the maxillary teeth. The cone is directed to a point midway between the molar teeth and at right angle to the film. Both these views provide a cross-sectional view of the jaws respectively.

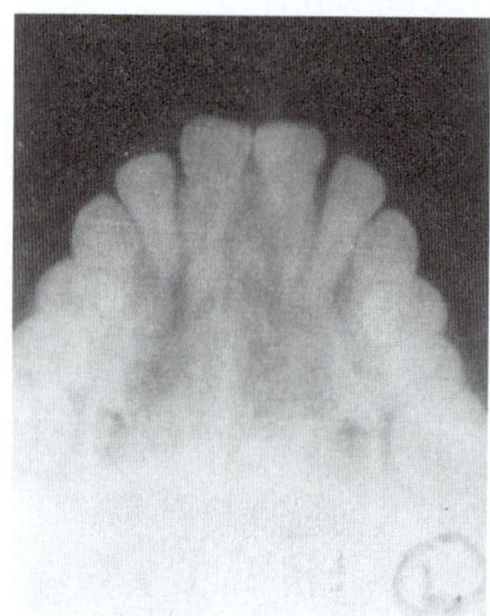

Fig. 3.2 (a) Occlusal view - Maxilla

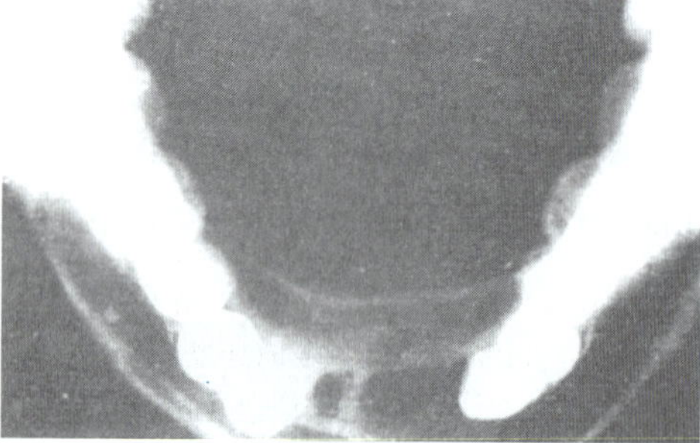

Fig. 3.2 (b) Occlusal view - Mandible.

C. Lateral view of the skull (Fig. 3.3a)

The lateral projection shows the profile of the skull. The images of the posterior borders of the mandible are superimposed while orbits are not superimposed.

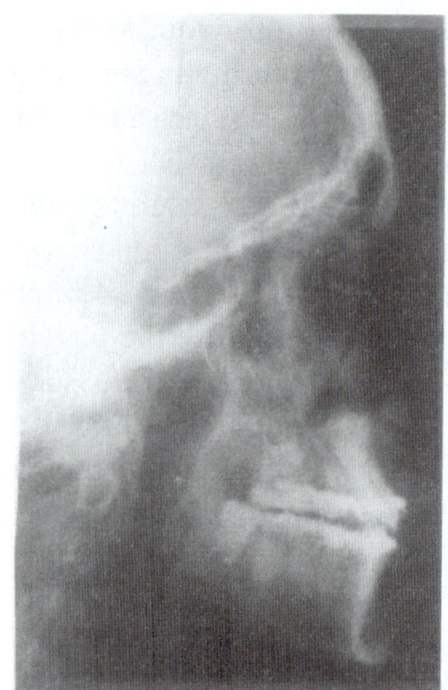

Fig. 3.3 (a) Lateral view of the skull.

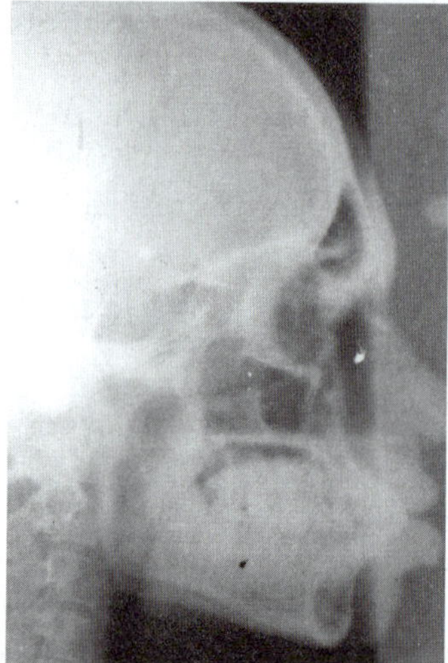

Fig. 3.3 (b) Lateral cephalogram.

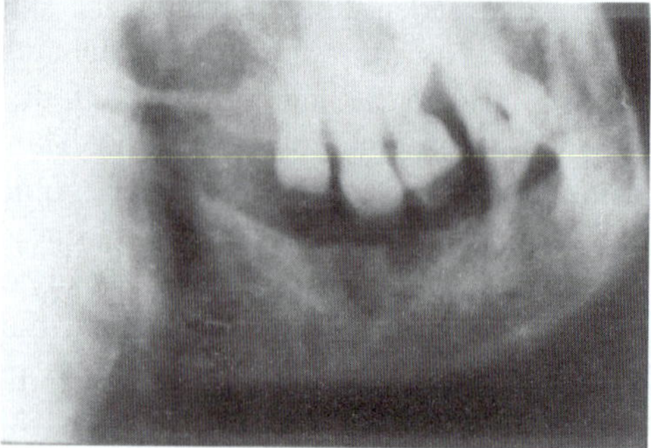

Fig. 3.3 (c) Lateral oblique view - Mandible.

Sella turcica can be clearly seen because it is a solitary structure in the midsagittal plane. Styloid and coronoid processes are clearly visible, while the skull base overlaps the temporomandibular joint. Therefore, modifications may be necessary, to view a few areas e.g. lateral oblique view of the mandible (Fig. 3.3 (a) and (c)), T.M. Joint view etc.

Cephalometric radiograph (Fig. 3.3b)

Aim of this view is to obtain the standardized and reproducible views of the facial skeleton in the lateral and posteroanterior projections. In a correctly taken view, the central X-ray beam passes through the ear plugs which are exactly superimposed. Conventionally, the film-focus distance is 6 feet and object-film distance is 5 feet 6 inches. In the lateral radiographs, both the sides of the facial skeleton overlap one over the other. Since the radiographic equipment is standardized all over the world, radiograph taken in one place is comparable to the view taken for the same patient in an another place. The view is useful to measure the distance between any two locations in the radiograph as the actual distance.This view is very helpful in the diagnosis, treatment planning and postoperative evaluation in reconstructive surgery of the facial region.

D. Posteroanterior view (Fig. 3.4)

This is one of the commonly used views. The patient's forehead and nose are positioned against the film. The image of the top of the petrous temporal is slightly above the superior margin of the orbit. Floor of the nasal cavity is flat and appears as a radioopaque line.

The middle third of the face can be conveniently studied in the occipitomental projection (Waters's view) (Fig. 3.4a). McGregor and Campbell advocated a system for the analysis of this view by following "five curvilinear lines of interpretation" of the facial bones (Fig. 3.4b).

Line 1: It is an imaginary line that starts from frontozygomatic suture line and runs along the super orbital margin to the frontonasal suture line. It crosses the glabella, follows the supraorbital region of the opposite side and terminates at the frontozygomatic suture line on the opposite side.

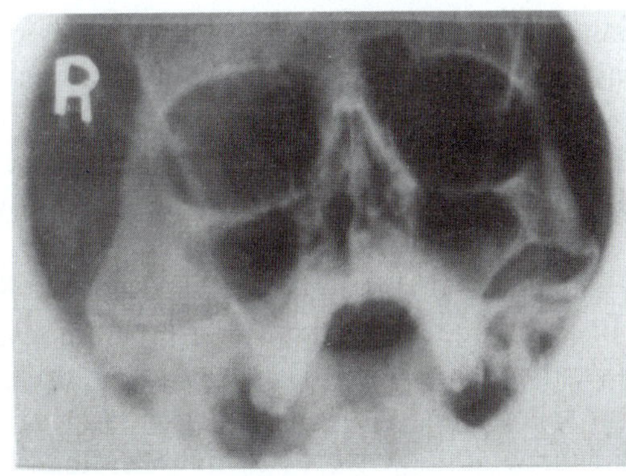

Fig. 3.4 (a) Maxillary sinus view-skull (occipitomental - 30°) Waters's view. True P.A. view skull.

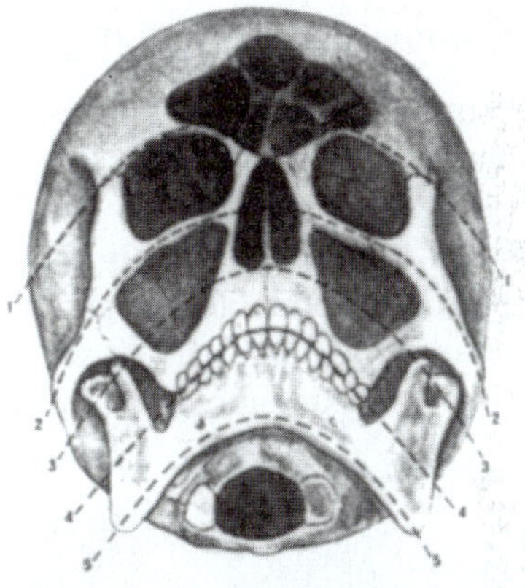

Fig. 3.4 (b) Maxillary sinus view - skull (Occipitomental - 30°). Five curvilinear lines.

Line II: It starts from the condyle of the mandible and passes across the mandibular (sigmoid) notch and coronoid process to the lateral wall of the maxillary sinus and then continues crossing the medial wall of the antrum at the level of floor of the nose and follows a similar course on the opposite side.

Line III: It starts from the condyle of the mandible and passes across the mandibular (sigmoid) notch and coronoid process to the lateral wall of the maxillary sinus and then continues crossing the medial wall of the antrum at the level of floor of the nose and follows a similar course on the opposite side.

Line IV: It passes along the occlusal plane.

Line V: This line corresponds to the lower border of the mandible.

Evaluation of this radiograph based on these five lines will help to diagnose any pathology, in the facial region. The maxillary sinus appears almost triangular and the anterior edge of the foramen magnum is covered by the mandible. This projection is useful to study the facial skeleton, orbits and maxillary sinus.

E. Orthopantomograms (OPG) (Fig. 3.5a, b)

This is a simplified extraoral procedure that visualizes the maxillofacial region in a single film. The main diagnostic advantage of orthopantomogram is that it covers relatively large area that is radiographed. The intraoral radiograph reveals the teeth, alveolar ridges and part of the supporting structures. But orthopantomogram covers the entire

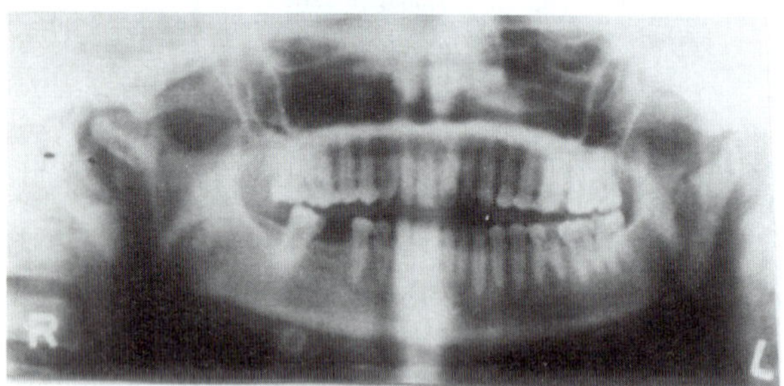

Fig. 3.5 (a) OPG - adult.

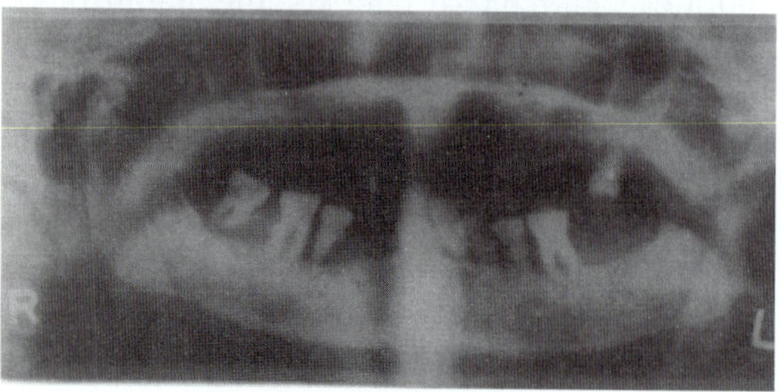

Fig. 3.5 (b) OPG - old age.

mandible from one condyle to the other. The maxillary region superiorly extends to the orbital region. Hence, the main advantage is the wide coverage and relationship of various anatomical structures. Unfortunately, they show magnification and geometric distortion. Some may even lack definition. The external placement of the film results in the increase of the object-film distance. It utilizes the principle of curved surface laminography in which anatomical structures in a selected plane are recorded while the intervening parts are blurred and this plane is called "focal trough". Even though this view lacks definition and details of the periapical region, they contribute so much information which no other conventional view offers. This presents many valuable information in one radiograph like teeth and associated structures, entire mandible, maxillary region extending to the orbital rim and posteriorly covering the T.M. joint region. This becomes very informative in case of maxillofacial trauma and pathology. It produces very little discomfort and requires minimum of patient's cooperation. The patient remains in a well supported stable position. The amount of radiation is well below when compared to other views of comparative nature. The information provided in this view is not available in the other routinely used views.

Disadvantages

(1) Overlapping: The lower anterior region cannot be properly visualized due to the overlapping and the "ghost image" of the spinal column.
(2) The image is dimensionally variable. Therefore, measurements are of no value from these radiographs.
(3) The cost is considerably greater than the conventional radiographic equipment.
(4) It requires more space.

Guidelines for positioning the patient

The area under investigation must coincide with the

focal trough of the equipment. Correct antero-posterior orientation is accomplished by positioning the patient in such a way that, incisal edges of the central incisors are placed into a notched incisal device. If anterior teeth appear blurred and reduced in width in the radiograph, this only indicates that the patient must have been positioned too far forward. If the image is too wide, the patient must have been placed too far backward. The patient must also be checked with regard to the midsagittal plane. Failure to do so will result in unequal magnification of the posterior region in the horizontal plane. If the patient is placed too far to one side, opposite side of the image becomes too wide.

The plane of occlusion must be horizontal. If the head is tilted backwards, image of the nasal floor will superimpose the apical region of the maxillary anterior teeth. If the head is tilted too far forward, lower anterior teeth appear outside the focal trough. This may give an impression as though roots are resorbed.

Even if the head is placed correctly, the tendency to remain behind the remainder of the body leads to severe overprojection of cervical vertebrae in the lower anterior region.

As already pointed out, the "ghost image" may hinder the interpretation of the OPGs. When present, they are always reversed. That means, objects on the left side will produce the ghost image on the right side.

Uses of OPG

(1) Mandibular morphology can be studied in a single film. Therefore, in cases of trauma, this view will provide valuable data of the fractures of all the parts of the mandible. Likewise, after the treatment, it helps to study the mandible completely. Various pathology involving mandible like impacted teeth, bony pathology like cysts and neoplasms, absence of teeth can be studied without the need for a second radiograph.

(2) Growth and development of the mandible including all aspects of dentition can be visualized.

(3) Temporomandibular joint profile can be studied. Apart from the condyle, articular eminence and articular fossa, even articular disc can be viewed. It becomes a very valuable diagnostic aid when mandibular deformities can be studied along with dental malocclusion and the possible involvement of temporomandibular joint due to parafunctions like bruxism, clenching etc.

(4) Maxillary sinuses and mastoid region can also be assessed in this view.

(5) During and after the orthodontic treatment, it helps to assess the overall periodontal space, paralleling of roots, integrity of the alveolar crests and the presence of any root resorption.

(6) Use of OPG among ambulatory dental population, to detect patients at-risk of stroke, has been reported in the literature. Atheromatous plaque in the extracranial carotid vasculature is recognized as the major contributing factor for cerebrovascular embolic and occlusive diseases. This can be identified by the presence of calcifications in the area of carotid vasculature. The identification should prompt mandatory referral of the patient to the physician for further evaluation. The discovery of atherosclerotic calcifications in the carotid bifurcation area has prognostic significance in the progressive evolution of a cerebral infarction.

F. Guide to radiographic interpretation of bone lesions

A good radiograph is only a diagnostic aid. Correlation with clinical and histological information is necessary for the final diagnosis. A systematic assessment of radiolucent and radio-opaque changes in the jaws and their relationship to any histopathological evidence aids in correct differential diagnosis of the lesions. In general, pathological changes in bone are manifested radiographically as any of the following alterations:

(1) Increased radiolucency
(2) Increased radioopacity
(3) Combination of both
(4) Alterations in the bone pattern of trabeculae and haversian system.

Wherever radiolucent or radioopaque lesions are seen, (a) site, (b) shape, (c) size, (d) margin and (e) presence of any internal structures are to be noted. These phenomena are illustrated with a few examples of radiolucencies, radioopacities and combination of both.

Radiolucencies (Fig. 3.6)

(1) "Cystic" lesions. Shape is circular and well-circumscribed. Margin is well-defined, appearing as "white" radioopaque line. No internal structures could be identified. But the degree of radiolucency within this demarcated area indicates the nature of the content as to whether it is fluid or soft tissue.

(2) Giant cell lesions. Shape is irregular. Margin is scalloped and irregular with characteristic absence of the "white" radioopaque line as in "cystic" lesions. Internally, there are apparent loculations and septa.

(3) Ameloblastoma. Shape is irregular. Margin is smooth, curved with "white" line. Apparent loculation, larger than the giant cell lesions, but septa are curved.

(4) Rarefying osteitis. Shape is irregular and margin is diffuse. Internally, trabeculation is of varying density. The central area is radiolucent with no trabeculation. However, gradual increase in trabecular density towards the margin can be seen.

(5) Osteosarcoma. Shape is irregular and margin is diffuse. There is subperiosteal bone deposition at the margins where the external surface is perforated. Hence, the cross-section of the margins appear.

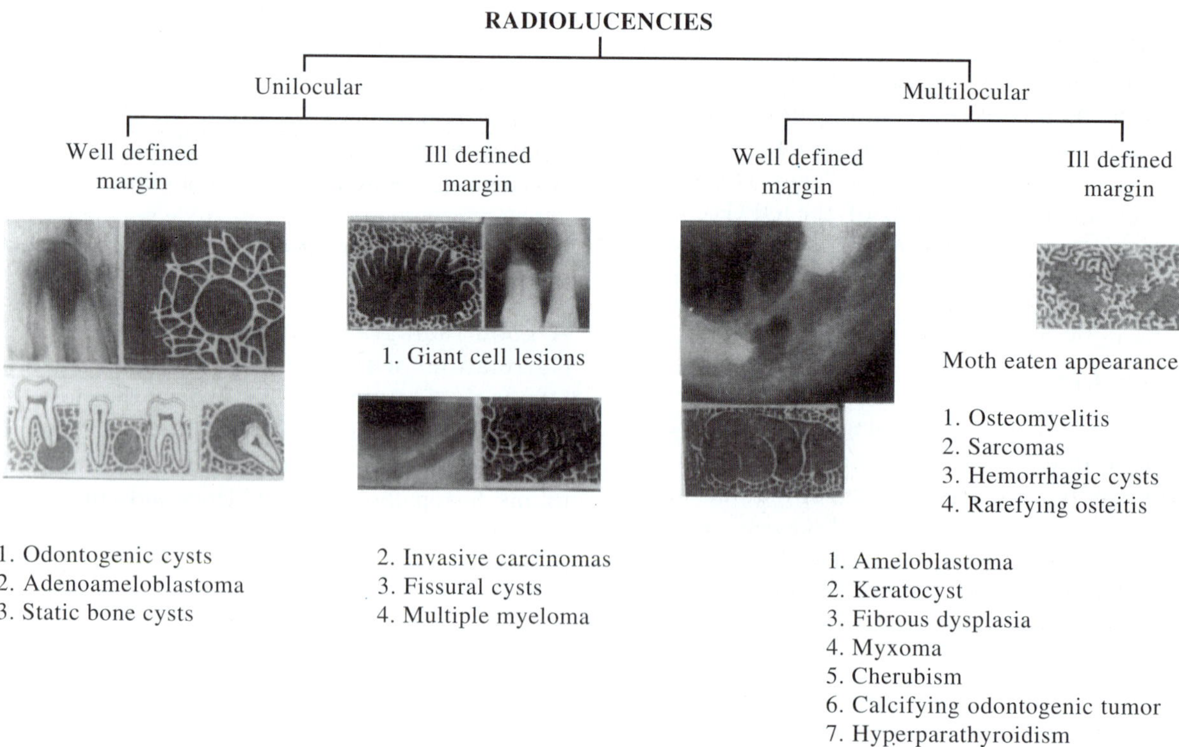

Fig. 3.6 Radiolucencies as seen in different types of lesions.

G. Radioopacities (Fig. 3.7)

(1) Retained tooth root. Shape is regular and the size of radiopacity is similar to that of the root present in the region. Margin is smooth and not continuous with the bony trabeculae. Root canal and periodontal space is identifiable,

(2) Osteosclerosis. Margin is irregular but well defined, continuous with bony trabeculae. The radiodensity is uniform.

(3) Osteoma. Shape is circular with smooth margin but not continuous with bony trabeculae. The narrow radiolucent zone between the lesion and periphery of the surrounding bone indicates the presence of the capsule.

H. Combined radiolucencies and radioopacities

Such an appearance is one of the most difficult lesions for differential diagnosis. Shape is irregular with diffuse margins. Radiolucency may be that of normal bone but increased radioopacities may be trabeculated. The histological appearance may suggest the extension of radioopacity along the cancellous spaces. This appearance may suggest any of the following conditions:

(1) Osteomyelitis
(2) Malignancy
(3) Osteoradionecrosis
(4) Fibroosseous lesions.

Whenever any attempt is made to diagnose the

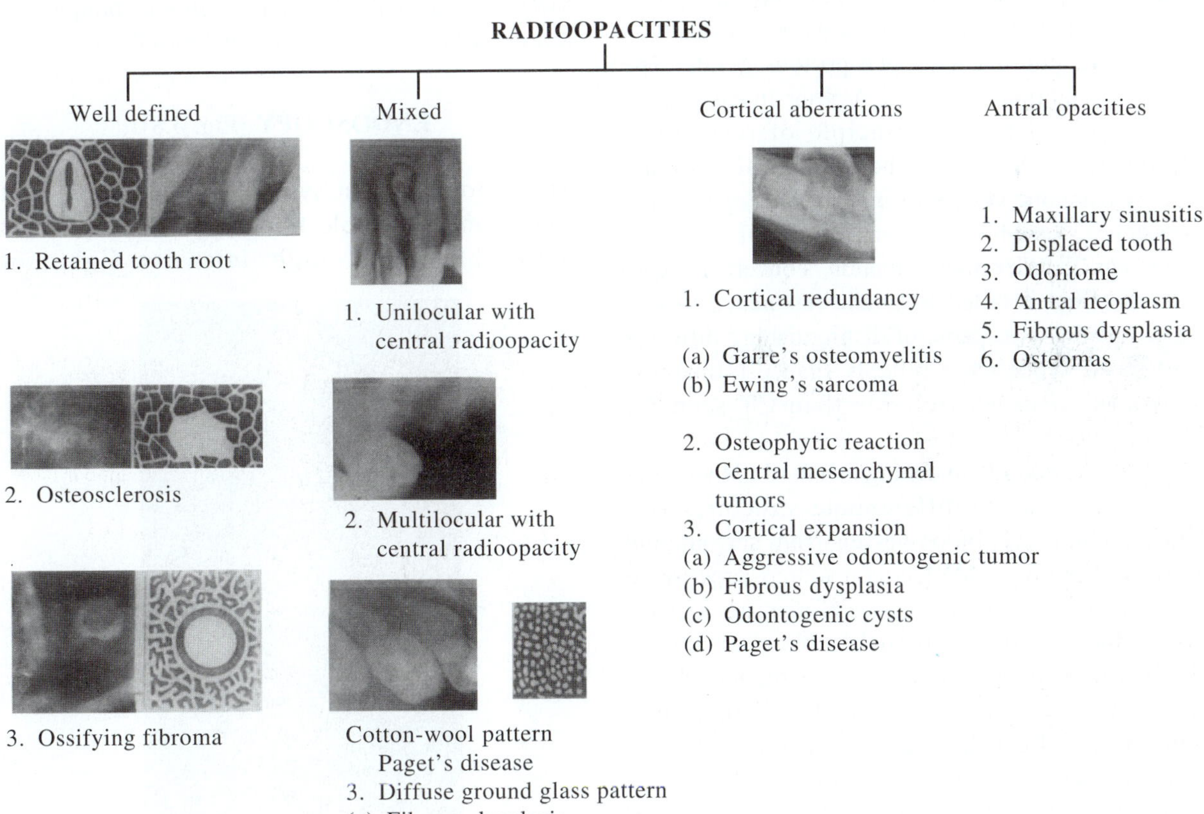

Fig. 3.7 Radioopacities as seen in different types of lesions.

bony lesions radiographically, it is necessary to examine the presence of any alteration in the bone pattern. One should carefully examine, whether

(a) there is any change in the density of the apparently normal bone.
(b) size and shape of the cancellous spaces.
(c) width of the trabeculae.
(d) any localized, symmetrical or diffuse distribution of any change.

I. Magnetic resonance imaging (MRI)

Human body contains nearly 70% of water with hydrogen as the principal component. The abundance of hydrogen and fat of the soft tissue provide an excellent source of hydrogen protons. During magnetic resonance imaging, the strength of the magnetic field affects the frequency or rate with which the spinning hydrogen protons gyrate. The behavior and quantity of the protons in each tissue are measured by the principle of resonance. Resonance is defined as the transfer of vibrating energy from one system to another. During imaging procedure, a sophisticated mathematical operation known as "Fourier transformation" converts the data into the final detailed magnetic resonance image. MRI imaging is capable of distinguishing different soft tissue types more reliably than CT imaging. However, it is less reliable than CT scan for imaging bone.

It has the ability to distinguish hard tissues from soft tissues and to differentiate structures like muscle, fat, nerve, blood vessels from surrounding tissues. Therefore, MRI is considered superior to other imaging techniques. Since X-rays are not used to produce the image, harmful effects associated with ionizing radiation are eliminated. In implantology, exact position of structures like inferior dental canal, mental foramen and floor of the maxillary sinus can be assessed with MRI. This is particularly helpful since MRI is a sectional imaging modality furnishing information about the three-dimensional relationship to these structures. Till date, main use of MRI in dental practice include the investigation of temporomandibular joint, where, features of the capsule, cartilage and the associated musculature can clearly be visualized. It is also helpful to evaluate the region for tumor pathology also.

But, in MRI, bony structures are not well defined because hard tissues contain less water and hence less hydrogen protons than soft tissue. It cannot record the dynamic functions like detection of disc perforations, etc. The biological effects are yet to be well defined as safe. Absolute contraindications include patients with cardiac pacemakers, cerebral aneurysm clips and embedded ferrous metals and pregnancy.

Therefore, it must be clearly understood that MRI is not a routinely used imaging technique and it does not replace the traditional radiology.

ENDOSCOPY (Fig. 3.8)

The fibrooptic light system is used as the light source and a flexible fibrooptic cable transmits narrow beam of high intensity light for

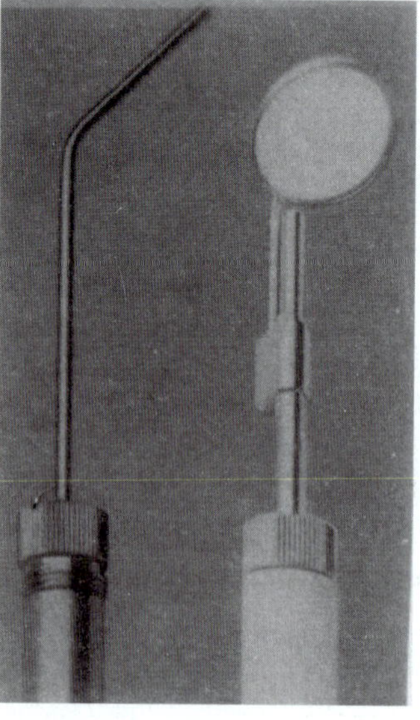

(a) (b)

Fig. 3.8 **(a)** Endoscope, **(b)** Illuminated mouth mirror.

transillumination. To start with, the light source was utilized to illuminate the oral cavity (Fig. 3.8b). This is also useful for many other purposes in the oral and maxillofacial surgery practice. For example, it is used for (a) locating retained roots in the edentulous jaw and displaced root into the maxillary sinus, (b) to view the intraarticular joint space through arthroscopy, (c) to examine the interior of the cystic bony cavities after cystostomy, (d) sinus endoscopy in orbital floor fractures and (e) sialoendoscopy of the submandibular and parotid salivary glands. (Detailed account of all these procedures are described under respective chapters).

ULTRASONOGRAPHY

Ultrasound imaging utilizes the reflection of pulses of higher frequency sound to display soft tissues and to differentiate between the tissue types, namely, soft, solid and cystic. Ultrasound can be used in three modifications:

(a) Doppler sonography
(b) A-Scan sonography
(c) B-Scan sonography.

Out of them, B (brightness) mode sonography has been useful while examining soft tissue of the head and neck region. The main advantages are that it is non-invasive, rapid, painless, inexpensive and easily reproducible, without any known deleterious biological effect. Clinical applications of this technique include examination of thyroid, parathyroid and salivary glands, larger vessels and masses of the neck. For example, it is very useful in the precise location of thyroid nodules for aspiration biopsy. In case of great vessels of the neck, this mode is useful to detect atheromatous plaques, aneurysms, stenosis, thrombosis and neoplasms. In salivary glands, cystic lesions can be differentiated from solid lesions. It has also been useful to detect the fractures of the orbital wall and the associated soft tissue prolapse. The value of the findings vary, depending on the soft tissue lesions and experience of the radiologists. Ultrasonic examination of the lesion can be done in 10 minutes at about the same cost as conventional radiography. The region may be scanned in transverse or longitudinal planes to create images analogous to tomography. Careful interpretations of the results can define the margins and its relations to adjacent structures. However, because this method has its own limitations, it is not one of the main diagnostic aids used in the field of maxillofacial surgery.

The use of digital image processing system in ultrasound diagnosis offers space-saving facility without compromising on quality. An interactive system finding leads to a more complete examination and evaluation, thereby increasing the reliability and objectivity of the examination. By digitizing the sonographic images, the visual data can be processed in a personal computer. Data of the computer assisted design (CAD) system can also be transferred to the CAM system. CAM offers the capability to produce models of the CAD data, leading to a model of the examined region. For example, outer surface of the ramus can be evaluated with the above mentioned CAD-CAM system. Bony structures cannot be penetrated by sonographic waves and therefore, bony surface directed to the scanner can be evaluated. The examination of the soft tissues present information on the total tissue surface examined and hence a "volume model" of the region is possible, thereby making the surgical planning somewhat easier. Thus, in the field of oral and maxillofacial surgery, treatment planning and documentation of the clinical data with 3D sonography is desirable. In spite of the advantages, this modality is not used routinely since it is highly technical and hence becomes an expensive proposition.

Computed technology has increasingly found applications in oral and maxillofacial surgery practice including the application of internet for Telediagnosis. Telecommunication-supported medicine permits the clinicians to investigate and to plan treatment through video-conferencing and electronic information exchange instead of patients being transported to the site of the clinician. The digitized patient information like electronically captured clinical images and other data are transmitted to the clinician thereby saving time, money and transport. Experience has shown that the clinicians could make a differential diagnosis based on the transmitted electronic data.

COMPUTERIZED AXIAL TOMOGRAPHY (CAT Scan)

This method of investigation is particularly valuable to demonstrate the relationship between the soft tissues, non opaque foreign bodies and bone. It is unique since, this is a non-invasive diagnostic technique capable of displaying the details of soft tissue relative to bone and air spaces of the nose and sinuses. Hence, this has given rise to entirely different scope to the diagnostic aspects of the maxillofacial region. But, some limitations exist:

(1) The equipment is expensive to install and to maintain.
(2) Patient's cooperation to keep the head and the body relatively motionless during scanning is essential. Hence, if necessary, sedation or anesthesia may be necessary.
(3) The presence of high density metallic objects within the area of scanning may cause artifacts.

The computerized tomography can be appreciated as a diagnostic method, as the visual display is found to be superior to the conventional radiographs. The radiographic diagnosis has been revolutionized with the introduction of CT scan. It is more sensitive to subtle differences than the conventional radiographs. It is capable of yielding abundant information for diagnosing pathological lesions as to its precise location and extent, so that, the most conservative and yet effective treatment can be rendered. This produces tomographic image which depends on the radioopacity of the tissues. The initial image appears on the screen. If necessary, it can be modified. The required image is then photographed from the TV screen. Plane and thickness of the slice is determined as per the requirement. In the maxilla, axial slices parallel to the occlusal plane at various levels are useful diagnostic aids. At present, three-dimensional reconstructions are possible with three-dimensional CT scans.

Applications

(1) A valuable adjunct in the radiographic examination of pathological lesions. Apart from identification of pathology, it is useful in the reconstruction of three-dimensional image of the lesion which helps in treatment planning. CT scan record regional lymph nodes. The ability to image low contrast structures can help to determine the contents of the pathologic space. It helps to identify perforation of the cortical bone or invasion of the adjacent soft tissues.

(2) Imaging of the paranasal sinuses is very effective. It is helpful to differentiate between fluid levels and soft tissues in the sinuses.

(3) Complex facial fractures are often difficult to image with conventional radiographs. With CT, three-dimensional images can be produced from a single scan. This helps in treatment planning.

(4) CT provides excellent imaging of the T.M. joint. Bony components are clear but imaging of the disc is inadequate (Magnetic resonance imaging is useful).

(5) It is very helpful for the pretreatment assessment of intraosseous implants. At present, CT is an ideal imaging modality of choice for the presurgical assessment of multiple implant sites.

DIGITAL RADIOGRAPHIC IMAGING

This is a new way of diagnostic imaging when compared to film-based imaging. The advantages include (a) less time-consuming and (b) requires lower dose. The features unique to digital imaging are: (a) image processing, (b) image reconstruction and (c) teleradiology.

Image processing makes the information in the image data which is more easily accessible to the naked eye. It defines the margins of the lesion thereby differentiating the lesion from the background.

Image reconstruction is used to produce three dimensional information, which is lacking in the conventional radiographs. The availability of three-dimensional data offers completely new array of possibilities. Both these procedures are different from the traditional film processing.

Teleradiology is an excellent example of the advantages of digital imaging. Electronic image transferred over a phone line or over the internet is faster than the traditional way of sending the radiograph by mail. Therefore, consultation with a colleague is almost instantaneous.

Digital imaging seems to be a promising new technology. Originally, it was used for research purposes and later used in intraoral radiography. Nowadays, extraoral systems are also available. Now, it has opened the door to new diagnostic information, not available with conventional film-based imaging.

The future of digital imaging

Digital technology has many applications in every day life. For example, fax machines, computers, video cameras and digital video discs. It is said that, "those who adopt the technology will have some frustrations because of learning curves and technology growing pains. Those who wait will only fall further behind and miss out on the incredible benefits, the digital imaging can bring."

Stereolithography

This is a method of organ-model production based on computed tomography scans which enables the representation of complex three-dimensional anatomical structures. For example, it is useful for the reconstruction of severe skull and facial bone defects while reconstructing unilateral bony defects, by mirror imaging of the contralateral side. Advantages include representation of complex anatomical structures, high precision, accuracy and the option to sterilize the models for intraoperative use.

COMPARATIVE ACCOUNT OF IMAGING TECHNIQUES

Conventional radiography, CT scan, MRI and other imaging techniques allow us to "look into" the body for diagnosing, monitoring and for guiding the treatment process of the diseases and injuries. They depend on the ability of the tissues to influence energy like X-rays or sound waves differentially so that, we can detect and record the variations to produce an image of the interior of the body. X-rays do not pass through tissues like bone and other hard tissues. Therefore these areas appear white (radio-opaque) in the radiographs. The areas more easily penetrated by the X-rays appear dark (radiolucent). This is the widely used conventional technique. Hallow structures like blood vessels, salivary and urinary systems do not appear distinctly in the radiographs. By introducing a contrast medium which can inhibit the passage of X-rays, these structures can be visualized. Examples of this contrast media technology are :

Angiography (blood vessels), myelography (spinal canal), I.V. Pyelography (urinary tract) sialography (salivary glands), barium meal (upper GI tract) and barium enema (lower GI tract). Multiple radiography within short span of time can lead to exposure of large volume of irradiation. To minimize this risk, techniques have been developed to use lesser amount of radiation to the operators and the patients by using lead shields.

Computed axial tomography (CT or CAT Scan) is a specialized form of radiography. It uses a rotating X-ray source and a computer to produce a series of finely focussed cross section images called Tomograms. Each tomogram is equivalent to a thin slice "cut" through the body. This is superior to conventional radiography techniques in their ability to visualize the soft tissues and become a critical tool for quickly assessing head and neck region.

Magnetic resonance imaging (MRI), like CT, produces a series of cross-section images of any area of the body. MRI, unlike CT, uses strong magnet and radio waves rather than X-rays to produce the images. MRI is considered superior to CT scan since patient is not exposed to X-rays. It produces images of higher contrast and detail. It is more expensive and time-consuming than CT. The patient is made to lie down on the table that moves into a large tube containing a cylindrical magnet. Loud knocking sounds are produced while images are being recorded. Patients who are claustrophobic may find this experience most distressing. These patients will be offered ear plugs to overcome the knocking sound. Recently attempts have been made to develop "open" machines.

Ultrasound imaging is an offshoot of sonar technology used to track submarines. During imaging, inaudible sound waves are bounced off internal structures. The images are produced based on the speed and intensity at which the sound waves return. This is commonly used to assess the heart (echocardiography) and during pregnancy to view the fetus. This is not useful to view the brain and lungs since the sound waves cannot penetrate the bones.

Radionuclide imaging is a nuclear medicine imaging technique. It requires inhalation, ingestion or injection of radioactive chemicals. A special camera is used to produce an image based on the varying degrees to which tissues absorb this radioactivity. These studies go beyond providing an image of structure and motion in their ability to detect metabolic activity. They are very useful to detect bone metastasis, monitoring of brain activity (Position Emission Tomography - PET) and to assess the damage of the heart muscle.

Present trend

This only proves that diagnostic methods have been revolutionized in the recent past with the patients and clinicians looking for more of "non invasive" and more efficient methods instead of the invasive methods wherever possible. For example, ECG may not reveal the changes in the interior of the vessels. Therefore, the "gold standard" of detecting the coronary disease is "angiography", where a cardiac catheter is inserted through the patient's groin and iodine based dye is injected into the coronary vessels. This reveals the road map of obstructions. Since, it is an invasive method, the clinicians and the patients prefer a reliable and non invasive diagnostic tools like CT scan and MRI. CT scan detects even a 20% narrowing (spasm) of the coronary vessel. Similarly, the treadmill test with ECG often gives false negatives. MRI helps to identify the exact location and dimensions of the plaque capable of presenting three-dimensional data. Ultrasound of the heart is no doubt reliable but cannot give early warnings. Hence CT scan and MRI are preferred even though they are more expensive. Early detection of these disorders can be helpful to reverse the changes and lifestyle of the patient.

ICD-DA(WHO)

(International classification of diseases)

"When any substantial volume of data has to be recorded, a coherent system of classifying and coding the data is essential. This becomes more relevent in the light of electronic media being used to retrieve data instead of a manual method. Therefore the Application of the International Classification of Diseases to Dentistry and Stomatology (ICD-DA) is used to provide a practical and convenient basis for the classification and coding of the data by the dental professionals. The principal objectives are: (a) to focus the attention of oral health personnel on detailed diagnosis for each patient using a comprehensive and consistent classification of oral diseases and oral manifestations of other diseases, (b) to provide a standard recording system and (c) to make possible the collection of data that will allow the prevalence of the oral diseases and to compare the data at an international level."

(If anybody wants to learn more about the details of ICD-DA, they are advised to refer to the WHO publications on this aspect).

CHAPTER 4

Basic Principles

ASEPSIS

Strict asepsis is the key word for trouble-free surgical practice. A detailed account on this aspect is given in Chapter 5.

DEVELOPING SURGICAL DIAGNOSIS

Tissues of the body respond to any injury in a predictable manner. Based on this predictability, surgeon has to plan the treatment in such a way that by observing the principles of surgical practice, task of the clinician becomes successful. Therefore, decision to perform surgery should depend on the surgical diagnostic steps. Such analytical approach in the surgical diagnosis becomes the stepping stone to successful surgical practice. The successful surgeon has to be a good *operating physician*.

PREOPERATIVE EVALUATION

The primary step is the presurgical evaluation of the patient. By using the appropriate data of the patient, the clinician develops the surgical diagnosis. Considering the fitness of the patient, the clinician is able to take an appropriate decision as to whether surgery is indicated or not.

TREATMENT PLANNING

Once the appropriate surgical diagnosis is made, the clinician's task is to solve three main problems to achieve success. They are—

HOW (surgical technique),
IF (indications),
WHEN (timing).

Out of this analysis, three definite possibilities of management emerge out. They are: Observation, Conservative treatment and Radical management.

Observation

Certain situations warrant observation of the patient. Performing surgery in such patients may put the clinician into difficulties.

Conservative treatment

A few other situations may necessitate conservative treatment. When not indicated, radical surgery should not be performed. Hasty decisions to perform radical surgery on such situations will only lead to disaster. It is said that a good surgeon is one who knows *"when not to operate"* or to manage conservatively.

Radical management

Surgery, at the appropriate situation will ensure success. Depending on the surgeon's experience and maturity of thought, correct decision has to be taken to perform surgery. Thus, treatment planning is designed to suit the specific oral, systemic and socioeconomic needs of the patient, based on correct preoperative evaluation, anticipated intraoperative and postoperative complications. Sometimes, failure to manage radically will lead to unsuccessful outcome.

BASIC SEQUENTIAL STEPS

The basic sequential steps in oral surgery are as follows:

(a) Preoperative evaluation
(b) Anesthesia
(c) Gaining surgical access
(d) Removal of bone
(e) Wound debridement
(f) Suturing
(g) Postoperative care.

(a) Preoperative evaluation

This is as important as the postoperative follow-up. A medically compromised patient and patients of extremes of age need careful evaluation regarding the health status. Various aspects of evaluation are furnished in Chapter 2.

(b) Anesthesia

Many of the oral surgical procedures are performed under local anesthesia. If the patients were to undergo surgery under general anesthesia, they must be evaluated for fitness to undergo surgery under general anesthesia. However, decision for fitness is usually taken by the anesthetist based on many factors like duration and type of surgery, health status of the patient and possible blood loss during surgery. The preoperative preparation of the patient depends on the type of anesthesia - general or local. Details of anesthesia are furnished in the chapter "Anesthesia and Pain Control".

(c) Gaining surgical access

The dentoalveolar surgical procedures require a mucoperiosteal flap to gain access to the surgical field. The following basic principles are to be followed for a satisfactory flap design:

(1) Incision must be made with a sharp blade. For most of the oral surgery procedures, BP blade No. 15 is used. Only for specific requirements like stab incisions (e.g., incision and drainage of an abscess), BP blade No. 11 is used (Fig. 4.1). A sharp blade cleanly incises the tissues without much of tissue damage. Such incisions heal well without wound dehiscence. Depending on the resistance by the tissue, blades lose the sharpness.

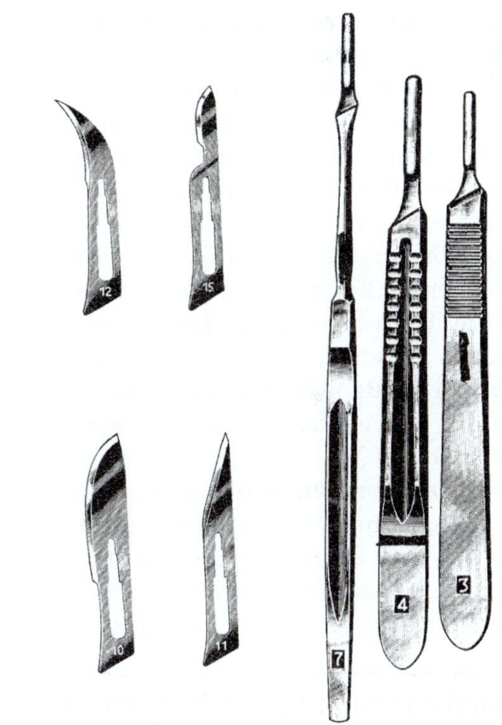

Fig. 4.1 BP blades-no. 12,15,10,11 & BP handles-no. 7,4,3.

(2) The incision must be firm and the stroke must be continuous and deep to the bone. Supraperiosteal incisions and multiple strokes result in tissue damage and troublesome hemorrhage since

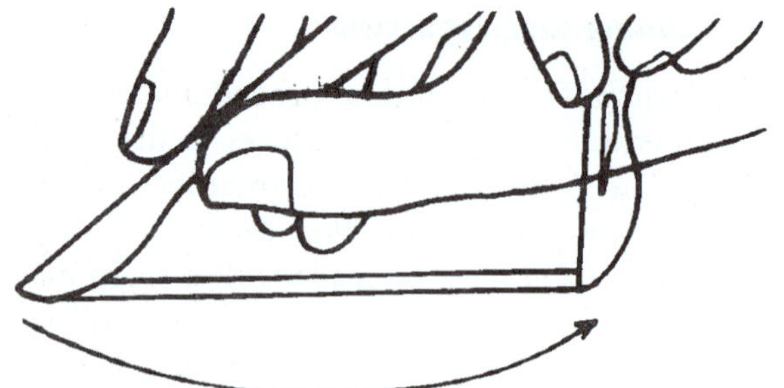

Fig. 4.2 Pen-grasp of the handle during incision.

Fig. 4.4 Semilunar incision must rest on the normal bone. **(a)** Correct, **(b)** Wrong.

the blood vessels are situated supraperiosteally. Incising the periosteum while reflecting the flap protects the supraperiosteal blood vessels. The flap also peels off cleanly. Short and interrupted incisions must be avoided. Pen grasp of the B.P. handle is advocated during incision.(Fig. 4.2).

(3) Incisions must be carefully planned in such a way that vital structures are not damaged. For example, incision placed parallel to the long axis of the vessels will not damage the vessels.

(4) Flap must be designed to provide adequate access to the surgical area. While doing so, base of the flap must be broad enough to ensure good blood supply at the free end of the flap. Unless the base of the flap includes a patent blood vessel, the apex of the flap should be narrower than the base. It is preferable to avoid acute angulation between the incisions (Fig. 4.3).

(5) Length-breadth ratio is an important factor to be borne in mind. It is preferable that length of the flap does not exceed the base (Fig. 4.3).

(6) The incision should always be made at right angle to the epithelial surface. If oblique incisions are made, the flap edges are susceptible to necrosis.

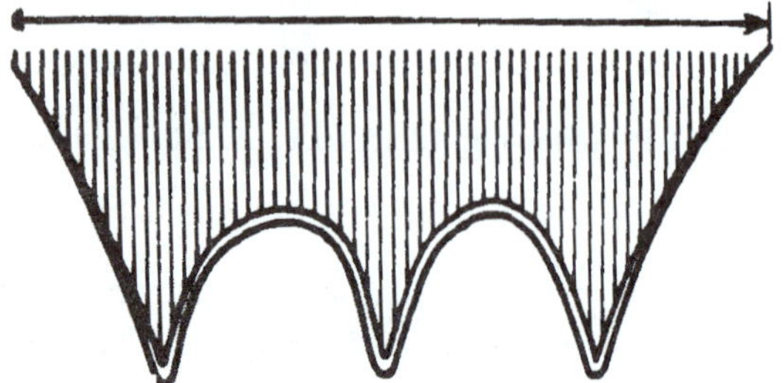

Fig. 4.3 Broad-based flap.

(7) The line of incision is planned in such a way that, after surgery, the line of closure rests on sound bone and not on the hematoma. Failure to do so will result in the wound dehiscence (Fig. 4.4).

(8) Whenever the incision is likely to involve the free gingival margin, adequate care is taken not to disturb the epithelial attachment. The incisions must be modified accordingly. Otherwise, during the wound healing, there is a distinct shift of the epithelial reattachment, exposing the cementum. To avoid this problem, several modifications of incisions have been proposed, to avoid disturbance to epithelial attachment.

(9) When the flap is raised from its bed, care is taken to avoid perforation of the flap. Such a hole will result in flap necrosis, distal to the button hole.

(10) Flap is designed in such a way that there is no tension during the flap retraction.

(11) The vertical limb of the incision should not be extended beyond the vestibular attachment. If it is extended, severance of the buccinator attachment leads to troublesome bleeding, swelling and postoperative hematoma at the vestibular depth that takes more time to resolve.

(12) Inadequate access to the surgical field results in forcible retraction and tearing of the flap. Long incisions take as much time to heal as the short incisions. Hence, the length of the incision depends on the access provided to the surgical field.

(13) Handling of the tissues during the

retraction of the flap is equally important. Gentle handling of the tissues is preferred during retraction with appropriate retractors. Failure to do so will result in tissue laceration, excessive postoperative edema and tissue damage caused by the rotatory instruments during surgery.

(14) Meticulous hemostasis through careful planning and execution during surgery is important. Excessive bleeding disturbs the delicate fluid balance. It also results in poor visibility of the surgical field. Bleeding under the flap may also result in subperiosteal hematoma, which interferes with the healing of the flap.

Intraoral incisions

Many types of incisions have been advocated for elevating an intraoral mucoperiosteal flap. In general, flaps can be grouped under three heads. (a) Random flaps, (b) Pedicled flaps and (c) Free flaps. Random flap indicates that flap is not based on a known blood vessel. Pedicled flap is based on a known blood vessel. Free flap means a flap which is totally severed from the bed so that during surgery, blood supply is newly established. The following are some of the commonly used random flaps.

(i) Envelop flap (Fig. 4.5). Incision along the free gingival margin is made to any desired length depending on the required exposure. Insertion of the periosteal elevator vertically under the interdental papilla facilitates reflection of the buccal or lingual mucoperiosteum. Once the interdental papilla is levered away, it becomes an easy task to elevate the flap. As already pointed out, since blood vessels are situated supraperiosteally, elevation of the flap subperiosteally protects the blood vessels from any damage. The presence of any gingival disease may present problems to establish the plane of cleavage. Since the mucoperiosteal flap contains inelastic periosteum, the flap can be accurately repositioned without any distortion. This is a convenient flap for exposing the alveolar crest prior to dental extraction.

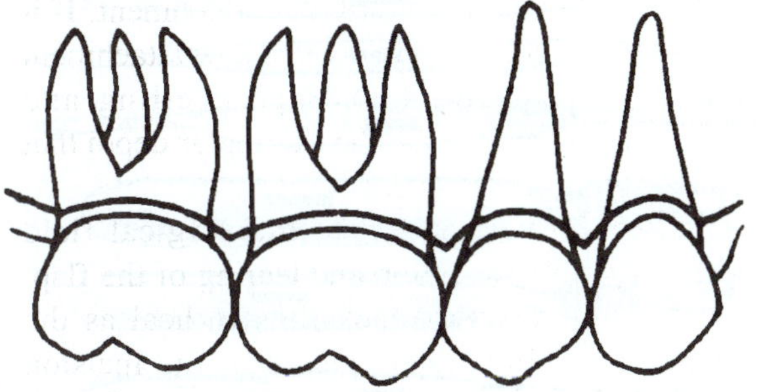

Fig. 4.5 Envelop flap.

(ii) Two-sided triangular flap (Fig. 4.6). If more of vertical exposure is required, the incision has to be extended more horizontally for a satisfactory envelop flap. Instead, a second incision can be added in the vertical direction, starting from one end of the crestal incision towards the buccal sulcus. The vertical limb can be a straight one or divergent towards the vestibular sulcus forming an obtuse angle at the free gingival margin. It can split the interdental papilla or placed on one side of the interdental papilla. Flap is raised in the usual way and held retracted. The two-sided triangular flap is easy to retract without any tension.

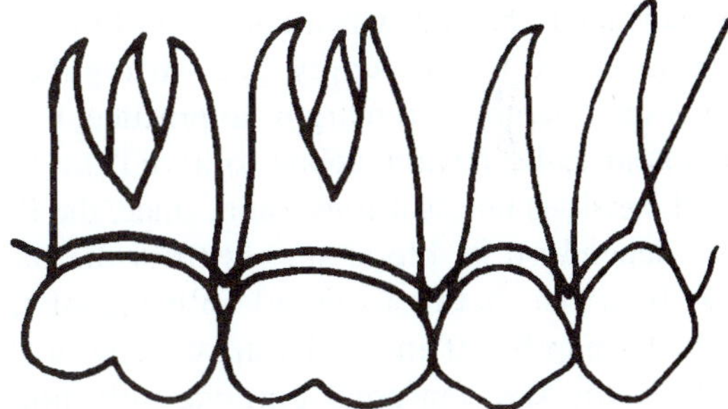

Fig. 4.6 Triangular flap.

(iii) Three-sided rhomboid flap (Fig. 4.7). This is very similar to two-sided flap except the addition of a second vertical incision towards the vestibule, thereby incisions should converge towards the free end of the flap to make the base broader. This also increases the surgical access. In this type of flap design, care is taken to make the base of the flap as broad as possible to ensure adequate blood supply. If the base is narrow or of

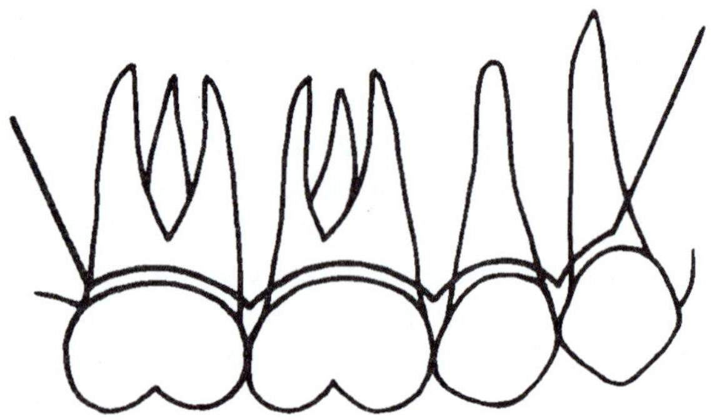

Fig. 4.7 Rhomboid flap.

disproportionate breadth when compared to the tip of the flap, the blood supply gets strangulated towards the free gingival margin. In practice, it has been found to be advantageous to avoid the two vertical incisions unless it is essential since, the flap has to depend on its blood supply from the base alone. It is also better to avoid splitting of the interdental papilla. If the incision is made at the middle of the free marginal gingiva, ugly notch results after healing. If the vertical incision starts mesial to the interdental papilla but within the area of embrasure, the interdental papillae will bear the suture.

Modification: Experience has shown that, whenever the incision involves the epithelial attachment, gingival retraction results during the postoperative healing phase. This leads to exposure of cementum and iatrogenic periodontal disturbances. Hence, it is preferable to plan a flap with the incision 2-3 mm away and parallel to the free gingival margin. Unfortunately, retention of such a strip of gingiva may reduce the surgical access.

When a portion of the unerupted tooth is visible, any epithelial attachment present in the gingival sulcus must be excised by making a reverse bevel incision of appropriate length before raising the flap. BP blade No. 12 is useful for this purpose.

Pedicle flaps: The above-mentioned flaps are examples of "random flaps", not based on a specific blood vessel pedicle. But, if a flap is based on a particular blood vessel, then it is known as pedicle flap. In oral surgery, such a flap is made use of in the palate, taking advantage of the presence of greater palatine vessels. If the flap is designed along the long axis of this blood vessel, the base of the flap will be located around the maxillary third molar. Two incisions are made parallel to the long axis of the vessel and also to the free gingival margin. Anteriorly, depending on the desired length of the flap, both the incisions converge and join with each other. So long as the flap contains the patent blood vessel, length-breadth ratio can be altered. Even if the length of the flap is extended anteriorly, blood supply to the flap is not strangulated. This is technically a far superior flap with high percentage of success.

In *edentulous mouth*, incisions are placed on the alveolar crest where buccal and lingual flaps have united during the healing phase. Relatively, this is an avascular area. Hence, bleeding is less, if incision is made in this area with the vertical incisions remaining the same as in dentulous mouth. For the same reason, incisions are made in the mid-palatine region in the anteroposterior direction. Based on these principles, applications of various intraoral incisions are described in the appropriate chapters.

Reflection of the mucoperiosteal flap (Fig. 4.8). Once incisions are made based on various criteria, the mucoperiosteal flap is raised from the bone by dissecting parallel to the surface. Wherever

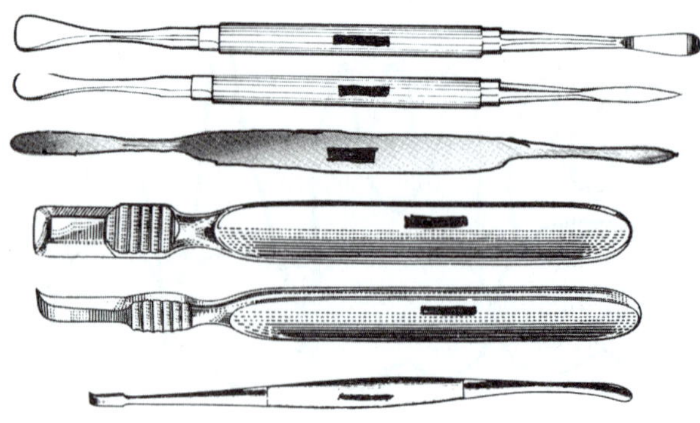

Fig. 4.8 Periosteal elevators.

tissue layers have similar properties, sharp dissection must be carried out. Otherwise, dissection will be difficult. But intraorally, mucoperiosteal flaps are raised subperiosteally, by blunt dissection with a periosteal elevator taking advantage of the well defined plane between the soft tissue (periosteum) and hard tissue (bone). Care must be taken to identify the difference in the periosteal attachment. For example, the interdental papilla is attached firmly to the alveolar crest of the interdental septum.

(1) When the flap is reflected, care should be taken not to damage important anatomical structures like infraorbital and mental neurovascular bundles, present inside their conical sleeve of periosteum around the respective foramina. Particularly, in atrophic mandible, mental foramen is vulnerable for damage because of its presence close to the alveolar crest.

(2) Muscular attachments require special attention during the flap reflection. For example, (a) anterior to and below the mental foramen, attachments of depressor labii muscle depressor anguli oris and platysma and (b) mentalis around the mental eminence will have to be detached. But, attachment of buccinator is easily disrupted and this should be avoided unless, additional access is required. If the incision disrupts the buccinator, troublesome bleeding and edema will result.

(3) The surgical access to the inner aspect of the mandible is made difficult because of the shape of the mandible. The difficulty is increased by the stronger muscle attachments. Mylohyoid attachment extends from third molar region to the midline. It is difficult to separate the muscle from the bone since, muscle slopes downwards and hence periosteal elevator may perforate the periosteum. If the muscle is not detached carefully, damage to the mylohyoid nerve may lead to cutaneous anesthesia around the chin. Similarly, elevation of the lingual mucoperiosteum near the third molar carries the risk of injury to the lingual nerve.

(4) When the flap is raised in the vestibule at the anterior aspect of the maxilla, perforation into the nasal cavity is possible. At the anterolateral aspect, care must be taken to preserve the infraorbital nerve. Still posteriorly, it is better to avoid damage to the posterior superior alveolar (dental) vessel so that, brisk bleeding can be avoided.

(5) Elevation of the mucoperiosteal flap in the palate needs careful consideration. Mucosa is tightly attached to the mid-palatine suture. The incision placed in the palate across the greater palatine vessel results in brisk bleeding. It may be difficult to arrest this hemorrhage by routine methods.

In general, oral cavity has abundant blood supply. Hence, flaps in the oral cavity can be

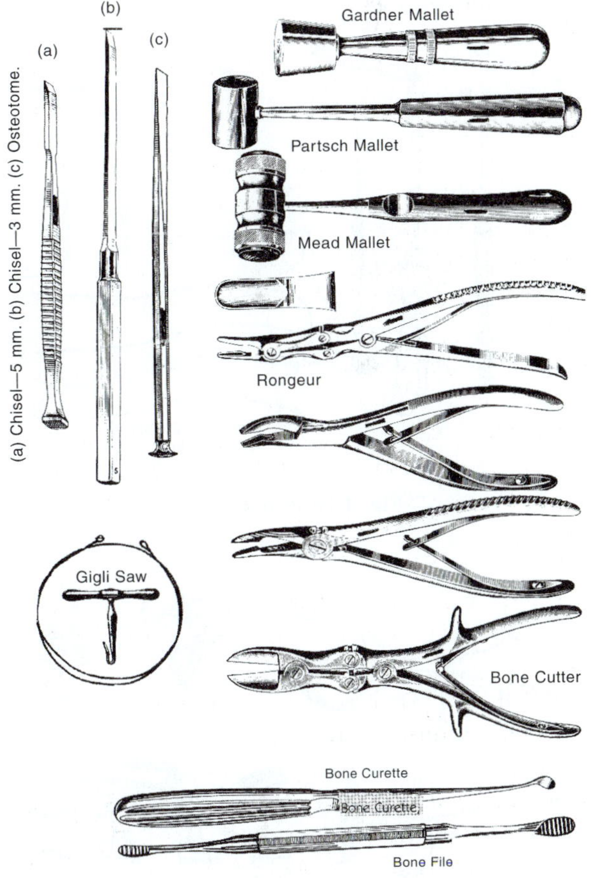

Fig. 4.9 Bone instruments.

mobilized more extensively than in any other part of the body. However, the longer the flap, the lesser is the blood supply for the terminal part of the flap (except in pedicle flaps).

(d) Removal of bone (Fig. 4.9 to 4.11)

This may be necessary either to gain access to the surgical field or to correct an existing bony defect. The extent of bone removal must be considered even before placing the incision so that, the suture line will rest on the sound bone and not over the hematoma. Hence, it is preferable to place the incision at least 5-6 mm away from the anticipated bony margin. In oral surgery, removal of bone is achieved with the following instruments or any combination of them:

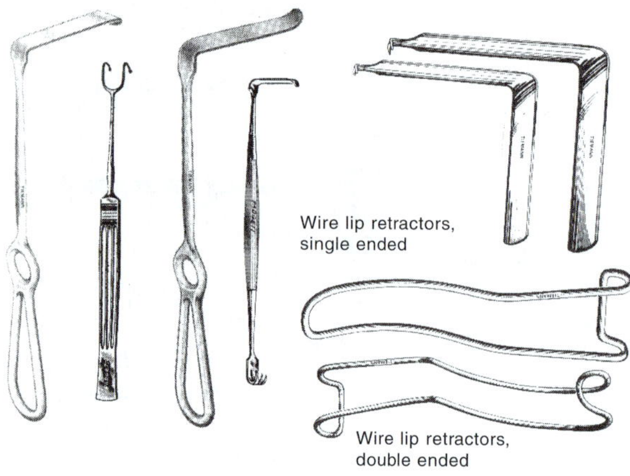

Fig. 4.10 Retractors.

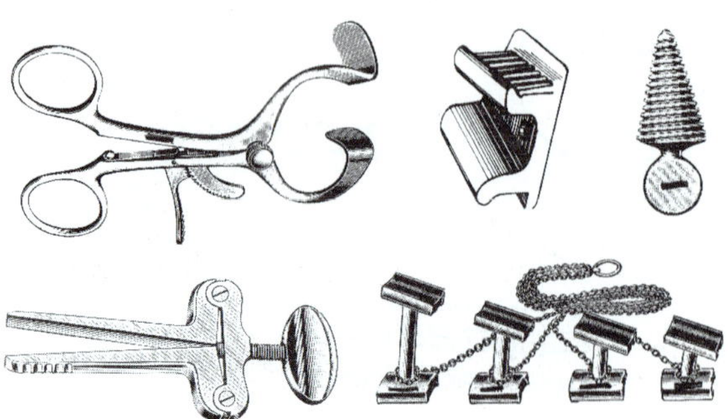

Fig. 4.11 Mouth gag and props.

(1) Chisel, osteotome, and mallet
(2) Rotatory instrument, e.g. surgical bur
(3) Clipping of bone with bone rongeurs
(4) Bone file
(5) Bone curette
(6) Gigli saw.

(1) *Chisel* and similar instruments along with a mallet are very convenient to remove the bone. Chisel cuts the bone efficiently, provided it is used properly. Chisel is a monobevelled instrument while, osteotome is bibevelled. Although, it is popularly used by the dental practitioners, conscious patients under local anesthesia do not prefer this instrument because of the metallic noise during malleting. In mandibular osteotomies, the jaw bone has to be stabilized by placing a mouth prop in the opposite side. The osteotome is useful to split the tooth in the "tooth division" technique.

(2) Rotatory instrument (*surgical bur*) (Figs 4.12 and 4.13). Dental engine in some form is

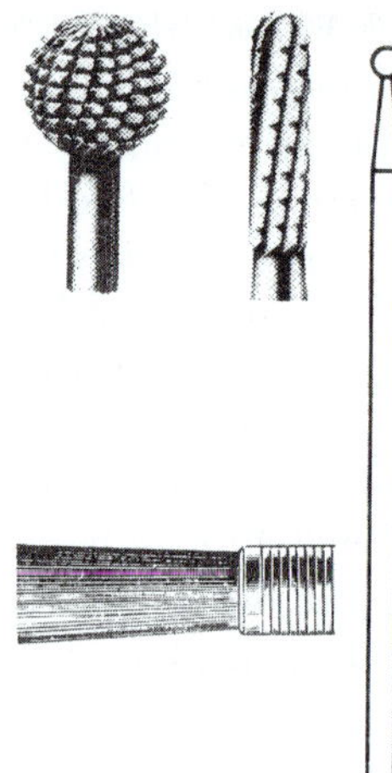

Fig. 4.12 Surgical burs and wire brush.

Fig. 4.13 Suction tip.

readily available with every dental practitioner. Perhaps, dental practitioners feel "at home" with bur than with any other instrument. Bur is used either to remove the bone or to cut a window. It is also useful to divide the tooth. When bur is used, proper retraction of the surrounding tissues is very essential to avoid injury. Bone cutting must be carried out with copious irrigation of saline to avoid thermal necrosis of bone. Efficient suction is necessary to keep the operating field clear. The conventional dental bur is not suitable since, blood clot tends to accumulate around the bur. The bur that is used for cutting bone should not allow clogging of blood clot. Even with a coolant, the speed of the rotatory equipment should be carefully monitored so that high speed drill is avoided. The pneumatic drills must be carefully used so that, forceful entry of air into the tissue spaces and the consequent emphysema is prevented. Under local anesthesia, rotatory instruments are acceptable to the patients.

(3) For clipping of bone, bone *roengeurs* are useful where sharp and irregular margins are to be eliminated. Finally, the surface of the bone can be smoothened with bone file.

(4) *Bone file*. Once adequate bone is removed, the specific surgery like removal of the unerupted tooth, cyst enucleation, etc. are performed. Then sharp edges of the bone is smoothened with bone file.

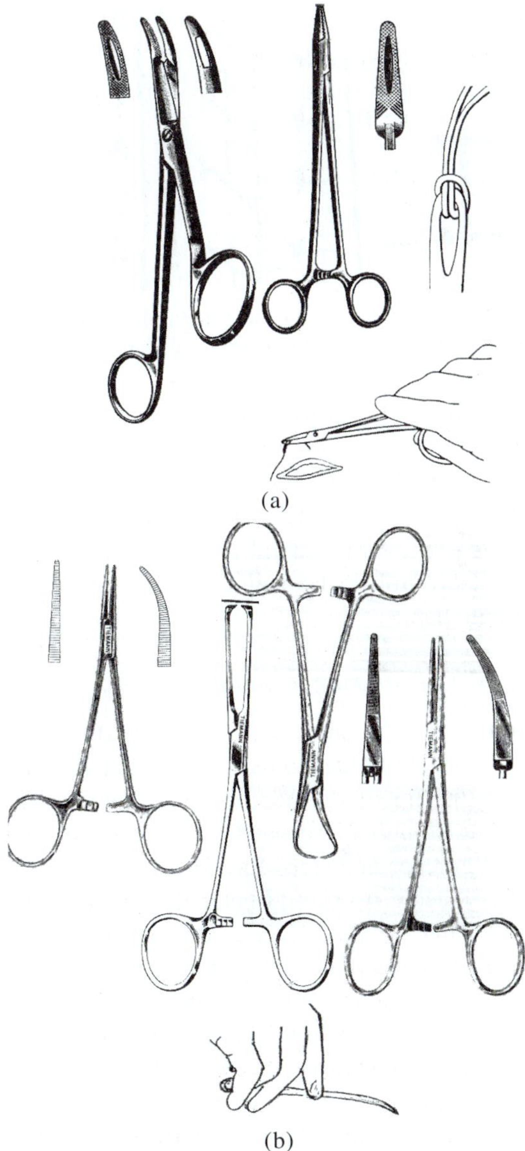

Fig. 4.14 (a) Needle holders, **(b)** Hemostats.

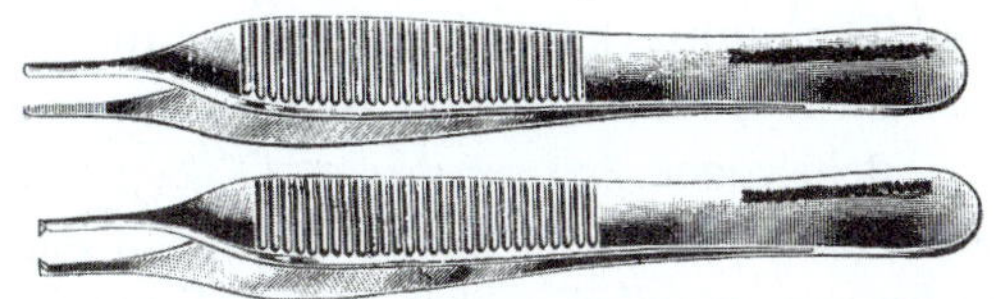

Fig. 4.15 Tissue forceps.

(e) Wound debridement

Before suturing the flap, the wound must be irrigated with saline so that no bone particles and foreign bodies remain in the surgical wound. If any area continues to bleed, hemostasis must be achieved before suturing the flap. Otherwise, accumulation of blood in the dead-space becomes a nidus for bacteria to grow. If the infection develops, it will delay the wound healing.

(f) Suturing (Figs 4.14, 4.15)

After the debridement of the surgical field and hemostasis, the flap is repositioned and held in

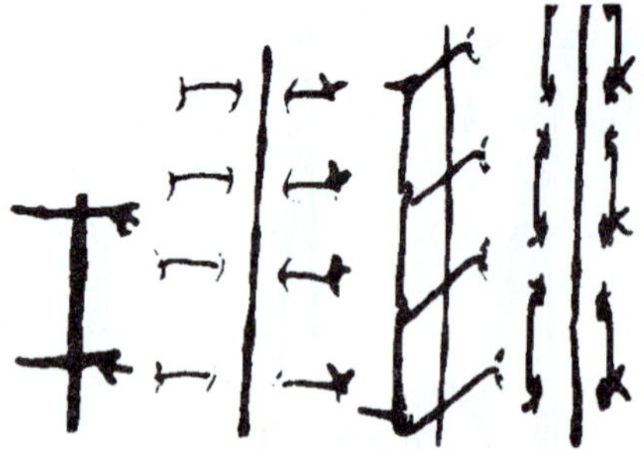

Fig. 4.16 Types of suturing. **(a)** Interrupted, **(b)** Vertical mattress, **(c)** Continuous, **(d)** Horizontal mattress.

contact with the adjoining wound margins by suturing so that wound heals by first intention. Suturing usually arrests oozing from the bed and wound margins. Care is taken not to suture the wound under tension. As a general rule, first bite is taken in the free mobile flap and sutured with fixed immobile flap.

Principles of suturing techniques

(i) Suture needle must be grasped with the needle holder, three-fourths distance from the tip of the needle. One must learn to distinguish the needle holder from artery forceps and sinus forceps.
(ii) Needle tip should enter the tissue at right angle to the surface of the tissue.
(iii) It should pass through the tissue depending on the shape of the needle.
(iv) Sutures should be placed 2-3 mm from the free margin of the wound and at equal depths.
(v) Sutures must be placed from thin to the thick tissue and mobile to the fixed tissue. If both are mobile, then it is left to the convenience of the operator.
(vi) The suture knot must rest on the bone, away from the wound, to avoid the wound dehiscence.

Instrumentation. A needle holder, a pair of tissue forceps, needles, suture material and a pair of scissors are required for the suturing procedures. It is left to the operator's choice regarding the selection of the type of the needle and the type of suture material, based on many criterias.

(1) "Eyed" needle with suture material of appropriate length is usually used in daily practice. Economically, it is less expensive. With usage, needle tip becomes blunt. If the needle and the suture material are not sterilized properly before use, it becomes a source of infection. Moreover, by repeated boiling, needle and the suture material get work-hardened and lose the strength. Needle breakage and repeated snapping of the suture material may interfere with suturing.

(2) Suture materials are classified as "resorbable" and "nonresorbable". The examples of non resorbable sutures are silk and synthetic materials like nylon, mersilene and prolene. Resorbable materials include cat gut (plain and chromic) and synthetic materials like Vicryl, Dexon. Monofilament material contains single strand. The term polyfilament suture is self explanatory. They are made up of multiple fibres - either braided or twisted.

With recent advances in surgical techniques and armamentarium, "atraumatic" sutures are frequently used. It may be expensive but the patient and surgeon derive many advantages by using the presterilized atraumatic suture materials. They are as follows:

(a) The needle is eyeless. Hence, the eye of the needle cannot traumatize the tissues. The cross-section of the needle, eye of the needle, and the suture material are the same and standardized. In the conventional needles with eye, the cross-section of all of them vary. If the eye of the needle is large, then the diameter at this place becomes considerably large because of the double fold of the suture material. Hence, when the needle tip pierces the wound, the opening is small at the time of entry. But, as the needle is drawn further, opening is enlarged considerably, when the eye of the needle passes through. Thus, tissues are traumatized, so that, it interferes with healing. That is why atraumatic materials are preferred.

(b) The suture material is presterilized by gamma radiation and hence sterilization is standardized. This reduces the chances of infection.

(c) Wound healing is good with a less conspicuous scar.

(d) Since, it is not subjected to repeated boiling, the question of needle breakage or snapping of the suture material does not arise.

For most of the intraoral suturing of mucoperiosteal flaps, cutting needles are used. They are flattened on the sides, so that near the tip of the needle, cross section is triangular. Hence, it helps in penetrating the tough issues. A portion of the needle shank is flattened to facilitate firm gripping by the needle holder. If this is absent, the needle rotates during its use.

Suturing within the oral cavity with restricted access can best be done by using a curved needle. Curved needle is well suited for efficient manipulation. The suture materials may be commercially available for ready use. In modern practice, suture materials made of synthetic polymers like polyglyconate and polyglactin on atraumatic needles are best used, since, these materials are less irritant to the tissues. They also possess higher tensile strength and their absorption is delayed. However, for economic reasons, black silk is still being used by many. The size of the suture material is with reference to its diameter. The smallest size that will provide the desired wound tension must be chosen. The higher the number, the smaller the suture. Likewise, the larger the diameter, the stronger the suture. In other words, 2-0 is thicker and stronger than 3-0. For intraoral purposes, 2-0 or 3-0 suture materials are mostly used depending on the region and use.

Needle holders resemble artery forceps, but it is characterized by the presence of short and stout beaks with serrated surfaces to prevent the needle from slipping during the usage. However, the handles are sufficiently long. Ideally, the needle is held clamped by the beaks of the needle holder of a position, nearly two-thirds of the distance from the tip of the needle. While the needle is passed through the tissues, the flap is gripped with a pair of forceps, with the free margin of the flap held everted. The needle should enter the tissues at right angle to the surface. The bite is always taken through the movable flap first so that, flap is adjusted towards the free end of the stationary flap. The point of entry of the needle should not be too close to the free margin to ensure that the suture does not cut through when the knot is tightened. After completing the knot, free ends of the suture materials are cut with scissors.

There are many types of *suturing techniques* available to the surgeon. Each method has advantages and disadvantages. Depending on the indications, the type of suturing is chosen to derive the maximum benefit. The frequently used types of suturing in oral surgery are as follows:

(1) Interrupted sutures
(2) Mattress sutures - horizontal and vertical types
(3) Continuous sutures.

In the oral cavity, one side of the wound constitutes the flap, which is elevated to gain access. The other side remains stationary, attached to the bone. To facilitate easy suturing, the edges of the fixed margin should also be raised for a sufficient distance. Suturing from the mobile to the fixed flap enables proper repositioning of the reflected flap. At the same time, for the sake of convenience, first bite is taken from the farther flap to the nearer flap.

Factors that determine the type of suture are:

(1) Type of the tissue
(2) Condition of the wound
(3) Healing process
(4) Anticipated postoperative course.

Different types of *suturing techniques* have been described depending on the differences in the points of entry and exit of the needle.

(1) **Interrupted sutures.** This is the most common method. Each suture is independent,

offering strength and flexibility in placement. The integrity of the suture remains intact even if one suture is disturbed or lost. Only disadvantage is the time required when compared to the other techniques. Needle enters the mucous membrane from the external to the tissue surface of the mobile flap. Then needle passes from the tissue surface through the fixed flap and comes out on the surface. Hence *both the points of entry and exit are on the outer surfaces of the flaps* respectively. Care is taken to ensure that both these points are equidistant from the free margins of the flaps. Unequal distribution should be avoided. Now, both the ends of the suture materials are tied either by hand or with instruments. Usually tying with hand results in wastage of suture materials when compared to tying with needle holder. At the time of tightening the knot, wound margins must be everted. If the knot is too tight, it will cut through the tissues resulting in ugly scar. Hence, tension must be distributed equally. The suture material is adjusted in such a way that the knots lie over the needle puncture point in any one side of the wound and not on the suture line. The suturing is done at regular intervals. The interrupted simple loop suturing continues to be the most common type of suture technique in oral surgery practice.

(2) **Mattress sutures.** This may be horizontal or vertical type. In this type, the *points of entry and exit are located in the same flap*. Point of entry is similar to the interrupted suture. The needle passes through the mobile flap and then through the fixed flap. Instead of placing a knot, the needle is passed in the reverse direction from the fixed flap through the mobile flap so that ultimately needle returns back near the point of first entry. In horizontal mattress type, point of entry and point of exit are situated equidistant from the free margins of the mobile flap. That means wider areas of the flap are sutured. In the vertical mattress suture, point of entry is situated away from the wound margin deep into the tissues while the point of exit is near the wound margin. Both these points are one above the other. Both the types are used wherever the wound margins are under tension. By avoiding the free margin of the flap, chance of the suture cutting through the flap is reduced.

(3) **Continuous sutures.** This is used to suture a wide area. The main advantages are: (a) ease and conserving the time of suturing, (b) distribution of tension over the entire suture line and (c) provision of watertight closure of the wound. It is less commonly practiced. This is very similar to interrupted sutures. But, instead of tying the knot, the needle is passed again through the mobile flap and the process is continued until the entire wound is sutured. The knot is placed at the end only. If the wound gives way in any one place, it disrupts the entire wound. To avoid this problem a few interrupted sutures are placed for reinforcement. This method also leaves an ugly scar.

(f) Postoperative care

(1) **Edema control.** Postoperative edema develops due to so many factors. They are: (a) too tight suturing, (b) suturing under tension, (c) dead space not obliterated, (d) rotatory instruments used without sufficient coolant, (e) forceful retraction during surgery and (f) surgical trauma. It is self-explanatory that edema can be minimized with the careful attention on all these factors. However, postoperative edema is inevitable. It can be minimized by advising the patient to have intermittent cold ice-packs on the external area of surgery at least for 1 or 2 days. Antiinflammatory drugs are also useful to reduce the edema.

(2) **Infection control.** Sterilization of instruments and adoption of strict aseptic techniques go a long way in establishing the control of infection. Preoperatively, attention to oral hygiene and application of antiseptics like chlorhexidine over the surgical fields will help in keeping the infection under control. Prophylactic or therapeutic antibiotic therapy is also helpful in this direction.

(3) **Nutrition.** Following oral surgery, oral feeding may be a problem. Hence, the patient may

have to be on liquid or semi-solid diet and should be told to have cold or warm but not hot diet. On the day of surgery, gentle mouth rinsing is permitted with restricted oral fluids. The routine oral hygiene measures are resumed only from the next day. Following major oral surgical procedures, the patient may have intravenous fluids and diet feeding is carried out through Ryle's tube. During the immediate postoperative period, patient is advised to have high protein, high calorie diet with adequate vitamins.

(4) **Suture removal.** Usually the wound margins are cleaned with antiseptics. The sutures are removed between fifth and seventh postoperative day. The knot is held by the forceps and lifted up. One of the sutures is cut off, close to the tissue, and the knot is pulled in such a way that the wound margins are brought nearer to each other. If the suture is pulled in the opposite direction, the wound will be gaped. If the suture is cut midway, the contaminated external loop is pulled through the wound that predisposes to wound infection.

Asepsis and Infection Control

GENERAL CONSIDERATIONS

The dental and paradental professionals are constantly exposed to a variety of microorganisms in blood and saliva of the patients. There is potential danger of these microorganisms causing infections like hepatitis-B, AIDS, tuberculosis, upper respiratory infections and many others. Hence, there is a need for protecting the patients and health professionals themselves from the hazards in the routine practice. Accidental inoculation of the infected materials must be prevented or at least minimized.

During oral surgery, the epithelial barrier that protects the underlying tissues is broken. Thus, the tissues of the patient become vulnerable to the microbes from the external environment. If the operators' hands and instruments carry infected material, microorganisms are liable to be deposited into the tissues. Therefore, instruments and the surgical environment must be free from microorganisms.

Asepsis is defined as the prevention of infection by eliminating pathogenic and vegetative microorganisms. *Sepsis* means breakdown of the living tissues accompanied by infection and inflammation. Antiseptics and disinfectants are the substances that prevent the multiplication of the microorganisms which are capable of producing sepsis. *Antiseptics* are substances which are applied to the living tissues. The term *"disinfectant"* is restricted to the substances applied on inanimate objects. The term *"sterility"* refers to the condition which is totally free from any viable micro-organisms. Therefore, it represents an absolute state. The question of degree of sterility in relative sense, therefore, does not arise. The ability of hepatitis-B virus to survive in the environment for many days at room temperature causes great concern to the clinician.

IMPORTANT FACTORS

Any discussion on asepsis and infection control can never be complete without identifying the following factors:

(a) Critical areas in relative terms - critical, semi-critical, and non-critical.
(b) Infective conditions of importance and their modes of cross-infection.
(c) Effective measures of infection control.
(d) Problems encountered in asepsis and infection control.

(a) Critical areas

As a rule, any instrument that penetrates the epithelial barrier should be sterilized. While instruments can be sterilized, many practical difficulties arise in sterilizing other than surgical environmental factors. Hence, to make the process of infection control feasible and meaningful, the items involving the surgical sepsis can be divided into three categories:

(i) **Critical:** This category includes all the items which may transmit the infected material into the blood stream and sterile areas of the tissues, e.g. all surgical instruments, implants, injection and suture needles, suture materials, handpieces, cutting areas of burs and blades. Absolute sterilization is necessary for these items involving destruction of microorganisms and spores.

(ii) **Semi-critical:** The items which are to be grouped under this category come in contact with the epithelial surface but not penetrating the epithelial barrier, e.g. endotracheal tubes, laryngoscopes and other fibre-optic-scopes, mouth mirror etc. which are not used in the surgical field. This group needs higher level of sterilization or disinfection since they may transmit microorganisms if there is any break in continuity of the epithelial surface. Hence, no chance is to be taken regarding the destruction of pathogenic and vegetative organisms.

(iii) **Non-critical:** Normally, items included under this category do not come in contact with the surgical field directly. Indirectly, these items can play an important role in cross infection. For example, pollution of the operating environment including equipment, light, etc. can lead to the accumulation of the microorganisms and contribute to the transmission of the infected material. Hence, such potentially contaminated areas require periodic attention for disinfection.

(b) Infective conditions

Mere presence of the microorganisms in the surgical field does not constitute sepsis. The manifestation of specific infections depends on the tissue reactions of the defense mechanisms of the host. Since all these factors are variable from time to time, it is the clinician's duty to keep the source of the infective process (microorganisms) under control. In spite of various preventive measures, sepsis develops. Attention will be focused on a few clinical conditions which cause great concern to the surgeons and the patients alike, in spite of routine aseptic precautions.

(1) Hepatitis-B
(2) AIDS (acquired immune deficiency syndrome).

Hepatitis (serum hepatitis)

Hepatitis-A causes infective hepatitis characterized by jaundice. Hepatitis-B causes serum hepatitis which is not characterized by jaundice. Since it is asymptomatic, many patients and members of the health profession continue to be the carriers. This constitutes a major, worldwide health problem. These carriers are potentially susceptible to dangerous consequences of viruses involving liver. Pathological consequences are not predictable due to its polymorphic nature. The defined population-at-risk are health professionals, transfused and dialyzed patients and drug addicts. A needle prick is enough to transmit the hepatitis-B virus. The mode of transmission may vary considerably. In many instances, persons who are positive carriers have become infected without any history of hepatitis and unable to recall any etiological episode. Therefore, the person is not only infected, but not aware of such infection. Such a person becomes a dangerous source of HBV transmission to other patients and health personnel. The professional consequences may be disastrous. The transmission of HBV is predominantly through contact with contaminated blood, blood products and saliva. Among the dental professionals, oral surgeons are especially at risk. It is now an established fact that HBV can be traced in biological cells. The carrier- state may persist throughout life. Such carriers are described to be "Australian antigen positive."

The clinical picture is extremely variable, ranging from asymptomatic (without jaundice) to a fulminating fatal disease. Hepatitis-B virus is not cytopathic. It is considered to be an attempt to eliminate infected liver cells by the immune system. This leads to the clinical symptoms.

Acute viral hepatitis is a systemic infectious disease, predominantly affecting the liver, resulting in hepatic cell necrosis and inflammation. The incubation period ranges from 40 to 180 days. The clinical picture consists of a prejaundice prodromal period followed by jaundice and ultimately resolution. The prodromal periods extend from 3 to 7 days. Such a patient suddenly develops fatigue, severe anorexia, nausea, vomiting, gastrointestinal disturbances, low grade pyrexia and headache. With the onset of the jaundice phase, prodromal symptoms gradually disappear. Extrahepatic manifestations like lymphadenopathy and splenomegaly may be present. Full clinical recovery may take 3 to 6 months. Relapse may occur during the convalescent period. It is said that, post hepatic syndrome usually affects intelligent patients. In a few patients, several episodes of remission and relapse develop alternatively.

Chronic infection leads to chronic hepatitis. Two types of chronic forms have been identified.

(1) Chronic persistent hepatitis as a benign form.
(2) Chronic active hepatitis as a regressive and destructive liver disease.

Recently, indirect but remarkable evidences linking HBV and liver cancer are available. Hence, evidence of an association between the carrier state of hepatitis-B virus infection and hepatocellular carcinoma is now sufficiently strong to justify immunization against this infection as a preventive measure.

Prevention: All efforts must be directed towards the preventive aspects of this disastrous condition.

(1) Higher level of hygiene and sanitation of the surgical environment is of great importance.

(2) Utilization of sensitive methods to detect the presence of HBsAg in blood is an indispensable tool to identify the carrier state of the person and the incidence of the disease in a given population.

(3) As a measure of precaution, all the dental students and dental professionals must be immunized against this condition. Prevention is better than an attempt to cure. Since there is no cure, immunogenic and protective hepatitis-B vaccine seems to be the effective method against this dreaded disease.

(4) Once the carrier status is identified in any person, appropriate measures must be taken to eliminate the carrier state by utilizing hepatitis-B immunoglobulin. Care must be taken to treat the patients who are known to be "Australian antigen positive".

(5) As a precautionary measure for the future, HBV blood stains must be destroyed by any known method like application of sodium hypochlorite solution or any other viricidal agent.

Acquired immune deficiency syndrome (AIDS)

Literature is becoming voluminous day by day regarding AIDS and its sequelae. Hence all the dental professionals and well informed patients are increasingly aware and concerned about this condition. An outline about this condition, the possibilities of the cross infection of the dental staff and patients and the precautions to be taken are furnished here.

AIDS is an infectious disease of the immune system. This is considered to be the final stage of the chronic, progressive disease, believed to be caused by AIDS virus known as human immunodeficiency virus (HIV). The envelope of HIV is made of lipids of the host cell membrane, proteins and glycoproteins, specific to HIV. Inside the envelope, nucleocapsid contains single stranded RNA molecule. AIDS virus is found in all the body fluids like blood, saliva, tear, urine etc.

Pathogenesis: AIDS virus (HIV) first enters the blood stream. Then, it attaches to the receptor on a cell surface of T_4 lymphocyte. The virus loses its envelope and enters the cell, thereby exposing the RNA core. After a variable period, new viruses are produced from T_4 cell surface and are released from the cell membrane into the blood stream. T_4 lymphocyte eventually dies.

Modes of transmission:

(1) Sexual transmission
(2) Through blood and blood products
(3) Perinatal transmission
(4) Nonsexual or noninfected contact with infected, dried or moist body fluids.

Clinical spectrum of the disease: Unfortunately, natural immunity is very rare. Hence, the disease progress leads to severe destruction of the immune system. The human infection by HIV leads to depletion of T_4 lymphocyte population and immunoglobulin concentration. The clinical features, therefore, exhibit an initial mononucleosis-like syndrome. Subsequently, other symptoms also appear. They are as follows:

(1) Lymphadenopathy is chronic and unexplained.
(2) Mucous membrane disease includes oral candidosis and oral leukoplakia.
(3) Hematological abnormalities are idiopathic thrombocytopenia and leucopenia.
(4) Recurrent, non healing dermatological lesions like herpes simplex and herpes zoster.
(5) Systemic features may be associated with AIDS e.g. Kaposi's sarcoma, Burkitt's lymphoma, Hodgkin's disease and leukemia.

Prevention and infection control. Several measures have been recommended to reduce the spread of AIDS virus from one person to the other.

(1) Proper medical history should be elicited from all the dental patients regarding their medications, recurrent illnesses, hepatitis, unintentional weight loss, lymphadenopathy and the presence of oral mucous membrane lesions.
(2) Gloves must be worn for the protection of the patients and professional personnel from coming in contact with blood, saliva, body fluids and secretions.
(3) Surgical masks and protective eye wear to avoid splashing of blood and body fluids.
(4) Disposable gowns, masks and coverings and their proper disposal after use.
(5) Hand washing with antibacterial and antiviral disinfectant soap is highly recommended.
(6) Very high level of sterilization of instruments by high pressure autoclaving is advocated.
(7) Decontamination of environment surfaces.

The development of an effective infection control programme is absolutely essential to prevent the spread of AIDS virus (HIV) from patient to patient, with or without the involvement of the intermediary health professionals. Failure to realize the importance of all these aspects will lead the professional to pay a very heavy prize for ones own negligence and ignorance. At present, there is no effective vaccine or drugs to treat this condition. Blood transfusion possess a substantial risk of HIV infection.

(c) Effective measures in infection control

Infection control has been found to be a "multi-faceted" discipline involving many factors, viz:

(1) Concept of asepsis and infection control.
(2) Personal protection through vaccines, masks, gloves, etc.
(3) Decontamination of used instruments.
(4) Sterilization of instruments.
(5) Asepsis of the operating environment.
(6) Surface disinfection.
(7) Aseptic surgical techniques.
(8) Postoperative aseptic techniques.

(9) Role of "disposables".
(10) Problems in infection control.

(1) **Concept of asepsis and infection control:** As already pointed out, asepsis deals with the elimination of the microorganisms to keep the possibility of infection under control. The very concept of cleanliness is the basis for infection control. The disinfection is accomplished by the application of an agent on inanimate objects concerned with surgical procedures to destroy the microorganisms. Decontamination involves many forms of measure of infection control starting from mechanical cleaning to sterilization of the instruments, equipment and office environment so as to reduce the potential danger of contamination. While doing so, it is very important that the disinfectant or decontamination procedures ensure asepsis without altering or interfering with the working efficiency of instruments and equipment. At the same time, these procedures are effective against all the pathogenic, vegetative and spore forms of the organisms.

(2) **Personal protection:** The method of protection against the hepatitis-B infection by immunization has already been dealt with. Regarding AIDS (HIV), the various measures to be taken as self protection have also been described. Because of the high risk involved in treating these patients, the use of masks and protective gloves have been advocated. This will prevent cross infection. Even though washing the hand is a sound procedure, use of gloves ensures adequate protection. Likewise, mask protects the health professionals from contracting any upper respiratory tract infections. Similarly, gowns also afford protection.

(3) **Decontamination:** Proper decontamination of used instruments is an insurance against cross infection. This forms part of general hygiene. As already pointed out, blood and saliva form the major contaminants. Hence, all the instruments must be thoroughly washed before sterilization. Mechanical dislodgement by effective cleaning continues to be the primary means of eliminating the viable microorganisms and other organic contaminants accumulated on the surface of the instruments and the operatory environment. The microbes have the variable ability to resist against disinfection. The resistant forms for the elimination by the routine methods of disinfection are the bacterial endospores and viruses. The use of chemical disinfectants and sterilants constitute a significant part of infection control.

(4) **Disinfectants** are chemical agents, capable of destroying or irreversibly inactivating the organisms present in various forms. *Sterilants* are chemical agents used to destroy the bacteria, their spores and viruses. They are used as reliable immersion disinfectants. No single agent or procedure adequately accomplishes the process of disinfection or sterilization of all the situations. Hence, selection and the ultimate effectiveness of any disinfectant or sterilant can be determined by the following factors:

(i) Number and type of microbes present.
(ii) Degree of their destruction required.
(iii) Resistance to the process by the microbes.
(iv) Nature and composition of the disinfectant solution.
(v) Required exposure time.
(vi) Potential adverse effects.
(vii) Type of the concentration used.
(viii) Quantity and type of the organic matter present.
(ix) The cost factor.

In general, instruments with smooth, nonporous cleansible surfaces are readily disinfected and vice-versa. Blood, saliva and other organic accumulation present on the surface of the instruments to be disinfected may prevent penetration or may inactivate the chemical agents. Some products may require exposure of the instruments for a long time. The choice of the disinfectant process also depends on the category and the relative potential for transmitting infection. For example, critical items require high degree of disinfectants while semicritical or noncritical items may not. Based on these criterias, a few guidelines can be drawn for the purpose of disinfection.

Critical items: Many of the sharp instruments, included under this category, may be damaged by high temperature. Hence they must be disinfected with high level disinfectants prior to their use. Otherwise, disposable materials must be used. Other instruments must be sterilized.

Semi-critical items: Most of the sharp instruments, included under this category, may be damaged by high temperature. Hence, disinfectants used for these items must at least destroy ordinary vegetative bacteria, fungi and a few viruses. In most of these items, meticulous mechanical cleansing, followed by an application of appropriate high level disinfectant is desirable. It will provide a reasonable degree of protection so that these items will be free of pathogens.

Non-critical items: Items like dental chairs, tables, light handles and wash basins do not come in association with the operating field. They offer little opportunity for the transmission of infected materials. They can be cleaned with a detergent and chemical disinfectant or with intermediate disinfectants. Sodium hypochlorite is an inorganic chlorine solution, which is considered to be an intermediate-level disinfectant. Because of its corrosive nature, degradation of plastic coated instruments, diminished activity in the presence of organic matter and being irritant to the skin, it has limited use in oral surgery.

Phenol compounds are also intermediate level disinfectants. In higher concentration, it destructs cell and precipitates cellular proteins. In lower concentrations, it inactivates essential enzyme systems. They are stable phenol compounds. They are good bactericides but weak sporicides. However, phenol compounds continue to be the disinfectants of choice in the field of oral surgery.

(5) **Sterilization:** This denotes total destruction of all the living organisms including spores and viruses. This is to render the surgical instruments inert by destroying all the pathogens. But, disinfection is an intermediate method used to reduce the number of pathogens through chemical germicides. If at all, any item is to be sterilized, disinfection should not be used. As a rule, any instrument which penetrates the tissues should be sterilized. According to the method of sterilization, time factor varies. For example, autoclave sterilization takes half an hour, while chemical sterilization may take nearly 12 hours. A steam sterilizer should be used, unless the object to be sterilized will be damaged by heat, pressure, moisture or otherwise inappropriate for steam sterilization.

Cold sterilization is the term used for chemical immersion sterilization. Unfortunately, the actual process of sterilization cannot be monitored by using this method. Hence, this is not the first choice of sterilization.

Flash sterilization is a method by which instruments are sterilized at 132°C for 3 to 5 minutes.

Pressure is an important component in autoclave sterilization. The saturated steam is an efficient form of sterilization. Prior to sterilization, the item must be thoroughly cleaned. Once a week, sterilizer load should be biologically monitored. Water sterilizers are not effective. As a general rule, any item which can be sterilized should be sterilized. Items which cannot be sterilized (which come under the category of semi-critical or non-critical items), must be draped or disinfected thoroughly. When the instruments are sterilized, sometimes, one may notice a brown/orange stain resembling rust. This represents a phosphate layer, which can be traced to the water source or detergents, dried blood or disinfectants.

Different methods of sterilization include dry heat, use of steam under pressure (autoclave), chemical vapor or immersion of the items in the chemical sterilants. Sharp instruments like blade and needles do not withstand heat. Now, many of these items including suture materials are available as disposable materials.

Handpieces form potential hazards, since they are contaminated with blood, saliva and other infected materials. When these rotatory instruments are in use, they in fact suck the contaminated materials inside the handpiece. Proliferation of water borne microbes inside the cooling water system takes place during stagnation between the treatment sessions. Hence, after each treatment session, the surface of the handpiece should be disinfected, after removing all the bloodstains and other contaminations. Then, bur is removed and cleaned. The interior of the handpiece is also cleaned so that blood and other contaminants are eliminated. The handpiece must be autoclaved and hygienically stored for further use. Sometimes, handpieces are sterilized by keeping it in a container having formaldehyde tablets. But, it is found to damage the high precision parts of the rotatory instruments. Hence, autoclave sterilization is the ideal method of sterilizing the handpieces.

(6) **Why disposable materials?** Dental and oral surgery procedures have undergone considerable metamorphosis in the recent past and it has become exceedingly technical in nature. Secondly, modern practice of oral surgery must take into account the revolutionary changes in the concept of cross infection. In this context, for safe practice, the importance of increasing orientation to disposable materials must be considered. In day-to-day practice, by utilizing the disposable injection needles, suture needles, and suture materials, gloves and syringes, the incidence of cross infection has been brought down considerably. Formerly, cross infection was considered to be due to streptococcal and staphylococcal infections. Today, these organisms no longer cause concern to the health professionals but hepatitis viruses and Gram negative bacteria might pose some problems. It is now an alarming fact that treatment in the oral cavity is regarded as a substantial source of transmission of infection. With regard to this difficulty, disposable materials represent the simplest, though not always economical path to maintain satisfactory level of hygiene. In every day practice, the great advantage of disposable articles is the availability of absolutely germ-free instruments and materials for ready use. The question may arise whether it is an economically viable proposition. By evaluating carefully cost-benefit analysis, everybody will come to the conclusion that use of disposables like needles, suture materials and syringes is advantageous.

The *prerequisites* for the disposable articles are:

(a) Economic factor: Possibility of manufacturing large quantities must be explored so that cost will come down.
(b) Utilization of inexpensive and easily processable basic materials like plastics etc.
(c) Possibility of large professional demand.

The *advantages* are:

(i) Time spent on cleaning and the associated hazards of handling contaminated materials are totally avoided.
(ii) The material is germ free.
(iii) Time for sterilization is saved.
(iv) Economy of mass production.
(v) Quality is ensured.
(vi) Prevents cross infection thereby protecting the health professionals and patients.
(vii) Since needles are for one time use, sharpness of the needles is assured.

The needles are considered to be the potential source of transmission of HBV and HIV from one person to the other. Hence, one time use of needles, syringes and suture materials are highly recommended. The sterile disposable gloves are also mandatory for all the surgical procedures in the oral cavity. The second group of items which need disinfection are: towels, cups, aspirator tips and waste containers. Hence, many professionals have started using these items in disposable forms for deriving the obvious benefits. In the recent past, oral surgeons in the urban centres have extended this benefit by using more and more of disposable materials. It is expected that the use of more and more of disposable materials will be made mandatory.

CHAPTER 6

Exodontia

GENERAL CONSIDERATIONS

Dental extraction has always been considered to be an unpleasant procedure for the patients due to "pain phobia". With the advent of safe local anesthetic drugs, techniques and standardization of the surgical procedures, extraction is no longer considered to be a painful experience to the patients.

OBJECTIVES

Extraction is one of the most common surgical procedures performed by a dental or an oral surgeon. The main objective is to severe the periodontal attachments carefully and lever the tooth out of the alveolar socket without damaging (a) the adjoining structures like neurovascular bundle, gingiva or alveolar bone and (b) anatomical areas like oral cavity, nasal cavity and the adjoining structures. While doing so, certain amount of trauma is inevitable. Hence, success in exodontia depends on how the trauma is kept to the minimum. The objective of the course is to provide a basis of knowledge for the successful practice. The skill and the practical wisdom of any clinician is directly proportional to the personal experience and the knowledge gained.

In general, according to the difficulties faced, the cases are classified into four types:

Type I : Easy patient, easy case
Type II : Easy patient, difficult case
Type III : Difficult patient, easy case
Type IV : Difficult patient, difficult case.

Every clinician should bear in mind this classification as a general rule, before undertaking even minor surgery.

BASIC REQUIREMENTS

(i) A good radiograph
(ii) Adequate anesthesia
(iii) Instruments
(iv) Adequate illumination
(v) Efficient assistance
(vi) Suction apparatus.

All the instruments and equipment must be periodically inspected to avoid any embarrassing moments during surgery. The maintenance includes sharpening of the instruments. Reasonable standard of sterilization and asepsis are essential.

PRINCIPLES

(i) To gain adequate access and to obtain secured grip on the tooth.
(ii) To apply controlled force in a predetermined direction.
(iii) To severe the dentoalveolar bondage with minimum trauma.
(iv) To safely deliver the tooth in toto out of the socket through an uninterrupted path of removal with minimal pain and discomfort to the patient.

The safe extraction of a tooth demands scrupulous application of these principles and a thorough knowledge of dentoalveolar anatomy.

Adequate access

The operator may experience difficulty if a good source of light is not available focussing on the surgical field. Access can be improved if anesthesia is adequate, bleeding is under control and the surrounding tissues are protected away from the surgical field. The grip is secured depending on the location and condition of the tooth surface on which the beaks of the forceps are applied. Since the enamel is brittle, the instrument should not be applied on the enamel or over the weak areas like dental caries or massive restorations. Similarly, application of the appropriate instrument will ensure secured grip on the tooth.

Application of the controlled force

The ability to apply the force for removal of the teeth should not be considered as a test for the physical strength of the operator. Injudicious application of force will result in fracture of the tooth or the jaw bone. In general, it is safe to stop the surgical movement of the forceps if any abnormal resistance is felt by the operator. On such occasions, a radiograph is mandatory to identify the underlying cause for the abnormal resistance. It may be due to (a) accessory roots, (b) unfavorable curvature of the roots, (c) fusion with the bone (ankylosis) or with the neighboring teeth or (d) locking with neighboring teeth.

To severe the tooth attachment with atraumatic technique

Depending on many factors, the attachment of the tooth can be severed by predetermined forces like rotational or pendulum movements. The rotational movement is by rocking in the longitudinal axis of the tooth. Pendulum movement is by rocking in the medial-lateral directions. The sole objective is to severe the periodontal fibers without damaging the adjoining structures. It must be least traumatic.

Safe delivery of the tooth

The objective must be to safely deliver the tooth in toto out of the socket through an uninterrupted path of removal with minimal pain and discomfort to the patient and without any associated complications.

Uneventful healing

Healing of the extracted socket must be without any discomfort and complications. This depends on the correct technique by the surgeon. But discomfort or complications may be due to the underlying systemic conditions like diabetes, vitamin deficiency or debilitating diseases of systemic origin.

INDICATIONS

In general, indications for removal of teeth are based on dentoalveolar pathology, feasibility or otherwise to restore the dental and periodontal structures, patient's willingness and motivation to undertake the types of treatment, economic implications and time factor. Universally, dental caries and periodontal disturbances account for nearly 85-90% of extractions of teeth.

(1) **Periodontal disturbances.** They form the common cause for dental extraction in India. When the teeth are periodontally involved, the clinician must decide whether to extract the tooth or not. The final decision depends on (a) the success of periodontal therapy, (b) patient's attitude towards the concept of conserving such teeth and (c) economic and time factors. Even if the patient desires to save the tooth, loss of more than 40% of periodontal support warrants extraction (Fig. 6.1).

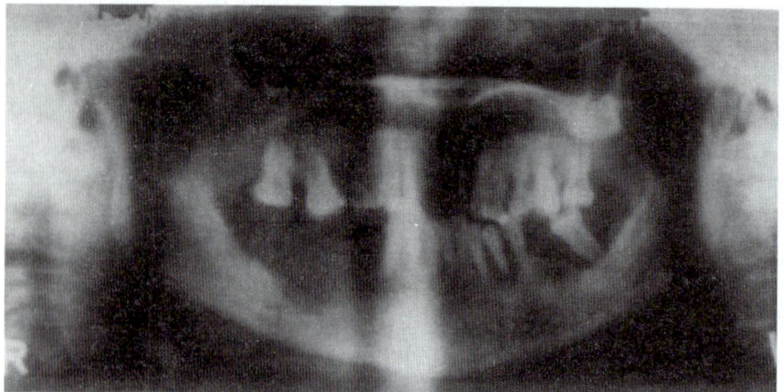

Fig. 6.1 Severe periodontal disease.

(2) **Dental caries.** When the tooth is extensively damaged by dental caries, the dental surgeon must evaluate the feasibility of conserving the carious tooth. Even if the patient and the dental surgeon desire to save the tooth, it is indicated for extraction if all the conservative procedures have failed. This may be either because of technical reasons or if the patient fails to cooperate. Sometimes, the sharp margins of the teeth repeatedly ulcerate the mucosa. Multiple carious teeth may lead to deteriorating oral hygiene. In such cases, removal of teeth will improve the oral hygiene.

(3) **Pulp pathology.** If endodontic therapy is not possible or if the tooth is not amenable for endodontic treatment, extraction is indicated.

(4) **Apical pathology.** If the teeth fail to respond to all conservative measures to resolve apical pathology, either because of technical reasons or because of the systemic factors, such teeth are indicated for extraction before the apical pathology widens with the consequent involvement of the adjoining teeth. (Fig. 6.2)

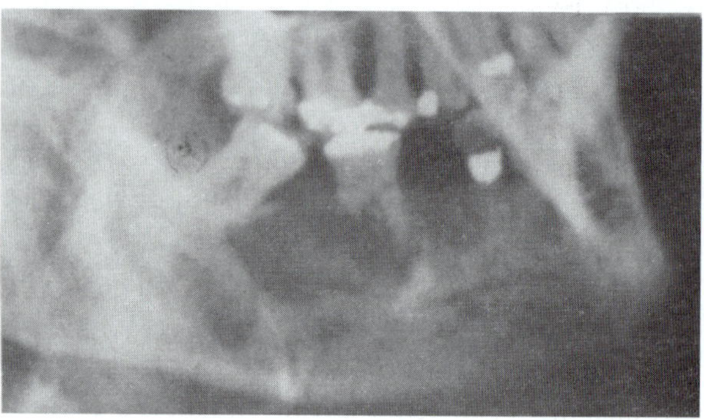

Fig. 6.2 Tooth involved in a cyst.

(5) **Orthodontic reasons.** During the course of orthodontic treatment, a few teeth may require extraction. They fall into any one of the following reasons:

(a) *Therapeutic extractions.* To gain space during the realignment of malposed teeth, extraction of teeth like premolars or molars are indicated.

(b) *Malposed teeth.* If the teeth in the dental arch are malpositioned, orthodontist may find it difficult to realign them. Under such circumstances, those teeth which are not amenable for orthodontic treatment are indicated for extraction.

(c) *Serial extraction.* During mixed dentition period, dental surgeon may have to extract a few deciduous teeth in a chronological order to prevent malocclusion as the child grows. As part of preventive dentistry, judicious extraction of a few deciduous teeth provides enough space for the eruption of permanent successors in a sequential way. This is known as serial extraction. However, before advising extraction, these teeth require proper evaluation and expert orthodontic opinion. Otherwise, instead of achieving stability of the dental arch, injudicious extraction can lead to undesirable esthetics like spacing between teeth or may even produce unacceptable facial profile. Therefore, decision for extraction of teeth for orthodontic reasons should be based on:

(a) Orthodontic assessment.
(b) Genetic evaluation, if needed.
(c) Evaluation of the soft tissues like lips, tongue etc.

(6) **Prosthetic considerations**. Extraction of teeth is indicated for providing efficient dental prosthesis. For example, to provide better design and success of partial dentures, a few selected teeth may have to be extracted. At the same time, caution is required if a patient requests the dental surgeon to extract a few remaining teeth to enable him to have complete dentures. It is a known fact that atrophy of the bone results in decreased denture bearing area and the consequent decreased denture stability. But, the retention of a few teeth like canines control the atrophy of the jaws. Likewise, intentional retention of a few teeth may be helpful to utilize them as abutments. Hence, careful evaluation by the prosthodontist is necessary for extracting teeth for prosthetic considerations.

(7) **Impactions.** Retention of unerupted teeth beyond the chronological eruption may sometimes be responsible for vague facial pain, periodontal disturbances of the adjoining teeth, temporomandibular joint problems, bony pathology like cysts and pathological fracture of the jaws. Impactions may predispose to anterior overcrowding of teeth. Careful evaluation of such patients including general condition and professional competence of the dental surgeon are some of the important considerations for removal of such impacted teeth. (Fig. 6.3)

(8) **Supernumerary teeth.** These teeth may be malpositioned or unerupted. Such teeth may predispose to malocclusion, periodontal disturbances, facial pain, bony pathology or may even predispose to esthetic problems. Unless retention of such supernumerary teeth are advantageous to the patients, they are indicated for extraction.

(9) **Tooth in the line of fracture.** (Fig. 6.4) This has been controversial over the course of years. The present concept is to extract the tooth in the line of fracture if (a) it is a source of infection at the site of fracture, (b) the tooth itself is fractured, (c) the retention may interfere with fracture reduction or with healing of the fracture. Formerly, all the teeth in the line of fracture were routinely removed. But now, a conservative approach is advocated and hence extraction of such teeth require guarded approach.

(10) **Teeth in relation to bony pathology.** They are indicated for extraction. For example, if they are involved in cyst formations, neoplasm or osteomyelitis, extraction is indicated. However, careful evaluation is required before extracting teeth involved in the cyst formations. If any chance exists for guiding the tooth to erupt to normal occlusion, efforts must be directed to conserve such teeth. Hence proper decision must be taken based on the individual case (Fig. 6.5).

(11) **Root fragments.** They may remain dormant for a long period. Hence, every patient must be carefully evaluated to decide whether

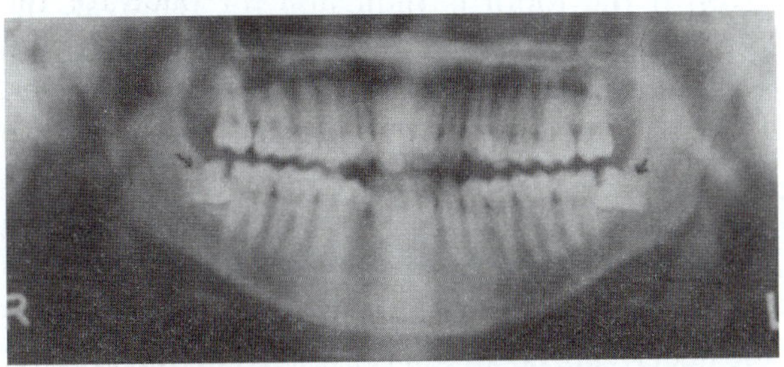

Fig. 6.3 Impacted mandibular III molar.

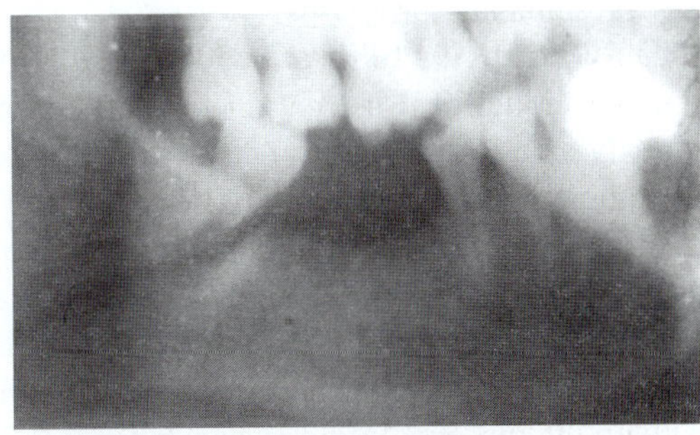

Fig. 6.4 Tooth fracture in the fracture-line.

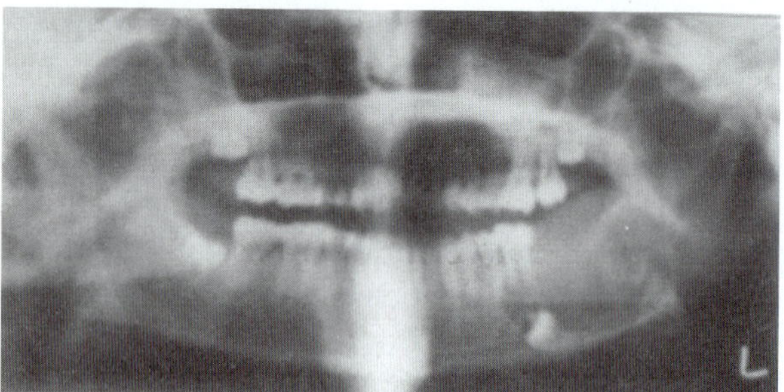

Fig. 6.5 Teeth in relation to bony pathology.

removal of root fragments is necessary. For example, roots may be at the submucosal level producing recurrent ulceration under the denture. Such ulceration may be painful or may undergo neoplastic changes. Such roots warrant removal. Sometimes, root fragments may be involved in the initiation of bony pathology like osteomyelitis, cyst or neoplasm. If such fragments are in close association with neurovascular bundle, the patient may complain of facial pain or numbness. Statistically, it has been observed that many broken root fragments remain asymptomatic. This has resulted in the controversy as to whether they are indicated for removal. As a general rule, very small fragments may be left alone and the patient is to be kept under periodical observation. All the other root fragments are indicated for removal. As the age advances, the patients become medically compromised. Hence, removal is indicated as soon as it is diagnosed, instead of waiting for the symptoms to appear, before general health of the patient presents any problems.

(12) **Teeth prior to irradiation.** Irradiation is one of the modalities of treating oral carcinomas. Previously as a prophylactic measure, all the teeth in the region of irradiation used to be extracted. But now, all the precautions are taken to conserve the teeth prior to irradiation. Hence, all the patients before irradiation must be carefully examined so that a decision is taken regarding the extraction of such teeth. If the oral hygiene can be maintained satisfactorily, routine prophylactic extraction of these teeth are not to be encouraged. Only teeth which cannot be maintained in a sound condition require removal.

(13) **Focal sepsis.** Sometimes, teeth may appear apparently sound. But radiological evaluation is a guiding factor to decide whether any teeth are to be considered as foci of infection. In such circumstances, weightage is in favor of the underlying systemic disorders like dermatological lesions, facial pain, uncontrollable ophthalmic problems etc. In such conditions, doubtful teeth are extracted instead of resorting to any conservative methods of management.

(14) **Esthetics.** Due to certain compelling reasons like marriage and job opportunities, some teeth may require attention for esthetic considerations. But due to time factor, it may not be possible to improve esthetics by any conservative orthodontic or surgical means. If so, such teeth are indicated for extraction, provided it is followed by immediate prosthetic restoration in a shorter duration.

(15) **Economic considerations.** Sometimes, the dental surgeon and the patient are faced with economic constraints even though technically conservation of teeth may be feasible. In such cases, extraction may be the only other alternative method of choice. However, the benefit of doubt is left to the discretion of the patient in such circumstances and extraction of teeth are indicated as a last resort.

CONTRAINDICATIONS

Even if the tooth is indicated for removal, the presence of certain factors make the tooth contraindicated for extraction. They may be *relative* or *absolute* contraindications. They can be considered relative, if the contraindication is provided with additional care, one can overcome the complication. In other words, given the situation, the patient is made fit to undergo extraction, once the underlying condition is treated. On the contrary, there are a few conditions which are absolute contraindications. These factors will be the impediments for extraction, even if care is taken. If extraction is carried out in the presence of such absolute contraindications, the outcome may be even fatal. Hence, it is essential to differentiate between these two types of contraindications. To avoid legal consequences, it is preferable to avoid extraction, if the contraindication is absolute.

The following conditions can be considered as *absolute contraindications*:

(1) Congestive cardiac failure
(2) Leukemia
(3) Uremia
(4) Cirrhosis liver
(5) Terminal stages of malignancy.

The *contraindications* may also be classified as *systemic* or *local factors*. The presence of absolute systemic contraindications indicate that this group of diseases exist in an uncontrolled state. No attempt should be made by the dental surgeon to thrust extraction on such patients. By doing so, the clinician will be inviting disaster, e.g. (a) metabolic disorders like uncontrolled diabetes, (b) uncontrolled cardiac problems, (c) leukemia (d) renal failure and (e) liver disorders like cirrhosis of liver. On the contrary, the following contra-indications are examples of relative contra-indications. That means, extraction is to be deferred, until the underlying conditions deserve attention to make the patient fit to undergo extraction. In such patients, the underlying condition is to be treated by way of precautions so that, complications can be avoided due to extraction.

(1) **Diabetes and hypertension.** Usually patients with these systemic problems are under medication to keep them under control. Hence, patients with controlled hypertension and diabetes can undergo extraction. However, it is good to investigate the state of these disorders in every patient and extraction should be carried out only after confirming that they are under control. Such precautions will be a sure way of preventing any potential complications subsequently.

(2) **Patients on steroid therapy.** If the patient gives history of cortisone therapy, then, dental surgeon has to take certain precautions. A physician's opinion must be taken. Otherwise, the normal precaution would be to safely double the dose of steroid, one or two days prior to extraction and to continue one or two days postoperatively. Then, the dose must be tapered gradually to the usual dose. Otherwise, the patient is liable to exhibit adrenal crisis due to stress.

(3) **Pregnancy.** The clinician should bear in mind the existence of the possibility of obstetric complications during the first and the last trimester. Hence, if possible, extraction can be carried out after obtaining the obstetrician's expert opinion.

(4) **Bleeding disorders.** The patients who give definite history of bleeding episodes need careful evaluation. It is not an absolute contraindication. Complications can be avoided, if the patient is properly evaluated and adequate precautions are taken. If necessary, close coordination with the hematologist is necessary to ensure uncomplicated recovery of the patient following dental extractions. Patients with anticoagulant therapy can undergo extraction after obtaining prior advice from the patient's physician/cardiologist.

(5) **Medically compromised patients.** In general, it is better to evaluate these patients preoperatively. Great caution should be exercised before treating this group of patients. Failure to do so may result in systemic complications. Sometimes, unwittingly drug interactions may pose problems.

(6) **Local contraindications.** These are relative contraindications. For example, extraction in the presence of active and uncontrolled infection will lead to the regional or systemic spread. Hence, it is preferable to control the infection and extraction can be safely carried out under the umbrella of antibiotic therapy.

(7) **Extraction of teeth in recently irradiated patients.** These cases deserve special mention. Irradiation of the jaws reduces blood supply due to fibrosis. Trauma with super added infection will

lead to the development of osteoradionecrosis of the jaw bones. Hence, it is better to defer the dental extraction in the irradiated patients to avoid this unpleasant complication. Similarly, extraction in the region of malignancy can result in metastasis.

PREEXTRACTION EVALUATION

Time spent on the preextraction evaluation of the patient is very valuable for a successful exodontic practice. If the operator takes it easy and proceeds with dental extraction without adequate pre-extraction evaluation of the patient, the clinician is bound to face very embarrassing moments. Hence, it is always wise to assess the patient on the following aspects:

(1) Systemic evaluation

(2) Local evaluation

 (a) Clinical

 (b) Radiological.

Systemic assessment of the patient including any difficulties encountered during previous extractions and general impression of the patient are very important. Examination of the oral cavity regarding the oral hygiene level has an important role to play in promoting smooth postoperative recovery. Any limitations in mouth opening is likely to cause hardships during extraction. Clinical examination of the tooth to be extracted and the adjoining structures will provide many vulnerable informations.

(1) **Access to the tooth.** Range of mouth opening, location, and position of the tooth in the dental arch are responsible for the surgical access to the tooth to be extracted. A malposed tooth may present difficulty in positioning the instrument for extraction.

(2) **Tooth mobility.** The usual tendency is to assume that a loose tooth extraction is easy without any possible complications. Although, it is true that technically its removal may be easy, dental surgeon must carefully diagnose the underlying cause for the tooth mobility. A loose tooth may be due to periodontal disease. But, sometimes, it may be because of the underlying pathology like neoplasm, etc. So, whatever necessary, a good intraoral periapical radiograph will be useful to properly assess the condition.

(3) **Anatomy of the crown.** Careful examination with proper illumination will reveal the condition of the crown for the presence of the following:

(a) Carious destruction of the crown.

(b) Shape, position, long axis and size of the crown.

(c) Presence or absence of the adjoining teeth and their condition.

(d) Nonvitality.

(e) State of the supporting structures.

(4) **Radiological assessment.** The clinical examination will not be complete without a periapical radiograph of the region. Some may request for a routine radiograph prior to dental extraction. Others may take it lightly and will make an attempt to extract the tooth. Radiograph is advised only when any difficulties are encountered. Both the extremes are to be discouraged. In general, the following factors must be borne in mind by way of precaution while asking for a preoperative radiograph:

(a) History of "difficult" or unsuccessful extraction.

(b) Crown with extensive caries, large restorations, nonvitality where diagnosis is in doubt and tooth is malposed.

(c) If the operator experiences abnormal resistance during forceps extraction.

(d) Any tooth which is in close proximity to important anatomical structures like neurovascular canal, maxillary antrum, etc.

(e) Attritioned teeth in elderly people.

(f) If tooth is partially or completely unerupted.

(g) Solitary tooth in the jaw without the adjoining teeth.

(h) Whenever underlying bony pathology is suspected.

(i) Any clinical condition which may predispose to abnormalities of tooth or alveolus like cleidocranial dysostosis, osteitis deformans, irradiated jaws, osteoporosis, and osteomyelitis.

Radiographic evaluation is likely to yield the following valuable information, necessary for safe exodontic practice:

(a) All the necessary features of the crown, needed for safe extraction.
(b) Any alteration in the number, size, shape and configuration of root curvature.
(c) Unfavorable root curvature.
(d) State of the alveolar bone and the root, sclerosis of bone or ankylosis.
(e) Presence of any apical and bony pathology.
(f) Proximity to anatomical structures, which will forewarn the operator about the possibility of nerve damage, oroantral fistula or fracture of the tuberosity of maxilla.

Hence, in general, preexisting assessment will help the operator in estimating the possible difficulties during dental extraction. It is better to take precautions rather than facing the intraoperative complications.

INSTRUMENTATION

The effective use of various instruments depends on the following:

(1) Understanding the design of the instruments
(2) Mechanical principles
    (a) Wedge principle
    (b) Lever principle of first order
    (c) Wheel and axle principle
    (d) Expansion of bony socket
(3) Path of delivery of the tooth
(4) Compression of the bony socket.

Extraction forceps (Fig. 6.6)

In general, the routine instruments used for extracting teeth can be conveniently classified as forceps and elevators. Forceps are those instruments

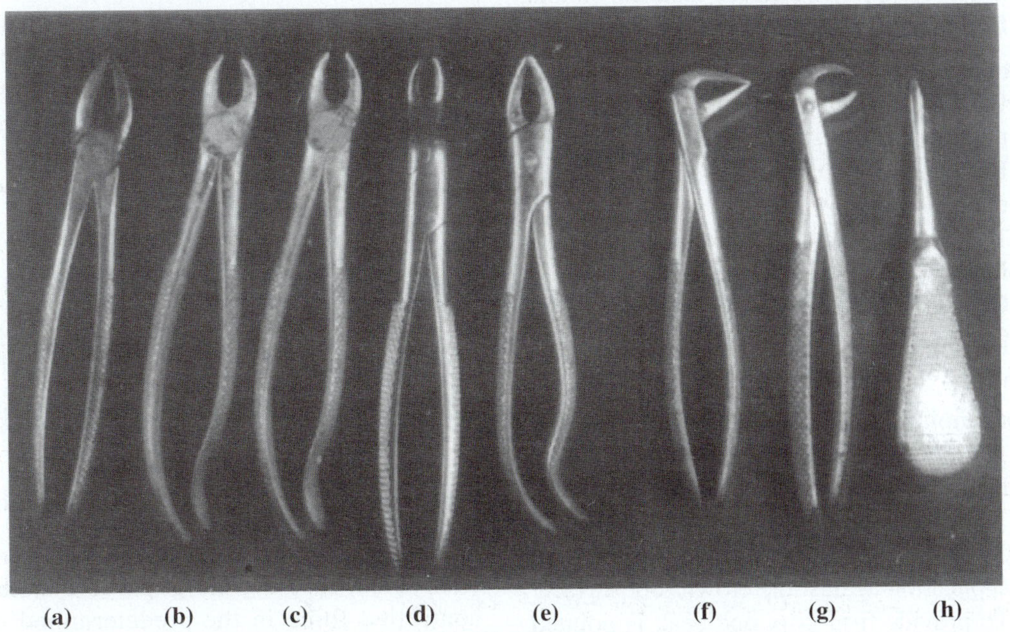

(a) (b) (c) (d) (e) (f) (g) (h)

Fig. 6.6 Extraction forceps for full mouth clearance: **(a)** Straight elevator, **(b)** Lower molar forceps, **(c)** Lower anterior forceps, **(d)** Upper root forceps, **(e)** Bayonet forceps, **(f)** & **(g)** Right and left upper molar forceps, **(h)** Upper anterior forceps.

used to grasp the tooth for removing it while elevators are those instruments designed for elevating the tooth out of the socket. Hence, forceps permits the controlled force on the tooth that allows dilatation of the alveolar socket, luxation and removal of the tooth. Every forceps has a pair of handles, a pair of beaks and a hinge. In this part of the world, English pattern is more popularly used by dental surgeons. The beaks constitute the working portion of the forceps.

Basically, the forceps used for upper and lower teeth differ in the design of the beaks. In the lower forceps, beaks are at right angles to the long axis of the handles while in the upper forceps, beaks are in the same line as handles or parallel to it. Based on these principles, English pattern extraction forceps are available for extracting the teeth.

(1) **Upper anterior forceps** (Ash no. 1)
   (a) Used for extracting upper incisors and canines.
   (b) Beaks are symmetrical and are placed in the same line as the handles.
   (c) Beaks are shorter than the handles, so that load arm is shorter than the working arm.

(2) **Bayonet forceps** (Ash no. 101-A)
   (a) Used for removing premolars and rarely for the upper roots.
   (b) Beaks are asymmetrical, placed parallel to the handles.
   (c) This arrangement facilitates the beaks to be inside the oral cavity more posteriorly.
   (d) One end of the handle is concave to provide better and secured grip for the operator's fingers.

(3) **Upper molar forceps** (Ash no. 94 & 95)
   (a) These forceps have asymmetrical beaks.
   (b) Beaks are broader than the anterior forceps.
   (c) The cross section of the beaks is concave/convex so that concave surface is meant for application against the crown/root surface.
   (d) To provide firm grip, one beak is pointed so that it can engage the bifurcation of the tooth. The other beak is rounded so that it adapts around the palatal root. Depending on the position of the pointed beak, the forceps can be identified as right and left.

(4) **Upper root forceps**
   (a) Designed for removing maxillary roots.
   (b) Beaks are symmetrical and closely approximate to each other.
   (c) To provide firm grip, the beaks are narrower to fit to the circumference of the root.
   (d) Beaks are slightly curved, corresponding to the curvature of the handles.

(5) **Lower anterior forceps** (Ash no. 74)
   (a) Beaks are similar to upper root forceps, in that they are narrower than the lower molar forceps.
   (b) Beaks are at right angles to the handles.
   (c) These forceps can also be used as lower root forceps although lower root forceps are also available with still narrower beaks.

(6) **Lower molar forceps** (Ash no. 73)
   (a) Beaks are at right angles to the handles.
   (b) Beaks are symmetrically pointed so that sharp pointed tips can engage the bifurcation, both at the buccal and lingual surfaces.
   (c) Beaks are more broader and stout.

These are the minimum instruments required for extracting the teeth. All these forceps are designed in such a way that they are applied with the beaks parallel to the long axis of the tooth. Failure to secure the grip in this way will result in the application of the force, leading to the fracture of the tooth.

Mechanical principles of instrumentation (Fig. 6.7)

Adaptation, securing the grip and transmission of controlled force in the predetermined direction depend on a few mechanical principles. Clear

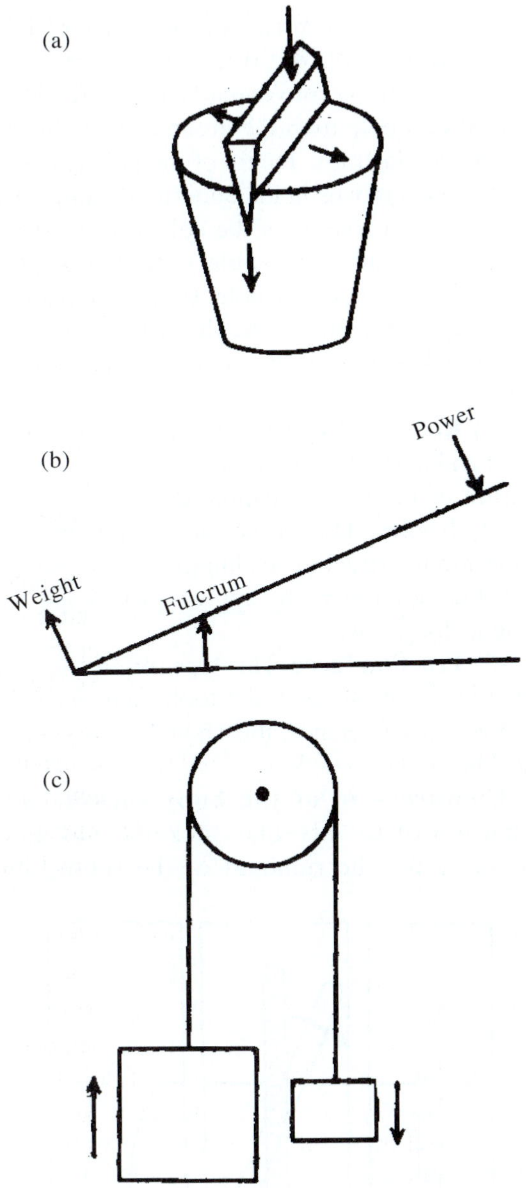

Fig. 6.7 Mechanical principles: **(a)** Wedge principle, **(b)** Lever principle, **(c)** Wheel and axle principle.

understanding of these basic physical principles is absolutely essential to do the extraction satisfactorily.

(1) **Wedge principle.** It is an established physical principle that a wedge can be used to split, expand, or displace the portions of substance that receive forceps. This principle is useful in the following way. The tips of the beaks are narrow and it broadens posteriorly. When the tip is forced between the mucoperiosteum and the tooth surface, the mucoperiosteum gets displaced. As the tips of the beaks are advanced still further, the bony socket is expanded so that the tooth is displaced out of the socket as the periodontal attachments are severed gradually.

(2) **Lever principle of first order.** The lever principle has three components - fulcrum, power, and weight. While extracting the tooth, controlled force is delivered in a predetermined direction. The power is represented by the handles and the weight is represented by the beaks which grasp the tooth. Lever is a mechanism by which modest force is transmitted at the long power arm, so that mechanical advantage is derived at the short, weight arm. This principle is used to advantage when elevators are used. This does not have much use in forceps extraction. However, it is used in combination with wheel and axle principle, with alveolar crest as the fulcrum.

(3) **Wheel and axle principle.** If the tooth is grasped with the beaks firmly and force is applied in the form of an arc, it is easy to deliver the tooth out of the socket. In the routine practice, one can derive mechanical advantage by introducing a pulley mechanism, e.g. to draw water from the well, wheel of the pulley rotates around the axle. Greater the diameter of the wheel, more is the mechanical advantage. Hence it is always better to hold the forceps handles as farther away as possible to increase the power arm.

Thus, it is found that the wedge action of the blades assists in the extraction by the dilation of the socket. The major movement of the opposing surfaces of a cone results in wedge factor due to the contact of two inclined planes with the root surface.

Each arm of the forceps represents each component of the lever with the hinge acting as fulcrum. It is found that length of the blades represents the mechanical advantage. Therefore, the farther the grip from the fulcrum and the shorter the blades, the greater is the mechanical advantage.

The wheel and axle motion of the forceps results in the bodily rotation of the tooth. This is responsible for the rupture of the periodontal attachment. This is perhaps the most important phase in the technique of extraction. During the extraction of upper teeth, axis of the wheel approximates the long axis of the handles. In the lower jaw, movement of rotation is perpendicular to the long axis of the handles. In fact, the ability to grip, lever and rotate provides a possible basis for classification of the forceps, according to the mechanical advantage.

PATH OF DELIVERY OF THE TOOTH

The above mentioned physical principles are useful to successfully extract a tooth. The primary motions applied to luxate and remove the tooth are as follows:

(1) **Apical pressure.** As already explained, beaks act as wedges between alveolar socket and tooth surface. Very little movement of the tooth in the apical direction takes place. Instead, this movement expands the bony socket and helps in securing a firm grip over a larger area of the tooth. Teeth with single conical roots may jump out of the socket during this phase like an orange seed jumping off the two fingers when pressure is applied.

(2) **Buccal force.** By keeping a continuous apical pressure, buccal force is added which expands the bony socket still further. During this movement, the forceps takes fulcrum from the crest of the alveolus.

(3) **Lingual apical pressure.** Simultaneously at the apical region, lingual apical pressure is exerted. By this movement, excess buccal expansion is controlled. Socket expansion is maximal in younger jaws but gradually decreases with advancing age.

Dilatation of the alveolar socket during extraction can be conveniently compared to the removal of a pole from the ground. When the pole is mobilized laterally, the tip of the pole embedded in the ground moves in the opposite direction. This results in the dilatation of the hole near the surface and enlargement of the hole near the tip of the embedded portion of the pole. If the pole is moved in the opposite direction, the dilatation of the opening takes place in the opposite direction (Fig. 6.8).

(4) **Rotational force.** This is applied by using wheel and axle principle in the form of an arc with fulcrum of the lever principle on the crest of the buccal alveolus. This is the most important phase in the tooth extraction technique. Upper anterior tooth can be removed by applying rotational force along its long axis.

(5) **Traction force.** This type of force is useful in the terminal phase of the tooth delivery out of the bony socket. Hence, this should be as gentle as possible.

Compression of the bony socket. Bony expansion of the alveolar socket is absolutely necessary for the removal of the tooth. Once

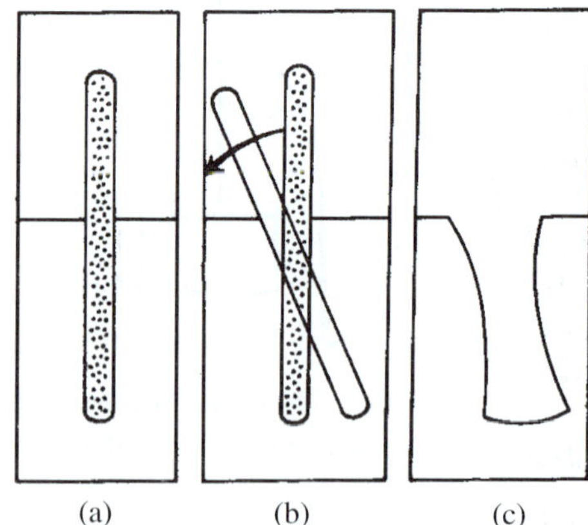

Fig. 6.8 Diagrammatic representation to illustrate the movement of a pole during rocking motion. **(a)** Pole at rest, **(b)** During movement, **(c)** Pressure effect seen.

extraction is completed, the expanded socket must be compressed as much as possible so that alveolar ridge will be of desirable shape and size after healing, which is necessary for providing adequate denture-bearing ridge.

EXTRACTION TECHNIQUES

General considerations

(1) **Light.** A well-illuminated operative field is one of the requirements for successful extraction.

(2) **Positioning of the patient.** This is an equally important consideration to carry out the extraction satisfactorily. Correct positioning avoids any occupational postural problems to the operator. Moreover, if mouth of the patient is too low or too high, the operator is forced to work with mechanical disadvantage. In general, the site of the operation is in level with the elbow of the operator or slightly at a lower level. The back rest of the chair is nearly vertical when upper teeth are removed and slightly reclined backwards while operating on the mandibular teeth.

(3) **Positioning of the operator.** The operator stands on the right hand side and in front of the patient during extraction of the teeth. When right mandibular teeth are removed, the operator stands on the right side and behind the patient. However, it is left to the choice and convenience of the individual operator with the development of seated dentistry.

(4) **Techniques.** The extraction of teeth is, in general, classified as "closed" and "open" surgical methods. They are also called "Intraalveolar extraction" and "Transalveolar extraction" respectively.

Intraalveolar extraction

(1) The tooth must always be grasped on the cementum and not on the enamel. Since enamel is brittle, the tooth is liable to fracture against any resistance during extraction. By placing the beaks on the root surface engaging cementum, more amount of the tooth substance is brought under the influence of the dental forceps. Proper clinical and radiographic evaluation help in placing the extraction forceps during the "closed" extraction technique.

(2) Another source of error is improper instrumentation. Beaks are designed to suit the anatomy of the crown of various teeth. Improper instruments placed along the wrong axis results in difficulty during extraction.

Hence, careful evaluation of the patient, correct choice and application of the instruments will reasonably ensure successful extraction of teeth.

Extraction of deciduous teeth deserve special attention. Following are some of them:

(a) Oral cavity of the child is small. Hence access is very limited.

(b) Deciduous molars enclose permanent tooth buds between the roots. Thus, they are liable for damage, dislodgement or accidental removal out of the crypt during extraction.

(c) Since deciduous teeth lack neck, carious extensions may involve the roots. Hence, firm grip of such carious teeth may not be satisfactory.

(d) Root resorption does not occur in an orderly fashion. Irregular resorption of teeth is responsible for the inevitable retention of root fragments inside the jaw bone during extraction.

(e) However, extraction technique is basically the same as that of removal of permanent teeth. But certain variations are advocated.

- (i) Choice of different instruments for extraction of deciduous teeth are desirable to suit the anatomy of the deciduous teeth.
- (ii) If wedge principle is applied in the usual way, underlying permanent tooth bud is liable to be injured. Hence, blade is shifted in such a way that its long axis coincides with the long axis of one of the roots.
- (iii) A firm lingual movement results in the tooth coming out of the socket without disturbing the tooth bud.

(iv) Even if a root breaks, a small fragment of the root can be left alone. It will undergo resorption or will get exfoliated as a natural course of event.

Transalveolar extraction

This is also known as "open" or "surgical" removal of teeth. It consists of gaining access by raising mucoperiosteal flaps and removal of bone so that the root fragment and unerupted tooth can be removed.

Indications

(1) Any tooth which resists the normal moderate force during the intraalveolar (closed) extraction.

(2) Unerupted tooth which cannot be removed by the routine closed extraction technique.

(3) Fractured tooth or roots which cannot be removed by routine forceps method (below the level of epithelial attachment).

(4) Hypercementosis or ankylosis as revealed by the preoperative radiological evaluation.

(5) Geminated, fused or dilacerated teeth.

(6) Teeth with complicated and unfavorable curvatures of roots.

(7) Extraction for the provision of immediate denture.

The following sequence is to be followed during the *transalveolar extraction* of teeth and roots.

(a) Anesthesia
(b) Access through mucoperiosteal flap
(c) Removal of bone
(d) Tooth division, if necessary
(e) Removal of tooth or roots
(f) Arrest of hemorrhage
(g) Wound debridement
(h) Toilet of the alveolar socket
(i) Suturing of the flap
(j) Suture removal
(k) Postoperative follow-up.

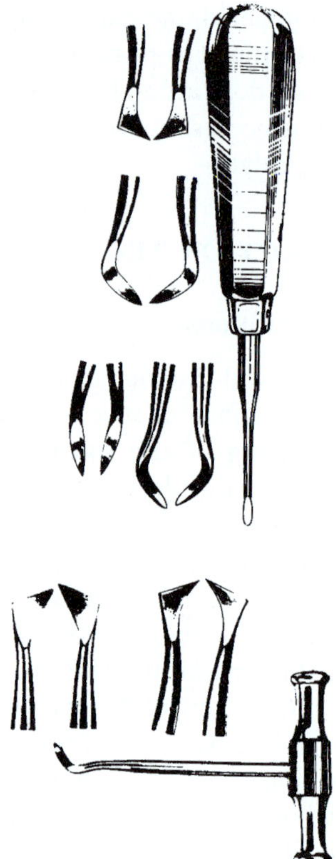

Fig. 6.9 Elevators.

Use of elevators (Fig. 6.9)

Elevators are the instruments used to elevate the tooth or root from the alveolar socket. All the above mentioned physical principles are applied during its use. The wedge is useful to dilate the socket and also to gain a point of application of the elevator. Then, lever principle is utilized in association with wheel and axle principle for the delivery of the controlled force in a predetermined direction. The effectiveness of the respective elevator is strengthened by the design of the handle to provide firm grip. Its efficiency depends on the design of the blade. The effectiveness of the elevator depends on the economy of instrumentation. The economy is in terms of relative mechanical advantage of the instrument.

Basically, to satisfy these needs, elevators are

designed on two basic patterns. In general, all the elevators have a handle, shaft, and a blade. In the straight pattern, all these three components are placed in one plane. In the other design, blade and shaft are in one plane and the handle is placed at an angle to them. There are so many elevators available commercially but a few are widely used because of their efficiency and convenience.

The elevators deliver the force based on various mechanical principles to drive the tooth or root along its path of delivery or line of withdrawal. It represents the direction along which the tooth move out of the alveolar socket with economy of force and economy of instrumentation. Hence, successful use of an elevator depends on the determination of the convenient path of its delivery. Such a line of least resistance is determined by a few factors.

(1) Root pattern and root curvature.
(2) Presence of any obstruction along the path of delivery.
(3) Appropriate point of application of the elevator is determined by the line of withdrawal of the tooth. The bone must be used as fulcrum and not the adjoining tooth.

A word of caution: Since some of these instruments have excellent mechanical advantage, operator must use them very carefully.

Types of elevators

The elevators which are widely used in the dental practice are as follows:

(1) Straight elevator (No. 18 and 19)
(2) Winter's cross-bar elevators - right and left (No.12 L and 12 R)
(3) Cryer's elevator.

(1) **Straight elevator** is used
(a) to elevate the mandibular third molars
(b) to luxate the last tooth in the dental arch
(c) to luxate the teeth in the case of multiple extractions. It is better to avoid this instrument in luxating or removing the maxillary teeth.

(2) **Winter's cross-bar elevators** form a pair. This is indicated to remove one of the mandibular roots where the other root has already been removed. In such cases, the tip of the elevator is introduced to the depth of the empty socket with the concave surface of the elevator facing the root to be removed. By applying wheel and axle principle with rotatory movement, the interradicular septum and the other root are elevated out of the alveolar socket. Hence, the same elevator is used for elevating the distal root on the right side and the mesial root on the left side. The other elevator is used for removing the other two corresponding roots. When both the roots are intact, tip of the elevator can be applied at the bifurcation from the buccal side and force is applied using lever principle and wheel and axle principle to elevate the roots.

(3) **Cryer's elevator** is an useful instrument to elevate or luxate the maxillary teeth or roots. The design of this elevator is such that less force is conveyed during its usage. Hence, fracture of the maxillary bone is less common.

It is seen that straight elevators are inserted parallel to the root surface. Hence parallel application is advocated for the controlled transmission of the force. In comparison "offset" elevators have the handle at an angle to the shaft, e.g. Cryer's elevator. They are used to remove erupted maxillary III molars and maxillary root fragments. The winter's cross-bar elevators are powerful instruments like straight elevators. Hence caution is necessary to avoid injury to the jaw bone and adjacent tissues during their use.

SEQUELAE OF DENTAL EXTRACTION

During development, alveolar bone develops as the tooth erupts. It mainly provides attachment and support to the teeth. Following extraction, the changes take place in the reverse order with resorption of the alveolar bone to form the residual alveolar ridge. The alveolar ridge must be in proper shape to facilitate denture construction.

Indiscriminate removal of alveolar bone results in reduction in the size of the alveolar ridge. Sometimes, during extraction, if the tooth breaks, the dental surgeon faces the dilemma to remove it or to leave it in situ.

The following is the sequence of events that follows if a fractured root fragment is left in situ:

(1) After the intermittent phases of resorptive and reparative processes, the fractured dentine surface is covered by acellular cementum. Then, a periodontal space develops along the new cementum, which is morphologically similar to the fibers of the normal periodontal fibers. But it differs in that the direction of the fibers are parallel to the root surface very similar to periodontal tissues of the developing tooth in a non-functional situation.

(2) Loss of morphology of the pulp with progressive fibrous replacement of pulp.

(3) Obliteration of the lumen of the root canal by laying down of laminated acellular cementum along the walls of the canal.

(4) Simultaneously, progressive resorption of the alveolar bone leads to the root fragment occupying more superficial position intraorally.

(5) Overlying prosthesis may exert pressure on it resulting in the development of a communication between the periradicular space and oral cavity.

Thus, it can be noticed that if the pulp is vital at the time of root fracture, the root remnant does not behave like a foreign body. The factors to be considered on the management of such root remnants are as follows:

(a) Vitality.
(b) Size and position of the root.
(c) Proximity to anatomical structures.
(d) Time lapse after the radicular fracture.
(e) Systemic status of the patient's age, physical and physiological status.

Hence, vitality and physiological size of the root and its close proximity to structures like maxillary sinus, neurovascular bundle are significant. If the foreign body response is seen, then the possibility of its resorption cannot be ruled out. Age factor is significant since it is related to the health status of the patient. As the age advances, degree of bone resorption as related to life expectancy. Physical status must be evaluated before taking any final decision regarding its management.

Localization

Once a decision is taken to remove the root, it must be clinically and radiologically evaluated. It is easy to localize in the dentulous jaw but it is relatively a difficult proposition in the edentulous jaw since intraoral periapical radiographs present two-dimensional picture and may even be misleading. Hence, many methods have been developed for its localization.

Impression of the alveolar ridge is taken and a cast is prepared. Wax sheet is adapted over the denture bearing area similar to denture base. Stainless steel wires are bent in different shapes and impregnated in different regions of the ridge for establishing the landmarks. The wax base is processed in clear acrylic. Intraoral x-rays are taken with this denture base in position. The relative position of the roots in relation to the wire landmarks in the denture base can form the guideline for its localization. This may be an useful method to place the incision but accurate localization may not be possible.

Based on the experience of this method, a similar method can be practiced by placing two or three small sterile suture needles in the suspected region as markers in the radiographs. Irrespective of the method - whether an acrylic template with wires impregnated or suture needles, intraoral radiographs taken, with the template or needles placed intraorally, help in the location of broken root. However, it is the responsibility of the dental surgeon to take a suitable decision as to whether to remove the root or to leave it behind. In case the root is left in situ, it must be properly recorded and the patient must be informed accordingly to avoid any medicolegal complications that may arise at a later date.

Impacted Teeth

GENERAL CONSIDERATIONS

Impacted tooth is one that fails to erupt and will not eventually assume its anatomical arch relationship beyond the chronological eruption date. All impacted teeth are unerupted or partially erupted. But any unerupted tooth can be termed as impacted only when root formation is complete and yet retained in an unerupted position. For example, during the eruptive phase, the angulation of the mandibular third molars are mesiooblique and maxillary third molars are distooblique. With the anteroposterior dimensional increase of the jaw bones, the teeth erupt and assume an upright posture. Such teeth should not be diagnosed as impactions.

ETIOLOGY

Chronology

Although any tooth in the dental arch can be impacted, only a few are predisposed to impaction than others in the following order of incidence. They are mandibular III molars, maxillary canines and premolars. It is extremely rare to find that I, II molars, incisors and deciduous teeth are impacted. This can be explained on the basis of the chronological order of eruption of these teeth. In general, any tooth erupting late, chronologically, can get impacted more frequently.

Lack of space

A few teeth are predisposed to impaction than the others due to lack of space. This may be due to the discrepancy between the dimensions of teeth and the dental arch. If so, the concerned tooth erupting late chronologically, within the insufficient available space, will present itself clinically as an impacted tooth. For example, mandibular III molar is impacted if the space between II molar and anterior border of the ramus is insufficient. Similarly, maxillary canine is impacted if the space between lateral incisor and first premolar is not sufficient. The same is true if II premolar has to occupy the space available between I premolar and I molar. Canine root being the longest, the crown has to cross the longest distance before erupting into the oral cavity. Such a problem of lack of space gets accentuated with increase in the mesiodistal dimension of the tooth and the progressive decrease in the arch-length as a process of evolution. On the contrary, I molar and incisors erupt early in the chronological order with ample space to accommodate them. Hence, in the event of impaction of these teeth, lack of space cannot be considered as the predisposing factor.

Obstructions

During the eruptive phase, if the crown encounters any obstructions like retained deciduous teeth, thick scar band, dense bone, odontome, cyst or odontogenic tumor, the concerned tooth remains unerupted beyond the chronological age. (Figs 7.1, 7.2)

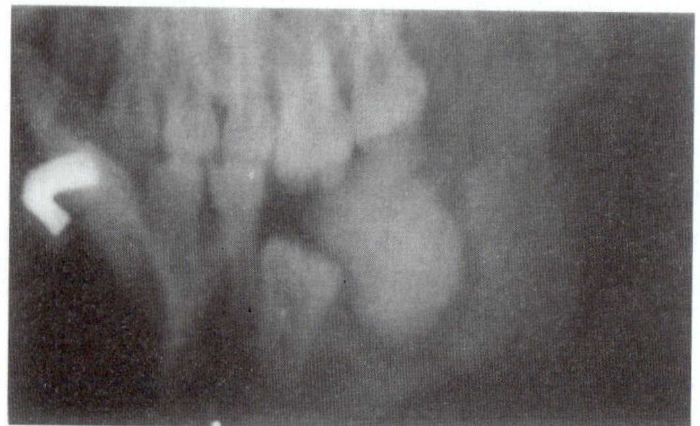

Fig. 7.1 Odontome obstructing the eruption of the mandibular I molar.

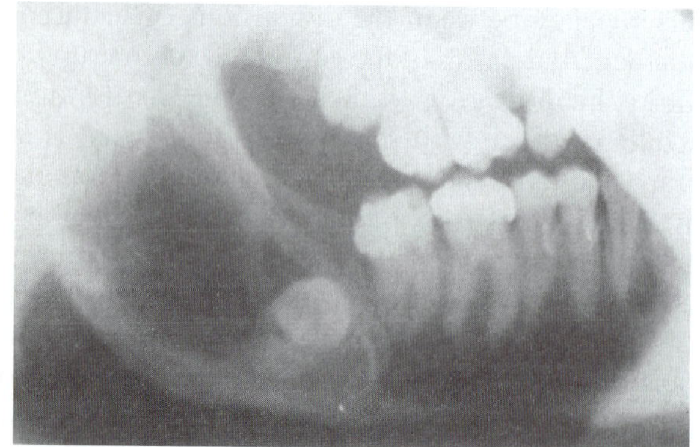

Fig. 7.2 Dentigerous cyst involving unerupted mandibular III molar.

Dilaceration

Deciduous anterior teeth involved in trauma transmit the traumatic force to the underlying permanent tooth bud. This leads to a shift in the long axis of the crown but the root formation proceeds in the predetermined direction. This may result in dilaceration of the root with different long axis of the crown and root respectively. This is responsible for the failure of eruption of the incisors or canines.

Non eruption

It necessarily does not mean that the tooth is impacted. Careful evaluation may reveal that it may be congenitally absent. Delayed or non eruption may be due to hormonal imbalances and other systemic causes. It can also migrate to the neighboring region (Fig. 7.3).

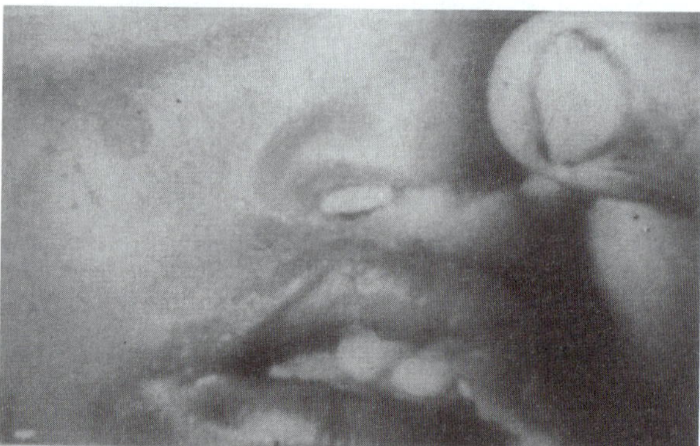

Fig. 7.3 Migrating incisor tooth erupting in the nasal cavity.

TO REMOVE OR NOT

Surgical removal of an impacted tooth is the frequently performed oral surgery procedure in dental practice. Whether an impacted tooth is to be removed or not can only be determined after careful evaluation of the patient. This consists of precise history, clinical examination, adequate knowledge of the regional anatomy, radiographic and physical examination and socioeconomic factors of the patient. On the basis of the decision taken, the treatment plan can then be formulated. Other important factors to be considered in this regard are as follows:

(1) Choice of anesthesia - whether local or general anesthesia or with sedation.
(2) Should it be an office procedure or the patient is to be hospitalized?
(3) When and by whom the surgery is to be performed?
(4) What surgical approach is ideal for the patient?
   (a) Buccal or lingual approach.
   (b) Chisel or bur to be used for the removal of bone.
(5) Should all the impacted teeth or only one is to be removed at a time?
(6) Consequences of removal or non removal of the impacted tooth.
(7) Cost-benefit analysis.

Indications for removal

(1) Nearly 75-80% of the patients are adults with partially or completely impacted teeth who develop *pericoronitis*.

(2) Need and the urgency for its removal depends on whether tooth is asymptomatic or not. Even if it is asymptomatic, decision is to be taken carefully depending on its adverse effects on health.

(3) Second molars are mostly involved with *caries or periodontal problems*, consequent to food impaction (Fig. 7.4). Root resorption may be due to the pressure effect.

(4) Recurrent *infection* around the pericoronal flap may predispose to temporomandibular joint problems.

(5) Removal of the impacted tooth is advocated as part of *preventive* dentistry to avoid problems at a later date since young patients tolerate the surgery very well with shorter convalescent period. As the age advances, the patients become medically compromised and hence complications are common.

(6) Pain or paresthesia like nonspecific earache and dental *pain* may be relieved by removal of such impacted teeth.

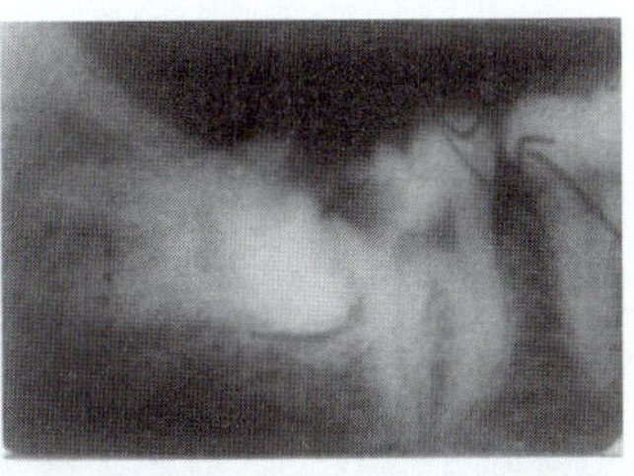

Fig. 7.4 (a) Dental caries in II molar with impacted III molar.

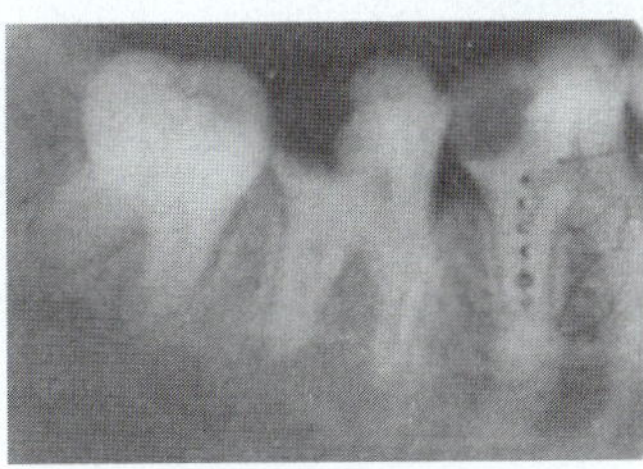

Fig. 7.4 (b) Dental caries in I & II molar. III molar impacted.

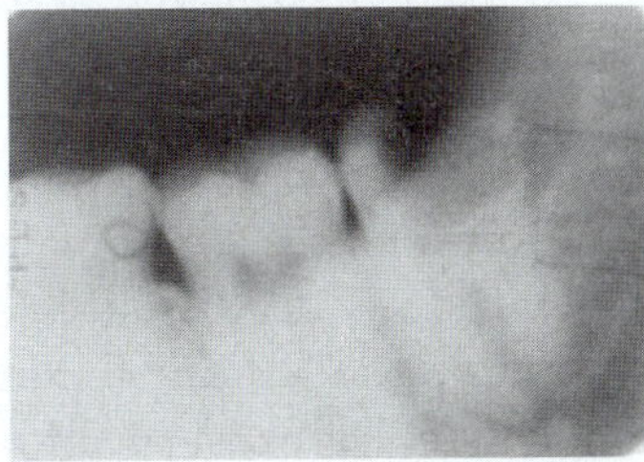

Fig. 7.4 (c) Caries in impacted III molar.

(7) These teeth may become *foci of infection* particularly for intractable ophthalmic problems, joint pain, general malaise, dermatological disorders etc.

(8) *Trauma* like recurrent cheek bite may be responsible for the development of premalignant and malignant lesions of oral mucosa.

(9) Due to pressure effects on the distal end of the arch, *orthodontic problems* like malocclusion and anterior overcrowding may develop during the adolescent period.

(10) Impacted teeth are frequently encountered with pathology like follicular *cyst or ameloblastic changes*. Presence of impacted mandibular III molar teeth with associated follicular 'cystic' and other lesions may weaken the bone and thus predispose

to fracture of the jaw bone (Fig. 7.5).

(11) Sometimes, removal of mandibular III

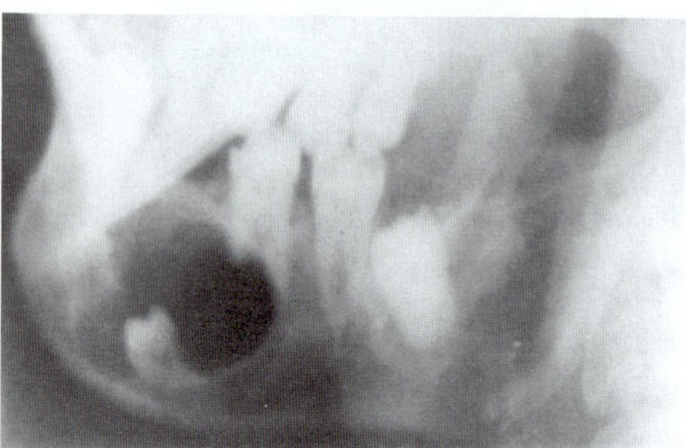

Fig. 7.5 A large lesion with an unerupted tooth weakens the bone.

molar tooth before root formation is indicated for *autotransplantation* to replace the lost I molar.

(12) The decision to remove an unerupted tooth in an edentulous jaw is always difficult to make. For *prosthetic considerations*, such a tooth may have to be removed to avoid or to manage frequent ulcerations under the denture. Many dental practitioners may not be aware of the existence of such impacted teeth until it becomes symptomatic. Rarely, it may even be a random radiological finding. Sometimes, partially erupted ones may be retained to serve as abutments for constructing fixed bridge prosthesis. Otherwise, all such teeth must be removed.

Contraindications

(1) **Health consideration.** Surgical removal is contraindicated if the patient is not fit to undergo minor oral surgery due to systemic disorders.

(2) **Prosthetic consideration.** Sometimes, partially erupted tooth has to be retained since such a tooth could be utilized as an abutment for a fixed partial denture.

(3) **Availability of adequate space.** Apparently an unerupted tooth may simulate an impacted tooth, but sometimes it is worth taking a chance to retain if adequate space is available for its eruption.

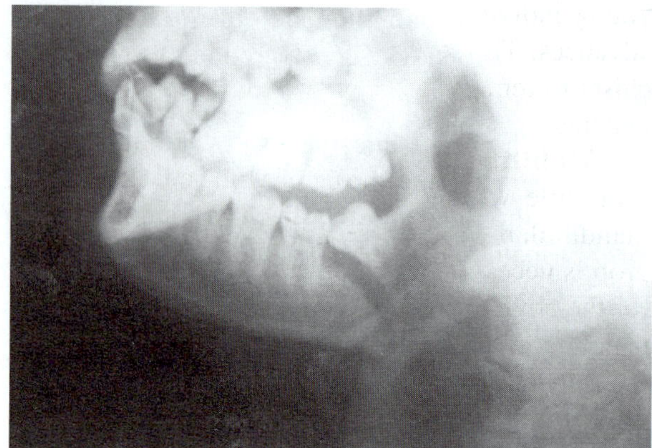

Fig. 7.6 The radiograph showing an unerupted III molar in the fracture line.

(4) **Socioeconomic reasons.** The patient may not be willing for removal due to fear of or for socioeconomic reasons.

Hopefully, the governing principle for the removal of an impacted tooth or not to remove is observed to preserve optimal oral health.

APPLIED ANATOMY

Location. Most of the impacted teeth are buried in the tissues with difficult access and may not be readily accessible.

Thick oblique ridge. Thick ridge on the buccal side resists buccal traction of the mandibular third molar.

Bone trajectories and grains. This is related to mechanical stress, run longitudinally parallel to the long axis of the bone. This is significant when chisel is being used for removal of bone to avoid inadvertent fracture involving wider areas of the mandible.

Mucoperiosteum. Extensive stripping of mucoperiosteum beyond the muscle attachment at the vestibule results in troublesome hematoma, swelling and postoperative discomfort. Likewise, extensive surgery on the lingual side leads to pharyngeal edema and dysphagia.

Bone and aging. Bone is relatively soft in

young individuals and becomes brittle as the age advances. This factor decides the choice of bur or chisel to remove bone in relation to the age of the patients.

Mobility of the jaw bones. Maxilla is immobile while mandible is mobile. So, when mandibular bone is removed with chisel, mouth prop is necessary to render the mandible immobile for the obvious reason. For the maxillary bone, this is not necessary.

Muscle attachments. Vestibule is formed by the attachment of buccinator buccally and mylohyoid lingually. Along the anterior border of the ramus, tendinous insertion of temporalis is present as two prongs along the external and internal oblique ridges. The labial vestibule is formed by the attachment of buccinator and orbicularis oris.

Blood vessels. Palatally, maxillary mucoperiosteum encloses large-sized greater palatine vessels. They are parallel to the dental arch situated supraperiosteally. Hence incisions placed across the dental arch are likely to damage these vessels. Such bleeding will be difficult to control. Distal to the mandibular III molar, a foramen is present, where a large-sized blood vessel may be encountered when the incision is extended distal to the mandibular III molar. In mandibular I molar region, care must be taken not to injure the facial vessel while extending the vertical incision down the vestibule. Such a bleeding will be difficult to arrest intraorally. In general, vessels are situated supraperiosteally. Therefore, incision on the attached mucosa must be subperiosteal to avoid bleeding.

Nerves. Mandibular (inferior dental) canal is closely related to the apices of mandibular molars. Lingual nerve is present on the lingual aspect of mandibular III molar. Hence, the possibility of damage of lingual and inferior dental nerves should not be overlooked.

Periodontal considerations. As far as possible, any incision involving the epithelial attachment must be avoided so that iatrogenic periodontal problems will not develop. Careful consideration on this aspect has led to the description of modifications of the standard incisions. More details are furnished where incisions are described.

MANDIBULAR III MOLAR

Classifications of impaction

Winter's classification (1926)

Winter described a method to classify the impaction of mandibular III molar taking into consideration the long axis of the impacted tooth in relation to the long axis of the second molar. This allows the description of vertical, mesiooblique, horizontal and distoangular impactions by working out the possibility of the direction and degree of obliquity of the impacted tooth. Later, Howe focussed the attention on the importance of vertical depth of wisdom tooth in the jaw by describing the "Winter's lines". The details are given under the heading "radiological interpretation".

Pell and Gregory's classification (1933) (Fig. 7.7)

The impacted mandibular third molars were classified very similarly to that of Winter's classification by utilizing the three-dimensional tilts of its long axis. There can be three possibilities depending on (a) relationship of the teeth to the ramus of the mandible, (b) relative depth at which it is placed and (c) the long axis of impacted tooth in relation to the II molar.

(1) *Availability of space between second molar and ramus (horizontal plane):*

Class I - Sufficient space exists between the distal aspect of second molar and anterior border of ramus to accommodate the mesiodistal diameter of the impacted tooth.

Class II - Space between the distal aspect of second molar and anterior border of the ramus is less than the mesiodistal diameter of the impacted tooth and hence partially buried in the ramus.

Class III - No space is available and hence the entire tooth is buried in the ramus.

(2) *Relative depth of the third molar (vertical*

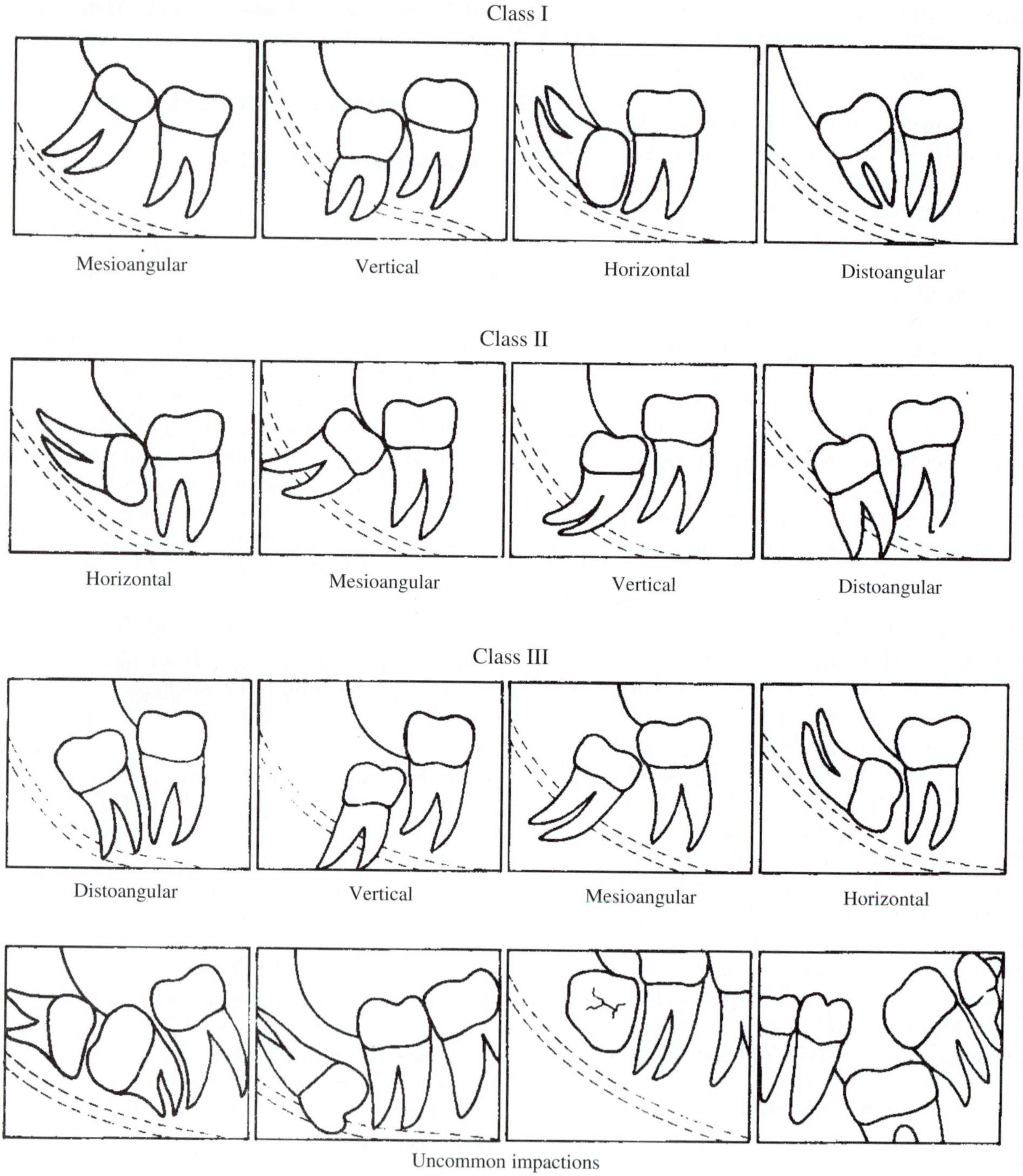

Class I

Mesioangular | Vertical | Horizontal | Distoangular

Class II

Horizontal | Mesioangular | Vertical | Distoangular

Class III

Distoangular | Vertical | Mesioangular | Horizontal

Uncommon impactions

Fig. 7.7 Diagrammatic representation of various types of impactions of mandibular III molar.

plane): (Fig. 7.8).

Position I - The highest point of the impacted tooth is in level with the occlusal plane.

Position II - The highest point of the impacted tooth is lower than the occlusal plane but above the cervical line of the second molar tooth.

Position III - The highest point of the impacted tooth is below the cervical line of second molar tooth.

(3) *Long axis of the impacted tooth in relation to the long axis of the second molar (angulation):* (Figs. 7.9, 7.10, 7.11).

Vertical, mesiooblique, horizontal, disto-angular, inversion, linguoversion and bucco-version. Thus, various possibilities can be worked out with various combinations. Examples of some rare impactions are illustrated in Figs. 7.12 to 7.14.

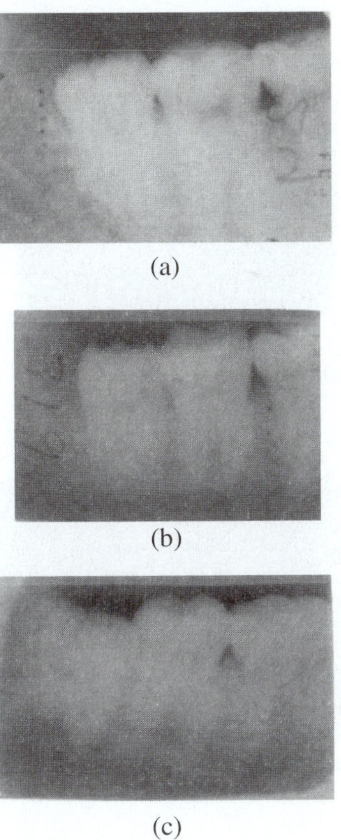

(a) (b) (c)

Fig. 7.8 a, b, c Vertical impactions.

Preoperative evaluation of the impacted mandibular III molar

Clinical

Treatment planning is based on thorough clinical evaluation of the patient with reference to the general and local factors, relevant to the possible postoperative sequelae. The systemic evaluation is identical to any other surgical procedures. In general, retrusive mandible, restricted mouth opening and small oral commissure are responsible

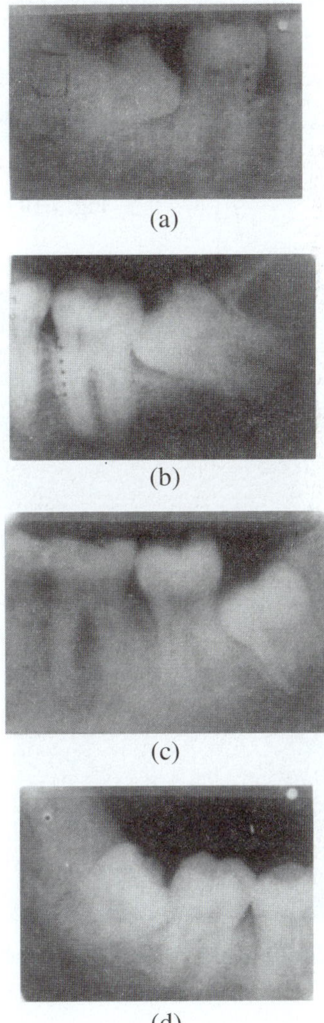

(a) (b) (c) (d)

Fig. 7.9 a, b, c, d Mesiooblique impactions.

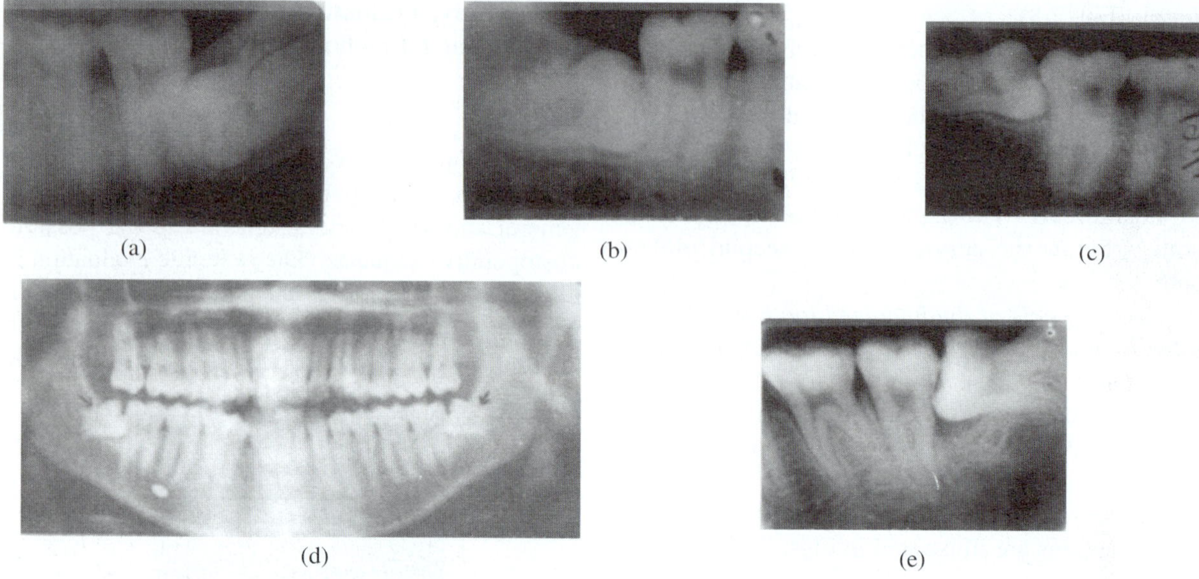

(a) (b) (c)

(d) (e)

Fig. 7.10 (a), (b), (c), (d), (e) Horizontal impactions.

(a) (b)

Fig. 7.11 (a), (b) Distoangular impactions.

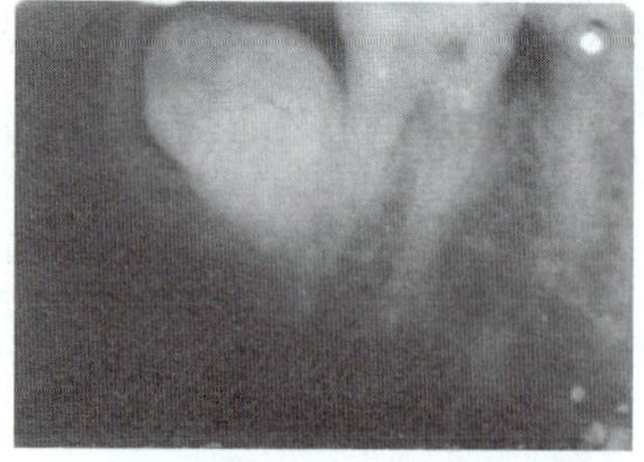

Fig. 7.12 Distoversion of III molar.

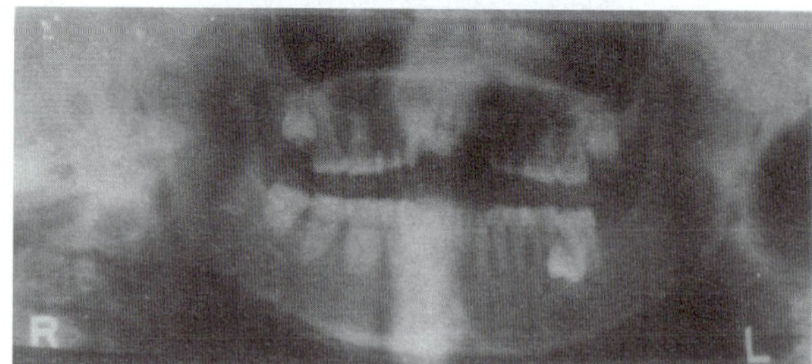

Fig. 7.13 (a) Inversion of the molar.

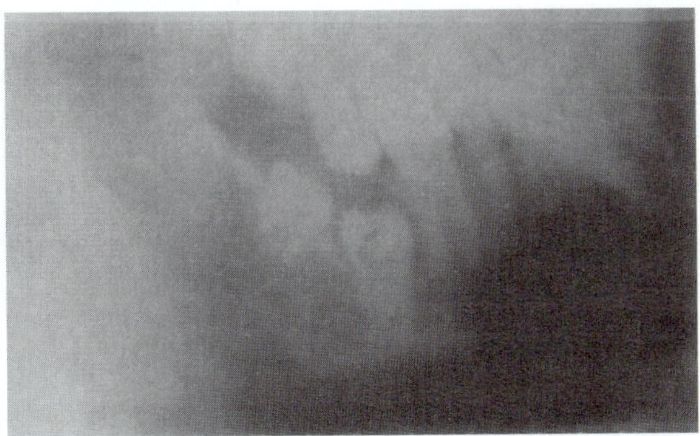

Fig. 7.13 (b) Impaction of II & III molar.

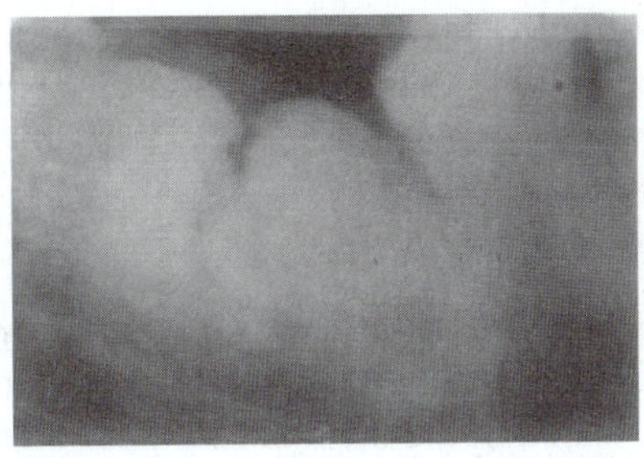

Fig. 7.13 (c) Impaction of II & III molar with crowns of the teeth facing each other. Occlusal view of mandible showing unerupted canine migrating from the right side.

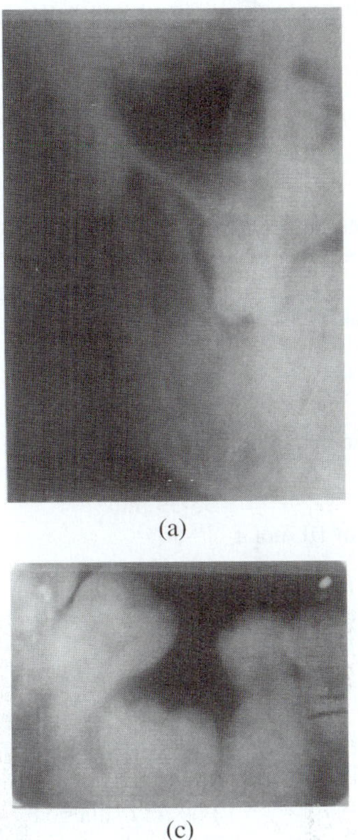

(a)

(c)

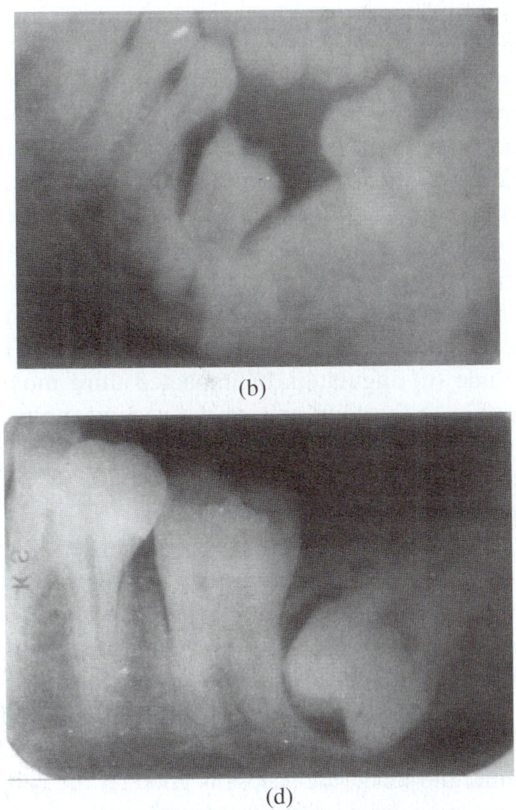

(b)

(d)

Fig. 7.14 Rare impactions: **(a)** Unerupted mandibular III molar lying near the sigmoid notch, **(b)** Unerupted mandibular I molar, II molar already extracted, **(c)** Unerupted mandibular I molar, **(d)** Inversion of unerupted mandibular III molar.

for the poor access to the surgical field. Conversely, protrusive mandible and large mouth opening will greatly increase the access.

Radiological assessment

(1) **Technique.** A standard periapical radiograph of the mandibular third molar region is mandatory. The patient is seated in the dental chair with mandibular occlusal plane parallel to the ground floor in the mouth-open position. Intraoral film is inserted and retained in the lingual vestibule, resting on the lingual surfaces of the molars. Ideally, anterior edge of the film should correspond to the mesial surface of the first molar and the superior edge should be marginally above the occlusal plane of the mandibular tooth. However, if third molar is horizontally placed, anterior edge of the film should correspond to the distal surface of the first molar. The x-ray cone is placed in such a way that the central rays pass through the distal cusps of second molar tooth at right angle to the x-ray film. In this way, buccal and lingual cusps of second molar will superimpose one over the other.

(2) **Types of impaction.** They must be identified as described under classification. They include (a) angulation of impacted third molar in relation to the long axis of the second molar, (b) type of impaction in relation to horizontal and vertical planes. The position and depth within mandible are also important factors.

(3) **Access.** Surgical access identified as easy or difficult can be determined by recording the inclination of the external oblique ridge, represented by the radioopaque line. For example, access is excellent if it is horizontal while access is poor if it is vertical. Similarly, if the radioopaque line representing the external oblique ridge is situated behind the tooth, the access is good. If the ridge is along or in front of the impacted tooth, access is poor.

(4) **Existing pathology.**

(a) Dental caries in II and III molars.
(b) Periodontal disturbances.
(c) Presence or absence of I molar.
(d) Any fusion of crowns between II and III molars.
(e) Conical and fused roots of II or III molars.
(f) Any associated dental pathology like odontome, cyst or neoplasm.
(g) Flexibility of the orofacial muscles.

Presence of dental caries, altered morphology of roots, type of the surrounding bone, presence of hypercementosis and difficult access predispose to breakage of the food during the removal of the impacted teeth. Presence of any existing pathology like cyst or tumors may predispose to pathological fracture of the mandible. Its proximity to inferior dental canal is a warning to the surgeon about the possibility of the nerve damage.

(5) **Scoring details for Wharf assessment** (Table 7.1)

Table 7.1 Scoring details for Wharf assessment

	Category	*Score*
1. Winter's classification	Horizontal	2
	Distoangular	2
	Mesioangular	1
	Vertical	0
2. Height of the mandible	1-30 mm	0
	31-34 mm	1
	35-39 mm	2
3. Angulation of III molar	1°-50°	0
	60°-69°	1
	70°-79°	2
	80°-89°	3
	90° +	4
4. Root shape	Complex	1
	Favorable curvature	2
	Unfavorable curvature	3
5. Follicles	Normal	0
	Possibly enlarged	1
	Enlarged	2
6. Path of exit	Space available	0
	Distal cusps covered	1
	Mesial cusp also covered	2
	Both covered	3
	Total	33

The six factors chosen for the scoring are:

(a) Winter's classification
(b) Height of the mandible
(c) Angulation of II molar
(d) Root shape
(e) Follicle
(f) Path of exit of the tooth during removal.

The scoring by this method helps the beginners to anticipate problems and to avoid difficult impactions. Unfortunately, the pitfall of this method is that, details of the surgical procedure are not considered. It is related to radiological features alone.

In this type of assessment, the total scoring to individual cases are directly related to the corresponding difficulties that one is liable to encounter during the removal of the impacted tooth. At any rate, this serves as a warning for the surgeon, by way of precaution.

(6) **Position and depth.** They can be determined by a method originally described by George Winter. Similar to cephalometric radiograph, a tracing of the intraoral periapical radiograph is taken. Three imaginary lines are drawn, known as "Winter lines".

"White line" represents the occlusal plane, joining the white enamel caps of the erupted molars. It is extended posteriorly over the third molar region. Perpendicular line drawn to the occlusal plane over the II molar represents its long axis. The axial inclination of the impacted third molar in relation to the long axis of II molar becomes quite obvious. For example, in vertical impaction, occlusal surface of the impacted tooth is parallel to the white line. In mesioangular impactions, occlusal plane of III molar meets the white line in front of the third molar. The maximum contour of the impacted tooth and its relationship to the white line will indicate the relative depth of its location.

"Amber line" represents the bone level, distal to the third molar and extended anteriorly along the crest of the interdental septum between the molars. The "amber line" represents the summit of the alveolar bone covering the impacted tooth. Hence, when the mucoperiosteal flap is reflected, the position of the impacted tooth above the amber line will be visible while the rest of the portion of the impacted tooth is embedded in the bone. This will indicate the extent of bone to be removed for the extraction of the impacted tooth.

"Red line" is drawn perpendicular from the amber line to an imaginary "point of application" of the elevator. Usually, cementoenamel junction on the mesial surface of the impacted tooth is taken as the point of application of the elevator. Thus, "Red line" indicates the depth at which the impacted tooth is located. Only in distoangular impactions, cementoenamel junction on the distal surface is taken as the point of application of the elevator.

It is estimated that any impacted tooth with less than 5 mm long "Red line" can conveniently be removed with ease under local anesthesia. Increase in the length of the red line of every additional mm renders the removal of the impacted tooth three times more difficult. Depending on the difficulties, they are best removed safely under endotracheal anesthesia if the red line is more than 9 mm and if the impacted tooth is below the level of the apices of II molar. Careful planning is necessary as to whether II molar will have adequate bony support or whether extensive removal of bone may render the mandibular II molar weak (Fig. 7.15).

Buccoversion and **linguoversion** can be identified by the relative radioopacity of the

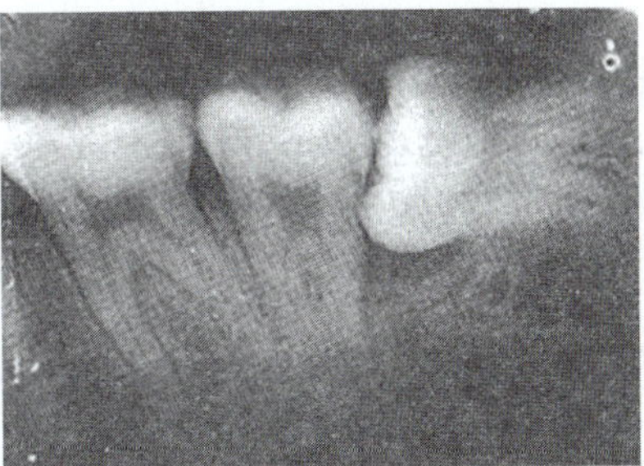

Fig. 7.15 Deep horizontally impacted III molar close to the neurovascular bundle has rendered II molar periodontally weak.

impacted tooth in relation to II molar tooth. The portion of the tooth near the x-ray film is more sharply defined and hence more radioopaque and vice-versa. "Tube-shift" method is more accurate for this purpose.

(7) **Crown of the impacted tooth.** Large bulbous crown with prominent cusps may present difficulty in smooth delivery. To avoid extensive bone removal, tooth-division technique is indicated.

(8) **Configuration of the roots of the impacted III molar tooth.** The **"point of application"** of the elevator and **"the path of delivery"** of the impacted tooth vary greatly depending on the configuration of the roots of the impacted tooth to be removed. Radiograph must be carefully examined with reference to the following factors:

(a) Fused or separate roots
(b) Number of roots
(c) Straight or curved roots
(d) If curved, is curvature favorable or unfavorable?
(e) Long and slender or short and stout roots.
(f) Convergent or divergent
(g) Texture and type of investing bone, e.g. hypercementosis etc.

Unfavorable curvature indicates the need for the tooth division technique. Hypercementosis renders removal of bone more difficult.

Root of the II molar. If II molar roots are smaller in relation to the impacted tooth or if the roots of II molar are fused and conical, operator must be careful not to luxate the II molar during the elevation. Similarly, absence of I molar leaves the II molar unsupported. During elevation, inadvertent luxation or dislodgement of II molar should be avoided.

(9) **Bone texture.** The texture and density of the investing bone varies with individuals, age, sex, and systemic constitution. Bone is cancellous and elastic in the younger age group, while it tends to become dense and sclerosed as the age advances.

(10) **Relationship with inferior alveolar (dental) canal.** If the root apices are very closely related to the inferior alveolar (dental) canal, the patient should be sufficiently warned about the possible postoperative impairment of labial sensation. When in doubt, it is better to employ tooth division technique to minimize the possible nerve damage. During surgery, even if the nerve is damaged, close proximity between the cut ends and the patent canal will promote recovery of the sensation within few weeks to few months.

Prediction of injury to the inferior alveolar (dental) nerve

Even if the tooth is not related, injudicious elevation of mesioangular impaction may result in the root apex impinging on the inferior alveolar (dental) canal. Roberts and Harris (1973) pointed out that impaired labial sensation is an unpleasant postoperative complication which can also develop due to the damage of the mylohyoid nerve. Radiological preoperative assessment is very important to identify the proximity of the impacted tooth to the inferior alveolar (dental) canal. Howe and Poyton (1960) developed the criteria to diagnose the "true relationship" of the root apices of impacted mandibular III molars to the inferior alveolar (dental) canal. A review of literature reveals that four radiological signs are seen in the roots of teeth, while three changes are noticed in the appearance of the canal. Sometimes, they may not be related but may be superimposed in the radiograph.

Relationship of the root to the canal

I. *Related but not involving the canal.*
   (a) Separated
   (b) Adjacent
   (c) Superimposed.

II. *Related to changes in the roots.*
   (a) Darkening of the root (radiolucent)
   (b) Dark and bifid root
   (c) Narrowing of the root
   (d) Deflected root.

III. *Related to changes in the canal*

(a) Interruption (loss) of lines

(b) Converging canal (narrowing)

(c) Diverted canal.

I. *Related but not involving the canal*

Root apex may be nearer to the canal but intervening *bone separates* both of them. If the intervening bone is less, it is considered to be adjacent. In some cases, roots superimpose the canal. Hence, in a two- dimensional periapical radiograph, the root appears to be closely related. Careful examination will reveal neither the outline of the root nor the canal is disturbed. In all these three conditions, chances of nerve injury are relatively rare. In the following cases, where roots are closely related to the canal with associated changes in the roots or canal, postoperative impairment of labial sensation is a possibility.

II. *Related to changes in the roots*

(a) *Darkening of the root.* Throughout the length of the root, its density is the same. It is not disturbed when the image of the root apex and canal overlap. But the density of the root is altered when the root impinges on the canal. In such conditions, the related position of the root is said to be relatively radiolucent and appear dark. Such darkening of the root is due to the decreased amount of the dental structures and/or cortical lining of the inferior alveolar (dental) canal.

(b) *Dark and bifid root.* When the canal crosses the root apex, it can be identified by the double periodontal membrane shadow of the bifid root apex.

(c) *Narrowing of the root.* If there is any narrowing of the root where the canal crosses, it denotes the presence of deep grooving or perforation of the root or the involvement of the greater diameter of the root by the canal in some form.

(d) *Deflected root.* This is seen as a deviation of the root buccally, lingually or both when it reaches the canal. It may even be deflected to the mesial or distal aspect.

III. *Related to changes in the canal*

(a) *Interruption or loss of white radioopaque lines.* The dense root and floor of the canal are seen as two white radioopaque lines in the radiograph. Either of them or both may be disrupted in relation to the root structure. This is considered to indicate deep grooving of the root and loss of the dense cortical walls of the canal which is considered to be a "danger sign".

(b) *Converging canal (narrowing).* When the canal crosses the root apex, there is a reduction in its diameter. This narrowing or converging appearance of the canal is due to the displacement of the roof and floor of the canal towards each other resulting in an "hourglass appearance". This appearance indicates partial encirclement of the canal. This is also considered as a "danger sign".

(c) *Diverted canal.* The canal appears diverted when it changes its direction. This is due to an upward displacement of the canal passing through the root. During eruption, the contents are considered to be dragged along.

The nerve injury presents as anesthesia or altered sensation of the lower lip and chin. The degree of the disturbance varies from mild to deep anesthesia. The involved area extends medially to the midline and alternatively up to an imaginary line extending downwards and backwards from the angle of the mouth to the lower border of the mandible innervated by the mental nerve. Intraorally, it extends over the area innervated by the inferior dental nerve and its branches. Isolated submental anesthesia is due to mylohyoid nerve injury. Studies have revealed that any darkening of the root, diversion of the canal and interruption of the white line are found to be significantly related to the inferior alveolar (dental) nerve injury as compared to the other signs. However, mere absence of preoperative radiological signs does not appear to ensure that nerve injury will not occur during the surgery.

(11) **Other radiographic techniques.** (a) As a routine, radiographs in one plane will be enough

but, in some occasions, another radiograph in the third dimension may be useful. Donovan (1952) described an axial projection method. The conventional intraoral x-ray represents the two-dimensional picture of the impaction- superoinferior and anteroposterior-while this axial projection reveals the third dimension. Intraoral x-ray film is placed in the transverse direction, at an angle of 45° with one edge resting against the anterior border of the ramus and another edge distal to the second molar. The central-ray is passed extraorally at the angle of the mandible perpendicular to the film. However, this method is not popularly practiced.

(b) *In "tube-shift" technique,* two conventional intraoral periapical radiographs are taken to provide useful information on the position of the tooth. One film is exposed in the usual orthoradial position, while the other film is placed in the same position but exposed on the mesio or distoeccentric position. If the tooth is lingually placed and hence close to the film, no significant differences are noticed in both the films. If it is buccally placed, tooth shadow appears to move in the opposite direction. To illustrate this phenomenon, one may recall the imaginary movements of the objects while travelling in a vehicle or train. When one looks through the window, objects near the window appear to move in the opposite direction and farther objects in the same direction. This exemplifies the phenomenon very well.

(12) **Age considerations.** Opinions widely vary concerning the stage in which it is ideal to remove the wisdom tooth surgically. Some prefer to wait until symptoms develop while others want to perform early prophylactic "odontectomy" of the unmineralized tooth germ, even at the age of 9 to 11 years. Mandibular growth pattern and the expected available space for the third molar to erupt can accurately be predicted. Those teeth which are liable to be impacted are ideally indicated for prophylactic odontectomy soon after the eruption of the II molar.

Early removal is considered to have the following advantages:

(i) Root formation is yet to be completed.

(ii) Pericoronal space is wide (for these two reasons, removal is relatively easy).

(iii) The tooth is not related to the inferior alveolar (dental) canal.

(iv) General health of the patient is good in young patients. Hence healing is usually uneventful.

Disadvantages with advancing age:

(a) Root formation is complete with unfavorable morphology.

(b) Closely related to inferior alveolar (dental) canal. Hence, technically removal becomes difficult.

(c) The patient becomes medically compromised as the age advances. Consequently, operative and postoperative complications are more.

But, experience has shown that majority of the patients wait until symptoms develop. Most of the impacted teeth are removed during the third decade of life or later. Such therapeutic removal is practiced to treat inflammatory complications while early prophylactic extraction is done in the age group of 14 to 18 years for orthodontic reasons.

(13) **Iatrogenic periodontal disturbances.** Two years after III molar surgery, in 32% of cases, intrabony pocket was found to develop distal to II molar. It was also found that morbidity of periodontal tissues may be reduced, if the III molar is removed at an early age. Clinical examination of the patients prior to and after III molar surgery have been studied on the following aspects to determine the periodontal problems of II molar by recording the intrabony pocket.

(a) Smoking habits
(b) Health status
(c) Oral hygiene index
(d) Plaque and gingival index
(e) Radiographic examination.

The incidence of periodontal disturbance to II molar is found to be high in individuals over 30 years. Hence, the following measures have been advocated to reduce the incidence of such iatrogenic periodontal disturbances:

(a) Optimization of the surgical technique including modified incision and careful removal of bone distal to II molar.

(b) Early removal.

(c) Maintenance of enhanced plaque control postoperatively.

(14) **Timing of removal.** Swelling and pain on the second or third postoperative day make the review of the patient mandatory. Hence, it is better not to operate on any patient who is not available for examination between second and fourth postoperative days. The pericoronal infection should be treated and surgery must be undertaken electively during the next opportune occasion. In diabetic patients, it is better to perform surgery in the morning to facilitate better after care with longer period of observation.

(15) **Evaluation of factors that render third molar surgery relatively "easy" or "difficult"** are provided in Table 7.2.

Table 7.2 Evaluation of factors that render III molar surgery relatively easy or difficult

Factors	*Relatively easy*	*Relatively difficult*
1. Pell and Gregory's classification		
(a) Horizontal plane	Class I	Class III
(b) Vertical plane	Position I	Position III
2. Overlying impediment	Soft tissue	Bone
3. Crown	Small	Large
4. Roots		
(a) Formation	Incomplete	Complete
(b) Curvature	Favorable	Unfavorable
5. Follicular space	Large	Thin and small
6. Surrounding bone	Elastic and cancellous	Dense or cortical
7. Relationship		
(a) II molar	Distal space	No distal space
(b) Inferior alveolar Canal	Not related	Related
8. Oral sphincter	Large	Small
9. Health status	Satisfactory	Medically compromised

SURGICAL MANAGEMENT

Historical background

Prior to the discovery of the x-rays, surgeons advocated that only those teeth that can readily be examined clinically in the oral cavity be removed with a cow-horn forceps. This was because such impacted third molars are not readily accessible. Symptomatic teeth were treated by extraction of the II molars. Traditionally, maxillary III molars were also removed to relieve the occlusal trauma. John Tomes was one of the first to describe the method of gaining access through a mucoperiosteal flap. Later technical improvements were due to the development of improved facilities for assessment, advancement in the techniques of surgical removal, better understanding about aseptic measures and improved patient management of impacted third molars. Basically, surgical removal involves the following steps, irrespective of the techniques adopted.

(a) Anesthesia
(b) Incision and mucoperiosteal flap
(c) Removal of bone
(d) Tooth removal
(e) Wound debridement
(f) Arrest of hemorrhage
(g) Wound closure
(h) Postoperative follow-up.

Mucoperiosteal flap (Fig. 7.16)

An impacted tooth buried under the tissues can be elevated only after gaining adequate access and eliminating the impediments. To gain access, all the basic principles of a flap must be followed. Many types of incisions have been advocated. Practically all of them have a posterior and an anterior limb with or without an intermediate limb. The incision should not be extended too far distally to avoid (a) troublesome bleeding from the buccal vessels and anastomosing branches of lingual and facial arteries, (b) postoperative trismus due to the damage of temporalis muscle and (c) herniation of buccal pad of fat into the operating field which is very tempting to pull it out further. Similarly, the distal incision made along the occlusal plane or towards the lingual direction carries the risk of iatrogenic injury to the lingual nerve, that is present submucosally.

(1) *L-shaped flap.* This is the most commonly practiced design. Incision distal to the II molar is angled laterally from the lateral margin of the distolingual cusp of the II molar. The total length of the distal incision is around 2 cm. Anterior limb is the vestibular extension at the level of II molar. If wider exposure is desired, it can extend anteriorly up to the I molar but it carries the risk of damaging the facial vessels if it is extended beyond the vestibular depth. Both the limbs of the incision join at the distobuccal region of the II molar tooth. During the elevation of this flap severing of the distal attached gingiva at the junction of both the limbs can iatrogenically result in gingival recession postoperatively. This can be avoided, if the incision is made in such a way that it avoids the damage to the distal epithelial attachment of the II molar by rendering the junction of both the limbs as a smooth one-sweep curve. This will also avoid the extension towards the vestibule by extending the anterior limb curved anteriorly above the vestibular level. Instead of placing the junction between both the limbs at the distobuccal cusp of the II molar, distal incision can be extended in such a way that mesial limb starts at the midpoint of the buccal free marginal gingiva of II or I molar tooth. This is to avoid splitting the interdental papilla.

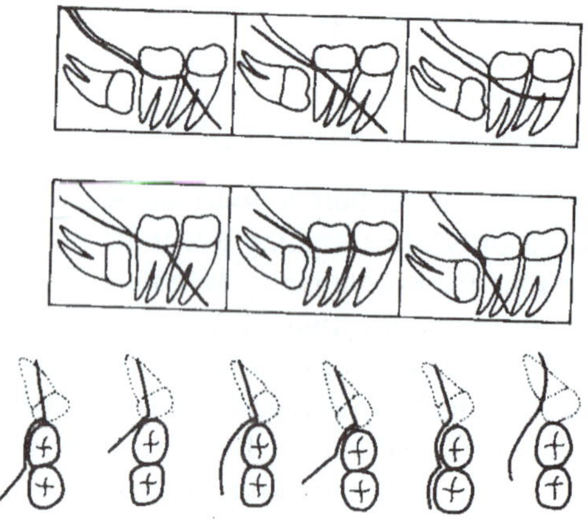

Fig. 7.16 Different types of incisions for surgical removal of impacted mandibular III molar. **(a)** Side view, **(b)** Superior view.

Another modification has been suggested by shifting the distal incision away from the distobuccal aspect of the II molar. In this type, the intermediate limb is vertical towards the junction of both the limbs.

Minor modifications include shifting the junction of both the limbs from distobuccal region of II molar to the midpoint of the distal region or even to shift lingually. Attempts have been made to leave behind a band of tissue with the epithelial attachment undisturbed.

(2) *Envelope flap.* The distal limb is similar to L-shaped flap. The difference lies in the anterior limb. It confines itself along the free gingival margin. Its anterior extension is directly proportional to the depth at which the impacted tooth is present. Hence, deeper the tooth, the longer the anterior extension.

(3) *Bayonet-shaped flap.* It has three parts - mesial, distal and intermediate or gingival limbs. The incision for this type of the flap is very similar to L-shaped flap. The junction between the two limbs is the intermediate gingival incision, around the distobuccal half of II molar tooth. In this type, more difficult is the tooth, more likely that the distal incision is placed more lingually. However, standard incision is at the midpoint of the distal surface of II molar. The intermediate gingival part varies considerably. If the mesial incision is angled forwards, it increases the access. It also provides better blood supply to the flap by providing a broader base.

If the impacted tooth is partially erupted, care is taken to eliminate the sulcus epithelium. This is done by introducing an intermediate limb around the partially erupted tooth. If it is not done, the intermediate limb carries the sulcus epithelium so that when the wound is sutured with the lingual flap, wound dehiscence develops. Hence, to achieve primary closure, this modification is necessary. Otherwise, primary suturing must be avoided under such circumstances.

(4) *General observations on the incision.* The success of any of these incisions depends on many factors. Following are some of the important factors:

(a) Surgical access.

(b) Healing of the sutured wound in terms of the patient's discomfort: Incidence of dry socket increases if the distal incision extends beyond the external ridge.

(c) Extensive studies on the role of the flap design on periodontal health have demonstrated that the incision that does not involve the epithelial attachment decreases the incidence of pocket formation distal to II molar.

(d) The incision must be located in such a way that suture line must rest on the normal bone. If it rests on the blood clot or empty cavity, wound margin breaks down.

(e) When part of the crown is clinically visible, epithelium present in the gingival crevice must be eliminated by a reverse bevel incision with BP blade No. 12. Failure to do so results in wound dehiscence.

However, the ultimate choice of the flap design considered for gaining access to the impacted third molar should be more with the operator rather than on any other criteria.

(5) *Elevation of the flap.* Irrespective of the flap design, the main intention of the operator is to elevate a satisfactory mucoperiosteal flap so as to adequately expose the impacted tooth and the overlying bone. If the incision has been made deep down to the bone beyond the attached gingiva, periosteal elevator can be inserted and the flap is released away from the bone. Wherever the tissues are adherent, a pair of scissors is useful to severe the attachment. For raising the envelope flap special instrument may be necessary to elevate the flap since it is difficult to enter into the correct plane with the attachment. It depends on how one gains entry below the periosteum by blunt dissection. Otherwise, perforation or button-hole develops in the flap. One must be careful while the distal limb of the flap is undermined beyond the required region in the ramus, particularly towards the internal oblique ridge. If the distal limb is placed at the centre of the retromolar fossa, tissue planes at this region do not divide that easily. At this point, any dissection with a sharp instrument may damage the lingual or mylohyoid nerve. Hence, the operator must not underestimate the importance of careful elevation of the mucoperiosteal flap. Experience has shown that mortality is not encountered in third molar surgery but clumsiness certainly increases the morbidity.

Once the flap is adequately reflected, proper retraction is essential. To meet the increased demand of the assisting hands, a great deal of ingenuity has played a part in popularizing self retaining retractors. For example, a retractor component could be attached to the mouth prop so that when the mouth prop is in position, the self retaining retractor plays its role by effectively retracting the flap.

Another useful modification is a small retractor, very similar to a thimble of the tailor. The *"thimble"* could be worn by the operator on the left index finger so that the flap can be retracted without much difficulty (Fig. 7.17). More often curved tip of the Howarth periosteal elevator itself can be utilized as an effective retractor.

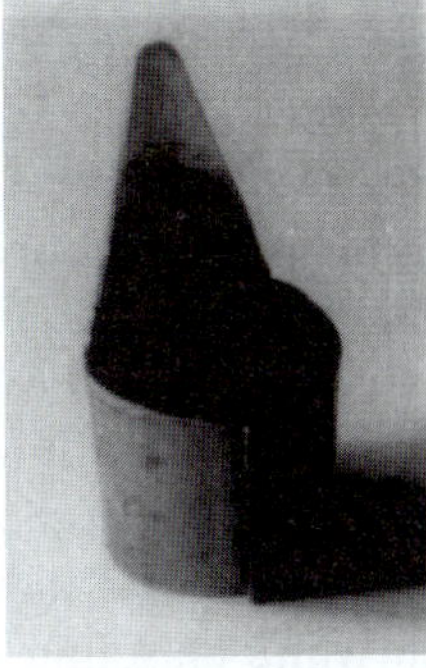

Fig. 7.17 Thimble as a modified retractor in III molar surgery.

Bone and tooth removal

Evaluation of the impacted tooth by the Winter's lines greatly helps the operator to determine the amount of bone that has to be removed. Amber line will indicate the extent of bone covering the crown. Adequate removal of bone to expose the crown of the impacted tooth is carried out with chisel, bur or combination of both. Redline will determine the point of application of the elevator and the depth at which the tooth is placed. The quantum of bone removal depends on the technique used.

Bur technique. A suitable mucoperiosteal flap exposes the impacted tooth and the bone covering the tooth. An adequately sized, rose head bur is used to make a "gutter" around the distal and buccal aspect of the impacted tooth. When the bone is removed at the distolingual region, lingual flap should be properly protected with a periosteal retractor. Failure to do so is likely to damage the lingual flap or the lingual nerve. More amount of bone is removed around the point of application to engage the elevator. Throughout the procedure, copious amount of normal saline is irrigated to avoid thermal necrosis of bone. To keep the operative field clear, an efficient suction is used constantly. Usually Ash No. 18 or 19 straight elevator is used for elevating the third molar. The principles of using an elevator has already been described under exodontia. After the removal of the tooth, a large vulcanite bur is used to burnish the sharp bony edges. The wound is irrigated well before suturing the wound. Contraangle handpiece modified for third molar surgery is also available (Fig. 7.18).

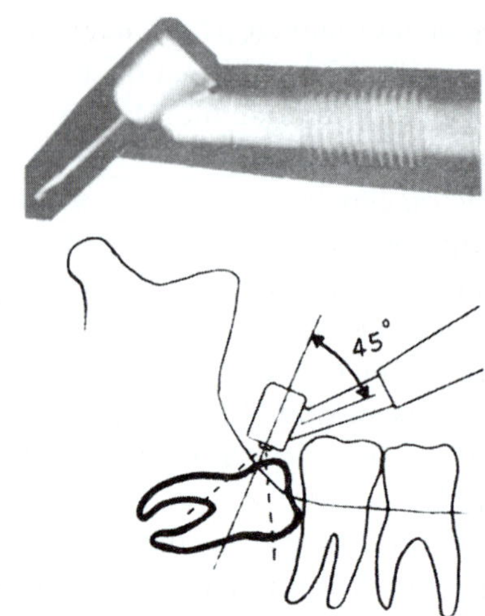

Fig. 7.18 (a) Modified handpiece with 45° head-to-shank angle makes the access to the mandibular III molar region easy, **(b)** Bur technique.

Chisel technique through buccal approach. A convenient mucoperiosteal flap is raised to expose the impacted tooth and the bone covering it. It is mandatory to make the mobile mandible immobile by placing a mouth prop on the opposite side molar region. The patient is then asked to bite on the mouth prop while chiseling of the bone is done, keeping in mind the direction of bone trajectories and grains. It is parallel to the long axis of the bone. The curved trajectories at the third molar region run anteriorly parallel to the oblique ridges. To restrict the bony cut to the desired extent, a vertical limiting cut is made by placing a 3 mm or 5 mm chisel vertically at the distal aspect of the II molar with the bevel facing posteriorly. After making a vertical groove, the limiting cut is completed by shifting the chisel anteriorly with the bevel resting on the bone, thereby making a deep vertical groove. Its approximate height is 5-6 mm. Then the chisel is placed at an angle of 45º at the lower edge of the limiting cut in an oblique direction. This will result in the removal of a triangular piece of buccal plate distal to the II molar. If necessary, bony cut can be enlarged to uncover the impacted tooth to the desired level. Finally, distal bone must be removed so that when the tooth is elevated, there is no obstruction at the distobuccal aspect.

Point of application of the elevator is created by removing a triangular piece of bone at the junction of the vertical limiting cut and the oblique bone cut. The distolingual bone is then fractured parallel to the external oblique ridge and hinge it lingually on the soft tissues if necessary. The fracture should not be parallel to the internal oblique ridge since such a fracture may extend up to the coronoid process.

Tooth division technique. If the tooth occupies a large area, as in horizontal impaction, a suitably modified flap is raised by extending in the anterior direction to expose the impacted tooth. If the entire tooth is to be elevated, large amount of bone is required to be removed. To avoid the removal of large amount of bone and to avoid the disturbance of the adjoining anatomical structures, tooth division technique is utilized. In the usual way, chisel is used to expose the buccal aspect of the crown. Then, bur is used to make a vertical groove on the cervical region of the crown. The cut is completed with a sharp osteotome. Thus, the crown separates from the root. Then root is removed with an elevator. If the roots are unfavorably curved, the roots are also divided at the bifurcation and removed separately. After the tooth removal a careful wound toilet is essential. This technique was described by Kelsey Fry.

Tooth division permits less bone removal and consequent smaller dead space. However, healing of bone does not depend on the extent of bone removal. Bone removal is never critical. *"Bone belongs to the patient and the tooth belongs to the surgeon."* This implies the tooth division technique.

Lateral trephination technique. This procedure is indicated for removing the unerupted III molar in the age group of 9 to 16 years. This modified S-shaped incision is made from retromolar fossa across the external oblique ridge. It then curves down along the reflection of the mucous membrane above the vestibule, extending up to the I molar anteriorly. Such an incision leaves behind a 5-mm cuff of attached mucosa at the distobuccal region of the II molar. The mucoperiosteal flap is elevated and held in the retracted position. The buccal cortical plate is trephined over the III molar crypt. The same bur is used to make vertical cuts anteriorly and posteriorly. A chisel or an osteotome is applied in the vertical direction over the bur holes. Then the buccal plate is fractured out, exposing the third molar crypt completely. Elevator is applied to deliver the tooth out of the crypt. Any follicular remnant present in the crypt is carefully scooped out, avoiding injury to the inferior alveolar (dental) canal at the lower part of the crypt. After smoothening the sharp bony margins and irrigating the wound, flap is sutured in position.

Lingual split bone technique was evolved and introduced by Kelsey Fry and later popularized by T. Ward. This method is useful to remove any impacted III molar placed lingually. The incision is very similar to any other technique. The mucoperiosteal flap is raised by any standard method. In the mandible, grains run along the long axis of the bone. Hence, grains are curved in the III molar region. In the usual way, a vertical limiting cut is made distal to the II molar on the buccal bone. This helps to establish the point of application of the elevator.

Now, in this technique, next is to remove the distolingual bone, by placing a 5-mm chisel distal to the III molar with the bevelled side facing upwards and cutting edge *parallel to the external oblique ridge*. If it is placed parallel to internal oblique ridge, osteotomy cut extends up to the coronoid process. The chisel is then driven into the depth depending on the desired level. The chisel is removed and replaced with the bevelled side downwards. The direction of the cut is now altered from downwards to inwards, that is, towards the lingual plate. By twisting the chisel, the bone splits obliquely backwards. The lingual plate breaks anteriorly at its thinnest point where crown of the III molar is nearest to the lingual surface. Now, a wedge-shaped piece of bone is removed. With an elevator, the tooth is elevated and delivered in the lingual direction. Then, the flap is sutured. The operator must be careful to avoid damage of the lingual nerve.

Position of the operator

Usually, the right handed operator is positioned to the right of the patient. The incision is made in the anterior (posteroanterior) direction, irrespective of the side of the surgery. More often, the direction of the incision is made to suit the convenience of the operator and the relative position to the patient. Killey recommended the incision for the buccal approach by starting just above the sulcus and then towards the third molar to avoid the accidental damage to the blood vessels. Warwick James operated with patient's head positioned between his knees and incised in an anteroposterior direction. Probably, he must have found that incising towards him was easier. Thus, incision depends on one's own convenience rather than any anatomical necessity.

Cost-benefit analysis

This is a term familiar to the business community. Of late, health professionals have started realizing the importance of cost-benefit in terms of providing health care to the patients. In the field of oral surgery, nearly 75% of the fees is derived from the surgical removal of the impacted third molars. The cost-benefit analysis of surgical removal of mandibular third molar is more appropriate. Hypothetically, if a flowchart is drawn on the basis of the number of possibilities and consequences, then the process of decision making will be within manageable limits. While doing so, the discussion will be restricted to well defined indications for the removal of impacted mandibular III molars of the "population at risk."

Consequences of removal

(1) 10-30% of cases develop dry socket postoperatively when compared to a low incidence after the routine dental extraction (2-4%).

(2) Damage to inferior alveolar (dental), lingual and mylohyoid nerves with impaired sensation are noticed in 2-3% of cases.

(3) Iatrogenic pocket formation distal to the II molar is relatively very high. This depends on the type and area of bone removal behind the II molar tooth. Studies have revealed that periodontal healing is impaired in individuals over 30 years. Therefore, optimization of the surgical technique and maintenance of enhanced plaque control may be beneficial.

(4) The postoperative complications like infection, pyrexia, pain and swelling between the second to fifth postoperative days are seen in nearly 50% of cases.

(5) Damage to the adjacent teeth may occur.

(6) General effects: III molar surgery increases the anxiety of the patient acting as a powerful stressing stimulus.

(7) Deeply placed impacted tooth in an edentulous jaw predisposes to fracture of the mandible.

(8) Increased fibrinolytic activity of blood, raised ESR, leucocytosis, increase in pulse rate, BP and urinary adrenaline are noticed during surgery.

Consequences of not removing an impacted tooth

(1) If the impacted tooth continues to be symptomless, the patient may be convinced that it need not be removed at all. But as the age advances, patient's general health deteriorates. With such medically compromised status, healing is likely to be adversely affected.

(2) With increasing age, bone becomes brittle and sclerosed. Hence, surgical procedures become more difficult and tedious. Difficulties with anesthesia, management of postoperative infections and many other complications are encountered.

(3) Retention of such teeth may predispose to infection (space infections and osteomyelitis), fracture mandible, cystic and neoplastic formation. Hence, biological prediction could become unpredictable.

The incidence of pathological lesions in relation to the impacted tooth does not seem to depend on the age. But, the postoperative complications are directly proportional to the degree of impaction and

RETROSPECTIVE ANALYSIS

1. Buccal vs Lingal Approach

	Criteria	*Buccal*	*Lingual*
1.	Access	Relatively easy in the conscious patient	Relatively difficult in the conscious patient
2.	Instruments	Chisel and mallet or Bur	Only chisel and mallet
3.	Procedure	Tedious	Easy
4.	Operating time	Time consuming	Less time consuming
5.	Technique	Easy to perform, hence traditionally popular	Technically difficult, hence not popular among all dental surgeons
6.	Bone removal	Thick buccal plate	Thin lingual plate
7.	Postoperative pain	Less	More due to the damage of lingual periosteum
8.	Postoperative edema	Obviously more	Less
9.	Dry socket	Incidence is high due to the damage of external oblique ridge	Incidence is negligible since socket is eliminated

2. Chisel vs Bur

	Criteria	*Chisel and Mallet*	*Bur*
1.	Technique	Difficult	Easy
2.	Patient's acceptance	Not tolerated well when performed under local anesthesia	Tolerated well under local anesthesia
3.	Chance of fracture of the bone	Relatively high	Less possibility
4.	Healing of bone	Good	Delayed due to overheating and inefficient cooling, aggravated by inefficient cutting of bone resulting in thermal necrosis.
5.	Postoperative edema	Less	More If airotor is used. Chances of emphysema are also more
6.	Dry socket	Incidence is less	Very high
7.	Postoperative infection	Less	More
8.	Advantage/Disadvantage	Difficult to remove deeply buried impactions; Impaction in edentulous jaws and in elderly patients.	Relatively easy to remove deeply buried impactions, impactions in edentulous jaws and in elderly patient.

age. Hence, early removal is preferred even though it is symptomless instead of facing the situation in a difficult circumstance. Thus, it becomes a difficult task for the dental surgeon to advice the patient appropriately as to whether to remove the tooth or not when it is symptomless. Germectomy is easy to perform but extremely difficult to motivate the patient. Similarly, it is equally difficult to perform or convince the patient as the age advances. Hence, one has to be very careful in assessing the relative importance. Equal care must be taken to impress on the patient regarding the transitory complications to avoid any possible medicolegal complications.

REPORT OF A WORKSHOP ON THE MANAGEMENT OF PATIENTS WITH THIRD MOLAR TEETH

In August 1993, American Association of Oral and Maxillofacial Surgeons convened a two-and-a-half-day workshop on the management of patients with impacted third molar teeth. The participants analysed objectively the literature and developed recommendations for the management of third molar teeth. They also identified the research questions and strategies on this aspect. The main discussions include (a) natural course, (b) identifications for care, (c) perioperative management, (d) wound healing and (e) complications. Summary of the recommendations of the workshop is furnished here:

A. Natural course

(a) **Is the change in third molar tooth position in adults predictable?** Accurate prediction in position/eruption in a given individual is not possible. Uprighting of unerupted third molars commonly occurs upto 25 years. Teeth in vertical position mostly proceed to full eruption. They may change position and if so, it may or may not be favorable. Such retained teeth should be monitored professionally - more frequently up to 25 years.

(b) **When a decision can be made that third molar is impacted?** It can continue to change position after skeletal growth is complete and fully formed. All horizontally impacted teeth in the ramus and those unerupted beyond the middle of third decade will remain impacted.

(c) **Under what circumstances do the third molars cause resorption of the second molar?** It occurs more frequently with horizontal and mesioangular impactions and progresses as the age advances.

(d) **What are the risks of such retained teeth?**

- (i) Cysts and tumors
  - (a) teeth-related lesions like dentigerous cysts
  - (b) associated lesions like keratocyst, odontogenic tumors and carcinoma.
- (ii) Infections like periodontitis, pericoronitis, osteomyelitis and space infections.
- (iii) Periodontal defect distal to the II molar.
- (iv) Dental caries and root resorption of II molar.

(e) **Is third molar tooth position a predictor for pericoronitis?** Pericoronitis is positively correlated with angulation, degree of eruption and anatomic factors. Vertical and distoangular impactions [soft tissue or partly covered by bone] are at highest risk. Horizontal full bony impactions have the least risk.

(f) **Do third molars adversely affect periodontal health?** Soft tissue partly covering the unerupted teeth serves as a reservoir for periodontal pathogens. Removal of such partly erupted teeth reduces the number of pathogens and plaque around adjacent teeth.

B. Indications for care

Note: Third molars are differentiated as "erupted", "partially erupted" and "impacted".

"erupted" - entire clinical crown visible.

"partially erupted" - so positioned that a portion of the clinical crown is visible.

"impacted" - so positioned that it will probably not erupt.

For removal

(i) Tooth non restorable due to caries, fracture or periodontal lesions.
(ii) To facilitate the management of periodontal disease.
(iii) Acute or chronic infections like pericoronitis, cellulitis or abscess.
(iv) To facilitate prosthetic orthodontic treatment.
(v) Tooth involved in the resection.
(vi) To facilitate orthognathic surgery.
(vii) Prophylactic removal for patients with focal sepsis before surgery like organ transplants, implants, chemotherapy or radiotherapy.
(viii) Pathology associated with the tooth follicle.
(ix) Resorption of adjacent tooth.

C. Perioperative assessment

It includes preoperative patient evaluation, risk assessment, operative management and post-operative care with the objective of minimizing known risks and complications.

Preoperative assessment: It should be appropriate to the patient's medical condition, type of anesthetic to be used and the operative procedure to be performed. It must include (i) review of the patient's medical/dental history, (ii) physical examination, (iii) preoperative risk assessment and (iv) an imaging examination appropriate to the patient's condition.

(1) **What is the proper means of preventing alveolar osteitis?** There is no definitive evidence that any technique eliminates alveolar osteitis. Literature and clinical experience supports the use of topical antimicrobial agents in the tooth socket to decrease the incidence of alveolar osteitis. Use of chlorhexidine mouth rinses may also be effective in reducing the incidence.

(2) **What is the role of intraoperative lavage?** Lavage of the tooth socket with saline appears to be effective in reducing its incidence.

(3) **What is the role of perioperative steroids?** Administration of steroids has shown to reduce the incidence of postoperative swelling, pain and trismus.

(4) **What is the role of perioperative antibiotics?** There is insufficient evidence to determine whether routine systemic antibiotic therapy decreases the postoperative incidence of pain, swelling, infection and alveolar osteitis.

(5) **What can be recommended regarding pain management?** Perioperative/appropriative use of steroids appears to decrease the postoperative pain. Use of long acting local anesthetics also appears to be advantageous in decreasing postoperative pain.

(6) **Is primary closure or closure leaving a gap distal to the second molar preferable?** Tight, primary-watertight-closure appears to increase postoperative pain and swelling.

(7) **Further studies are required** concerning (a) effectiveness of analgesics, (b) relationship of temporomandibular joint and third molar, (c) effectiveness of polyglycolic acid and polylactic acid sutures in the extraction sites and (d) the type and effectiveness of cold therapy for the management of postoperative pain and swelling.

D. Wound healing

(1) **Is there a preferred flap design for the removal of third molar?** Two well controlled prospective studies have shown no difference between flap designs that provide anterior vestibular release and those that do not.

(2) **What are the risk factors of alveolar osteitis?**

(a) Smoking and bacterial contamination.
(b) Increased age.
(c) It is not clear whether principal risk factor is decreased vascularity or increased exposure to bacterial contamination.
(d) Literature concerning the influence of gender and oral contraceptives is not

definitive.

(e) Information concerning whether there is any relationship to the day of the menstrual cycle and type of birth control medications with the incidence of alveolar osteitis.

(f) Experience of the surgeon, amount of surgical trauma and the duration of surgery are factors that appear to influence the incidence of alveolar osteititis.

Unfortunately, a consistent definition of alveolar osteitis currently does not exist.

(g) Is pericoronitis a risk factor for operative morbidity?

Pericoronitis appears to be a risk factor for alveolar osteitis and postoperative infection.

(3) **What is the natural course of neurosensory deficits after surgery?** Deflection of the canal, loss of lamina dura of the canal, shadowing of the roots and to a lesser extent, narrowing of the canal are seen as significant radiographic indicators of increased chance of nerve injury. Neurosensory deficit after third molar surgery disappears within 4 to 6 months in nearly 75% of cases.

(4) **When should third molars be removed to minimize problems of wound healing?** The least morbidity arises with early removal before complete root development.

(5) **What are the factors that may influence healing following third molar removal?**

(a) Plaque accumulation on the distal surface of II molar.
(b) Periodontal defect distal to the II molar.
(c) Pathological widening of the follicle.
(d) Smoking.
(e) Age more than 25 years.
(f) Presence of infrabony defect distal to the II molar, increased mesioangular inclination, increased contact area of the third molar with II molar and resorption of the II molar roots. Any three of these factors lead to increased risk of poor healing. Each risk factor may lead to an increased depth of the infrabony pocket of 0.5 to 1.0 mm per factor. Perioperative periodontal scaling has no effect on wound healing after the removal of third molar.

E. Complications

Potential complications were identified and the following format for evaluation was established.

(a) Frequency
(b) Significance
  (i) reversibility
  (ii) degree of mobility
  (iii) disability
  (iv) complexity of management.

Risk of neurosensory injury

(1) **Frequency**

(a) Reports indicate that incidence of injury to the inferior dental nerve of 1.0 to 7.1%.
(b) Incidence to the lingual nerve is lower - 0.02 % to 0.06 %.
(c) Injury to buccal nerve and mylohyoid nerves is not routinely reported.

(2) **Significance**

(a) *Reversibility:* Most of the nerve injuries are reversible.
(b) *Degree of morbidity:* Density and persistence of unpleasant sensation like pain and burning will effect morbidity.
(c) *Disability:* Minimal for majority of patients.
(d) *Complexity of management:* Data on timing of surgical correction and outcome assessment is lacking. Microsurgical repair of the damaged nerve is potentially complex.

(3) **Variables in neurosensory risk**

(a) Relationship of the tooth to the nerve
(b) Bone density
(c) Dilaceration of roots
(d) Flap design

(e) Thickness of the lingual plate
(f) Anatomic variation
(g) Use of a local anesthetic
(h) Mechanical trauma - burs, chisels, retractors
(i) Surgical approach. Eg. Lingual approach.

(4) **Risk of major infection after third molar surgery**

Major infection in this context is defined as one requiring I.V. antibiotic therapy with or without hospitalization.

Infections can be classified into four categories:

(i) *Categories:*
  (a) Immediate major
  (b) Immediate minor
  (c) Delayed major
  (d) Delayed minor.
(ii) *Frequency:*
  (a) Immediate major - extremely low
  (b) Immediate minor - low
  (c) Delayed major - lower than immediate major
  (d) Delayed minor - low.
(iii) *Significance:*
  (a) Reversibility - usually complete
  (b) Degree of morbidity - varies with severity
  (c) Disability - usually short-term
  (d) Complexity of management - varies with severity.
(iv) *The overall frequency of infection* has been reported to be 0.06% to 4.3%.

(5) **Indications for surgical repair of sensory nerve injury**

Literature is insufficient to answer this question.

(6) **Association between TMJ problems and 3rd molar surgery**

(i) Frequency: extremely low - sufficient data not available.
(ii) Significance:
  (a) Reversibility - generally reversible
  (b) Degree of mobility - minimal
  (c) Disability - usually short term and minimal
  (d) Complexity of management - usually minimal involving symptomatic care.

(7) **Specific complications**

(a) Alveolar osteitis (dry socket)
(b) Fractured maxilla
(c) Fractured mandible
(d) Hemorrhage
(e) Postoperative sequelae (unusual)
(f) Airway obstruction
(g) Oroantral fistula
(h) Displaced teeth during surgery.

(a) *Alveolar osteitis*

Frequency : incidence reported 1% to 30% - variable.

Significance:

Reversibility - reversible

Degree of morbidity - short term (manifestations are locally severe, hygiene is a problem, diet is altered.)

Disability - short term

Complexity of management - generally uncomplicated.

(b) *Fractured maxilla*

Frequency - low. Usually tuberosity is involved.

Significance:

Reversibility - reversible

Degree of morbidity - minimal

Disability - minimal

Complexity of management - simple.

(c) *Fractured mandible*

Frequency - extremely low. It increases with age, physical and medical status, and complexity of the procedure.

Significance:

Reversibility - reversible

Degree of morbidity - significant.

Disability - short term - minimal with loss of masticatory efficiency and decreased jaw function.

Long-term - rare. Some degree of neurologic deficit and non union.

Complexity of management: moderately complex, increases with long-term disability.

(d) *Hemorrhage*

Frequency - 0.2 to 1.4 %

Intraoperative - rare

Immediate postoperative - rare

Delayed - rare

Significance:

Reversibility - readily reversible

Degree of morbidity - very low

Disability - low

Complexity of management - usually simple.

(e) *Postoperative sequelae (unusual)*

(excessive swelling, severe dysphagia, severe pain, severe trismus)

Frequency - low

Significance:

Reversibility - readily reversible

Degree of morbidity - low

Disability - short-term but severe

Complexity of management - self limiting and reversible.

(f) *Airway obstruction*

Frequency - extremely rare

Significance:

Reversibility - extremely low

Degree of morbidity - moderate to grave

Disability - short term but severe

Complexity of management - moderate to complex.

(g) *Oroantral fistula*

Frequency - extremely low

Significance:

Reversibility - reversible

Degree of morbidity - low

Disability - low

Complexity of management - low to moderate.

(h) *Displaced teeth*

(Antrum, submandibular space, airway, GI tract, infratemporal space.)

Frequency - low.

Significance:

Reversibility - reversible

Degree of morbidity - low

Disability - low

Complexity of management - low to moderate.

UNERUPTED MAXILLARY III MOLAR (Figs 7.19 and 7.20)

UNERUPTED CANINE (Figs 7.21 to 7.23)

General considerations

Ectopic eruption and impaction/non eruption of permanent canine is a frequently encountered clinical problem. Diagnosis and management of this problem is very important from esthetic point of view. Unlike mandibular and maxillary third molars, possibilities of retention of unerupted canines must be carefully evaluated since permanent maxillary canine tooth is regarded as the *"corner stone"* of the dental arch. Hence, absence of canine in its position in children over 13 years, without any history of extraction, must be carefully investigated. All possible efforts must be taken to eliminate the impediments for its eruption and also to guide the tooth into its occlusal position. Any delay to get the tooth into its functional position may mean that extraction is the only available mode of treatment. Such teeth should always be investigated systematically.

Incidence ranges from 0.92 to 1.8 %. Its clinical absence reflects the esthetic value. Its role in occlusion during mandibular lateral excursion is equally well known. Chronologically, permanent canine erupts in the preexisting available space between the lateral incisor and first premolar. It has the longest period of development from the deepest area, which explains the fact that maxillary canine has the longest root.

During its eruptive phase, the crown has to

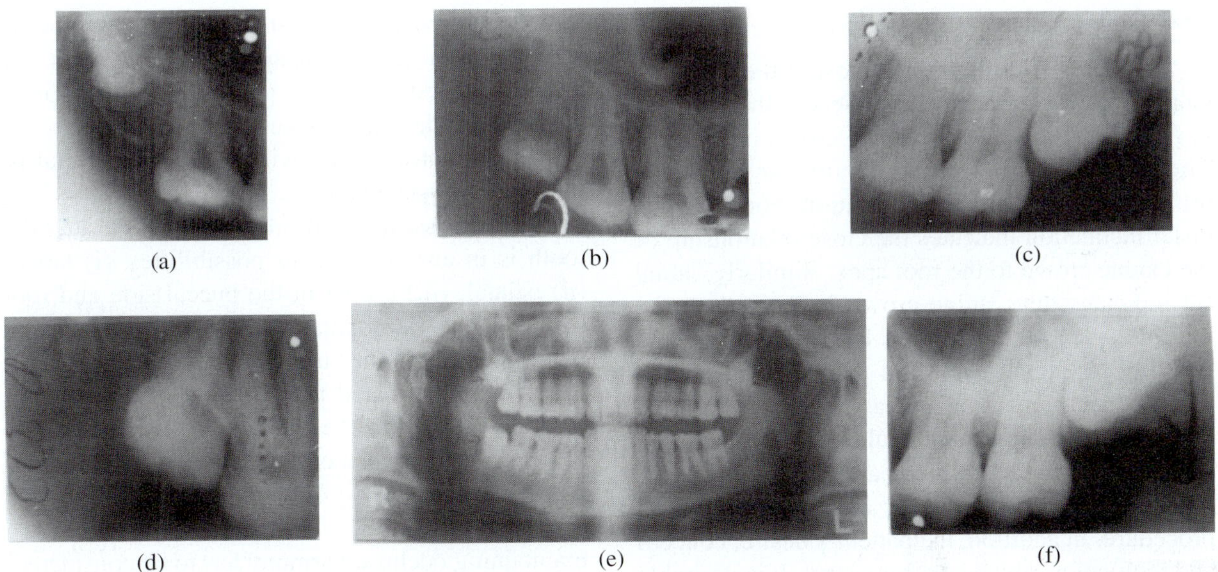

Fig. 7.19 Maxillary III molar impactions.

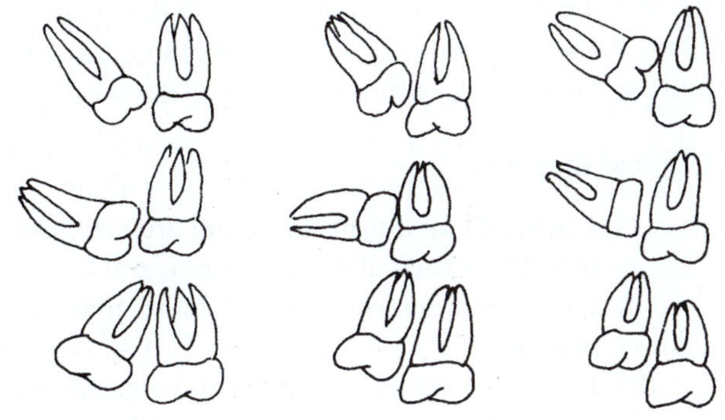

Fig. 7.20 Different types of impactions of maxillary III molars.

travel the most devious path of longest distance before it reaches its functional occlusal position. Hence, lack of space at the appropriate time to ensure normal eruption seems to be the most probable predisposing factor for its non eruption. The canine lags behind during its crown formative phases. Displacement from its normal path of eruption most commonly occurs in a palatal direction. Lack of resorption of deciduous canine is also considered to be responsible although failure of eruption seems to be a consequence of rather than the cause of impaction.

Etiology

(1) Generalized cause include endocrine deficiencies.

(2) The local causes - either individually or combination of the following factors (multifactoral etiology).

(a) Tooth size - arch length discrepancies.
(b) Early loss or prolonged retention of deciduous canine.
(c) Dilaceration.
(d) Ankylosis.
(e) Abnormal position of the tooth bud.
(f) Canine in relation to alveolar cleft.
(g) Cystic or neoplastic formation in relation to the developing canine.
(h) Early correction of distally tipped and flared lateral incisor.

Assessment

Clinical examination. In most of the cases, on palpation, a bulge could be noticed either labially or palatally. It may be due to the crown or the root. The angulation of the lateral incisor may also provide a clue regarding its location. For example, distal inclination indicates the close relationship of the canine crown to the root apex. Similarly, labial tilt indicates that canine crown is located on the buccal aspect of the root. If it is retroclined and possibly in lingual occlusion then it indicates the palatal displacement of the canine. But its relative position in the dental arch could be confirmed only with radiographs. The medical and dental history are elicited as required for any minor surgical procedure. In addition, the patient's desire, concern and motivation are equally important. It is desirable to discuss with the patient, the possible modes and duration of the treatment before taking any decision.

Radiographic examination. It is necessary to locate the true position and direction of the unerupted tooth with radiographs in two planes - horizontal and vertical- for the accurate localization. In the horizontal plane, the standard periapical or anterior occlusal radiograph reveals the detailed picture of the unerupted canine and the structure of the surrounding bone. A lateral radiograph may be necessary to estimate as to how high the tooth is placed in the maxilla.

In the vertical plane, occlusal view reveals the palatobuccal position of the tooth and its relation to the dental arch. The central ray is projected along the long axis of the incisors. The better method would be to utilize the parallel method advocated by Clark in 1909 to demonstrate the buccopalatal position. It is also known as the tube-shift method. In this method, two periapical radiographs are taken with the films placed in the same position. One film is exposed in the usual way. Another film is exposed with the x-ray cone moved horizontally in any one direction. Both the films are compared. The tooth is considered to be placed palatally if the tooth shadow appears to have moved in the same direction since it is farthest from the x-ray tube. If it is buccally placed, it appears to move in the opposite direction. This phenomenon has been described under mandibular III molar.

Orthopantomogram will also be beneficial to locate the impacted tooth.

The **assessment** will ultimately reveal that the tooth is in any of the four possibilities: (i) labial, (ii) palatal, (iii) crown in the buccal side and root in the palate (labiopalatal) and (iv) crown in the palate and root in the buccal direction (palatolabial). It has been estimated that 76% to 93% are found palatally or within the dental arch. Recently, CT scan has been advocated to detect the resorption of the roots.

Malocclusion. The role of canine in maintaining occlusal harmony has to be considered. The availability of space, presence of deciduous canine or supernumerary tooth are taken into consideration while determining the complexities of the treatment involved to correct the malocclusion. Thus, the assessment is determined by three factors: patient, location of canine and malocclusion.

Clinical features

(1) Clinically absent in the dental arch beyond the chronological age of eruption.
(2) Displacement of adjacent teeth may be present.
(3) Presence of swelling in the buccal or palatal mucosa over the unerupted tooth.
(4) Formation of fistula in the region of the unerupted tooth.
(5) Transformation into follicular cyst.
(6) Resorption of adjacent roots or alveolus leading to mobility.

Root morphology. The root is often hooked or curved which may be responsible for fracture at the root apex during its removal. The usual radiograph reveals the curvature of the root but it will not be obvious if the long axis and the x-ray beam are in the same plane. The root apex lies in the direction of eruption of canine tooth. It is reasonable to deduce that the presence of deflection of the apex is the result rather than the cause of impaction.

Treatment possibilities

Prevention of canine impaction. When the clinician detects early signs of ectopic eruption or noneruption, attempt should be made to prevent the impaction and its potential sequelae. One such measure is *serial extraction* as early as 8 to 9 years of age. It has been estimated that in 91% of cases, removal of deciduous canine will normalize the position of canine if crown of canine is distal to the midline of the lateral incisor. The success rate is estimated to be around 60% if the permanent canine is mesial to the midline of the lateral incisor tooth.

Once the evaluation reveals that the canine tooth is displaced, several options are open for treatment. The management depends on many factors. They are:

(a) Age of the patient.
(b) Stage of tooth development.
(c) Position of the impacted tooth.
(d) Evidence of root resorption of permanent teeth.
(e) Patient's motivation to undergo the treatment.

The various possibilities of treatment are:

(i) To leave the tooth in situ.
(ii) Surgical removal of the unerupted canine and prosthetic replacement.
(iii) Surgical removal of the unerupted canine and mesial movement of the I premolar in its position.
(iv) Surgical exposure of the crown.
(v) Surgical repositioning.
(vi) Surgical autotransplantation.

The surgical repositioning and transplantation procedures are best left to expert oral surgeons to assess the need and to carry out the procedure if indicated.

No treatment (to leave the tooth in situ). So long as the deciduous canine is in its position, the patient may not be willing to undergo any type of treatment. But the patient must be educated regarding the possible complications of leaving behind the impacted canine in situ. For example, it may predispose to resorption of roots of the adjacent permanent teeth or may be involved in cystic changes of the tooth follicle. Sometimes, resorption may be rapid. In the event of the decision being taken to leave the tooth in situ, it must be periodically monitored radiographically at intervals. If the patient is not medically fit to undergo the surgical procedure, then it is better to defer the surgery.

Surgical exposure of the crown. The objective of this procedure is the suitable exposure of the crown for the application of traction. Radiological and clinical evaluation is done to carefully assess the various aspects concerning the indications, possible sequelae of surgical exposure and the type of impediment for the tooth to erupt in the normal sequence. Once an appropriate decision is taken, the surgical exposure can be achieved by surgically removing the hard and soft tissues present in the path of its eruption in such a way that the appropriate anchorage point is readily available.

The unerupted tooth is exposed by placing a cruciform incision with its center over the anticipated location of the crown of the unerupted tooth. The resultant four triangular flaps are raised adequately and excised so that crown is exposed, which is lying in a bony cavity. Hemostasis can be achieved by the application of pressure. If necessary, sufficient bone is removed which obstructs the path of eruption. The tip and maximum contour of the neck around the cingulum is also exposed carefully without damaging the adjacent dental structures in such a way that the bony cavity is also saucerized. While doing so, adequate care is taken to sufficiently expose the labial surface of the tooth. To prevent epithelialization around the exposed crown, a surgical pack can be inserted.

This is not without problems since the health

of the periodontium deserves special mention. The pocket depth and the level of alveolar bone on the mesiopalatal aspect of surgically exposed palatal canine are important factors. Normally, such an exposed tooth erupts by itself without any necessary aids like pins or brackets for the traction. The application of traction itself has been a subject of controversy. Hence, the operator should carefully assess the need for such a traction.

Even though problems related to the failure of normal eruption are encountered frequently, it has long been recognized that it should be possible to predict and prevent them by the timely intervention. If an ectopic eruptive path is confirmed clinically and radiologically, interceptive measures will involve extra action of the deciduous canine, surgical exposure, transplantation or removal. Usually, the timing and type of surgery are dictated by orthodontic considerations. It is very important to recognize that surgery follows orthodontic planning rather than preceding it.

Surgical removal

It is indicated if:

(1) The impacted canine is located very far from the occlusal plane.
(2) No other methods are possible to retain the tooth.
(3) The patient is not willing to undergo orthodontic treatment for longer duration.
(4) Leaving behind may result in resorption of adjacent dental structures.
(5) Pathological changes in the crypt like infection, periodontal disturbances and cyst formation.
(6) The required space does not exist for the canine tooth in its functional position.
(7) Because of the unfavorable anatomy of the tooth, other methods like repositioning is not likely to be successful, e.g. curved roots, etc.

The prognosis for the long term retention of deciduous canine must be assessed and the patient must be appraised of further treatment in case it is lost eventually.

Procedure. The operator has to decide as to whether to gain access by **labial or palatal approach** or both, depending on the location of the tooth. The incision for the labial approach is very similar to the incisions made for apicoectomy. If it is placed high, a semilunar incision is made, taking precautions to ensure that the postoperative suture line will rest on the normal bone of 5-6 mm and must be maintained between the free gingival margin and the maximum convexity of the incision

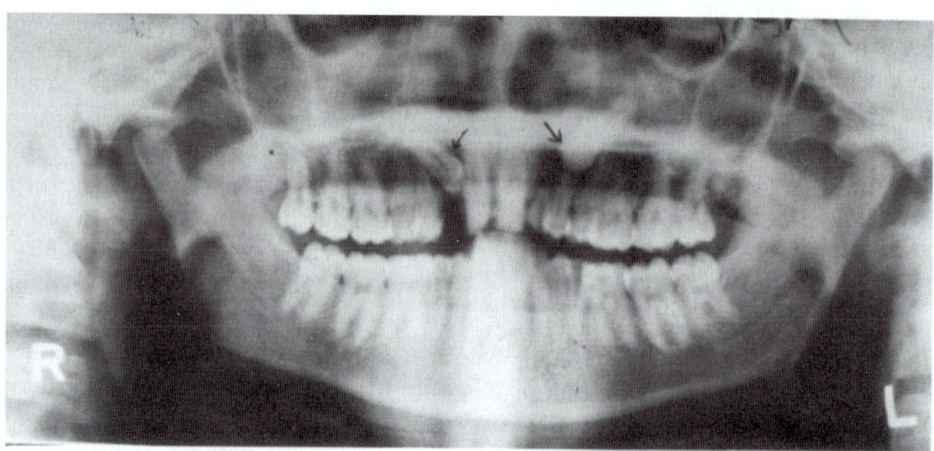

Fig. 7.21 Canine impaction: Arrows indicate lateral maxillary canine impactions seen in an orthopantomogram.

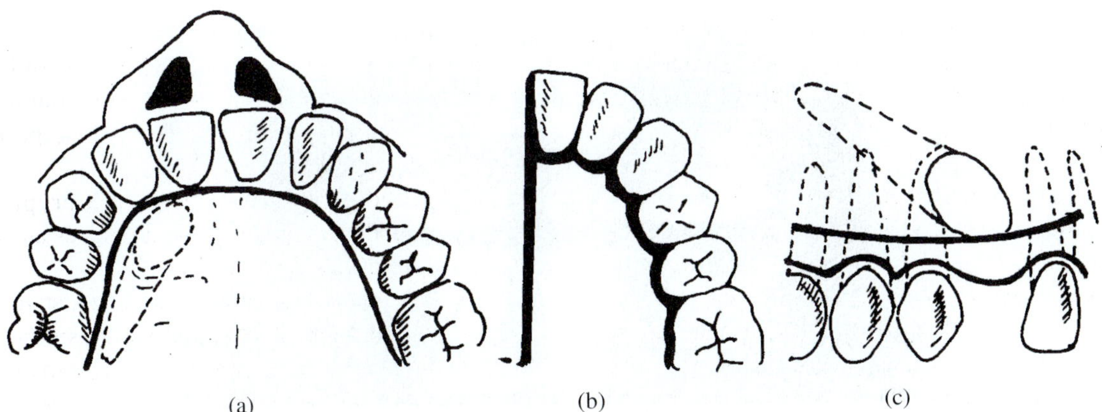

Fig. 7.22 Surgical approach to impacted canine. **(a)** Palatal approach of impacted canine with modified incision without involving free gingival margin, **(b)** Palatal incision along the free gingival margin, **(c)** Exposure of impacted canine-labial approach.

line. However, if the position of the tooth warrants the placement of the incision closer to the free gingival margin, it is safe to avoid semilunar incision. Instead, the rectangular flap will serve the purpose.

If palatal approach is necessary, incision is placed along the palatal free gingival margin between the premolars so that palatal mucoperiosteal flap is raised to expose the palatal bone anterior to the premolars. If need be, it can be extended still posteriorly to the desired extent. The operator may encounter some resistance along the midline. Brisk hemorrhage is found near the incisive foramen that can be easily arrested with pressure pack. To avoid iatrogenic periodontal problems modified approach can be made by placing the incisions parallel to the dental arch, leaving behind a 5-6 mm strip of palatal mucoperiosteum. This leaves the periodontium undisturbed. In case where the tooth is situated across the alveolus, it will necessitate composite labial and palatal approaches.

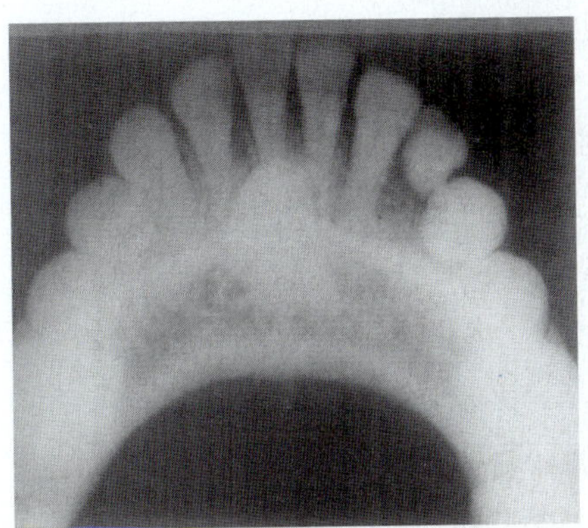

Fig. 7.23 Migration of mandibular canine to the midline.

Palatal versus labial impactions:

(a) The incidence of palatal impaction usually exceeds labial impaction in the ratio of 2:1.
(b) Nearly 80% of palatal impactions have sufficient space for eruption into the dental arch while, only 15 to 20 % of labial impactions have sufficient space for eruption.
(c) Labially positioned canines may erupt on their own without surgical exposure or orthodontic treatment. Palatal impactions seldom erupt without any intervention.
(d) Palatally impacted canines are more inclined in a horizontal direction while, labially impacted canines are inclined in the vertical direction.

Removal of the impacted tooth. Once the flap is raised, the tooth can be located by the presence of a bulge overlying the tooth. Then, sufficient bone

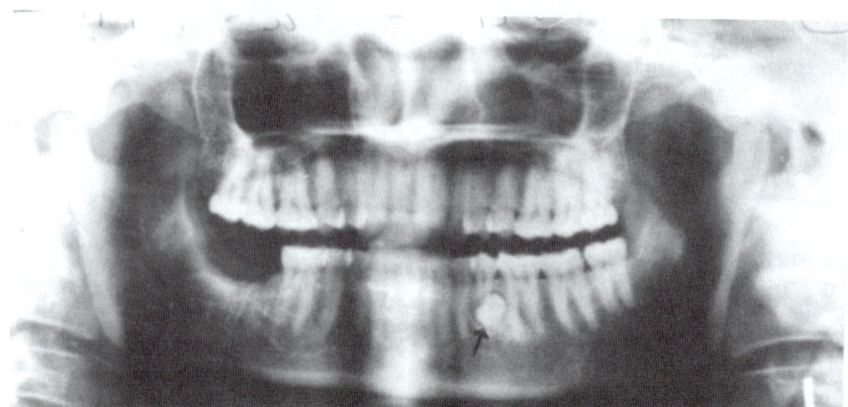

Fig. 7.24 (a) Impacted mandibular premolar.

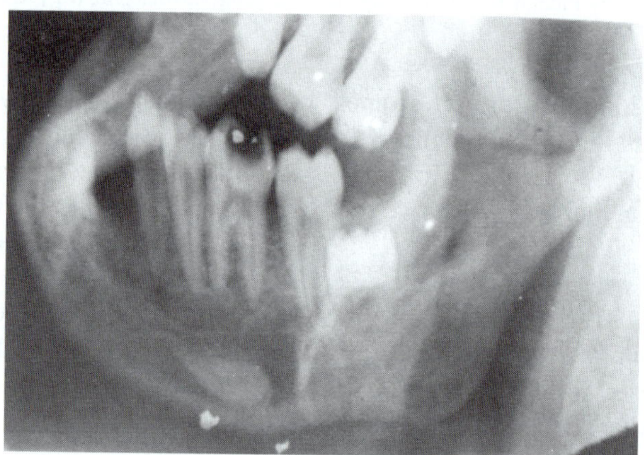

Fig. 7.24 (b) Migrated premolar deeply buried.

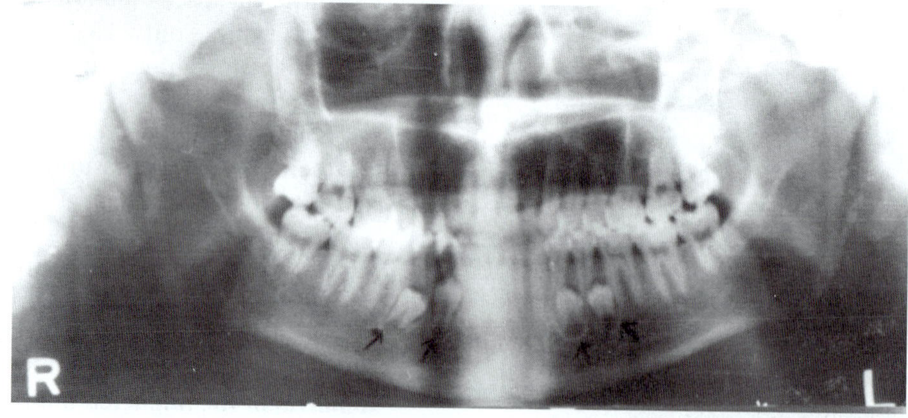

Fig. 7.24 (c) Two supernumerary premolars on either side of the mandible.

is removed with bur or chisel. Bur is found to be more useful than the chisel in such situations to expose the entire crown. Care should be taken not to injure the roots of the adjacent teeth while exposing the cusp of the unerupted tooth. Once the maximum contour of the tooth is exposed, particularly around the cingulum, Cryer's elevator is applied at the appropriate point of application as determined by the curvature of the roots and the path of delivery of the tooth. If the root curvature is unfavorable, then it is preferable to divide the tooth so that crown and the root could be removed separately. During the elevation of the tooth, care must be taken not to place the fulcrum on the neighboring teeth. If the root apex fractures during the elevation, the small buried root apex can be left in situ. Equal attention must be directed to remove the tooth follicle and loose bone or tooth fragments from the bony crypt and to smoothen the sharp bony margins.

Wound closure. The flap is sutured back to its original position and a pressure pack is applied to arrest the bleeding and also to mould the flap. In the labial approach, suturing is never a problem provided incision has been made properly. In the palatal approach, mattress sutures are placed at the interdental space with the suture knots placed on the labiobuccal side. If the modified palatal incision is made, then, it is easy to suture the wound.

Usually, the healing of the wound is uneventful. But sometimes, wound healing is troublesome due to the hematoma formation beneath the palatal flap. This is overcome by adapting a thin sheet of Stent's impression compound over the palatal flap. This avoids hematoma formation by exerting a sustained pressure to hold the mucoperiosteal flap firmly against the palatal bone.

A more refined technique would be to construct a splint in clear acrylic resin preoperatively and apply it in position postoperatively. Clear acrylic is to be preferred to ensure that ischemic necrosis of the flap is avoided by identifying the pressure points through the transparent splint. Because of the nonsticky surface, it is easy to keep the oral cavity clean. Sutures are removed on the seventh postoperative day. The teeth adjoining the operative field are tested for the loss of vitality periodically. If needed, necessary treatment is instituted.

Orofacial Infections

GENERAL CONSIDERATIONS

Intact dentition, periodontal structures and oral mucous membrane constitute the *first line of resistance* within the oral cavity against the invasion of microorganisms into the body. This is supported by the host immune and cellular defense of mechanisms. The oral cavity is constantly flooded with microorganisms in the salivary fluid environment, but they remain non pathogenic. Sometimes, oral microflora which remains in commensal state with the host may exhibit parasitism. Thus, dynamic balance between the host and the resistance factors are responsible for the non pathologic state of the oral microbes in a healthy individual. Once microorganisms begin to dominate over the host resistance, infection sets in. If the infection is of rapid onset, it is said to be acute. If organisms are not virulent enough to produce acute state or if there is partial resolution of acute infection, the condition develops into a chronic state. Most of the inflammatory swellings in and around the maxillofacial region are due to odontogenic infections. Once microorganisms invade across the first line of resistance, they react with the host immune and cellular defense mechanisms of the body and manifest as acute or chronic infection. Therefore, the clinician must be aware of the role of three factors—*host, environment* and the *microorganism* for the maintenance of the delicate homeostasis. The host defense mechanisms are the major factors to determine the outcome of any infection. Pathogenic potential depends on the virulence and quantity of the organisms. The term virulence refers to the degree of harmful effects on the host. It depends on the capacity to produce harmful toxins and invasiveness of the organisms. Quantity refers to the number of organisms and their capacity to multiply. Increase in the pathogenic organisms may lead to the increase of the virulence factors. Under normal circumstances, the host factors (local, humoral and cellular) predominate over the microbial factors (virulence and quantity). The more they predominate, the greater will be the host reserve. Whenever microbial factors increase or host factors decrease, pathogenic potential of the microorganisms increases. Once this occurs, host reserve will diminish and will result in the development of infection.

FACTORS INFLUENCING THE SPREAD OF INFECTION

Sometimes, a few factors determine the further progress of the condition including spread of infection to the neighboring regions along the path of least resistance. These factors are as follows:

(a) State of the oral microorganisms
(b) Host and its environment
(c) Disturbance to the delicate balance between the oral microflora and the host resistance
(d) Anatomical factors.

State of the oral microorganisms

(1) **Change in the oral environment.** Due to the change in the oral environment, the organisms begin to multiply resulting in large number of microorganisms. Quantitative increase may raise the virulent factors in the infected site.

(2) **Virulence.** This refers to the qualities of microbes that may become harmful to the host. This is an important factor to determine the progress of the infection. The biochemical environment of the host ultimately determines the susceptibility of the host to the organisms. Thus, virulence becomes the cumulative effect of the parasite's physiological and metabolic functions that may favor the survival, multiplication, growth and the consequent pathological changes in the host tissues.

(3) **Mediators.** The virulence and invasiveness of microbes depend on the toxins, enzymes and other metabolic byproducts. The systemic reaction may truly reflect the degree of virulence due to the mediators of the organisms. For example, streptococcus releases toxins containing spreading factors like fibrinolysin and hyaluronidase. Staphylococcus releases toxins that may aid in localizing the infection and formation of pus. Gram negative bacteria like *Escherichia coli* and *Pseudomonas* complicate the defense mechanism.

Host and its environment

The general body resistance varies between the individuals and between the times in the same individual. Likewise, age, sex, debilitating conditions like diabetes, malnutrition, chronic nephritis, hepatitis, AIDS and immunity status of the host directly influence the onset and spread of infection. The reserve resistance factors of the host can be considered under categories like (i) local defenses, (ii) humoral and (iii) cellular components.

(1) **Local defense.** Epithelial lining, secretion and drainage system, microbial flora and local mucosal immune system constitute the local defenses of the oral and maxillofacial region. The term refers to the integrity of the primary line of defense like intact teeth, healthy periodontal structures and oral mucous membrane in the salivary environment with the efficient drainage system. Any alteration or disturbance to the local defenses results in the penetration of microbes across this primary barrier. For example, subperiosteal abscesses may develop following the surgical removal of teeth and periapical surgery. When the intact mucous membrane is reflected to gain access, microbes enter this barrier in spite of strict asepsis during surgery. They begin to colonize subperiosteally around the dead space or blood clot. Wherever blood supply is interfered, the commensals gain the upper hand and behave as parasites. In a healthy oral environment, the emergence of pathogens is under control. The environment becomes conducive to infection, once this delicate balance is disturbed. So long as salivary secretion and the flow are efficient, the ability to mechanical cleansing and swallowing help in maintaining satisfactory oral hygiene. Similarly, drainage system is maintained through lymphatics. The disturbance to this delicate balance leads to change in the oral environment that aids in the establishment and spread of infection.

(2) **Humoral and cellular components.** The complement system and immunoglobulins are the components of humoral defense found in the serum.

Both are complementary to each other. This humoral defense is known as antigen-antibody reaction. Some of the important benefits derived by the body are: (a) chemotaxis, (b) bacteriolytic activity, (c) phagocytosis, (d) neutralization of toxins and (e) activation of the complement. The chemotaxis is important to mobilize the polymorphs towards the zone of infection. Bacteriolytic activity helps to control the microbial multiplication. Phagocytosis includes engulfing the foreign bodies like live and dead bacteria and digest them. The five classes of immunoglobulins are (a) IgG (present in intra and extravascular fluids in significant concentrations), (b) IgA (present in secretions), (c) IgM (largest of the immunoglobulins present in serum), (d) IgD (no specific biological activity has been assigned to it) and (e) IgE (least abundant of all in serum, involved in the development of immediate hypersensitive reactions). They enhance the phagocytosis by coating the surface of the bacteria to enable the polymorphs to engulf more effectively and destroy them, known as *opsonization*.

(3) **The cellular components** of the defense are mainly (a) polymorphs (phagocytes) and (b) lymphocytes. Monocytes found in the blood stream take over the function of phagocytosis in later stages. Similar cells, derived from the tissues are known as macrophages. Ultimately, monocytes take over the responsibility of engulfing the leucocytic debris, which help in the resolution of infection, although phagocytosis is initiated by polymorphs. The cell membrane of the phagocyte invaginates around the microbe and forms a vacuole. The vacuole utilizes the powerful oxidation-reduction reaction, depletion of nutrition and destruction of microorganisms. Usually, polymorphs predominate during the acute phase while monocytes and macrophages predominate during the chronic phase.

The lymphocytes coordinate with monocytes during the chronic stage. There are two types of lymphocytes— B-lymphocytes and T-lymphocytes. Morphologically, both the types are indistinguishable. Functionally, they have some important functions in the resistance to infection. However, they differ in their location and certain functions.

(a) Both the types of cells regulate the actions of phagocytes.

(b) Interferon enhances the lysis of bacteria by phagocytosis.

(c) Macrophages inhibiting factors restrict the macrophages from moving away from the site of infection so that they are retained where they are needed most.

(d) T-cells secrete mitogenic factors which stimulate B-cells to proliferate so that antibody response to antigenic stimulation occurs. Thus, the lymphocytes, in general, are responsible for the modulation and control of phagocytosis.

B-cells predominate in bone marrow and the germinal centres of the lymph nodes while, T-cells predominate in spleen, thymus and deep centers of lymph nodes. Functionally, B-cells are primarily involved in fighting against the extracellular pathogens that are not able to survive inside the phagocytes. These cells differentiate as plasma cells that are capable of secreting specific antibodies. T-cells are responsible to fight against the intracellular pathogens like viruses and microorganisms which are able to survive inside the phagocytes. These cells are responsible to control the multiplication of neoplastic cells known as cell-mediated immunity.

Disturbance to the delicate balance between the oral microflora and host resistance

It leads to the establishment of infection. The local response of the host against the invasion of pathogens is known as inflammation. If the microorganisms succumb to the resistance of the host, resolution takes place. Otherwise, infection continues and spread to the neighboring regions depending on the anatomical factors.

Anatomical factors

Tissues of the head and neck are invested in fascial planes separated by loose connective tissue. Although these fascial planes tend to localize the infection within their limits, they constitute imperfect barrier to the spread of infection. Spaces between these planes communicate with each other. Anatomically, the first barrier to infection from the bone is the periosteum. Once pus tracts along the path of least resistance and this barrier is penetrated, the infected materials tend to spread along the various fascial planes, blood vessels and lymphatics. It is not uncommon to come across the spread of infection from one space to the other. It is essential to identify the pathway of infection and to form the basis for identifying the exact site for the surgical drainage of pus. The following are some of the general principles to be kept in mind regarding the spread of infection.

PRINCIPLES RELEVANT TO SPREAD OF INFECTION

Spread of infection within the dental structures

The microorganisms and infected material from dental caries spread along the path of least resistance and penetrate into the pulp and periapical tissues resulting in the inflammatory changes in the pulp. The dead tissues of the pulp become a good medium for the multiplication of microorganisms. Bacteria therefore multiply and spread beyond the dental structures into the periapical region.

Spread into the bone

The response of the alveolar bone to the invading organisms is very similar to that of pulp. The central marrow spaces, surrounded by unyielding calcified material of the alveolar bone responds in the form of inflammatory reaction that confines itself to the central area. Depending on the outcome of inflammatory response, the spread of infection takes place along the marrow space of the bone even before involving the cortical plates. Even the involvement of the cortical plates depends on the relative thickness at various situations. When the perforation of the cortical plates take place, further spread depends on the muscle attachments. A few examples will illustrate this aspect.

(a) In the mandibular molar region, buccal plate is thicker, reinforced by external oblique ridge while lingual plate is thinner. Hence, chances of infection perforating the buccal plate are less in this region. Even when the lingual plate is perforated, further spread depends on the muscle attachments. If the perforation is above the attachment of mylohyoid muscle, infection spreads to the floor of the mouth intraorally. If it perforates below the attachment of the mylohyoid, the infected material enters the submandibular space.

(b) The bone at the apical region of the maxillary premolars and molars forming the floor of the maxillary antrum is very thin. Apical infection therefore spreads into the maxillary sinus easily from the maxillary posterior teeth.

(c) If the infection perforates the maxillary and mandibular buccal plates, further spread is guided by the attachment of buccinator muscle and muscles of facial expression. Perforation towards the oral aspect of these muscular attachment leads to the spread of infection intraorally. Otherwise, the infection spreads on the facial aspect.

(d) Similarly, distal to the mandibular third molar, buccinator and superior constrictor of pharynx with pterygomandibular raphe cross the anterior border of the muscle in the buccolingual direction. If the pericoronal infection involves a distoangular impaction beyond this muscle barrier posteriorly, the infected material tracks in the posterior direction and enters the space between the masseter and ramus (submasseteric space).

(e) In maxilla, outer cortical plate is thin. In a few areas, it is perforated by the periosteal nutrient vessels. But the palatal plate is thicker. Therefore, the infection perforates the outer plate of the maxilla with greater ease and present themselves in the soft tissues of the face either extraorally or intraorally depending on the muscle attachments. The incidence of the palatal perforation is relatively less.

(f) *Lymphatic spread*. The dental infection readily spreads through the lymphatic channels and

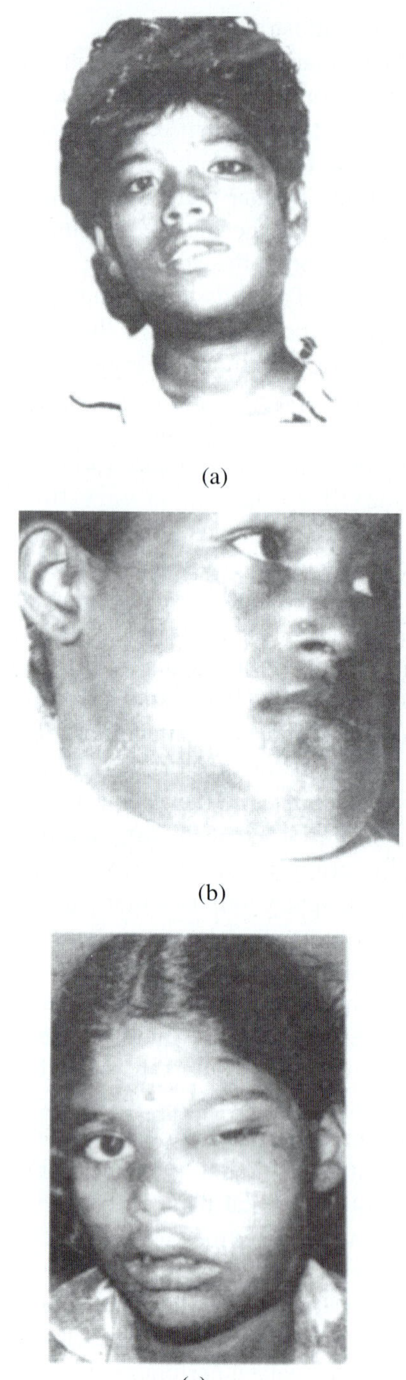

(a)

(b)

(c)

Fig. 8.1 Space infections: **(a)** Alveolar abscess, **(b)** Abscess extending to the floor of the mouth, **(c)** Abscess extending to the infraorbital region.

ultimately drain into the submandibular nodes before reaching the jugulodigastric group of lymph nodes.

(g) Hematogenous spread along the venous channels may give rise to certain problems. For example, infection arising from the maxillary teeth can spread through the anterior facial vein or pterygoid plexus of veins in the retrograde direction and pass through the emissary veins before reaching intracranial cavernous sinus. Fortunately, this route of spread is relatively rare. It occurs only when the normal route of venous drainage is blocked.

Spread into the soft tissues (Fig. 8.1)

Many muscles and fascia exist around the jaw bones. Muscles are less susceptible to invasion of bacteria. Anatomically, around the various muscles, loose fibrous connective tissues are present, limited by tough condensation of fibrous connective tissue called fascia. Thus, muscles and fascia form the barrier to the spread of infection across them. Instead, infected material spread along the surfaces of these structures involving loose fibrous tissue. This has led to the concept of "tissue spaces" which exist between various fascia. They are either potential spaces or may contain important structures like salivary glands, lymph nodes, nerves and blood vessels enclosed in loose connective tissue. The clear understanding of the concept of various "tissue spaces" is essential. Infections in each space exhibits well-defined clinical features. They also tend to spread from one space to the other sequentially, in an orderly fashion. As already explained, when the infection perforates the cortex, it enters the perialveolar soft tissue spaces depending on the factors like attachment of muscles etc.

Stages in the spread of infection

(a) **Stage of initiation.** It refers to the initial period wherein microorganisms enter the adjoining tissue spaces and multiply without manifesting any inflammatory tissue reaction. This period may range from several hours to a few days. If at all the tissue reaction takes place, it will be very mild.

(b) **Stage of triggering infection.** During this stage, microorganisms release the toxins and other metabolic byproducts into the tissue spaces so that inflammatory reaction could be noticed. The spread of the infected material is facilitated by toxins like fibrinolysin, hyaluronidase called *cellulitis*. The intensity depends on the microorganisms and the type of toxins liberated by them. If spread is fast, the infection appears in the tissue space as a diffuse, indurated, tender, red swelling. Parenteral antibiotics help to control the infection effectively at this stage.

(c) **Stage of abscess formation.** Once the inflammatory process sets in, cellular response can be strikingly noticed. This involves phagocytes that engulf the dead and dying bacteria and necrosed tissue. Depending on the presence of microorganisms, formation of pus leads to the development of abscesses. Because of the accumulation of pus, the swelling becomes fluctuant. The more superficial it is, fluctuation can be elicited easily. In case of infections predominantly by organisms like streptococci, cellulitis spreads very fast. It is characterized by the absence of abscess formation. Such type of spread of infection may be life threatening.

(d) **Stage of resolution.** Pus and other infected materials always spread along the path of least resistance or fascial spaces. In 10-15 days time, the infected materials may drain out of the tissue spaces in the natural course of the lesion. If it is evacuated by natural or by surgical means, the process of resolution sets in. This is supported by the immune system through the antibodies and activated 'T' lymphocytes. Histologically, this process is usually described as "round-cell infiltration". Simultaneously, macrophages eliminate the necrosed material through phagocytosis. The stage of resolution is usually aided by surgical drainage of the infected materials.

DIAGNOSIS

Symptoms

Most of the symptoms are of systemic origin and hence indicate the potential serious state of this condition. Hence, each patient must be thoroughly evaluated and investigated.

(a) *Pyrexia* is a reliable indicator of the seriousness of infection. If the oral temperature is elevated beyond 100ºF, it is significant. There may be a variation between the infected and non infected side of the mouth. Axillary temperature is unreliable. If needed, rectal temperature can be recorded (usually 1 degree Fahrenheit higher than the oral temperature).

(b) *Malaise* seems to be the other sensitive indicator. It is a feeling of weakness, lack of energy, loss of appetite and vague discomfort.

(c) *Dehydration* may be due to the interference of the normal food and fluid intake. Rise in body temperature significantly accelerates the water loss by evaporation. Average fluid intake is 2400 ml/day but due to pyrexia and dehydration, it may increase up to 3600 ml/day. Clinically, the dehydrated person feels that the lips and oral cavity are dry. There is significant decrease in salivary flow.

(d) Swelling of the involved region and the regional lymph nodes are common.

(e) Difficulty in swallowing and to open the mouth may be superadded.

Signs

(a) Pyrexia can be recorded objectively.
(b) Dehydration can be confirmed by the appearance of dry skin and decreased salivary flow.

Routine investigations

(a) WBC total count is elevated in serious infections. The differential count of WBCs will indicate the nature of infection whether it is acute or chronic. The relative percentage of various leucocytes becomes very significant. Normally, polymorphs are 55-65%. Its increase signifies the presence of acute infection. Consequently, there is a proportionate decrease of lymphocytes. On the contrary, marked increase of lymphocytes (normal 25-35%) and decrease of polymorphs indicate the presence of chronic infection. In a normal person, eosinophil count ranges between 0-5%. Any rise in the eosinophil count signifies the presence of allergic manifestations.

(b) Erythrocyte sedimentation rate (ESR) is sensitive by its rise in chronic infections. Perhaps, it is useful to detect low grade chronic infections. The normal range is 0-20 m/hour.

Special investigations

Any infected material from the infected site must be carefully collected and sent for microbiological evaluation. The culture obtained is very useful to identify the microorganisms responsible for the infection by gram staining. The investigation can be carried out on the infected material. The culture is useful to make a rational choice of antibiotics. It is estimated that many organisms found in the oral cavity are anaerobic. Hence, it is better to perform aerobic and anaerobic cultures on all the specimens collected from oral infections whenever the patient does not respond to the conventional antibiotic therapy.

SPECIFIC INFECTIONS

(1) **Periapical abscess**

This is commonly termed as alveolar abscess. This lesion results due to the spread of dental and periodontal infection to the periapical region manifesting itself as *alveolar abscess*. Depending on the period of onset, it may be acute or chronic. During the early phase, the abscess confines itself within the bone at the periapical region. If the infected material accumulates, the rise in the pressure results in burrowing the cancellous bone and bone marrow along the path of least resistance until the pus reaches the surface and invades the soft tissue spaces. Early decision to drain helps the condition to resolve quickly. More often, removal of the offending tooth accelerates the process of resolution. In single-rooted teeth, drainage can be established through endodontic route.

(2) **Pericoronitis**

Pericoronitis is defined as the inflammation of the soft tissues of varying severity around an erupting or partially erupted tooth with breach of the follicle. It results in establishing a communication with the oral environment. Even though this can occur in relation to any tooth, mandibular third molar is more often involved. Statistically, this condition seems to be the third odontogenic infection and one of the common causes for the removal of the impacted III molars. Usually, misplaced III molars erupt in the lateral direction that is the non functional region of the dental arch with unfavorable drainage. It is termed as pericementitis. In early part of 20th century, it was also known as folliculitis. Later, Kay described this condition as pericoronitis. It may develop at any age but it is more common between 16 and 24 years of age.

Teething. It is not the same as pericoronitis. Every erupting tooth under normal conditions develop local inflammation and tissue degeneration. This condition could be termed as supracoronitis to differentiate the inflammation of the follicle as pericoronitis.

Pathogenesis. It is widely believed that factors that predispose to pericoronitis are emotional stress, fatigue, upper respiratory tract infections, second trimester of pregnancy and menstruation. Impinging maxillary molars aggravate this condition by traumatizing the pericoronal soft tissues of the mandibular III molars. Repeated occlusal trauma leads to edematous swelling thereby disturbing the drainage of the inflammatory exudate. Any of these conditions may upset the delicate balance by lowering the general resistance of the patient.

During the eruptive phase, significant collagenase activity in the operculum is present. The pericoronal pocket with soft tissue debris is found to be an ideal anaerobic incubator-like environment for the microorganisms. With the associated osteitis, distal bony pocket increases the infection. Depending on the local condition, virulence of the organisms and varying degree of resistance to infection, edema spreads by the action of the toxins. Pathology of pericoronitis is similar to the abscess formation or cellulitis. The spread of infection is guided by the resistance of the surrounding tissues like fascia, muscle etc.

Clinical features. On the basis of the patient's history, it is convenient to group them as acute, subacute and chronic phases.

Acute phase. In the early stage, it is very similar to teething. The patient is aware of the eruption of the tooth and discomfort aggravated by traumatic occlusion at the mandibular retromolar region. Severe throbbing pain radiates to the adjacent regions. Development of some degree of restricted mouth opening may be due to the stimulation of pain receptors, extraoral swelling and dysphagia. On examination, the patient becomes ill with pyrexia, increase in pulse and respiration rate (TPR). Regional submandibular lymph nodes are enlarged and tender. Halitosis is present. Pyrexia is associated with tachycardia, leucocytosis and malaise. Intraorally, swelling and redness with purulent discharge from pericoronal space could be noticed. Increase in edema may lead to rapid separation of muscles of mastication and the consequent trismus. Dysphagia indicates that infection has spread into sublingual and parapharyngeal spaces. Sloughing or ulceration may be noticed around the operculum.

Subacute phase. During this phase, systemic features become less acute. The patient experiences continuous dull pain, persistence of intraoral swelling, jaw stiffness, regional lymphadenopathy and pus discharge from the follicular space. Ulceration of the operculum becomes more pronounced. Pus tracks submucosally along the mandibular groove formed by external oblique ridge resulting in perimandibular, pterygomandibular and submasseteric abscesses. With the advent of wide range of antibiotics, the incidence of spread of infection to parapharyngeal spaces has become less prevalent.

Chronic phase. This phase is characterized by the complete absence of all the systemic features except during acute exacerbation. Usually the patient complains of dull pain and discomfort with unpleasant taste in the oral cavity. Intraoral periapical radiograph may reveal a crater-like bony defect around the third molar.

Pathogenesis of pericoronitis is summarized in the form of a flowchart (Page 134).

Diagnosis. Diagnosis does not present any problem with proper history and careful clinical examination. It is advantageous to record the patient's body temperature, pulse and respiration rate. Special investigations include radiographic examinations, total and differential counts of leucocytes. If facilities exist, bacteriological examination is done to determine the nature of causative organisms so that it is helpful to confirm the sensitivity to various antibiotics. Whenever a fungal infection is considered, special request must be made to the microbiologist since it requires anaerobic methods of culture.

Differential diagnosis:

(1) During the early phase, pulpitis and periodontitis are the obvious sources of confusion when pain is the main feature.

(2) In the later stage, limitation of mouth opening with jaw stiffness can mimic temporomandibular joint dysfunction.

(3) If the swelling is diffuse, one is liable to confuse with tonsillitis.

(4) Acute exacerbation might occur in a pre-existing cyst of odontogenic origin in the III molar region.

(5) Very rarely, malignancy may have to be ruled out if the patient is elderly in the age group of 40 and above with superadded infection.

PATHOGENESIS OF PERICORONITIS

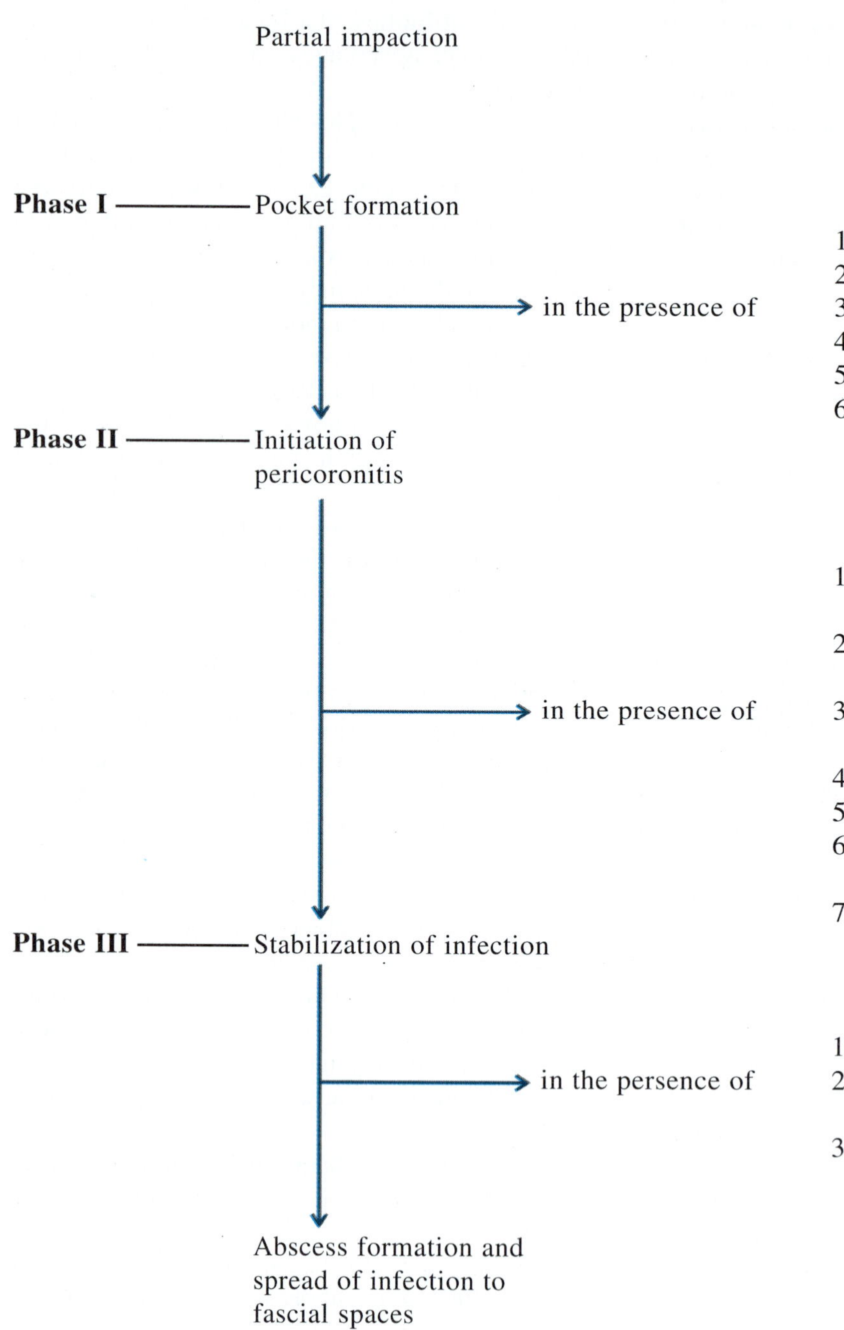

1. Inadequate oral hygine
2. Retention of plaque
3. Occlusal trauma
4. Retention of food debris
5. Gingival infection
6. Reduced general resistance.

1. Mucosal edema of pericoronal flap
2. Retention of plaque and food debris
3. Action of toxins, enzymes and antigens
4. Regional lymphadenopathy
5. Jaw stiffness and dysphagia
6. Systemic factors like pyrexia, malaise
7. Diffuse facial swelling.

1. Pyrexia
2. Increase in the severity of all the above clinical features
3. Pericoronal pocket with exudation of pus.

Management. The present day management of pericoronitis has been well systematized. One should evaluate carefully to determine whether the retention of the wisdom tooth is likely to serve any useful purpose. It does not mean the eruption into normal occlusion alone. In certain occasions, such a tooth can be retained to serve as an abutment for a bridge construction.

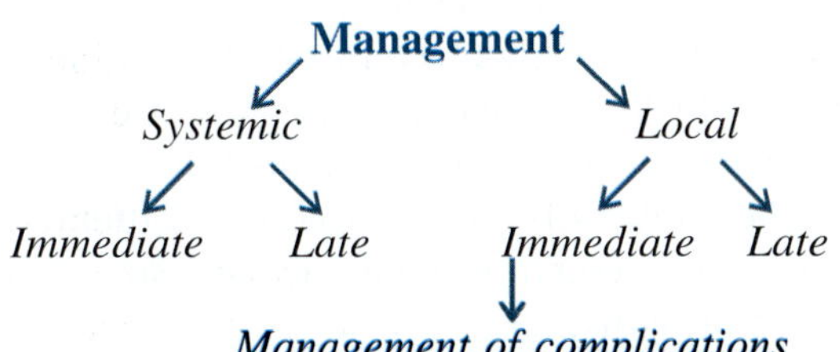

Management can also be divisible into three phases:

Phase I - Pocket formation
Phase II - Mucosal edema
Phase III - Abscess formation.

General treatment.

(1) All toxic patients must be advised absolute bed rest.

(2) Soft, nourishing high protein diet must be prescribed.

(3) Appropriate antibiotic therapy must be instituted. Penicillin is the drug of choice while metronidazole is a reasonable alternative.

(4) Suitable analgesic should be prescribed depending on the severity and intensity of pain.

Local treatment.

(1) Traumatic occlusion, if any, may be relieved by removal or grinding of the maxillary third molar.

(2) Improvement of oral hygiene and general health are equally important.

(3) If the abscess has developed, drainage must be established.

(4) After irrigating the follicular space with hydrogen peroxide, caustics like trichloroacetic acid, chromic acid or ammoniacal solutions of silver nitrate are usually applied. Then, one drop of an astringent like Talbot's solution of iodine can be applied. Talbot's solution contains iodine, zinc iodide, glycerine and water.

(5) Frequent warm saline gargling is soothing to the patient. External application of heat should be avoided since it promotes spread of infection towards the facial skin.

(6) After the resolution of the infection, appropriate decision must be taken as to whether III molar must be removed or to be retained after pericoronal flap excision. If the molar tooth cannot be retained, possibility of utilizing the III molar tooth germ for transplantation, to replace a badly carious and broken down first molar tooth, must be considered.

(7) Operculectomy (flap incision) is indicated if the tooth has erupted and flap is covering the tooth. This is advocated after the acute symptoms have fully subsided.

(8) Mandibular movement is eccentric during closing. This is an attempt by the patient to avoid traumatizing the inflamed gingiva.

(9) The patient may also complain of difficulty to open the mouth. Muscular spasm due to reflex irritation may be the cause for trismus.

Preventive measures.

(a) Extraction of damaged I or II molar at an early stage creates more space for the III molar.

(b) Extraction of III molar at an early age (prophylactic odontectomy).

Periodontal abscess

Usually, this lesion results due to chronic periodontitis. The infection starts from the gingival cervices. This may or may not be associated with non vital teeth. Radiography is very helpful to establish the diagnosis.

Acute cellulitis

If the local resistance or the nature of the bacteria prevents the spread of infection, abscess develops. Otherwise, spreading type of infection called cellulitis develops. If the physiological response fails to resist the spread of infection, the patient may develop severe systemic reactions like elevated body temperature and erythrocyte sedimentation rate[ESR], rise in leucocytes count and alteration of differential count. Correspondingly, pulse rate also increases. Electrolyte in balance results in malaise. The prognosis depends on the appropriate surgical intervention and medications. If the infection spreads deeper into the tissue spaces, diagnosis may be difficult.

TISSUE SPACE AND FASCIAL PLANES

The systematic survey and the exact location of infection help in diagnosing the various space infections. Shapiro defined the fascial spaces as the potential spaces between the layers of fascia. They are normally filled by loose connective tissue. The fascial compartments in relation to the dental infections are described here.

(a) Canine space
(b) Buccal space
(c) Masticator space
(d) Submandibular and sublingual spaces
(e) Submental space
(f) Pterygomandibular space
(g) Pterygopalatine space
(h) Lateral pharyngeal space
(i) Retropharyngeal space
(j) Mediastinitis.

Fascial planes

The oral and maxillofacial region is well compartmentalized by the fascial layers. Surrounding or separating the muscles of the region, fasciae and fascial planes offer an anatomically defined potential spaces, filled with loose connective tissue. When the space is invaded by infection, the connective tissue breaks down and the infection spreads from one space to the other.

The deep cervical fascia includes (a) superficial investing layer, (b) carotid sheath, (c) pretracheal layer and (d) prevertebral layer. These fascial layers may be divided anatomically into superficial and deep layers. The superficial fascia surrounds platysma. In the neck, deep fascia is arbitrarily divided into anterior, middle and posterior layer. They can be identified as supra and infrahyoid components. Below the hyoid, anterior layer of the deep fascia arises from the vertebral spinous processes and encircles the neck. At the posterior border of the sternomastoid muscle, this anterior layer splits to surround this muscle and splits again to enclose the infrahyoid strap muscles. This layer attaches superiorly to the hyoid bone. Inferiorly, it attaches to sternum forming the suprasternal space (space of burns).

The middle layer passes behind the strap muscles. Inferiorly, it follows these muscles under the sternum, fuses with the great vessels of the mediastinum and fibrous pericardium. Superiorly, it fuses with hyoid bone and thyroid cartilage.

Posterior layer lies deep to the trapezius muscle and spreads across the posterior triangle of the neck to the posterior border of the sternomastoid muscle. It splits to form an anterior layer forming the anterolateral wall of the carotid sheath and a posterior deep portion which also contributes to the carotid sheath. This fascial sheath contains internal jugular vein, common carotid artery and vagus nerve.

The neck fascia creates numerous fascial spaces in the neck. The terminology of these spaces varies among various authors. The visceral compartment is of great importance and it is divided into anterior and posterior portions. Anterior part of the compartment is called pretracheal space and surrounds the trachea. Posterior part is retropharyngeal space which lies behind the pharynx.

The fascial spaces above the hyoid bone are formed by the anterior and posterior layers of the deep fascia, (middle layer is absent). Anterior layer of the deep fascia extends to the mandible and zygomatic arch passing across the muscle of the floor of the mouth (mylohyoid and anterior belly of the diagastric muscle). This anterior layer of the deep fascia splits posteriorly to form a capsule around the submandibular gland. It splits to enclose masseter, medial pterygoid and ramus of the mandible. It also splits to enclose the parotid gland. The posterior layer encloses the vertebral muscles. The suprahyoid area is identical to infrahyoid area.

Each fascial space infection is considered as a separate clinical entity. General principles remain the same in the management of all the space infections. The following must be borne in mind:

(a) The treatment of the fascial spaces infection depends on adequate and dependent drainage.
(b) These spaces are communicating to one another and therefore infection spreads from one space to another.
(c) Primary as well as secondary spaces involved in the infection must be drained.
(d) Anatomy may be grossly distorted by the swelling of the infectious process.

Canine space

This space is involved in odontogenic infection more commonly and in the nasal infection less commonly. Infection from the maxillary canine may present itself as a swelling in the labial sulcus and rarely as a palatal swelling. Levator labi superioris originates high in the canine fossa. It intermingles with fibres of orbicularis oris and attaches with the angle of the mouth. If the infection from the maxillary canine perforates the labial cortex above the attachment of this muscle, the infection can be located in the "potential" canine space. The pus from this area can be drained by placing an intraoral incision higher than the maxillary labial vestibule. If it is not drained, it can find its way out through the facial skin or the ascending infection may spread to the cavernous sinus. If the infection cannot be controlled, extraction of the offending tooth i.e. canine tooth will solve the problem.

Buccal space

Buccinator muscle is closely related to the apices of the posterior teeth by its attachment to the lateral aspect of the maxillary and mandibular alveolar bone. It is this muscle attachment which decides the direction of spread of infection from these teeth. If the infection from the maxillary teeth perforates the buccal plate above the muscle attachment and in case of mandibular infection, perforating below the buccal alveolar plate, infection will enter the "potential space" under the buccinator muscle. The boundaries of the space are (a) buccopharyngeal fascia and buccinator muscle medially, (b) skin of the cheek laterally, (c) zygomatic arch superiorly, (d) lower border of the mandible inferiorly, (e) labial musculature - zygomatic and depressor anguli oris muscles - anteriorly and (f) posterior attachment of the buccinator muscle - pterygomandibular raphe - posteriorly. Buccal space contains (Stenson's) parotid duct, buccal pad of fat and facial artery. The infection of this space can be identified by the presence of a cheek swelling associated with damaged posterior tooth. Since it will be difficult to establish intraoral drainage through mucosa, submucosa and buccinator muscle, it can be drained through a cutaneous incision placed inferior to the point of fluctuation. Then blunt dissection should be carried out extensively upto the boundaries of the space all-round. It may also be possible to drain through aspiration. Care should be taken to avoid damage to facial nerve and Stenson's duct. Surprisingly, this space can accommodate a very large volume of infected material.

Masticator spaces (Fig. 8.2)

These spaces exist in relation to all the muscles of mastication. They are formed by the splitting of the investing layer of deep cervical fascia, attached to the lower border of the mandible. This fascial sling contains mandible and all the four muscles of mastication. The outer sheath encloses temporalis and masseter while inner sheath encloses medial

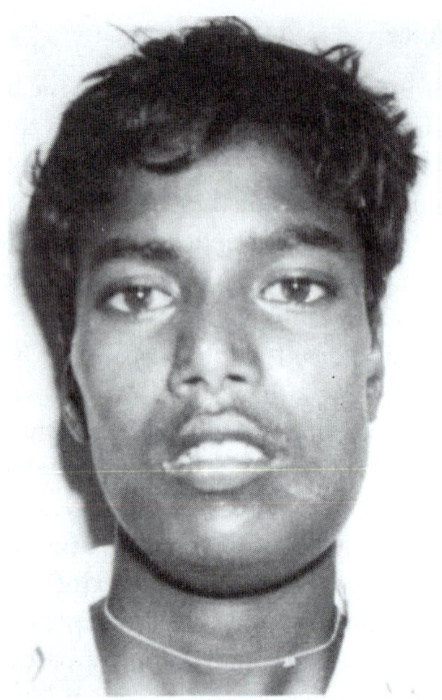

Fig. 8.2 Submasseteric space infection (clinical photograph).

pterygoid and lateral pterygoid muscles. The temporal fascia splits into two well defined layers. The superficial layer attaches to the lateral portion of the zygomatic arch while, deep layer fuses with the periosteum. Thus, the *temporal space* is divided into superficial and deep portions. The superficial portion is between superficial temporal fascia and the lateral surface of the temporalis muscle. The deep portion is between medial surface of the temporalis and periosteum of the temporal bone.

Below the zygomatic arch, the lateral surface of the masseter is covered by the fascia which splits to cover the parotid gland as the *parotid space*. Anteriorly, all the spaces communicate subperiosteally. Posteriorly, this space is bounded by parotid space laterally and lateral pharyngeal space medially. Superiorly, it is bounded by parotid and lateral pharyngeal spaces and communicates with temporal pouches. Thus, the masticator space infections are mostly dental in origin. It is very important to differentiate the masticatory space infections from lateral pharyngeal space infections. Usually, infection of this space results from (a) mandibular molars, (b) infection of the pterygomandibular space due to septic needles during the inferior dental nerve block anesthesia and (c) trauma to mandible involving molar teeth. Clinically, the hallmark of the infection of the masticatory space is trismus disproportionate to the swelling.

Submasseteric space infection

This represents one of the complications following the spread of dental infection. Consideration of anatomy of masseter muscle and its anatomical surroundings are necessary to understand this clinical entity. Masseter occupies the lateral aspect of mandibular ramus in three layers. Potential spaces exist between the adjacent areas of masseter and ramus and in between the muscle layers. Anteriorly, the muscle is crossed by the pterygomandibular raphe with buccinator running anterolaterally and superior constrictor posteromedially.

Etiology

(1) Pericoronitis associated with vertical and distoangular impaction of mandibular third molar may result in infection extending across the buccinator diaphragm to enter the potential space and gets localized there.

(2) Pus from the periapical region of one of the molars can penetrate the buccal plate below the buccinator to burrow subperiosteally, reaching the submasseteric region.

(3) Infection of the extracted socket of third molar or contaminated needles during local anesthetic injections may lead to suppuration with the pus accumulating in the space between masseter and ramus and also in between muscle layers.

(4) Pus can also pass into submasseteric and intramasseteric spaces from other regions of the masticator space.

(5) Infection from mandibular molars may spread intraosseously reaching the ramus. Then, it can perforate the lateral cortex to form subperiosteal abscess. Once the periosteal barrier is broken, the

infected material reaches submasseteric and intra-masseteric areas.

(6) Infection may occasionally spread from the adjacent spaces like lateral pharyngeal or parotid spaces.

Clinical features

(1) Swelling is moderate and diffuse over the lateral aspect of the ramus. It may be firm but rarely compressible because of the tense masseter muscle.

(2) Trismus without corresponding edema is easily a conclusive feature.

(3) The character of pain is not so definitive. It varies depending on the severity of infection. Discomfort with tenderness may be present. However, marked degree of limitation of jaw movement seems excessive and inconsistent with the swelling present.

(4) The swelling does not encroach on the submandibular or postauricular regions. However, unilateral regional lymphadenopathy may be present.

(5) Systemic features like pyrexia, malaise and toxicity may be present.

(6) Intraorally, induration or slight prominence of the soft tissues along the anterior border of masseter and retromolar region may be present.

(7) Radiological examination: Osteolytic changes in the ramus are proportional to the chronicity of the lesion. Mottled bone rarefaction develop at the angle or in the ramus. Subsequently, the destruction of bone is progressive with eventual sequestration.

(8) In chronic stage, abscess may burst spontaneously on the facial skin. If the posterior body of the muscle is breached, the depression between the ramus and parotid gland is the region where abscess spreads and may form a sinus discharging pus.

Differential diagnosis

(1) Acute swelling of parotid gland due to the similarity in the location, e.g. Mumps, pyogenic parotitis.

(2) Furuncle at the external auditory canal.

(3) Facial trauma over the ramus without fracture because of the accumulating hematoma.

(4) Preauricular lymphadenopathy.

Treatment

(1) Correct diagnosis is mandatory for the satisfactory treatment.

(2) Chronologically in the prodromal stage of the developing infection where pus is suspected, intraoral aspiration is a reliable, simple and safe procedure. The material must be submitted for the microbiological evaluation.

(3) If the infection has invaded the muscle substance, incision and drainage is the treatment of choice. The incision extends intraorally along the anterior border of the ramus and the external oblique ridge up to the molar tooth. With the instrument kept close to the ramus, abscess is drained by Hilton's method. Efficient suction is very useful to evacuate the contents. Very rarely, extraoral incisions are employed at the angle of the mandible.

(4) Antibiotic cover is essential depending on the microbiological investigations.

(5) If drainage is established, local bone necrosis of the ramus is self-limiting. If the condition fails to resolve completely, it is to be treated as a case of osteomyelitis of the ramus.

Pterygomandibular space

This is a potential space bounded laterally by the medial surface of the ramus, medially and infero-obliquely by lateral surface of the medial pterygoid muscle and superoobliquely by the lateral pterygoid muscle. Pterygomandibular raphe with superior constrictor and buccinator on either side, cross the anterior boundary of this space.

Submandibular and sublingual spaces

The space between symphysis menti and hyoid bone in the midline bounded by anterior belly of the digastric laterally is called submental space. Mylohyoid forms the floor and deep fascia forms the roof. It contains anterior jugular vein and submental lymph nodes.

The submandibular space is located lateral to the submental space. Posteroinferiorly, the space is bounded by stylohyoid and posterior belly of the digastric muscle. Anteroinferiorly, it is bounded by the anterior belly of the digastric muscle and above by the lower border of the mandible. Floor is formed by mylohyoid and hyoglossus muscles. Superficially, the roof is formed by platysma and deep fascia. The space is enclosed by the investing layer of deep fascia. The superficial layer is attached to the lower border of the mandible and deep layer to the mylohyoid line. In other areas, both these layers fuse around the periphery of the submandibular gland and becomes continuous with the fascia covering anterior belly of the digastric and mylohyoid muscles. The contents of this space are superficial part of the submandibular gland, facial artery and mylohyoid muscle. The contents of this space are superficial part of the submandibular gland, facial artery, mylohyoid nerve and vessels and submandibular lymph nodes. The deep portion of the gland continues around the posterior border of mylohyoid muscle into the sublingual space.

The sublingual space is present above the mylohyoid muscle. The roof is formed by oral mucous membrane. Laterally, it is bounded by the alveolar process of the mandible above the mylohyoid line. Medially, it is bounded by genioglossus and geniohyoid muscles. This space contains submandibular duct and deep portion of the submandibular gland, lingual and hypoglossal nerves and terminal branches of lingual artery.

Ludwig's angina

This term refers to cellulitis involving bilaterally three fascial spaces - submandibular, submental and sublingual spaces. The patient has a typical open mouth appearance. Floor of the mouth is characteristically elevated and tongue is protruded making the respiration difficult. This infection usually extends from mandibular teeth into the floor of the mouth by perforating the lingual plate below the attachment of the mylohyoid muscle. This is characterized by the induration, absence of fluctuation, not pitting on pressure. The tissues may even become gangrenous with sharp limitation between the affected and normal tissues. This infection is often caused by streptococcus hemolyticus, mixed with many types of aerobic and anaerobic microorganisms. Systemic reactions like pyrexia and malaise develop. There is increased salivation, inability to open the mouth and swallow. Cervical tissues become board-like. In general, the patient becomes toxic with edematous larynx. The floor of the mouth appear elevated with protruded tongue and difficulty to breathing. Therefore, one should remember the first written description of this clinical entity - it is to be *Feared*, it is rarely *Fluctuant* and it proves *Fatal*, if it is not diagnosed and treated properly.

Lateral pharyngeal space

This is situated around the pharynx and hence known as parapharyngeal space, lying lateral to pharynx, medial to masticator and submandibular spaces. It extends from the base of the skull to the hyoid bone. This space is bounded (a) medially by superior constrictor of the pharynx, (b) laterally by mandible, retromandibular portion of the parotid and medial pterygoid muscle, (c) anteriorly by the pterygomandibular raphae, (d) posteriorly by prevertebral and visceral layers of deep fascia, (e) inferiorly by the attachment of the capsule of submandibular gland to sheaths of stylohyoid and posterior belly of digastric muscles and (f) superiorly by the petrous part of the temporal bone. Styloid process divides the space into two compartments-anterior and posterior compartments. But they are not completely separated from each other. Anterior compartment contains lymph nodes, ascending pharyngeal and facial arteries and loose areolar tissue. The posterior compartment contains carotid sheath (internal carotid artery, internal jugular vein, glossopharyngeal, vagus, accessory and hypoglossal nerves, and cervical sympathetic trunk). This compartment does not contain any lymph nodes.

The infection involving this space is very serious and poses threat to life. Infection from the masticator space spreads into this space. If the infection is a rapidly spreading cellulitis, it is similar to Ludwig's angina. The complications are: (a) respiratory arrest due to acute laryngeal edema, (b) thrombosis of internal jugular vein, and (c) erosion of internal carotid, ascending pharyngeal or facial arteries. If hemorrhage occurs, it invariably proves fatal.

Retropharyngeal space

The middle layer of the deep fascia encloses esophagus and trachea. Thick strand of connective tissue extends from the esophagus laterally to the carotid sheath. This results in an anterior neck compartment known as pretracheal space and a posterior retropharyngeal space. The posterior compartment lies behind pharynx and esophagus. Inferiorly, it extends to upper mediastinum and superiorly to the base of the skull. Posteriorly, it communicates to the posterior mediastinum and anteriorly retropharyngeal space is bounded by the pharyngeal wall. The infection of this space spreads from nasal and pharyngeal infections through the adjoining spaces or through lymphatics. The characteristic features of the space infection are- dyspnea, dysphagia, esophageal regurgitation and pyrexia.

Mediastinitis

Infection spreads from neck deep spaces into the mediastinum. Rarely, it may also extend from odontogenic infections through the perivascular space around the carotid sheath. This will develop as a late complication. The main features are - fever associated with substernal pain, progressive septicemia, abscess formation in the mediastinum, pleural effusion, empymea, evidence of compression of the mediastinal veins resulting in decreased venous return and pericarditis. Ultimately it may prove fatal.

Infratemporal fossa

The infection from maxillary molar teeth usually spreads into pterygopalatine and infratemporal fossa. Posterior to the maxillary sinus, pterygo-palatine fossa is situated. It communicates with infratemporal fossa through pterygomaxillary tissue. Its upper end is continuous with inferior orbital fissure that contains infraorbital nerve - a continuation of the maxillary nerve. The pterygopalatine fossa also communicates with pterygoid canal. Superiorly, this fossa is closely related to optic and abducent nerves that may be involved in the infection of this fossa. Infratemporal fossa is located behind the ramus and below the level of zygomatic arch. It is medially bounded by lateral pterygoid plate, posteriorly by the parotid gland and anteriorly by maxilla. Superiorly, the roof is formed by greater wing of the sphenoid, perforated by foramen ovale that transmits mandibular nerve. Laterally, this space is continuous with temporal spaces and inferiorly with the region deep to the body of the mandible. The infection of both the spaces is rare. However, infection may result from maxillary molar teeth or due to infection following local anesthesia with improperly sterilized needle or from masticatory spaces and lateral pharyngeal spaces. Clinically, involvement of these areas is characterized by pain and trismus. Eye may be closed and proptosed. Paralysis of sixth nerve and optic neuritis may develop.

Cavernous sinus thrombosis

Infection from the "dangerous zone" of the face may spread along the deep fascial veins in the retrograde direction. Although it is unusual, infected thrombus from this region ascends along the vein against the venous stream due to the absence of valves in the angular, facial and ophthalmic veins. The infection may spread along the pterygoid plexus of veins reaching through emissary veins into the cavernous sinus. The cavernous sinus thrombosis can be usually diagnosed by

(a) The site of infection.
(b) Early signs of obstruction seen in the retina, conjunctiva or eyelid.
(c) Paresis of III, IV and VI cranial nerves due to inflammatory edema causing ophthalmoplegia.
(d) Evidence of meningeal irritation.

Thrombosis of the sinus can be confirmed by a test known as Tobey-Ayer test. It can be performed by compressing the internal jugular vein with the fingers. On the side of thrombosis, there will be no rise of CSF pressure. Infective thrombosis occurs less likely in the superior sagittal sinus than in lateral or cavernous sinus. Clinical features include headache, pyrexia, vomiting and papilledema. Treatment includes intravenous chloramphenicol. Since this condition is life-threatening, appropriate treatment must be undertaken immediately.

Parotid space

This space is formed by the splitting of the investing layer of deep cervical fascia. The contents of the space are parotid gland, extra and intraglandular lymph nodes. External surface of the gland is covered by thick fascia with septa dividing the gland into lobules. The internal layer of the fascia is thin and incomplete where the space communicates with lateral pharyngeal space. Posteriorly, it is in close relation to middle and external ear. Inferiorly, the fascia is thick and reinforced called stylomandibular ligament. This separates parotid from submandibular space. When this space is involved, it is present as a hard and smooth swelling in front and below the external ear.

Imaging in space infections

Infratemporal and pterygopalatine fossae are situated very deep in the maxillofacial region. They contain very important structures like maxillary artery, pterygoid venous plexus, maxillary and mandibular nerves and Meckel's ganglion. Conventional radiographs of the region may not be useful. Therefore, imaging by computed tomography (CT) has been tried, since boundaries can be defined in this technique. The following anatomical boundaries are defined:

Infratemporal fossa:

Anteriorly	-	Lateral wall of maxilla
Posteriorly	-	Lateral pterygoid muscle
Medially	-	Pterygomaxillary fissure and lateral pterygoid plate
Laterally	-	Ramus of the mandible
Roof	-	Skull base
Floor	-	Inferior level of lateral pterygoid muscle.

Pterygopalatine fossa:

Anteriorly	-	Posterior wall of maxilla
Posteriorly	-	Pterygoid process
Medially	-	Vertical plate of palatine bone
Laterally	-	Pterygomaxillary fissure
Roof	-	Skull base
Floor	-	Pterygopalatine canal.

The masticator space is divided by the mandible into medial and lateral compartments. The medial compartment of the masticator space includes infratemporal, pterygopalatine and pterygomandibular spaces. Precise location of the condition is essential to carry out the treatment.

MANAGEMENT OF SPACE INFECTIONS (Fig. 8.3)

General principles

The general care of these patients must be directed (a) to inhibit (bacteriostatic) or to destroy (bactericidal) the microorganisms and (b) to promote the physiological defense mechanisms of the body by attending to the physiological needs of the patient. In general, the following sequence of management is advocated for the orofacial infections.

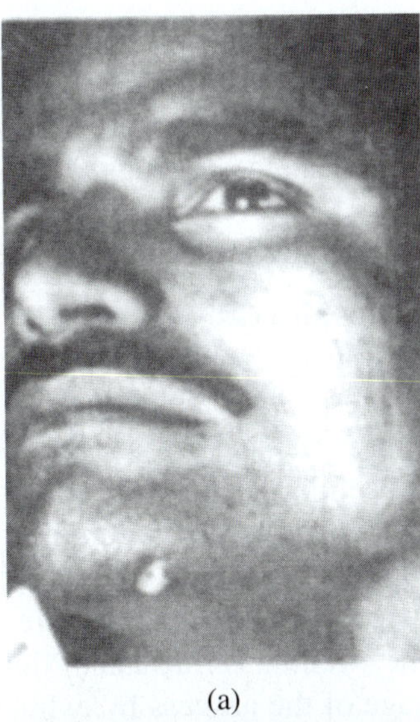

(a)

(b)

Fig. 8.3 Space infection with sinus discharging pus. **(a)** Preoperative, **(b)** Postoperative.

(1) **Maintenance of the airway.** This is very important in conditions like Ludwig's angina and lateral pharyngeal space infection. The clinician must be alert to identify any respiratory embarrassment. Correct positioning of the patient is an important emergency measure to relieve the respiratory embarrassment. Patients must be placed on the side to avoid this complication. If necessary, airway patency can be maintained by endotracheal intubation. In extreme cases, tracheostomy may have to be performed to save the life of the patient as an emergency procedure. Therefore, it is important to classify the patients with compromised airway.

Class I - Occult respiratory distress: Cases of mild to moderate supraglottic or lateral pharyngeal edema and patients with mild to moderate trismus who do not have severe infection interfering with the airway as in pericoronitis.

Class II - Obvious respiratory distress: These patients develop stridor, labored breathing but alert and cooperative. Since hypoxia would not have developed, the situation permits the clinician to plan the management of the airway. The patient may keep the mouth open for breathing.

Class III - Total respiratory obstruction: These patients develop hypoxia, delirious or may become unconscious. If the airway is not restored by intubation, cricothyroidotomy or emergency tracheostomy, the patient may even develop cardiac arrest.

(2) **Empirical antibiotic therapy.** Primarily, immediate empirical antibiotic therapy must be instituted before the microbiological investigation of the lesion. This is directed towards most of the causative organisms responsible for this infection. This is known as "gun-shot" therapy.

Culture of microorganisms. It is essential to obtain a culture of the causative microorganisms if there is no response with the initial empirical antibiotic therapy within 2 or 3 days. This can be done by drawing blood from the patient or by taking a swab from the infected material to culture the organisms. Sometimes, culture of the organisms in such patients after antibiotics therapy may distort the true microbial picture. However, culture is useful to isolate the responsible organisms for the infection as the appropriate antibiotic therapy can be instituted.

(3) **Establish drainage** at the most dependent area to decompress the swelling and to reduce the burden to the defense mechanism of the body. Since

the infected wound is capable of generating pus and other infected materials continuously, it is better to place a drain so that sustained drainage is possible. Moreover, the drain prevents the wound margins to close. Blocking of the opening promotes accumulation of the infected material. The surgical procedure of incision and drainage is most effective only when it is carried out at the most fluctuant part of the swelling.

(4) **Supportive therapy and care of the patient.**

(a) *Control of pyrexia.* The nature's way of combating the microorganisms is to elevate the body temperature as a response to endogenous pyogenes. This is detrimental to the growth and multiplication of the microorganisms. It also increases the blood flow to the infected region and raises the basal metabolic rate (BMR). It enhances the activities of defense mechanism through enzymes, antigen-antibody reaction and inflammatory cell response. However, abnormal raise of the body temperature above 102°F is likely to be harmful to the host because of undue stress. Unfortunately, hyperpyrexia results in dehydration, depletion of stored energy and stress on cardiovascular system of the body. Hence all the efforts must be directed to maintain the body temperature within limits. The rise of temperature above 102°F denotes bacteremia that is usually accompanied by rigor and delirium.

(b) *Hydration.* Dehydration is directly proportional to the level of pyrexia. Hence, requirement of fluid has to be carefully monitored to ensure proper fluid balance. Wherever possible, adequate oral intake of fluids must be encouraged. If it is not possible, I.V. fluids therapy must be started. It has been estimated that rise in every degree of the body temperature results in the corresponding increase in the body's metabolic requirements by nearly 10-12 %. The I.V. therapy is useful to provide the nutritional requirements. Therefore, the I.V. fluid must provide proteins, vitamins and high caloric value of dietary supplements. If the patient is not able to have oral feed, nasogastric tube can be an alternate route.

(c) *Pain.* This is also directly proportional to the infective process and damage to the tissues. Pain and swelling can be brought under control with anti-inflammatory and analgesic drugs.

Treatment of specific infections

(1) **Alveolar abscess.**

(a) Caries or periodontal infection is the etiology from which bacterial invasion progresses beyond the tooth involving periapical region. In case of doubt, radiograph is useful to identify the etiology.

(b) Root canal therapy or extraction of the offending tooth is the treatment of choice.

(c) Incision and drainage of the abscess is indicated if the swelling is fluctuant. Priority is given for the drainage of the abscess by extraction unless it is planned to conserve the tooth.

(2) **Periodontal abscess.** Usually this develops as a result of chronic periodontitis starting from gingival region but extending along the periodontal space. Hence it may or may not be associated with the non vital tooth.

(a) Relief of pain is by relieving the pressure with incision and drainage of the fluctuant abscess.

(b) Radiographs are useful to assess the damage of the periodontal tissues. If the involved tooth is to be saved, debridement of the root surface and elimination of the granulation tissue may be necessary to promote tissue regeneration.

(c) Appropriate antibiotic therapy is the treatment of choice.

(3) **Submandibular space.** The patient develops trismus and induration of the floor of the mouth. Tongue is edematous and appear elevated. If left untreated, it may lead to the development of osteomyelitis of the mandible. It is best drained through submandibular area. Trecheostomy is done only if required.

(4) **Retropharyngeal space.** Swelling is present in the posterior pharyngeal wall. If the patient develops dysphagia and respiratory obstruction, the treatment must be undertaken as an emergency life saving measure. Sometimes, spontaneous rupture into

the pharynx may lead to the spread of infection into the mediastinum.

(5) **Parapharyngeal space.** The patient will develop swelling in the lateral pharyngeal wall and the parotid region. Spontaneous rupture of the abscess spread into the pharynx and may involve carotid sheath.

Emergency tracheostmy may have to be performed to maintain breathing.

Prevention of cross infection in dental practice

The present-day dental practitioners have been advised to wear gloves for their own protection. This is mainly to reduce the incidence of cross infections. It seems to be a sensible precaution since it may lead to the reduction of upper respiratory tract infections and also to minimize the inhalation of polluted air. Sterilization methods need a careful evaluation because of the inadequacy of boiling water sterilizers. This can be overcome by using autoclave in dental practice.

Recently, the possibility of contracting infectious diseases during the dental treatment has been attracting wide attention. The likelihood of contracting AIDS (Acquired Immune Deficiency Syndrome) or HIV infection has wide implications in dental practice and the interaction between dental, medical and auxiliary professionals. All these factors have resulted in the usage of disposable materials in every day practice. There is an urgent need for the awareness among the dental professionals to safeguard the patients, staff and themselves from the risk of cross infection.

INFLAMMATION OF BONE

General considerations

Bone is a connective tissue containing deposits of calcium salts in the ground substance. It acts as a reservoir of calcium phosphate to mobilize calcium in case of need. The normal bone is organized as lamellar plates, relatively hypocellular and stress oriented. It may be cortical or cancellous. Cotical bone makes up 80% of the skeleton found in the outer shell of the bone. It is composed of tightly packed osteons to form the Haversion system. It is made up of small concentric lamellar cylinders surrounding a central vascular channel connected by haversion canals. The canals contain vessels, nerves and possibly lymphatics. The cancellous bone is less dense, more elastic than cortical bone. It is found in the interior of the bone.

Pathological bone is woven with more osteocytes than lemellar bone. It is the product of rapid bone formation, resulting in an irregular, disorganized pattern of collagen orientation and osteocyte distribution. It is found in adults at ligaments' and tendons' insertion. It may also occur in response to bone injury and changes in mechanical stimulation.

Osteoblasts form osteoid, non-mineralized component of bone matrix. They initiate mineralization of osteoid material.

Osteocytes maintain bone, comprising 90% of all cells in the mature skeleton. They originate as osteoblasts which have been trapped within osteoid, formed by surrounding osteoblasts forming lacunae. They have single nucleus and an increased nucleus-cytoplasm ratio. They are smaller in size and play an important role in controlling the extracellular concentration of calcium and phosphate.

Osteoclasts act in opposition to osteoblasts. Their main role is to resorb bone. They are multi-nucleated, irregularly shaped giant cells.

Matrix

Matrix is made up of organic components (40% dry weight in mature bone) and inorganic components (60% dry weight).

Organic components

(a) *Collagen.* It is composed of type I collagen. It provides bone's tensile strength, comprising 90% bone matrix. Collagen molecules align themselves longitudinally. Cross-linking leads to decreased solubility and increased tensile strength.

(b) *Proteoglycans*. It contributes to the compressive strength of bone.

(c) *Osteocalcin*. It is produced by osteoblasts, to make up 10 to 20 % of the collagenous protein of bone. It attracts osteoclasts. Therefore its function is associated with bone remodelling.

(d) *Interleukin*. Interleukin - 1 is a powerful stimulant to bone resorption. It is mitogenic to osteoclast precursors. Interleukin - 6 is mainly responsible for the acute phase protein response. It potentiates the bone resorbing effects of Interleukin-1.

Inorganic components

(a) *Calcium hydroxyapatite:* It provides the compressive strength to bone. It makes up most of the inorganic matrix, responsible for the mineralization of the matrix. The term mineralization refers to the transformation of hydroxyapatite from a soluble to solid form. Primary mineralization occurs in gaps in collagen while, secondary mineralization occurs at the periphery.

(b) *Osteocalcium phosphate:* It comprises of the remaining inorganic matrix.

Remodelling of bone

It is affected by mechanical function according to Wolff's law which attempts to predict bone adaptation in the face of an altered loading environment. Generally it occurs in response to stress. Compression causes negative potential which stimulates osteoblast activity and bone formation. Tension causes positive potential leading to osteoclast stimulation. Bone is dynamic. Coordinated osteoblast and osteoclast activity results in continuous remodelling of both cortical and cancellous bone throughout life.

Bone circulation

The blood supply is derived from the following sources:

(a) Nutrient artery which enters the bone and runs along the long axis. This is a high-pressure system.

(b) Periosteal vessels run from periosteum to the cortex and supply the superficial part of the cortex. They are large and abundant in childhood but scarce in old age. This is a low-pressure system.

(c) Wherever muscles are attached to the bone, blood supply is derived through the muscle attachments.

Periosteum is a double layered membrane. The outer layer is fibrous and the inner layer is osteogenic. Fibrous layer is protective while the inner layer is osteogenic in nature.

Bone marrow

Red marrow is the tissue in which blood cells develop. It contains 40% water, 40% fat and 20% protein. In later stages of growth in the adult, when rate of blood cell formation has decreased, red marrow slowly changes to yellow marrow.

Yellow marrow is made up of 80% fat, 15% water and 5% protein. Under appropriate stimulus it can revert to red marrow.

OSTEOMYELITIS

(Figs 8.4 to 8.7)

The jaw bones are generally resistant to infection. The inflammatory exudate induces resorption of the overlying cortex and penetrates the periosteum. The inflammation of bone results as a result of an element of ischemia along with bacterial infection. The pathological resorption of bone is mediated by (a) prostaglandin, (b) osteoclast-activating factor and (c) monocyte factor. Wherever bone destruction takes place, there is always an associated local bone regeneration. Such a combined bone destruction and bone formation is an important feature of most of the bony pathology.

Osteomyelitis is defined as a diffuse inflammation of the soft tissues of the bone involving cancellous bone marrow and periosteal components. This condition is classified as acute or chronic osteomyelitis. Topazian broadly classifies the osteomyelitis into suppurative and non suppurative types. Suppurative type may be infantile, acute and chronic. Non suppurative type includes chronic sclerosing (focal or diffuse), Garre's osteomyelitis, actinomycotic and radiation osteomyelitis. Inspite of intimate relationship between teeth and medullary cavity, the low incidence of osteomyelitis is attributed to the host resistance and high vascularity of the jaw bones. However, in the presence of alterations in host defenses, osteomyelitis may develop in patients with systemic diseases like diabetes, leukemia, anemia, agranulocytosis, malnutrition and chronic alcoholism. Conditions which may alter the vascularity of the bone like radiation, fibrous dysplasia, Paget's disease and osteoporosis may predispose to this condition.

Pathogenesis

This clinical entity develops due to hematogenous spread or due to spread from a focus of infection. Primarily, odontogenic infections or trauma to the bone initiate this condition. Due to the excellent blood supply, thin cortical bone and relative lack of medullary bone in maxilla is said to be responsible for the low incidence. On the contrary, mandible resembles a long bone - it has well-defined periosteum, cortical bone and medullary cavity. The bone marrow contains reticuloendothelial cells, erythrocytes, granulocytes, cancellous bone, osteoblastic precursors with good vascularity. It is lined by endosteum containing large number of osteoblasts. Cortical bone has a distinctive architecture with haversion system. Central canals communicate among the adjoining aversion systems and periosteum to provide a complex vascular and neural network that provide nutrition to the bone. This helps in the regeneration, repair and functional demands of the bone. The bone is covered by the periosteum containing an inner layer of osteogenic cells and an outer fibrous layer.

Therefore, any compromise to the blood supply is a critical factor. Anatomically, it is found that coronoid receives blood supply through temporalis while, condyle gets vascularity through lateral pterygoid muscle. Mandible gets blood supply from inferior dental vessels (endosteal) while, secondary vascularity is from the periosteal vessels. Mandibular venous drainage is provided by two routes - upwards to the pharyngeal plexus through inferior dental veins and downwards to the external jugular vein.

The process of osteomyelitis is initiated by acute inflammation. Increase in the intramedullary pressure results in the vascular compromise. Tissue necrosis may lead to the formation of pus which travels along the haversion system and nutrient canals and finally form a subperiosteal abscess. Forcible elevation of the periosteum results in the reduction of vascularity of the adjoining cortex. Compression of the neurovascular bundle promotes osteomyelitis-mediated- mandibular anesthesia. This helps to differentiate between alveolar abscess from acute osteomyelitis. Accumulation of more pus in the medullary cavity may lead to its spread to the neighboring soft tissues . Ultimately it may find its way out through mucosal or cutaneous fistulae. If the entity does not resolve, it may develop into a chronic condition. Formation of granulation tissue and new blood vessels will lead to lysis of bone. Such dead pieces of bone get isolated from the normal bone by the granulation tissue. This dead bone is called *sequestrum*. Rarely there is an attempt to form new bone called *involucrum*. This is perforated by revascularization process and through such channels called *cloacae*, pus escapes towards the epithelial surface. Radiographically, sequestrum appears radioopaque than normal bone and the zone containing granulation tissue appears radiolucent.

Formerly, staphylococcus strains were attributed as the major causative organisms for this condition. Recently, with the liberal use of antibiotics, there has been a decline in the staphylococcal infections. This has resulted in the

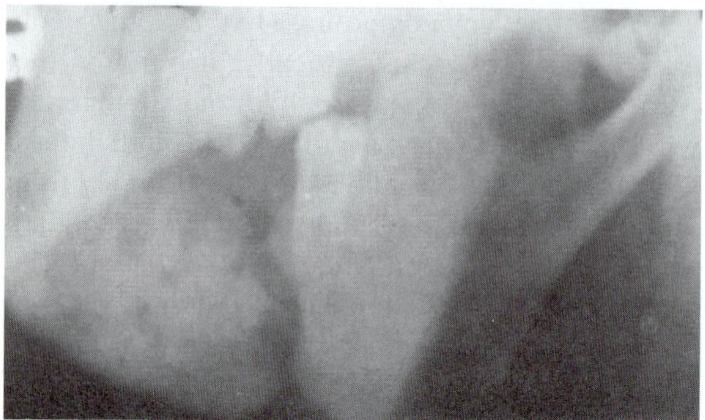

Fig. 8.4 Chronic osteomyelitis–mandible—III molar region.

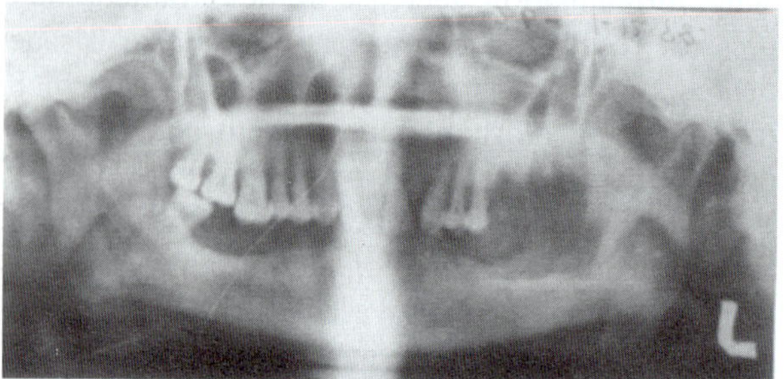

Fig. 8.5 Chronic osteomyelitis–mandible (Ramus).

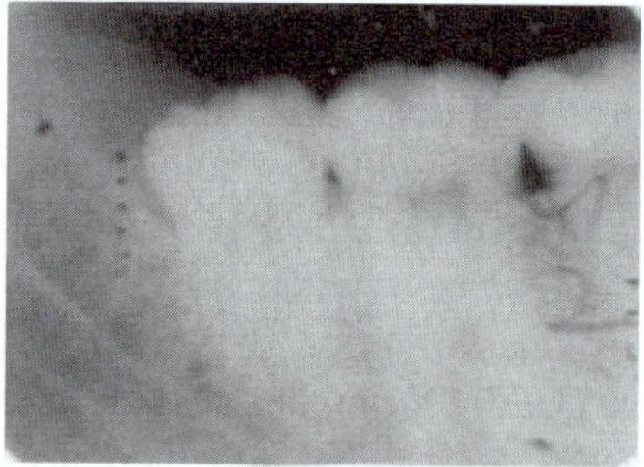

Fig. 8.6 Distoangular impaction predisposes to submasseteric space infection.

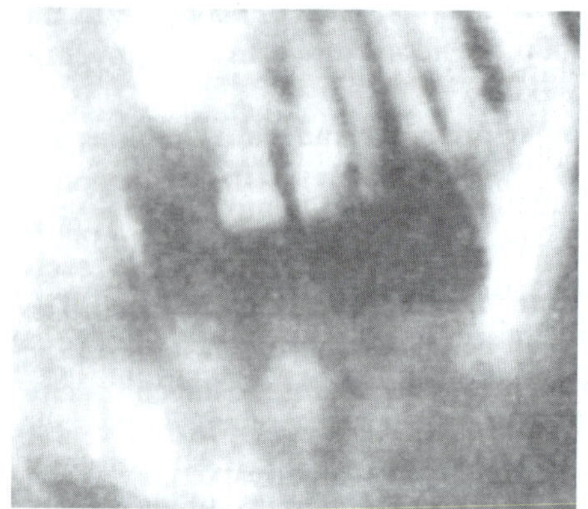

Fig. 8.7 (a) Sequestrum.

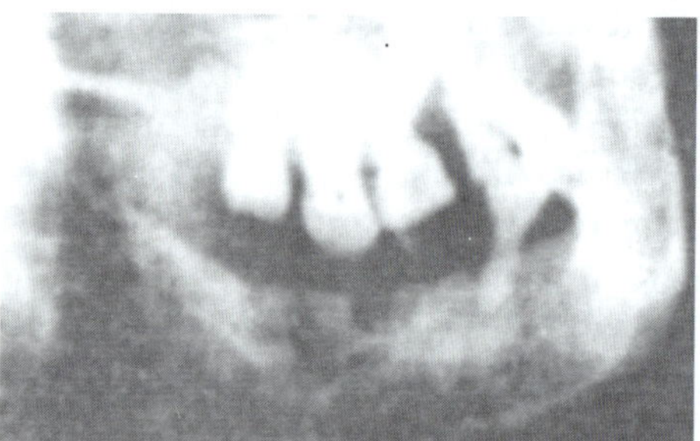

Fig. 8.7 (b) Osteolytic lesion–mandible.

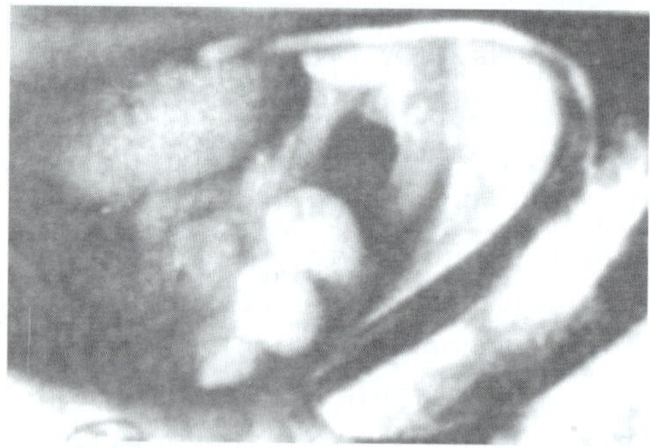

Fig. 8.8 Dry socket (alveolitis in the alveolar socket).

development of osteomyelitis due to the causative organisms not previously associated with this condition like anaerobes. This is characterized by the development of foul-smelling pus and necrotic tissue. Multiple organisms of varied morphology can be identified from this area.

Osteomyelitis in infancy

This is one of the rare types of infection involving maxilla in a few weeks old infants. It is otherwise called maxillitis. The causative organism is found to be staphylococcus aureus, believed to have been acquired from contaminated nipple or breast of the mother. The entry of the organism is possible only through a break in the oral mucosa of the infant. If the condition is diagnosed early and appropriate antibiotic therapy is instituted to the infant, the condition resolves. With the spectrum of antibiotics, the incidence of this condition has become rare.

Acute osteomyelitis

It is more common in mandible than in maxilla. It starts with infection involving medullary portion of the bone. Usually the periapical infection spreads to the medullary area and starts diffusing along the path of least resistance. The natural defense mechanism resists such a spread but the onset of acute osteomyelitis is associated with lack of resistance of the patient. With the advent of antibiotics with wider spectra, the incidence of this condition has reduced considerably.

Clinical features

(1) Deep boring, continuous pain.
(2) Intermittent paresthesia of the lower lip which helps the clinician to differentiate this condition from alveolar abscess.
(3) Edema of the overlying tissue which is tender.
(4) Systemic features like pyrexia and malaise.
(5) Radiological changes are absent.
(6) Microbiological investigation reveals the nature of microbial flora and antibiotics to which they are sensitive.

The treatment consists of instituting appropriate antibiotic therapy. Either the condition resolves or leads to the chronic stage, depending on the microorganisms and resistance of the host. Wherever necessary, incision and drainage at the point of fluctuation should be carried out.

Chronic osteomyelitis

This is characterized by minimal pain. If the pus is not drained, it perforates the cortex and forms the subperiosteal abscess. The failure to drain the pus results in the accumulation of pus and the consequent elevation of periosteum from the bone. Once subperiosteal abscess forms, the subperiosteal blood vessels are stretched and ultimately the vessels break resulting in ischemia of the associated cortical plate. This is because the subperiosteal blood supply is severed. The destructiveness of the osteomyelitis is also due to the pressure exerted by the pus and the lysis of the suppurative material. If the antibiotics have exerted the bactericidal effect, the growth of microorganisms is controlled resulting in resolution. If the organisms are resistant to antibiotic therapy, they multiply and release the toxins depending on their virulence. Due to ischemia, an island of cortical bone becomes devitalized and becomes favorable for the precipitation of the ionized calcium, mobilized by the surrounding osteolytic process. Such a devitalized piece of bone appears sclerosed and becomes a foreign body. This is known as "Sequestrum".

Study of the blood supply to the mandible in various age groups has revealed that blood supply is derived from subperiosteal and endosteal blood vessels. As an aging process, the inferior dental and the peripheral periosteal vessels gradually narrow down resulting in decreased blood supply. This problem is not encountered in maxilla. Hence, mandible in the elderly age group are more prone to osteomyelitic changes than maxilla.

The mandibular premolar and molar regions are mostly involved. The patient feels that the area supplied by inferior dental nerve has become numb. This is, perhaps, due to thrombosis of the inferior dental vessels exerting its pressure over the inferior dental canal. The involved teeth may be tender and found loose in the involved bony segment. Depending on the chronicity of the condition, multiple sinuses develop in the alveolar process intraorally and over the corresponding facial skin discharging pus. The regional lymph nodes enlarge.

Radiography. Radiographs of the involved region during the first two weeks appear normal. As the osteomyelitic changes take place, the affected region appears mottled due to the widening of the medullary space and enlargement of Volkman's canal. As the condition progresses, the attempts to isolate the sequestrum by the formation of granulation tissue around the sequestrum can be seen. Hence, sequestrum appears radioopaque in the radiograph, separated by a zone of radiolucency. Since the zone of radiolucency is irregular, the picture is described as a characteristic "moth-eaten appearance", coinciding with the establishment of chronic osteomyelitis. Because of the osteoblastic layer of the periosteum, a layer of subperiosteal new bone formation called "involucrum" is formed, appearing in the radiograph as a fine, linear laminated opacity, parallel to the cortical surface. This further adds to the loss of the radiographic definition of the normal bone architecture. Involucrum may be noticed in children and adolescents but absent in adult mandible. Later on, fragments of sequestra may get separated by the well- demarcated radiolucent zones.

At present, imaging sciences like tomograms, CT and bone scintigraphy.are made use of to diagnose this clinical entity even during the acute phase. In the early stage, bone scintigraphy is considered the most sensitive diagnostic method. Conventional radiographs and tomograms show bony destruction and periosteal changes two or three weeks after the onset of the condition. CT provides simultaneous depiction of bony and soft tissues with improved resolution of space and density. MRI is a diagnostic imaging technique based on nuclear magnetic resonance that has exclusively been used for soft tissue imaging.

Recently, scintigraphy is being used more for the imaging of bone (Radionuclide scanning). This procedure helps to determine the presence of reactive bone. Conventional radiography is helpful if at least 50% of bone mineral is altered. Therefore, scintigraphy is useful to diagnose the early cases of osteomyelitis, even before the radiographic bone changes develop. Hence, this technique is considered as the "gold standard" for locating osteomyelitis in its initial stage. However, it is found that this method fails to differentiate between osteomyelitis and bone tumors with increased bone metabolism.

MRI shows structural changes in the bone marrow without exposing the patient to radiation. But, it is of lower diagnostic sensitivity than CT or conventional tomograms. Since, prognosis depends on early diagnosis and treatment, the ability to identify the inflammatory bone and soft tissue changes with MRI assumes great significance. However, it provides no major advantages over bone scintigraphy.

Treatment

(1) The earlier the condition is diagnosed, the better will be the chances of resolution. The empirical *antibiotic therapy* is started depending on culture and antibiotic sensitivity tests and lysis of the infective material within a closed space in the bone. The sequestrum and the devitalized tissues form good nidus for the bacteria to grow and multiply. The resistant strains of staphylococci are responsible for the development of the typical "hospital infection". Hence, *sequestrectomy* and *curettage* of the infected area clear up the osteomyelitic region effectively. Since there are multiple areas of radiolucency, the entire area is made into one cavity and self-cleansing. Thus, the cleaned up bony cavity and the removal of overhanging bony margins render the bony cavity broad. This is known as *saucerization.*

The clinical and radiological evidences reveal that the medullary cavity is extensively involved without the perforation of the cortex by the infective process, multiple holes can be made for instituting effective drainage and also to release intraosseous pressure. If needed, the outer cortex can be removed. Partial or total removal of cortex is known as *decortication.* This must be used judiciously. After the removal of the cortex, the soft tissue approximation increases the vascular supply of the bone. By doing so, antibiotic therapy is also made more effective.

(2) The number and timing regarding the decision to extract the involved teeth requires the discretion and proper judgement of the clinician. Depending on the need, the cavity is packed with appropriate dressing like roller gauze impregnated with iodoform or Whitehead's varnish. Periodically, the dressing is to be changed to keep the wound clean and granulating and also to prevent the wound getting infected.

(3) Very rarely, if the involvement and osteolytic damage of the bone is extensive and when all the conservative methods have failed to yield satisfactory results, consideration to resect the involved bone and subsequent reconstruction with autotransplantation of bone may have to be done.

(4) In specific infective types of osteomyelitis like tuberculosis, syphilis or actinomycosis, the specific antibiotic therapy is required for a long period.

(5) *Hyperbaric oxygen*: This is very useful in the management not amenable to the conventional antibiotic therapy and other modes of treatment of osteomyelitis of the mandible. The rationale behind hyperbaric oxygen therapy is mainly to increase the level of arterial and venous oxygen tension within the infected tissues. (a) This will help to increase the vascular supply to the region, (b) It will result in bactericidal or bacteriostatic effect on aerobic organisms, (c) This will also promote fibroblastic, osteoblastic and osteogenic activity of the bone, (d) This will, in turn, improve the quantity and quality of the production of granulation tissue, (e) It is also expected to promote resorption and replacement of the devitalized bony tissue, (f) This form of therapy is indicated in the management of osteoradionecrosis, (g) It is contraindicated in neoplastic tissues and chronic pulmonary disorders. Oxygen toxicity is known to affect the retina, respiratory and central nervous system, (h) This is best used only as an *adjunct therapy* to antibiotic and surgical therapy.

(6) Choice of appropriate *antibiotic therapy* for orofacial infections:

(i) Evaluate the infection and the patient's host defense mechanisms:
   (a) Physiological
   (b) Pathological
   (c) Immunological.
(ii) Establish effective surgical drainage and eliminate the etiology.
(iii) Assess the need for an antibiotic.
(iv) If needed, then choose the appropriate antibiotic.
   (a) Identify the causative organisms through culture.
   (b) Determine the antibiotic sensitivity of the causative organisms.
   (c) Select the least toxic antibiotic with the narrowest spectrum.
   (d) Prefer bactericidal rather than bacteriostatic agent.
   (e) Prescribe the drug known for its efficacy rather than to experiment with a newly introduced drug.
   (f) Carefully record the history of the patient's drug allergies and untoward reactions.
   (g) Determine the renal and liver status of the patient before therapy.
   (h) Cost-benefit aspect must also be considered.

OSTEORADIONECROSIS

General considerations

This is a potential sequelae following irradiation of the oral cavity while treating oral malignancy. In a way, this is preventable. The initial reaction of the endothelium to irradiation is followed by fibrosis and constriction of the blood vessels. Hence, radiotherapy of the oral cavity is known to alter the vascular supply to the orofacial region and salivary flow. It also produces extensive mucositis. Thus, the combination of *decreased blood supply, salivary flow* and *poor oral hygiene* promote the development of cervical dental caries. At present, this is considered as a metabolic and tissue homeostatic deficiency created by radiation-induced cellular injury, characterised by the sequence: radiation - formation of hypoxic, hypovascular and hypocellular tissue - tissue breakdown - result in a chronic non healing wound. Microorganisms are considered as contaminants.

Thus, the spectrum of changes in the mandibular region following irradiation may be grouped under three categories:

(1) Atrophic changes (have already been dealt with)
(2) Aseptic osteoradionecrosis of the bone
(3) Superadded sepsis.

The aseptic radionecrosis can be considered as an advanced stage of altered physiological state in which mandibular region is no longer viable. Osteoblasts tend to become radiosensitive more than osteoclasts. Hence, following radiotherapy, disproportionately greater lytic activity with extensive depletion of the osteocytic population results in the degenerative changes in the bone.

Pathogenesis

It is observed that there are three factors that play an important role in the development of osteoradionecrosis of the mandible. They are as follows:

(1) History of irradiation of the region
(2) Trauma to the tissue overlying the mandible
(3) Infection.

In other words, mandible is rendered vulnerable due to irradiation changes. If the mucoperiosteum is intact, the underlying bone is well protected. A definite episode of trauma to the mucoperiosteum like extraction of a tooth will expose the underlying bone to the oral environment. Through this opening, sepsis enters the devitalized bone. The bacterial invasion resulting in infection of the bone where the altered nature of the bone with impaired defense mechanism lead to the onset of osteoradionecrosis.

Prevention and management

(1) It is noticed that the situation is further complicated by the presence of teeth. Hence the teeth in the line of irradiation were used to be prophylactically removed to provide intact mucoperiosteum.

(2) With the advent of modern techniques, conservative measures are taken to preserve these teeth so that osteoradionecrosis does not set in later. In the recent times, perhaps, the following steps have been responsible to reduce the incidence of this condition.

(a) Deep x-ray therapy resulted in its high incidence. Following cobalt therapy with the selective target, the intervening tissues like teeth and mucoperiosteum are spared.

(b) Selectively, if the salivary glands are spared in the course of radiation, salivary flow is not altered.

(c) Maintenance of good oral hygiene is necessary. Calculi around the teeth must be removed prior to irradiation. Otherwise, dental calculi may absorb radiation and start secondarily emitting later. Hence, dental prophylaxis is necessary prior to irradiation.

(d) Care should be taken to avoid any form of trauma to oral mucoperiosteum like dental extraction, denture irritation etc. during the postirradiation phase.

(e) Prophylactic hyperbaric oxygen therapy: Histopathologic studies have suggested that the radiation-induced obliteration of the inferior dental artery seems to be the dominant factor in the onset of this condition, leading to an ischemic necrosis of bone. Because of this concept, treatment of this lesion has changed considerably in the recent past. It is focused on revascularization of the irradiated tissues. The rationale for the use of hyperbaric oxygen therapy in this condition is to revascularize the irradiated tissues and to improve the fibroblastic cellular density thereby limiting the amount of nonviable tissue to be surgically removed, enhancing wound healing and also to prepare the tissues for reconstruction, when indicated.

(f) Unlike osteomyelitis, this condition takes longer duration for the osteolysis. Very rarely, sequestrum separates in the normal course of time, it may even take many years. Hence, extreme caution is necessary before instituting any form of radical treatment. Very rarely, curettage, sequestrectomy etc. is performed. Depending on the resolution of the lesion, bone grafting may be undertaken at a later date. Larger lesions can best be treated with combined hyperbaric oxygen therapy, surgery and antibiotic therapy.

CHAPTER 9

Maxillofacial Injuries

GENERAL CONSIDERATIONS

Maxillofacial injuries may be limited to superficial abrasions of the soft tissues of the face or may involve the facial skeleton with associated injuries of the cranium, chest and other parts of the body. For the convenience of clinical study, face is divided into three parts (Fig. 9.1). Lower third of the face is formed by mandible. Middle third of the face includes maxillae and associated bony complex. The arbitrary line drawn joining the frontozygomatic, frontomaxillary and frontonasal suture lines along the supraorbital margin divides the middle third from the upper third of the face. Etiology, clinical features and the management widely differ in all these three areas of the face. Functionally and esthetically, trauma of the facial skeleton results in the disturbance to

(a) mouth and jaws
(b nose and respiratory tract
(c) orbit and vision
(d) skull and brain

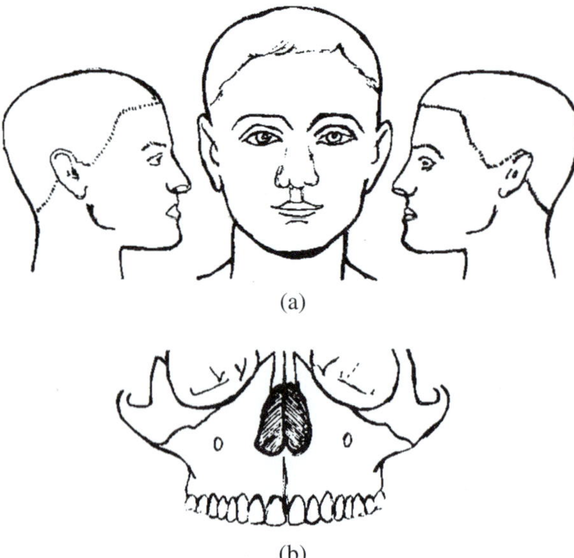

Fig. 9.1 (a) Face - front and side views, **(b)** Midfacial skeleton.

(e) facial complex as a whole.

Due to the complex anatomy of the region and overlapping of many health specialties, a teamwork is essential to treat the facial trauma. However, oral surgeon should take the primary responsibility of the patient.

ETIOLOGY

Some of the most severe injuries are caused by Road Traffic Accidents (RTA). But many other etiological factors may also be responsible for facial trauma.

(a) Road traffic accidents (RTA)
- Four wheelers (car, bus, etc.)
- Two wheelers (scooter, cycle, etc.)

In all these cases, the injured person may be driving the vehicle or may be a passenger. In case of the driver of four wheelers, associated chest and other injuries need attention. In two wheelers, pillion riders are more severely injured than the person who drives. Sometimes, the injured person may be a pedestrian injured by the vehicle. In the recent times in India, two wheelers are involved more due to decreased stability on the road.

(b) Fist fights
(c) Industrial accidents
(d) Sports injuries, e.g. hockey, football, cricket and boxing injuries
(e) Train accidents
(f) Occupational hazards, e.g. fall from a height while at work
(g) Gunshot injuries
(h) Miscellaneous injuries.

PRIMARY CARE (LIFE-SAVING MEASURES)

Every patient with facial trauma must be examined for any evidence of intracranial involvement. Proper clinical examination is mandatory to determine the general condition of the patient. At times, one may encounter life-threatening emergency situations. The prime concern must be to keep the patient alive before instituting any definitive treatment for the maxillofacial injuries. The following are some of the important conditions that require attention.

Airway maintenance

Respiratory obstructions can lead to asphyxia in an unconscious patient. The factors responsible to cause respiratory obstruction are the following:

(a) Aspiration of salivary secretions, blood, vomitus, foreign bodies like loose teeth, dentures etc.

(b) In bilateral parasymphyseal fractures, tongue and its attachments drag the symphyseal fragment posteriorly resulting in the tongue falling back, thereby obstructing the airway.

(c) Large hematoma, edema around the pharynx and emphysema can lead to airway obstruction.

The steps to be undertaken to maintain patent airway are the following:

(i) Oral cavity and nasopharynx must be cleared of blood clot, salivary secretions and foreign bodies.

(ii) Steps must be taken to stabilize the tongue with a stay suture so that it is prevented to fall back. It relieves the obstruction of the airway.

(iii) Metallic airway can be placed to maintain the patency of the respiratory passage. The patient must be placed on the face down position.

(iv) If the airway obstruction is present in the pharynx, an emergency tracheostomy may be necessary. It is also possible to open the airway through the cricothyroid membrane (*coniotomy*).

Control of hemorrhage

Usually, this is not a life-threatening emergency in facial injuries unless there are associated injuries or any major vessel is involved in trauma.

Neurological problems

The head and spinal cord are vulnerable to injuries in facial trauma. Because of the close association between facial and intracranial injuries, it is rather mandatory to make a routine neurological examination of the patient before treating facial trauma. A patient with head injury is a constant source of anxiety to those responsible for the management. To understand the various aspects of head injuries, the following clinical situations are defined.

Cerebral concussion

A transient state (due to head injury) of instantaneous onset, manifests widespread symptoms without any evidence of structural cerebral injury, followed by amnesia of the actual moment of the head injury.

The neurological involvement can be determined by the extent of facial injuries and level of consciousness. Hence, the initial neurological examination must include the following aspects:

(a) Level of consciousness
(b) Examination of cranial nerves
(c) Evidence of any special injuries
(d) Presence of amnesia.

The level of consciousness forms one of the most significant factors to be considered. One must differentiate between an alert, conscious patient and a comatose, unconscious patient.

Between these two stages, the patient may be in any one of the intermediate stages. While *coma* indicates that the person is not responsive, *semiconsciousness* indicates that the person is unconscious but responds to painful stimuli. *Lethargy* indicates that the person is sleepy but who can follow the verbal commands. The level of consciousness indicates the degree of intracranial involvement.

Pupillary changes

A bright torch light must be used to detect any of the following pupillary changes.

(a) Difference in the changes between the eyes
(b) Fixed and dilated pupil
(c) No reaction to light

Injury to the cranial nerves can be examined by proper neurological examination. Damage to I cranial nerve leads to anosmia (loss of smell). Damage to the II cranial nerve leads to loss of vision. Injury to III, IV and VI nerves result in the involvement of the ocular muscles. Trigeminal nerve damage can be diagnosed by the loss of sensation of the facial region. VII nerve damage is represented by the involvement of the muscles of facial expression.

Examination of the motor system provides the necessary information to localize the various sites of brain injuries, e.g. absence of body movements, convulsions, responses to various stimuli and limb movements. Hemiplegia indicates the possibility of pressure effects on the motor cortex. But delayed hemiplegia may occur due to subdural or epidural edema or hematoma. Response to various types of stimuli, pupillary reflex and reflex of the tendons must be properly recorded.

Amnesia

It is the term that refers to loss of memory. Some may not be able to remember the events before or after the accident.

Hemorrhage

Any severe external bleeding should be viewed with concern. Appropriate measures must be taken without any delay.

Shock

Shock is not the usual complication in the isolated facial injuries. Invariably, it may be a neurogenic or primary shock. Steps must be taken to maintain the records of temperature, pulse and BP of the patient periodically.

Anoxia

Brain is particularly vulnerable to hypoxia. It may be (a) *anoxic anoxia* (from airway obstruction by tongue, laryngeal spasm or aspiration of blood or vomitus or inadequate ventilation), (b) *anemic anoxia* (from blood loss). Therefore, steps must be taken for the provision of a free airway, replacement of lost blood and maintenance of the systolic blood pressure above 100 mm Hg.

Control of infection

Although wound infection and its control are of general nature, particular steps must be taken to prevent the onset of tetanus and gas gangrene, apart from bone and wound infection. In case of intracranial involvement, neurologist must decide the nature of antibiotics. Hence, antibiotic therapy is generally considered to be a multi disciplinary responsibility in these patients.

Control of pain

In general, analgesics must be administered minimally. If a narcotic like morphine is given to a patient with a probable head injury, it may hinder or interfere with diagnosis. For example, (a) it may stimulate the nucleus of III nerve causing miosis, thereby masking the neurological signs which are very vital to diagnose cerebral hemorrhage, (b) as a respiratory depressant, it aggravates the respiratory problem, (c) it may stimulate nausea and vomiting. Under these circumstances, narcotics are contraindicated in facial trauma.

EVALUATION OF THE PATIENT

Detailed evaluation of the facial injuries is undertaken on completion of the life-saving emergency measures. Consultations with a neurologist and a physician are necessary before undertaking specific treatment of facial fractures. The evaluation, proper treatment, planning and the management of maxillofacial injuries require adequate knowledge of anatomy of the region and special training. Accurate diagnosis is the stepping stone to success in the management of these patients.

General examination

Every patient with facial trauma must be examined for fractures of other parts of the body so that appropriate specialists could be consulted. If possible, treatment planning should include sequence of treatment of various fractures when the patient is anesthetized.

History

A proper history should be elicited from the patient. If the patient is unable to describe the details of the incident, efforts must be directed to gather information about the loss of memory, loss of consciousness, if any, history of vomiting, medications given etc.

Clinical examination (Figs 9.2 - 9.4)

(a) Presence of *contusion* will provide valuable information regarding the type and directions of force of the trauma.

(b) Development of *facial asymmetry*, abnormality or edema after the injury.

(c) *Occlusion*: Detailed examination of teeth and occlusion are absolutely essential. If the fracture involves tooth-bearing area of the jaws, occlusion will be altered. This provides information regarding the displacement of fragments. Sound dentition will be useful for immobilization of jaws.

(d) If *ecchymosis* is present around the tooth or at the floor of the mouth, it is suggestive of fracture.

(e) *Loss of function*: Fractured jaws result in

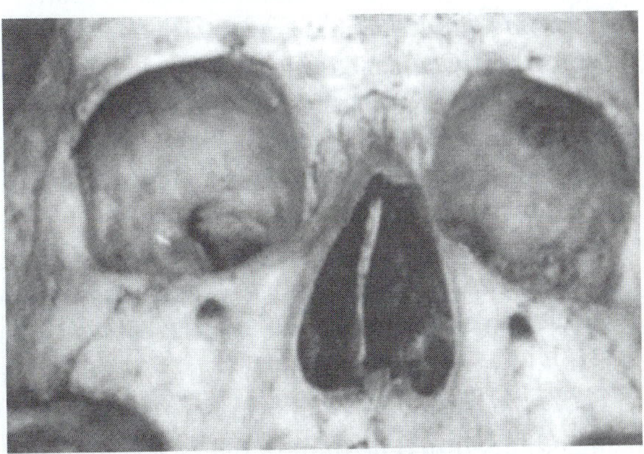

Fig. 9.2 Photograph of adult facial skeleton.

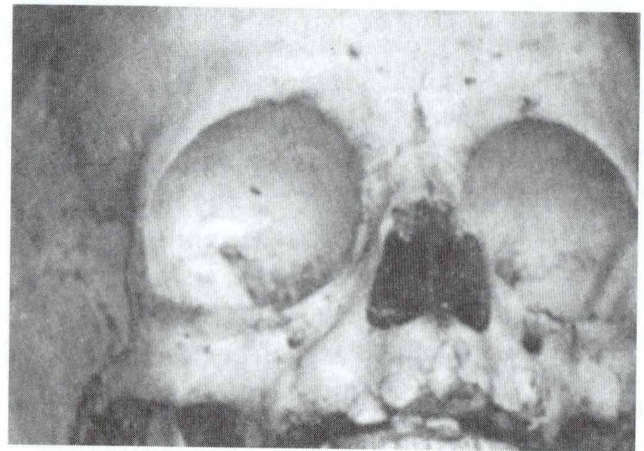

Fig. 9.3 Photograph of facial skeleton of a child.

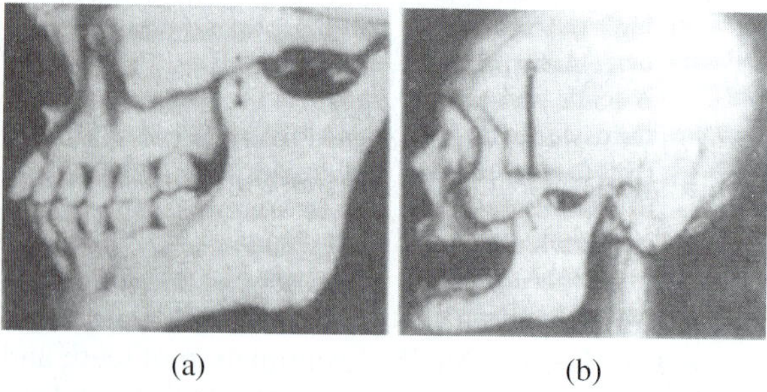

(a) (b)

Fig. 9.4 Side view of facial skeleton **(a)** Dentulous, **(b)** Edentulous.

difficulty to move the mandible.

(f) *Anesthesia*: Loss of sensation over the face indicates that fracture involves the corresponding sensory nerve, e.g. inferior alveolar nerve, infraorbital nerve, etc.

(g) *Bleeding* from the ear, nose and mouth.

(h) *CSF rhinorrhea* (CSF leak through the nose). CSF otorrhea (CSF leak through the eye).

(i) *Neurological* examination including eyeball movements, muscles of facial expression, presence of headache and pain.

(j) Any *abnormal mobility* or crepitus.

(k) *Radiological* examination.

Depending on the type of fracture, radiographs must be advised.

Mandible fractures can be diagnosed from lateral oblique view, PA view and occlusal view of the mandible. If middle third of the face is involved, maxillary sinus view is the best view. In the recent times, CT scan is utilized to diagnose the complicated fractures including intracranial injury.

HEALING OF FRACTURES

Historically, fracture has been considered to heal by secondary intention (by callus formation). During 1970s, a team of Swiss orthopedic surgeons proposed that *primary healing* can occur if callus formation is prevented by the close approximation, rigid fixation and immobilization of fractured fragments. Accordingly, philosophy of the management of fractures changed dramatically. Hence, it is absolutely essential to review the details of healing of fractures under varied circumstances so that role of various types of fixations in fracture healing can be understood properly.

Healing by secondary intention (by callus formation) (Fig. 9.5)

Weinmann and Sicher described the process of healing of fractures in six stages.

(1) **Hematoma formation.** Soon after the bone is subjected to increased strain of high order, fracture occurs. This results in break in continuity of bone and rupture of blood vessels from cortex, medulla, periosteum, surrounding muscles and

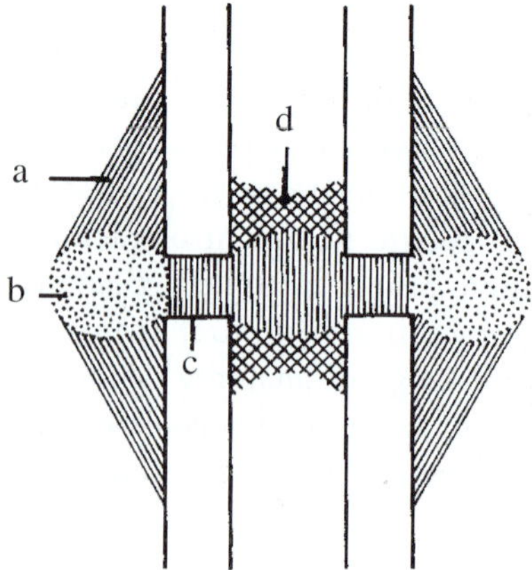

Fig. 9.5 Healing of fracture by callus formation: **(a)** Anchoring callus (periosteal), **(b)** Bridging callus, **(c)** Uniting callus, **(d)** Sealing callus.

adjacent soft tissues. The resultant pooling of blood at the site of fracture forms a *hematoma*. The spasm of endosteal and other blood vessels with clotting process arrest the hemorrhage. Hematoma surrounds the fractured bone ends and extends into the marrow space. This process continues for 6-8 hours after the accident. There is an immediate acute traumatic inflammatory phase.

(2) **Organization of hematoma.** The hematoma contains remnants of periosteum, bone, muscle, fascia and bone marrow. New capillaries invade the fibrin network of the blood clot in 24-48 hours. Polymorphs and macrophages soon take part in demolition, digestion and removal of the devitalized tissues from the hematoma. Osteoclasts resorb bony spicules and bone fragments. The giant cells are believed to have been formed by the fusion of macrophages. Simultaneously, fibroblasts also invade the blood clot. Early organization of hematoma is characterized by the proliferation of blood vessels. The tortuous course of new capillaries retards the blood flow, resulting in stasis and proliferation of mesenchyme with the associated rise in calcium level of the capillary bed. By this, most of the debris would have been removed and bone ends are rendered smooth. The ingrowth of undifferentiated fibroblastic cells and vascular endothelial elements form the *granulation tissue*.

(3) **Formation of provisional (fibrous) callus.** Within 10 days, hematoma is organized and replaced by granulation tissue. At this stage, fibroblastic cells reveal their differentiation potential. Many of them secrete the characteristic ground substance, *"osseomucin"*, which is deposited between the collagen network. The ground substance and coarse collagen fibers form the matrix known as *osteoid tissue*. But minerals are yet to be deposited. The granulation tissue is replaced by the formation of loose connective tissue and partial obliteration of the capillaries. This stage is known as *fibrous callus*.

(4) **Primary (bony) callus formation.** After 10-15 days, calcium deposition commences but the calcium content of the callus is very low. Hence, it is very soft and will not be visible in the radiograph. At this stage, depending on the location and function, the callus has been termed as *anchoring callus*, bridging callus, uniting callus and scaling callus. At this stage, mechanism of calcification is not properly understood. Probably, high content of alkaline phosphatase present in the osteoblasts may be an important factor. The local pH is acidic which helps calcium to become solution after the osteoclastic resorption of fractured ends. Once pH rises to alkaline tide, alkaline phosphatase may be able to react more easily with hexose monophosphate to produce local saturation of phosphate.

Anchoring callus. This callus is formed on the external surface of the bone between the anchoring callus and the two fracture ends. Since this is cartilaginous in nature, it is questioned as to whether this type of callus occurs in mandible fracture.

Uniting callus. This is seen at the interfragmentary gap. However, it does not form until callus forms in other areas. By the time uniting callus is formed, extensive bone resorption can be noticed at the bone ends. Hence, it can be noticed that this type of callus is formed at the fracture site and also in the areas of bone resorption.

Sealing callus. This forms across the fractured ends, filling the bone marrow spaces. This is also called endosteal *callus*.

(5) **Secondary callus.** It is matured bone replacing immature bone of the primary callus. Since degree of calcification is more, it is visible more in the radiographs. But it differs from bone with the development of pseudohaversian system that can withstand the active use. This process is seen from 20-60 days. Fixation can be conveniently removed during this stage. It is found that bone forms in electronegative regions and resorption occurs in the electropositive regions. Thus, alkaline phosphatase of osteoblasts plays an important part in osteogenesis while acid phosphatase and lysosomal enzymes of osteoclast act in acid pH and helps in *autolysis*. Formation of definitive callus is

the final stage of healing.

(6) **Remodelling of bone.** During this phase, remodelling takes place by the resorption of callus except for the ones present in the interfragmentary gap. If bone is not subjected to functional stress, true matured bone will not form. True haversian system oriented to stress factors replaces non-oriented pseudohaversian system of secondary callus. Thus the bone is moulded and sculptured to conform to the size of the remainder of bone.

Primary healing of bone (without callus formation). During 1970s, some Swiss surgeons claimed that the traditional gap healing of fractures occur when the fragments are incompletely immobilized. Mobility leads to resorption of bone ends, formation of external callus, internal callus and differentiation of fibrocartilage in the interfragmentary gap. But, bone repair takes place differently under perfectly stable conditions. Their extensive studies revealed that stable fixation of fractured fragments results in primary healing where neither connective tissue nor fibrocartilage form before new bone is laid down.

Bone consists of three elements: *periosteum, endosteum* and *cell population* within the haversian system. All these structures can be activated by injuries like fracture. They respond either by bone resorption, bone formation or ultimately by connective tissue and cartilage formation (*callus*). Bone resorption, connective tissue formation and cartilage production are related to the mechanical stimuli caused by the movements of the ends of the fragments. But if such movements are prevented during the first four weeks of healing, very little callus forms along the periosteal surfaces of the fragments and also within the marrow cavity. In bone repair with stable internal fixation, the process is initiated by the ingrowth of tiny thin walled blood vessels accompanied by loose network of mesenchymal cells. The most remarkable observation is the appearance of osteoblasts along the surface of the ends of fragments without the initial bone resorption along the surface. Even slight movements of fragments will destroy this delicate granulation tissue and damage the vessels and bone forming cells. Thus, the first stage of primary healing under rigid fixation is characterized by longitudinal reconstruction of the fracture site by the haversian remodelling. Hence, contact healing takes place by haversian remodelling. Simultaneously, it leads to the union and reconstruction of ends of the fragments. Interfragmentary compressions of the fractured ends can hasten the primary healing process. Persisting mechanical instability of the bone fragments obviously exhibits degenerative changes but does not mineralize. Simultaneously, vascular invasion and fibrocartilage resorption come to a standstill. Consequently, no bony union is possible. Thus, a study of fracture healing under varied circumstances explains the role of various types of fixation of fractures. To explain this phenomenon, the term welding is comparable to primary union and soldering with callus formation.

TOOTH IN THE LINE OF FRACTURE (Fig. 9.6)

With considerable changes in the philosophy of the management of maxillofacial trauma over the course of time, management of tooth in the line of fracture has remained controversial. Historically, such teeth are condemned due to the high incidence of complications. Many considered them as nidus for infection. In the process, even the vital teeth have been sacrificed to avoid any untoward sequelae like

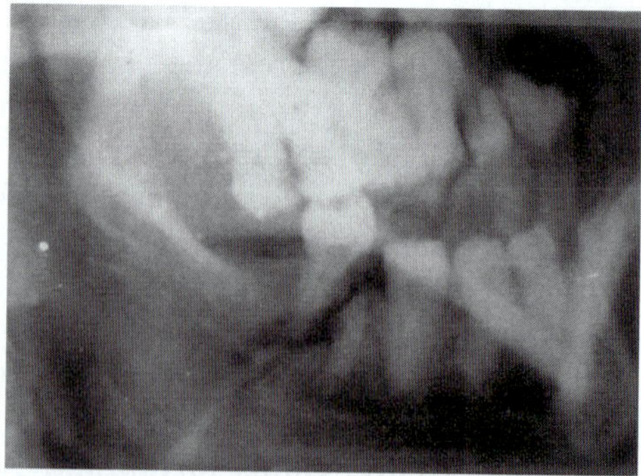

Fig. 9.6 Lateral view of the mandible - fractured tooth in the line of fracture.

osteomyelitis, delayed union or non-union of fractures.

With advancement of modern surgical techniques and control of infection, attempts are made to retain such teeth except when they are severely infected or mobile. They found significant increase in osteomyelitis when molars were retained, when compared to single rooted teeth. Later, on the basis of retrospective studies, it was advocated that all devitalized teeth and roots should be removed. Now, in a selective approach with appropriate case selection, antibiotic therapy are preferred.

Frequency and character of complications to different types of fractures were correlated and classified according to the degree of periodontal involvement. Teeth with exposed root apices or root surfaces were found to have poor prognosis. Timing and types of fracture treatment also influence the decision to retain or to remove the tooth. Inadequate immobilization of fragments is found to be one of the main factors for infection. Hence, early treatment with complication-free stabilization of fractured fragments are important prerequisites to avoid infection. Supportive antibiotic therapy is indicated but early treatment is more important. Likewise, lacerated gingival margins, shattered alveolar walls and root fractures adversely affect healing of fractures.

In fractures, at the angle of the mandible, significant number of impacted third molars deserve special attention. Decreased incidence of complication has been noticed when such teeth are best left alone provided they are not mobile and do not interfere with reduction of fractures. Wherever it is associated with pericoronal infection, it is better to remove them.

Therefore, any decision has to be based on the variable like (a) condition of teeth, (b) alveolar socket, (c) clinical situation, (d) timing and type of treatment. Of late, there seems to be a distinct shift towards conservative approach, with increasing understanding of biomechanics of the mandible and fracture healing. It is an accepted fact that susceptibility to infection is directly proportional to the mobility of the teeth and the bone fracture since mechanical instability increases the incidence of infection. Therefore, on the basis of the present knowledge, the following useful guidelines have been suggested:

(1) Teeth in the fracture line, which are intact, neither mobile nor involved in inflammatory changes may be left in situ.

(2) Teeth that hinder the reduction of the fractured fragments may be removed.

(3) Teeth with exposed root surfaces or root apices and mobile must be removed.

(4) Timing of the treatment is a decisive factor. No sooner the treatment is instituted, chances of infection become less.

(5) In case of fractures involving the angle of the mandible, impacted third molars deserve special mention. During open reduction, if they are removed, complication rate increases considerably. Hence, as a rule, completely unerupted molar be left in situ, provided it does not interfere with reduction of fractured fragments. On the contrary, all third molars, in the line of fractures must be removed if they are involved with pericoronal infection.

(6) Since periodontal and alveolar damage delay the healing of fractures, careful assessment is essential for the successful management of teeth.

PRESTRETCHING OF THE WIRE

Loosening of the wires in the mouth during the course of treatment is a common occurrence. Patients make postoperative visits to tighten or to replace such wires used for intermaxillary fixations. Prestretching is advocated to avoid such problems. Studies conducted to test the alterations of mechanical properties of stretching the wires have revealed that the differences in the physical properties between stretched and unstretched wires exist because disorderly crystalline pattern is being rearranged as the wire is being stretched. Slipping along the orderly planes that were in the initial crystalline pattern of the wire becomes more difficult. Prestretching is a form of *"cold working or strain hardening"*. It decreases the elasticity and deformation of the wire but results in increased strength and minimal deformation. Therefore, it is always preferable to prestretch the wires before use.

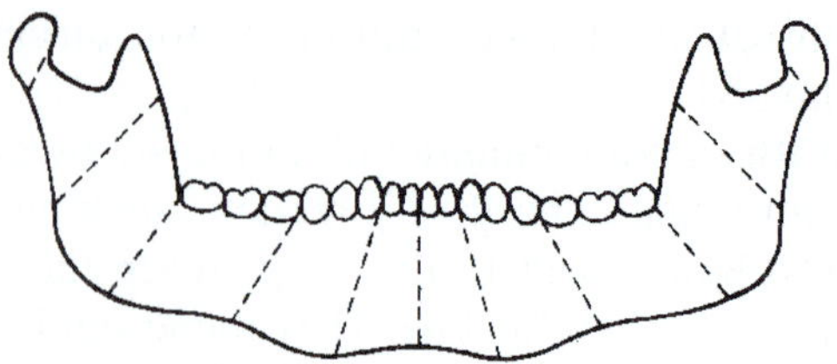

Fig. 9.8 Common sites of fracture in mandible.

APPLIED ANATOMY OF THE MANDIBLE

General features

Mandible is a sturdy, horse-shoe shaped mobile bone, located prominently among the facial bones. The configuration of the mandible varies in different areas. Basically, the bone has a lateral and a medial compact bone with an area of central spongiosa. Ramus is relatively thinner than the body. The cortex is thick in the angle and mental foramen region, laterally reinforced by the external oblique ridge and lingually by internal oblique ridge. These bony trajectories transmit and disperse the masticatory forces towards the middle cranial fossa by virtue of its articulation with the temporal bone.

Areas of weakness (Figs 9.7, 9.8)

(a) *Presence of teeth or foramen.* Wherever the body of the mandible is occupied by more amount of tooth substance, that area becomes a zone of weakness. For example, root of the canine tooth is the longest among mandibular teeth. Similarly, the presence of unerupted third molars or canines constitute the areas of weakness. The premolar region is weak by the presence of the mental foramen. Thus, canine, premolar and third molar regions are the areas of weakness.

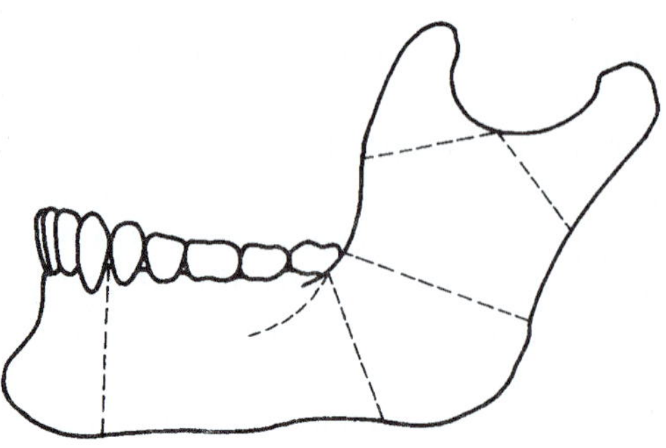

Fig. 9.7 Areas of weakness in the mandible predisposing to fracture.

(b) *Symphysis.* Mandible is in two halves at birth but unite at the end of the first year. Throughout life, this line of fusion continues to remain relatively weak. However, the lower part of symphysis is reinforced by the bony ridges which run towards the angle and coronoid process.

(c) *Alveolar bone.* Body of the mandible has two components - basal bone and alveolar process. The alveolar bone itself is variable in thickness. The junction between these two components constitutes a *"line weakness"*, predisposing to fracture of the alveolar process without involving the basal bone.

(d) *Angle.* It is the junction between horizontal body and vertical ramus of the mandible. The curved transition zone between these two parts constitutes a major area of instability at the point where trajectories change the direction. Apart from being weak anatomically, it forms a source of weakness on physiological considerations also. Consideration of muscle attachments and their function will reveal that the direction of all the muscles attached anterior to the angle is in downward and backward direction. On the contrary, the resultant pull of the muscles, attached posterior to this zone, is upwards and forwards. Thus, angle becomes the junction between two diametrically opposite groups of muscle pull resulting in weak area. This is a very significant factor with reference to the displacement of the fractured fragments also.

(e) *Ramus.* It is roughly rectangular in shape.

The presence of mandibular (sigmoid) notch and the inferior dental foramen, predispose to a natural cleavage plane. But even if the fragments are multiple, a cushion-effect is provided by the masseter and medial pterygoid muscles from either side.

(f) *Condyle.* It articulates with the temporal bone to form temporomandibular joint. Any trauma involving the condyle will naturally disrupt the joint. The displacement is guided by the attachment of lateral pterygoid muscle. The resultant force of this muscle leads to the displacement of the condyle in a forward and medial direction. Superiorly, at the depth of the glenoid fossa, condyle is seperated from the middle cranial fossa by a paper thin sheet of bone. In the event of the fragment being driven upwards, it can land inside the middle cranial fossa. But it is a rare occurrence. Mandible, through its slender condyle, act as a natural shock absorber in preventing the intracranial injuries.

Biomechanics of the mandible

The masticatory functions of the mandible are governed by the power and direction of the muscles of mastication supported by the accessory muscles. When the muscle functions are physiologically coordinated, tension forces are at the superior border and compression forces are grouped at the inferior border. In case of fractures at the angle, this can cause distraction at the alveolar crest region. Hence, biomechanical factors and forces must be taken into account in the rational treatment of fractures. Based on these biomechanical characteristics, an osteosynthesis line could be drawn as a guidance for ideal fixation of fractured fragments. It corresponds to the line of tension at the base of the alveolar process. However, in the anterior region, in addition to the subapical line, another line is drawn near the lower borders. The principal factors involved in the mandibular fractures are dynamic (due to trauma) and static factors (mandible). The common causes responsible for the dynamic factors to set in motion are the etiological factors, characterized by the direction and severity of trauma. For example, simple unilateral or greenstick fractures occur due to trauma of less intensity. On the contrary, if it is heavy, the fracture will be compound and comminuted. The direction and the site of trauma determine the location of fractures and the type of displacement of the fragments.

The static factors of the mandible include physiological age, mental and physical condition, presence of muscles around the mandible. Predisposing factors are the anatomical weaknesses. Chances of fracture are less if the person is young but it occurs frequently due to heavy calcification. If the person is mentally and physically relaxed at the time of injury, incidence of fracture is less. Although coronoid is a bony process that can be involved in fracture, displacement is very rare due to the splinting effect of tendinous attachment of temporalis muscle.

Blood supply

Centrally, blood supply is derived from the main nutrient vessels (inferior dental vessels). Peripherally, it is provided all around by the periosteal vessels by all muscles at the points of attachment. As the age advances, nutrient blood supply gets reduced, probably due to the narrowing effect of the aging process. On such eventuality, the bone has to depend on its peripheral sources. This fact must be taken into consideration when contemplating on open reduction procedures involving extensive stripping of the periosteum which may deplete the blood supply.

Dentition and fracture

This needs careful evaluation. In fact, teeth are necessary for the efficient immobilization of jaws. Occlusion is always taken as guidance for the reduction of fractures. But the role of the tooth in the line of fracture in the management of fracture has remained controversial. Hence, it has been dealt with separately.

Nerve supply

Management of craniofacial injuries demands a thorough knowledge of all the cranial nerves. In mandibular fractures, impairment of functions mainly involves the mandibular nerve and its branches. Break in continuity of the inferior alveolar (dental) nerve will result in numbness and anesthesia of the corresponding half of the lower lip. Knowledge of the anatomy of the nerves of the face is necessary to minimize the postoperative morbidity of nerve damage.

CLASSIFICATION OF MANDIBULAR FRACTURES

Mandibular fractures can be classified based on the following criteria:

(1) Anatomical locations
(2) Fracture in relation to the site of injury
(3) Condition of the fractured bone fragments at the fracture site
(4) Types of displacement of the fractured fragments
(5) Fracture with reference to dentition.

(1) Anatomical locations

(a) Symphysis
(b) Canine region
(c) Mental foramen region
(d) Body
(e) Angle
(f) Dentoalveolar region
(g) Ramus
(h) Condyle
(i) Coronoid process.

(2) Site of injury

Fracture is said to be *direct* if it occurs at the site of impact. If it occurs away from the site of injury, it is known as *indirect* fracture. Usually this classification is useful to record the combinations of the fractures occurring at the site of injury and the associated fractures.

(3) Bone fragments at the fracture site

This type of classification is based on the condition of the bone fragments at the site of fracture. It also gives an indication about the severity of trauma and the communication with the external environment.

(a) *Simple.* If the overlying tissues of the bone are intact and the fragments are not exposed to the external environment, it is said to be simple.

(b) *Greenstick.* This is an incomplete fracture of flexible bone seen in children. Only one cortex of the bone is fractured and the other cortex is bent and exhibits minimal mobility when palpated. Such a type of fracture is termed as greenstick.

(c) *Comminuted.* When the bone is involved in violent trauma, the fragments are multiple, crushed and splintered. Such high-impact injuries are said to be known as comminuted fractures, e.g. gunshot injuries.

(d) *Compound.* If the fractured fragments communicate to the external environment through the wound, then it is called compound fracture. If such fragments are comminuted, then such a fracture is called *compound comminuted fracture.* As a rule, fractures involving the tooth-bearing segments are always compound because of breach of the attached mucoperiosteum that establishes a link between the fractured fragments and the external environment through the gingival sulcus and periodontal space. However, in edentulous mandible, it is usually simple.

(4) Type of displacement of the fractured fragments (Figs 9.19 to 9.22)

In angle fractures, the direction of the fracture line is taken into account to determine the need for any fixation of the fragments. It is considered to be *favorable*, when the muscle pull approximates the displaced fragments. In such cases, direction of the muscle pull is at right angle to the fracture line. If it is *unfavorable*, the muscle pull distracts the fragments away from each other and result in displacement. This classification is very useful to record the direction of the fracture line in relation to the direction of the muscle pull, when viewed horizontally and vertically. (For details see page 173).

(5) Fracture with reference to the dentition

Dentition and its status form important criteria for the successful management of mandibular fractures. On the basis of the dentition, fractures can be classified. Dentition is used as the best guide to reduce the fracture and also to utilize them as fixation points for immobilization. If dentition is not available for immobilization, alternate methods of fixation and immobilization may have to be thought off. Based on the status of dentition, fractures of the jaw can be classified as fractures of:

(a) Dentulous jaw
(b) Dentulous jaw with posterior edentulous fragment
(c) Edentulous jaw
(d) Jaws in children.

PRIMARY (LOCAL) TREATMENT

Careful assessment is mandatory to determine:

(1) Whether any treatment should be provided before undertaking the specific treatment.

(2) Whether the patient is fit to travel, if it is necessary to be transported for any specialist's consultation. If there is a possibility of any delay in instituting the specific treatment for the fractures, then it is essential to provide some form of immobilization. The following are some of them:

(a) Adhesive plaster can be applied under the chin and carried over the vertex so that adequate support to the mandible can be provided. Care must be taken to prevent the adhesive plaster from sticking to the facial skin and hair.

(b) Barrel bandage can be applied around the vertex and the lower jaw. To provide satisfactory anchorage, bandage is wrapped around the forehead and back of the head. A safety pin or adhesive plaster can be used to retain the bandage in position.

(c) Elastic chin bandage is an effective and comfortable form of bandage.

(d) Four-tailed bandage is one of the effective forms of support to the fractured mandible. If it is not properly applied, backward pressure can result in respiratory embarrassment. If may also aggravate the displacement of fractures. If at all any surgery like primary suturing or arrest of hemorrhage is performed, the keynote of this preliminary surgery is simplicity and conservation.

Management

The objectives are :

(1) **Management of systemic complications.** Various aspects of systemic management has already been dealt with. This must be accorded top priority before commencing the local fracture treatment.

(2) **Surgical considerations.** Following trauma, the bone exhibits break in continuity. Depending on the direction of trauma and contraction of the attached muscles, bone fragments are displaced. The main objectives of management are: (a) precise diagnosis, (b) early reduction of the fracture, (c) adequate fixation of the fragment in the reduced position, (d) immobilization of the jaws in the occlusal position during the healing period. The aim is to achieve a satisfactory anatomical union of the fractured bone fragments.

(3) **Physiological considerations.** The union must be achieved in such a way that the restoration of jaw function is achieved to the maximum extent possible. To achieve optimal functional result, it is necessary to prevent the "joint disease", consequent to the immobilization of the jaws. Joint disease is a symptom complex involving the bone and the temporomandibular joint following immobilization.

(4) **Esthetic considerations.** The surgeon must always aim at restoring the facial contour to a satisfactory extent.

(5) **Time factor.** It should be the objective to achieve the full benefits of treatment within the limited time constraints. Time factor is equally

important so that the patient can return back to normal life as early as possible.

(6) **Minimum morbidity.** All the efforts must be directed to minimize or to avoid any residual morbidity. The important morbidities to be avoided or minimized are:

(a) Loss of tissue
(b) Occlusal disturbances
(c) Disturbed jaw movements
(d) Disturbances to the union of the fractured fragments
(e) Reduced intake of the diet resulting in weight loss
(f) Permanent disabilities like nerve injuries, deformities, etc.

(7) **Economic factor.** Keeping the time factor in mind, care must be taken to reduce the period of hospitalization and convalescence so that the patient spends less time and money before returning back to normal life at the earliest possible time.

Clinical diagnosis

It is absolutely essential to get as much information as possible by the careful clinical examination of the patient. At the same time, too much of handling of the injured patient must be avoided since it may do more harm than good.

(1) **History of facial trauma.** The history of the involvement of facial trauma in any form should be recorded.

(2) **Inspection.**

(a) *Hemorrhage.* Posttraumatic bleeding starts from endosteal, periosteal and surrounding soft tissues.

(b) *Pain.* The patient who has sustained injuries of the jaws experiences considerable discomfort due to pain. It tends to aggravate if the patient attempts to move the jaw.

(c) *Swelling.* At the site of injury and fracture, inspection will reveal the swelling due to edema or hematoma. This may result in facial asymmetry.

(d) *Altered occlusion.* Subsequent to trauma it is considered to be one of the very characteristic clinical intraoral signs of fracture.

(e) *Sublingual ecchymosis.* Presence of sublingual submucosal hematoma is pathognomonic of a compound fracture. The tear of the lingual mucoperiosteum results in the accumulation of blood clot.

(f) *Disturbed function.* The patient will be unwilling to move the mandible and may also have difficulty in breathing and swallowing.

(g) *Halitosis.* This may be due to the disturbed function and poor oral hygiene. As time passes, it may even become worse.

(h) *Paresthesia.* At the site of fracture, tear or injury to the sensory nerves may result in the loss of sensation of the areas of distribution of the nerve. Inferior alveolar (dental) nerve damage results in the numbness of the lower lip. Hence, the presence of numbness over the corresponding half of the lower lip confirms the fracture of the mandible.

(3) **Palpation.**

(a) The exact site of fracture can be diagnosed by careful palpation of the jaw region.

(b) All the inspection findings can be confirmed.

(c) The area will be tender.

(d) Abnormal mobility can be elicited through bimanual palpation (Fig. 9.9). Such abnormal movements of the fractured ends result in crepitus.

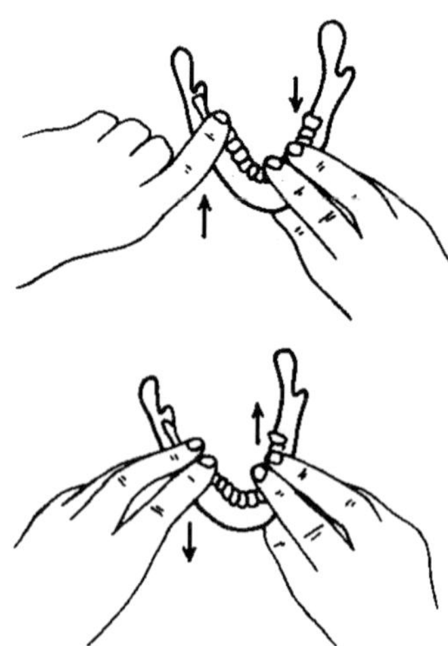

Fig. 9.9 Clinical examination of the mandible bimanually to elicit abnormal mobility.

As far as possible, crepitus must never be elicited unless it is absolutely essential. Examination must be done as gently as possible.

Radiographic diagnosis (Figs 9.10, 9.11)

Radiographs taken following facial injuries can sometimes be misleading. The interpretation of the radiographs of the facial skeleton is very difficult due to the difficulties encountered in standardizing the techniques and also due to the multiplicity of overlapping of structures. Hence, they must be considered as valuable aids but not in place of clinical examination. Each radiograph is designed to reveal a certain area. Knowledge of normal appearances and variations is essential before diagnosing the abnormalities. In conformity with the definition of fracture, classical radiological features confirm the break in continuity of radioopaque bony outline by an abnormal radiolucency, representing the fracture line.

The most useful radiograph is *panoramic radiograph* since it represents the entire mandible in a single radiograph. But the anterior region is superimposed by the cervical vertebrae. Hence, symphyseal region will be obscured in this view. In case facilities do not exist for panoramic radiography, lateral oblique view of the mandible can be taken. This view shows the area from premolar to the subcondylar region. Hence radiographs must be taken for both the sides separately. It is always a good practice to take another x-ray at right angles to the first view. For example, occlusal view of the mandible reveals the third dimension of the body of the mandible. For

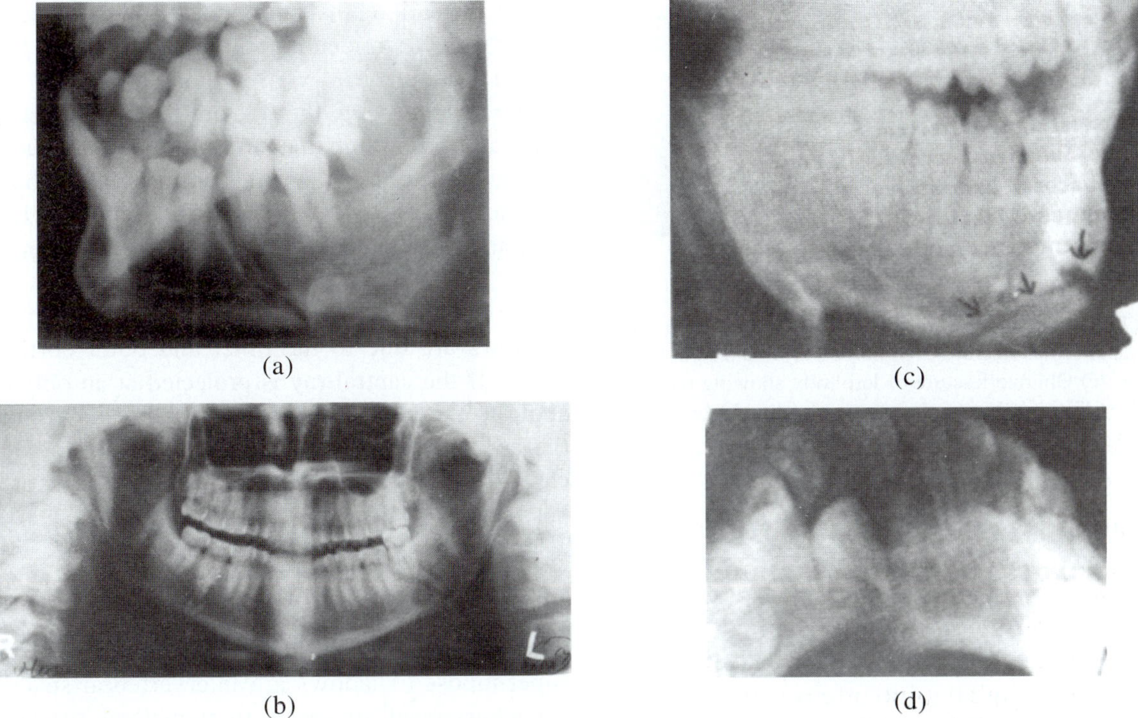

(a) (b) (c) (d)

Fig. 9.10 Fractures of mandible–radiographs **(a)** Fracture line between II premolar and I molar, **(b)** Fracture between II and III molar. III molar prevents the displacement of the ramus, **(c)** Isolated fracture at the lower border, **(d)** Fracture line involving incisor tooth bud.

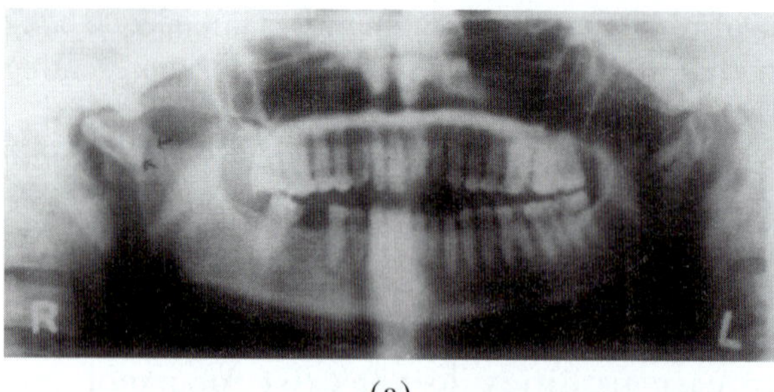

(a)

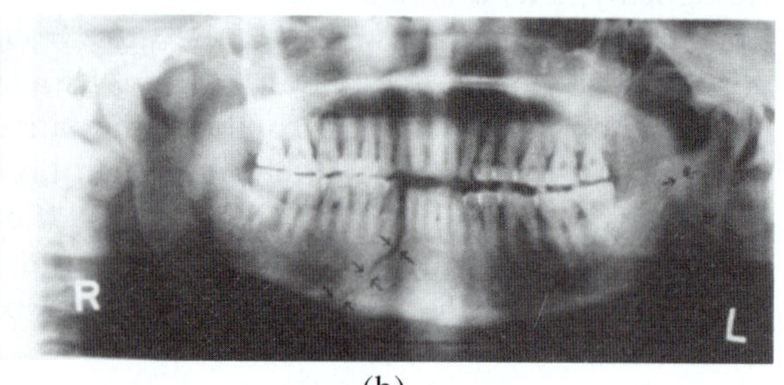

(b)

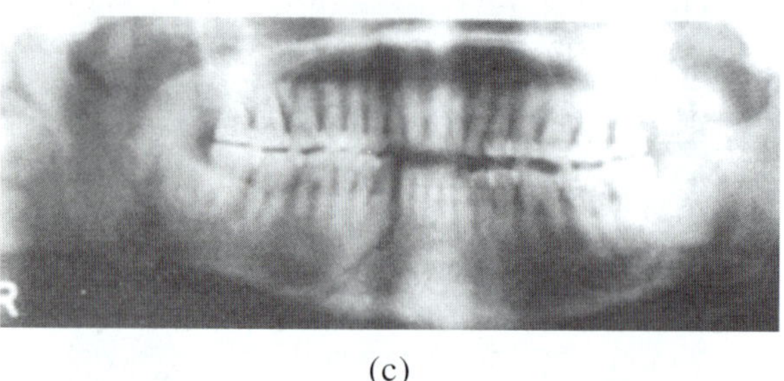

(c)

Fig. 9.11 Orthopantomographs showing fracture lines: **(a)** Bilateral condylar fractures, **(b)** Left condyle and right body fracture, **(c)** Oblique fracture of left body showing the step deformity at the lower border, fractures at right body and left angle.

the injuries involving angle, ramus and condyle, posteroanterior view is useful.

Intraoral periapical radiographs are useful to diagnose the relationship of the tooth in the line of fracture. Special views may have to be taken for the temporomandibular joint in case of condylar fractures. Of late, *CT scan* is becoming increasingly popular to get the comprehensive and precise picture of the injured facial skeleton.

The radiographic findings are helpful to confirm:

(1) The sites of fracture.
(2) Direction and displacement of the fragments.
(3) Condition of the teeth adjoining the fracture line.
(4) Severity of the damage of the bone.
(5) The presence of any bony pathology involving the fractured fragments like impacted tooth, cysts or neoplasms.

A definite system of examining the radiographs must be followed.

(a) The *angle of the x-ray* projection must be borne in mind while interpreting the bony structures in the radiographs.

(b) *Normal radiological appearance* of the involved region must be visualized and correlated with the clinical and radiological findings.

(c) Attention must be focussed at the suspected *site of fracture* to identify the fracture lines.

(d) When the x-rays pass through the *interfragmental gap*, the fracture line will show as dark radiolucent line in contrast to the radioopaque outline of the bone. If the ends of the fractured bone overlap, x-rays pass through bone ends of less thickness of bone. Hence, a lighter shadow can be seen.

(e) *Double fracture lines*. (Fig. 9.12). The main shadows are due to the inner and outer cortical plates. If the central ray is projected at an oblique angle to the plane of fractures, the breaks in both the cortical plates do not coincide. Then in such cases, double fracture lines may be seen. The area between the two fracture lines may be mistaken as a separate detached fragment of bone.

(f) Certain *normal structures like suture lines* closely simulate fractures. Hence, care must be taken to exclude them. The examples of superimposed shadows are intervertebral spaces, nasopharyngeal air space, linguopalatal airspace, hyoid bone and soft tissues of the neck. Likewise, mental foramen can be mistaken for a cyst.

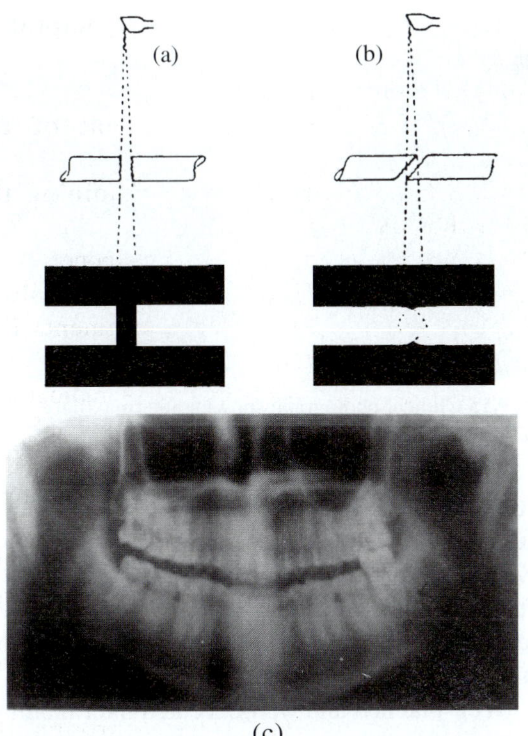

Fig. 9.12 Double fracture lines: **(a)** Normal interfragmentary gap, **(b)** Diagrammatic representation of double fracture lines in lamellar fractures, **(c)** Radiograph showing double fracture lines at the left body involving III molar tooth.

METHODS OF IMMOBILIZATION OF THE JAWS

Many inexpensive and uncomplicated equipment and methods of treatment are available for the immobilization of the jaws. It is left to the individual clinician to choose the most suitable method (and hence a matter of judgement), keeping in mind the needs and circumstances under which the patient is being treated.

Intermaxillary fixations (IMF)

(1) **Direct wiring** (Fig. 9.13). The prestretched soft stainless steel ligature wire is passed around suitable teeth and twisted tightly. The twisted ends of the adjacent corresponding upper and lower

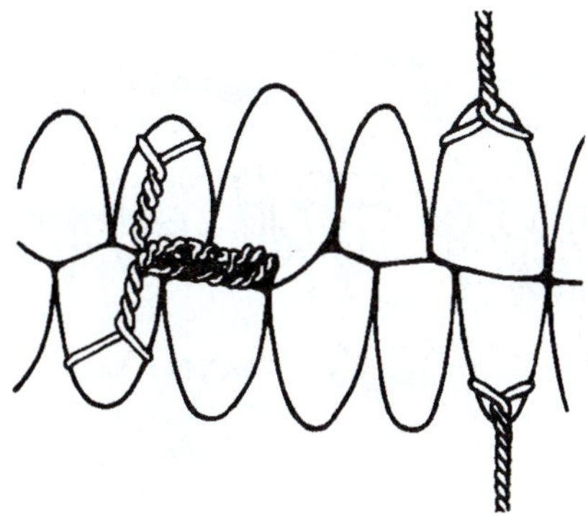

Fig. 9.13 Intermaxillary direct wiring.

individual wires are twisted together until the mandibular teeth are brought into correct occlusion with the maxillary teeth. This method is fairly quick. Since wires are twisted twice from each jaw, further tightening may result in breakage of the wire. In such case, the entire wiring procedure will have to be repeated. The ends of the twisted wires are bulkier and are liable to injure the lips and cheek mucosa. This may be useful in emergency management.

(2) **Ivy-eyelet wiring** (Fig. 9.14a, b). A prestretched 20-25 cm long, stainless steel ligature wire is grasped with two artery forceps, one on either end. An eyelet is formed by twisting around the shank of a bur. The ends of the wire are cut off so that both the ends are equal in length. Care is taken to ensure that the length of the eyelet and the two strands of wire is at least 10 cm long. Now the eyelet is ready for use. 10 to 12 such eyelets are prepared preoperatively.

Both the wire ends of the eyelet are passed through the interdental space of the selected region from buccal to lingual side. One end is passed through the mesial interdental space from the lingual to the buccal side. At this stage, the distal end of the wire is passed through the distal interdental space and then through the eyelet so that both the ends of the wires are near the mesial interdental space. Ends of both the wires are grasped close to the teeth with artery forceps. With continuous traction they

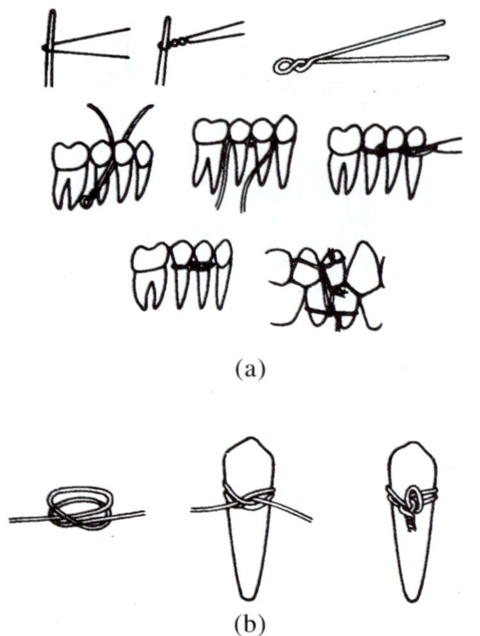

Fig. 9.14 Intermaxillary **(a)** Ivy-eyelet wiring, **(b)** Eyelet wiring in an isolated tooth.

are twisted two or three times, while the eyelet is drawn towards the interdental space. The distal end of the wire is passed through the eyelet to prevent the eyelet from slipping through the interdental space. The excess wires are cut off and the short remaining stump is bent and pushed into the interdental space so that tip does not injure the oral mucosa.

In case of an isolated tooth without the adjoining teeth, the eyelet can be fixed by passing one end of the wire of the eyelet around the tooth and brought it out of the eyelet. Now both the wires are grasped and tightened. The excess of the twisted wires is cut off, bent and adjusted downwards so that the tip of the cut end does not injure the mucosa (Fig. 9.14b).

Suitable interdental spaces are utilized for placing the eyelets so that wires are distributed uniformly. Elastic bands or strands of wire are placed between the upper and lower eyelets according to the method used to reduce the displacement (Fig. 9.15). Ultimately, in order to balance the forces uniformly

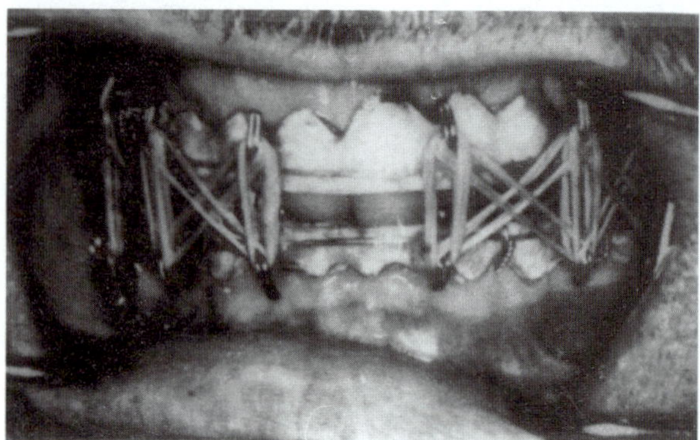

Fig. 9.15 Clinical photograph showing intermaxillary wiring fixation with rubber elastics.

between the jaws, the pattern of fixation of intermaxillary wires between the upper and lower jaw will resemble V-W-V (or inverted) pattern from left molars to right molars. Thus, to get this pattern, eyelets are uniformly distributed in the following manner:

Well-planned and well-executed intermaxillary wiring with eyelets provide stable fixation of the jaws. This method is suitable when sufficient number of opposing teeth are present in both the arches. Perhaps, the main disadvantage is that the procedure is time consuming. In case the patient is treated under general anesthesia, eyelets may be placed in advance under local anesthesia to save the anesthetic time. If so, reduction and placement of tie-wires between the eyelets alone are done under general anesthesia. Care must be taken to remove the throat pack before placing the tie-wires for intermaxillary fixation. The endotracheal tube must be left in position until the patient recovers from anesthesia completely. The wire cutter must be available for use in case, patient develops respiratory embarassment during the recovery phase.

(3) **Arch-bar wiring** (Fig. 9.16). If sufficient number of teeth are not present or not suitable for eyelet/direct wiring or when more rigid type of immobilization is required, arch bar wiring is indicated. This can be done either by Risdon's arch

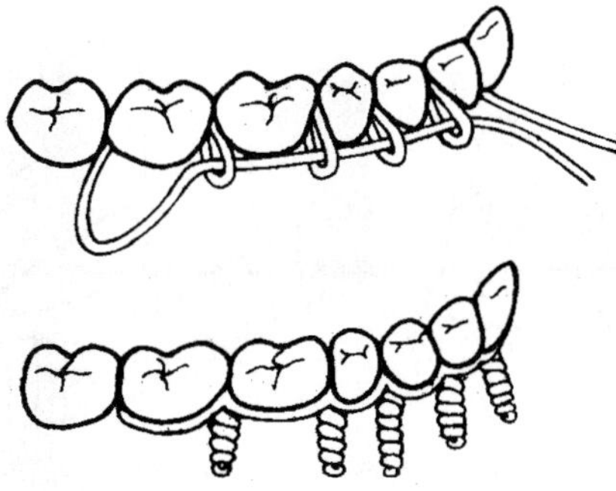

Fig. 9.16 Continuous wiring.

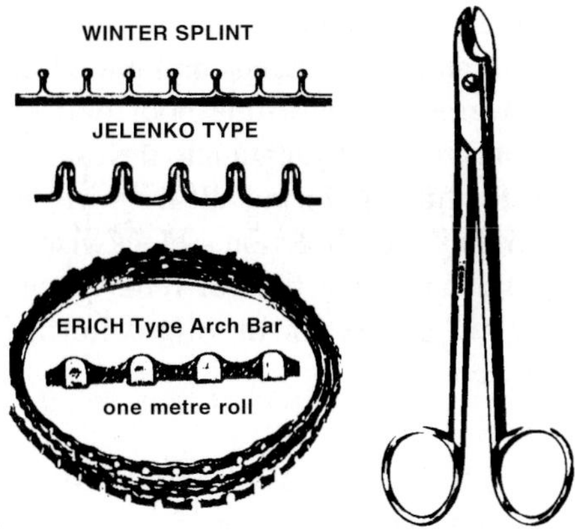

Fig. 9.17 Arch bars and wire-cutter.

bar wiring or with preformed arch bar. Risdon's arch bar wiring is done by passing two prestretched long wires around both the second molars and both the wires are twisted with an artery forceps to full length. Ends of both the twisted wires are held by artery forceps and twisted together near the midline. The excess of wires is cut off and the ends are bent downwards in such a way that tips of the wires do not injure the mucosa. The arch bar is fixed with separate strands of wire around alternate teeth by interdental wiring. Arch bar wiring is done in both the jaws. Then intermaxillary fixation is done between upper and lower arch bars. Wires are tightened to immobilize the jaws in occlusion. By combining the principles of eyelet and Risdon's arch bar wiring, a continuous loop wiring has been suggested.

Preformed arch bar or half round wire of appropriate length is adapted over the buccal and labial surfaces of the teeth. The arch bar is fixed with stands of wire on alternate teeth by interdental wiring. Fractured jaw is reduced as per the occlusion. Then the mandible is immobilized by intermaxillary wiring (Fig. 9.17).

If the body of the dentulous mandible is involved in fracture, intermaxillary fixation (IMF) by any one of the above three methods is done and retained for a minimum period of 3-4 weeks. Once occlusion is established, that itself will take care of reduction, fixation and immobilization. Throughout the wiring procedure, care must be taken to twist the wires either in the clockwise or anticlockwise direction.

During the periods of immobilization, suitable instruction must be given to the patient on the following aspects:

(1) High caloried, high protein liquid diet at 3 or 4 hourly interval.
(2) Attention to oral hygiene after every meal.
(3) In case the intermaxillary wires get loosened, patient should call on the oral surgeon for tightening the wires.
(4) Even if there is no complaint, the patient should be reviewed once a week.

Removal of wires. In 3-4 weeks time, the fractured fragments unite clinically.

(1) The intermaxillary tie-wires are first removed.

(2) Then, jaw movements must be checked for pain. The presence of any abnormality in the jaw movements or in occlusion must also be checked.

(3) If necessary, bimanual palpation can be carried out to check the clinical union at the fracture site.

(4) If the clinical union is satisfactory, the remaining wires can be removed. Otherwise, wires are placed again. The eyelets can be removed by twisting the wire ends in the opposite direction and one wire is cut off close to the tooth. Then, the wire

is released from the eyelet. Now, the eyelet is grasped with an artery forceps and pulled out with a sharp movement. Due to the poor oral hygiene, these patients will need attention to the oral hygiene.

(5) At the time of wiring, all the wires must be tightened in any one direction - clockwise or anti-clockwise so that at the time of removal of wires, the movement can be in the opposite direction without any confusion.

FRACTURES AT THE ANGLE OF THE MANDIBLE (Figs 9.18 - 9.22)

The term *'angle of the mandible'* may mean different under different situations. For example, *anatomical angle* denotes the union where inferior border of the mandible joins the posterior border of the ramus. *Clinical angle* represents the junction between the alveolar bone and the ramus of the mandible where internal oblique ridge originates.

Surgical angle is the junction between ramus and the body where external oblique ridge originates. Fracture at the angle of the mandible has some of

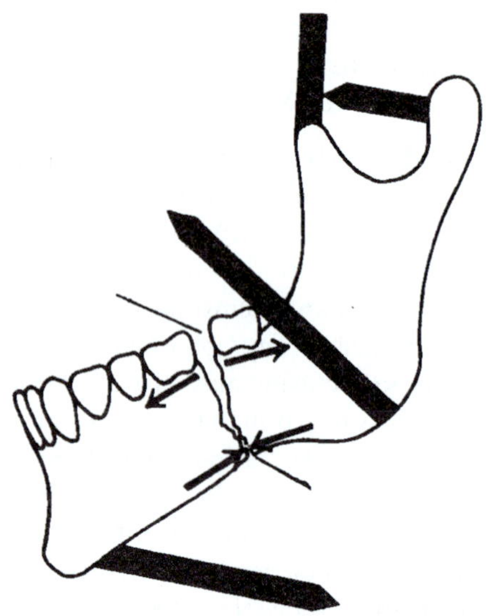

Fig. 9.18 Biomechanics of fracture–mandible showing the sides of traction and compression.

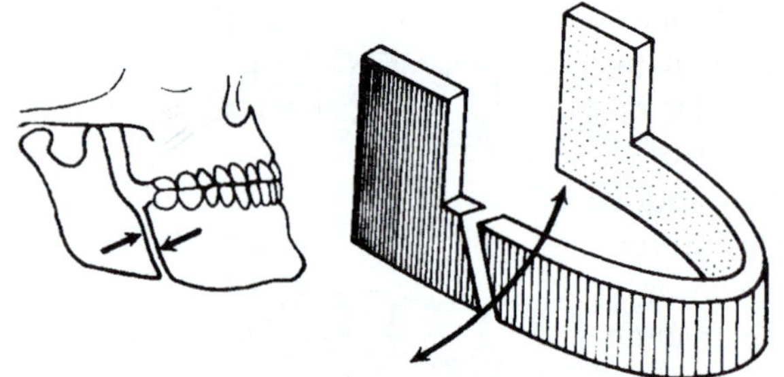

Fig. 9.19 Horizontally favorable fracture (HF). Displacement not possible.

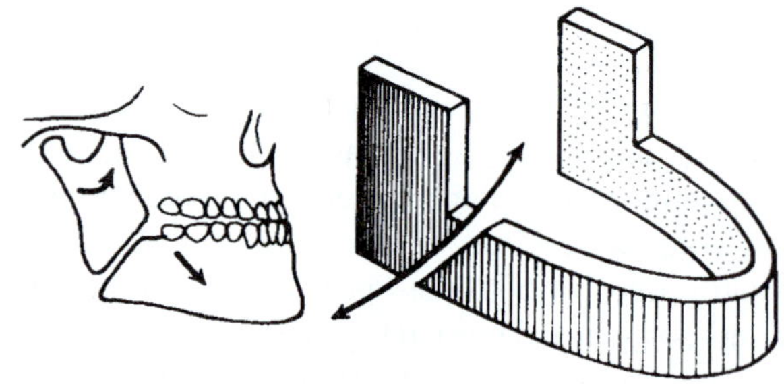

Fig. 9.20 Horizontally unfavorable fracture (HUF). Ramus gets displaced upwards and forwards.

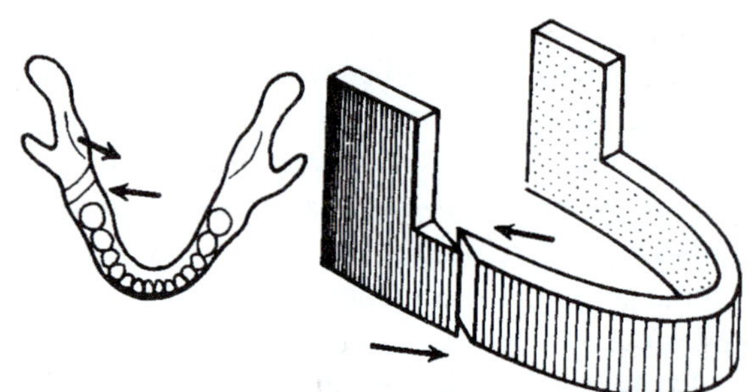

Fig. 9.21 Vertically favorable fracture (VF). Medial displacement not possible.

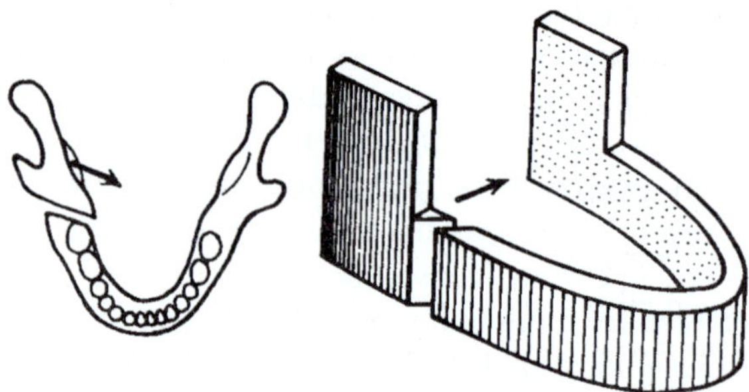

Fig. 9.22 Vertically unfavorable fracture (VUF). Medial displacement occurs.

these factors in common. The fracture line usually starts at the junction of the posterior end of the alveolar process and body with the ramus of the mandible. From this point, it may extend downwards in different directions but very rarely anatomical angle is involved. As it extends downwards and backwards from the surgical angle, the fracture line usually terminates at the inferior border of the mandible, anterior to the masseter. Whenever III molar is impacted or partially erupted, the fracture line extends through the bony crypt or the alveolar socket. Otherwise, it is behind the third molar leaving the posterior fragment edentulous.

(1) Biomechanically, lingual side of the mandible in the II and III molar region is the site of maximum tensile strain when the force is applied from the anterolateral direction on the same side. Weakness exists at this place by the abrupt change in the direction of forces from the body to the ramus in two different planes. In the horizontal plane change in the direction is at 90 degrees at the upper border while in the vertical plane, it changes nearly 20 degrees. Such a change in the direction of the forces is due to the unshaped alveolar process joining with the divergent ramus.

(2) Partly erupted or impacted III molar occupies more space. Hence, bone is deficient in that region. Biomechanically, strength of the mandible at this point is at the upper border, reinforced by the oblique ridges.

(3) Insertion of medial pterygoid and masseter muscles offer a source of strength to the ramus. Hence, the fracture line passes through the mesial root of the III molar in the buccal plate. But on the lingual plate, it usually extends posteriorly behind the distal surface of the III molar tooth.

Displacement of fragments

Elevator group of muscles exert an upward, forward and medial pull while depressor group of muscles exerts a downward and backward pull in an intact mandible. When the fracture line is in the region of the third molar, these two muscle groups become independent in their action. The resultant muscle forces lead to the development of compression at the lower border of the fracture line and tension at its upper border. This factor is of great significance while selecting an ideal location for fixation of fractures. Following unilateral fracture at the angle, posterior edentulous fragment becomes the lesser fragment while body of the mandible maintains its continuity with the opposite side and hence it is the larger fragment. In such a case, all the mandibular teeth are in occlusion due to the powerful reflex contraction of the muscles at the opposite side. On the fracture side, ramus moves independently.

The direction of the fracture-line plays a decisive role in the displacement of the fractured ramus to recognize the role of different directions of the fracture line at the angle of mandible. With reference to the displacement of the posterior edentulous fragment, a method has been described to determine whether ramus is prevented to swing upwards by the larger anterior dentulous fragment or not. Based on this criteria, angle fractures were classified by the British oral surgeons as favorable and unfavorable fracture when the angle of the mandible is viewed in the horizontal and vertical planes. The various possibilities are as follows:

Horizontally favorable (HF) (Fig. 9.19)
Horizontally unfavorable (HPF) (Fig. 9.20)
Vertically favorable (VF) (Fig. 9.21)
Vertically unfavorable (VCF) (Fig. 9.22)

To differentiate the favorable and unfavorable fractures when viewed horizontally, the situations of mandibular movements are simulated by drawing an imaginary line in the form of an arc crossing the fracture line, with the condyle as the centre of the circle (arc is defined as part of a circle). (Figs 9.19 and 9.20) This represents the possible range of movements of the ramus. If the fracture line and arc of the circle are parallel to each other, then anterior fragment is not likely to obstruct the movement of the ramus. This was considered to be unfavorable. On the contrary, if the arc crosses the fracture line, then it implies that the anterior fragment will prevent the ramus to swing upwards due to the physical obstruction caused by the body of the mandible and hence considered to be favorable. Since this sequence of events is to be viewed horizontally, they are called *horizontally unfavorable* and *favorable* fractures respectively. In this type of displacements, masseter and medial pterygoid are the muscles that play a major role.

When the angle fracture is viewed from above in the vertical plane, the displacement of the posterior fragment can be noticed in the medial direction by the contraction of medial pterygoid and mylohyoid muscles. The configuration of the fracture line in the buccolingual direction dictates such a medial displacement of the ramus. If the lingual plate is longer than the buccal plate of the body of the mandible at the site of fracture, ramus is prevented to move medially (Fig. 9.21). In fact, muscle contraction results in close approximation of the fragments. This is called *vertically favorable*. If the fracture line runs in such a way that lingual plate is shorter than the buccal plate of body of the mandible, ramus is easily pulled medially and hence fragments are distracted away from each other. This is called *vertically unfavorable* (Fig. 9.22). From the clinical point of view, the term "unfavorable" forewarns the operator, focussing the attention that interfragmentary gap is widened and hence there is a need to bind the fragments by any suitable method of fixation.

Management

From the above discussions, it is quite evident that favorable fractures are treated by immobilization of the anterior dentulous fragment with maxillary teeth in proper occlusion. The posterior edentulous fragment is mechanically prevented to get displaced. If it is horizontally unfavorable but vertically favorable, the posterior fragment may be displaced upwards and laterally. If it is horizontally favorable but vertically unfavorable, the fragment may be medially displaced. In either conditions, the displacement is minimal. But if it is horizontally and vertically unfavorable, maximum degree of displacement is encountered.

HF and VF	-	No displacement
HUF and VF	-	Minimal displacement
HF and VUF	-	Displacement is minimal in the medial direction, disturbing the superior constrictor fibers. Patient will experience dysphagia.
HUF and VUF	-	Maximal displacement.

The policy of the management of the tooth in the line of fracture has considerably changed from radical to conservative line of management. Sometimes, non-retention of such a tooth may render the fracture unfavorable. Radical treatment is warranted, only when the fracture is associated with fracture of the tooth and the fracture site communicates to the exterior.

Methods of fixation

(1) **Posterior extension of the saddle.** This is one of the non-surgical methods to control the posterior fragment from swinging upwards. This method was tried in patients who are not fit to undergo even minor surgery. This has been abandoned because of the ulceration of the mucous membrane below the acrylic plate saddle.

(2) **Transalveolar wiring of the upper border.** Kelsey Fry advocated this method to control the posterior fragment. As already pointed out, the fragments are distracted more at the upper border than the lower border at the point of tension. Hence, it is the ideal place for the fixation of fragments. The approach is very similar to dentoalveolar surgery by raising a mucoperiosteal flap. Hence, this method is very popular among the oral surgeons. Once the alveolar process is exposed, holes are drilled on both fragments. Prestretched soft stainless steel wire is passed through the holes and the fragments are fixed in the form of mattress suture. The transalveolar wire may be placed across the socket. Stability is less if the wiring is done only

on the buccal plate since the gap widens on the lingual side. The only disadvantage is its instability in case of muscle contraction. In such cases, wire will cut through the thin alveolar bone. The greatest advantage is that it can be done as an intraoral office procedure under local anesthesia.

(3) **Transosseous wiring at the lower border** (Fig. 9.23). In contrast to the upper border wiring, transosseous wiring at the lower border can withstand the contraction of the powerful musculature. But the fixation is to be carried under general anesthesia. Since this involves exposure of the lower border of the mandible through extraoral approach, strict aseptic precautions must be undertaken. It is relatively a major procedure involving an external approach. Postoperative morbidity like scar and injury to the branches of facial nerve are common. Period of hospitalization is more with this procedure. Care must be taken not to do any fixation in the region of the inferior dental canal (Fig. 9.23). Intraosseous wiring should not involve neurovascular canal. It must be either below or above, but not through the canal.

Technique

(1) Oral cavity must be totally excluded from the surgical field to avoid contamination of saliva.

(2) The patient should preferably be operated under general anesthesia.

(3) Skin incision is made along one of the neck creases. While doing so posteriorly, it should not extend beyond one finger breadth below the ear lobule to avoid damage to the facial nerve. To avoid mandibular branch of the facial nerve, incision is extended one finger breadth below the lower border of the mandible. The incision is made through platysma and deep fascia. The anterior extension of the incision is guided by the location of the fracture site. Usually, access to the fracture site is adequate if incision is placed in such a way that the incision is centred around the fractured area. The incision must be of adequate length since too short an incision will provide inadequate access to the surgical field.

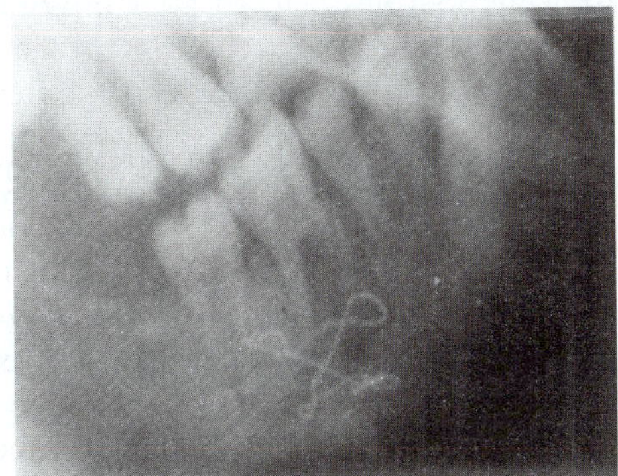

Fig. 9.23 Wires must not involve neurovascular canal. Wrong technique resulting in osteomyelitis.

(4) Infiltration of any standard 2% local anesthetic solution with adrenaline is useful as a hemostatic. It also helps in defining the fascial planes during dissection and also to control postoperative pain.

(5) Branches of facial vein are divided and ligated. Facial artery is identified below the deep facia, anterior to masseter. Then, the fascia is incised lightly. Facial artery, as it passes through the tissues, is seen to bulge through the incision. A small length of the artery is defined and a pair of artery forceps is applied and the vessel is divided between the two clamps. Then they are ligated with 3-0 catgut. Similarly, anterior branch of the posterior facial vein is also ligated.

(6) Now, by further dissection, inferior border of the mandible is defined. An incision is made on the periosteum to expose the fractured fragments adequately. Care is taken not to perforate the oral mucous membrane or to injure the contents of mental foramen.

(7) After exposing the bone ends adequately, appropriate point is chosen to drill holes. Care is taken to drill the hole in the posterior fragment higher than the anterior fragment without injuring the inferior dental canal. To avoid injury to the underlying soft tissues, blade of the periosteal elevator is placed on the medial aspect of the bone. Rowe's bone holding forceps is useful (Fig. 9.24)

for holding the fragment and drilling the hole through one blade which has a hole.

(8) Prestretched soft stainless steel wire is used for fixation. Before fixation, occlusion must be maintained with intermaxillary fixation.

Intraosseous wiring can be done by passing the wire through the posterior mobile fragment. If the operator experiences difficulty to bring the wire out of the anterior fragment, a loop of wire can be passed through the anterior fragment from lateral to the medial side. Beneath the bone, the loop is opened out and the free end of the long wire is threaded. Now the loopwire is pulled out from the medial to the lateral side of the anterior fragment. After positioning both the fragments in proper alignment with mandible in occlusion, artery forceps is used to clamp on both the wires close to the holes and before it is over the anterior hole twisted tightly. The excess of the twisted wire is cut off with a wire cutter close to the hole and twisted further. Care is taken not to over twist. The cut end of the projecting twisted wire is pushed into the anterior hole so that soft tissues are not injured by the sharp end of the wire. This fixation relies on a single strand of wire for its stability. Sometimes, hinging on the point of fixation of the anterior fragment, posterior fragment may swing up. To avoid this problem, the wire fixation can be reinforced by employing another interfragmentary fixation in the form of a figure-of-eight wiring at the lower border of the mandible. To avoid slipping, two small grooves like letter x can be made at the lower border where the two limbs of figure-of-eight crosses each other. The ends of the twisted wires can be inserted into the hole of the posterior fragment. This reinforcement will provide adequate stability to the posterior fragment.

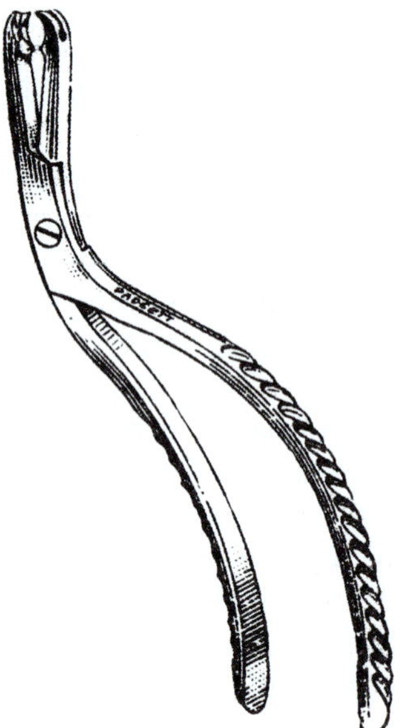

Fig. 9.24 Bone holding forceps.

Obwegeser modified this technique by utilizing a single strand of wire for both the components of the wiring. But it is difficult to pass the same wire to ensure adequate fixation because the wire ends become loose. To overcome this difficulty, surgeons proposed two holes in each fragment, one above the other so that figure-of-eight wiring can be done.

Whatever be the type of interosseous wiring, the decision on which type of wiring technique to be used is difficult to make since no two fractures can be identical. Many individual variations exist. The variables are:

(a) Position of fracture.
(b) Degree of comminution.
(c) Nature of the edges of the fractured fragments.
(d) Presence or absence of infection at the fracture site.
(e) Time that has elapsed after injury at the time of surgery.
(f) Surgical skills of the surgeon.

Irrespective of the type of interosseous wiring done, the important factors that ultimately decide the success of fixation are:

(i) Stability of the fixation of fragments.
(ii) Establishment and maintenance of proper occlusion.
(iii) Good approximation of the fractured edges without any foreign body at the inter-fragmentary gap.

(9) *Debridement* of the wound is done with saline irrigation so that no loose fragments of bone or soft tissue are lying in the wound. The wound is closed in layers. The periosteum, fascia and platysma are approximated with interrupted cat-gut sutures. Interrupted black silk sutures are placed on the skin edges for the final closure of the wound. To avoid scar, it is preferable to use atraumatic 4-0 silk suture or its equivalent on a cutting needle. Care is taken to equally distribute the sutures and also to evert the skin edges. There may not be any need for placing a drain unless the circumstances warrant.

(10) Finally, the wound is gently rolled with a piece of gauze from one end to the other to squeeze out any residual fluid collected in the surgical field.

(11) Then, a layer of vaseline gauze is spread over the sutured wound. The greasy surface is non sticky and hence, it is easy to change the dressing postoperatively. Such a non-greasy surface is repellant to the accumulation of any fluid on the wound margins. This will considerably reduce the incidence of postoperative infection.

(12) A pad of cotton wool is placed over the wound to apply gentle and uniform pressure before a crepe bandage is applied. If intermaxillary wiring is released, after the patient recovers from anesthesia, it is reapplied to restore the occlusion.

(13) Usually, the wound healing is uneventful. The patient is advised suitable antibiotics, analgesics and antiinflammatory drugs. The patient is reviewed after 48 hours for change of dressing and removal of drain, if any.

(14) On the fifth postoperative day, the sutures are removed. If edema is still marked, alternate sutures are removed and rest of the sutures are removed on the seventh postoperative day.

(15) The patient is advised regarding the diet, postoperative care of the oral cavity including maintenance of oral hygiene, apart from drugs like antibiotics and analgesics. The patient is recalled once a week for check-up whether any wire is loosened or broken. 3-4 weeks postoperatively, the intermaxillary wiring is removed.

(16) The stainless steel wire used for interosseous fixation is left in situ permanently unless osteomyelitic changes in the bone necessitates its removal.

Morbidity. The morbidities associated with extraoral open reduction and internal fixation have been studied and quantified to demonstrate the possible predisposing factors. Morbidity is directly related to the type of fracture, tooth in the line of fracture, presence of infection and the operative delay. Any surgical procedure has the potential for complications. The advent of antibiotic therapy, modern surgical armamentorium and refined techniques have minimized the incidence of complications. Among the sites of fracture, angle fractures are found to heal with residual problems.

FRACTURES OF EDENTULOUS MANDIBLE (Fig. 9.25)

They are mostly simple fractures without any tear in the mucoperiosteum. They usually heal well without much complications. If the displacement is minimal, the patient can be made comfortable with four-tailed bandage around the jaws with the patient's dentures in position. However, if the displacement of the fragments is more, then treatment is necessary by any one of the following methods:

(1) Gunning-type of splint with circumferential wiring (Fig. 9.25c and d).
(2) Open reduction and interosseus wiring.
(3) Open reduction and plate fixation.
(4) Extraoral pin fixation.

Gunning splint

A gunning splint can be fabricated by taking impression of the alveolar ridges. The patient's dentures can also be suitably modified. Even if they are broken at the time of the accident, it can be repaired and used. If the dentures are available for use, anterior teeth can be removed. Two or three

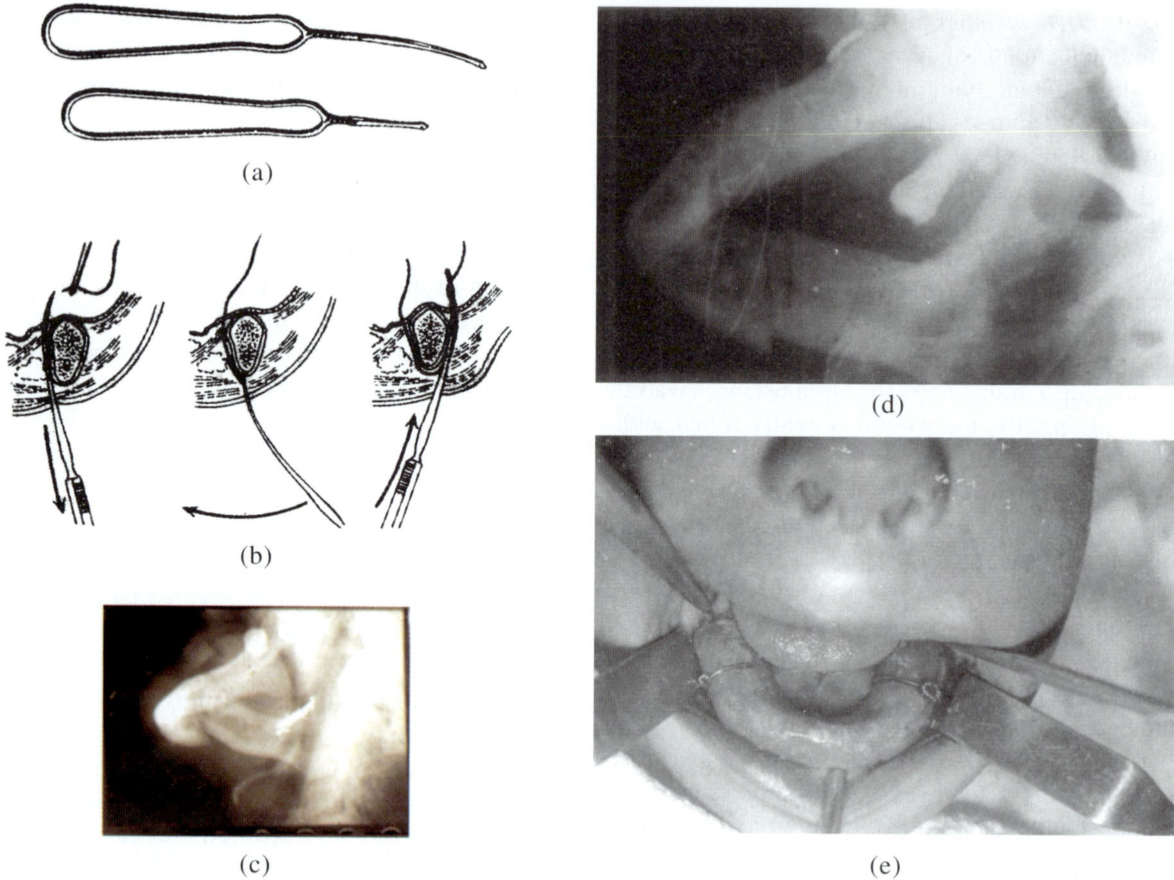

Fig. 9.25 (a) Oral surgery awl: The longer one for the mandible (circumferential wiring) shorter is for the maxilla (peralveolar wiring), **(b)** Technique of circumferential wiring for the edentulous mandible fracture, **(c)** Fractured edentulous mandible, **(d)** Circumferential wiring in position, **(e)** Circumferential wiring in a child during mixed dentition.

hooks can be fixed with cold cure acrylic on either side of the denture. The flange of the dentures may be reduced to accommodate the posttraumatic edema. Two or three holes are drilled on the palatal aspect of the upper denture for the fixation by transalveolar wiring. Dentures are advantageous since the patient's bite is readily available.

If the old dentures are not available, fresh impressions are taken reproducing the alveolar ridges in the displaced position. The plaster cast is taken to the laboratory, sectioned at the fractured site and the fragments are fixed in the realigned position with sticky wax. A fresh base is prepared for the realigned model and gunning splint is prepared. Then it is washed thoroughly with soap and water and kept immersed in an antiseptic solution for a few hours before use.

Technique. Surgery can be performed either under general or local anesthesia. The patient's skin and oral mucous membrane are swabbed with antiseptics and the face is draped. The impression surface of the splint is adapted with Guttapercha. The under surface of the splints is immersed in hot water so that Guttapercha becomes soft. The fragments are reduced and in the reduced position, the gunning splint is adapted on the ridge. Now the splints are ready for fixation. The lower splint is fixed by circumferential wiring while the upper splint is fixed by peralveolar wiring.

Circumferential wiring

Appropriate points are chosen to pass the wires, taking care not to injure the mental neurovascular bundle and facial vessels. Usually one in the midline and one on either side at the premolar-molar region are placed. The oral surgery awl is passed at the labial vestibule intraorally so that the tip of the awl comes extraorally near the skin. BP blade No. 11 is used to make a stab incision to enable the tip of awl to emerge through the skin. A soft stainless steel wire is threaded and drawn so that the free end of the wire is drawn intraorally. Once awl is withdrawn out of the tissues, awl is passed along the lingual vestibule close to the bone where the wires are placed labially. Awl is driven and brought out through the same skin incision. The stainless steel wire is threaded and drawn towards intraoral direction. Three such strands of wires are positioned at the selected points circummandibularly. Both the ends of the wire are secured by artery forceps and pulled alternatively in to-and-fro motion until the wire is in close contact with the bone and no soft tissue is entrapped between the bone and wire.

Now, the splint is placed on the alveolar ridge of the mandible in the reduced position and held securely by the assistant. Both the ends of the wire are crossed over the splint by holding them with artery forceps and twisted so that the splint is securely fixed on the alveolar ridge. The excess of the twisted wires is cut off and their free ends are bent inwards so that injury to the oral tissues is avoided. More often, circummandibular wiring alone is sufficient to fix the mandibular fragments. The postoperative marginal discrepancy in the bite and between the fragments is ignored. Bone remodeling and dentures construction will overcome the residual deformities due to any alteration in the alignment of the fragments.

During mixed dentition period, roots are resorbed. Body of the mandible has multiple unerupted tooth buds. Therefore, intermaxillary wiring and interosseus wiring are contraindicated. Therefore, circumferential wiring can be done.

Peralveolar wiring

If it is decided to fix upper splint also, it is carried out by peralveolar wiring. As in mandible, the impression surface of the upper splint is adapted with softened Guttapercha. When it is soft, splint is adapted over the maxillary alveolar ridge. Oral surgery awl is driven across the alveolus at the canine eminence, as high as possible to accommodate the flange of the splint and also to allow the awl to be driven in a downward and inward direction towards the palatal aspect of the alveolar process. Corresponding to the points of exit, holes are prepared in the palatal plate of the splint. Awl is driven through the alveolar process to draw the stainless steel wire. The free ends of the wire are crossed over the splint similar to circumferential wiring and securely fixed. Now, the bite is checked. Any discrepancy can be overcome by the application of Guttapercha. The buccal hooks in the splint are used for intermaxillary fixation (Fig. 9.25e).

Plate fixation (plate osteosynthesis) (Figs 9.26 and 9.27)

This is one of the established methods of fixation. Even though wire osteosynthesis provides satisfactory fixation, it has to be supplemented with immobilization of jaws for a minimum period of four weeks. Prolonged immobilization of the mandible leads to considerable difficulties like difficulty in eating, speech, joint problems in addition to social inconvenience. Many special circumstances may arise in which maxillo-mandibular fixation is not desirable or contraindicated. Special procedures have been devised to avoid or to reduce the need for intermaxillary fixation by providing adequate stabilization of the fractured fragments. In Europe, use of plates and screws in various forms have been advocated. Time immemorial, the plates and screws have been sporadically used and discontinued due to certain inherent problems. There has been a constant urge to refine the techniques of plate fixation. It has been pointed out that any treatment method that does not rely on intermaxillary fixations must ensure the restoration and maintenance of correct occlusion. Every system of plate fixation has advantages and disadvantages. The indications of plate fixations, in general, are not absolute. However,

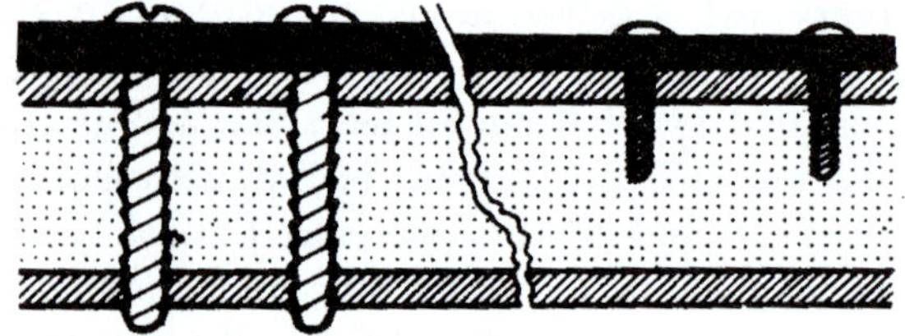

Fig. 9.26 Bone plating: cortical and monocortical.

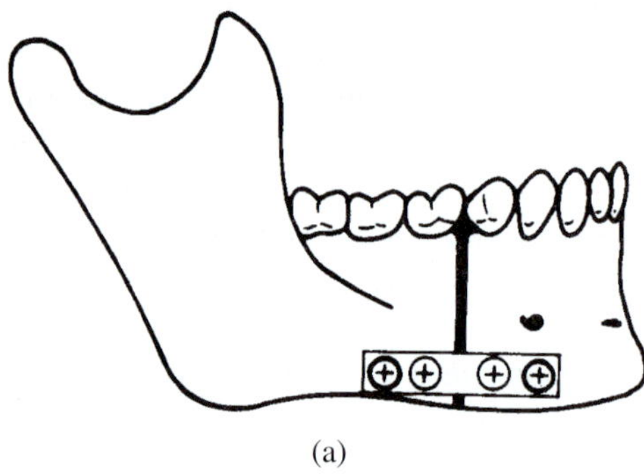

(a)

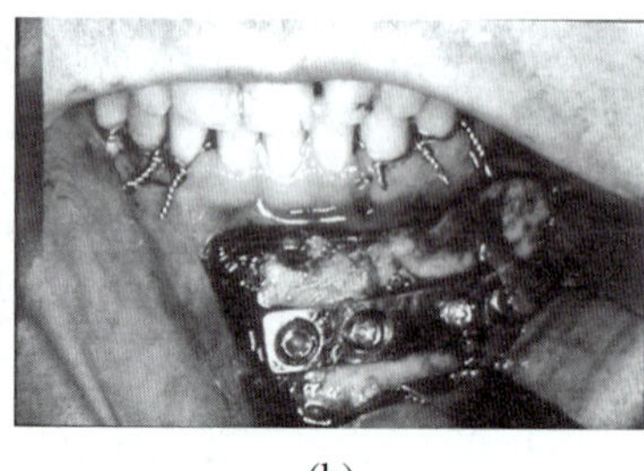

(b)

Fig. 9.27 (a) Plate osteosynthesis for the fracture mandible, **(b)** Clinical photograph with dynamic compression plate fixation.

they have been found to be useful in a few special circumstances.

(1) In cases where intermaxillary wiring is contraindicated, any appropriate method of plate fixation is preferable to dispense with immobilization of jaws, e.g. mentally deficient persons, epileptics, patients with head injuries, elderly, uncooperative and asthmatic patients.

(2) Plate fixation is preferred in patients who desire to reduce the convalescent period to return back to work quickly.

(3) Complicated fractures with loss of bone segment and the atrophic mandible that need adequate reinforcement of the mandible.

Contraindications

(1) Plate fixation is not indicated in fractures that are grossly displaced, extensively comminuted and heavily contaminated.

(2) The presence of pathological abnormalities in bone.

(3) Mixed dentition period.

In general, bone plate osteosynthesis should neither be considered as a replacement for other types of fixation nor to be condemned for the possible complications. The plate may be a non-compression or compression type. The non-compression technique is done with monocortical screws while compressional technique is done with bicortical screws (Figs 9.26, 9.27). Since the techniques are fundamentally different, one method under each type of plating will be described.

Compression plate osteosynthesis (Figs 9.27 and 9.28)

General principles

The use of plates and screws to treat mandibular fractures is nothing new to the oral surgeons. But inconsistency in the results has been responsible for abandoning the plate osteosynthesis sporadically and to gather momentum periodically.

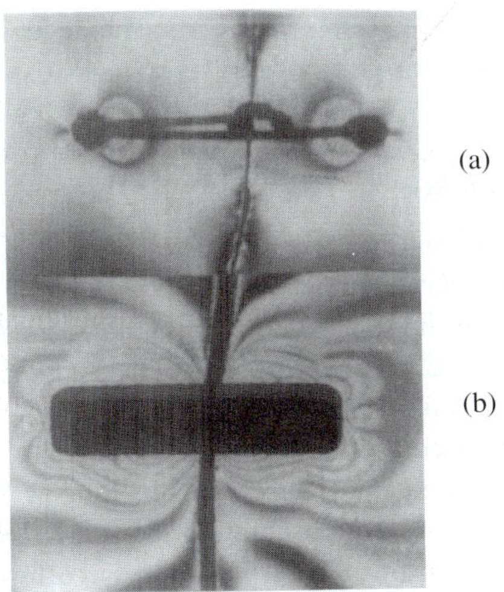

Fig. 9.28 (a) Wire osteosynthesis, **(b)** Plate osteosynthesis showing the distribution of forces.

The simplest and popular method of internal fixation has been the *wire osteosynthesis*. But the operators found that (a) fragments are not stable three dimensionally, (b) intermaxillary fixation is mandatory, (c) interfragmentary pressure cannot be controlled, (d) the wires lack adequate rigidity, directional control and surface contact to maintain rigidity under functional stress. Fragments in mandibular fractures are subjected to strong mechanical forces and hence the need for stable fixation. Experiments and clinical experience proved that susceptibility to infection depends on the mobility of the fragments. It was observed that consolidation of bony fragments can be accelerated when the ends of fragments are pressed against each other. This prompted the propagation of compression plates to produce interfragmentary compression. In 1958, compression plates, functioning on the principles of inclined plane between the screw and the hole of the metal plate, were developed. During 1970s, it was adapted to the maxillofacial injuries.

The splints, wire osteosynthesis and monocortical plates are not found to be strong enough to provide stable fixation independently without intermaxillary fixations (IMF). Hence, two or more methods need to be combined to achieve the required stability. For example, intermaxillary immobilization is absolutely essential when any other fixation is used. There are a few situations where intermaxillary wiring is not acceptable, (e.g. extremes of age, uncooperative and mentally retarded patients, fractures involving the joints, patients with respiratory disturbances, etc.). Some patients may desire to reduce or to avoid the period of immobilization. Under these circumstances, an urgent need was keenly felt to develop a suitable method of fixation that can provide stable internal fixation without an additional intermaxillary immobilization.

This prompted the European surgeons to develop a rigid, stable compression plate fixation system association of osteosynthesis (AO). This system was believed to provide a functionally stable fixation, a satisfactory dental occlusion and jaw relationship irrespective of the state of dentition. This system advocates that immobilization of jaws could be dispensed with so that disadvantages associated with intermaxillary immobilization are avoided. They include speech and communication difficulties, poor oral hygiene, possible damage to the periodontium, impaired nutritional intake, weight loss and joint problems due to the disuse of muscles of mastication. (a) Advancement of biotechnology of plates and screws, (b) refinements in design, (c) use of highly biocompatible implant materials, (d) better concept of biomechanics of repair of bone and (e) modifications of surgical technique have been responsible for the revival of interest in the plate osteosynthesis.

It was found that even the screws with 2 mm diameter has contact surface area seven times greater than that of 0.5 mm stainless steel wire. The compression at the fracture site promotes rapid healing and greater resistance to separation. It also provides intimate apposition and mechanical stability of the fragments. Once the fragments are reduced and rigidly immobilized, optimal bone repair depends on preservation and maintenance of intact blood supply and avoidance of infection. This environment promotes primary healing of bone. Osteogenic elements and capillary blood supply are readily found to traverse the fracture site, resulting in direct longitudinal bone healing with less remodeling in 3-4 weeks. When the inter-fragmentary gap is more than 0.8 mm, primary healing does not occur. Instead, secondary bone healing occurs by callus formation due to the absence of precise anatomical reduction or due to the micromobility of fragments during the healing process.

Problem of occlusion

The primary aim of treating these mandibular fractures should be to reposition the teeth in centric occlusion. But in plate osteosynthesis, accurate repositioning of the fragments are given primary importance. This necessitates occlusal rehabilitation postoperatively. Hence, attention must be focussed to avoid any occlusal disturbances. If there is any minor discrepancy in the alignment of fragments, it will be remodeled by osteoblastic activity.

Biomechanical factors

As already described, biomechanical forces at the angle of the mandible result in *tension forces* on the alveolar margin and *compressive forces* on the lower border of the mandible. If the plate is placed at the lower border of the mandible where the compressive forces already exist in the mandible due to the activity of the muscles, no useful purpose is served. But anatomically, alveolar border is an unfavorable location because of the presence of teeth. For this purpose, AO system has modified the dynamic compression plates for treating mandibular fractures.

Axial compression

Generation of axial compression at the fracture site results in (a) close approximation of bone ends, (b) three-dimensional stability responsible for promoting primary healing and (c) immediate restoration of function of the fractured bone. Infection of the fractured bone ends is found to be related to the mobility of fragments. Functional dynamic forces generated by the masticatory forces during function may exceed the static forces contributed by the plate leading to loosening of the screw and loss of plate stability.

Plate stability

This factor is mainly related to the quality of the screw-placement and the "pullout" strength. The stability of the screw depends on the tissue reaction and trauma during its insertion. Thermal necrosis of the bone around the screw due to the use of dull drills at rapid speed without saline irrigation as a coolant and the consequent failure of regeneration of healthy bone may result in loosening of the screw. Once that happens, interfragmentary compressive forces and rigidity of the fragments are lost. The other factors responsible for the screws to become mobile are (a) quality of bone where screws are placed, (b) whether screws are mono or bicortical, (c) diameter of the screw and (d) the dynamic loading force placed on the compressed fracture site. It has been proved beyond doubt that successful and predictable utilization of the compression plates and screws depend on proper case selection and adherence of specific technical details.

Once the phenomenon of primary healing was properly understood, maxillofacial surgeons of Switzerland and Germany developed compression osteosynthesis designed for the maxillofacial region, as adjunct to stability and healing. Plates and screws of AO system need to be removed eventually. Plates made of vitallium, chrome cobalt alloy by Luhr are left in situ for longer duration. The screws of Luhr system is self-tapping and bicortical while screws of AO method are bicortical used in tapped screw holes. They are supposed to maximize the screw to bone surface area contact. This system also advocates the use of lag-screws individually or in combination with plates. Description of the compression plate osteosynthesis technique as advocated by AO system is described below.

Operative technique.

(1) Under nasoendotracheal general anesthesia or local anesthesia, the fracture is reduced by means

of intermaxillary rubber-elastics applied between the maxillary and mandibular arch bars. The centric occlusion is thus established preoperatively.

(2) Formerly extra oral submandibular Risdon's approach but now intraoral approach is used for the exposure of the fractured site.

(3) With body of the mandible in centric occlusion, posterior fragment is reduced and the fractured bone fragments are approximated with the help of special reduction tongs and held in the reduced position.

(4) An appropriate mandibular dynamic compression plate (DCP) with lateral screw holes is selected. This plate has two lateral oblique holes. When the screw with spherical head is driven into the two inner holes, they provide interfragmentary compression. It is possible by means of the two outer holes to produce additional compression at the alveolar margin of the fractured fragments. These two outer oblique holes take over the function of the tension band plate in the alveolar region. The problem of gaping that may develop is thus overcome by the two lateral oblique holes. The plate is contoured properly with a plate-bending pliers. The problem of gaping that may develop lingually in the fractured fragments can be avoided by slightly over bending the plate called *"compensatory bending"*. This provides interfragmentary compression on the third dimension on the lingual side. Now, the plate is ready for fixation with two holes on either side of the fracture-line.

(5) The DC plate clamp is applied to hold the plate on the lateral surface of bone at the selected location between the inferior border of the mandible and inferior dental canal.

(6) Drilling through the inner holes on either side of the fracture line is done with the hand-brace drill, operated pneumatically with 600 revolutions per minute. Thermal damage of the bone is avoided by using this special drill. Then the holes are tapped with the corresponding drill. It also has a provision to reverse the revolution so that drill bit can be removed without disturbing the tapped bone. The wound is irrigated with saline to reduce the heat and also to wash away the bone particles. The soft tissue around this region should be well protected during drilling to avoid any injury. Care is taken to drill the hole through both outer and inner cortical plates. The appropriately selected screw is driven into the tapped hole and tightened.

(7) The same procedure is repeated through both the lateral holes in both the fragments. When the screws are tightened, the bone approximates both at the alveolar border and at the lingual side. Thus, three-dimensional interfragmentary compression is provided.

(8) As far as possible, intraoral approach is preferred to expose the fracture site. Difficulties may be experienced for the plate fixation in angle fracture. In this case, the screw holes can be drilled through transbuccal drill guide, passed through a skin stab incision.

(9) After irrigation of the wound, the wound is closed in the usual way. The intermaxillary rubber bands can be retained for 2 or 3 days until the edema subsides. It is advisable to put the jaw into function as early as possible.

Osteosynthesis using lag screws (Fig. 9.29)

(1) Niederdellman (Germany) described this technique. This is applicable when there is a lamellar fracture with broad surface contact between the bone fragments. Osteosynthesis is accomplished using a 2.7 mm thick cortical screw. This procedure can conveniently be performed through intraoral approach.

(2) After establishing the centric occlusion, the bone fragments are exposed and reduced.

(3) Fragments are held in the reduced position with the DCP clamp. A gliding hole is drilled through the outer cortex using 2.7 mm thick drill.

(4) Then the drill sleeve is inserted and the inner cortex is drilled using 2.0 mm thick drill. The inner hole is tapped.

(5) The screw is driven inside until it has a firm grip in the inner cortical bone. When the screw is

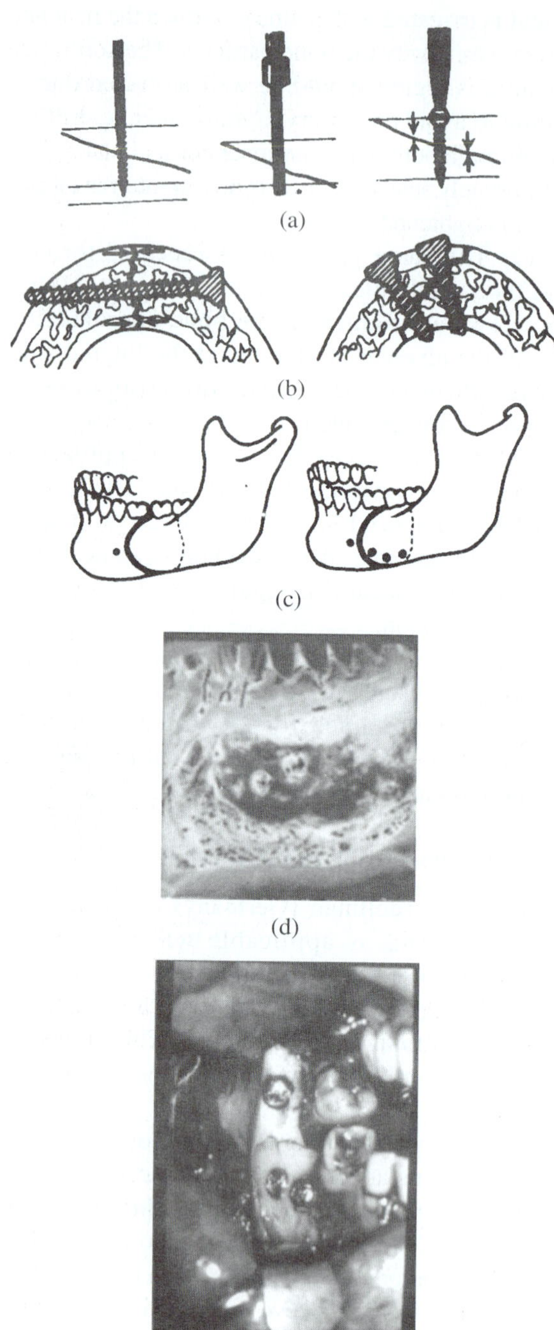

Fig. 9.29 (a), (b), (c) Osteosynthesis using lag screws in lamellar fractures, (d) Lamellar fracture treated with 2 lag screws, (e) Fracture of the ramus treated with 3 lag screws.

tightened, the inner fragment is drawn towards the outer fragment and gets fixed.

Miniplate osteosynthesis (Non-compression technique) (Fig. 9.30)

Biomechanical principles. Based on mathematical and experimental studies carried out by Champy at Strasbourg (France), an osteosynthesis line has been suggested. The U-shaped body of the mandible has an outer and an inner cortex with the central medullary space. The outer cortex is strong and thick, particularly at the symphysis. In the molar region, outer cortex is reinforced by the presence of external oblique ridge from the mental foramen to the coronoid process. These reinforced ridges provide good anchorage points for the screws. Around the symphysis, it is thicker near the lower border while at the molar region, the thickest cortex is in the upper border. Presence of the inferior dental canal must be taken into account. Taking anatomical and biomechanical factors into consideration, an ideal osteosynthesis line for the mandibular body can be drawn. It corresponds to the line of tension at the base of the alveolar process. Along this osteosynthesis line, plates can be fixed with monocortical screws. Anteriorly, a line drawn at the subapical region is the place along which plate could be fixed with monocortical screws. In addition, another line is drawn near the lower border to neutralize the tension forces. Behind the mental foramen, plate can be fixed at the subapical region but above the inferior dental canal. At the angle of the mandible, the plate can most favorably be fixed on the broad surface of the external oblique ridge as high as possible or horizontally parallel to the lower border of the mandible.

Biophysical properties of the material used. The choice of materials depends on the various bending and tension force, anatomical factors and biocompatibility of the material. Plates, screws and instruments should be of the same material to avoid any possible oxidation reduction phenomenon with the consequent effects on tissues.

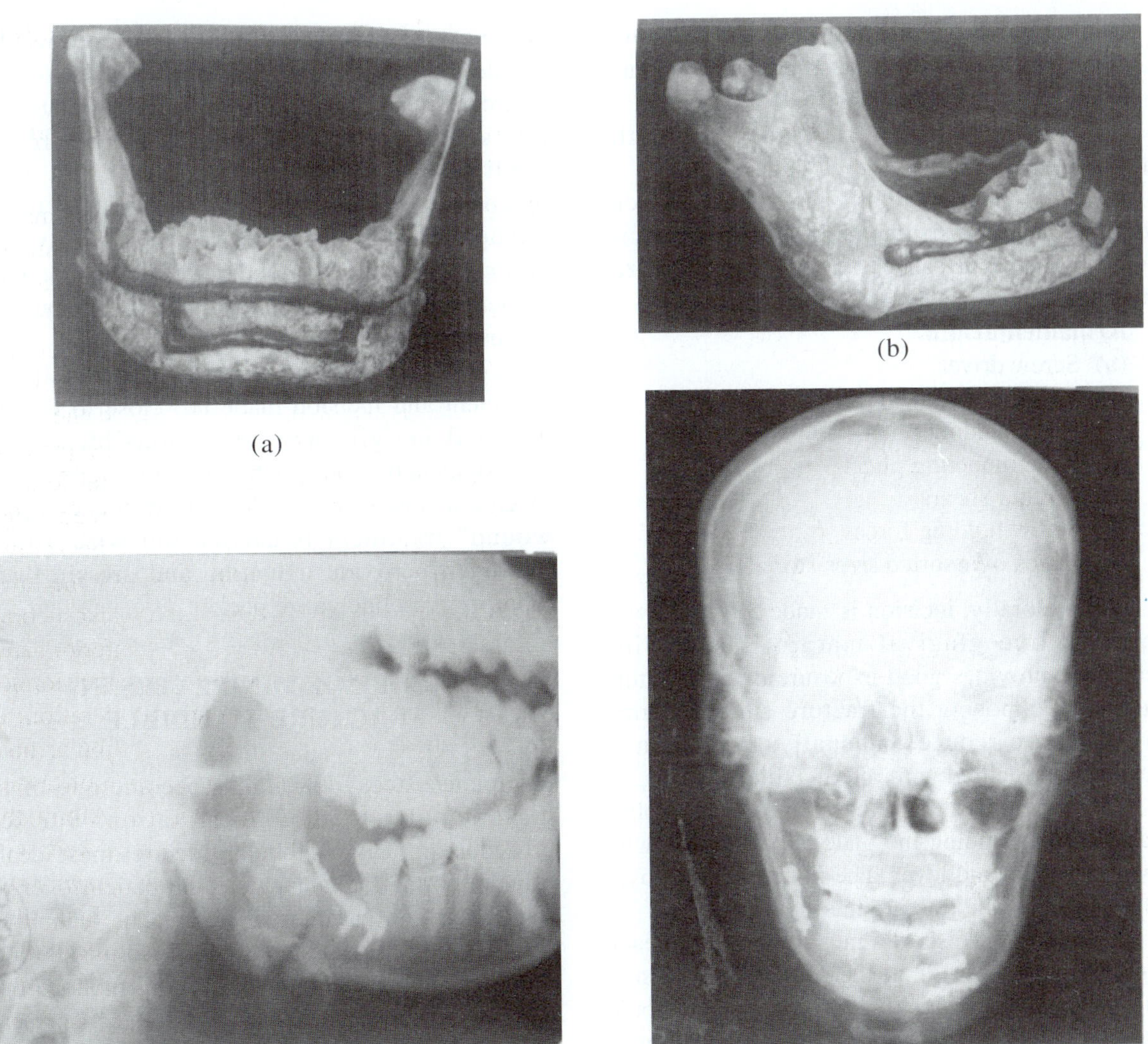

(a) (b) (c) (d)

Fig. 9.30 Osteosynthesis line for placing miniplates (Champy): **(a)** Front view-mandible, **(b)** Side view-mandible, **(c)** Fracture-angle of the mandible. Fixation with a miniplate, **(d)** Miniplate fixation at the body and angle of the mandible.

Technique

(1) Insertion of plates can be done through extraoral, intraoral or combination approaches. Depending on the location of fractures, the choice of the approach is made. The fracture at the body and angle can be fixed through intraoral approach. Extraoral approach will be necessary only for the fracture of the ramus or condyle.

(2) The drilling must be monoaxial and precise to avoid conical bur holes. Otherwise, adequate anchorage will not be available for the screws.

(3) The instrumentation must be perfect in such a way that the diameter of the drill and the screw must be the same. The screws are self-tapping. Hence, drilling must be done slowly to avoid thermal necrosis and micro fracture of the bone.

(4) While threading the screw in the bone, maximum contact between the screw and bone must be ensured.

(5) Plates must be fixed only along the osteosynthesis line.

(6) This precise technique requires a co-ordinated set of instruments stored in a special container so that it can be conveniently sterilized before use.

Armamentarium.

(a) Screw driver
(b) Plate bending lever
(c) Plate bending plier
(d) Plate modeling pliers
(e) Cutting shears
(f) Screw holding forces
(g) Plates of assorted sizes stored in a rack.

(7) Intraorally, incision is made 5-6 mm away from the free gingival margin. "Degloving technique" provides good exposure of the fracture site. After exposing the fracture site, fractured fragments are reduced manually. Occlusion is checked and secured with intermaxillary wiring.

(8) Along the osteosynthesis line, the miniplate is adapted by bending the plate appropriately with modeling pliers and lever. The plate is placed over the bone across the fracture line.

(9) At least two screws must be placed in each fragment. During drilling, the plate is held firmly with the appropriate instrument. The speed should not exceed 1000 revolutions per minute. Drilling is done ideally, perpendicular to the surface of the bone. Only after placing the screw in one hole, the next hole is drilled. Screws are driven precisely to fix the miniplate in position.

(10) In angle fractures, plate should be placed on the oblique line in the proximal fragment, corresponding to the line of tension. If the screw fails to gain a firm grip, position of the plate may be altered.

Complication.

(1) *Postoperative infection.* Strict asepsis, precise technique, appropriate armamentarium and adequate antibiotic coverage will reduce the incidence of infection. Inadequate fixation of fragments leads to infection. Fixation of plate with one screw on either side of the fracture and application of the plate outside the ideal osteosynthesis line provide instability to the fixation. If possible, time lapse must be avoided between injury and the time of treatment. Good oral hygiene measures, wound care and maintenance of occlusion are the prerequisites.

(2) *Wound dehiscence.* Delay in instituting the treatment and incision made too close to the free gingival margin may be responsible for the development of wound dehiscence during the fourth to eighth postoperative days. If it occurs, "open wound" treatment is carried out with diluted hydrogen peroxide irrigation and dressing with iodoform/vaseline gauze pack.

SCOPE OF MINIPLATES IN FRACTURE MANDIBLE

Miniplate osteosynthesis has become one of the most popular methods of fixation. Surgical procedure to treat mandibular fractures must ideally offer important advantages to the patient over the traditional conservative methods. The techniques must be simple and preferably be performed through intraoral approach. In this direction, monocortical plates based on biomechanical principles represents one of the standard and satisfactory methods of fixation. But contrary to the expectations intermaxillary fixation is needed. Prevalence of postoperative infections is high. Costwise, it is expensive than wire. Yet, monocortical plates have a place in the treatment of fractures.

An evaluation of internal fixations

A review of the various fixations used for treating these fractures will reveal that interosseous upper or lower border wire-osteosynthesis is considered to be "traditional and standard" techniques of fixation. But in the recent past, understanding of the biomechanics of fracture healing and advances in surgical techniques have resulted in the popularization of stable internal fixation techniques. The relative efficacy of various techniques can be evaluated based on the following primary predictors.

(1) *Successful treatment*. Success in this context is based on

(a) bony union
(b) restoration of satisfactory posttraumatic occlusion
(c) good jaw function.

(2) *Postoperative complications*

(a) infection
(b) malocclusion
(c) malunion
(d) facial nerve injuries
(e) non-compliance of the treatment, e.g. release of intermaxillary fixation before the stipulated period.

(3) *Period of hospitalization.*

(4) *Postoperative loss of weight.*

(5) *Relative effectiveness with reference to*

(a) age of the patient
(b) number and type of fracture (simple, compound, etc.)
(c) dental status of the patient
(d) medical history
(e) time elapsed between the time of injury, admission and treatment.

(6) *Duration of intermaxillary fixation.*

(7) *Duration of posttreatment follow-up and its need.*

(8) Treatment acceptability by the patient with reference to psychological reaction of the patient towards the course of the treatment - due to pain, swelling, trismus.

(9) *Cost-benefit analysis:* On the basis of studies conducted so far, the following are some of the relevant factors to be borne in mind with regard to the choice of fixation between the traditional and stable internal fixations.

(i) The most common complication with wire-osteosynthesis has been infection due to the mobility of the fragments at the fracture site.

(ii) In wire osteosynthesis, intermaxillary fixation is mandatory. Consequently

(a) Special attention is required to maintain good oral hygiene.
(b) Periodontal disturbances may develop.
(c) Unsatisfactory nutrition leads to weight loss.
(d) Hospitalization and/or convalescent period is prolonged.

(iii) Patients with rigid fixation may develop malocclusion and transient palsy of the mandibular branch of the facial nerve. But they are attributed to frequent technical errors.

(iv) Rigid internal fixation is technically a demanding procedure. The complication rate is relatively high due to errors. This tends to come down once the operator masters the technique.

(v) This procedure has a few marked advantages.

(a) It does not require signified postoperative cooperation from the patient.
(b) Convalescent period is markedly reduced.
(c) The risk of non-union or infection is very low.
(d) This procedure is very advantageous to patients who require early mobilization of the jaws and special nutritional requirements.

(vi) More often, one important factor constantly remembered by the patient but usually ignored by the clinician is the cost-benefit factor. Bone plates and screws are expensive. Surgery may be more time-consuming. Because of the difference in cost, there is an obligation on the part of the clinician to take the potential clinical and economic advantages into consideration before choosing any method of fixation in the treatment of fractures.

The following are some of the other methods of fixations of fractured mandible. (Fig. 9.31)

(a) Extraoral pin fixation
(b) Pyriform aperture wiring
(c) Circumferential wiring.

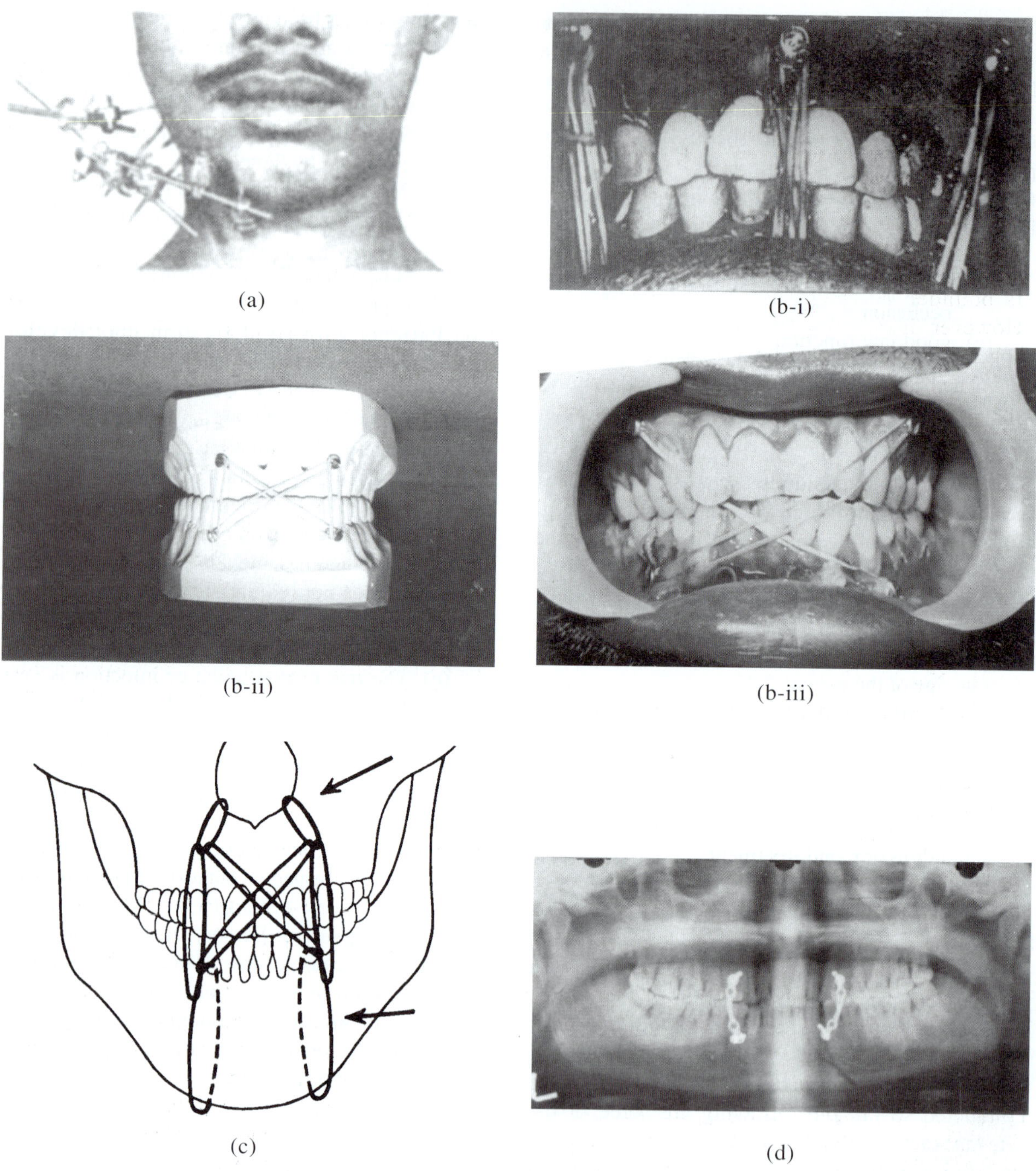

Fig. 9.31 (a) Extraoral pin fixation for fractured mandible, **(b)** Screws as fixation points are useful in children and edentulous jaws, **(c)** Pyriform aperture wire and circumferential wires used as anchorage points for intermaxillary fixation, **(d)** Supramucosal maxillomandibular plate fixation.

FRACTURES OF THE MIDDLE THIRD OF THE FACE

Applied anatomy (Fig. 9.32)

The middle third of the face is bounded superiorly by a transverse line joining the frontozygomatic, frontomaxillary and frontonasal sutures along the supraorbital margins. Inferiorly, it is limited by the occlusal plane of the maxillary teeth. Posteriorly, it is bounded by the sphenoethmoidal junction. However, it includes the pterygoid plates of the sphenoid bone posteroinferiorly.

The bones which constitute the middle third of the facial skeleton are grouped as paired and unpaired.

Paired	*Unpaired*
1. Maxillae	1. Vomer
2. Palatine bones	2. Ethmoid
3. Zygomatic bones	3. Sphenoid
4. Zygomatic processes of temporal bones	
5. Lachrymal bones	
6. Nasal bones	
7. Inferior chonchae	

The middle third of the facial skeleton is formed by a complex articulation of all these bones with maxillae.

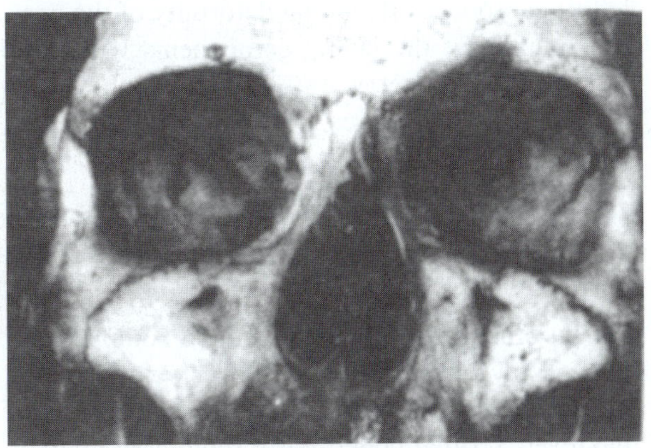

Fig. 9.32 Facial skeleton–front view.

Structural formation

Maxilla is roughly triangular when viewed anteriorly. The alveolar process forms the base of the triangle. At its apex, they are joined by ethmoid to form anterior cranial fossa. Laterally, they are joined by zygomatic processes and posterolaterally separated from the greater wing of the sphenoid by inferior orbital fissure. The structure of the facial skeleton is such that the entire middle third of the face is driven by the frontal force in a backward and downward direction along the sloping base of the skull.

In contrast to mandible, bones of this part of the facial complex are thin and fragile. However, architecturally they are designed with bony reinforcements to withstand and distribute the masticatory forces to the base of the skull. They are also designed to take part in the formation of the oral, nasal, sinus and orbital cavities. This part of the facial skeleton articulates with the base of the skull (frontal bone and body of the sphenoid) like an inclined plane sloping downwards and backwards at an angle of 45 degrees to the occlusal plane. Large area of mucosa lining the various cavities provide periosteal blood supply.

Classification

Due to the complex nature of the skeletal involvement, it is more convenient to group them based on two criteria (a) involvement of dentition, (b) whether located centrally or laterally. While considering these fractures, it is also possible to indicate the fractures of varying combinations.

(1) **Fractures not involving occlusion**

A. *Central region (nasoethmoidal complex)*

I degree, involving nasal bones and/or septum.

II degree, involving nasal bones and frontal processes of maxillae.

III degree, involving I, II and ethmoid bone (nasoethmoid).

IV degree, involving I, II, III and frontal bones (frontonasoethmoid).

B. *Lateral region (zygomatic complex)*

I degree, involving zygomatic arch.

II degree, involving I and zygomatic bone.

III degree, involving I, II and maxilla without involving dentoalveolar segment.

(2) **Fracture involving dentition**

I degree, involving dentoalveolar segment.

II degree, involving low level fractures (Le Fort I)

III degree, involving middle level subzygomatic fractures (Le Fort II).

IV degree, involving high level, suprazygomatic fracture (Le Fort III)

Suprazygomatic fracture is also called *craniofacial dysjunction.* The fractures under this category may be unilateral or bilateral with various combinations of fractures.

General clinical features

As classification indicates, these fractures vary from minor injuries to severe fractures affecting the entire middle third of the facial skeleton. Hence, clinical features vary depending on the severity of injury (Fig. 9.33 a, b).

(1) **Blocking the patency of airway.** This can occur due to the blockage of airway by the blood clot. Fractured fragments may be driven posteriorly, forcing the soft palate and tongue against the posterior wall of the pharynx, thereby reducing the pharyngeal space and consequent blockage of airway.

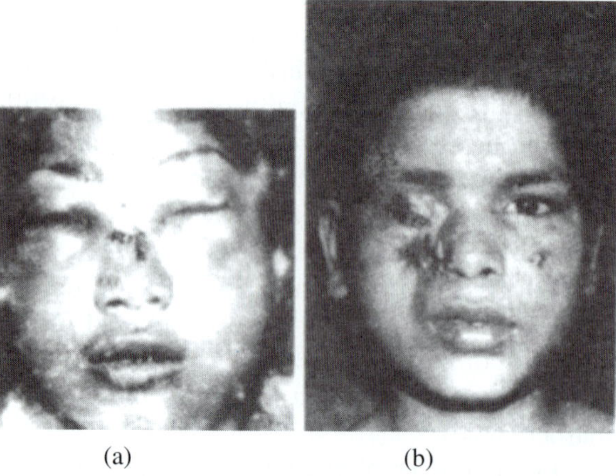

(a) (b)

Fig. 9.33 Clinical photographs: **(a)** Fracture of the middle third of the face, **(b)** Gun shot injury of the maxillary region.

(2) **Facial edema.** The typical edema consequent to trauma to the middle third of the facial skeleton presents a ballooning effect. Such edema usually masks the diagnosis of the underlying injury.

(3) Periorbital and subconjunctival *ecchymosis* usually develop after the edema sets in.

(4) **Epistaxis.** Bleeding from the nasal cavity and nasopharynx. It usually stops after sometime.

(5) **CSF rhinorrhea.** Depending on the damage of the cribriform plate and involvement of the anterior cranial fossa, cerebrospinal fluid leak occurs. This is usually arrested if the fracture is reduced.

(6) **Disturbance to occlusion.** It is seen only when the fracture involves dentition. In such cases, premature occlusion of the last molars result in anterior open bite and a sense of gagging.

(7) **Abnormal mobility.** Depending on the nature of the injury, abnormal mobility of the fractured fragments could be elicited.

(8) **Facial deformity** is very conspicuous. For example, central third involving dentition will result in dish face deformity and elongation of the face. The fracture of central third without involving dentition produces flattening deformity of the nose. The fracture of the lateral components will result in facial asymmetry and flattened cheek. In zygomatic arch fractures, trismus develops.

NASOETHMOIDAL FRACTURES

Clinical features

(1) Fractures of the nasoethmoid complex may involve any of the following bones - nasal bones, frontal bone, ethmoids, frontal processes of maxillae, lacrimal bones, nasal septum and vomer. Depending on the degree and direction of trauma, any or all these bones may be displaced. The

direction of displacement corresponds to the direction of trauma. If it is from the front, characteristic flattening deformity results. If it is from the lateral direction, nasal deviation occurs.

(2) Bleeding due to tear of the nasal mucous membrane results in epistaxis, followed by blocking of the nasal passage.

(3) Subcutaneous hemorrhage results in circumorbital and subconjunctival ecchymosis, more pronounced around the medial canthus of the eye.

(4) Disturbance of the frontonasal and frontoethmoidal regions results in cerebrospinal fluid rhinorrhea, leaking through the cribriform plate of ethmoid.

(5) The involved area is tender and unstable on palpation.

(6) Prominent epicanthal folds.

(7) Telecanthus.

(8) Evidence of lacerations at the site of injury. Since it is prominently located, nasal pyramid is more often involved in facial injuries.

Treatment

Aims

(a) To relieve the blocking of nasal passage so that functional airway is restored.

(b) Early restoration of the proper shape of the nose. Delay in treatment may result in early malunion of the fragments.

Management

(1) *Anesthesia.* Under local or general anesthesia, reduction can be done. Roller gauze soaked with 5% Xylocaine packed into the nasal cavity provides satisfactory anesthesia. It can be supplemented by external infiltration.

(2) *Reduction.* More often, this fracture is treated without adequately assessing the damage preoperatively. Generally, there is a wrong belief that the entire nasal bone is detached and displaced from its base. But in reality, it is the lower part of the nasal bone that is usually fractured. Very rarely, base of the nasal pyramid is detached from the frontal bone as in frontonasoethmoid fractures. Hence, close reduction and internal splinting may have to be done in severe injuries.

Closed reduction of the fragment is carried out with a pair of Walsham's nasal disimpaction forceps. Final centralization of the displaced nasal septum is carried out with Ash's septal forceps. (Fig. 9.34)

Technique. Walsham's forceps are available in pairs - right and left side. Each forceps has a smaller and a larger blade. The smaller blade is inserted into the nostril. The larger blade, covered by a soft rubber tube to protect the skin is applied externally. When the handles are closed, blades grip the side of the nose firmly up to the medial canthus, ensuring that the blades grip parallel to the frontal process of maxilla. Medial or lateral rotation will result either in-fracture or out-fracture of the nasal pyramid. During this manipulation, the base of the nasal skeletal framework should be given counter-pressure with the opposite hand to mould the fragments and also to provide additional stability to the head. After satisfactory manipulation, Ash's septal forceps is

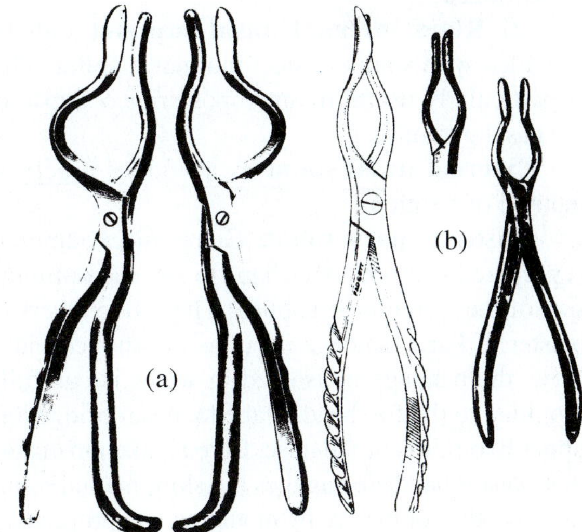

Fig. 9.34 (a) Rowe's maxillary disimpaction forceps, **(b)** Walsham's nasal and septal forceps.

introduced into the nasal floor. Septal cartilage is realigned with a forward traction.

(3) *Fixation and immobilization*. Usually, immobilization is not necessary if the displacement is not severe. However, if it is necessary, it can be achieved either with intranasal or extranasal splintage.

Intranasal splint

(1) **Ribbon gauze pack.** This is one of the procedures considered to be adequate. Ribbon gauze is soaked with paraffin or bismuth iodoform paraffin paste and packed into the nasal cavity carefully in layers from superior nares downwards. It is allowed to remain in position for a few days.

But, unfortunately, this method has many disadvantages.

(a) Airway is blocked.

(b) It is a potential source of infection, particularly when CSF rhinorrhea is present.

(c) Over packing may result in postoperative telecanthus. However, it is of great value in arresting persistent bleeding from the nasal cavity. This is definitely indicated as an intranasal lateral stabilization of the septum that has been repositioned.

(2) **Rigid internal nasal support** can be provided with stainless steel intranasal splint. This is particularly useful in anteroposterior collapse of the nasal pyramid.

External nasal splint is a widely practised method of fixation.

Plaster of paris splint: Gauze piece template is prepared in a butterfly-shape to suit the optimum size of the splint to be applied. Then, five layers of plaster of Paris bandage is cut as per the template. Now, the bandage moistened in water is carefully moulded to the forehead, glabella, nasal bridge and upper two-thirds of the nose. Care is taken to ensure that plaster bandage engages the skin, medial to the inner canthus of the eye by moulding it appropriately. Once plaster of Paris sets, the splint is properly secured to the forehead and cheek with adhesive tape. The splint is usually left in place for 2-3 weeks. It is better to apply a fresh splint once edema subsides. Otherwise the original splint may become ill-fitting.

ZYGOMATIC COMPLEX FRACTURE
(Figs 9.35 - 9.38)

Recognition of various types of the zygomatic fractures and the stability after reduction are the prerequisites for proper treatment. In order to understand the nature of the complex problems involved, certain basic principles need to be understood.

Applied anatomy

Articulation of zygomatic bone is tripod in nature. It unites with (a) frontal bone superiorly, (b) temporal bone posteriorly and (c) maxilla anteroinferiorly. Coronoid process moves deeper to this bone during the normal mandibular movements. Temporal fascia is attached along the superior border while masseter is attached along its inferior border. It takes part in the formation of the lateral wall of the orbit. At the lateral wall, *Whitnall's tubercle* provides attachment to *Lockwood's suspensory ligament.* The vertical position of the globe depends on this suspensory ligament.

Classification

The classification is an attempt to correlate the displacement with reference to the site of impact and the consequent stability of the fractured zygoma. It may rotate around its vertical or longitudinal axis and may be displaced medially, laterally, posteriorly or inferiorly. The post-reduction stability depends on the direction of rotation. Waters' view skull (maxillary sinus view) is the best view to evaluate these fractures. Based on this, these fractures are classified as follows (Fig. 9.35):

Group I No significant displacement
Group II Zygomatic arch fractures

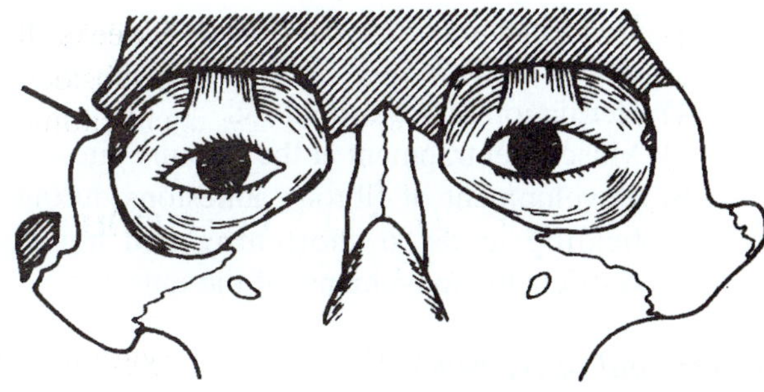

Fig. 9.35 Zygomatic fracture above the Whitnall's tubercle.

Group III Unrotated body fractures
Group IV Medial rotation
Group V Lateral rotation
Group VI Complex fractures

Rowe and Killey classified these fractures in the following manner:

Type I No significant displacement
Type II Zygomatic arch fractures.
Type III Rotation around vertical axis
(a) Internally
(b) Externally
Type IV Rotation around longitudinal axis
(a) Medially
(b) Laterally
Type V Displacement en-bloc
(a) Medially
(b) Inferiorly
(c) Laterally
Type VI Displacement of orbitoantral partition
(a) Inferiorly (blow-out)
(b) Superiorly (very rare)
Type VII Displacement of the orbital rim segments.
Type VIII Complex comminuted fracture.

Stability after reduction is closely related to the type of fractures. It is stable in (a) zygomatic arch fracture (Type II), (b) lateral rotation around vertical axis (Type III-b) and (c) posterior displacement (Type V-c).

Fractures are not stable in

(a) Medial rotation around longitudinal axis (Type IVa)
(b) Medial displacement (Type Va)
(c) Lateral displacement (Type Vb)
(d) Inferior displacement (Type Vd)
(e) Complex fractures (Type VII). In these unstable fractures, fixations are required for stability.

Clinical features

(1) *Flattening of the cheek*. It can be observed by viewing the face from above.

(2) *Periorbital edema and ecchymosis*. Invariably, these are constant features. While edema is generalized around the orbital region, ecchymosis is around the attachment of orbicularis oculi muscle.

(3) *Subconjunctival hemorrhage (Blood-shot eye).* This is significant of zygomatic injury. This is noticed in the outer quadrant seen disappearing under the eyeball. Its posterior limit cannot be visualized. Due to the direct oxygenation of hemoglobin, subconjunctival ecchymosis remains red in color.

(4) *Unilateral epistaxis*. This is due to filling of blood into the maxillary sinus and escape through the ostium resulting in epistaxis.

(5) *Infraorbital anesthesia.* If infraorbital nerve is involved in fracture, the patient complains of anesthesia of the corresponding upper lip, lateral portion of the nose and the upper teeth which stays for a few months.

(6) *Trismus.* Difficulty to open the mouth develops if the displaced zygoma blocks the coronoid process mechanically.

(7) *Diplopia*

(a) If the fracture occurs above the *Whitnall's tubercle* (above the attachment of Lockwood's suspensory ligament), downward displacement of the eyeball results in the alteration of the optical axis. It results in double vision (diplopia). If the fracture occurs below the attachment of the suspensory ligament, suspensory mechanism is left undisturbed and hence no diplopia occurs.

(b) When there is severe comminution of the orbital floor, periorbital fat herniates into the maxillary sinus resulting in enophthalmos. Entrapment of the extraocular muscle (lateral rectus and inferior oblique) restricts the movement of the eyeball. Such restrictions due to the muscle entrapment can be confirmed by *forced-duction test*. This is done by grasping the globe of the eye with a pair of forceps and elevating it. Failure to rotate the eyeball upwards confirms the diagnosis.

Isolated orbital floor fractures without the involvement of the orbital rim are known as *"blow-out"* fractures. This is possible because the floor is made up of paper-thin bone. Anatomically, the globe is seen to protrude outside the orbital rim slightly. Any blunt injury by an object bigger than the globe tends to transmit pressure on the globe. The pressure increases inside the orbit by the compression of the eyeball so that the weak floor alone gives way. The inferior rectus and inferior oblique muscles herniate into the maxillary sinus through the breach of the floor. This presents a typical "hanging-drop" appearance in the maxillary sinus radiograph. Within the first week of injury, if the herniation is not relieved, the damaged soft tissue heals in the same position resulting in severe shortening of these muscles. That is why optical axis is altered, resulting in diplopia. In such cases, it is very difficult to correct diplopia once the healing is completed. Hence, proper diagnosis soon after injury holds the key for its successful management.

Such problems are not seen in children because of the resilience of the bone. Diplopia, in general, can occur due to many causes that interfere with the functioning of extraocular muscles. The causes can be grouped under (a) *physical interference,* (b) *functional interference* and (c) *neurological causes*.

Physical interference

(1) Extravasation of blood and the ocular muscles.
(2) Bony spicules.
(3) Disturbance to the attachment of inferior oblique muscle.
(4) Herniation of periorbital fat.
(5) Muscles entrapment at the fracture site.
(6) Development of fibrous adhesions during healing leads to shortening and hence restricts the movements of the muscles.

Functional interference

Disturbance to the inferior rectus and inferior oblique muscles following the displacement of the globe interferes with function of the eyeball.

Neurological interference

(1) Supranuclear impairments of third, fourth and sixth cranial nerves.
(2) Nuclear lesions of these cranial nerves.
(3) Intracranial infranuclear injuries.
(4) Arteriovenous fistula compressing cavernous sinus.
(5) Superior orbital fissure or intraorbital damage.

Radiographic evaluation

Waters' view skull (maxillary sinus view) is the most suitable view for these fractures. However, posterior displacement is not shown in this x-ray since displacement occurs in the same direction as the x-ray beam. Likewise, rotation of zygoma may not be adequately evaluated. Rotation around the longitudinal axis can be identified by Caldwell-Luc view and rotation around the vertical axis in the submentovertex view. The submentovertex view is equally indispensable in (a) zygomatic arch fractures, (b) posterior displacements and (c) medial and lateral rotations around the longitudinal axis. Radiological evaluation can never be a replacement for proper clinical examination. It is indispensable to diagnose the type of zygomatic fractures. Very rarely the suture lines are mistaken for the fracture lines in the radiograph. Sometimes, such cases are diagnosed as fractures without displacement. This aspect is of great medicolegal importance.

Management

Asymptomatic fractures without or with minimal displacement may be left alone. Arch fractures need reduction. No fixation is usually necessary. However, many of the zygomatic fractures that are unstable after reduction necessarily need fixations. There are several methods described in the literature for reduction and fixation of the zygomatic fractures.

Reduction

(1) *Non-operative treatment.* Many fractures with minimal or without displacement will not require any surgical intervention. So, proper decision must be taken based on (a) displacement of fragments producing any facial disfigurement, (b) presence of diplopia and (c) difficulty to open the mouth.

(2) *Use of towel clamps.* In war injuries, they are treated as an emergency measure by applying towel clamps externally for reduction. Since there is no control of the fragments during such reduction and also due to the unstable nature of many of these displaced fragments, it is not used routinely.

(3) *Gilles temporal approach.* Originally, Sir Harold Gilles introduced this method to elevate the depressed zygomatic arch fractures. Later, this approach was used for treating the other fractures of zygomaticomaxillary complex. The surgical anatomy of the zygomaticotemporal region facilitates this approach successfully. The temporal fascia is attached along the upper border of the zygomatic arch while temporalis muscle passes below the arch to gain the attachment to the coronoid process. Hence, the tissue plane that exists between the temporal fascia and the muscle is utilized for introducing the zygomatic elevator so that the instrument gains access to the undersurface of zygoma without a facial scar.

Technique. The temporal region of the affected side is preoperatively shaved where superficial temporal artery bifurcates. The external auditory meatus is plugged with cotton to prevent any fluid or foreign body entering inside. 2 to 2.5 cm long incision is made parallel to the anterior branch of the superficial temporal artery. Dissection is carried out until temporal fascia is exposed which can be identified as white glistening membrane. Then, the fascia is incised. Howarth, periosteal elevator is introduced and passed downwards and forwards until the elevator easily slips below the depressed zygoma. Once the correct plane is established, the periosteal elevator is withdrawn. Now it is replaced with a suitable zygomatic elevator (Fig. 9.36).

Originally, the Bristow's orthopedic periosteal elevator was used for this purpose. Later on, Rowe modified a special type of elevator. It has a blade and an oval handle, very similar to the Bristow's elevator. At present, many types of zygomatic elevators are available in the market. The operator

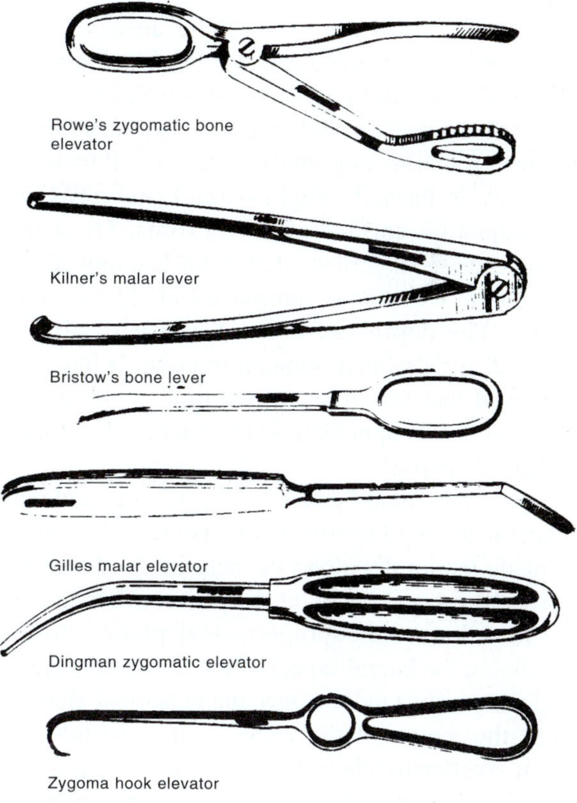

Fig. 9.36 Different types of zygomatic elevators.

must choose the elevator that does not need fulcrum or support from the skull bone during the elevation of the depressed zygoma. Pressure on the parietal bone may result in depressed fracture of the skull bone. While elevation is carried out, an audible snapping sound is heard if the zygoma is reduced. The elevator is moved under the zygomatic bone to iron out the depression. Once satisfactory elevation is achieved, the elevator is withdrawn. Catgut sutures are placed to close the incision of the temporal fascia. Scalp wound is closed with black silk mattress sutures to secure adequate hemostasis. Postoperatively, care is taken to ensure that pressure is not exerted on the elevated zygoma until the bone fragments are united clinically. During the immediate postoperative phase, a cross mark is made on the facial aspect of the cheek with methylene blue to serve as a warning for the nurses and other attendants.

(4) *Intraoral approach.* The access to the undersurface of zygoma can also be gained through intraoral vestibular approach. An incision is made along the buccal vestibule around maxillary molars posterior to the zygomatic buttress. Periosteal elevator is passed subperiosteally towards the infratemporal surface of the zygoma. Once this plane is defined, periosteal elevator is removed and zygomatic elevator is introduced along the same plane. The depressed bone is elevated with an upward, forward and outward traction. It has been observed that less force is required to elevate the zygoma in this approach when compared to Gillcs temporal approach.

Recently, modification has been suggested with a lateral coronoid approach. In this method, incision is made intraorally along the anterior border of the coronoid process. A blunt dissection is carried out further along the supraperiosteal plane, closely following the lateral aspect of the coronoid process and temporalis tendon. Once the periosteal elevator is in the region of the zygoma, it is withdrawn. Then, zygomatic elevator is introduced in position and the depressed bone is elevated. Occasionally, one may encounter the herniation of the buccal pad of fat. It will be tempting to pull out the fat further and further. It is better to reposition rather than excising it.

These procedures can be carried out under local anesthesia. The greatest advantage is the absence of external scar. However, care should be taken not to introduce infection from the oral cavity.

(5) *Percutaneous approach.* This was originally introduced as an emergency method by inserting a hook or towel clip through the facial skin over the depressed zygoma. Once the hook engages the deeper aspect of the bone, the fracture can be reduced by a strong outward traction. The exact location of the application of the hook is at the intersection of a perpendicular line dropped from the lateral canthus of the eye and a horizontal line extended posteriorly from the margin. One has to take care that the hook is not inserted deep into the inferior orbital fissure and also to avoid bleeding from the orbital veins. Although it looks like a simple procedure, considerable experience and adequate knowledge of anatomy of the region are required to avoid serious complications.

Fixations (Figs 9.37, 9.38)

It has been found that zygomatic arch fractures are best treated by reduction alone. They are usually stable and hence no need for any fixations. But the fractures involving the body of the zygoma with displacement requires some method of fixations.

(1) *Antral approach.* The zygomatic bone forms the apex of the maxillary sinus. When this bone is fractured, the bony fragment telescopes which can be reduced by Caldwell-Luc approach through the maxillary sinus. Since the zygoma is unstable, an antral pack is provided to prevent the displacement of bone into the antrum. The antral pack is expected to exert counter pressure thereby preventing the bony displacement. It is also used to provide support for orbital floor-fractures. This method used to be popular but now it has been replaced by a few direct methods of fixation. Unfortunately, the antral pack is not under the control of the operator. Under

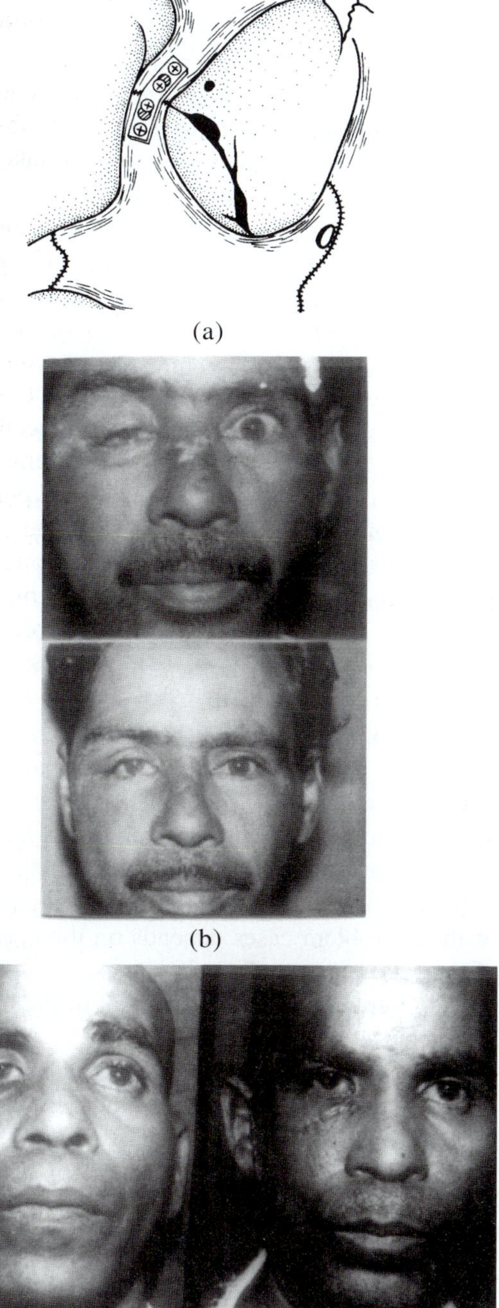

(a)

(b)

(c)

Fig. 9.37 (a) Miniplate fixation for zygomatic fracture, **(b)** & **(c)** Pre and postoperative clinical photographs of the patients with fractured zygoma.

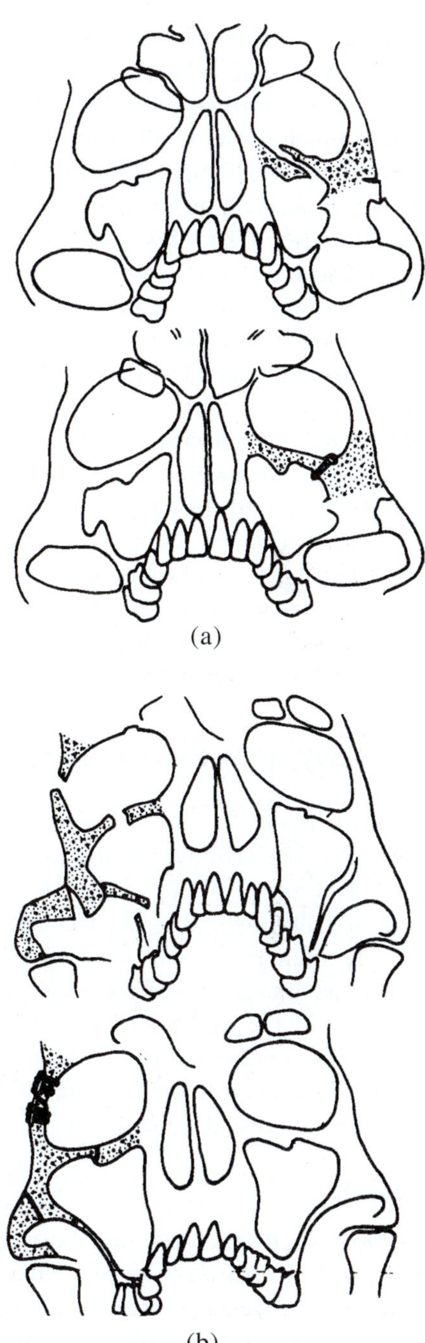

(a)

(b)

Fig. 9.38 (a) Lag screw fixation for fractured zygoma: (i) Preoperative. (ii) Postoperative, **(b)** Plate fixation at the frontozygomatic region for the fractured zygoma: (i) Preoperative. (ii) Postoperative.

packing results in inadequate fixation while over packing may damage the orbital contents.

(2) *Direct fixation through open reduction.* Clinically and radiologically, the fractured zygoma is properly evaluated. Under general anesthesia, incisions are placed along the natural crease, in accordance with Langer's line to expose frontozygomatic and zygomaticomaxillary fracture-lines. Either through Gilles temporal approach or through intraoral approach, depressed zygomatic fragment is elevated under direct vision. Then, holes are drilled through the full thickness of the bone on either side of the fracture-lines. Periosteal elevator is kept underneath the bone as a guard so that deeper tissues are not injured during drilling. 26-gauge stainless steel ligature wire is used for the interosseus wiring. Instead of interosseus wiring, osteosynthesis plates can also be used for fixation of these fractures. After the debridement, wound is closed in layers with interrupted sutures.

BLOW-OUT FRACTURES

Fractures of floor of the orbit without the involvement of the orbital rim are called *"pure blow-out"* fractures. If the orbital rim is also involved, it is known as *"Impure blow-out"* fractures. In such fractures, the orbital fat and muscles herniate into the maxillary sinus, producing enophthalmos. If the inferior rectus and inferior oblique muscles are also involved in herniation, the movements of the eyeball are restricted. Failure of such upward rotation leads to diplopia.

Management

Diagnosis of such fractures can be confirmed clinically by *"Forced duction test"* and by the *"Hanging drop"* appearance in the maxillary sinus radiograph. Delay in the treatment will lead to persistent diplopia. The prognosis becomes poor, depending on the delay. The floor of the orbit must be surgically explored to release the adhesions at the orbital floor. Autogenous bone grafts or Teflon sheets are placed at the floor to prevent the herniation again.

Otherwise, floor of the orbit can also be explored through *Caldwell-Luc approach.* After repositioning the bone fragments, the floor of the orbit can be provided support by an antral pack soaked with whitehead's varnish. This must be retained for 20 to 25 days. Care must be taken to ensure that undue pressure is not given at the posteromedial aspect of the sinus around the optic nerve.

Isolated blow-out fracture of the orbital floor is relatively rare. If the diplopia persists even after the edema subsides, a tomogram should be advised. If there is limitation of ocular rotation and if the forced-duction test and tomogram are positive, then exploration of the orbital floor is justified. Even then, an ophthalmic opinion must be obtained before submitting the patient for surgery. Whenever possible, a "Hess chart" must be advised prior to surgery since this is the best baseline for further assessment of the patient.

The clinician who is responsible for the primary care of the patient often faces a dilemma regarding borderline cases. As the experience increases in the interpretation of clinical and radiological features of such patients, the proportion of such doubtful cases will decrease. Ultimately, successful management of these problem cases depends on the application of the following surgical objectives:

(1) Reduction and replacement of the fractured fragments and the orbital contents.

(2) Stabilization by appropriate methods of fixation for restoration of the stable orbital floor.

(3) Restoration of orbital movements.

(4) Preservation of the volume of the orbital contents including periorbital fat.

General observations on the orbital fractures

(1) Appreciation of applied anatomy and applied physiology is absolutely essential to understand the precise nature of these injuries and rational approach to their treatment.

(2) There are many avoidable complications in the management of orbital fractures.

(3) The success of the treatment is directly proportional to the quality of the patient's care.

(4) Similarly, delay in instituting appropriate treatment will yield inferior results with far reaching implications.

(5) Most of the zygomatic fractures with rotational displacements are unstable and hence require fixations.

(6) The patients with orbital fractures must therefore be referred to the specialist for treatment without delay.

(7) All ocular injuries must have the benefit of ophthalmic consultations.

LE FORT FRACTURES (Fig. 9.39)

Detailed account of Le Fort fractures are outside the scope of this book. Therefore, a brief outline is provided here on Le Fort fractures. They involve the midfacial skeleton disturbing dental occlusion. Le Fort I and II are subzygomatic while Le Fort III are suprazygomatic fractures. They may be unilateral or bilateral without midpalatal split. In 1901, Le Fort, a French anatomist, believed to have studied the pattern of fractures of maxilla by subjecting 40 cadaver faces to trauma of differing amounts of energy from different directions with sandbags. He observed that the fracture-line involving the maxillae invariably fell into one of the three predictable patterns. These lines roughly correspond to the weak areas of the midfacial skeleton. Later, this monumental work became the basis for describing them as Le Fort fractures.

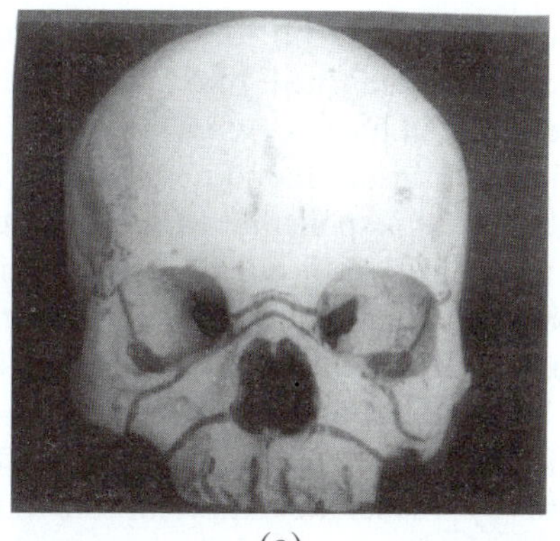

(a)

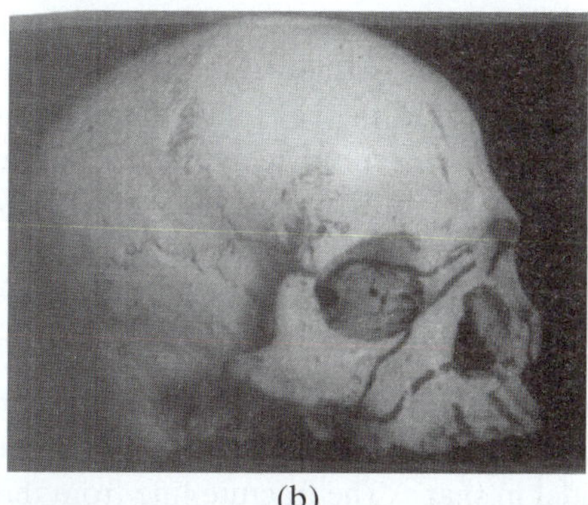

(b)

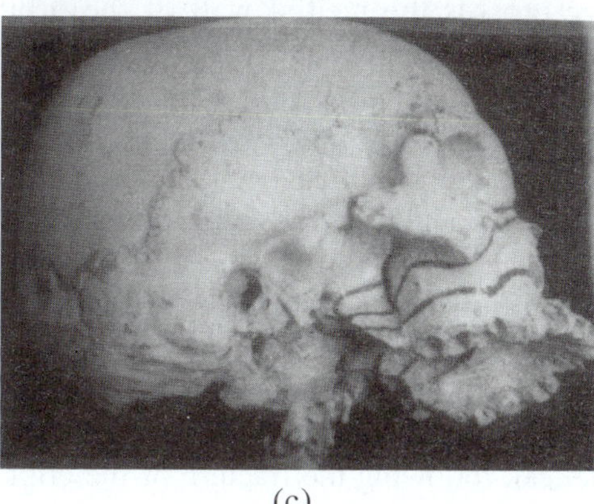

(c)

Fig. 9.39 Le Fort fracture lines **(a)** Front view, **(b)** & **(c)** Side views.

Le Fort I fractures (Guerin's fracture)

They are called horizontal fractures because of the horizontal direction of the fracture line and low level fractures since they involve the lower portion of maxilla. The fracture line runs along the apex of all the maxillary teeth involving the lower third of the nasal septum, lower thirds of the pterygoid plates and the associated portions of the palatine processes. Usually, displacements of the fractured maxillae may be due to (a) the direction of the traumatic force, (b) the contraction of medial pterygoid muscles. But in low level fractures, the muscle factor does not play any role in the displacement. That is why absence of the posteroinferior displacement of the fractured fragment may be responsible for an inexperienced clinician to miss the diagnosis during the preliminary examination. Radiographic examination is helpful to confirm the diagnosis. However, these fracture lines should not be confused with cervical vertebral shadows or with intervertebral shadows. Recent surveys reveal the important role of CT scan in the diagnosis and the management of midface injuries. If early diagnosis is made, it will be helpful to plan out the treatment so that the possible complications due to the delayed treatment and repeated anesthesia could be avoided. CT scan also helps to avoid multiple radiographs, thereby reducing radiation damage to the patient.

Le Fort II fractures

They are known as pyramidal or midlevel fractures for the obvious reasons. The mobile fragment is pyramidal in shape. The fracture line from the nasal bridge crosses the medial wall of the orbit and lachrymal bone. Subsequently, it recrosses the orbital rim at the junction of lateral two-thirds and medial one-third in the region of the infraorbital foramen. The fracture line passes along the zygomaticomaxillary suture line on the lateral wall of the maxillary sinus. It extends posteriorly crossing the pterygoid plates. The fracture-line runs below the zygomatic region. The entire midface is edematous with subconjunctival hemorrhage and CSF rhinorrhea. The nasal discharge of CSF is due to the leak following the fracture of the cribriform plate of ethmoid. If it dries up when collected in a dry cloth, then it is mucous discharge (due to starch). If it does not dry up, then the neurosurgical opinion is mandatory to rule out the base of the skull fracture and the possible spread of infection intracranially. Such a patient will give history of loss of consciousness. *Battle's sign* is characterized by ecchymosis along the course of posterior auricular artery in the mastoid region and rise of body temperature.

Le Fort III fractures

They are otherwise known as transverse or high level fractures. They are also responsible for craniofacial dysjunction. These fracture lines run parallel to the base of the skull separating the midfacial skeleton from the skull base. The fracture line crosses the ethmoid, lesser wing of the sphenoid and may even involve optic foramen to reach the pterygomaxillary fissure. Thus, it is supra-zygomatic. The patient develops a characteristic facial deformity anterior open bite, CSF rhinorrhea, base of the skull fracture, epistaxis, bleeding through the ear (otorrhea) and elongated face.

In general, Le Fort fractures are diagnosed on the basis of the clinical examination and radiographic evaluation. Any patient with a suspected midfacial trauma must be examined for any possible injury to the cervical spine. If there is any cervical pain, alteration in the cervical contour or any neurological deficit of the extremities, a neurological opinion must be obtained to rule out any cervical injury. On the whole, all the midfacial fracture patients must be examined for the following important clinical features:

(1) Pain or tenderness
(2) Facial deformity
(3) Ecchymosis
(4) Epistaxis
(5) Otorrhea
(6) Anesthesia
(7) Malocclusion
(8) CSF rhinorrhea
(9) Abnormal mobility of the facial skeleton
(10) Limitation of the mouth opening
(11) Gagging sensation in the throat
(12) Amnesia, loss of consciousness, etc.

Brief outline of the management

Reduction and disimpaction of maxillae are done with a pair of maxillary disimpaction forceps. The wider blades are inserted inside the mouth. The smaller unpadded blades are inserted along the nasal floor. The operator stands at the head end of the patient, grasping the handles of the forceps. Traction is applied in a downward and forward direction to disimpact the mobilized maxillae.

In the midfacial fracture, fixation is achieved in two forms:

(a) **Craniomaxillary (direct)**
(b) **Craniomandibular (indirect)**

Craniomaxillary fixations are direct while craniomandibular fixations are indirect in nature. In both fixations, anchorage point is cranium. If maxilla is fixed with cranium, it is direct. If mandible is fixed with cranium, maxilla gets sandwitched and here it is indirect. Depending on the level of the fracture, anchorage point is taken for fixing the fractures. These fixations are broadly grouped as external and internal fixations. Previously, all the midface fractures used to be fixed with external anchorage provided on the Plaster of Paris head cap. Although fixation looks stable, as the days progress by Plaster of Paris (POP) head cap becomes unstable. This renders the fixations unstable. At present, many types of internal fixations are being used, e.g. direct transosseous wiring, plate osteosynthesis, internal suspension with wires (Adam's wiring) etc. Adam described the method of internal suspension by means of a subcutaneous wire in 1942. The main disadvantage is the upward and backward pull of the reduced maxilla. Ideally, it should be upward and forward. Immobilization is provided with intermaxillary wiring, retained for a period of four weeks. Direct fixation is more accurate then the indirect fixation.

Complications

(1) Disfigurement of the face is common if the reduction and fixation are not satisfactorily carried out or as a result of nonunion or malunion of the fractures.

(2) Ophthalmic complications.

(a) Diplopia if the blow out fractures are unrecognized.
(b) Diminished vision due to optic nerve damage.

(3) Deranged occlusion like persistent anterior open bite.

(4) Restriction in mouth opening.

(5) Persistent periorbital edema due to the traumatic block of lymphatic drainage of the periorbital region.

(6) Intracranial infection like meningitis.

(7) Very rarely, posttraumatic diabetes insipidus may develop.

PITFALLS IN THE TREATMENT OF MIDDLE THIRD OF THE FACE

The overall treatment of midfacial trauma involves specialized knowledge and expertise in a complex anatomical region. The responsibility is shared by a number of surgical specialties. For the benefit of the specialist who takes over the primary responsibility of such cases of midfacial trauma, a few problems need careful attention by way of caution.

(1) Problem of airway and its maintenance for general anesthesia.
(2) Failure to treat bony injuries before repairing the soft tissues.
(3) Relying on centric occlusion without stable fixation of midfacial fractures.
(4) Vital structures likely to be discarded indiscriminately during the initial treatment.
(5) Consultations with other specialists.

With lesser trained personnel taking the responsibility of the patient during the initial phase of the treatment, some of the following errors are likely to increase unless care is taken to identify and institute the appropriate treatment.

(a) *Hematoma of the nasal septum* are often unrecognized during the early phase since it may

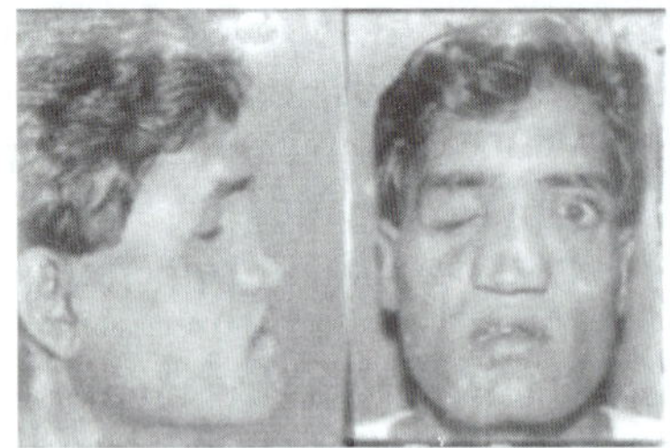

Fig. 9.40 Front and side view of malunited midface fractures.

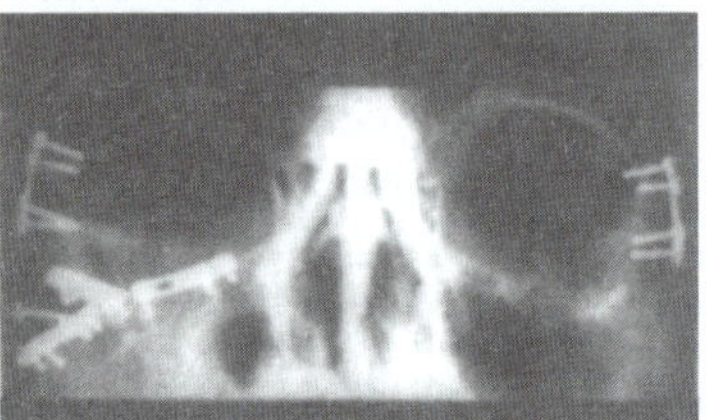

Fig. 9.41 Plate fixations for Le Fort II and III fractures.

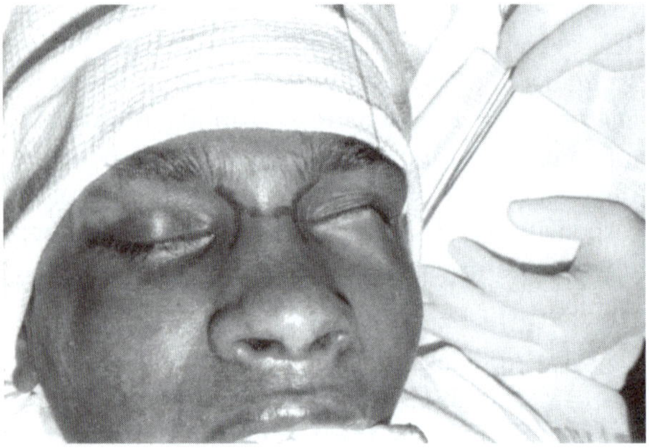

(a)

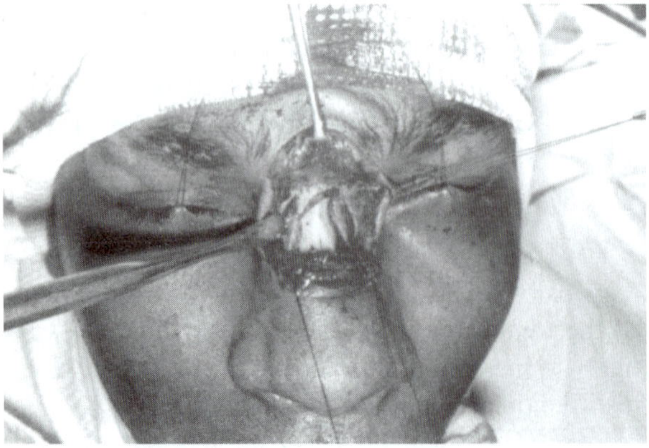

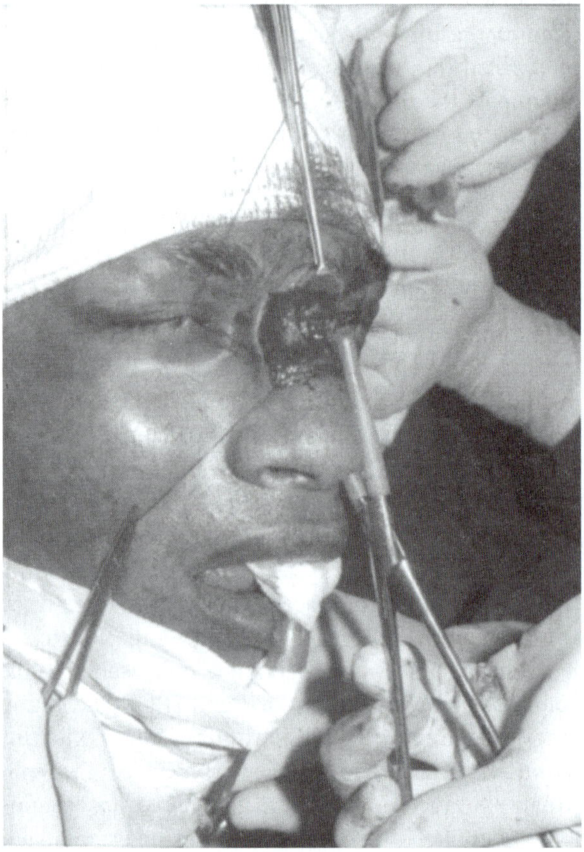

(c)

(b)

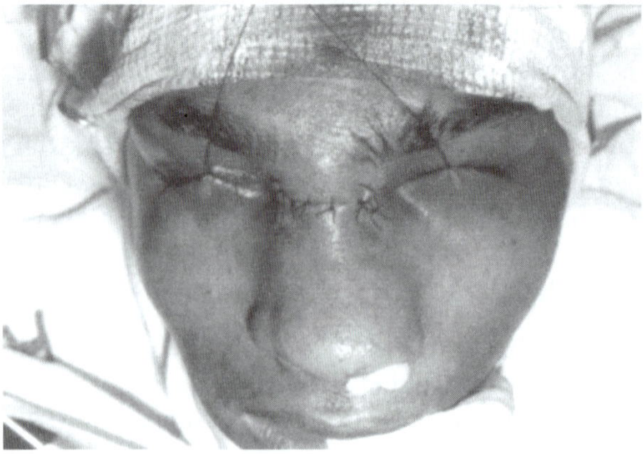

(d)

Fig. 9.42 Nasal fracture. **(a)** Incision, **(b)** Displaced fracture, **(c)** Fracture reduction, **(d)** Wound closure.

be mistaken for edema. They are usually associated with fractures of the septal cartilage without the associated fracture of the nasal bones. Hematoma inside the orbital cavity can result in serious complications like loss of vision. Ecchymosis and edema of the eyelid usually obscures this problem. Hence, early evaluation of the vision and eyeball movements must be made. Every midfacial trauma is a potential head injury. Hence intracranial problems like hematoma or concussion should be recognized during the early phase itself.

(b) The magnitude of the bony injury are sometimes overlooked and hence not appreciated in the radiographs taken during the early phase. Sometimes, bleeding into the sinuses interferes with the contrast quality of air, that is helpful in the diagnosis of midfacial injuries. Hence, it is obligatory to evaluate the magnitude of the bony injuries by careful palpation of the facial skeleton and occlusion. Examination should not be limited to mere observation of the face and examination of radiographs.

(c) In severe injuries of the midface, maintenance of patent airway during anesthesia is very important. If the maxillae are reduced but not immobilized in occlusion, they become unstable during the postoperative period. Hence, a decision must be taken whether an elective tracheostomy is necessary to facilitate proper reduction and immobilization of jaws without disturbing the occlusion.

(d) Treatment of soft tissue injuries without reduction and fixation of fractures is not a sound practice. Usually, it is very tempting to suture the soft tissue (bleeding) wounds under local anesthesia even before the clinical and radiological assessment of the fractures. If the necessary treatment of the fractured bones are undertaken later, already sutured soft-tissue wounds are jeopardized resulting in poor esthetics. If no attempt is made to restore the distorted facial skeleton, esthetic result is more pronounced.

(e) If centric occlusion alone is taken into account without stable fixation of the midfacial fractures, such fixations become unsatisfactory. Hence, immobilization in centric occlusion should be done only after satisfactory reduction and fixation of the midfacial skeleton.

(f) Sometimes, damaged vital structures like lip and rim of the ala of the nose are discarded indiscriminately during the initial phase of treatment. Wherever possible, they should be preserved.

(g) The neurological, ophthalmological, orthopedic, thoracic and cardiovascular consultations are essential for the proper management of severe facial trauma. Failure to do so will result in morbidities and sometimes mortality.

CHAPTER 10 Cysts of the Oral Cavity

GENERAL CONSIDERATIONS

Cysts are pathological cavities lined by epithelium, filled with amber colored serosanguinous fluid containing cholesterol crystals. They may involve hard and soft tissues of the oral cavity. Cysts may be of odontogenic or non-odontogenic origin. A few lesions may resemble cysts but do not fulfill these criteria. Based on these factors, cysts of the oral cavity can be classified as follows:

CLASSIFICATION

Congenital

(1) Thyroglossal cyst
(2) Dermoid cyst

Developmental

(1) *Non-odontogenic*

(a) *Fissural cysts* (Fig. 10.1)
- (i) Median cyst of the jaw
- (ii) Nasopalatine (incisive canal) cyst
- (iii) Nasoalveolar (nasolabial) cyst
- (iv) Globulomaxillary cyst

(b) *Mucous retention cysts*
- (i) Ranula
- (ii) Mucocele

(c) *Solitary bone cyst*

(d) *Aneurysmal bone cyst.*

(2) *Odontogenic*

(a) *Derived from dental lamina*
- (i) Keratocyst
- (ii) Primordial cyst
- (iii) Calcifying odontogenic cyst.

(b) *Derived from reduced enamel epithelium*
- (i) Eruption cyst
- (ii) Dentigerous cyst (follicular) coronal or lateral type (Fig. 10.3).

(c) *Derived from epithelial rests of malassez (periodontal)*
- (i) Periapical
- (ii) Lateral
- (iii) Residual.

Cyst-like lesions

(1) Hemorrhagic cyst (traumatic bone cyst)

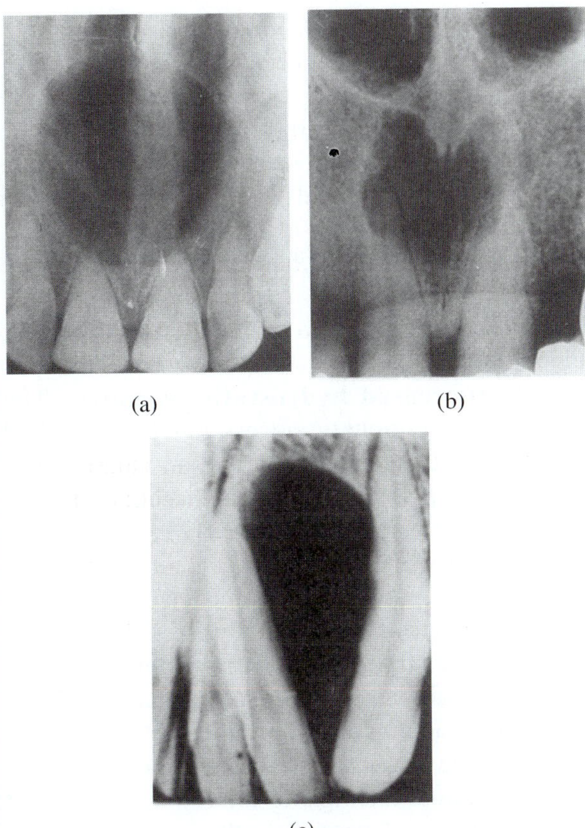

Fig. 10.1 Fissural cysts **(a)** Median palatine cyst, **(b)** Incisive canal cyst, **(c)** Globulomaxillary cyst.

(2) Static bone cysts (idiopathic or Stafne's defect)

(3) Neoplasms of the bone presenting a radiolucent appearance, e.g. ameloblastoma, angioma, myxoma, fibroma, giant cell lesion etc.

(4) Fibrous dysplasia

(5) Metabolic dysfunctions, e.g. hyperparathyroidism.

(6) Histiocytosis-X (disease of reticulo-endothelial system)

Detailed descriptions of these cysts can be found in any of the standard textbooks in oral pathology. However a brief account is furnished.

(1) Fissural cysts are believed to have developed from the enclaved epithelium. The lining is thin and friable. Hence, care is needed for the complete surgical excision. Prognosis is good if the lining is completely removed. They are usually asymptomatic. Only when they enlarge, swelling is clinically visible.

(2) Odontogenic cysts are derived either from dental lamina, reduced enamel epithelium or epithelial rests of Malassez. Cysts arising from the dental lamina have greater potential for recurrence if the surgical excision is not complete. Relatively cells derived from the epithelial cell rests have better prognosis. They tend to grow slowly. The terminology of the cysts are characteristic. Apical (dental) cyst is located at the apex of the tooth. Dentigerous cyst is seen in relation to the crown of an unerupted tooth. It is also called Follicular cyst because it develops in relation to the follicle of the developing crown. Primordial cyst derives its name since they develop in place of a tooth. Keratocyst is so named since it contains keratin flakes. Calcifying odontogenic cyst is called by the name since it is an odontogenic cyst with areas of calcification. Residual cyst is called by this name because, cyst is inadvertently left behind while extracting the tooth in relation to an odontogenic cyst.

(3) Cyst-like sessions are not true cysts by the definition. Cyst lining is lacking in this group of lesions. They are called so because they appear in the radiographs as radiolucencies.

Initiation of cyst formation

In general, there are two phases of a cyst (a) initiation of cyst formation, (b) enlargement or expansion of the cystic cavity. The mode of development is taken into consideration for the classification of cysts of the oral cavity. They are also classified based on other criteria. It has been found that the cysts with similar nature of origin have some striking resemblance in their clinical behavior. Hence, the classification based on its origin is also useful for clinical purposes. This classification furnishes the guidelines for the origin and pathogenesis of these cysts although they are based on various hypotheses.

Many theories have been formulated regarding the mechanism of cyst formation. Some of the important factors responsible for cyst formation are as follows:

(1) Proliferation of the epithelial remnants.
(2) Intracystic fluid accumulation.
(3) Resorption of bone as the fluid accumulates and epithelial lining proliferates.

The phenomenon of multiplication of epithelial cells has been identified but the initiating factor for its proliferation is only a matter of hypothesis. In case of odontogenic cysts, the epithelial "*cell rests of malassez*" lying dormant are believed to proliferate and provide the epithelial lining to the cysts. In case of developmental cysts, epithelial cells lying dormant at the fusion lines may multiply and line these cysts. Infection is considered to be the precipitating factor as a source of irritation. Once the cavity is lined by epithelial lining, it assumes the role of a semipermeable membrane allowing tissue fluid to enter the cavity but preventing the fluid to pass out of the cavity. Such continuous intracystic fluid accumulation accounts for the increased *hydrostatic pressure* above the capillary blood pressure. It is aided by increased *osmotic pressure* that attracts the fluid into the cavity. Both these factors are responsible for building up internal pressure as an important factor for the establishment and growth of the cyst. Cystic fluid is also being considered as an inflammatory exudate containing proteins with higher molecular weight. The other components include cholesterol breakdown products of RBCs and exfoliated epithelial cells.

Enlargement of cysts

Once cysts are initiated and defined, they continue to grow and enlarge in size irrespective of their nature and pathogenesis in the enlargement of the cysts. The following mechanisms may be involved:

(1) Increased hydrostatic pressure.
(2) Increased osmotic pressure.
(3) Increase in the surface area of the lining-"*mural factor*".
(4) Displacement of surrounding soft tissues or resorption of bone.

Depending on the type of the cyst, these mechanisms play their relative roles for the enlargement which ultimately define the characteristics, clinical features, postoperative behavior and prognosis of all the cysts. Hence, a brief account of the mechanism of enlargement of cysts is essential for the clear understanding of the clinical behavior and to formulate the treatment planning.

(1) **Increased hydrostatic pressure.** The principle of lymphatic access has been studied extensively. Cysts enlarge due to an imbalance of hydrostatic pressure between the contents and surrounding tissue fluids. This imbalance results in the increased osmolarity of the contained fluid. Any cavity in the body that becomes separated from lymphatic access may be subjected to osmotic imbalance resulting in pressure differences. The fluid contents of the cysts vary considerably. The cyst lining acts as a semipermeable membrane. Based on the characteristics of the fluid content of the cyst, nature attempts to dilute the cystic fluid by the passage of tissue into the cyst through the cyst lining. This adds to the total volume of fluid that is responsible for increased hydrostatic pressure. However, this depends on the osmotic pressure of the cystic contents.

(2) **Increased osmotic pressure.** It is believed that cyst lining act as a semipermeable membrane and the osmotic theory of cyst enlargement is readily and widely being accepted. Recent hypothesis states that the cystic fluid is an inflammatory exudate containing proteins with high molecular weight. Irrespective of the fact whether it is an inflammatory exudate or protein molecules entering from the surrounding tissue fluid through the cyst lining, the role played by increased osmotic pressure in the enlargement of cysts is widely accepted. Presence of large intracystic molecules like globulins, fibrinogen and fibrin degradation products are responsible for the sustained increase in osmotic pressure. However, cyst enlarges even

though it contains less fluid. This observation has led to the acceptance of another mechanism of expansion known as mural factor.

(3) **Increase in the surface area of the lining (mural factor).** In a few cysts like primordial cysts and keratocysts, the keratin plays important role than *hydrostatic and osmotic factors*. In such cases, instead of uniform expansion, cyst enlarges with finger-like projections into the surrounding cancellous bone. Perhaps, this factor determines the recurrence and the aggressive nature of the growth of a few cysts which closely resemble neoplasms in their clinical behavior. A resting epithelial cell may be activated by infections due to the action of chemical irritants. Consequently, multiplication of the epithelial cells can lead to two types of cysts. In one type, cyst lining is derived from degenerating epithelium. In the other type, cells exhibit a process of maturation and not degeneration as proved by histochemical studies. Hence, their clinical behavior widely differs. These factors must be borne in mind, during the management of cysts which enlarge by this mechanism. Because of this nature of growth, treatment also must be more radical with ample safety margin to prevent recurrence.

(4) **Resorption of bone.** The cystic lining has been experimentally found to release the "bone resorbing" factors. This observation has led to the identification of factors with osteoclastic activity like prostaglandin E2 and E3. Perhaps, difference in the quantity of release of prostaglandin is responsible for the difference in the mode of growth, typical of a few cysts. However, mechanism of prostaglandin production is not definitively known. In addition, collagenase present in the cyst wall may have some role in this mechanism.

Clinical significance of classification

Many classifications of cysts are based on clinical and radiographic features. Adjacent structures like teeth, neurovascular bundle and anatomical spaces are important considerations. Mere anatomical locations of cysts should not be considered important when compared to the nature of the cyst and precise diagnosis. The clinical behavior must correlate with diagnosis of the lesion that will have direct bearing on the nature of its management. A few cysts have been clearly identified as "recurrence-prone" cysts. These cysts are found primarily to contain keratinizing lining. They are non-inflammatory in origin, believed to arise from the residues of the dental lamina. Relative frequency of its occurrence in younger age group of patients is another factor for serious consideration. The aggressive clinical behavior suggests the increased mitotic activity at the cellular level nearly seven times more than the cysts of inflammatory origin.

DIAGNOSIS

Since most of the cysts are asymptomatic during the initial phase, they are discovered as a random finding during routine clinical and radiological examination (Fig. 10.2 a & b).

(1) Cyst should be suspected if the swelling is found to be a smooth, rounded and painless expansion of the jaw bone.

(2) Teeth in relation to the lesion is an important factor for correct diagnosis. Absence of the tooth in its position in the dental arch in young patients suggests that the lesion could be dentigerous cyst. In elderly persons, clinical absence of the tooth with a history of extraction leads to the diagnosis of residual cyst.

(3) If the swelling of similar nature is in relation to a non-vital, carious or fractured tooth, then the diagnosis is dental (periapical) cyst (Fig. 10.2 c & d).

(4) If these swellings are painful and tender, they should be suspected as infected cysts.

(5) If the swelling is hard, fast growing at the angle of the mandible producing facial asymmetry in the younger age group, provisional diagnosis of keratocyst or primordial cyst must be made.

Thus, diagnosis should be provisionally made based on the physical findings and history. If the

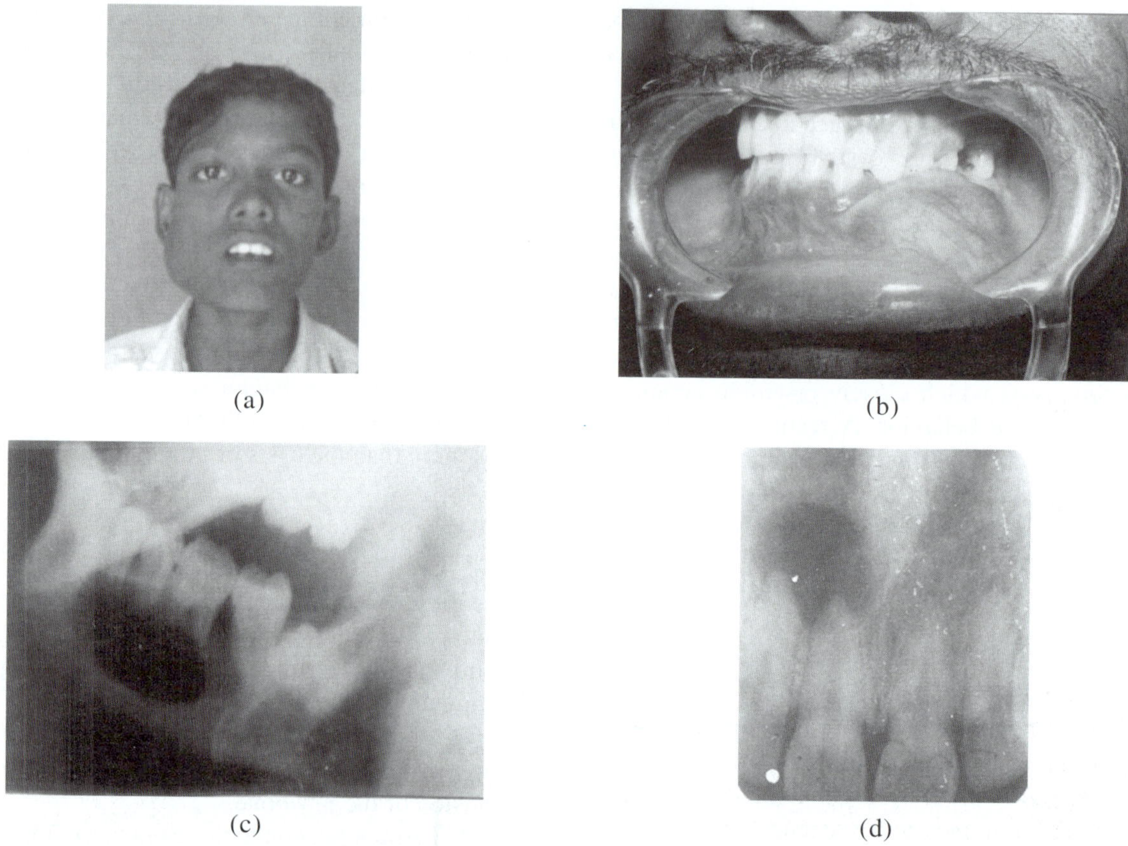

(a) (b) (c) (d)

Fig. 10.2 (a) & (b) Facial and intraoral photographs, **(c)** Dental cyst seen as a large circumscribed unilocular radiolucency in premolar and molar regions of the mandible, **(d)** Radiolucent lesion at the periapical region of maxillary incisors.

swelling has expanded considerably, clinical examinations may reveal *"egg-shell crackling"*.

On the basis of the provisional diagnosis, radiological examination and a few other investigations may be necessary to confirm the diagnosis.

(a) Aspiration

It is one of the easy investigations that the clinician can undertake before referring the patient for further evaluation. Once the needle enters the "cystic" cavity, the nature of the swelling could be confirmed depending on the nature of the contents, aspirated from the "cystic" cavity. If it is solid, aspiration is negative. Aspiration of "cystic" fluid and demonstration of cholesterol clinch the diagnosis. Dentigerous cyst and periapical cysts yield clear, straw-colored fluid containing cholesterol crystals. If the syringe is held under a beam of light, these crystals are bright and glistening. Keratocysts yield creamy white suspension of keratin. Aspiration of fresh blood gives a warning signal for a vascular lesion.

(b) Estimation of proteins in the cyst fluid

It underlines the role of early diagnosis in allowing

a proper surgical approach to the lesions like keratocysts. Diagnosis is usually confirmed through biopsy. But sometimes they are notoriously unsatisfactory. Hence, the fluid that is aspirated can as well be analyzed for estimation of proteins. Simple paper electrophoresis will reveal that fluid from keratocysts will be low in soluble protein content. The fluid can be centrifuged to estimate soluble protein. If the protein level is less than 4 gm/100 ml, then it is possible that the lesion is an odontogenic keratocyst. If the level is more than 4 gm/100 ml, then the fluid is probably derived from the other types of cysts.

(c) Cytology smear from the aspirated fluid

It is also found useful to detect the presence of keratinized squamae. Considering the clinician's assessment, a reasonably accurate preoperative diagnosis is possible.

(d) Radiological evaluation (Figs 10.3 -10.5)

In fact, the radiological evaluation is essential for diagnosing these lesions as cysts. Usually for apical lesions, periapical radiographs are essential. For larger lesions, lateral oblique view of the mandible and orthopantomograms are useful to define the

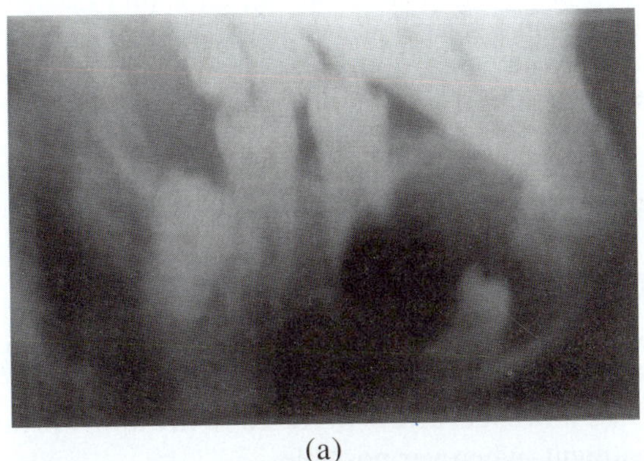

(a)

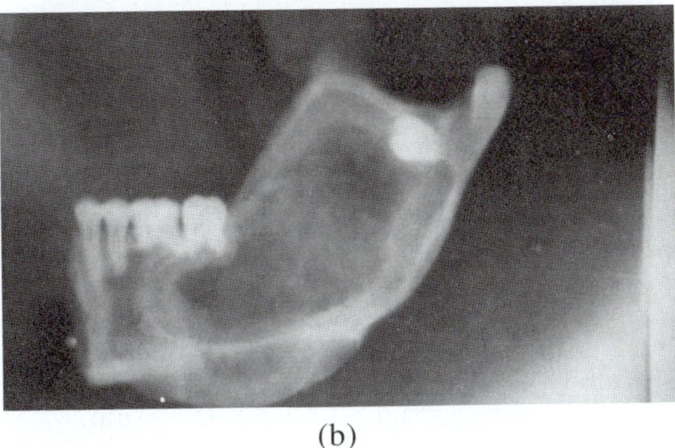

(b)

Fig. 10.3 Dentigerous cyst involving **(a)** An unerupted premolar tooth near the lower border of the mandible, **(b)** Unerupted third molar near the condyle.

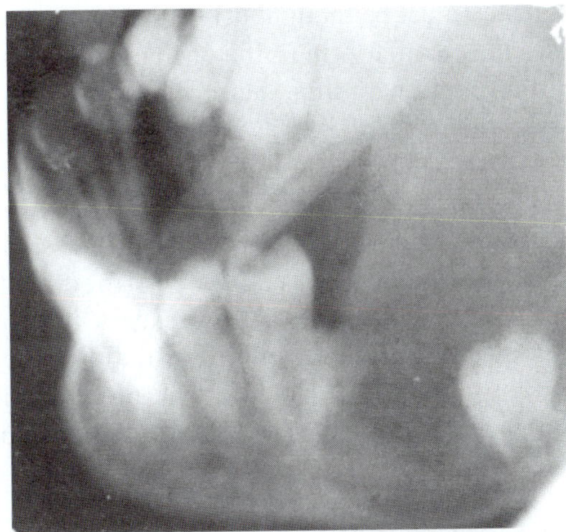

Fig. 10.4 Dental cyst in the body of right mandible.

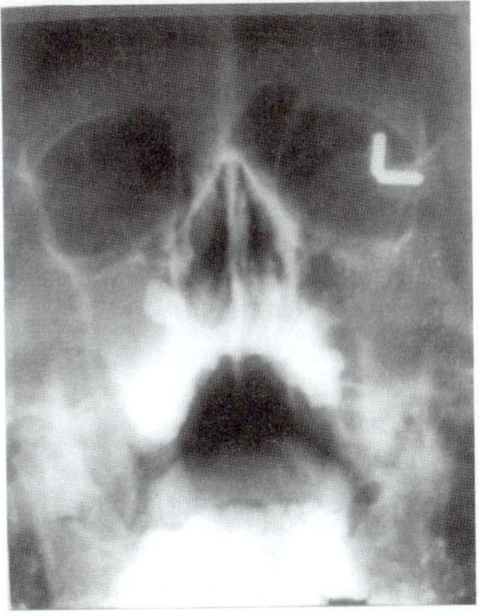

Fig. 10.5 Cyst in relation to left posterior teeth involving maxillary sinus.

size, site, extension and the marginal outline of the cystic lesions. Cysts are described as *well-circumscribed radiolucent* lesions. The neurovascular bundle in the mandible is seen to be displaced by the cysts. As the cyst grows, radiolucency increases due to the destruction of the cortical bone and not due to cancellous bone destruction. Chronic infection of the cystic sac results in a noticeable zone of sclerosis of the bone at the periphery of the cystic cavity. This is responsible for the well-circumscribed appearance. If the bone resorption is irregular, the possibility of malignancy must be thought off. If the cystic cavity invades the maxillary sinus, the opaque image forms part of a sphere with thin, dense, linear outline. As the cyst enlarges in size, it displaces the adjacent teeth with or without resorption of roots. Keratocyst, at the angle of the mandible, may extend backwards towards the ramus and coronoid process. The radiolucency is more readily confined to the medullary cavity. If the cyst presents irregular enlargement, it produces multiple radiolucencies resembling a multilocular cyst. The presence of a tooth inside the cystic cavity confirms the diagnosis of dentigerous cyst.

(e) Histopathological examination

In spite of all these investigations, histopathological evaluation only provides conclusive evidence to confirm the diagnosis. If the cyst is small, excision biopsy of the lining is indicated. If the cyst is very large and is in association with anatomical areas, incisional biopsy is performed to confirm the diagnosis. It is better to keep the opening patent so that cavity is kept in a decompressed state. Depending on the diagnosis, treatment is undertaken.

MANAGEMENT

The untreated cysts tend to increase in size gradually. If it is allowed to grow indefinitely, it will weaken the jaw bone. Trivial injury or attempted dental extraction may result in pathological fracture.

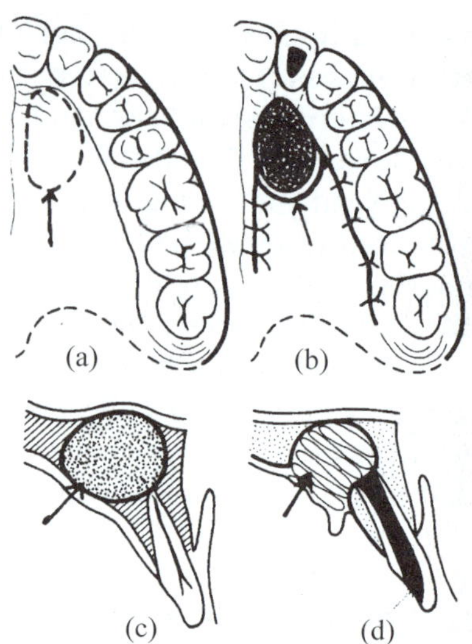

Fig. 10.6 (a) Palatal view of the incisor region with dental cyst involving lateral incisior-preoperative, **(b)** Palatal view after the enucleation of the cyst, root canal filling of lateral incisor with bony cavity packed with roller gauze, **(c)** Preoperative side view, **(d)** Postoperative side view.

Principles of management

(1) Decompression of the intracystic pressure.

(2) Elimination of the cystic lining.

(3) Preservation of teeth with appropriate treatment, wherever possible.

(4) Preservation of the neighboring anatomical structures like inferior dental canal, nasal cavity, maxillary sinus and teeth.

(5) Prevention of the recurrence of the cyst.

(6) To monitor the involved teeth during the postoperative phase until regeneration of bone is complete (Figs 10.6).

OPERATIVE PROCEDURES (Figs 10.7 – 10.11)

The epithelial lined pathological cavities can be treated in any one of the following methods:

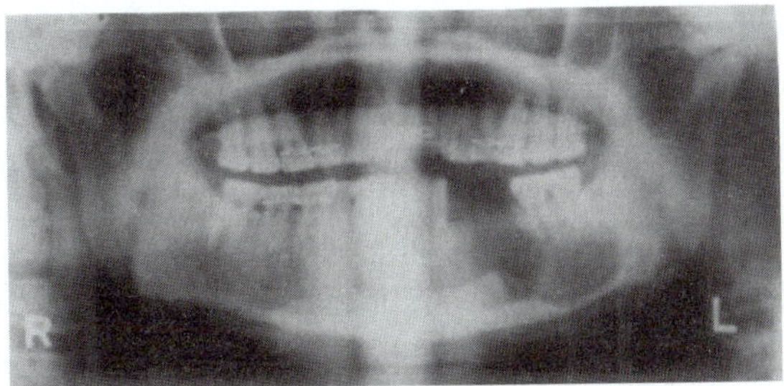

Fig. 10.7 Marsupialization.

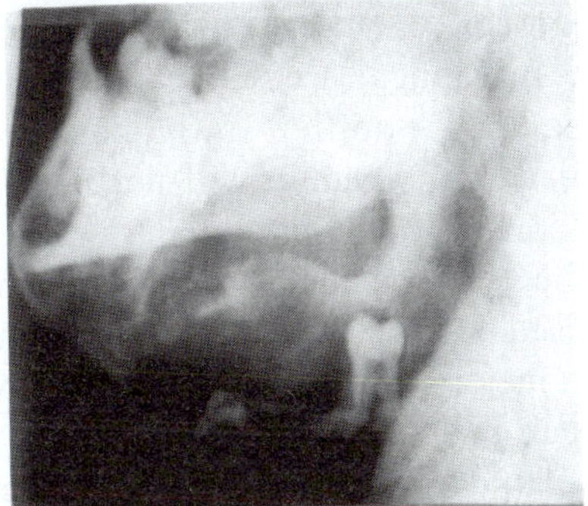

Fig. 10.8 Cyst–Mandible–Preoperative.

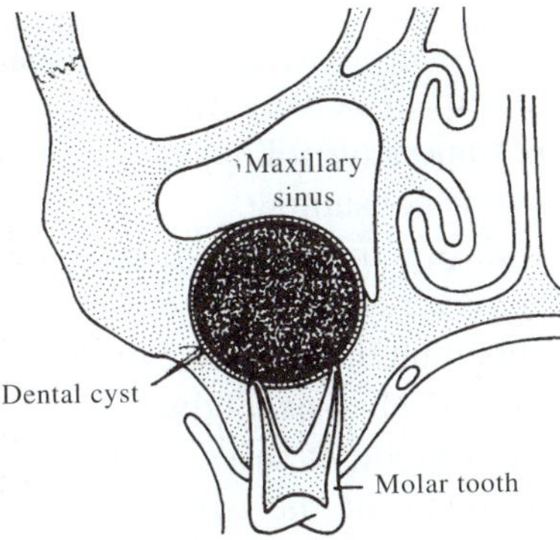

Fig. 10.9 Dental cyst in relation to molar tooth, pushing the antral wall into the maxillary sinus.

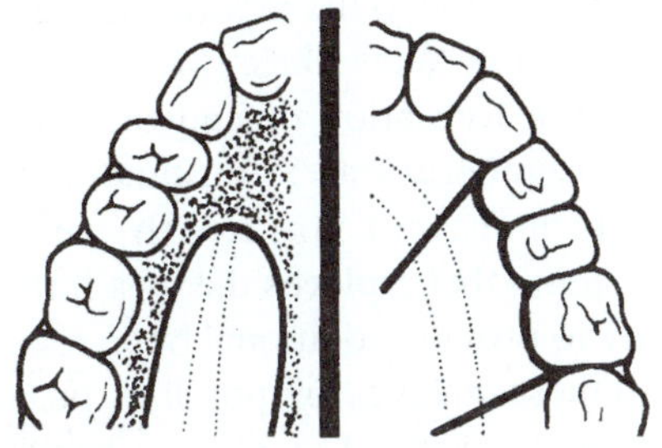

Fig. 10.10 Correct and wrong incisions in the palate.

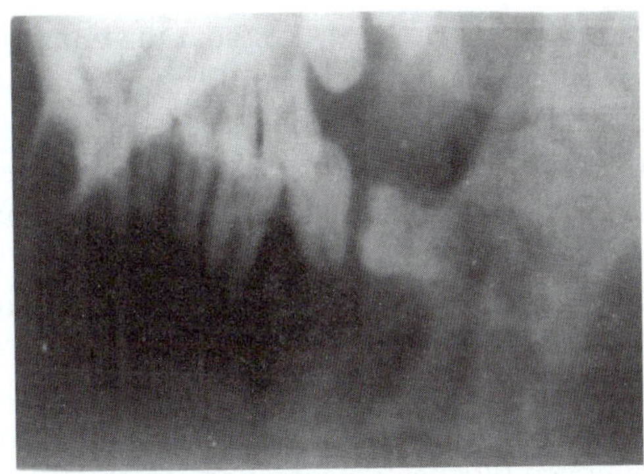

Fig. 10.11 Cyst involving II & III molars.

(1) Enucleation of the cyst and primary closure.

(2) Marsupialization of the cyst and healing by secondary intention (granulation) (Fig. 10.7).

(3) Modification by a two staged procedure.

I phase	:	Marsupialization
II phase	:	Enucleation and primary closure after the cavity shrinks.

Marsupialization

This word takes its origin from the term "marsupial". Healing of the cyst by this method resembles marsupials like kangaroo. The design of this technique ensures the patency of the opening created on the cyst wall for the purpose of decompression until the cavity is obliterated by the filling up of the cavity by bone regeneration in layers. As layers of bone are formed, the cavity becomes shallower until the floor of the cavity gradually comes to the surface. Based on these principles, the marsupialization procedure is done in the following manner:

(1) Preoperatively, the extent of the cystic cavity is evaluated by clinical and radiological examination. This is useful to design the mucoperiosteal flap and the bony window (Fig. 10.13).

(2) Incision is made deep to the bone and the

soft tissue flap is elevated to expose the bony wall.

(3) A window is created on the bony wall with a chisel and mallet or with bur.

(4) The fluid content of the cyst is evacuated.

(5) The cyst lining and the soft tissue around the opening are sutured together.

(6) The cavity is packed with ribbon gauze soaked with Whitehead's varnish.

(7) The cavity is periodically irrigated and pack is renewed once in 2 or 3 days until the entire cavity is obliterated by bone regeneration.

Both these procedures - enucleation and marsupialization - are fundamentally different in many ways. Consequently, indications, contraindications, technique, advantage and disadvantages also differ.

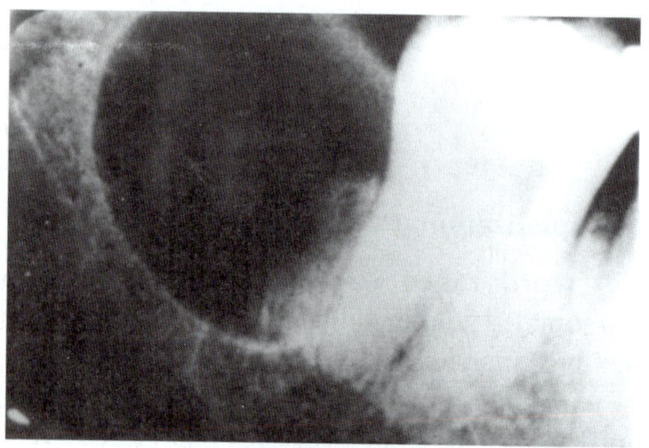

Fig. 10.12 Primordial cyst

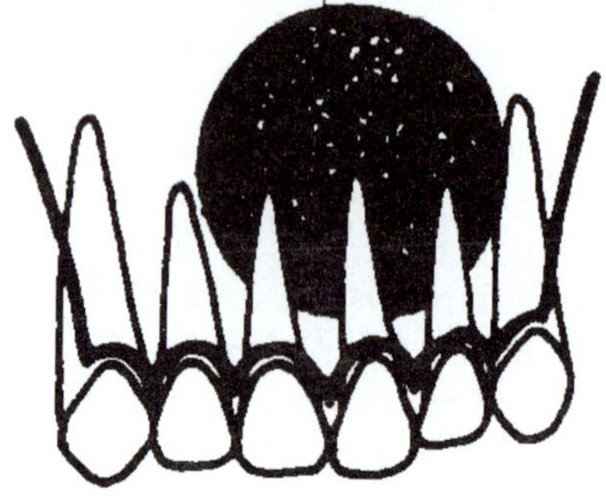

Fig. 10.13 A large dental cyst involving the four anterior teeth–Flap design.

Indications for marsupialization

(1) If cyst is very large, possibilities of leaving behind a part of the lining from inaccessible areas exist. Depending on the extension, bone is weakened so that pathological fracture may occur. Hence, in such cases, marsupialization is indicated.

(2) In younger patients, dentigerous cysts may involve unerupted teeth. Marsupialization permits the eruption of unerupted teeth.

(3) Similarly, when the cyst is too large involving anatomical areas like maxillary sinus, neurovascular bundle and nasal cavity, marsupialization procedure will not interfere with these anatomical structures.

(4) The elderly patients are mostly medically compromised. Hence, these patients may not be fit to undergo major surgery like enucleation of a large cyst. In such patients, marsupialization is an ideal procedure that can be completed as an office procedure under local anesthesia.

Disadvantages

(1) Marsupialized cystic cavities require periodical postoperative follow-up for a long period. Hence, it is time consuming.

(2) By doing this procedure, pathological process is allowed to continue even after surgery. This is an important disadvantage of this procedure.

However, if this procedure is carried out (wherever indicated), it serves the purpose well. Once the contents of the cyst are evacuated, it results in the decompression of the cavity. Hence, there is a tendency for the remaining part of the cyst lining to contract due to the myofibroblasts present. As the contraction takes place, the resultant space is filled by the formation of endosteal bone as a process of regeneration. Simultaneously, there appears a marginal ingrowth of normal mucoperiosteum that replaces the cyst lining. It has the capacity to provide additional bone regenerative factors. All these changes are possible, provided the opening remains patent. Larger the opening, faster is the healing and obliteration of the cavity. It is necessary to irrigate the cavity to prevent any stagnation of food debris. It also prevents premature closure of the opening. It is surprising to note that a substantial part of the cystic cavity obliterates during the healing process.

The antagonists of this procedure vigorously advocate the cyst enucleation because of the inherent advantages of total elimination of pathological lining and healing by primary intention. But in reality, this may present many practical difficulties as the size of the cyst is of greater dimension.

Enucleation and primary closure

This procedure essentially consists of complete removal of the cyst-lining and primary closure of the wound so that bony cavity is allowed to obliterate by the regeneration of bone. On an average, such a healing is completed in 6 to 9 months period depending on the size of the cyst cavity.

(1) Mucoperiosteal flap is raised to gain access into the cystic cavity. Incision is planned in such a way that the future suture line rests on the normal bone so that mucoperiosteal flap heals well.

(2) After the flap is elevated, the area of bony expansion is identified. At the thinned out bony wall, a window is made to gain entry into the cyst. If the cyst wall is of equal thickness, a series of holes are made in an oval fashion and all the holes are joined by a fissure bur. The other way is to use chisel and mallet to make an opening through the wall. Depending on the need, the window can be enlarged with Rongeur's forceps. Thus, the cystic sac is widely exposed.

(3) A plane of cleavage is utilized between the cyst lining and the bony wall to dissect out the cystic sac in one piece along with the contents, out of the bony wall and it is subjected to histopathological examination.

(4) If any tooth or root is involved in the cyst the necessary treatment for that tooth is carried out either by extraction or by apicoectomy with apical seal.

(5) Now, the cavity is cleaned and the bony margins are smoothened. After the hemostasis is achieved, the flap is repositioned.

(6) The wound margins are closed with interrupted sutures. The cavity fills up with blood clot. In due course of time, the blood clot gets organized and leads to the regeneration of the bone.

(7) Sutures are removed on the 6th or 7th postoperative day. The routine antibiotic therapy and analgesics will take care of postoperative infection and pain respectively. In the normal course, the cavity should heal slowly.

Modified procedures

In order to overcome the disadvantages of both these procedures and also to derive the advantages respectively, a moderate approach has been suggested wherein the procedure is done in two stages. During the first stage, cyst is marsupialized and it is allowed to shrink in size. In the second stage, the patient is taken up for cyst enucleation once the cyst shrinks to a manageable size. The stage at which enucleation is to be done is only relative. Hence, the decision is left to the choice of the operator and convenience of the patient. The benefit of decompression is derived during the early phase. During the second stage, cyst lining is totally eliminated. This, a compromised procedure as suggested by Waldron, is called Waldron's procedure.

Present concepts

If the cyst is small, it is enucleated. If the operator has doubt about the possibility of leaving behind part of the cyst lining either because of inadequacy of surgical capability of the operator or because of the extensive nature of the cyst, Waldron's procedure is practiced. This is a very valuable procedure if the cyst is too large and involves the anatomical structures like maxillary sinus. The

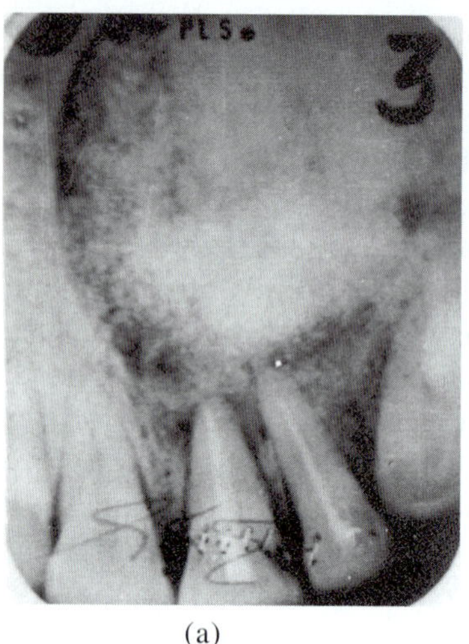
(a)

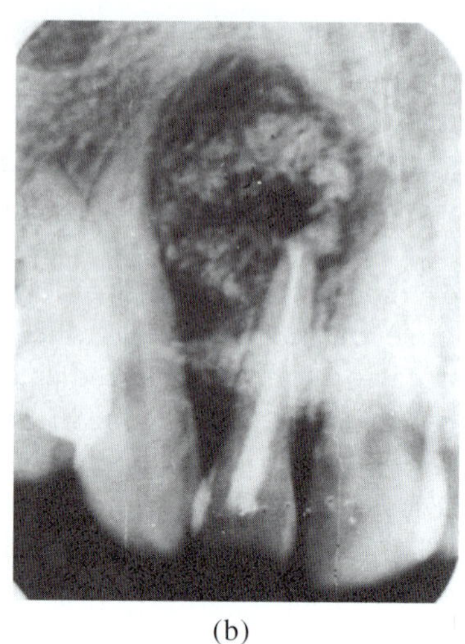
(b)

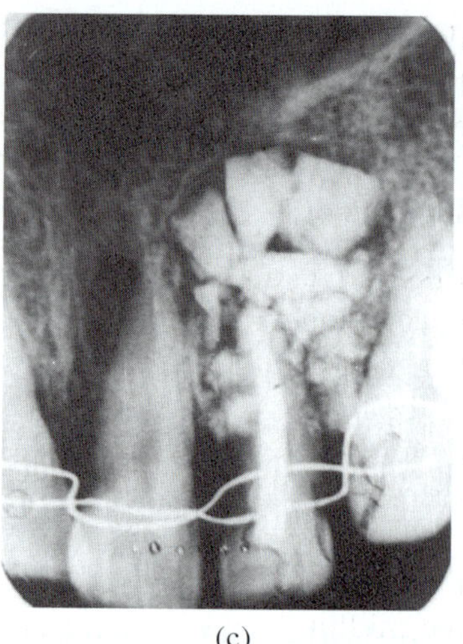
(c)

Fig. 10.14 (a), (b), (c) Root canal filling, cyst enucleation, cavity filled with bone substitutes and primary closure.

operator can avoid the creation of oroantral fistula, oronasal fistula, and damage to important structures by adopting this modified procedure. Since indications and timing of both the stages are purely relative, there are no contraindications for this procedure.

Enucleation and bone grafting

In practice, it has been found that highly vascular periosteum and endosteum of the jaws possess remarkable capacity for regeneration of bone. Even if a surgeon is confident of enucleating the cyst in toto, the cyst enucleation may not be successful in case the cavity is too large. Hence, too large a hematoma is liable to break down during the healing process. To overcome this, surgeons have attempted to fill the bone cavity with cancellous bone chips or bone substitutes before the primary closure. This increases the osteogenic potential of the cavity considerably. Wherever autotransplantation of bone is not feasible, surgeons have attempted to utilize a variety of materials like absorbable hemostatic materials, stored bone of various types and many other bone substitutes with variable success (Fig. 10.14). Although definite indications exist for these procedures, operator must carefully select the methods depending on the individual cases and the surgical skills of the operator.

In general, cysts of the oral cavity, irrespective of their origin, location and clinical features, are treated by any of the four techniques-namely (a) enucleation, (b) marsupialization, (c) Waldron's procedure, (d) enucleation with packing of bone or bone substitutes.

CLINICAL VARIATIONS

Thyroglossal cysts

Thyroid gland development originates from the junction of anterior two-thirds and posterior one-third of the tongue. The point of origin is called *foramen cecum*. The thyroglossal duct is a transient structure of developmental origin extending from the dorsum of the tongue to the area where thyroid gland develops. Once thyroid develops, thyroglossal duct epithelium is supposed to disappear. If persistent epithelium of thyroglossal duct is stimulated, thyroglossal cyst may develop and occupy any of the locations between the tongue and thyroid gland. Clinical features, location and histopathology, confirm the diagnosis. Treatment is enucleation.

Fissural cysts (Fig. 10.1)

Fissural cysts grow very slowly. They are uncommon cysts of developmental origin. They are believed to develop from the epithelial remnants at the fusion lines of various processes during the development of face. These cysts are termed accordingly depending on the respective locations.

(1) **Median cysts of the jaws.** The mandibular mesenchyme migrates from both sides and fuse in the midline to form the mandibular arch. At the fusion line, if the persisting epithelium is stimulated, cysts can develop between the two roots of incisors. They can be mistaken for residual apical cysts of deciduous dentition or later periodontal cyst. Vitality test will prove that it is of non-odontogenic origin.

(2) **Nasopalatine (incisive canal) cyst.** This is the most common type of the fissural cyst. It may develop at the junction between the primary palate (upper lip) and both the lateral palatine processes of maxilla. The incisive canal is formed at this location for the passage of long sphenopalatine nerves and vessels. The cyst at this location produces a cavity, posterior to the interincisor space of maxillary teeth. As the cyst enlarges in size, it appears as a swelling in the region of the incisive papilla. Radiologically, it appears in the midline of the maxilla as a well-defined ovoid or heart-shaped radiolucency, behind the central incisors. Histologically, cyst is lined by oral epithelium (stratified squamous epithelium) or respiratory epithelium (pseudostratified columnar epithelium) or both. The connective tissue contains large nerves and blood vessels.

(3) **Nasoalveolar cyst.** It arises at the labial sulcus under the ala of the nose. As it grows in size, nasolabial fold gets obliterated and bulge is seen in the inferior meatus. They are located outside the alveolar bone (extraosseus). Probably epithelium at the junction of median and lateral nasal processes may be the cells of origin. Due to its enlargement pressure resorption of the labial aspect of the alveolus is possible. Radiographically, it cannot be recognized unless any radioopaque material is injected inside the cyst cavity.

(4) **Globulomaxillary cyst.** It is a rare developmental entity arising from the epithelial remnants at the junction of maxillary and median nasal process. It can be confused with periodontal cysts arising from lateral incisor. It has a characteristic pear shape seen at the interdental space between vital maxillary lateral incisor and canine teeth. Since these cysts have thin and friable lining, complete enucleation may not be possible.

All these fissural cysts can be surgically enucleated. They usually do not recur, if they are excised completely.

Odontogenic keratocysts

These lesions are unique among the odontogenic cysts because of the characteristic microscopic features, aggressive behavior and high recurrence rate. The reported incidence is around 7 to 10% among the odontogenic cysts. It appears to be common among males. The term "odontogenic keratocyst" was coined originally for the odontogenic cysts that demonstrated keratinization of the epithelial components. WHO defined this lesion as "a synonym to primordial cyst, arising from the tooth-bearing areas of the jaws, more common in mandible, characterized by a thin, fibrous capsule and a line of keratinized squamous epithelium rarely exceeding 5 cells thick and having no rete pegs." This lesion represents a specific type of non-inflammatory odontogenic cysts believed to originate from the primordial epithelium - dental lamina - with distinctive histopathological features, aggressive behavior and remarkable potential for its recurrence. The odontogenic cysts are classified according to the nature of stimuli responsible for the epithelial proliferation. While epithelial cell rests are the sources of inflammation in the inflammatory radicular cysts, follicular cysts develop by passive pooling of fluid between the follicle and the crown of an unerupted tooth. But odontogenic keratocysts are distinguished from other odontogenic cysts by the histological appearance. The epithelial cells exhibit increased mitotic index but very similar to ameloblastoma. Epithelial cell rests of the dental lamina are believed to be the cell of origin in the pathogenesis of keratocysts. Dental lamina has the ability for proliferation, keratinization and infiltration into the connective tissue during odontogenesis. Some research workers have hypothesized that basal cells of oral epithelium could be the cells of origin for the lesion. Protein and immunoglobulin content of their fluids and higher prostaglandin content of the cyst wall are responsible for the difference in their clinical behavior. The epithelium is parakeratinized or orthokeratinized. Keratocysts with orthokeratin lining have a much lower incidence of recurrence than with parakeratinized lesions.

This lesion occurs in all the age groups but more common during the second and third decades of life found at the angle and ramus of the mandible. They usually remain undetected and may be discovered through random radiological examination. By that time, the lesion would have become extensive. Usually, they remain symptomless until secondarily infected. The cyst extends along the medullary space of the mandible without producing much of cortical expansion. Radiologically, it may present unilocular or bilocular radiolucency. Multilocular lesions are differentiated from ameloblastoma only by histopathological examinations. It may also be associated with unerupted tooth resembling a dentigerous cyst. When no tooth is involved, it may be diagnosed as primordial cyst. Sometimes, the involved roots may undergo resorption.

The lining is characterized by its thick creamy white caseous material. It resembles pus but lacks the characteristic foul smell. It increases rapidly in its extension. It is notorious for its aggressive growth and recurrence. The clinical behavior is very erratic.

The high incidence of recurrence is attributed to the following factors:

(1) Cyst lining is thin and fragile. Hence, during enucleation, part of the lining may be left behind.

(2) Many satellite daughter cysts may exist which may not be clinically identifiable. Each satellite cyst is capable of growing independently. Under these circumstances, small monocystic lesions are indicated for enucleation. Large and recurrent cysts need more radical procedures. Ameloblastic or malignant transformation of the cyst lining have also been reported in the literature. Hence, it is preferable to extensively study the cyst lining from various parts of the cyst histopathologically (serial sections). Patient must be periodically reviewed clinically and radiologically. The patient must be warned about the possibility of recurrence even after exceptionally long intervals.

(3) The lesions with bony expansion or perforation through the cortical plate may result in recurrence due to the difficulty to excise the thin cyst lining completely.

(4) Keratocysts associated with basal cell syndrome are reported to have higher recurrence rate.

(5) These cysts with orthokeratin lining recur when compared to the cysts with parakeratinization.

Primordial cyst

Primordial cyst is an epithelial lined cyst in the jaws not associated with unerupted teeth. It is believed to develop prior to the development of a tooth. Incomplete removal may result in recurrence of the cyst. The cyst lining has a great potential for ameloblastic change.

Calcifying odontogenic cyst

Calcifying odontogenic cyst is a rare lesion presenting as unilocular or multilocular cyst. In both the forms, dental primordial tissues may be induced to develop multiple small odontomes. Hence, some may include this lesion as a variety of odontogenic tumors. This lesion commonly occurs in the anterior part of the mandible during the second decade of life. It usually presents itself as a painless swelling with intraosseous lesion producing a hard bony expansion. Lingual extension may occur. In its initial stages, it is accidentally discovered as a random radiological finding seen to originate from the interdental space, resulting in displacement or resorption of roots. Histologically, the epithelial lining is 5-8 cells thick. Basal layers of cells are cuboidal or columnar. The nuclei are seen away from the basement membrane. Sometimes, this lesion may be diagnosed as keratocyst. “Ghost cells” appear with tendency to calcify. Unlike keratocysts, this lesion can be treated by enucleation successfully since recurrence is rare.

It has been found to exhibit extreme diversity in its clinical and histopathological features and biological behavior. Although majority of these lesions are cystic in architecture and appear to be non-neoplastic, some of them appear as solid lesions and apparently neoplastic in nature. Because of the diversity, there has been confusion and disagreement in the terminology. In 1971, WHO described this lesion as a “non-neoplastic” cystic lesion. In 1992, WHO deleted the term “non-neoplastic” and classified the lesion as a benign odontogenic neoplasm.

To resolve this controversy, these lesions are suggested as “cystic” and “solid” with solid lesions as neoplastic lesions. Such a view will help the practitioner to carryout an appropriate treatment of these lesions - whether cystic or solid. All solid lesions deserve the treatment very similar to ameloblastomas.

Traumatic bone cyst

Traumatic bone cyst is an incidental radiological finding. They are also called hemorrhagic cyst, simple bone cyst, progressive bone cavity and extravasation cyst. There is a lack of agreement on the terminology of this lesion. Similarly, etiology is yet to be completely explained. Several hypotheses have been suggested. The occurrence of microtrauma may lead to subsequent intramedullary hemorrhage, then osteoclastic activity and the elimination of trabeculae in the medially bone. This is the most widely accepted pathogenesis and hence called traumatic bone cyst. They are asymptomatic, most common in children and adolescents. Very rarely, cortical expansion has been reported in the literature. The teeth in the region remain vital. Root resorption or mobility never occurs. Two types of such lesions have been identified:

(1) Latent
(2) Progressive

Radiologically, it may appear as unilocular or multilocular, well demarcated radiolucency with scalloped margins, extending between the teeth. Diagnosis can be confirmed only during surgery since aspiration proves negative. Once a window is made, the cavity is seen characteristically empty. Histopathology is not possible since empty cavity is encountered during surgery. The treatment is as follows:

(1) Surgical exploration.

(2) Curettage to stimulate intraosseous bleeding.

(3) Gelfoam packing of the cyst or bone grafting or injection of autogenous blood into the cavity to stimulate osteogenesis.

(4) Primary closure of the wound.

Endodontic Surgery

GENERAL CONSIDERATIONS

Endodontic surgery is defined as a surgical aid to treat endodontic problems. Aetius, a Greek physician, was the first to incise an acute apical abscess. Hullihan (1839) later refined and popularized it. G.V. Black (1886) and others described "root amputation" as a radical cure for the chronic abscess in root filled teeth. Today, endodontic surgery in root filled teeth has a definite role to eliminate periapical pathology. As it is common with all the successful techniques, part of the success is due to its simplicity. All periapical lesions do not require surgery. Similarly, root canal therapy alone cannot be the treatment of choice. There seems to be a mistaken belief that "small lesions" are to be managed conservatively while "large lesions" are best treated surgically.

The International Classification of Diseases (ICD-WHO) lists five entities of periapical disease. Chronic apical periodontitis and radicular cyst are diagnosed primarily, based on radiographic features while clinical manifestations are predominant for the other three - (i) acute periodontitis, periapical abscess (ii) with or (iii) without sinus. The standard radiology textbooks describe the radiographic features of the first two lesions as an increased area of radiolucency in relation to the root apex. Sclerotic reactions are sometimes diagnosed on the basis of increased radioopacity. Recently, the common periapical radiographic changes are described in the following manner:

(1) Widening of periodontal space
(2) Discontinuity in lamina dura
(3) Thickening of lamina dura
(4) Periapical rarefying osteitis
(5) Periapical condensing osteitis
(6) Rarefying and condensing osteitis.

With the availability of a wider spectrum of antibiotics, rapid strides in the precise techniques of root canal therapy and better understanding of the nature of periapical pathosis, there is no scope for speculation on the role of endodontics or endodontic surgery since one does not replace the other. Surgery should not be considered as a "cover-up" for the lack of skill of root canal therapy. The endodontic surgical procedures could be classified in the following manner:

CLASSIFICATION

(1) *Incision and drainage*
(2) *Periapical surgery*

(a) Curettage
(b) Apicoectomy
(c) Retrograde filling

(3) *Postoperative evaluation - alternate methods*
(a) Reimplantation
(b) Endodontic implants

Incision and drainage

This procedure is carried out to drain the pus and toxins from the periapical region under antibiotic cover so that the patient is relieved of discomfort, pain and swelling. Healing process is directly proportional to the drainage of toxic material. The surgical intervention avoids the spontaneous drainage and the resultant cutaneous fistula. The success depends on the timing of the procedure. The optimum time to intervene is when the abscess is soft and fluctuant. It is preferable to drain under block anesthesia since infiltration will result in failure of anesthesia, increased pain and spread of infection.

Periapical surgery

This includes root amputation, curettage and retrograde filling. To gain entry into the inaccessible *"apical delta"*, root amputation is necessary. To avoid percolation of infected material from the root canal into the apical region, effective retrograde filling is essential. In practice, all these three procedures (root amputation, curettage and retrograde filling) are carried out as part of apicoectomy.

Indications

(1) *Predisposing factors for the failure of conservative root canal therapy*
(a) Unfavorable curved root apex.
(b) Root resorption.
(c) Accessory root canals.
(d) Apical third root fracture.
(e) Cyst formation.

(2) *Failure following root canal therapy*
(a) Inadequate or overfilled root canal.
(b) Fragmentation of the instruments inside the root canal.
(c) Persistent postoperative discomfort.
(d) Lateral perforation at the apical third of the root.
(e) Persistent periapical radiolucency.

(3) *Inaccessibility to "conservative root canal therapy"*
(a) Porcelain jacket crown or postcrown.
(b) Anatomical defects like dens in dente.
(c) Calcified root canal.
(d) Nonvital teeth used as abutments for bridges.
(e) Broken R.C.T. instruments in the root canal.

Contraindications

(1) *Anatomical considerations*
(a) Surgical inaccessibility, e.g. molars (palatal roots).
(b) Short root (amputation will further reduce the tooth anchorage).
(c) Inadequate or poor bony support due to advanced periodontal disease.
(d) Proximity of the root apex to anatomical structures like mental foramen, inferior alveolar canal, nasal or antral floor.

(2) *Systemic disorders*
(a) First trimester of pregnancy.
(b) Uncontrolled diabetes, heart disease, hypertension, kidney, liver and hemorrhagic disorders.
(c) Focal sepsis consideration.
(d) Emotional and uncooperative patients.

Surgical anatomy

(1) Reflection of mucoperiosteal flap should not be extended beyond the muscle attachment (vestibule) above the root apices to avoid troublesome postoperative hematoma.

(2) Proximity to nasal or antral floor must be remembered since over-zealous removal of bone may result in oronasal or oroantral fistula.

(3) Proximity to mental foramen and inferior dental canal may predispose to postoperative paresthesia due to nerve damage.

Surgical pathology

Fish (1936) in his hypothesis, identified four distinct zones around a focus of infection. A clear understanding of this concept is essential to conceive the rationale of endodontic surgery.

(a) *Zone of infection* around the focus of infection is characterized by accumulation of polymorphs. Microorganisms are present in this area.

(b) *Zone of contamination* surrounds the zone of infection where lacunae appear empty due to autolysis of dead osteocytes. This zone is characterized by marked round-cell infiltration.

(c) *Zone of irritation* presents an area of activity to promote repair. There is considerable dilution of toxins in this zone, characterized by the presence of histiocytes and osteoclasts.

(d) *Zone of stimulation* is filled with fibroblasts and osteoclasts where toxins are mild enough to be a stimulant.

The *zone of infection* is inside the root canal at the root apex and the other three zones are at the periapical alveolar bone. The success of endodontic treatment depends not only on the surgical skill of the operator but also on the logical approach based on sound endodontic principles. The main aim of the root canal filling is to cleanse the root canal and obturation of the apical constriction. With the elimination of the microorganisms at the zone of infection, the surrounding zones of contamination and irritation gradually recede. This emphasizes the importance of an effective apical seal of the apical constriction, acting as a physiological barrier. By presenting the toxins from the root canal to react with the apical alveolar bone, the defense mechanism helps to resolve the periapical pathology. In this direction, endodontic surgery is helpful to eliminate the zones of contamination and irritation and also to establish an effective apical seal.

Preoperative assessment. Since the patient is to undergo a surgical procedure, the patient's condition should be evaluated for fitness to undergo surgery. The success depends on thorough preoperative assessment of the individual case for fitness to carry out periapical surgery. Some of the important factors to be considered are as follows:

(1) Careful examination of the periapical radiograph to identify (a) the nature of the periapical region like curved apex, (b) presence of foreign bodies like excess root filling and broken instruments, (c) erosion of the root apex, (d) shape and size of the periapical radiolucency, (e) bony support of the tooth and (f) length of the root.

(2) In young patients, healing of the wound will be fast but age is reflected in the degree of apical development.

(3) Periodontal condition of the affected tooth.

(4) Presence of chronic sinus.

(5) Presence of traumatic occlusion and associated gingival recession.

(6) Pulpal and periodontal status of the adjoining teeth.

Preoperative preparation of the mouth

(1) In acute or subacute stage, surgery must be restricted to drainage.

(2) Preoperatively, root canal is opened and the root canal treatment is done in the routine manner.

(3) When the infection passes into the chronic phase, canal is biomechanically prepared and the appropriate root filling is done immediately before surgery. Although it is tempting to do the root canal filling during surgery, it is better to carry out earlier since toxic materials will be carried into the operating site if surgery and root filling are done together.

P = 100 × (1 - C/L)

(*Note*: C represents length of the root resected in mm, L represents length of the root in mm before the root resection. The cut surface of the retained root must be bevelled towards the labial plate. This helps in the insertion of the retrograde filling. (Fig. 11.9) Care is taken to avoid damage to the adjoining sorts.

The tissue removed from the periapical region must be examined histopathologically to determine the nature of the lesion.

(4) **Retrograde filling.** Proper cleaning, preparation, disinfection of the root canal and appropriate root filling of the apical third of the root canal that seals the apical foramen adequately are the essential requirements for the success. But timing of the root filling in relation to endodontic surgery is debatable. Irrespective of the root filling before or after root section, preparation and sterilization of the root apex is essential. Retrograde filling is done during periapical surgery to achieve an apical seal. This is to overcome the problems like impracticability of coronal approach, procedural accidents, inaccessibility by routine methods and to prevent the leakage of toxins into the periapical tissues from the root apex. (Fig. 11.10).

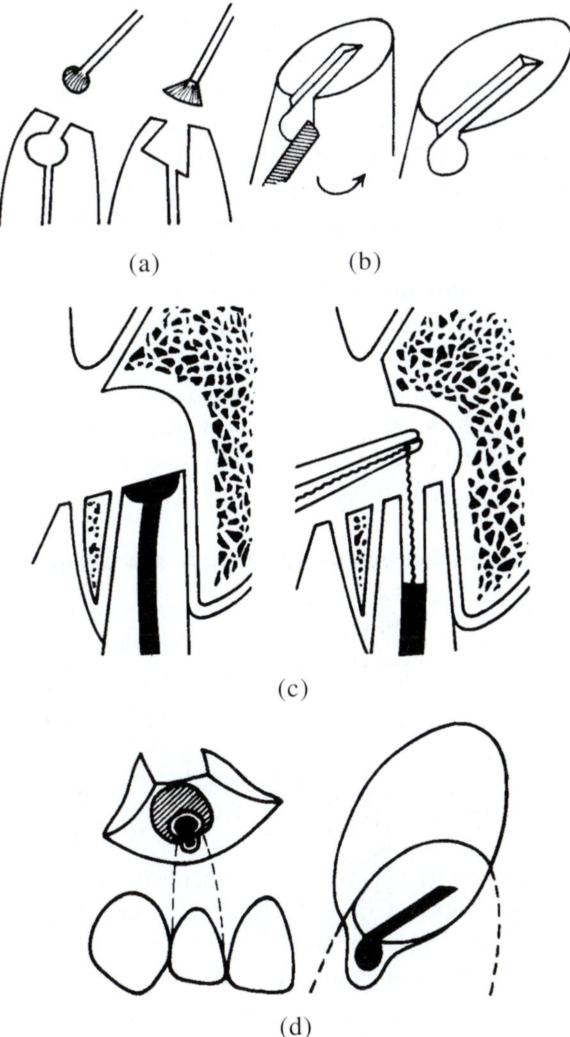

Fig. 11.10 (a) – (d) Retrograde filling - root preparation.

The difficulties commonly encountered during the retrograde root canal filling may arise from

(a) Restricted vision of the operative field.
(b) Difficulties during filling and condensation of amalgam in ideal dry conditions.
(c) Limitation of accessibility of the root canal.

After root resection, an inverted cone bur is used to undercut the cavity for the retention of the amalgam.

Electrolysis around the zinc contents of silver amalgam is caused by electric flow between zinc and other metals of amalgam. Zinc carbonate is precipitated at the periapical region which is responsible for retardation of the healing process. Hence, zinc-free silver amalgam is the material of choice for the purpose. Once the curettage and debridement of the bony cavity has ensured that all the pathological tissues have been eliminated, the area is irrigated with warm saline. Sharp bony margins are smoothened and apical seal is examined with a sharp probe for any defect. If any medicaments are applied to treat the cut ends of the dentinal tubules, care must be taken to apply the medicaments only on the root surface.

For the past few years, the surgical microscope has received increased attention by the endodontists and endodontic surgeons as means to increase their ability to carry out their surgical and non-surgical procedures.The rationale seems to be to reduce the high surgical failure rate. It is claimed that it is cost-effective and capable of improving the surgical success rate. As in many areas of microscopic surgery, it aims at good visualization and magnification.

(5) **Suturing.** Following irrigation, the wound is curetted gently to promote bleeding since blood clot is the best possible wound dressing. The mucoperiosteal flap is repositioned and sutured with interrupted sutures. As far as possible, traumatic occlusion should be eliminated by selective grinding of the opposing teeth.

Wound healing following periradicular surgery

Surgery of the periradicular region is mainly to eliminate the etiological factors of endodontic origin causing periradicular pathology. Thus, pathological injury is being corrected through intentional surgical trauma initiated for the purpose of eliminating the etiology, based on the predictability of the surgical wound healing. This is the response of the living tissues, involving a complex series of biological events - some occuring simultaneously and others in due course of time. In general, wound healing depends on the traumatized tissue and type of the wound. The tissues involved are - mucoperiosteal tissues (gingiva, alveolar mucosa, periosteum), periradicular tissues (bone, gingival and periodontal ligament) and radicular tissues (cementum and dentine). Tissues of periodontium receive three types of surgical trauma during periradicular surgery - incisional wounds are made with blade, blunt dissectional wounds are made with periosteal elevators and excisional wound with rotatory instruments in removing bone and resecting the root end. Therefore, the entire wound healing in response to periapical surgery is diverse and complicated. Following are some of the important relevant observations:

(a) Wound healing responses to endodontic surgery are not the same as in periodontic surgery. Submarginal rectangular flap is less predictable. Great care has to be exercised in approximating, stabilizing and compressing the flap following surgery.

(b) Dissectional wound results from the elevation of the mucoperiosteal flap from the bone. Healing is slower than incisional wound.

(c) Connective tissue healing appears to be directly related to the speed with which epithelial healing occurs. Elevated periosteum is destroyed by the reflective forces. The cells of the cambial layer does not survive and collagen of fibrous layer becomes depolymerized. Crestal bone osteoclastic activity occurs if it is involved during the flap reflection.

(d) Maintaining the vitality of root attached, tissues greatly enhance rapid wound healing by initiating flap reflection and elevation in the vertical incision, using undermining elevation to reflect the flap and by preventing the dehydration of the tissues with frequent irrigation.

(e) While eliminating the endodontic problems, operator should ensure that periodontal problems are not initiated. In other words, flap design and incision shall be submarginal rather than intrasulcular for better healing.

Postoperative follow-up

(1) Suture is removed on the seventh postoperative day. Postoperative edema and pain are inevitable. A suitable antiinflammatory and analgesic preparation should be prescribed. Sometimes, discoloration of skin due to extravasation and breakdown of the blood can result in ecchymosis which is more common in fair skinned persons. If proper care is taken, transient paresthesia, oroantral or oronasal fistulas do not develop.

(2) Patient should be reviewed at regular intervals. Condition of the tooth should be evaluated clinically and radiologically at periodical intervals of one, three, six, nine and twelve months to

determine the rate of healing, regeneration of bone and the persistence or enlargement of periapical radiolucency.

(3) It is worthwhile to recall the patient periodically to evaluate the prognosis of the tooth after apicoectomy. Symptomless patients must be advised to seek advice if any of the following clinical features develop, indicating the possible failure of surgery:

(a) Appearance of sinus.
(b) Evidence of infection like swelling, pain etc.
(c) Increased tooth mobility.

After 8-9 months, all the operated patients must be radiologically investigated even if they are symptomless. The following are some of the possibilities:

(i) Following surgery, even in the presence of substantial amount of bony defect, the bone is expected to heal with the reformation of cancellous bone. Failure can be identified by the presence of increased or persistent radiolucency. Such persistent radiolucencies need further investigation.

(ii) If the symptoms are mild or negligible, another radiograph is taken after two months. If the radiolucency is not increased in size, such a tooth must be kept under observation for some more time.

(iii) If such radiolucencies are associated with symptoms, another surgical intervention may be necessary. But even after repeated surgery if tooth shows no signs of any improvement, attempt must be made to rectify the errors before any other methods of management are considered for treatment (Please refer page 226).

Prognosis of periapical surgery

Various factors considered in relation to the prognosis include:

(a) Presence of preoperative symptoms.
(b) Size of the preoperative periapical lesion.
(c) Quality of the root canal filling.
(d) Its timing relative to the surgery.
(e) Presence of a retrograde filling.
(f) Type of the retrograde filling.
(g) Technique and skill of the surgeon.
(h) Tooth involved.

Note: Apical surgery in posterior teeth imposes technical limitations.

Age of the patient - better healing in younger patients.

Reasons for the failure of apicoectomy procedure

(1) Incomplete apical seal has been found to be one of the most common reasons for the failure. It may be due to (a) the presence of an accessory root canal, (b) contamination of the apical seal, (c) insufficient apical seal, (d) incompletely resected root tip and (e) accessory root away from the apex.

(2) Damage to the root like lateral perforation, root fracture, etc.

(3) Postsurgical migration of the epithelial attachments towards the root apex, damage to the periodontal, alveolar, gingival tissues and the consequent drainage of pus along the root surface result in the development of deep periodontal pockets. As a consequence, distance between the epithelial attachment and the root apex reduces. Consequently, tooth becomes mobile.

(4) The following are some of the etiological factors for the wound to breakdown:

(a) Inadequate apical seal.
(b) Occlusal interference.
(c) Necrosis of the pulp of the neighboring teeth.
(d) The possibility of incomplete elimination of periapical delta.
(e) Inadequate saucerization of the bony cavity.
(f) Difficulty in eliminating the large area of the dead space over the resected root apex.

In practice, prognosis seems to depend on the successful elimination of apical pathology and placement of an effective apical seal. The etiology in each case should be properly evaluated. If necessary, the operation may be repeated. If the wound breaks down because of the large dead space, it is better to pack the cavity with gauze soaked in whitehead varnish. The dressing should be repeated periodically until the bony cavity granulates completely (healing by secondary intention).

(5) The usefulness of endodontic surgery while considering pulpless teeth as foci of infection is still debatable. Although conclusive proof is wanting, benefit of doubt should be given to the patient and hence every cause must be considered on merits of the case. While treating such pulpless teeth, retention of such teeth through endodontic surgery must be carefully considered in terms of general health of the patient.

(6) Prognosis is relatively good if the procedure is done properly. To evaluate the bone repair, an immediate postoperative periapical x-ray must be taken as a guide.

(7) Comparison of the success rate shows that 85% of the cases treated with ultrosonic techniques and 68% of the cases treated through the use of rotatory instruments were successful. Likewise, the difference between the success rate for maxillary teeth is around 80% when compared to the success rate in mandibular teeth which is around 65%. This is because of the greater difficulty involved in performing surgery in mandibular teeth.

In the diagnosis, treatment planning and follow-up of the periapical lesions, radiograph is the most accurate aid in endodontics. But the real extent of a lesion and its spatial relationships to important anatomical landmarks are not easily visualized. In order to improve the quality of the information, when dealing with periapical lesions, possibility of using computerized tomography may be considered. Repair of periradicular tissues consists of a complex regeneration involving bone, periodontal ligament and cementum. If cortical plate is perforated, healing will be periosteal in nature and it will occur from the outside of the lesion to inside. Conventional periapical radiograph may not reveal this factor, while follow-up with CT scan will confirm that repair of the periapical tissues has commenced with regeneration of the external cortical repair. This reveals the usefulness of CT scans in the periapical lesions.

Postoperative evaluation - alternate methods

Careful preoperative assessment will reveal the presence of any of the problems for apicoectomy. If so, the following procedures can be considered as the possible alternate methods:

(1) Reimplantation
(2) Endodontic implants.

Reimplantation

The term refers to the intentional removal of a tooth and its reinsertion into its socket after endodontic therapy and root section in vitro.

Indications

(1) This is limited to posterior teeth where apicoectomy is not feasible or inaccessible.

(2) If internal or external resorption has perforated the root apex, root resection cannot be performed satisfactorily.

(3) Where the root canal in posterior tooth is sharply curved, it cannot be treated by conventional methods.

Procedure

(1) Under local anesthesia, tooth is atraumatically removed and the socket is curetted under strict aseptic conditions.

(2) The removed tooth is endodontically treated, root filled; root resections and retrograde filling are done by another operator. Care must be taken to prevent drying of the tooth. Cutting of the tooth substance is done under the irrigation of sterile saline. Care must be taken to avoid damage to the periodontal ligament.

(3) The treated tooth is replaced into the socket. The tooth is immobilized with any appropriate

method of wiring, using the two adjacent teeth for anchorage.

(4) Postoperatively, adequate relief must be provided for any possible traumatic occlusion of the tooth.

(5) The splint is left in situ for a period of at least 8 weeks. By taking precautions like: atraumatic removal of the tooth, satisfactory technique, minimum damage to periodontal ligament and if the tooth is kept out of the mouth for a minimum period, prognosis is excellent. Resorption of the root is inevitable. The process is rapid depending on the damage of the periodontal ligament. If the tooth remains in position for a period of 5 years, prognosis is considered to be excellent.

Endodontic implants (Fig. 11.11)

The endodontic implant is a rigid structure which extends through the root canal into the periapical osseous tissue, to lengthen the existing root anchorage and to provide stability to the tooth.

In contrast to the other implants, endodontic implants are not exposed to the oral environment. The area of bone prepared for the implant bed is not extensive. The angulation of the implant can easily be established through the root canal. They act as stabilizers when the loss of periodontal support is more than 40%, consequent to apicoectomy procedures or root fracture. These metallic extensions extend through full length of the root into the apical alveolar bone mainly to increase the crown-root ratio. They also provide better anchorage and stability to such mobile teeth. Prognosis tends to be poor if the root fracture involves the epithelial attachment resulting in the infection of the alveolar bone. General principles of dental implants are illustrated separately in the chapter "Introduction to Dental Implantology".

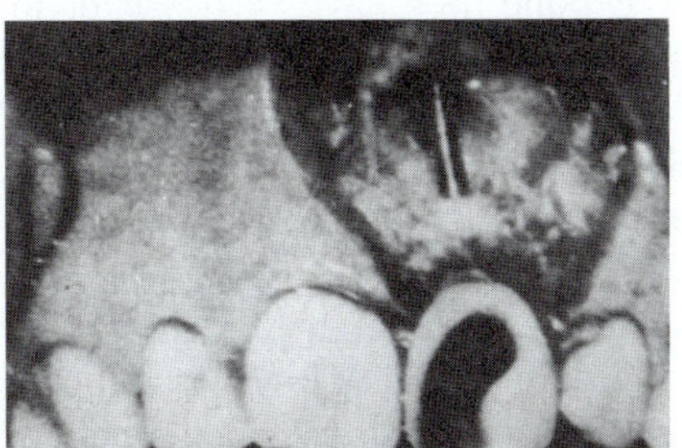

Fig. 11.11 Endodontic implant.

Indications of endodontic implants:

(1) To reinforce the management of transverse root-fracture.

(2) To stabilize the overdenture abutment.

(3) To stabilize during the autotransplantation.

(4) In teeth with severe periodontal disturbance and extensive bone loss, endodontic implant is used as an aid to pulp-periodontal therapy.

The crucial factor affecting the longevity of an implant is the nature and degree of the forces acting on the implant. When the stress distribution pattern in the tooth with intact supporting alveolar bone was analysed, it was found that most of the stresses were distributed along the cervical third and middle third of the root, reducing towards the root apex. It was also found that stresses were concentrated in the region of bone loss. But in the case of endodontic implant, the stress was higher on the lingual aspect of the tooth. Hence, it is evident that an endosseous implant alters the stress distribution pattern within the supporting bone when placed in a tooth with supporting bone loss. Since this is a technique-sensitive procedure, the practice of endodontic implants requires specialist knowledge and training. It should never be practiced unless one possesses special training and skill to perform this procedure.

CHAPTER 12

Orthodontic Surgery

Orthodontic surgery broadly refers to the role of surgery in achieving the objectives of orthodontic treatment. It includes (a) surgical aids to orthodontics and (b) orthognathic surgery.

SURGICAL AIDS

Usually, the patient requiring orthodontic treatment is evaluated first by the orthodontist, to assess the need and to determine the overall orthodontic treatment plan. While doing so, if any surgical procedures are considered to help the orthodontic treatment, these are known as surgical aids to orthodontics. These preorthodontic surgical procedures do not correct the malocclusion by themselves. Following surgery, orthodontic treatment has to be undertaken to complete the treatment. The following are some of the common surgical aids to orthodontic treatment:

(1) Serial extraction
(2) Therapeutic extraction
(3) Unerupted teeth
  (a) Surgical exposure
  (b) Surgical removal
  (c) Transplantation
(4) Removal of impediments
  (a) Extraction of submerged deciduous molars
  (b) Removal of odontomes
  (c) Management of dentigerous cysts obstructing the eruption of teeth
(5) Diastema
  (a) Relief of abnormal frenal attachments
  (b) Removal of mesiodens-erupted or unerupted
  (c) Excision of dense interdental alveolar bone
(6) Corticotomy

The surgical aids to orthodontics are very well within the scope of minor oral surgery as office procedures. But orthognathic surgery must be undertaken only by a competent oral and maxillofacial surgeon. Hence, a detailed account is presented on surgical aids. However, only an outline of orthognathic surgery is included, enough for the dental practitioner to advise the patient awaiting corrections of malalignment of teeth and jaws.

Serial extraction

This is an interceptive orthodontics by which sequential extractions of deciduous teeth reduce the severity of malocclusion and hopefully reduce the extent of mechanical intervention. The clinicians who employ this method are mainly concerned with (a) sequence and timing of extraction, (b) variable effects of growth during the process of serial extraction and (c) appropriate time and method of the appliance therapy. While it is considered to be beneficial in selected areas, serial extraction by itself can only be an aid to guide the eruption of teeth during the mixed dentition period. As early as 1743, this procedure was described in the French literature as a guide for the eruption of teeth. Hence, it was also termed as "guidance of eruption". Early removal of deciduous teeth, in a sequential manner, is expected to provide the benefit for the subsequent alignment of erupting and erupted teeth. Tweed's report on the failure of orthodontic treatment due to arch length deficiency led to the evolvement of rationale for utilizing serial extraction of teeth. This is known to allow physiologic unassisted movement of rationale for utilizing serial extraction movement of the adjacent teeth into more favorable positions. This also reduces the time and complexity of active appliance therapy. The normal dental development, eruption and exfoliation of teeth provide the guidelines for the timing of extraction in a sequential and pre planned manner.

These *guidelines* are as follows:

(1) Among the development yardsticks, timing of serial extraction must be considered in relation to the dental clinical age rather than chronological age of the patient.

(2) As a planned programme, every patient who undergoes serial extraction requires continuous monitoring of the craniofacial growth and dentoalveolar development.

(3) It must be considered only as a supplementary and not as the only treatment procedure.

Indications

- (a) Arch length deficiency and tooth size discrepancies.
- (b) Crowded state during the mixed dentition period.
- (c) Lingual eruption of incisors.
- (d) Abnormal eruption, direction and sequence.
- (e) In Angle's class-I malocclusion, it benefits in carefully selected cases. In class-II and III cases, this programme must be approached with great caution.

Technique

There is no single technique since it is only a long-range guidance programme. The three stages of serial extraction therapy are:

- (a) Extraction of mandibular deciduous canines.
- (b) Removal of I deciduous molars.
- (c) Removal of erupting or erupted premolar tooth.

With the exfoliation of deciduous canine, the immediate purpose is to permit the eruption and the alignment of lateral incisors. I deciduous molars are generally removed 12 months after deciduous canines between 9-10 years. If the diagnostic study confirms the inherent arch-length deficiency, the removal of I premolar permits the canines to drop distally into the space created by extraction. The three periods of physiologic "raising of the bite" are (a) 6 years, (b) 12 years and (c) 18 years, corresponding to the eruption of I, II and III molars respectively.

Therapeutic extraction

Depending on the arch length deficiency and the crown size, the orthodontic decision to therapeutically extract the premolar or molar teeth is taken, so that adequate space could be gained for realigning the teeth. More often, I premolar is removed as part of orthodontic treatment plan.

Unerupted teeth

Surgical exposure

The importance of early recognition and proper diagnosis of any abnormality concerning the eruption of teeth needs emphasis. Correct diagnosis will reveal the etiological factor that is responsible for the non-eruption of teeth. Clinical and radiological examination will reveal the presence of overlying thick fibrous band or bone in relation to the crown of incisor or canine tooth. Even after a reasonable period, beyond the chronological age of eruption of the corresponding teeth, if the tooth fails to erupt, overlying soft or bony tissue is excised so that the tooth is sufficiently exposed. Appropriate radiograph will reveal the direction of the tooth and the stage of root formation. Unless reasonable chance exists for its eruption in the normal path, surgical exposure is not likely to serve any useful purpose. Any tooth in the dental arch may require this procedure. But it is usually done for the maxillary incisors and canines because of the esthetic importance.

Technique

Based on clinical and radiological examinations, the exact position of the crown is located. With cruciform incision made on this area under local anesthesia, four triangular flaps are raised enough to expose the crown. The resultant flaps are excised. Bleeding, if any, is arrested by pressure pack. In order to prevent the soft tissues to grow over the exposed area, a periodontal pack is applied. This pack also helps to define the area where epithelial attachment is established around the tooth. During the surgical exposure, if bone is to be removed, care is taken not to damage the neighboring teeth. Properly assessed and adequately exposed incisors and canines usually erupt into the anatomical position without much difficulty. If any devices like pins are placed to apply orthodontic forces, care is taken to ensure that application of excessive traction is not followed by pulpal death or failure to erupt. In the case of incisors, entire incisal edge, cingulum, mesial and distal convexities must be exposed. In canines, the anatomical neck of the tooth is exposed, aided by removal of the distobuccal bone that may be present along the path of its eruptive movement. Elimination of such obstruction will readily provide a satisfactory channel of eruption.

DIASTEMA

During the mixed dentition period, usually a natural interincisal space exists between the two maxillary incisors. As the permanent canines erupt into the anatomical position, the space closes spontaneously. If any such space persists between any two adjacent teeth, it is known as diastema. The term median diastema refers to the persistence of the space between the two maxillary central incisors.

Etiology

(i) Smaller sized teeth in large jaws: For example, a peg-shaped lateral incisor or its absence may be responsible for such spacing.

(ii) Diastema also develops due to the presence of a supernumerary tooth between the central incisors, called mesiodens. It depends on the size, location and path of eruption of mesiodens at the interincisal space.

(iii) Presence of a cyst or an odontome separates the incisors.

(iv) Abnormal attachment of labial frenum to the incisive papilla is considered to exert its influence as a wedge. It may also interfere with the formation of transseptal cervical, gingival and alveolar crest bundles of periodontal ligament between the two maxillary central incisors. The transseptal fibers are known to have a binding effect between the teeth. Its absence may predispose to interdental spacing.

(v) Thick, dense, interdental alveolar septum may also have its effect as a wedge. An intraoral periapical radiograph will readily demonstrate the underlying pathology.

(vi) Abnormal habits like tongue thrusting and lip biting may lead to the proclination of the incisors resulting in spacing.

(vii) Heredity may play an important role as a predisposing factor for diastema.

As already pointed out, surgical elimination of the etiological factor alone may not be sufficient to correct the diastema. Appropriate orthodontic therapy is mandatory. In spite of active closure of this space, it is the relapse which puzzles the surgeon. However, the remedial measures in properly assessed cases at the optimum time still continue to yield satisfying results in the management of median diastema.

Treatment

It depends on the etiological factor. The most common cause is the abnormal labial frenum that separates the two maxillary incisors. Frenectomy is performed as an adjunct procedure to orthodontic therapy. This procedure is mainly designed to eliminate the fibrous tissue present over the midline suture. Under local anesthesia, this procedure can easily be performed. The upper lip is held in the extended position to make the frenum tense and also to facilitate dissection. A stay suture is placed on the frenal attachment to the incisive papilla. Then, incision is placed on either side of the frenum deep to the bone, with the palatal ends of both incisions joined together in such a way that the fibrous attachment is severed. The detached frenum along with the underlying fibrous tissue is dissected out up to its attachment to the lip. After undermining both sides, the wound is approximated with interrupted sutures. The gap on the alveolar bone is covered with zinc-eugenol mix or a periodontal pack. It is left in-situ for a week until the area granulates. If the intraoral x-ray shows dense alveolar bone or the presence of a mesiodens, the interdental space is exposed with a vertical incision. Bur is preferred to remove the bone or to gain access around the unerupted supernumerary tooth. After removing the mesiodens or bone, the wound is closed with interrupted sutures.

Repositioning. This procedure involves rotation of the unerupted canine tooth about its apex. By doing so, the long axis of the tooth is shifted from oblique to vertical direction. The crown shifts while the root apex does not so that neurovascular bundle entering into the apex of the canine tooth is left undisturbed. If the crown of the tooth does not reach the occlusal plane, it is left as it is, hoping that the tooth will erupt into its anatomical position in due course of time.

Transplantation. This involves the surgical removal of the unerupted tooth from the bed and placing it in its anatomical position. It is ideal and wise to transplant the unerupted tooth with open apex because of its increased vascularization. Preoperatively, it is wise to assess as to whether sufficient space exists to accommodate the crown of the permanent canine tooth. Steps must be taken to stabilize the tooth during healing stage with a splint. After 6-8 weeks, splint is removed. Traumatic occlusion, if any, must be checked and relieved.

MANDIBULAR DEFORMITIES

Introduction

An understanding of the mandibular development and growth helps to appreciate the complex background of the mandibular deformities. Primarily, mandible develops through membranous ossification and forms the body and ramus.The secondary centres of ossification are believed to be present in the condyle and coronoid process. The primordial mandible depends on organogenesis and cellular differentiation for its basic outline. Organogenesis designs the broad outline while differentiation fills in the details so that the final definitive structure is eventually accomplished by the combined efforts of organogenesis and differentiation through careful coordination. The hereditary factors imparted to the first branchial arch manifest with postnatal growth of the mandible. Further growth is due to cellular proliferation of the articular surface of the condyle. This results in thrusting the jaw downwards and forwards. The growth is essentially appositional, aided by modeling of bone. Major appositional growth occurs along the posterior border of the ramus while resorption along the anterior border provides the required space for the eruption of successive molars. Condylar growth increases the height of the ramus while body grows downwards and forwards in harmony with other bones of the facial skeleton. At the coronoid and gonial angle, there is appositional growth. Developmental changes in the cranial base exert definite influence on the position of the developing mandible. The constancy of the gonial angle of the mandible is indicative of harmony of all the contributing influences. The ultimate configuration of the mandible seems to be derived from a combination of three main factors:

(i) Prenatal development and postnatal growth of teeth and alveolar bone.
(ii) Appositional growth at coronoid and gonial angle.
(iii) Inherent bony growth potential.

Variations in skeletal morphology (Fig. 12.1)

Diversity of skeletal pattern of the mandible exists

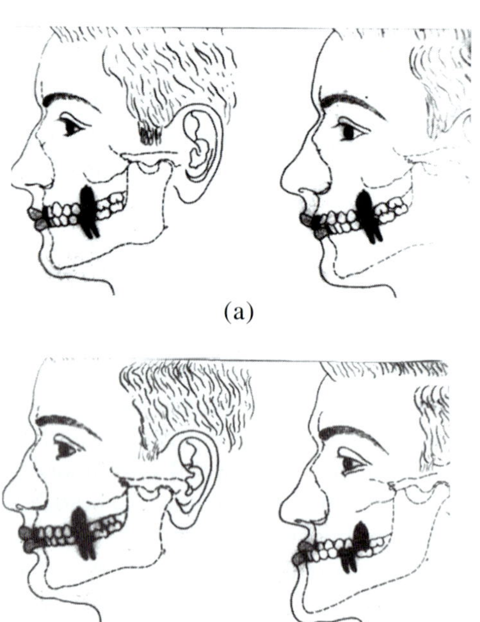

Fig. 12.1 Variations in skeletal morphology with facial soft-tissue contour. **(a)** Cl I & II divi. 1 (i), **(b)** Cl II divi. 2 & Cl III.

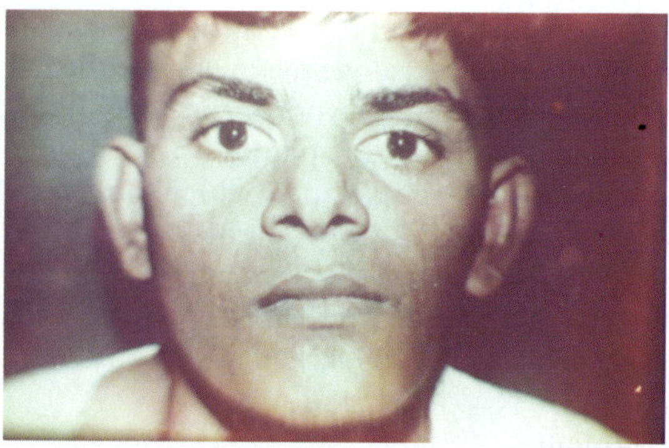

Fig. 12.2 (a) Mandibular excess–unilateral.

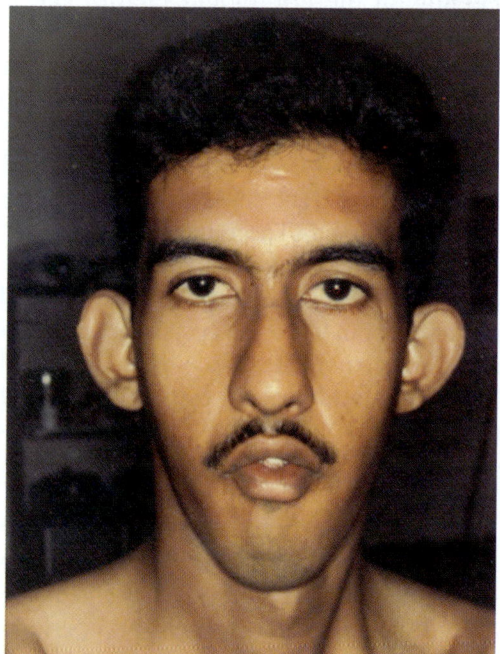

Fig. 12.2 (b) Mandibular excess–bilateral (vertical).

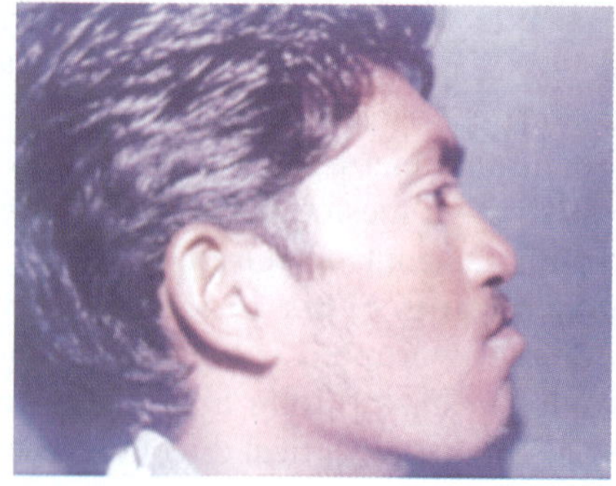

Fig. 12.2 (c) Mandibular excess (side view).

in health and disease. Considerable variations of normal facial pattern exist between different ethnic groups of the population and also within each individual group. "True facial harmony" is a factor probably determined in each locality. But, in general, symmetry and proportionate balance of features constitute essential requirements for most of the esthetic demands. Excess, deficiency or asymmetry in growth of the bone beyond the limits commonly observed, constitute deformity. Irrespective of the etiological factors involved in the production of mandibular deformity, the basic alterations in the normal contour of the mandible can be resolved into one of the following categories:

(i) **Mandibular excess (protrusion)** (Fig. 12.2c)
  (a) Unilateral (Fig. 12.2a)
  (b) Bilateral (Fig. 12.2b)

(ii) **Open bite deformity**
  (a) With mandibular excess (Fig. 12.3a, b).
  (b) Without mandibular excess (Fig. 12.3 c).
  (c) With maxillary excess (Fig. 12.3d).

Fig. 12.3 (a) Mandibular excess with open bite (side view).

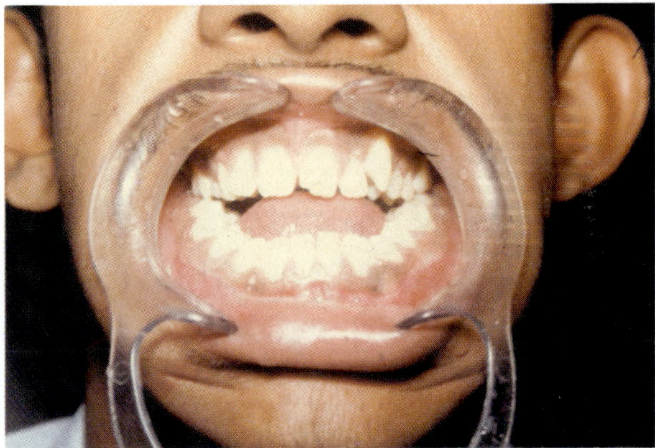

Fig. 12.3 (b) Mandibular excess with open bite (front view).

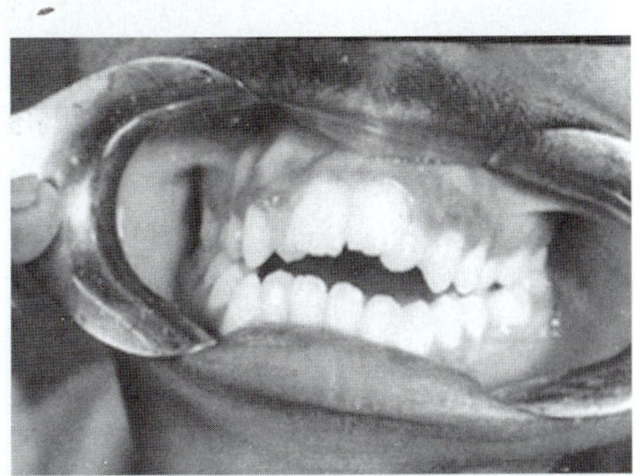

Fig. 12.3 (c) Open bite without mandibular excess.

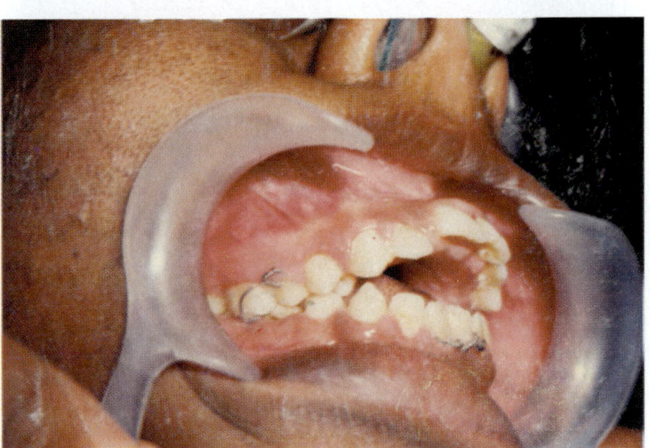

Fig. 12.3 (d) Open bite with maxillary excess.

(iii) **Mandibular deficiency (retrusion)**
- (a) Unilateral (Fig. 12.4a, b)
- (b) Bilateral (Fig. 12.5a, b)

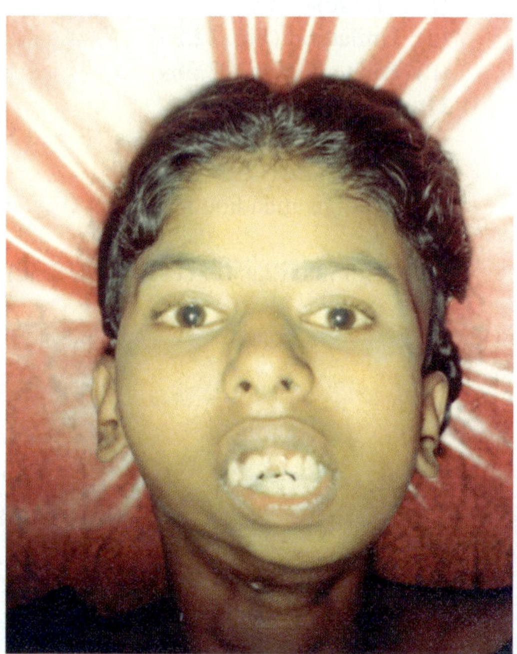

Fig. 12.4 (a) Mandibular deficiency (unilateral ankylosis).

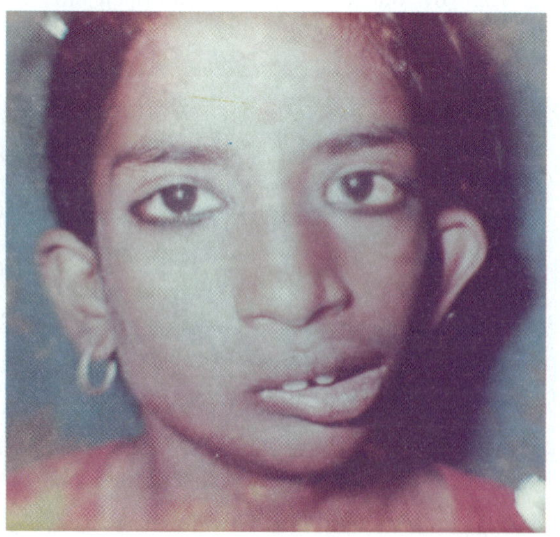

Fig. 12.4 (b) Developmental deformity-Mandibular deficiency (unilateral).

(iv) **Combination with maxillary deficiency** (Fig. 12.5c)

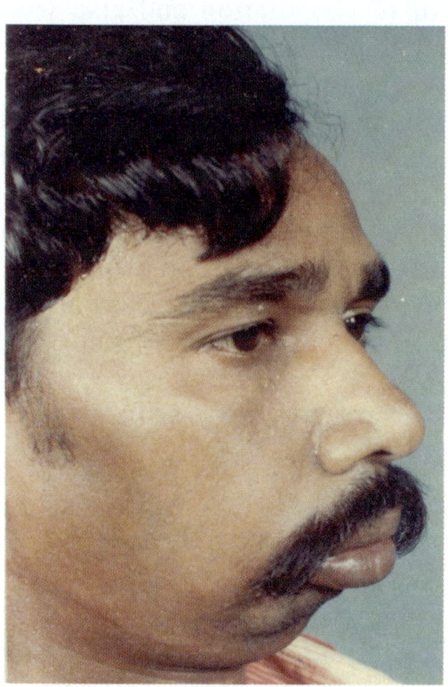

Fig. 12.5 (a) Mandibular deficiency–bilateral (side view).

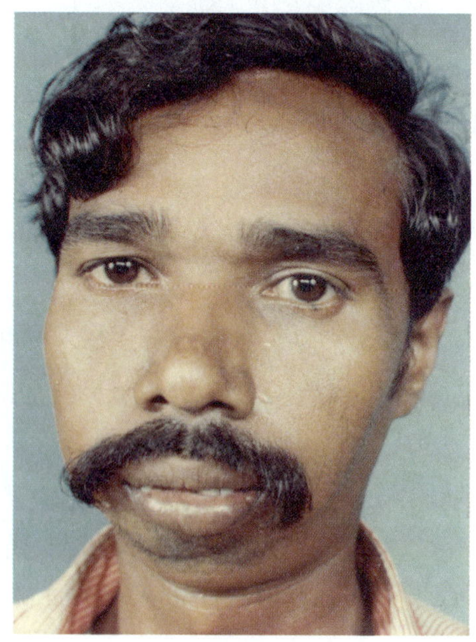

Fig. 12.5 (b) Mandibular deficiency-bilateral (front view).

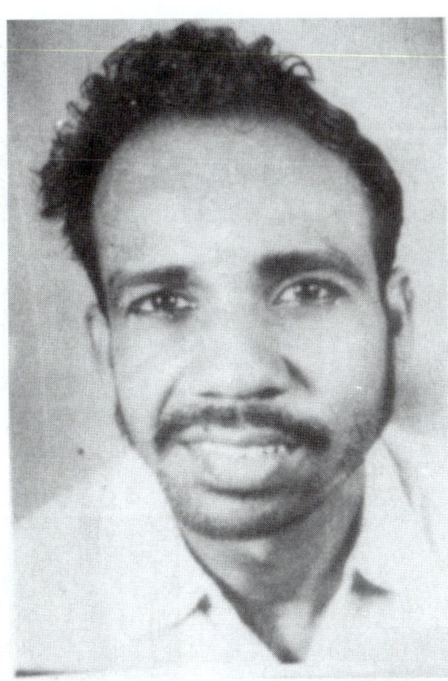

Fig. 12.5 (c) Unilateral mandibular and maxillary deficiency (Combination with maxillary deformity).

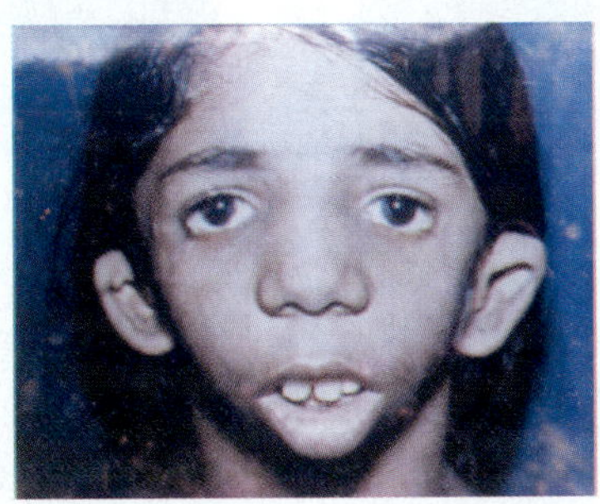

Fig. 12.5 (d) Bilateral mandibular and zygomatic deficiency (Treacher-Collin syndrome).

(v) **Bilateral mandibular and zygomatic deficiency** (Fig. 12.5d).

Etiology

The morphological characteristics of the human mandible appear to have arisen from evolutionary changes, associated with relegation of prehensile function from jaws to hands, selective changes in orofacial musculature, accompanied by development of speech and facial expression. The multiplicity of factors responsible for the deviation of normality may be grouped as under.

(i) **Congenital anomalies**
   (a) Macrognathia - unilateral or bilateral
   (b) Micrognathia - unilateral or bilateral
   (c) Apertognathia - unilateral or bilateral
   (d) Agenesis of the condyle - unilateral or bilateral.

(ii) **Inherited anomalies of development**
   (a) Variations like Angle's class II or III deformity
   (b) Condylar hyperplasia - unilateral or bilateral
   (c) Skeletal open bite (apertognathia).

(iii) **Initiating factors for the acquired anomalies**
   (a) Trauma to condyle
   (b) Infection involving the condyle
   (c) Radiotherapy inhibiting the condylar growth
   (d) Abnormal habits.

(iv) **Initiating factors for the pathologic anomalies**
   (a) Extrinsic due to pressure from neoplasms
   (b) Intrinsic like fibrous dysplasia, cherubism
   (c) Endocrine abnormalities like acromegaly, gigantism.

Diagnostic modalities

Precise determination of all the disharmonies rests with the following modalities:

(1) Clinical evaluation (Fig. 12.6, 12.7)
(2) Dental analysis (Fig. 12.8)
(3) Cephalometric analysis (Fig. 12.9, 12.10)
(4) Model analysis

The overall status of the teeth, periodontal and oral structures through clinical and radiographic examination are of great importance in treatment planning.

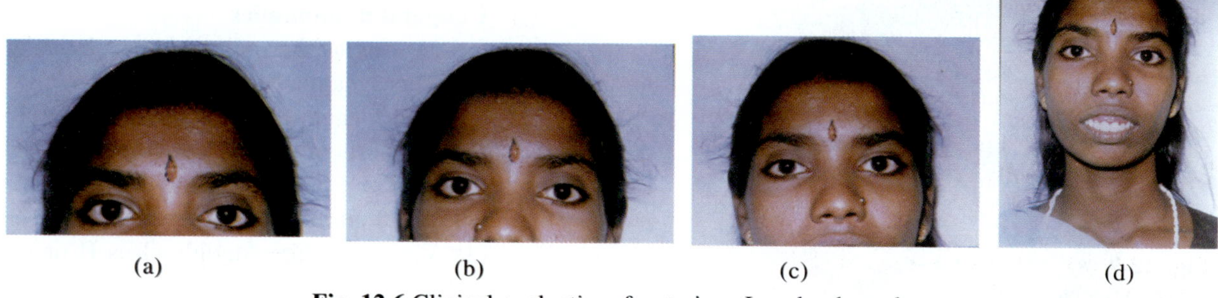

(a) (b) (c) (d)

Fig. 12.6 Clinical evaluation–front view. Level a, b, c, d.

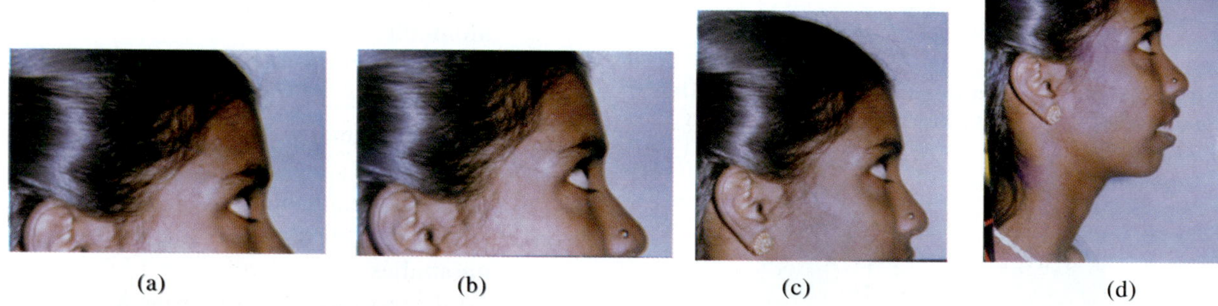

(a) (b) (c) (d)

Fig. 12.7 Clinical evaluation–side view. Level a, b, c, d.

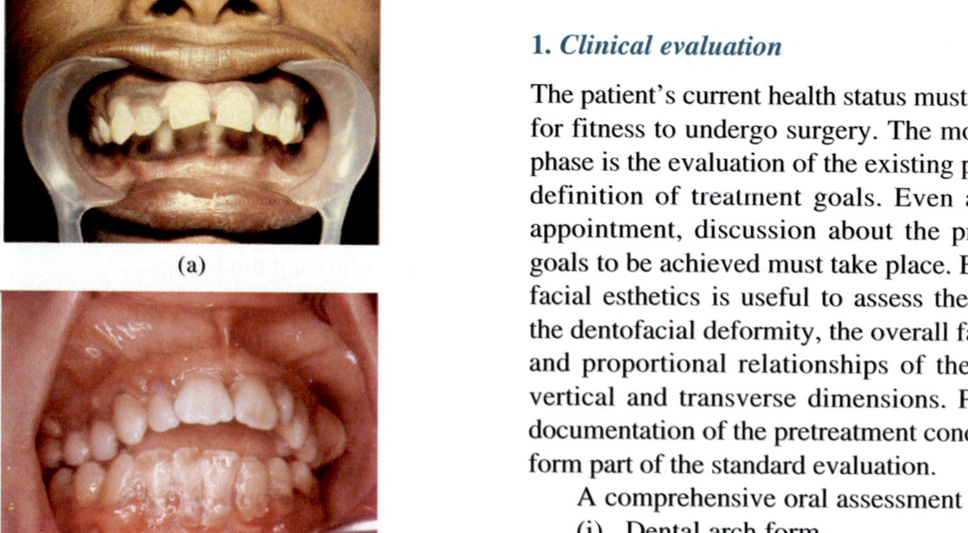

(a)

(b)

Fig. 12.8 Dental analysis **(a)** closed bite, **(b)** open bite.

1. *Clinical evaluation*

The patient's current health status must be evaluated for fitness to undergo surgery. The most important phase is the evaluation of the existing problems and definition of treatment goals. Even at the initial appointment, discussion about the problems and goals to be achieved must take place. Evaluation of facial esthetics is useful to assess the presence of the dentofacial deformity, the overall facial balance and proportional relationships of the face in the vertical and transverse dimensions. Photographic documentation of the pretreatment condition should form part of the standard evaluation.

A comprehensive oral assessment includes:

(i) Dental arch form,

(ii) Symmetry,

(iii) Dental alignment,

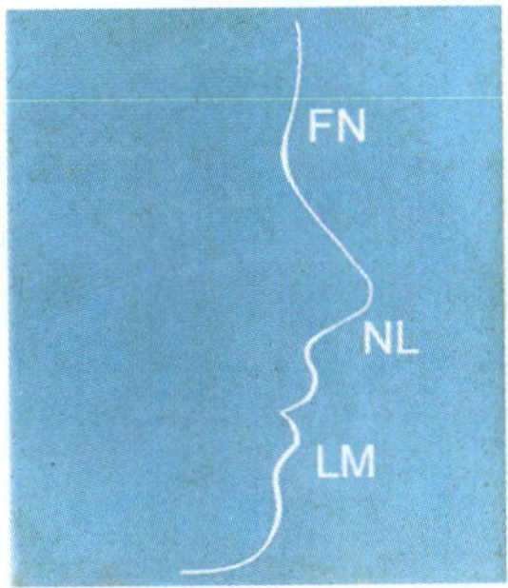

Fig. 12.9 (a) Soft tissue contour. FN - Frontonasal curve, NL - Nasolabial curve, LM - Labiomental curve.

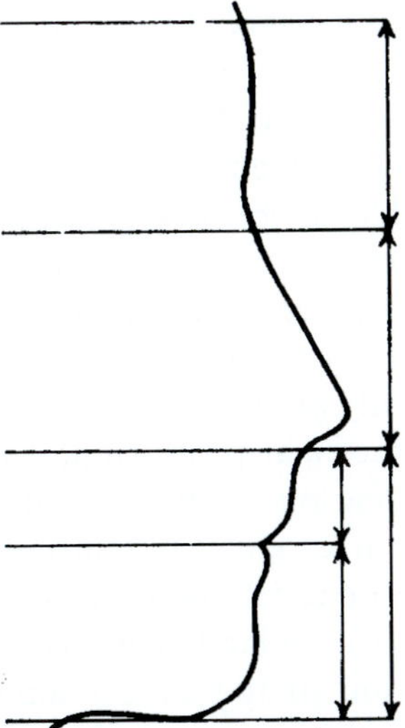

Fig. 12.9 (b) Soft tissue contour.

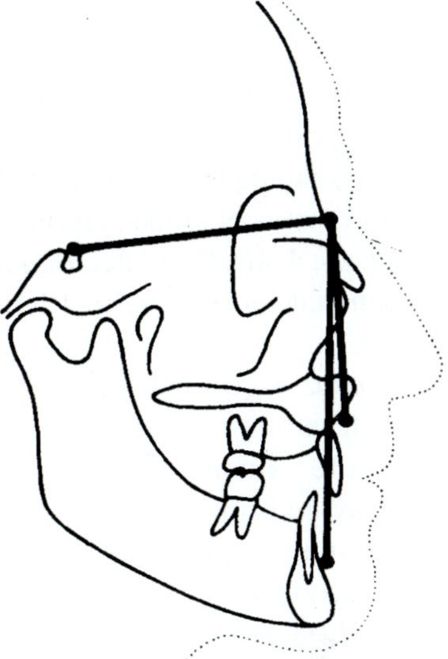

Fig. 12.10 (a) Lateral cephalogram.

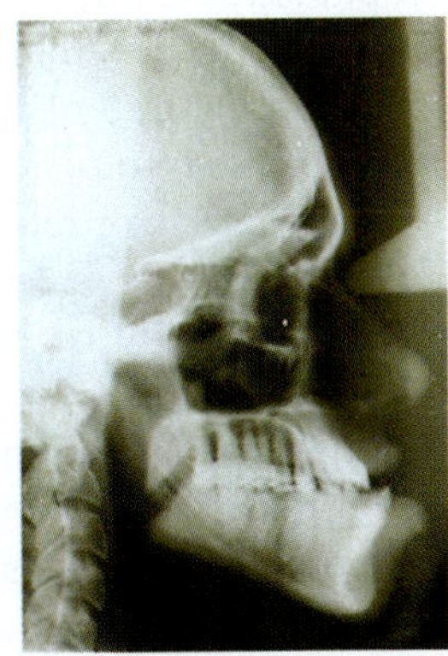

Fig. 12.10 (b) Mandibular excess.

(iv) Occlusal abnormalities in the vertical, transverse and anteroposterior dimensions,
(v) Temporomandibular joint function and muscles of mastication, and
(vi) General oral hygiene status.

The general clinical impression of the following conditions should be confirmed with appropriate radiographs:

(a) Condylar hyperplasia
(b) Macrognathia
(c) Micrognathia
(d) Skeletal open bite
(e) Asymmetry.

(a) **Condylar hyperplasia** is considered as an inherited condition. If it is bilateral, it will result in mandibular excess with or without skeletal open bite. If it is unilateral, facial asymmetry develops.

(b) **Macrognathia.** The mandibular excess may be due to macrognathic mandible or due to muscular and skeletal elements of the mandibular components of the first branchial arch. If both the muscles and bones are hypertrophied, the gonial angle is within the normal range; but the lower jaw is an enlarged replica of the usual pattern. If the pterygomasseteric sling is normal or reduced in length but bone growth is abnormal, the bone growth conforms to a reduced muscular environment. An obtuse gonial angle with short ramus and elongated body will be observed. When muscular component alone is large, muscular hypertrophy occurs. Unilateral macrognathia may be due to proportionate enlargement of muscles and bone on one side.

Thus, mandibular excess may be due to bilateral condylar hyperplasia stimulated by the abnormal response to the hormonal environment. Macrognathia may be primarily skeletal, muscular or involving both the factors. This may be related to an error of organogenesis at a very early stage of intrauterine life. Mandibular excess may be due to aberration of one or more of the following factors: (a) heredity, (b) hormones, (c) growth of the cranial base, (d) appositional growth, (e) bone resorption, (f) alveolar process development and (g) functional activity. As a first step, it should be evaluated whether the excess (protrusion) is true or relative as a result of hypoplasia or retroposition of the upper jaw. The mandibular excess is called mandibular prognathism. It may be classified as follows:

Type A. Bimaxillary prognathism. It is not considered to be a reflection of the overgrowth of the craniofacial skeletal complex but secondary to the relationship of horizontal and vertical cranial base component. This may be considered to be a true prognathism of genetic origin.

Type B. Maxilla is of normal length but mandibular length is in excess. This is an absolute mandibular prognathism due to the mandibular growth beyond the normal limit.

Type C. Shortened and underdeveloped maxilla, but mandible is within normal limits (pseudoprognathism). This is a relative or apparent mandibular prognathism secondary to the growth deficiency of maxilla. The lower occlusal plane and increased gonial angle are evident.

Type D. Dental intermaxillary relation is normal but prognathic appearance is due to the increased length of the basal bone with mental prominence.

Type E. Maxilla is of normal length and mandible is prognathic. The lower third of the face is elongated with open-bite relationship.

When viewed in profile, the relative length of ramus and body can be observed. The upper lip is often obscured by the apparently overfull lower lip and appears relatively thin and weak. Normally, the length from the outer canthus of the eye to the level of the corner of the mouth should be equal to the length from the lower limit of the alar margin to the undersurface of the chin. But in prognathic mandible there is considerable increase in the length of the lower third of the face. The shape of the chin is also variable in its prominence.

Intraorally, variable degree of Angle's class III type of malocclusion will be present. Reverse overjet and overbite with retroclination of the lower anterior teeth due to the pressure of the lower lip is characteristically present.

In asymmetrical protrusion, clinical picture varies depending on whether it is due to condylar hyperplasia, macrognathia confined to skeletal element only or involving osseous and muscular components. Condylar hyperplasia involves the accommodation of the excess amount of bone between glenoid fossa of one side and the anterior limit of the mandible. The lower border of the mandible on the affected side is bowed downwards. The chin is thrust forwards, towards the opposite side. The ramus on the affected side exhibits concavity on its lateral aspect. This imbalance of growth between the two sides causes twisting of the vertical axis of the chin. If the skeletal macrognathia is confined within normal muscular pattern, it is manifested by elongation of the body alone since pterygomasseteric sling restricts the ramus. Such inequality in the length of tooth-bearing segment of the jaw results in deviation of the midline towards the normal side without the twisting of the vertical axis of the chin and very little bowing of the lower border of the mandible. If both osseous and muscular components are involved, angle is markedly displaced downwards on the affected side. The growth of the enlarged half of the lower jaw, simultaneously with the normal half, enables the dentoalveolar segment to accommodate itself to the upper jaw. Hence, cross bite does not develop. Some amount of twisting of the vertical axis of the chin occurs but not to the extent noticed in condylar hyperplasia.

(c) **Micrognathia.** Minor degree is probably represented by Angle's skeletal or dental class II malocclusion. It may usually exhibit disproportion between inherited bony and muscular tissues. Probably, variations are seen in Frankfort-mandibular plane and the gonial angle. Marked degree of micrognathia exhibits a disproportionate reduction in the skeletal and muscular components to make the lower jaw smaller.

Symmetric retrusion of the mandible may be striking by the lack of prominence of chin. It varies from mild developmental reduction to gross alteration of profile that may be due to bilateral destruction of condylar growth in early childhood. This may lead to almost total absence of the mental prominence. Due to the relative prominence of the nose and middle third of the face, the facial appearance is described as "bird-face deformity". The profile of the face appears to slope backwards from the lower lip down to the neck as a smooth line. The vertical height of the lower third of the face is shortened considerably in association with corresponding reduction in the soft tissue cover.

Intraorally, mandibular teeth are markedly retropositioned. Since the tongue-space is reduced considerably, the tongue exerts its pressure and proclinates the lower anterior teeth markedly. They are situated on the reduced apical base and hence fanned outwards and forwards in an attempt to achieve the contact with the corresponding upper teeth. The jaw movements may be absent in ankylosis of temporomandibular joints. In case where joint is functionally normal, incisal clearance may be restricted but adequate, while lateral excursion and protrusion are limited.

In asymmetrical retrusion, the same clinical features can be noticed unilaterally. The lower third of the face on the normal side is flattened with compensatory length of the body of the mandible due to the unopposed condylar growth. Hence, the midline of the mandible is deviated towards the affected side with reduction in the height of the ramus and length of the body of the mandible. The failure of the balanced forward and downward growth of the chin can be seen. Intraorally, midline of the lower incisor teeth is deviated towards the affected side. The reduction in the height of the ramus results in a marked upward slope of the occlusal plane on the affected side accompanied by a tilt in the transverse occlusal plane.

(d) **Skeletal open bite (apertognathia).** It may or may not be associated with mandibular excess. More often, it is also associated with true hypoplasia of the middle third of the facial skeleton. Tongue appears large for the oral cavity. Anterior part of the tongue spreads over the incisal and occlusal surfaces of mandibular teeth during deglutition and speech. Sometimes, the macroglossia is an inherent disproportion between relative size of the tongue and the mandible. Secondary distortion of the alveolar and basal bone develops due to the different inherent patterns of the skeletal and muscular morphology.

This is an uncommon condition characterized by relatively short ramus, increased gonial angle and sometimes with varying degree of hypoplasia of the premaxillary region of the middle third of the facial skeleton. This condition occurs with or without mandibular prognathism.

At rest, there is incompetent lip seal. During deglutition, there is pronounced tongue-thrusting with the whole of the anterior portion of the tongue spreading outwards so that occlusal and incisal edges of the lower teeth are covered except the last two molars. When teeth are in occlusion, several teeth do not come in contact. The divergence between the upper and lower teeth increases progressively in the anterior direction so that interincisal distance between the anterior teeth is striking. This may result in speech disorders.

(e) **Asymmetry.** It may be due to unilateral hyperplasia or hypoplasia of the condyle.

2. *Cephalometric analysis*

The field of cephalometrics to anybody, who is not involved in active orthodontics or growth and development studies, represents a no-man's land of obscure concepts and a few geometric uncertainties. Lot of literature is available on cephalometrics and craniofacial measurements, but easily masterable analysis used by the clinical surgeon is not readily available. The diagnosis can be made by a simplified orthodontic analysis based on a few bony points readily available on any standard cephalogram.

Advantages:

(i) Successful treatment is based on careful diagnosis. In this direction, cephalometric analysis is an aid in the diagnosis of skeletal and dental problems.

(ii) It can be a tool for simulating surgery.

(iii) It also allows the clinician to evaluate the patient postoperatively.

This analysis is primarily designed to harmonize the position of teeth with the existing skeletal pattern. A specialized cephalometric appraisal system called COGS (cephalometrics for orthognathic surgery) has been developed. This system describes the horizontal and vertical position of the facial bones by the use of a constant coordination system. The size of the bones are represented by direct linear measurements, and the shapes by angular measurements. The chosen landmarks and measurements can be altered by various surgical procedures. The COGS appraisal describes dental, skeletal and soft tissue variations. This systematized approach to measurements, converted into computerized way of measuring, is used.

The radiographic reference points are as follows:

S (Sella turcica)	Geometric midpoint of the pituitary fossa.
N (Nasion)	Deepest concavity of the frontonasal suture in the midsagittal plane. The inclination of SN line remains essentially unchanged throughout life. Hence, it can be used as a constant reference point against which maxillo-mandibular deviations can be measured.
A (Subspinale)	Point of deepest concavity on the maxillary alveolar ridge (at the midline) in the midsagittal plane.
B (Supramentale)	Point of deepest concavity on the mandibular alveolar ridge at the midline.
Gn (Gnathion)	The most anteroinferior point on the convexity of the mandibular body at the midline.
MP (Mandibular plane)	A plane constructed from menton to the angle of the mandible.
Me (Menton)	The lowest part of the contour of mandibular symphysis.
Go (Gonion)	The most posteroinferior point on the convexity of the mandibular angle. This can be located by bisecting posterior ramus plane and the mandibular plane angle.
Pog. (Pogonion)	The most anterior point on the convexity of the mandibular body at the midline.
ANS (Anterior nasal spine)	The most anterior point of the nasal floor and the tip of

	the premaxilla in the midline.
PNS (Posterior nasal spine)	The most posterior point on the contour of the palate.
AIS	Line drawn through the incisal tip and root apex of the maxillary central incisor as it appears in the radiograph.
BIS	Line drawn through the incisal tip and root apex of the mandibular central incisor as it appears in the radiograph.
SNA angle	The degree of variation from the prescribed norm indicates maxillary prognathia or retrognathia.
SNB angle	The degree of variation from the prescribed norm indicates the mandibular prognathia or retrognathia.
ANB angle	Indicates maxillomandibular relationship.

The baseline for comparison of most of the data in the analysis is a constructed plane (*Frankfort's horizontal plane*) by drawing a line from S to N. Most of the measurements will be made from projections, either parallel, perpendicular or at an angle to horizontal plane.

Horizontal skeletal profile. This refers to a few simple measurements made on the skeletal profile to assess the amount of disharmony. This is made parallel to the horizontal plane. This is very practical since most of the surgical procedures are primarily made in the anteroposterior direction.

(i) *The N-A Pog angle* gives an indication of the overall facial convexity but not a specific diagnosis as to whether maxilla or mandible is at fault.

(ii) A perpendicular line from HP (horizontal plane) is dropped through N. Horizontal position of A is measured to this perpendicular plane (N-A). This measurement describes the apical base of maxilla in relation to N. It enables the clinician to determine if anterior part of the mandible is protrusive or retrusive.

(iii) N-B is also measured in a plane parallel to HP from the perpendicular line dropped from N. This measurement indicates the horizontal position of the apical base of the mandible in relation to N. Thus, the clinician has the quantitative assessment of the anteroposterior position of the mandible and the degree of mandibular horizontal dysplasia.

(iv) *N-Pog.* It is measured in the same manner as N-A and N-B. It indicates the prominence of the chin. Hence, it is easy to determine whether the discrepancy is in the alveolar process, chin or mandible.

Vertical skeletal discrepancy. It may reflect an anteroposterior complex dysplasia of the face. The vertical skeletal cephalometric measurements are grouped into anterior and posterior components. The anterior component is again subdivided into measurements of (a) middle third facial height (distance from N to ANS that is measured perpendicular to HP) and (b) lower third facial height (from ANS-G, that is, measured perpendicular to HP). The posterior maxillary height is the length of a perpendicular line dropped from HP intersecting PNS. Vertical skeletal measurement of the anterior and posterior components of the face will help in the diagnosis of anterior, posterior or total maxillary hyperplasia or hypoplasia, clockwise or anticlockwise rotations of maxilla and mandible.

Thus, cephalometric appraisal is one of the steps in orthodontic diagnosis and treatment planning. It gives the insight into the quantitative nature of dental skeletal dysplasia. COGS analysis uses linear dimensions to describe the size and position of facial bones. It also helps to diagnose the nature of facial dysplasia and abnormalities in the position of teeth. However, one should be aware of the limitations of two-dimensional cephalometric analysis.

3. *Model analysis*

Clinical and cephalometric evaluation chiefly determines the nature of the anomaly. But model analysis discloses finer points of a functional nature. It also determines the limits of surgical correction. The guiding principle, in determining how the models are to be sectioned, as a mock surgery, and repositioned, is to solve the problems at the point of greatest abnormality. Although, one may occasionally strike a compromise to reach the most acceptable results, correction at the site of greatest deviation remains important. Plaster models must be mounted on the simple hinge-type of articulator. It is always better to have at least two sets of models mounted to allow for replanning of the surgery. Line measurements made on the models at the sites of proposed osteotomies give an accurate idea about the extent and direction of surgical fragment manipulation.

Mock surgery of dental models has become a routine practice for diagnosis and treatment planning. All techniques contain potential errors that can lead to inaccuracy and difficulties. The most difficult aspect in performing model surgery is the repositioning of the maxillary cast during bimaxillary surgery. One is obliged to decide in treatment planning, whether esthetic or functional considerations are the most important factors in any chosen case. In outlining the surgical particulars on the models, one should keep the relevant anatomic facts in mind.

Treatment

Limitation of orthodontic treatment. Since this cannot alter the relationship of the basal bone of the jaws, surgical correction must be undertaken for the correction of severe basal bone deformities. Secondly, as the age of the patient advances, success of orthodontic correction narrows down. It is a known fact that orthodontic treatment is time consuming. In such cases, surgery is performed to achieve the desired result in a shorter period.

Criteria for a satisfactory surgical correction. Ideally, the dentofacial deformity should be converted into an acceptable standard of normalcy without any significant impairment of function of orofacial structures. Permanent postoperative stability of the new jaw relationship should be achieved with satisfactory union of bones within a reasonable period of time. The surgery should not result in any morbidity like damage to sensory or motor nerve supply. It is preferable that no externally visible scar develops postoperatively.

The treatment can be considered sequentially under three district phases irrespective of the procedure.

(1) Presurgical treatment phase.
(2) Surgical treatment phase.
(3) Postsurgical treatment phase.

Choice of the suitable surgical procedure

No single procedure is applicable to correct all the jaw deformities. That is why every part of the mandible has been utilized to perform osteotomies. Just because one is familiar with a particular technique, that should not be the reason to exclude all the other osteotomy techniques. With the wide choice available to the operator, it is mandatory that every patient be properly evaluated so that, with proper treatment planning, the appropriate surgical technique is chosen to suit the specific requirements of the patient. The success of the osteotomy also depends on gaining adequate access. Depending on site of osteotomy, surgical access is gained.

Surgical access in orthognathic surgery (Fig. 12.11 and 12.12)

If osteotomy is to be performed in the basal bone of the mandible, it can be surgically exposed up to the first molar region through intraoral degloving vestibular approach. The labial vestibule is injected with normal saline containing adrenaline to define the plane of surgical dissection and also to provide hemostasis. Then, the lower lip is retracted with the

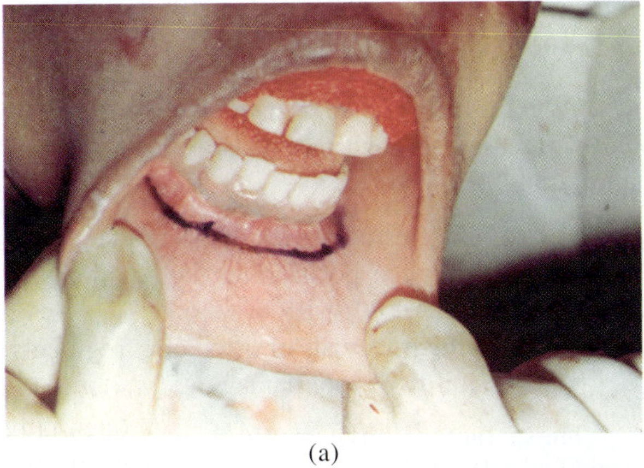

(a)

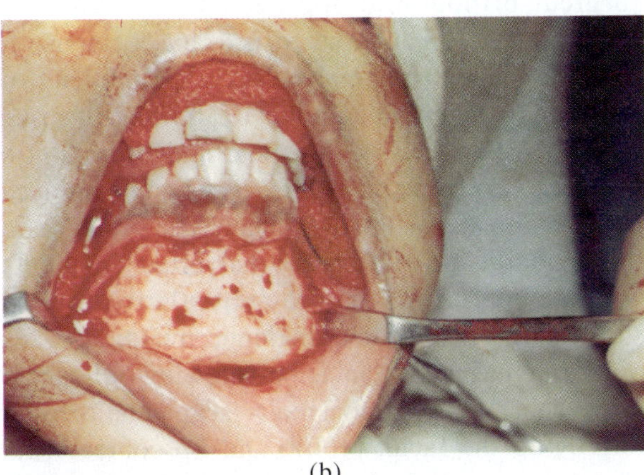

(b)

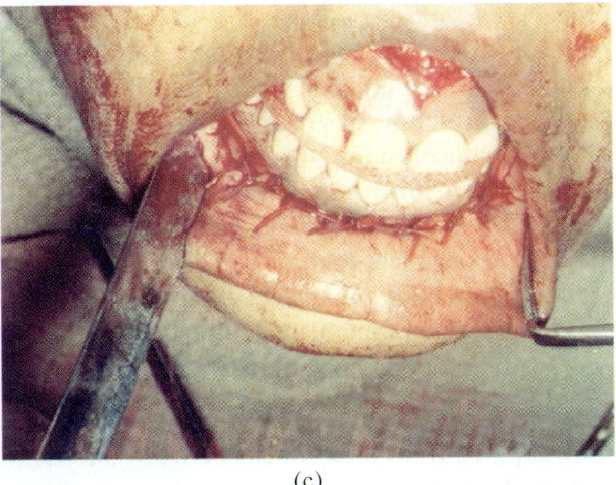

(c)

Fig. 12.11 Surgical access (intraorally) for the mandible **(a)** Incision, **(b)** Surgical exposure, **(c)** Sutures in position.

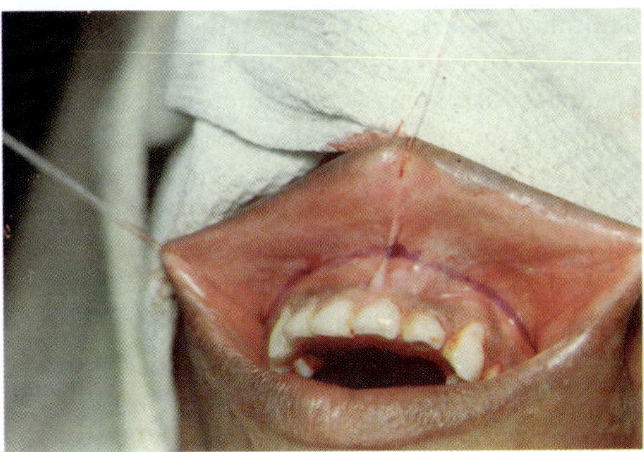

Fig. 12.12 Surgical access (intraorally) to maxilla.

help of traction sutures applied on the lower lip. A clean sweep incision is made on the labial and buccal mucosa, a few mm away from the vestibule. Along the incision, dissection is carried out towards the mandibular periosteum. Now, another incision is made on the mandibular periosteum and it is raised with a periosteal elevator. If the incision is made at the depth of the vestibule, the scar contraction may lead to the obliteration of the depth of the vestibule. When this incision leaves behind a fringe of mucosa on the alveolus, it facilitates suturing of the wound easily. If the incision is made at the depth of the vestibule, it is difficult to penetrate the suture needle through the attached mucosa of the mandible, during suturing. In addition, saliva does not penetrate into the wound. Instead, saliva is retained in the trough of the vestibule. That is why incision away from the depth of vestibule is preferred for this approach. The only difficulty encountered is brisk and troublesome bleeding.

The access to the angle and ramus of the mandible can be gained by the extraoral submandibular (Risdon's) approach. To avoid the externally visible scar, alternatively, intraoral incision can also be used. The description of the submandibular approach has been described in the chapter on maxillofacial injuries. In case of jaw deformities, one may find that bony landmarks are distorted. Therefore, it is preferable to identify few landmarks like gonial angle, inferior and posterior borders of the mandible and sigmoid notch. Surface markings are also made for the facial vessels at the anterior border of the masseter muscle and also for the mandibular branch of the facial nerve. Although the standard procedure is followed to expose the angle of the mandible, a few variations need to be remembered while placing the incision. An obtuse angle is a characteristic feature of prognathic mandible. To produce a desirable angle of the mandible, the incision line must be lower than normal towards the posterior aspect with the mandibular teeth placed in occlusion. Likewise, in retrognathic mandible, incision must be opposite of what is applicable for prognathic mandible.

Ramus can also be exposed by placing a vertical mucosal incision intraorally along the anterior border of the ramus of the mandible. If needed, the incision can be extended lower down towards the buccal vestibule, as in third molar surgery. By doing so, lateral and medial surfaces of the mandible can be exposed through intraoral approach.

Access to the neck of the mandible can be through submandibular Risdon's approach or through preauricular approach.

Interalveolar corticotomy (Fig 12.13)

While corrections of severe dentofacial deformities are being carried out successfully, it is a paradox that small segment osteotomies still continue to be unreliable procedures. If the diastemas are large, associated with proclination of maxillary anteriors and lip incompetence, interalveolar corticotomy procedures are being performed with variable prognosis.

Disadvantages of orthodontic therapy in these cases are:

(i) Limitation in adult patients, with less bone support for the roots.
(ii) High incidence of relapse.
(iii) Prolonged treatment time.
(iv) Socioeconomic factors.

Osteotomies of smaller dentoalveolar segments and immediate repositioning have the following limitations:

(i) Possibilities of nonvitality of the teeth.
(ii) Difficulty in positioning the segments as desired.
(iii) Avascular necrosis of osteotomy segments.
(iv) Possibility of root damage.

These factors have resulted in a combined surgical orthodontic approach with a view to eliminate the avascular necrosis of the segments. It has been found that interalveolar corticotomy in two stages followed by orthodontic treatment will strike a balance between the surgical and orthodontic treatment. Cortical cuts will weaken bony resistance is the rationale for this treatment. The orthodontic force bodily moves the dentoalveolar segments without interfering with the vascularity. It also shortens the period of orthodontic treatment. This procedure has the advantage of allowing orthopedic movement of the dentoalveolar segments, thereby improving the facial profile and lip competence. There is no critical age for carrying out this procedure.

Indications:

(i) Correction of Angle's class-II division I malocclusion.
(ii) Retrusion of mandibular anterior with adequate chin can be corrected by moving the segment forward.
(iii) Correction of Angle's class-II division-II.
(iv) Closure of interdental diastema, resistant to orthodontic correction.

The two-stage dentosseous osteotomies, with time gap of two or three weeks between the stages followed by the application of orthopedic force, have a few distinct advantages:

(i) Technically safer and easier.

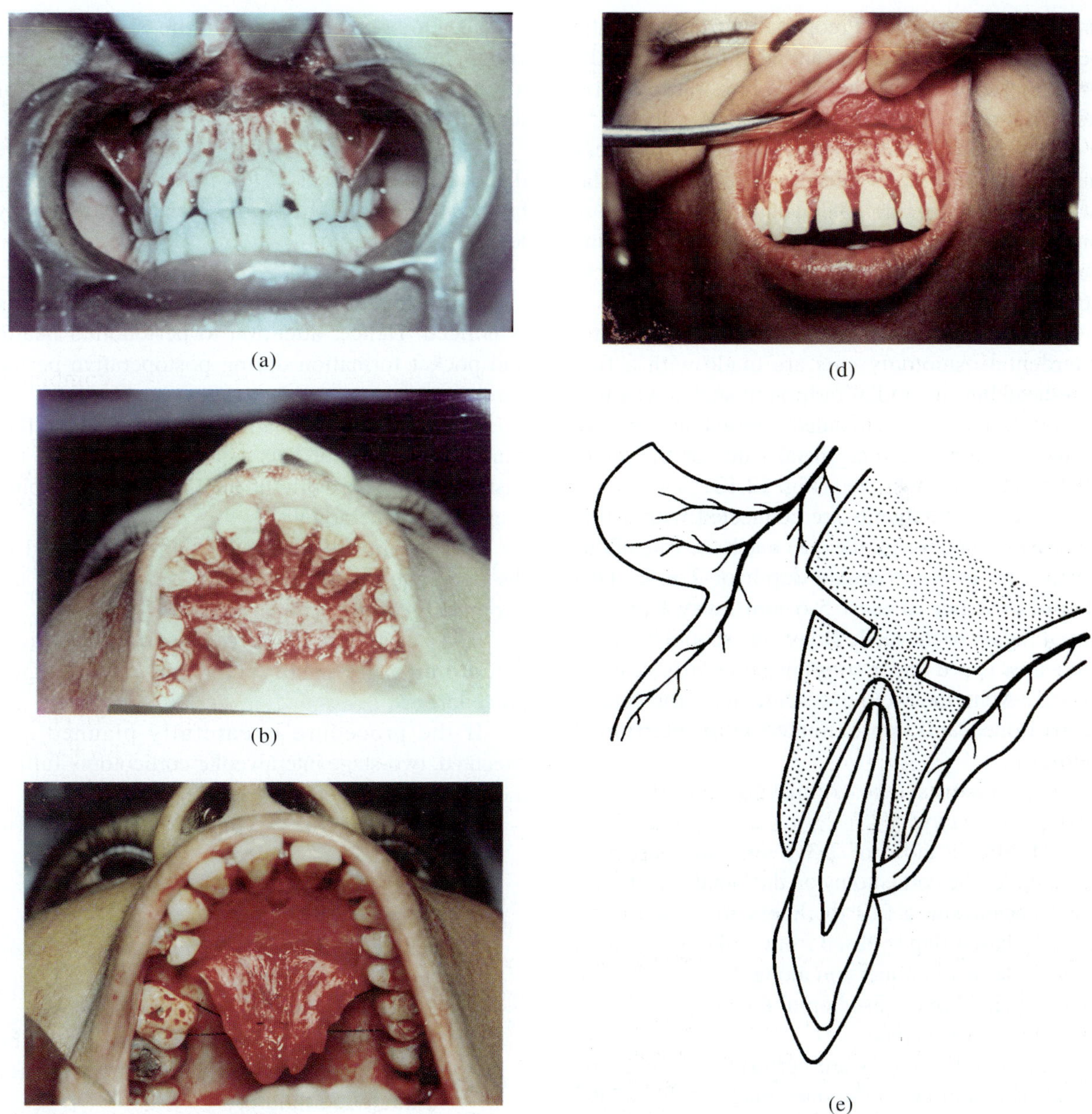

(a) (d) (b) (c) (e)

Fig. 12.13 Correction of maxillary protrusion. Interdental alveolar corticotomy **(a)** Labial ostectomy lines, **(b)** Palatal ostectomy lines, **(c)** Photograph showing palatal exposure, **(d)** Labial ostectomy photograph, **(e)** Diagrammatic representation showing interference with blood supply following alveolar corticotomy procedures.

(ii) Biologically safer procedures.

(iii) Absence of avascular necrosis, damage or devitalization of teeth or ankylosis.

Surgical technique. After the routine preoperative evaluation of the patient for fitness to undergo the surgery, the patient is prepared to undergo the procedure. Preoperatively, gingival and periodontal status must be attended to improve the oral hygiene. Wherever needed, endodontic treatment procedures can be performed.

(a) Under local anesthesia, full thickness mucoperiosteal flap is raised palatally from molar to molar on either side. The incision is placed along the free gingival margin. Anteriorly, nasopalatine neurovascular bundle is severed and clamped to achieve hemostasis.

(b) After careful evaluation, longitudinal interdental osteotomy cuts are made with a fine rose-head bur in a radial fashion in such a way that damage to the roots is avoided. These bony cuts are made on the mesial and distal sides of the teeth, which are to be mobilized (Fig. 12.13).

(c) These bony cuts are connected with a fine tapering fissure bur till the cuts reach the cancellous portion to an approximate depth of 2 mm. This should be made at least 5-6 mm away from the apical region of the teeth. Bony cuts should be made with slow speed under constant saline irrigation.

(d) After the wound debridement, the flap is repositioned and approximated with interrupted sutures.

(e) Sutures are removed on the 7th postoperative day.

(f) After a lapse of 2-3 weeks, the patient is taken up for the corticotomy on the labial side. Under local anesthesia, a full thickness mucoperiosteal apically-based flap is raised from molar to molar on either side, with an incision along the free gingival margin. The flap is raised up to the bony margin of the anterior nasal spine.

(g) Osteotomy cuts are performed through the labial plate similar to the ones made at the palatal side.

(h) Flap is repositioned with interrupted sutures.

(i) Sutures are removed on the seventh postoperative day.

(j) On both occasions, suitable antibiotic and analgesics are prescribed to the patient.

(k) On an average, it takes 30-45 minutes for each surgical procedure.

(l) Once the healing of the soft tissue is complete, orthodontic treatment is started. It takes about 8 weeks for the successful closure of diastema.

It will be seen that movement of the dentoalveolar segment is slow in the first four weeks but becomes rapid afterwards. Relapse is relatively less in these cases.

Complications:

(i) Postoperative periodontal pocket formation is noticed. Hence, attention to periodontal health and pocket formation during postoperative period is necessary.

(ii) Hematoma formation under the palatal flap can be troublesome. This can be prevented by the sustained pressure with the application of the splint prepared preoperatively.

(iii) Vitality of the teeth is directly related to the operative disturbance of the vascularity at the periapical region.

(iv) Avascular necrosis with subapical osteotomies are relatively rare in two staged procedure.

If the procedure is carefully planned and executed, two-stage interalveolar corticotomy fulfills the following objectives:

(a) Hastens the course of orthodontic treatment.
(b) Results are stable and long lasting.
(c) Less complications.
(d) This can even be adopted as a salvaging procedure for orthodontic failures.
(e) Biologically a sound procedure.
(f) Age is not a contraindication. It can be performed as an outdoor procedure for orthodontic failures.
(g) Easy to perform with excellent patient acceptance.

INTRAORAL SEGMENTAL OSTEOTOMIES (Figs 12.14 to 12.18)

Correction of deformities involving dentoalveolar

segments were originally developed as an adjunct to orthodontic therapy. These segmental osteotomies are performed in maxilla and mandible involving a few teeth. A few popular and widely used techniques are described here.

Mandibular anterior segmental osteotomy

Through standard intraoral vestibular approach, the involved dentoalveolar segment is exposed. The subperiosteal flap is elevated sufficiently to expose the chin prominence from one mental foramen to the other. As per the preoperative model surgery, a horizontal bony incision is made with bur. Care is taken to place this bony incision at least 5-6 mm away from the apex of the lower anterior teeth. If the alveolar segment is required to be retropositioned, first premolar on either side is extracted. Ostectomy is performed in the premolar region up to the horizontal osteotomy level. Now, the osteotomy is performed and the alveolar segment is mobilized taking care that the lingual pedicle is left intact. Now, the mobilized segment is repositioned in the desired place and fixed with appropriate fixation. The soft tissues are sutured in position. A pressure bandage dressing is applied externally to avoid excessive postoperative edema.

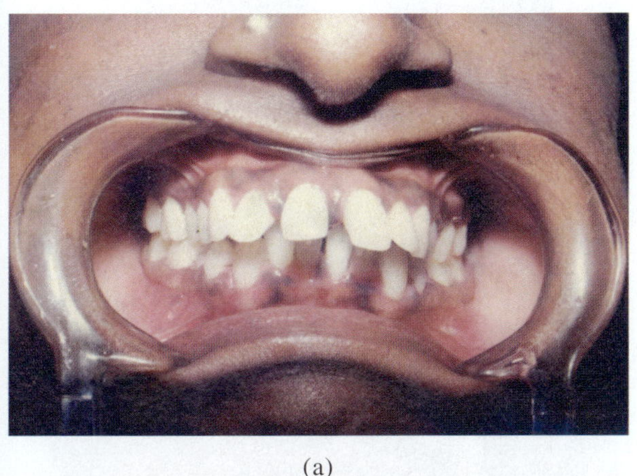

(a)

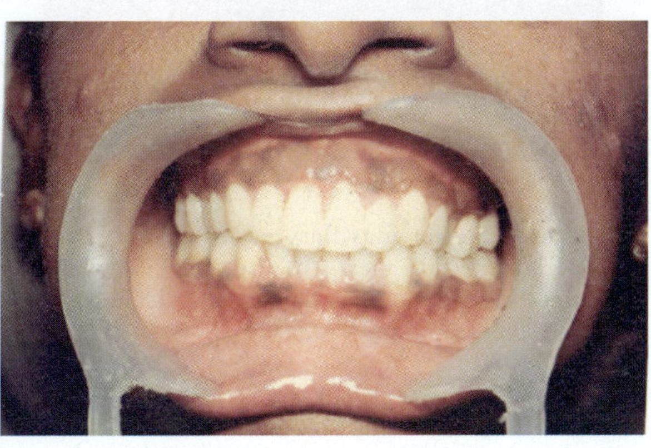

(b)

Fig. 12.14 (a), (b) Pre and postoperative photographs (intraoral).

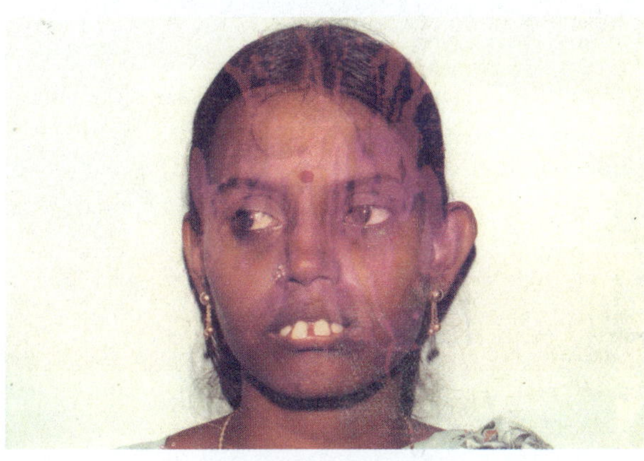

(c)

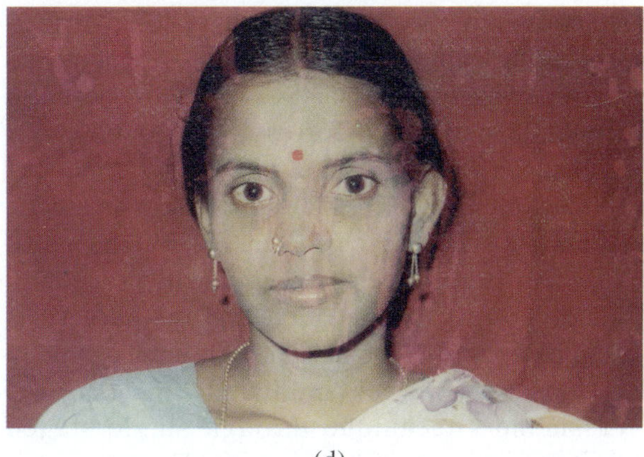

(d)

Fig. 12.14 (c), (d) Pre and postoperative photographs (intraoral).

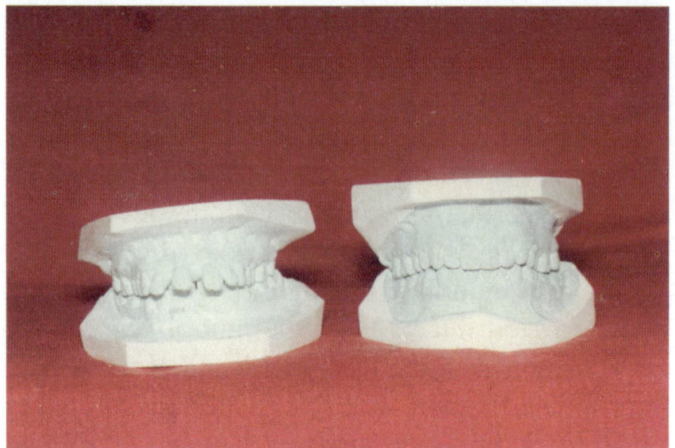

Fig. 12.15 (a), (b) Front view.

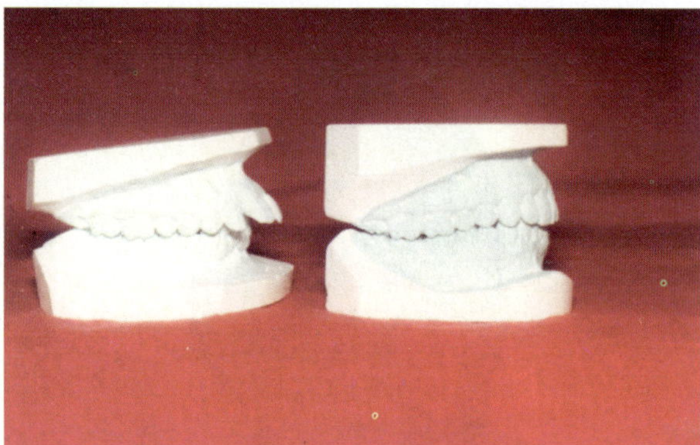

Fig. 12.15 (c), (d) Side view.

Anterior maxillary osteotomy

Sometimes, this procedure may have to be done in association with anterior mandibular osteotomy to have better result. Since this is one of the procedures frequently performed for esthetic reasons, this technique is described here.

Wassmund described the single stage technique through labial approach. Later, for better results, Schuchardt preferred the two staged procedure. Palatal side is operated first and the surgery is completed through labial approach after a month. In 1962, Wunderer modified the original Wassmund's technique through single staged procedure by palatal approach. However, for everyday practitioner's convenience, one procedure is described which provides reasonable success.

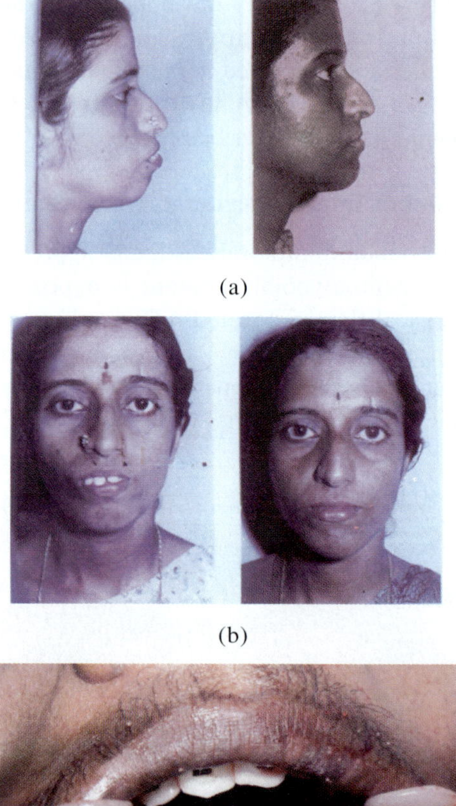

(a)

(b)

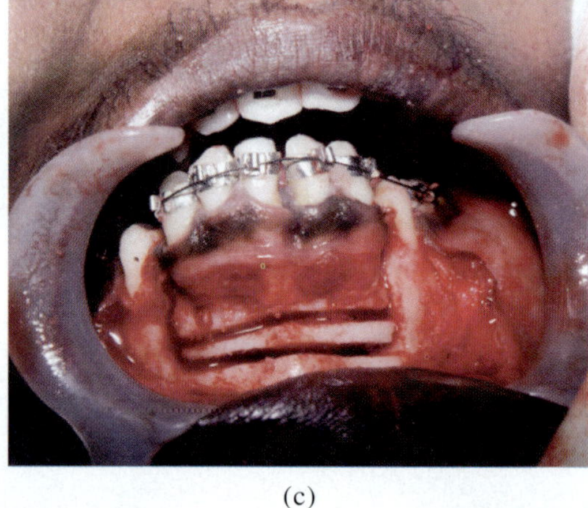

(c)

Fig. 12.16 Anterior maxillary osteotomy **(a)** Pre and Postoperative - side view, **(b)** Pre and Postoperative-front view, **(c)** Anterior mandibular sub-apical osteotomy to correct the deep bite.

Technique. Under general anesthesia, this procedure is conveniently performed. Infiltration of saline with adrenaline in the labial vestibule provides adequate hemostasis and helps to define

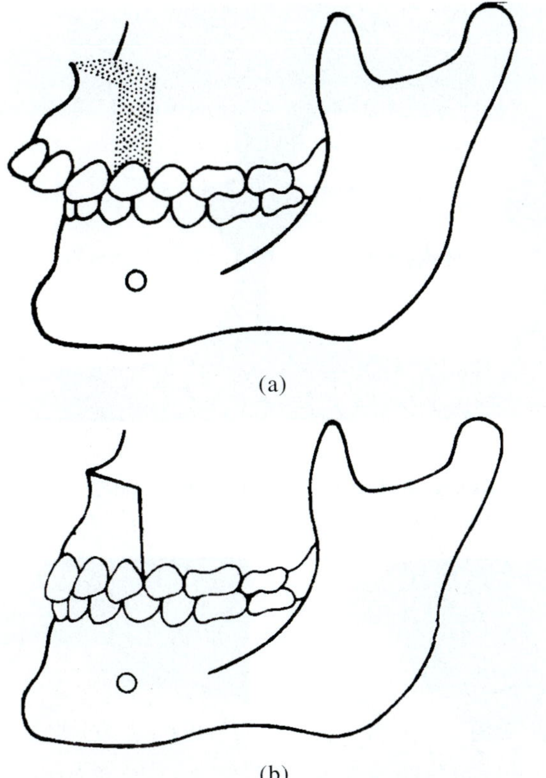

(a)

(b)

Fig. 12.17 Maxillary anterior osteotomy for correction of Angle's Class II division I malocclusion: **(a)** Preoperative, **(b)** Postoperative, after set back.

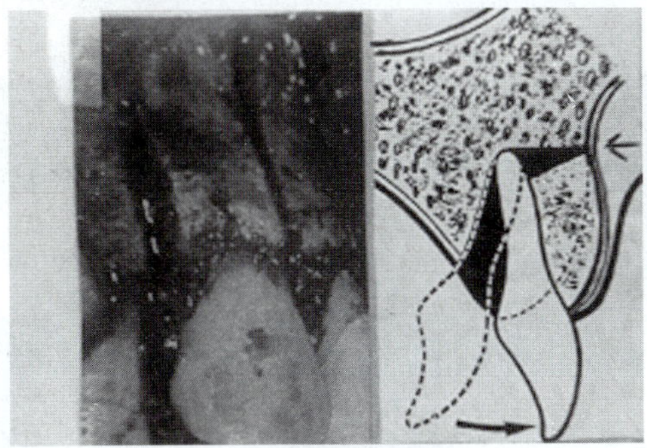

Fig. 12.18 Segmental single tooth osteotomy.

the plane of dissection. As described earlier, incision is made on the labial mucosa and not on the vestibular mucosa. This incision usually extends from premolar of one side to premolar region of the other side. The dissection is carried towards the bone. Another incision is made on the periosteum and elevated so that labial alveolar bone, pyriform aperture and anterior nasal spine are exposed. The area is packed with gauze strip to achieve hemostasis. Now, both the first premolars are extracted. Two parallel osteotomy cuts are made vertically mesial and distal to the first premolar region without damaging the periodental attachment of the adjoining teeth. The labial alveolar bone is removed. Now, a horizontal bony cut through the labial plate is made 5-6 mm above the apex of anterior teeth with tapered fissure bur. The area is packed with gauze and attention is on the palate.

In the first premolar region, palatal mucoperiosteum is tunneled bilaterally in a V-shaped manner so that both the oblique cuts meet at the midline. Care is taken to introduce the periosteal elevator to protect the palatal flap before the bone cut is carried out on the palatal cortex with a tapered fissure bur. Equal attention must be paid not to damage the endotracheal tube while cutting the bone deeper. Now, a narrow osteotome is used to complete the osteotomy at the palatal and labial cortex. Once bony fragment is mobile, a gauze piece is placed over the mobile dentoalveolar fragment and the segment is down fractured towards the palatal side. By doing so, the entire osteotomy site is under direct vision from the labial side. The fragment is then repositioned as per preoperative planning. Bony obstruction, if any, could be removed either with big rose head bur or Rongeur's forceps. The osteotomized segment is repositioned in such a way that desired occlusion is obtained. Now, the segment is fixed appropriately and the wound is sutured.

MANDIBULAR OSTEOTOMIES
(Figs 12.19 to 12.27)

Osteotomies of the madible has been successfully performed in practically all the sites of the mandible. For example, it starts from condylar

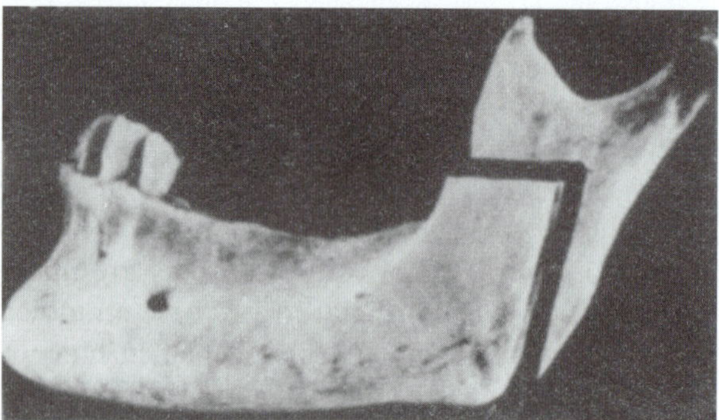

Fig. 12.19 Mandibular Ramus Reverse L osteotomy.

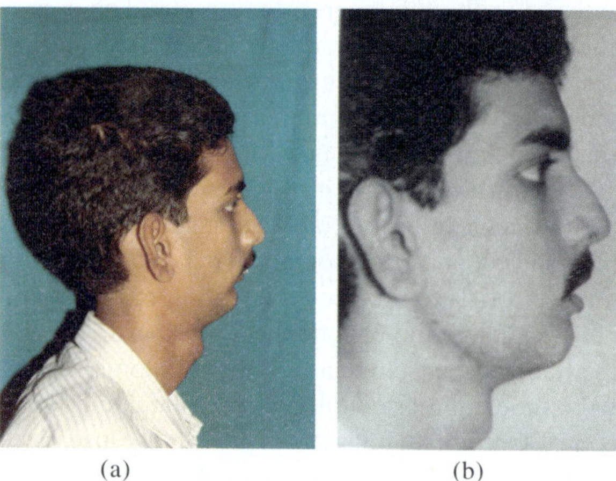

(a) (b)

Fig. 12.20 Mandibular advancement **(a)** Preoperative, **(b)** Postoperative.

region, to ramus, angle and body of the mandible. Initially, most of the procedures were performed by the general surgeons and therefore they were extra-oral procedures. Once oral surgeons started taking over the responsibility of these patients, they developed intraoral techniques.

Extraoral vertical ramus osteotomy (Fig. 12.24)

The objective of this procedure is to vertically section the ramus from the sigmoid notch to the lower border of the mandible through submandibular approach. The bony cut extends to the angle just posterior to the inferior dental foramen

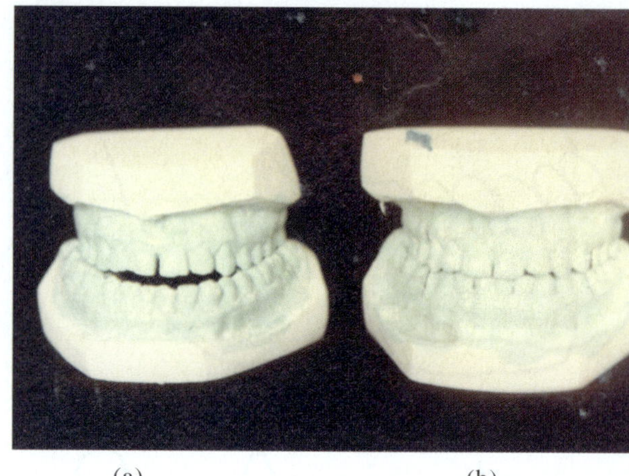

(a) (b)

Fig. 12.21 (a, b) Pre and postoperative models to correct anterior open bite.

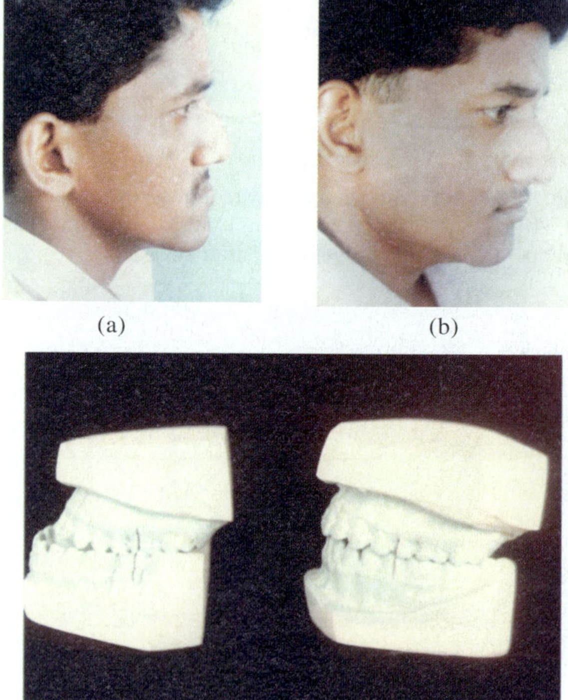

(a) (b)

(c)

Fig. 12.22 Mandibular excess **(a)** Preoperative, **(b)** Post-operative, **(c)** Dental models pre and postoperative.

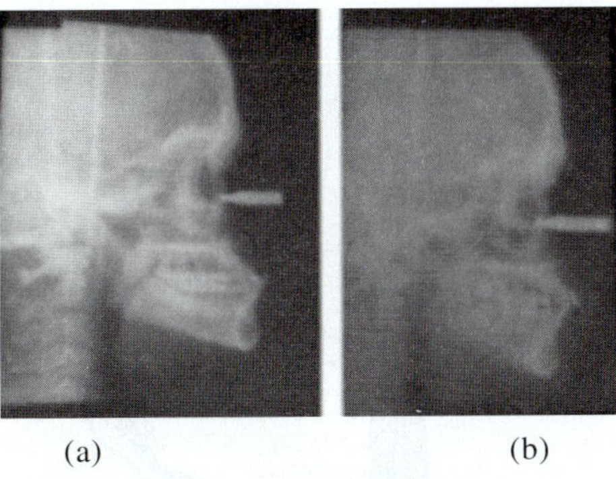

(a) (b)

Fig. 12.23 Pre and postoperative cephalometric radiograph showing correction of mandibular excess.

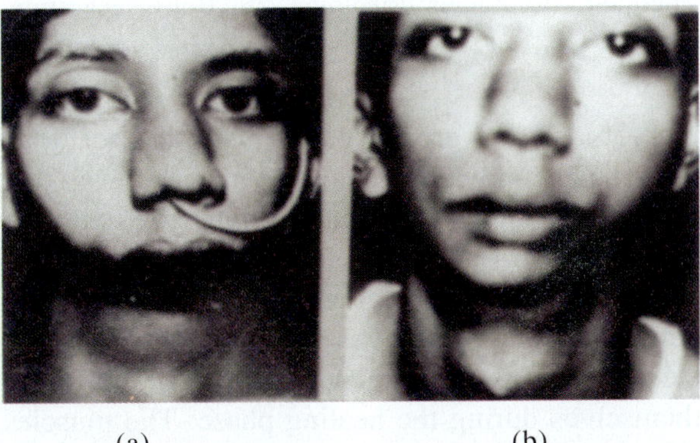

(a) (b)

Fig. 12.24 Mandibular advancement with bone graft (front view) **(a)** Preoperative, **(b)** Postoperative.

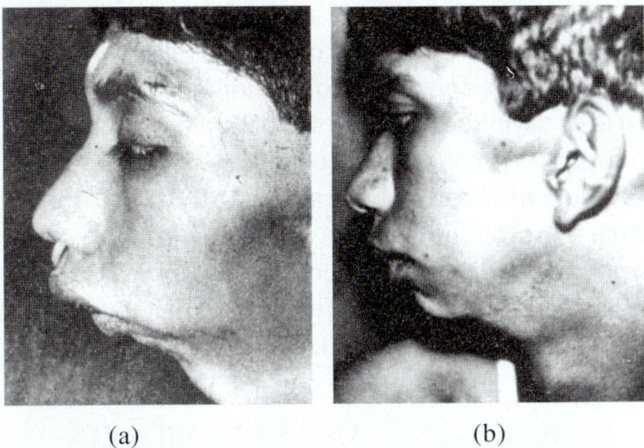

(a) (b)

Fig. 12.25 Mandibular advancement (side view) **(a)** Preoperative, (b) Postoperative.

so that nerve injury is avoided. This is a satisfactory procedure to correct mandibular excess as well as deficiency. In case of mandibular excess (prognathism), a segment is removed while in deficiency (retrognathism), a bone graft is inserted at the osteotomy site. Functional and cosmetic results are also good. No temporomandibular joint manifestations are observed. The only disadvantage seems to be the external scar.

Intraoral sagittal osteotomy (Fig. 12.26)

The objective of this method is to split the vertical ramus sagittally. The main advantage seems to be the versatility of this procedure. Therefore, practically all types of mandibular deformities are being corrected by this technique. Once incision is made along the anterior border of the ramus through intraoral approach, periosteum lateral to the ramus is elevated up to the posterior and inferior border. Specially devised long bladed Obwegeser's retractor is inserted to retract the lateral flap. Likewise, medial flap is also elevated and retracted, avoiding damage to the inferior dental neurovascular bundle. Superiorly, this dissection is carried up to sigmoid notch. Now fiber optic light source is available to these retractors for better illumination of the operating field. A horizontal medial bony incisions are made on the medial cortex of the ramus above the inferior dental foramen. Then the bony cut is extended along the anterior border of the ramus with rose head bur to facilitate the splitting of the ramus sagittally. It is extended along the lateral cortex down to the inferior border of the mandible in the molar region. The ramus is split with a broad osteotome. Now the medial and lateral cortex of the ramus are mobilized in a predetermined direction. Inferior dental neurovascular bundle is retained intact within the medial cortex of the ramus. Functional length of muscles and the consequent difficulties to the adaptability of the orofacial muscles greatly influence the outcome of surgery. For example, temporalis muscle places severe restriction on the

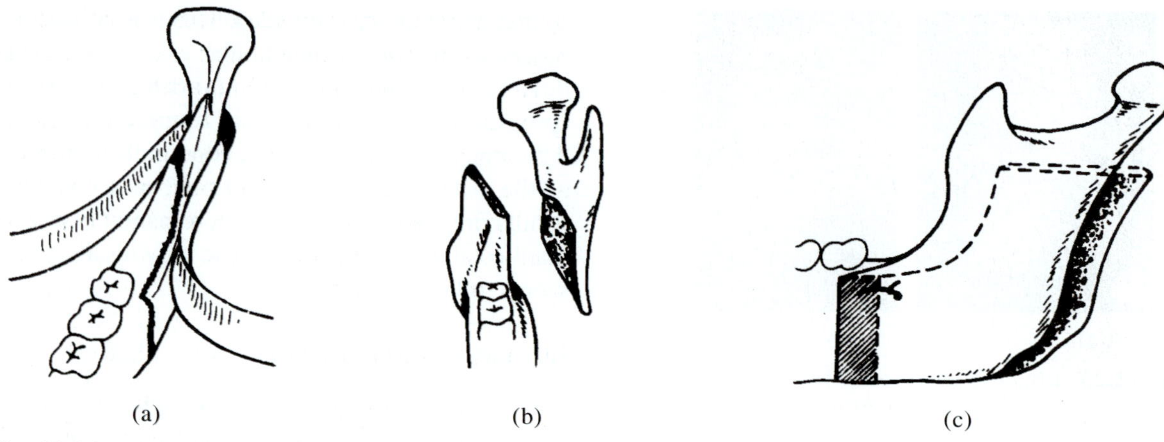

Fig. 12.26 Intraoral ramus-split osteotomy (Obwegeser's technique): **(a)** Ramus osteotomy, **(b)** Bony separation, **(c)** Fixation of osteotomized segments.

posterior repositioning of the prognathic mandible. On the contrary, lateral pterygoid influences the least. It may, at the most, distract the head of the condyle by its pull. The masseter and medial pterygoids have greater capacity to distract bone ends in subcondylar osteotomies in such a way that the patient can develop anterior open bite, with the posterior teeth acting as fulcrum. But these two muscles have no deleterious effect following vertical osteotomies of the ramus since muscles are elevated during surgery and allowed to reposition themselves during the healing phase. The muscles attached between mandible and hyoid bone supplement the action of the principal muscles of mastication.

The complex lingual musculature by virtue of their pressure effect can result in the relapse following the corrections of mandibular excess. This is also supplemented by the suprahyoid group of muscles. The problem becomes more acute in case of patients with abnormal habit like tongue-thrusting. Therefore, while planning the orthognathic surgery, attention must be paid to the musculature and their influence on the stability of the osteotomized segment.

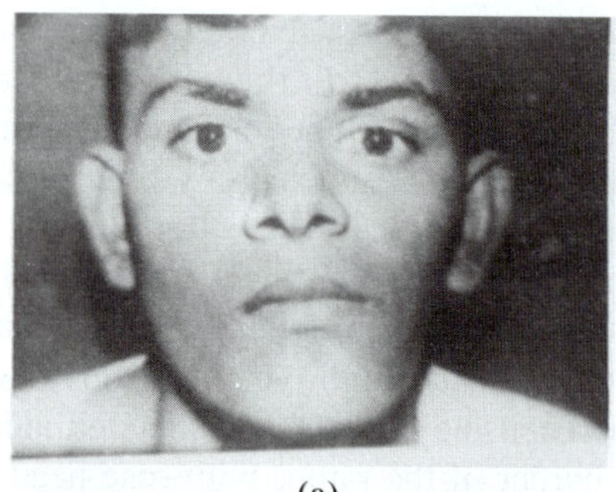

(a)

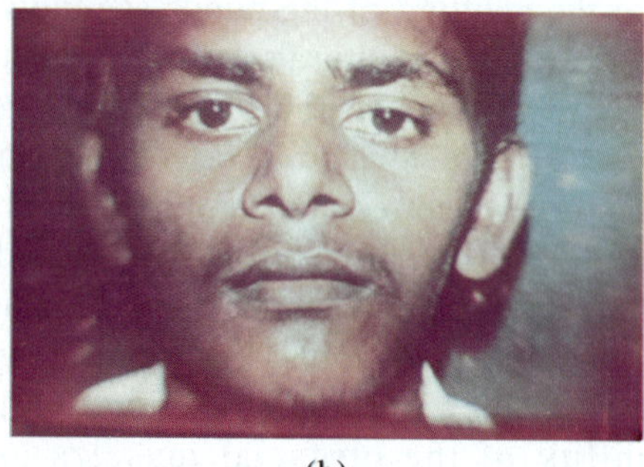

(b)

Fig. 12.27 Mandibular excess - unilateral **(a)** Pre-operative, **(b)** Postoperative.

MICROGENIA AND GENIOPLASTY (Fig 12.28)

A careful evaluation of patients with retruded chin will reveal that not all the patients require osteotomy

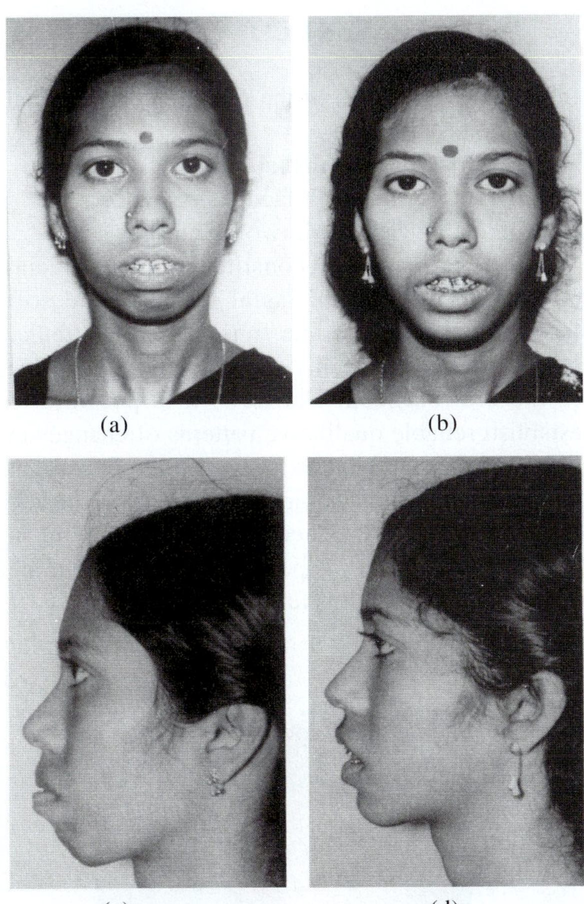

Fig. 12.28 Clinical photographs - Cl II division I occlusion with microgenia **(a)** Preorthodontic - Interdental corticotomy, **(b)** Postorthodontic, **(c)** Presurgical with mandibular microgenia, **(d)** Post surgical.

and advancement of the mandible. Wherever occlusion is satisfactory, there is no need to alter the occlusion. But the position of the chin is considered to be the foundation that determines the overall harmony of the facial profile. A variety of implants have been utilized to augment the deficient chin with varied success. Autogenous onlay bone grafts require an objectionable second operation. Both graft and synthetic implants are not successful because of the associated bone resorption. Bone grafts resorb while bone under the bed of the synthetic implants resorb. Either way, the facial profile is altered. More often, synthetic implants migrate due to the action of the chin muscles and may even get exfoliated. Therefore, to achieve stable improved facial profile, genioplasty provides the answer. Many methods of genioplasty have been described in the literature.

Careful preoperative evaluation is a prerequisite for this procedure. The complexity of the development of chin is evident in the anthropological, osteological, myological and cephalometric discussions. Ricketts described *chin, point-B,* and *mandibular incisor* as keystone TRIAD. Following the preoperative analysis, mock surgery is performed to determine the osteotomy plane and the desirable postoperative facial profile. The techniques used are as follows:

(1) Sliding advancement genioplasty.
(2) Horizontal osteotomy for the correction of macrogenia.
(3) Horizontal sliding osteotomy for asymmetry.
(4) Horizontal osteotomy with ostectomy.
(5) "Sandwich" horizontal osteotomy.
(6) Step osteotomy.

All these procedures can be carried out through intraoral approach.

Formerly, osteotomy was performed with Bur. Now, it is performed with precision by using Pneumatic osteotomy drills. (Fig. 12.29).

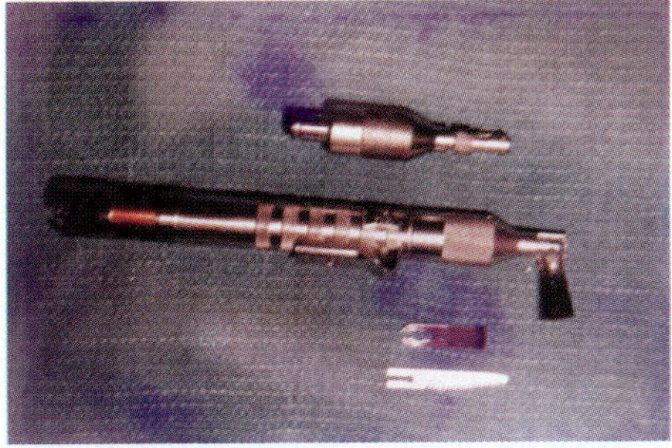

Fig. 12.29 Pneumatic osteotomy drills.

CRANIOFACIAL SURGERY

Although this is outside the scope of this book, the concept of craniofacial surgery is to be understood by the practitioner so that it will be helpful to refer the patient to the appropriate centre. For the past 10 years, enthusiastic oral and maxillofacial surgeons collaborated with the pediatric and neurosurgeons to perform corrective surgery on patients with craniofacial malformations. Now it is possible to surgically correct any of the skeletal deformities involving the entire skull. Surgical access to the upper one third of the facial skeleton is possible with transcranial incisions. Incidentally, this approach has been found to be very useful in managing maxillofacial trauma and to gain access to the T.M. joint. Figure 12.30 illustrates the concept of craniofacial surgery.

PRESENT CONCEPT

In general, objectives of the management of facial disharmonies are:

(i) Correction of dental malocclusion.
(ii) Improvement of facial appearance.
(iii) Long-term stability of the results.

They reflect three constituents of the facial complex — dentition, facial skeleton and soft tissues of the face. Some time back, mandibular osteotomies were the only surgical options available to the oral surgeon. But now, it is possible to establish reliable qualitative patterns of changes in the facial contour. On this basis, the present concept of facial disharmonies have been reviewed in the following manner. Since a detailed account is certainly outside the scope of this book, an outline of the present concept is furnished here.

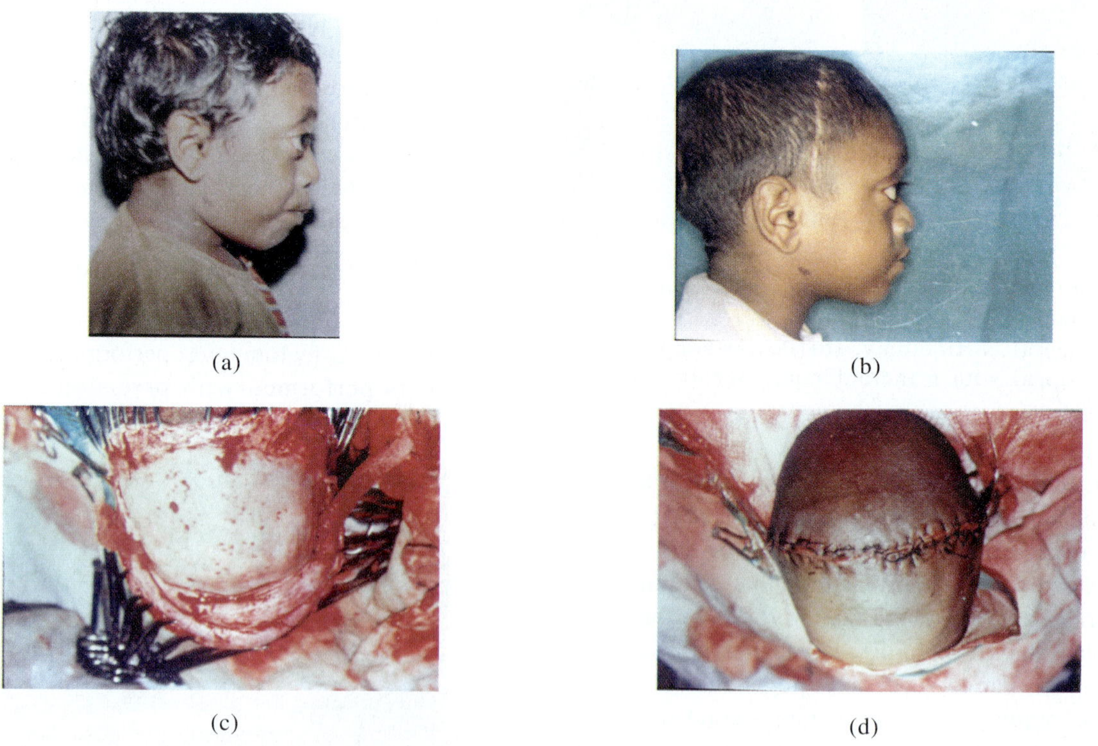

(a) (b) (c) (d)

Fig. 12.30 Craniofacial surgery - Transcranial frontal bone advancement **(a)** Preoperative, **(b)** Postoperative, **(c)** Frontal bone surgical exposure with bicoronal flap, **(d)** Bicoronal flap suture.

1. Symmetrical disproportions

A. Anteroposterior plane
   (a) Mandibular excess
   (b) Mandibular deficiency
   (c) Maxillary excess
   (d) Maxillary deficiency
B. Vertical plane
   (a) Mandibular excess
   (b) Mandibular deficiency
   (c) Maxillary excess
   (d) Maxillary deficiency
C. Transverse plane
   (a) Mandibular transverse excess
   (b) Mandibular transverse deficiency
   (c) Maxillary transverse excess
   (d) Maxillary transverse deficiency.

2. Asymmetrical disproportions

Transverse facial asymmetry. So, it is quite evident that the shift in emphasis from occlusal rehabilitation to esthetic improvement has been most obvious. During the follow-up of the patients postoperatively, it could be observed that, particular procedures produce predictable results in terms of facial esthetic changes. There has been an increase in the utilization of personal computers to undertake predictive planning. It has been the teaching that, it is better to wait until the facial growth is completed - until the age of 18 years is crossed. Recently, a technique called *distraction osteogenesis* has been found to be useful to achieve a controlled three-dimensional bone lengthening during the growing phase.

Distraction osteogenesis is a relatively new technique. It is anticipated to become an invaluable tool in the management of facial deformities in the years to come. The ability to induce callus and then to gradually and progressively distract the proximal and the distal ends of the bone without disrupting the vascular supply is known as distraction osteogenesis. Distraction process is very similar to orthodontic tooth movement where surface lining osteoblasts are responsible for laying down new bone. McCarthy and others have described four distinct components of the distracted zone.

(a) Radiolucent central zone comprising fibrous tissue.
(b) Bone formation along the stretched fibrous tissue.
(c) Remodelling area where bone spicules are lined by osteoblasts and osteoclasts.
(d) Area of mature bone which remodels in a year or so.

The area where bone lengthening is required, initially, an osteotomy is carried out subperiosteally. A latent period of 5 to 7 days is allowed before initiating distraction process.

Fixations are attached to the bone on either side of the osteotomy site. After achieving the desired lengthening, bone is allowed to consolidate under function into cortical and medullary phases. The following morbidities have been described in the literature following this procedure:

(a) Localized edema.
(b) Necrosis of the skin.
(c) Pin-tract infection.
(d) Unpredictable ossification of the expanded zone.

The rate and rhythm of distraction are important in determining the prognosis of the procedure. They are

(a) **Rate:** Below 0.5 mm per day may lead to premature union and above 1.5 mm per day may lead to non-union.

(b) **Rhythm:** Patient is instructed to activate the appliance four times a day to give separate lengthenings of 0.25 mm each giving a total of 1mm per day. This, relatively slow distraction, is painless. When clinical lengthening is less than 10% of the initial bone length, overlying soft tissue can adapt easily. It seems that vessels, nerves and muscles all have some ability for such adaptations.

Advancements in this technique include
(a) Intraoral lengthening devices,
(b) Widening and lengthening of the mandible,
(c) Advancement of maxilla.

Further studies and clinical experience alone will reveal the clinical indications and the possible limitations of this procedure.

Robinson emphasized that any learner of orthognathic surgery must learn any one technique first and then can make changes later, as they desire. But in practice, if a person masters one technique, then the tendency is to do the same procedure irrespective of the deformity to be corrected. Many feel that teaching in orthognathic surgery must provide the basis for an outline in surgical techniques. In other words, teaching must not be stereotyped. Thus, pendulum swings between the two extremes. During the training phase, one must understand the basic principles of various procedures in orthognathic surgery. But when it comes to practice, simpler methods can be practised with success while complicated procedures must not be undertaken unless one is trained properly to perform them. As Gilles put it, *esthetic surgery is an attempt to surpass normal*. Therefore, one must take all precautions to keep the incidence of morbidities as low as possible, especially in the field of orthognathic surgery.

Preprosthetic Surgery

SCOPE

This branch of oral surgery has gained considerable importance in the recent past as an important breakthrough in the growing challenge to the prosthodontist in providing satisfactory dentures. Perhaps, this has been largely due to:

(a) An increasing demand by the patients for better quality of dentures,

(b) An increasing awareness of the role of preprosthetic surgery by the prosthodontist, and

(c) An active role of the oral surgeon to make the denture-bearing area of the oral cavity conducive to satisfactory prosthetic service.

Unfortunately, many patients endure their discomforts with their dentures at considerable expense of money and time until they assume and console themselves as "dental cripples". It is in this context that well-established preprosthetic surgical techniques can play a major role to regain faith in the expertise of the prosthodontists. In fact, some timely surgical interventions will render the denture more effective. The basic procedures can be undertaken by any dental practitioner leaving the major reconstructive preprosthetic procedures to a specialist oral surgeon.

In spite of the advances in prosthetic technology with new denture materials, an appreciable number of patients continue to experience difficulties in wearing their dentures. Such problems of the denture-bearing area may be due to many factors. For example, a well-fitting denture can become ill-fitting due to biological aging of oral tissues. Hence, it is absolutely essential for every member of the dental profession to possess adequate knowledge of biological considerations which will aid in prosthodontic practice. Sometimes, for elimination of the denture, "displacing" factors may be the only way to make the denture satisfactory. It is equally essential for the oral surgeon to understand the actual needs of the prosthodontist who in turn should understand the aims, scope and limitations of preprosthetic surgery which can be considered as a tripod with the patient, prosthodontist and oral surgeon as the three components. At the same time, the dental practitioner must realize that a poor surgical result will leave the patient in a worse situation. Hence, practice of preprosthetic surgery can be successful, depending on the team approach and on the realization of the special features of this branch of surgery. The scope of preprosthetic surgery includes the following:

(i) *Ridge preservation* procedures as a preventive measure.
(ii) *Corrective or recontouring* procedures of the defects and abnormalities.
(iii) *Ridge extension* procedures:
  (a) *Relative* methods, e.g. sulcus extension (vestibuloplasties).
  (b) *Absolute* methods, e.g. ridge augmentation methods.
(iv) *Reconstructive* procedure like correction of abnormal ridge relationships.
(v) Provision of *accessory aids:*
  (a) Creating favorable under-cuts.
  (b) Dental implants.
  (c) Onlay denture.
(vi) *Modified denture construction* procedures, e.g. immediate denture where construction of the denture precedes surgery.

Each method has a definite and positive role to play under specific circumstances in denture construction. The field of preprosthetic surgery is highly technical. Hence, it demands superior skill of the surgeon. The aging of soft tissues of the medically compromised patients will be difficult to work with because of the scarring and friability of the atrophic mucous membrane. Even the placement of incisions must be well planned in advance so that the ultimate scar does not break down under the influence of the denture pressure during function. If this factor is not kept in mind, elimination of one unfavorable factor will be replaced by the creation of another undesirable factor. Hence, preprosthetic surgery is utilized to rectify the biological obstacles and also to improve the denture-bearing area of the oral cavity for improved efficiency of the denture. But, the practitioner must always bear in mind that it can only be an aid to denture construction but can never be a substitute for a satisfactory dental prosthesis.

OBJECTIVES

It is to provide an ideal denture-bearing area which will provide maximum comfort and retention of dentures during function.

(a) The anatomical base should be healthy, firm and smooth.

(b) The supporting surfaces must be of adequate size, covered by healthy mucoperiosteum of even thickness.

(c) Sufficient space must exist between the alveolar ridges to accommodate the dentures without any gross abnormalities of the jaws and their relationship.

Variation in ridge atrophy of the jaws

A well-fitting denture constructed on an apparently satisfactory alveolar ridge can develop into an ill-fitting denture over the course of a few years due to the onset of a number of defects and abnormalities. It has been estimated that, on an average, 0.1 mm of bone resorbs per year in the anterior region of maxilla while it is nearly 4 times more in the mandible. When this 4:1 ratio is projected for a period of 20-25 years, it will be found that 2 to 2.5 mm of bone resorption can occur in maxilla. But it is nearly 8-10 mm of bone loss in the mandibular ridge. This clearly demonstrates that the demand for preprosthetic surgery is more in mandible than in maxilla.

Usually, hard and soft tissues of the oral cavity including frenal attachments and bony prominence may not have any significance relevant to the practice of prosthetic dentistry when teeth are present. But, after full mouth extraction, the very same structures may become obstacles for the functioning of dentures. The surgical aids are therefore necessary to restructure the oral cavity in such a way that prosthetic rehabilitation will restore the masticatory efficiency, speech, dental, facial and esthetic functions in the best possible manner. The corrective and reconstructive preprosthetic surgery has undergone tremendous advancement over the past 25-30 years. Obwegeser from Switzerland stimulated the oral surgeons to face the challenge of prosthetic rehabilitation successfully.

EVALUATION

This aspect comprises 'Triad' - *patient, prosthodontist and oral surgeon.*

The patient is the one who is to wear the denture. In practice, we come across patients who feel unhappy with the dentures even though they are well-designed, properly constructed and esthetically good. Likewise, a few others wear the denture happily, however poorly designed, constructed and ill-fitting it may be. This can be attributed to the psychological make-up of the patient towards one's own environment. However, the patient should be carefully evaluated for the need of preprosthetic surgery taking into consideration the positive and negative factors helpful for the successful construction of the denture. It is a good practice to radiologically survey the jaws with panoramic x-rays to plan the treatment properly. Proper assessment of the patient must include the age, health status, motivation, awareness of the operative procedures and the discomforts associated with surgery. A non-motivated patient becomes a problem if surgery is thrusted on him.

The prosthodontist must carefully evaluate the supporting oral hard and soft tissues, including the problems and difficulties of the patient. This is absolutely essential in the diagnosis and treatment planning including the provision of the plaster casts, construction of appliances and other adjunct procedures necessary preoperatively. The prosthodontist must also have adequate knowledge of the scope and limitations of preprosthetic surgery.

The oral surgeon is the person to plan and perform the surgical procedures on the denture-bearing area. But it is always a good practice to consult the prosthodontist. Perhaps, his responsibility starts even before commencing the extraction of teeth, considering the importance of preserving and preparing a good base for the denture. On the basis of evaluation, the oral surgeon should take a decision as to what is good for a particular patient under the given circumstances. During the process, one must ensure that no new problem is created consequent to surgery.

A thorough evaluation is essential regarding the following factors while undertaking any preprosthetic surgery:

(1) Chief complaints of the patient.
(2) The patient's expectations of the surgical and prosthetic treatment.
(3) Esthetic and functional needs of the patient.
(4) Outlook towards one's own environment.
(5) The patient's adaptability.
(6) Past history of any prosthetic treatment.
(7) General health status.
(8) Attitude towards maintenance of oral hygiene.
(9) Intraoral examination.
    (a) Amount and contour of the alveolar ridge and basal bone.
    (b) Quality of the mucosa covering the denture-bearing area.
    (c) Depth of the vestibule.
    (d) Presence and location of abnormal fibrous and muscle attachments.
    (e) Jaw relationship.
    (f) Any pathological lesions present in the hard and soft tissues of the oral cavity.
    (g) Alveolar ridge
        (i) Inspection, palpation and radiological examination of the denture-bearing area.
        (ii) Bony ridge form and contour.
        (iii) Bony undercuts or bony protuberances.
        (iv) Buccal vestibule.
        (v) Palatal vault.
        (vi) Tuberosity area.
        (vii) Location of mental foramen and the mylohyoid ridge.
        (viii) Interarch relationship.
        (ix) Appropriate radiographs.

Panoramic radiographs provide most of the required informations like bony pathology, impacted teeth, retained roots, bony pattern of alveolar ridgc, size and pneumatization of maxillary antrum.

(x) Resorption of alveolar bone.

(xi) Muscular and mucosal attachments.

REQUIREMENTS OF AN IDEAL RIDGE (Fig. 13.1)

(i) It should have desirable vestibular depth.

(ii) It must provide adequate bony support for the dentures.

(iii) Ideally, alveolar ridge should be as large as possible, broad and U-shaped.

(iv) The ridge should be covered by adequate keratinized mucosal lining of uniform thickness and compressibility but immobile so that denture stability is ensured.

(v) The ridge should be free from any unfavorable hard and soft tissue protuberances or undercuts.

(vi) It should be free from abnormal muscle attachments or scar bands which may disturb the peripheral seal of the denture.

(vii) The relationship between maxillary and mandibular ridges must be satisfactory three-dimensionally-*anteroposteriorly (horizontal), transversely* and *vertically*.

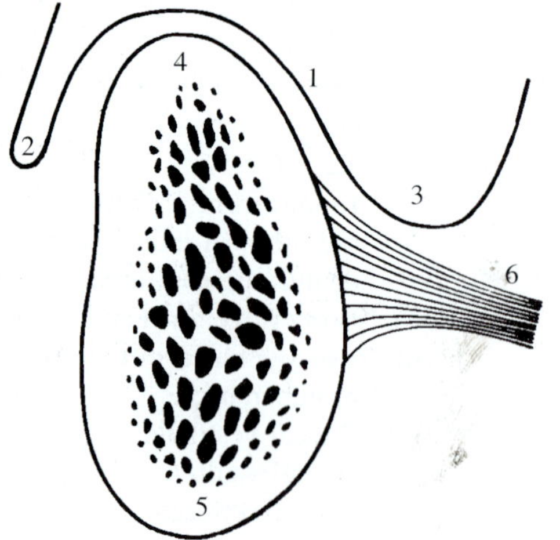

Fig. 13.1 An ideal mandibular alveolar ridge (diagram). 1. Masticatory mucosa over the alveolar ridge. 2. Vestibule. 3. Lining mucosa. 4. Alveolar ridge. 5. Basal bone. 6. Attachment of the muscles at the floor of the mouth.

On completion of full mouth extractions, the patient has to wait for a reasonable period before the denture is inserted. Prior to the denture construction, the dental practitioner must ensure that the entire denture-bearing area of the prospective prosthetic patient must fulfill these criteria.

The alveolar ridges may break down due to the following factors:

(a) Atrophy of the alveolar bone following dental extraction due to the preoperative periodontal problems or due to pressure under prosthesis.

(b) Mucosal and bony atrophy associated with faulty metabolism and aging process.

(c) Occlusal disharmonies.

(d) Deformation of denture bases.

PREVENTIVE MEASURES (RIDGE PRESERVATION)

There are many preventive measures that can be adopted even during the extraction of teeth, as an aid to denture construction.

(1) Preventive measures start even when the decision is taken to make the patient edentulous. The factors which influence the fate of natural teeth are:

(a) Quality of the oral tissues,

(b) Their resistance to dental diseases,

(c) Patient's attitude,

(d) Quality and regularity of the patient's care of oral hygiene and general health.

In most of the cases, decision to retain the natural teeth or not can easily be made. But a few borderline cases exist in which any decision is difficult to make. Such considerations are: (a) pattern of bone resorption, (b) bony support of the teeth and (c) presence of any pathological changes in the jaws. Perhaps, retention of molars or canines for the provision of onlay dentures is a worthwhile proposition.

(2) Raising the quality of dental extraction seems to be a simple and yet the most effective way. Radiological survey reveals that nearly 25% of the edentulous jaws contain retained or burried roots. Intelligent use of radiographs is helpful to anticipate the breakage of roots during dental extraction so that the necessary precautions can be taken. Proper preoperative evaluation and meticulous techniques of dental extraction will considerably reduce the incidence of burried roots. Usually, the retained roots work their way out until they reach the surface and ulcerate the mucous membrane under the denture.

(3) During the dental extraction, the alveolar socket, which expands, must be carefully compressed back into its place. The sharp margins, if any, must be trimmed after completing the dental extraction. Generous removal of bone will lead to significant reduction in the size of the ridge.

(4) If the soft tissue flaps have the tendency to gape open, sutures must be loosely applied to preserve the desired shape of the alveolar ridge. Tooth division technique helps to avoid large areas of bone removal.

(5) During the dental extraction, a little forethought will help to eliminate the probable prosthetic difficulties like irregular alveolar ridge, bulbous tuberosity, unfavorable undercuts and fibrous bands. Interdental papillae and crests of the septal bone sometimes lead to multiple prominences along the ridge. If necessary, they may be trimmed and margins are sutured.

(6) (a) Retained root remnants in edentulous jaws, (b) unerupted teeth and (c) pathological lesions like odontomes, granulomas and cysts are more often found lying dormant and asymptomatic in edentulous jaws. It has been found that retained roots form nearly 25% of them. Sometimes, radicular fractures during extraction may be inevitable due to many predisposing factors. It is ideal to remove all such fractured root fragments. Sometimes, it is better to leave it behind in situ since its removal may involve the excision of large amount of bone. In young adults, it seldom gives rise to any problem. But in elderly patients, it has to be removed if it is superficially placed. The term "root apex" refers to the radicular portion, not exceeding 6 mm. Forcible removal of the palatal root apex may result in its displacement to the maxillary sinus. In such cases, it is wise to leave it alone. Over the course of time, if it works its way out under the denture, it can be removed.

Experience has shown that the mere presence of a root fragment in edentulous jaw does not warrant removal. The operator has to assess the justification of removal by proper evaluation. As a rule, all the root fragments associated with any pathology should be removed. During the removal of burried teeth, care must be taken to ensure the preservation of maximum amount of alveolar bony ridge. For example, tooth division technique is useful to avoid removal of large areas of bone.

Panoramic radiographs furnish useful and consolidated information in a single radiograph. Taking full mouth radiographs is time-consuming and causes inconvenience to the patient and the operator.

Whatever be the localization method, removal of deeply embedded roots in an atrophic edentulous jaw in elderly patients must be undertaken only by an experienced operator since it involves risks. Apart from difficulties in localization, it is found that elderly patients cannot withstand prolonged surgical procedures. In such elderly patients, oral cavity presents a challenge to the operator. The tissues are friable and atrophic as an aging process. They heal very slowly. Risks of jaw fracture and damage of the neurovascular bundle in atrophic jaws during surgery are important possibilities that one should always bear in mind.

RIDGE CORRECTIVE PROCEDURES

These oral surgical procedures are to be considered as corrective methods, to be carried out on the alveolar ridge, to achieve the criteria of an ideal ridge. They are mainly aimed at altering, improving or even replacing the tissues of the denture-bearing area. When they are done during dental extraction or before inserting the denture for the first time, they are called primary procedures. They can be considered as corrections on soft tissue or bone. Certain corrective procedures carried out after the patient has started using the denture are known as secondary procedures. These procedures are done in soft tissue or bone.

A. SOFT TISSUE

Labial frenectomy

High attachments of labial frena and fibrous bands can cause denture instability by interfering with the peripheral seal of the denture during function. Moreover, if the periphery of the denture impinges the labial frenum, the overlying mucous membrane is traumatized. Since these ulcers are painful, the patient prefers not to wear the denture. As an urgent measure, the corresponding area of the denture can be trimmed to prevent such ulceration. If the problem continues to persist, repeated trimming of the denture may result in its breakage. Hence, it is preferable to perform frenectomy to avoid such recurrent problems.

Labial frenal attachment consists of thin bands of fibrous tissue and a few muscle fibers covered by mucous membrane. It usually extends from the upper lip to the crest of the alveolar ridge. Sometimes, it may extend on to the maxillary incisive papilla.

Under local infiltration anesthesia, the upper lip is everted and stretched with a stay-suture. A vertical, long, elliptical incision is made on either side of the fibrous band. The incision is extended down to the alveolar bone and anterior nasal spine. The frenum and the underlying muscular components are dissected away from the periosteum deep to the vestibular sulcus. Once the bleeding is controlled, an interrupted suture is placed with an atraumatic catgut suture fixing the wound margins to the underlying periosteum at a covenient predetermined depth in the vestibule. The rest of the areas are closed with interrupted sutures. If the alveolar ridge cannot be covered, the defect is left unsutured to granulate and epithelialize. Guttapercha can be adapted over the flange of the acrylic denture so that sulcus is maintained in the new position. Reattachment of the lip is thus prevented so that obliteration of the sulcus does not occur. Some prefer to lengthen the suture line by performing Z plasty or V-Y procedures. If 2 or 3 bands are present at the frenal attachments, then, a horizontal incision is made supraperiosteally along the vestibule and the wound is allowed to granulate and epithelialize as a localized vestibuloplasty. Unfortunately, these procedures may produce scar contraction, resulting in obliteration in the sulcus depth. The denture flange can be extended by adapting guttapercha but its role to resist scar contraction is questionable.

Lingual frenectomy

This procedure will be necessary if the attachment of the lingual frenum is high enough to displace the lower denture during function. Too much of trimming will make the denture weak. The chances of breakage of the horseshoe-shaped denture at this point is very high. In addition, another problem with lingual frenum is the interference with speech. This clinical condition is known as *ankyloglossia*. It consists of very dense fibrous connective tissue bands, covered by mucous membrane. Occasionally, it may contain superficial fibers of genioglossus muscle, thereby the free movement of the tongue is restricted.

The tongue is highly muscular. Hence, the movement of the tongue should be controlled during the surgical excision of the lingual frenum. The patient's cooperation is required to perform this procedure under local anesthesia. For this reason, general anesthesia is preferred by many. The tip of the tongue is fixed with a stay suture and stretched in an upward and backward direction so that the floor of the mouth is elevated. Very similar to the labial frenectomy, a narrow, elliptical, long incision is made on either side of the frenum. The frenal attachment is excised along the undersurface of the tongue, lingual vestibule and on to the lingual alveolar periosteum. Care is taken to avoid the injury to the papilla of the submandibular duct. Sufficient amount of muscle fibers, fibrous bands and the strip of mucous membrane are trimmed away to mobilize the tongue adequately. More bleeding will be encountered than in labial frenectomy. After securing hemostasis, the first suture is placed with atraumatic catgut at the depth of the vestibule, fixing the wound edges to the underlying periosteum. The wound margins are approximated with interrupted suture. The denture flange is extended by adapting Guttapercha.

Mobile soft tissues on the alveolar ridge

The mobile and unsupported soft tissues are often found in the anterior maxillary alveolar ridge due to ill-fitting dentures. There may be associated resorption of bone. This mobile soft tissue is compressible and hence the denture becomes very unstable. During the early phase, the patient experiences increasing instability of the denture. Consequently, the rocking movement of the denture during function results in gradual resorption of the underlying bone and may even be exposed in the midline anterior to the nasal spine. The overlying mucous membrane gets traumatized due to denture pressure resulting in a painful ulcer. In course of time, such unsupported alveolar tissues increase in size and may even prolapse towards the palatal direction, thereby clinically exhibiting mobile alveolar ridge in the anterior maxillary region. Usually, tuberosity is not involved in this process. As a corrective measure, such compressible, mobile, alveolar soft tissues need not be excised to make the denture stable and to arrest further resorption of bone.

Under local infiltration anesthesia, a linear wedge excision of the excess soft tissues along with the alveolar crest is done. To facilitate approximation of the wound margins, submucous excision of the fibrous tissue on either side is done adequately, limiting such dissection to the mobile alveolar soft tissue. The wound edges are approximated with interrupted sutures taking care not to obliterate the labial sulcus.

Denture granulomas

Howe classified the denture granulomas into three groups on the basis of size and situation of the base of these lesions.

Class-I Granulomas of the masticatory mucosa.
Class-II Granulomas of the lining mucosa.
Class-III Granulomas at the vestibule, obliterating the sulcus.

Usually, surgical defects in class-I heal well with minimal scarring. In class-II lesions, wound should not be closed under tension. Sometimes, wide undermining of the adjacent mucosa may be necessary. Class-III lesions will require epithelial cover.

Enlarged tuberosity

Idiopathic fibrous hyperplasia found in relation to the maxillary posterior teeth may persist even after the removal of these teeth. Such enlarged tuberosity may render the denture unstable, thereby reducing the masticatory efficiency. This bulky fibrous tissue is seen more on the palatal aspect. A three-dimensional reduction of such enlarged tuberosity is required to provide adequate denture space at the posterior region. Presurgical radiographs may be necessary to determine whether the underlying bone is also involved.

Under local infiltration anesthesia, a wedge of soft tissue from the first molar to tuberosity region is excised. Then, a cushion of soft tissue from the undersurface of the palatal mucoperiosteum is also trimmed so that wound margins can be approximated without any tension. Brisk bleeding may be encountered if care is not taken to avoid the damage of greater palatine vessels while dissecting the undersurface of the palatal flap.

Enlarged retromolar pad

This is very similar to the enlarged maxillary tuberosity, preventing the posterior extension of the denture base. Under local anesthesia, an elliptical incision is made around this hyperplastic region and the excess tissue is excised. Thinning of the flaps may be necessary. Care should be taken not to remove excess tissue on the lingual side to avoid damage to the lingual nerve and vessels. The wound is closed with interrupted sutures. This is relatively a rare condition when compared to enlarged tuberosity of the maxilla.

B. BONE

Shaping the unsuitable bony ridge

It is a well-known fact that during contouring of the ridge, excision of excessive amount of alveolar bone often results in excessive resorption. Conservative reduction of the alveolar bone preserves more bone. Hence, over-enthusiastic reduction of the bone must be avoided to correct irregular or sharp ridges, unsuitable for the construction of dentures. The surgery should be restricted to the elimination of the irregular or sharp ridges and unfavorable undercuts.

The term *alveolectomy* refers to the trimming and removal of the labiobuccal alveolar bone along with minimum amount of interdental and inter-radicular septal bone.

Interseptal alveolectomy consists of excising the interdental septa and compressing the fractured labial or buccal palate towards the palatal or lingual plate, hinging on the labial mucoperiosteum. This considerably reduces the size of the alveolar socket with minimum loss of bone. If the height of the ridge is high, required bone can be trimmed only then.

Alveolectomy

Indications

(1) Patients with dense, cortical alveolar bone, which offers resistance during dental extraction.

(2) If the bony ridge continues to be irregular even after 2-3 months of extraction, recontouring of the ridge is necessary. Usually, this radical procedure is reserved for patients whose alveolar ridges are not suitable for providing the prosthesis.

(3) Patients who undergo extraction of isolated teeth with prominent alveolar bone.

(4) This radical procedure is a prerequisite for providing an immediate denture for esthetic purposes.

Treatment planning. Before surgical intervention, careful treatment planning is essential. To determine the extent of bone removal, a preoperative template should be prepared. A plaster cast is prepared with a good impression of the denture-bearing area. The clinical findings are carefully examined on the plaster cast and marked with a pencil. A mock surgery is performed on the model, taking into consideration the area of the ridge which requires excision and the extent of bone to be removed. Once the shape of the ridge is satisfactory, a template is prepared in clear acrylic to cover the entire denture bearing area. Preoperatively, acrylic template is cleaned with soap and water and left immersed in any cold sterilizing solution for a few hours. Now, the template is ready for use at the time of surgery.

Under local infiltration anesthesia, a suitable mucoperiosteal flap is raised to expose the irregular surfaces of the bony ridge. The flap design depends on the timing of surgery-whether surgery is performed on the edentulous ridge at the time of extraction. If it is on the edentulous ridge, incision is placed along the crest of the alveolus which is relatively avascular area. Depending on the surgical exposure, an oblique relief incision is made on the labial side to provide a broad base to the flap. If the procedure is to be performed at the time of extraction, incision is made along the free gingival margin taking care to excise the epithelial attachment to facilitate its removal along with the extracted tooth. The underlying alveolar bone is exposed with such an envelope flap. Irrespective of the flap design, bone is exposed and the required bone is removed by any one of the accepted methods of bone removal. Excessive reflection of the flap should be avoided. Depending on the irregularity of the alveolar ridge, recontouring is done with bone Roengeurs' or with chisel and mallet. Sometimes a big rose-head bur or flame-shaped metallic acrylic trimmer can be useful for the purpose. After achieving the desired recontouring of the bone, flap is repositioned back over the ridge to determine the excess of the flap to be trimmed. Excess, if any, is trimmed with a pair of scissors. Then the template is tried as a guidance for bone removal. Areas of bone still require to be removed as per the treatment planning and they can be identified easily by observing the pressure points from the blanching of the mucous membrane by applying pressure over the template in position. Such areas should be trimmed further until the template, in clear acrylic, is in uniform contact with the denture-bearing area. The bone surface is made smooth with bone file. After copious irrigation of the surgical field, to remove the loose bony particles, the flap is approximated with interrupted sutures. The sutures are removed between fifth and seventh postoperative day. Usually, the wound healing is uneventful.

Intraseptal alveolectomy. This is yet another method of socket reduction. But it has the advantage of retaining as much of compact labial bone as possible which usually resists resorption of bone postoperatively. This is more significant due to the fact that the cancellous bone undergoes more resorption under pressure. Therefore, the labial plate of bone is retained without disturbing its blood supply. Hence, the result of this procedure is expected to be more long lasting. This method is possible only at the time of extraction of teeth and not on the edentulous ridge. So, this method is widely used for providing immediate dentures. Preparation of template may not be very useful in this procedure.

Under local infiltration anesthesia, incision is placed along the free gingival margin, with epithelial attachment and the interdental papillae left attached to the respective teeth. An envelope flap is raised conservatively. Then, extraction of teeth is carried out starting from canine towards the midline bilaterally. This is only an attempt to preserve the integrity of the labial plate without disturbing its blood supply and soft tissue attachments. After completing the extractions, a wedge of labial alveolar bone is removed on either side, distal to the canine region. This will establish discontinuity between the anterior labial plate with its posterior counterparts. This will facilitate easy fracturing of the labial cortical plate without much difficulty. The Roengeur's forceps is introduced into the socket. The interradicular septa are trimmed and removed by keeping the flat surface of the blade held as close to the labial plate as possible. This will result in severing the communication between labial and palatal cortical plates. A gauze piece is placed over the labial plate and fractured with digital pressure. Some advocate the fracturing of the labial plate by placing any convenient instrument at the canine socket on either side and pressure is applied towards the labial direction to create a horizontal fracture of the outer cortex. Whatever be the method, it is left to one's own convenience, so long, as tear of the mucous membrane is avoided during the fracturing of the labial plate. Thus, collapse of the socket is achieved. The edge of the palatal mucoperiosteum is elevated marginally so that free ends of both the labial and palatal plates are trimmed and moulded, and the future alveolar crest is smooth and not irregular.

If an immediate denture is being provided, the denture must be prepared in clear acrylic so that it will serve the function of a template. Any blanching, noticed through the clear acrylic, forms the guide to relieve the pressure points. The wound margins are approximated with interrupted sutures.

This method is simple and quick but indicated only when extraction could be done with minimal disturbance to the alveolar socket. If the alveolar bone is dense and cortical, the operator may experience considerable difficulty in performing this procedure. However, this method cannot be applied in moulding edentulous ridges and in cases where intrabony pathology exists.

Elimination of unfavorable undercuts

Genial tubercles, mental tubercles and mylohyoid ridge may become unfavorable prominences due to the severe atrophy of the mandibular alveolus.

Resection of genial tubercles. Muscles attached to the superior genial tubercles form a fold of mucous membrane between the opening of the Wharton's duct and the ridge. Since it is superficially placed, this fold interferes with lingual flange of the denture by disturbing the lingual periphery seal. The denture is displaced whenever tongue is lifted. This results in frequent ulceration of the lining mucosa. The shelf-like bony prominence present in the intercanine region results in the obliteration of the lingual vestibule. Because of the presence of the bony tubercle, deepening of the lingual vestibule at this region is not possible.

Hence, vestibuloplasty can be carried out after resecting this bony prominence leaving behind a zone of mucosa with the underlying fibroelastic tissue between the opening of the submandibular salivary duct and the ridge. The surgical access could be gained by a midline incision. In this region, superior genial tubercles are exposed and chiseled out. It is advantageous to fix the genioglossus muscle with a catgut suture before chiseling the tubercle to prevent it from disappearing into the floor of the mouth. The cut surface of the bone is smoothened with a bone file. The excised tubercle is severed from the muscle and removed. The wound is closed with interrupted black silk sutures.

Resection of mylohyoid ridge. This is relatively a minor procedure under local anesthesia to remove the sharp shelf of mylohyoid ridge along with a portion of mylohyoid muscle attached to it. This procedure is designed to eliminate the unfavorable undercuts so that retention and stability of the denture are improved by the extension of the lingual flange deeper. By doing so, it is expected to resist the lateral movements of the denture.

In addition to block anesthesia, local infiltration is advantageous since it will assist in defining the plane of dissection from the bone. An incision is made in the transverse direction just anterior to retromolar pad across the alveolar ridge. On the buccal sulcus, the incision is extended anteriorly, just above the mucobuccal reflection. The flap is raised, exposing the ridge and the lingual shelf. By doing so, damage to the lingual nerve is avoided. Mylohyoid ridge and the muscle are then exposed. While the assistant supports the mandible from below, chisel is placed in a vertical direction on the ridge. A sharp tap separates the mylohyoid ridge from the lingual surface of the mandible. Bone pieces are held with a pair of forceps and dissected away from its soft tissue attachments. The sharp bony ridge is removed and the bone is smoothened with the bone file. The muscles and mucosal flap are replaced back and wound is closed with black silk interrupted sutures.

Excision of tori. Usually, tori are found in the palatal vault and the lingual aspect of the mandible bilaterally. If the denture is worn by the patient, it rests on the bony prominences and causes ulceration. This ulceration on a bony swelling makes the patient apprehensive due to cancer phobia.

Tori are developmental in origin occurring as exostosis. Grinding of dentures to provide relief on these areas will render the dentures weak. Hence, excision is the treatment of choice.

The palatal lesions can be exposed through a midline incision over the exostosis (Fig 13.2). If needed, one end of the midline incision can be extended in the form of Y, avoiding the contents of nasopalatine foramen. The overlying mucoperiosteum is often thin and hence difficulty may be encountered in raising this flap. On exposure, the torus will be found to be dense and cortical in nature. Moreover, the midline of the palate tends to be thin. Developmentally, this is a fusion line. Hence, care must be taken while chiseling the torus to avoid fracture or creation of the oronasal fistula. To avoid such a complication, it is preferable to use the fissure bur to make a few grooves. Then, chisel is used to remove the bony exostosis in pieces. Finally, the floor of the lesion could be smoothened with a large vulcanite bur. The flap is repositioned to determine the extent of the flap in excess, consequent to the removal of the bony prominence. The excess, if any, is trimmed to facilitate better approximation of the flap edges. The wound is closed with interrupted sutures. Due to the gravity, palatal flap tends to hang down, creating a dead space between the palate and the flap. This can be avoided by using a preoperatively prepared splint to obliterate the dead space and to prevent the collection of blood clot deep to the flap.

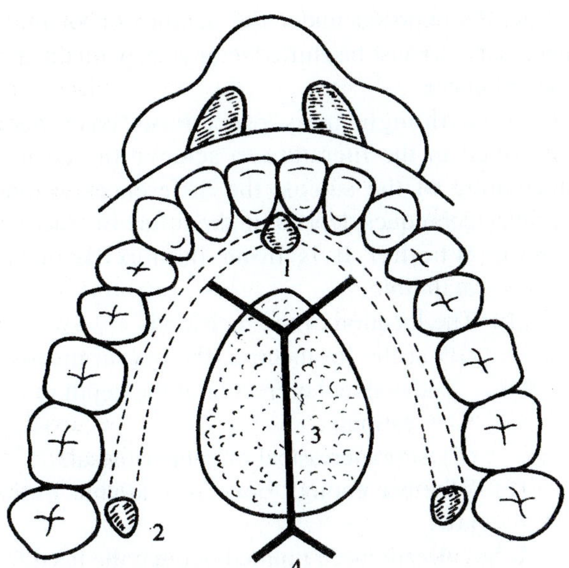

Fig. 13.2 Torus (palate) excision. 1. Incisive foramen. 2. Greater palatine foramen. 3. Torus palatinus. 4. Lines of incision to expose the torus.

Mandibular lesions can be exposed by making an incision along the crest of the ridge in the premolar region. The vertical component of the incision may be made anteriorly. Then, L-shaped mucoperiosteal flap is reflected. A 5 mm chisel is placed vertically at the base of the lesion along the superior border. With the bevel facing the bone, a gentle blow is usually sufficient to separate moderately sized mandibular torus. The base of the lesion is smoothened with a bone file and flap is sutured. If the patient is dentulous, horizontal component of the incision is placed parallel to the free gingival margin without disturbing the epithelial attachment. All the patients must be reassured that tori have no pathological significance.

Correction of the enlarged tuberosity. This is very similar to the soft tissue correction of the enlarged tuberosity. A radiograph is necessary to confirm whether the enlargement of the tuberosity is due to the soft tissue, bone or both. If bone is also found to be involved in the enlargement, a three-dimensional reduction to a desired level can be carried out. But the operator must keep in mind that overzealous reduction of the tuberosity may inadvertently expose the maxillary sinus apart from interference to the denture retention. As already pointed out, elimination of one problem should not create another problem. Hence, proper preoperative planning is mandatory to achieve the objective.

RIDGE EXTENSION PROCEDURES

Following dental extraction, resorption of the alveolar bone leaves behind a residual ridge termed as the denture-bearing area. After the denture is provided, alveolar bone resorption continues. After a few years, the reduction of the denture-bearing area due to the resorption during function leads to ulceration and further bone loss. Once the height of the alveolar ridge is reduced, there is a proportionate increase of the displacing forces of the dentures. Hence, the denture becomes unstable. Usually, grinding of the denture is done to reverse the chain of events. But depending on the preexisting periodontal disturbances and the quantum of denture pressure during function, ulceration and bone loss occur. In order to arrest the chain of events and to prevent further bone loss, deepening of the vestibule is considered to be a useful procedure. This alone will increase the retention and stability of the denture, provided, sufficient amount of alveolar bone is available for denture construction. In cases of extreme alveolar ridge atrophy, sulcus deepening may not be possible.

Vestibuloplasty

Vestibuloplasty, as a sulcus deepening procedure, is a relative method of ridge extension by deepening the vestibule without any addition of bone. Only the soft tissue attachments are shifted to a favorable zone in the jaw bones so that more of the denture-bearing area is available to increase the retention and stability of the denture. Careful assessment of the cases will reveal that all the cases do not respond favorably to the ridge extension methods. If adequate alveolar and basal bone are not available, repositioning of the buccinator, mylohyoid muscle and mental nerve may not yield the desired results. The ultimate goal is to expose more of the available alveolar bone by surgically repositioning the muscle attachments to a favorable zone. By this procedure, a larger denture-bearing area is made available, thereby contributing to greater denture stability and denture retention.

But it has been found that the achievements following surgery tend to reverse back in varying proportions to the preoperative status over the course of time depending on the procedure. Hence, there has been several attempts to improve the techniques to avoid obliteration of the vestibule so that the results will be of a permanent nature. Application of the following basic principles are essential to achieve satisfactory results in any of the ridge extension procedures.

(1) In vestibuloplasty procedures, the exposed soft tissues should be provided with an epithelial lining to avoid scar formation and the consequent contracture. If contracture develops, vestibule becomes shallow. The greater the thickness of skin grafts, the lesser the tendency for contraction. Hence, as far as possible, thin grafts must be avoided.

(2) Whenever vestibule is deepened, some degree of contraction is inevitable. Hence, the defect must be overcorrected to compensate for the post-operative contraction.

(3) If the epithelial lining is not readily available around the neighboring region, efforts must be taken to transplant the tissues to cover the defect even from any distal region rather than suturing the wound under tension.

(4) To avoid such troublesome contracture, it is preferable to plan the surgery in such a way that the defect lies over the bone rather than on the soft tissues.

(5) Surgery must be least traumatic since healing may be retarded in the aging friable tissue.

(6) Such ridge extension procedures must not leave any anatomical structures like blood vessels or nerves exposed under the denture pressure. If necessary, it must be shifted to any deeper area, e.g. mental nerve.

Even though many procedures have been described in the literature to achieve the desired deepening of the sulcus, the differences among various techniques depend on the following factors:

(a) Whether it is done in maxilla or in mandible.
(b) The location of the incision is
    (i) at the lip mucosa, the buccal mucosa, the alveolar crest or at the depth of the vestibule,
    (ii) supraperiosteal or subperiosteal.
(c) Whether enough bone is available in the jaw.

It has already been pointed out that the need for vestibuloplasty is greater in mandible than in maxilla.

(1) **Labial approach.** Incision is placed along the depth of the sulcus and dissection is carried out

supraperiosteally to the desired depth. The raw area is allowed to heal by epithelialization. Sulcus tends to obliterate as the healing proceeds. To overcome the scar contraction, skin or mucous membrane graft is provided to cover the raw area with varying success.

(2) **Kazanjian's method** (Fig. 13.3). Incision is modified by placing it through the lip mucosa to the desired length. Then, the labial mucosal flap is raised upto the depth of the vestibule. By severing the muscle attachments, deepening of the vestibule is achieved by extending the dissection supraperiosteally (Fig. 13.3b). Now, the mucosal flap is placed over the periosteum of the ridge and sutured at the depth of the vestibule (Fig. 13.3c). During the immediate postoperative period, vestibular depth apparently increases but later it obliterates due to the scar contraction of the soft tissue of the lip. Hence, the success in sulcus deepening is short-lived in this method.

(3) **Clark's method** (Fig. 13.4). Incision is made slightly labial to the crest along the alveolar

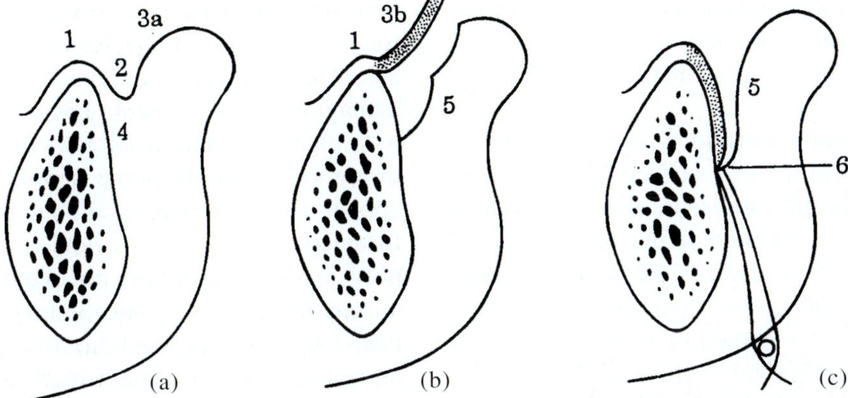

Fig. 13.3 Kazanjian's method of vestibuloplasty. Flap is raised from lip to cover the raw area of the alveolus. Raw area of the lip is allowed to granulate. 1. Masticatory mucosa overlying the alveolus. 2. Vestibular depth. 3a. Lining mucosa of the lip. 3b. Raised from the lip. 4. Alveolar bone. 5. Raw area of the lip allowed to granulate. 6. Mucosal flap fixed at the vestibular depth with stay suture.

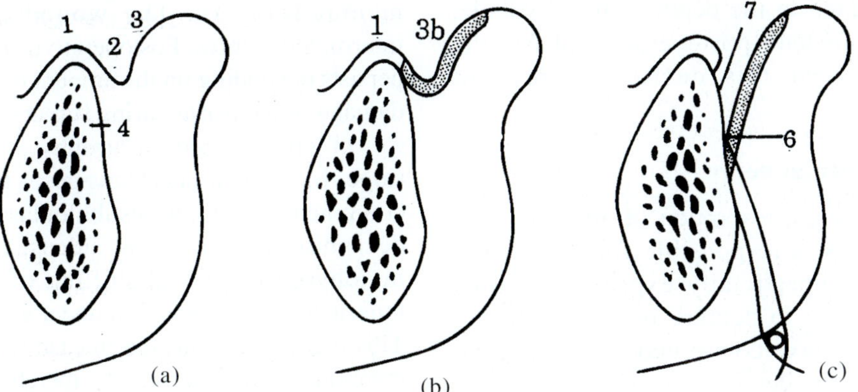

Fig. 13.4 Clark's method of vestibuloplasty. Flap is raised from the alveolus to cover the raw area of the lip. Raw area of alveolus is left to granulate. (1, 2, 3, 4, 5 and 6 stand for same labelling as in Fig. 13.3. 7- Raw area left on the alveolar bone).

ridge to a desired length. The dissection is carried out supraperiosteally and the muscle attachments are severed upto the predetermined depth of the sulcus. From the point of incision, the lip mucosa is undermined upto the vermilion border so that free edge of the mucosal flap can be anchored to the periosteum at the depth of the vestibule. The raw surface on the alveolar bone is allowed to heal by granulation. Since the raw area is situated on the alveolar ridge, possibility of contraction is reduced. The success in sulcus deepening is long-lasting than Kazanjian's method. But as the days progress by, the attachment of the lip musculature to the alveolar bone gradually shifts towards the alveolar crest, depending on the scar contraction, thereby obliterating the sulcus.

(4) **Obwegeser's method.** It is very similar to Clark's method but the raw surface of the ridge is covered with skin graft to ensure that the depth of the vestibule is maintained at the predetermined level and not shifted towards the alveolar crest. Instead of skin, mucosal graft has also been tried.

Whatever be the method of vestibuloplasty, it is preferable to deliberately over-extend the sulcus depth to compensate for the possible obliteration of the sulcus postoperatively, depending on the procedure. Preoperatively, acrylic denture with over-extended flange is prepared. Following surgery, Guttapercha is adapted over the denture flange and adapted to the depth of the vestibule. During the immediate postoperative phase, the patient must wear this denture to prevent contraction.

Lowering the mental nerve

As an aging process, resorption of alveolar bone takes place. This is responsible for the mental foramen being superficially exposed and thus become vulnerable to denture pressure. During function, mental nerve comes under the influence of the flange of the denture causing neuropraxia. Hence, the patient may develop paresthesia or anesthesia of the corresponding half of the lower lip. Sometimes, the patient may even develop neuralgic type of pain during mastication due to the pressure on the nerve. Digital pressure on the nerve trunk around the mental foramen precipitates the onset of similar pain. This problem can be avoided by lowering the mental nerve as part of vestibuloplasty. If the mucoperiosteal flap is raised to deepen the vestibule, the mental nerve will be exposed. Shifting the mental nerve is therefore absolutely essential for the successful deepening of the vestibule.

Procedure. By digital palpation, the mental nerve trunk at the point of its exit from the mental foramen is located. Either as an independent procedure or as part of the vestibuloplasty, mental foramen is exposed by placing the incision on the alveolar ridge above the mental foramen, without damaging the nerve trunk. Dissection is carried out with blunt ended scissors, between the muscle and the nerve, so that the nerve is mobilized sufficiently enough to expose the basal bone below the mental foramen. Nerve trunk is held retracted with skin hook or silk staysuture to avoid nerve damage during the drilling of bone. 3 mm chisel or rosehead bur is used to cut the bone to accommodate the nerve at a lower position. Chisel is preferable since bone piece can be cut and removed as one piece. During the removal of the lateral cortex of bone, one should remember that mental nerve branches off from the inferior dental nerve and passes backwards, upwards and laterally before emerging out of the mental foramen. The wound is closed with interrupted sutures. Postoperative anesthesia usually persists depending on the amount of manipulation or damage of the nerve during surgery.

In extreme case of atrophy of the mandibular ridge, Macintosh and Obwegeser have proposed a combined method of vestibuloplasty, simultaneous deepening of the buccal sulcus, resection of the mylohyoid ridge and shifting of the mylohyoid muscle to a lower position under general anesthesia. This method is indicated in case where the floor of the mouth bulges intraorally, thereby obliterating the lingual sulcus and displacing the lingual flange of the lower denture during function.

Changes in the soft tissue profile following mandibular vestibuloplasty

Mandibular residual ridge reduction results in the alteration of facial morphology following mandibular vestibuloplasty. This is characterized by reduction of anterior lower morphological facial height. Soft tissue profile changes can be recorded on lateral cephalometric radiographs taken pre- and postoperatively. Without the dentures, the edentulous patient's face appears as "overclosure" with unsupported lips, inversion of the vermilion border of lower lip, flattening of the labiomental groove and hence appear prognathic with empty chin.

It appears as though vestibuloplasty is inevitably followed by undesirable changes in the soft tissue profile. Studies have revealed that different types of vestibuloplasty give rise to soft tissue facial alterations conspicuously. During the first postoperative month, changes like increase in chin thickness are induced by surgery and reduction of the vertical dimension of the anterior face at rest. Probably, positional change of mentalis muscle is responsible for shortening of the lower lip compensated by the attempted closure of the upper lip and reduction of vertical dimension (overclosure). Detachment and lowering of mentalis muscle lead to loss of muscle tone and tissue congestion, responsible for the increase of chin thickness. Any surgical technique resulting in minimal relapse of sulcus depth should be chosen. Any attempt to overcome the relapse by over correction of the anterior sulcus depth should be kept to the minimum.

Maxillary pocket inlay vestibuloplasty. This surgical procedure is carried out under general anesthesia.

(1) Skin graft is obtained from the non-hairy region of the thigh and stored.

(2) Intraorally, incision is placed along the vestibule above the attached gingiva from one to the other zygomaticomaxillary buttress at the I molar region. Supraperiosteal dissection is performed to create pockets one on either side of the pyriform aperture.

(3) Dissection is continued superiorly to the level of the attachment of levator anguli oris muscle and medially upto the base of pyriform aperture. Care should be taken not to perforate the nasal cavity.

(4) Preoperatively, the patient's denture is modified with extended labial flanges. Guttapercha is added to these flange extensions to fit the newly created pouches. Before the graft is placed into the pouch, impression compound is used to take the impression of the pouches. The two labial flanges are covered with the raw surface of the graft facing outwards. Now, the denture flanges are inserted into the pouch. The denture is fixed in position with bilateral circumzygomatic wires. Wire fixations are removed after 7 days. After trimming the excess skin graft, the denture is reinserted. During the weekly review, flanges are adjusted without losing the bulbous character of the flange above the mucocutaneous junction. New denture can be constructed after 6 weeks. It is very important that grafted pouch should never be left empty for any time to avoid contraction and consequent difficulty in the reinsertion of the denture. Denture must be worn during the night also for nearly one year to avoid the active contraction.

The pocket inlay vestibuloplasty is advantageous since it increases the denture stability and retention by providing pocket sphincters to grip the denture flanges. This will also be helpful to restore deficiency in the region of nasolabial fold with improved contours.

RIDGE AUGMENTATION PROCEDURES

Factors predisposed to ridge atrophy

Physiologically, the function of the alveolar bone is to provide attachment and support to natural teeth. Hence, loss of teeth leads to resorption of the alveolar bone but the rate and its rapidity varies from person to person. It is common to find that the resorption of bone is retarded by the retention of a few erupted or unerupted teeth in-situ. Usually, alveolar resorption is uniform in the buccolingual and vertical directions. Sometimes, bone loss may be pronounced but the pathogenesis cannot be identified. Hence, arrest of further bone loss cannot be prevented.

Factors that may influence the bone loss

(a) Local factors,
(b) Disturbances in vascularization and
(c) Disturbances in bone mineral metabolism.

(a) They can be controlled by proper fitting and functioning dentures. The patient must be strictly warned that denture should not be worn during sleep at night.

(b) Disturbances in vascularization: The central blood supply to the mandible through inferior dental vessels tends to decrease as an aging process. Probably, it is due to atherosclerosis of the vessel that diminished vascularization occur. It is usually compensated to a certain extent by the periosteal blood supply from facial vessels. The denture pressure of excessive stripping of periosteum in such individuals interferes with the compensatory revascularization resulting in atrophy of the ridge.

(c) Disturbance in bone-mineral metabolism. Relationship between mandibular atrophy and metabolic bone loss has been extensively investigated with radiological and endocrinological studies to determine as to whether:

(i) any metabolic factor is responsible for the bone loss and
(ii) if it is positive, the nature of the disturbance in the bone-mineral metabolism.

The studies have revealed that characterized secondary hyperfunction of parathyroid glands by decreased mineralization and increased activity of osteoclasts indicate a shortage of calcium, probably of dietary origin. Calcium-phosphorus ratio must be 1:1 in the diet. If there is excess of phosphorus in the diet, there will be consequent increase of serum calcium, leading to secondary hyperfunction of parathyroid. Clinically, it is found that patients receiving calcium and Vitamin D for nearly one year after extraction have a significant reduction in the alveolar bone loss. With the marked increase in life expectancy of the population and improvement in living condition, it is estimated that every fourth person is expected to be with an average age of 60 years. This is the critical time when most of them would be using a complete denture for over 10 years. Many may need a change of the denture due to the biological changes in the alveolar ridges and oral mucosa. So far, atrophic ridges have not been considered as a major prosthetic problem because the incidence is relatively low. With the significant increase in geriatric population, it is now possible to group the population into various "dental generations". Accordingly, the generation which needs change of their complete dentures could be considered to enter into the "second prosthetic generation". If alveoloplasty is done at the time of extraction, such a localized trauma also predisposes to excess of bone loss. Similarly, if the denture is not properly constructed, improper ridge-adaptation may result in abnormal distribution of occlusal forces. Volume of alveolar bone present also varies with facial form. For example, the mandibular plane angle is low with more acute gonial angle. Such a mandible is capable of generating higher bite-force on the alveolar ridge. Hence, combined long-term result of all these local and systemic factors ultimately determine the alveolar bone loss, consequent increased interarch space and its influence on the surrounding orofacial structures. In turn, their influence can be noticed by the decreased denture stability and retention. Correspondingly, discomfort to the patient increases. As a cycle of these events, bone loss occurs still further. As already pointed out, mandible is more frequently involved in this process than maxilla. In order to break this cycle, restoration of the ridge to an optimum dimension is absolutely essential. Unfortunately, as the bone loss increases, no useful purpose will be served by performing any of the relative methods of increasing the height of the ridge like vestibuloplasty. Hence, there is a need to build up the ridge by absolute methods rather than relying on the relative methods. Augmentation methods are major preprosthetic, reconstructive procedures and they are best managed by expert oral surgeons.

Aims and objectives

(1) Restoration of optimum ridge height and width, vestibular depth, ridge form and optimum denture-bearing area.
(2) Protection of vascular bundle.
(3) Proper interarch relationship.

The existing interarch relationship markedly alters after the extraction of teeth. For example, in case of normal relationship (Angle's class-I), the pattern of alveolar bone resorption is such that maxillary ridge recedes and becomes smaller while receding downwards, and laterally in mandible which results in the three-dimensional enlargement of mandibular ridge. Hence, class-III relationship develops. It gets accentuated where class III relationship already exists in the dentulous state. This phenomenon must be properly understood even at the stage when planning is carried out to make the patient edentulous. Proper understanding ultimately enhances the success of the denture construction. Minor discrepancies can always be overcome by alterations in the dentures. Major discrepancies will have to be corrected either by augmentation or orthognathic surgery. Whatever method is adapted, one must ensure that the changes in the atrophic jaws, consequent to surgery, are of permanent nature. Improperly planned surgery on the grossly atrophied jaws will only aggravate the situation. At any rate, the problem should not get worsened. Hence, the patient must be evaluated properly to determine the factors responsible for the bone loss. Unless this is corrected, surgery will not be a successful venture.

The general outline of augmentation procedures is given here:

Mandibular augmentation

(1) Superior border augmentation
  (a) Bonegrafts.
  (b) Cartilage grafts.
  (c) Alloplastic grafts.
(2) Lower border augmentation
  (a) Bonegrafts.
  (b) Cartilage grafts.
(3) Interpositional grafts.
  (a) Bonegrafts.
  (b) Cartilage grafts.
(4) Visor-sandwich-osteotomy.

Maxillary augmentation

(a) Onlay bone grafting.
(b) Onlay grafting of alloplastic materials.
(c) Interpositional grafting.

Orthognathic surgery

(a) Mandibular osteotomies.
(b) Maxillary osteotomies.
(c) Combined procedures.

CHAPTER 14

Oral Surgery in Relation to Maxillary Sinus

INTRODUCTION

The existence of *maxillary sinus*, termed as *antrum of Highmore*, was known even before Highmore described it in 1651. But it was he who highlighted the possibility of its connection with nasal cavity. In 18th century, John Hunter was the first to observe that dental infection can spread to the neighboring areas and predicted the possible relationship between dental pathology and antral infection. Since then considerable interest developed, resulting in the overlap between the border land of ENT and dental specialties. Hence, it is essential to identify and define the scope of the dental surgeon in the prevention and the management of antral pathology of dental origin.

APPLIED ANATOMY

(1) **Size.** Maxillary sinus is the largest of the paranasal sinuses, occupying the body of the maxilla. They may be same or asymmetrical in size and shape (Fig. 14.1).

(2) **Shape and boundaries.** It is pyramidal in shape. The lower part of the lateral wall of the nose forms the base, with its apex projecting into the zygomatic process of downwards, forwards and

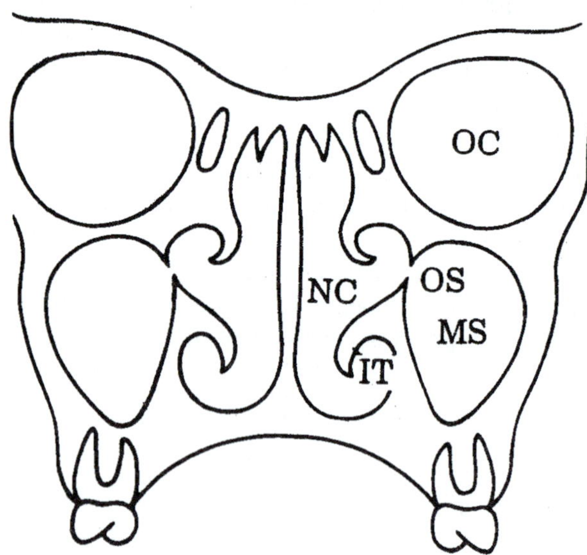

Fig. 14.1 Coronal section showing relationship of maxillary sinus to orbit and nasal cavity. MS-Maxillary sinus, NC-Nasal cavity, OC-Orbital cavity, OS-Osteum, IT-Inferior turbinate.

backwards respectively.

(a) Superiorly *roof*, orbital plate of maxilla (which is also the floor of the orbit).

(b) Inferiorly, *floor,* alveolar process of maxilla.

(c) Posteriorly, infratemporal surface of the maxilla.

(d) Anterolaterally, facial surface of the maxilla.

(3) **Ostium.** It is 3-4 mm in diameter, present in the middle meatus. The sinus opens at the posterior part of semicircular hiatus semilunaris. Sometimes, accessory openings may be present. Maxillary sinus indirectly communicates to the other paranasal sinuses through the lateral wall of the nose. It is situated at a higher level, in relation to the floor of the sinus.

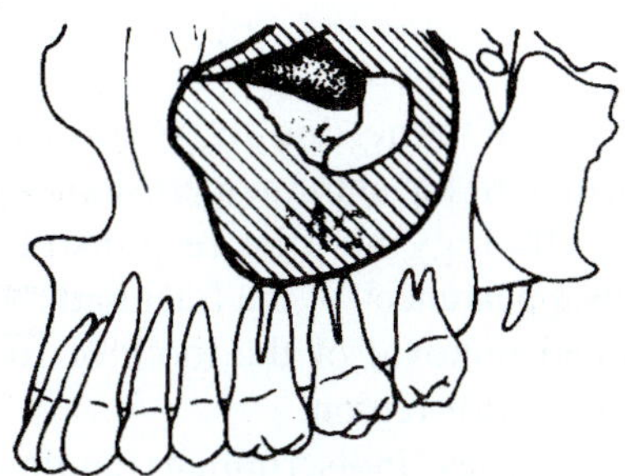

Fig. 14.2 Maxillary sinus and its relationship: Diagram showing side view of the maxillary sinus and its relationship to dentition.

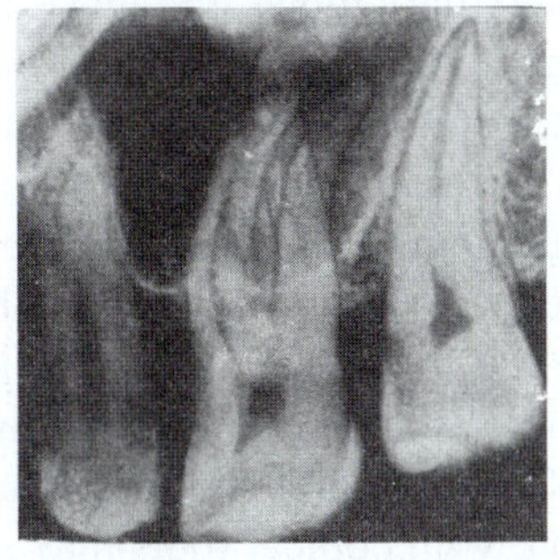

Fig. 14.3 Intraoral radiograph of the molar region showing the floor of the sinus as related to II premolar and molar teeth.

(4) **Relations.** Posterior-superior dental nerves are situated at the posterior wall and infraorbital nerve at the roof. At the floor, radiating bony septa are present between the roots of adjacent teeth. Rarely, root apices perforate the floor found in direct contact with the antral lining (Fig. 14.2). However, the number of roots related to the sinus are never constant.

(5) **Nerve supply.** Nerve supply to the antrum is derived from superior dental, infraorbital and greater palatine nerves. Due to their proximity to the antral lining, they are of clinical significance with reference to facial pain, impaired sensitivity and loss of sensation of maxillary teeth in various antral pathology.

(6) **Blood supply.** It is derived from internal maxillary artery via the terminal branches of infraorbital artery and its subsidiaries like posterior and anterior superior dental arteries.

(7) **Venous drainage.** Veins accompanying the arteries drain primarily into anterior facial vein and the angular vein to inferior ophthalmic vein.

(8) **Lymphatic drainage.** It is through the orbital foramen or through the ostium into submandibular nodes.

(9) **At birth.** It is a rudimentary shallow cavity, approximately 2 cm long, 1 cm broad and 1 cm high.

(10) **Growth.** It grows by a process of pneumatization. It reaches two-thirds of its adult size around 12 years and its adult size between 15 and 18 years of age. The floor is parallel to the nasal floor upto 12 years of age. It is situated higher, when it reaches its adult size. The greater the degree of pneumatization, the thinner the walls of the antrum. It is tubular at birth, ovoid during childhood and pyramidal during adulthood.

(11) **Histology of the lining.** The sinus is lined by the mucous membrane of the respiratory epithelium, i.e. pseudostratified, columnar, ciliated epithelium. Goblet cells are also present. The ciliary movement promotes the transportation of mucous towards the ostium, even though its location is unfavorable. In sinus infection, if the toxins prevent

the ciliary movements, secretions tend to accumulate and exert pressure on the exposed root ends which is responsible for the facial pain.

(12) **Functions.**

(a) The inspired air passes through the air sinuses before entering into the respiratory tract, so that, it is brought to body temperature. This is significant in climate with extremes of temperature.

(b) Simultaneously, it aids to filter the debris from the inspired air.

(c) Quality of the voice production depends on the status of the sinuses. It helps to enhance the resonance of speech. However, it is altered in the presence of antral pathology.

(d) Sinuses are located in front of the brain. This situation is considered to create "air padding" to provide good thermal insulation to the important nervous tissues like forebrain, olfactory region, etc.

(e) Sinuses increase the surface area of the skull.

(f) Pneumatization makes the skull bone and facial skeleton lighter.

The dental surgeon is mainly concerned with the extension of dental pathology into the sinus and the consequent alterations in its functions.

(13) **Age changes.** Often, antrum may extend into the alveolus between the roots into the zygomatic bone, tuberosity of the maxilla and infraorbital plate. Normally, it is related to molars but may extend from lateral incisors to third molars. In some places, roots are gloved by paper-thin lamella. Roots may lie in close contact with the antral lining where the intervening bone may be absent. In older persons, when teeth are lost and alveolar bone is resorbed, the antral walls become thin and tendency to revert to its infantile state can be noticed, showing an apparent increase in size.

(14) **Transillumination.** Since walls are relatively thin, transillumination is a useful accessory investigation if the antrum contains, (a) fluids like blood, mucous or pus, (b) polypoid or hypertrophied antral lining, (c) neoplasm and (d) fibroosseous lesions. This should be carried out in a dark room by placing a strong light source into the mouth with lips in closed position. The normal antrum shows a definite infraorbital crescent of light with bright glowing pupil. This is not seen if antrum is pathological. This test is considered to be less accurate than radiographic examination.

(15) **Nasal endoscopy** has become one of the popular methods of direct visualization of the interior of the maxillary sinus. This is also used to perform antral surgery by direct visualization.

Once the epithelial lining is removed surgically, nasal mucosa grows through the ostium into the antrum. During the immediate postoperative phase, the regeneration is of less specialized epithelial membrane of transitional type.

ROOT OR TOOTH IN THE MAXILLARY SINUS

Etiology

(1) Lack of bone due to greater degree of pneumatization of the antrum or erosion of bone due to apical pathology may be responsible for the sudden "disappearance" of the fractured root during the attempted removal of the tooth or root in the maxillary posterior region.

(2) Sometimes, indiscriminate and aggressive instrumentation, to retrieve the fractured palatal root of the maxillary first molar, may be responsible for pushing the root into the antrum.

(3) If a maxillary molar is solitary and isolated, the supporting alveolar bone tends to be dense and cortical as a response to increased occlusal load. However, the antrum often extends into the surrounding edentulous area. Hence, this may predispose to the fracture of the alveolus and slip into the sinus.

(4) Just like an orange seed popping out of the grasp of the finger, maxillary third molar or second premolar tooth with conical roots may slip into the antrum when it is grasped with forceps during extraction.

Diagnosis

The displaced foreign body may be inside the antral cavity or between the lining and sinus wall. To locate it, *"head shaking"* test is advocated. A routine intraoral periapical radiograph of the region is taken. After the patient bends forwards and shakes the head from side to side, another radiograph of the same region is taken. Both the radiographs are compared to find out whether the foreign body has changed its position or not. If it is inside the antrum, shift is possible. But it is not likely to move if it is between the lining and the bony wall. It is likely that the root is stuck with the lining in the antral cavity so that it may continue to maintain the same position. However, this test may not always be reliable. It is common to find that buccal roots may be pushed under the lining, while palatal root inside the antral cavity or under the palatal mucoperiosteum.

Whenever such a complication is suspected, the operator must quickly refer the patient for expert consultation. However, depending on one's capability and availability of facilities, any of the following simple methods can be tried:

(1) If the nozzle connected to a powerful suction is kept at the fistulous opening, the root can be recovered.
(2) If a long roller gauze is loosely packed into the antrum through the tooth socket and withdrawn in a jerky motion, the root is likely to come out along the gauze if it is lying loose in the antrum.
(3) If it is not successful, Caldwell-Luc procedure is the method of choice to retrieve the foreign body. Efforts must be made to remove it as early as possible so that the antrum is not infected.

FRACTURE OF THE TUBEROSITY

Predisposing factors

(1) If antrum involves the tuberosity, alveolar bone around third molar is thin. Extraction of such a third molar may inadvertently result in tuberosity fracture.
(2) Hypercementosis of the third molar.
(3) Divergent roots.
(4) Germination of second molars with unerupted third molar.

Management

Whenever tuberosity fractures during forceps extraction, the forceps should be immediately abandoned. A large mucoperiosteal flap is raised and tuberosity is dissected away so that both are removed. The wound is then closed with mattress sutures. However, if the fragment involves a large size and the mucoperiosteum is attached, it can be repositioned, splinted and treated like any alveolar fracture. But the healing is likely to be complicated by the breach of the antrum and the preexisting dental pathology for which extraction was attempted. Hence, retention of the fractured tuberosity should be considered only if the involved fragment is large.

OROANTRAL FISTULA

Oroantral fistula refers to the pathological communication between oral cavity and maxillary antrum. Fresh communications will lack the epithelial lining while long standing ones, known as chronic oroantral fistula, have epithelialized fistulous tract. Both are two different clinical entities and hence their management also differs fundamentally.

Etiology

1. Extraction of teeth

(a) **Incidence.** Statistically, maxillary second molars are situated close to the antral floor. But paradoxically, oroantral fistula develops more often, during the attempted removal of the palatal root of the first maxillary molars.

(b) **Age.** The sinus attains its normal size during 15 years of age. Hence, the chances of creating a fistula is less likely in children and young adolescents.

(c) **Size of the antrum.** It varies from person to person and even between the sides of the same person. As the age advances, sinus cavity enlarges in size by a process of pneumatization. Sometimes, root apices of maxillary molars are placed close to the antral floor with deficiency of bone between root apex and sinus lining in some areas. Due to aging or due to the presence of apical pathology, bone may resorb. Under physiological conditions, if abnormal communication develops following dental extraction, chances of spontaneous closure is good, if blood clot in the tooth socket is left undisturbed. But, if the clot is deficient or breaks down due to infection, the tract is lined by epithelium and it develops into a chronic fistula.

(d) **Shape of the tooth.** When an orange seed is grasped and pressed between the thumb and index finger, the seed jumps out of the grasp. Similarly, when a maxillary third molar tooth with conical roots is grasped above the cervical line (towards the crown) with an extraction forceps, it readily slips into the maxillary antrum and creates the communication. Therefore tooth must be grasped on the cementum and not the enamel, so that the tooth slips into the oral cavity and not into the sinus.

(e) **Degree of pneumatization.** With increase in the degree of pneumatization, the antral walls become very thin. The air space extends towards the alveolus with apices of adjacent teeth intruding into the sinus cavity. These roots will be covered by paper-thin lamella which constitutes the socket. Rarely, this bone may be absent. Hence, oroantral fistula is created inevitably during removal of such teeth.

(f) **Potential line of weakness.** More often, presence of an unerupted or partially erupted upper third molar, in close proximity to the maxillary tuberosity, forms a potential line of weakness. Extraction of second molar may result in fracture of tuberosity of maxilla involving second and third molar teeth. Consequently, oroantral fistula develops.

(g) **Root fracture.** If palatal root of the molar tooth breaks during extraction, injudicious instrumentation to remove the broken root leads to disturbance of normal physiological repair of the alveolar socket. This will be one of the precipitating factors in creating an oroantral fistula due to the loss of the blood clot.

(h) **Mouth rinsing.** Vigorous rinsing of the mouth following extraction of upper molars, lying very close to the maxillary antrum, may result in forcible removal of the clot. This will also predispose to the establishment of an oroantral fistula.

Thus, inspite of exercising great caution, oroantral fistula will continue to be created in dental practice by the dental surgeons during extraction of molar teeth due to various predisposing factors.

2. Surgical procedure

(a) *Surgical removal* of maxillary impacted teeth and apicoectomy of maxillary molars may lead to creation of antral perforations.

(b) *Radical surgical treatment* of large infected maxillary cysts may inadvertently result in oroantral fistula. If marsupialization is done in large cysts, where bony septa are deficient, the cyst lining becomes necrotic due to deficient vascular supply and eventually breakdown resulting in a large fistula.

(c) Following *Caldwell-Luc procedure*, some surgeons allow the vestibular incision to heal by itself without suturing. If the incision rests on normal bone, healing of the wound is spontaneous and uneventful. But if the incision line is left unsupported by bone, the wound breaks down creating a fistula.

(d) The fractured zygoma is treated by Caldwell-Luc procedure with one end of the antral pack left protruding out of the wound in the buccal sulcus. After the treatment is over, when the gauzepack is removed, the wound may persist leaving behind the fistulous opening. This is avoidable if gauze is brought out through the intranasal antrostomy.

(e) The antral neoplasms are sometimes surgically treated by a procedure known as fenestration. Such segmental resection of maxilla results in the creation of a large opening into the maxillary sinus.

Maxillofacial injuries. Penetrating injuries of the facial skeleton and gunshot wounds may be responsible for the creation of a persistent, large oroantral fistula although this is of rare occurrence in everyday practice.

Osteomyelitis of maxilla. This is an extremely rare clinical entity precipitated by the preexisting systemic conditions like diabetes, kidney disorders, leukemia, syphilis, Paget's disease and localized conditions like irradiated maxilla. Massive sequestration leads to the creation of a large fistula.

Malignancy involving maxillary sinus may erode the alveolar process resulting in loosening of teeth. Later on, exfoliation of these teeth and ulceration of the growth lead to the establishment of abnormal oroantral communications.

ACUTE OROANTRAL FISTULA

Symptoms

(1) History of recent surgery in the vicinity of maxillary sinus.
(2) Escape of air and fluids through the nose from the mouth.
(3) Unilateral epistaxis.
(4) Excruciating pain.
(5) Enhanced column of air, causing a change in the vocal resonance and consequently change in the voice.

Signs

(1) Physical examination of the site of extraction or surgery will readily confirm the presence of fistula. But, exploration with an instrument like silver probe should be avoided.

(2) The diagnosis can be confirmed by "noseblowing test". This is done by keeping a wisp of cotton over the fistulous opening intraorally and the patient is directed to blow through the occluded nostrils with the mouth kept open. If the fistula is present, air will pass through the defect, displacing the cotton fibers. If blood has got collected in the alveolar socket, air will bubble through the fistula.

(3) If water is flushed into the tooth socket or if the patient rinses the mouth to determine the patency of the communication, the response will be positive. This will also carry the risk of contamination of the antrum with oral microflora. Hence, this must be avoided. We have to rely on patient's history.

(4) In some cases, unilateral epistaxis can be noticed if the blood has accumulated in the sinus cavity.

(5) If the nozzle of a suction is placed near the newly created fistula, a sound very similar to blowing across the mouth of an empty bottle can be heard. If the sinus is healthy and empty, this sound is heard. But this sign is absent if the sinus is chronically infected.

Sequelae

Most of the fistulae spontaneously heal by themselves depending on the stability of the blood clot and on the adhesive tendency of the clot to the alveolar wall. If the alveolus is deep and narrow, spontaneous healing is likely. But they are likely to persist if

(a) extraction has been traumatic with gross soft-tissue damage,
(b) there has been disturbance to normal healing,
(c) the sinus is infected already,
(d) the diameter of the gap is wider than 5 mm and
(e) any of the predisposing factors are present.

Management

For all practical purposes, all the suspected cases should be considered as a fistula. Accordingly, the main aim must be to preserve the blood clot intact in the socket to promote normal healing so that ingress of oral microorganisms into the maxillary sinus is prevented.

Ideally, healing of the newly created fistula is possible by providing adequate support to the tooth socket. Many methods have been advocated to repair the bony defect. The choice of the technique depends on

(a) surgical experience and ability of the operator,
(b) facilities and operating time available at the disposal of the operator and the patient,
(c) general health of the patient and
(d) size of the fistulous opening.

As far as possible, the patient must have the benefit of doubt and hence deserves treatment at the hands of an experienced operator.

If the fistula has been created but complicated by the presence of any foreign body like root, tooth, etc or by the preexisting maxillary sinusitis, closure must be attempted only after retrieving the foreign body or after eradicating the sinus infection.

(a) Simplest method is to reduce the height of the alveolar bone so that mucoperiosteal flaps from either side are loosely sutured across the socket. The blood clot is provided adequate support by this procedure. It can be reinforced by placing a lyophilized collagen sheet across the socket prior to suturing.

(b) If the flaps cannot be approximated, a buccal advancement flap or a palatal mucoperiosteal pedicled flap of a combination procedure can be successfully utilized. But it must be undertaken only under ideal conditions by a specialist (details under chronic fistula).

Instructions

(1) Whatever method is utilized to cover the defect, additional support by way of an acrylic splint will be advantageous.

(2) The patient should be instructed not to rinse the mouth vigorously and not to blow the nose, but to do gently if it is absolutely essential.

(3) Suitable antibiotics and analgesics must be prescribed.

(4) As already pointed out, maxillary sinus opens at the middle meatus of the lateral wall of the nose situated at an unfavorable situation. Hence, decongestant nasal drops has a definite role to play.

(5) During the postoperative period, Tr. Benzoin inhalation or any commercial decongestant may be prescribed to help in the spontaneous healing of the fistula.

ACUTE SINUSITIS

Acute sinusitis may be a suppurative or non-suppurative inflammation of the antral mucosa. It is very similar to any epithelial tissue but pathology is modified by the following factors:

(1) Vascularity is very high.

(2) Antral mucosa lines the air chamber.

(3) Sinus opens in the middle meatus situated higher than the antral floor. Hence, very often osteum tends to get blocked and consequent drainage is affected.

(4) It is closely related to teeth and hence presents a picture overlapping between teeth and the antrum.

Etiology

Knowledge of anatomy of the *lateral wall of the nose* - particularly middle meatus - is essential to understand the etiology of sinusitis. The middle meatus is divided by an arc-shaped gap called Hiatus semilunaris that forms the entrance to a groove called infundibulum. Most of the paranasal sinuses open into the infundibulum - maxillary sinus opens into posterior and inferior end with frontal sinus in the superoanterior end and anterior- ethmoid between them. Patency of the infundibulum is of importance to the drainage of the sinuses. Therefore, this area forms the "bottleneck" of the entire drainage and proper ventilation of all the paranasal sinuses. This is compared to the patency of the pharyngotympanic tube for proper functioning of the middle ear. Any obstruction of this area can initiate a chain of pathological process in the following manner.

The blockage of the *infundibulum* leads to disturbance to the ventilation and drainage resulting in the stagnation of the secretion. This is followed by the damage of ciliary function of the respiratory epithelium and inflammation of the mucosa. This in turn contributes to further obstruction. Therefore, anterior ethmoid bone, where infundibulum is situated, is one of the key factors in infected sinusitis.

The following are some of the common causes for the maxillary sinusitis of odontogenic origin:

(1) Direct spread of infection from periapical abscess into the antral activity.
(2) Root fragment displaced into the maxillary sinus.
(3) Oroantral fistula.
(4) Infected cysts of odontogenic origin involving the antrum.

Pathogenesis

During the early phases of inflammation, initial vesodilation leads to increased production of mucous from the mucous glands. The mucous consequently exerts pressure within the lumen of the antrum.

Clinical features

(a) The patient gives history of "catching cold" 3 or 4 days earlier.
(b) Nasal block is secondary to rhinitis. It increases with upright posture and decreases while lying down.
(c) Increase in purulent, thick, discolored and foul smelling nasal discharge is a prominent feature.
(d) The patient develops cough secondary to the nasal discharge with the onset of pharyngitis.
(e) A sense of fullness and pain on the cheek on bending forward.
(f) Ear symptoms develop secondary to dysfunction of pharyngotympanic tube.
(g) The patient feels toxic with pyrexia.
(h) All the related maxillary teeth are tender on percussion.

Diagnosis

It can be made on the basis of these characteristic clinical features. Radiographic examination of the sinuses will be non-informative.

Treatment

(1) Since the patient is toxic and febrile, absolute bed rest must be advised to relieve the nasal block and pain.

(2) Nasal inhalation will be soothing to the patient.

(3) Plenty of fluids are necessary to keep the mouth well-lubricated and also to dilute the toxicity.

(4) Therapy: Paracetamol provides symptomatic relief while a broad spectrum antibiotics, active on Gram positive and Gram negative microorganisms, will take care of infection.

If the process of inflammation and repair go together simultaneously, it results in hypertrophy or scar formation. Thus, the ostium is narrowed considerably, resulting in insufficient aeration. Such a chronic inflammation of the sinus affects mucosa and bony walls.

CHRONIC OROANTRAL FISTULA

This is best treated by a specialist oral surgeon. Due to the persistence of the communication between the oral cavity and maxillary antrum, oral microorganisms migrate and infect the maxillary sinus. Hence, the main aim is to eliminate the co-existing maxillary sinusitis and the epithelial lining of the tract before closing the fistula. The easiest way to keep the sinus clean is to insert a well-fitting acrylic plate or a denture soon after oroantral fistula is identified. Antral wash 2 or 3 times a week through the fistulous opening and nasal decongestants are useful adjuncts. While prescribing antibiotics, it is important to consider that a mixture of aerobic and anaerobic organisms are present in chronic maxillary sinusitis. If such care is taken, oroantral fistula shrinks in size and may even close spontaneously. If closure does not occur in 3 months time, persistent fistula requires surgery.

Clinical features

(1) Persistent unilateral foul nasal discharge.

(2) Postnasal drip with the discharge trickle down the pharynx from the posterior nares resulting in foul smell and unpleasant taste.

(3) Possible systemic sequelae due to the swallowed pus in the form of pyrexia, malaise, headache, anosmia and morning anorexia.

(4) Pain which was the dominant factor in the acute phase diminishes considerably.

(5) Polyp projecting from the antrum into the oral cavity prevents the fistulous tract to heal spontaneously.

Investigations

Before undertaking the surgical management, the following investigations are mandatory to confirm the diagnosis:

(1) The patient is made to rinse the mouth gently with water mixed colored solution, which is readily available in any clinic, e.g. Mercurochrome or gentian violet. It finds its way into the sinus and come out through the nasal cavity. If plain water is used, it will be difficult to differentiate from the nasal discharge. Colored solution is easy to differentiate from the nasal discharge.

(2) An intraoral periapical radiograph is taken with a silver probe placed into the fistulous tract to determine the patency of the tract.

(3) Maxillary sinus radiograph of the skull with or without the probe inside the oroantral fistula is taken to study the associated antral pathology.

(4) Routine evaluation of the patient for fitness to undergo surgery is necessary to avoid postoperative complications.

Symptoms

The maxillary sinus opens in the middle meatus. The sinus is an aerated cavity in the bone, lined by mucoendosteum which is continuous with the respiratory nasal epithelium. This psuedostratified, ciliated, columnar epithelium aids in the drainage of antral secretions. With the development of sinusitis, the radiographs taken may show sinus opacification, fluid level or mucosal thickening, depending on the existing pathology. Ultimately, Caldwell-Luc procedure may be absolutely essential to eliminate antral pathology. Antral puncture and its role has been a subject of controversy. Escape of fluid from the oral cavity into the nostril is an annoying complaint when the patient rinses the mouth. Such passage of fluid is pathognomic of oroantral fistula. Unlike acute fistula, systemic features are characteristically absent.

Main objectives

(1) Elimination of antral pathology.
(2) Elimination of epithelial lining of the fistulous tract.
(3) Establishment of a stable two-layered closure of the fistula.
(4) Establishment of satisfactory drainage through inferior meatus of the lateral wall of the nose.

Management

Usually, if the fistula persists for more than 2-3 months, the fistulous tract would have been epithelialized. Then, chances of spontaneous closure are less. The following methods have been described for the surgical closure of oroantral fistula.

(a) Buccal advancement flap.
(b) Palatal pedicled flap.

(c) Combination of both.
(d) Modified closure with a double flap repair.
(e) Pedicled flap of buccal pad of fat.

The general principles are:

(a) Blood supply should be adequate so that the flap does not necrose,
(b) Suture line is well supported by normal bone,
(c) Wound is not sutured under tension, and
(d) All the basic requirements of a flap are fulfilled.

(a) Buccal advancement flap (Rehrmann's flap) (Fig. 14.4)

This method was originally described by Von Rehrmann in 1936. This is a widely used, technically simple method. This is based on the principle of periosteal release advocated by Berger. It provides satisfactory and a simple closure without tension. Care must be taken to avoid pressure of the flap over a sharp bony margin. Rich vascularity is present at the upper mucobuccal fold. Hence, infiltration with local anesthetic solution containing vasoconstrictor minimizes bleeding and reduces the troublesome postoperative hematoma. Incision is made around the fistulous tract with B.P. blade No. 11. The entire epithelialized fistulous tract and any associated antral polyps are dissected out with B.P. blade No. 15 and removed. Two divergent incisions are made on the buccal gingiva deep to the bone mesially and distally on either side of the fistulous margins. While extending the oblique incisions towards the vestibule, care must be taken not to injure the parotid duct opening. This broad-based flap is raised from the alveolar bone. To overcome the inelastic nature of the periosteum, the flap is turned over and on its under surface, a horizontal relief incision is made anteroposteriorly on the periosteum (Fig. 14.4c). This helps to mobilize the flap towards the palatal flap. Prior to suturing the flap across the fistula, maxillary sinus must be carefully explored for the presence of any evidence of infection. Fibrooptic light is useful to view the interior of the sinus cavity. The wound is sutured if the antrum and the lining are healthy. If there is any need to eliminate antral pathology, Caldwell-Luc procedure is desirable before the closure of the fistula. During surgery, hemorrhage should be completely arrested since hematoma at the suture line may result in the breakdown of the wound.

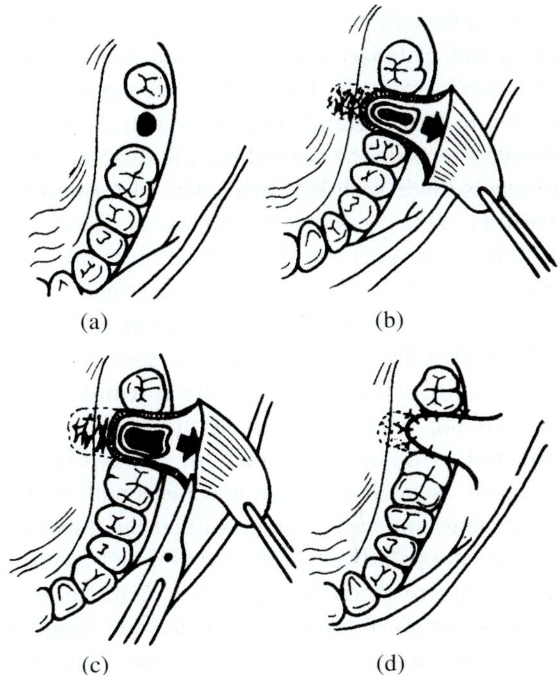

Fig. 14.4 Buccal advancement flap: **(a)** Oroantral fistula (OAF) in the II molar region, **(b)** Raising the buccal flap, **(c)** Oroantral fistula is deepithelialized. A relief incision is made only on the periosteum at the flap (arrow) so that buccal flap can be released more, **(d)** The flap extended further towards the palate and fixed.

(b) Palatal pedicled flap (Ashlay operation) (Fig. 14.5)

Palatal mucoperiosteum derives blood supply from greater palatine vessels. It emerges from greater palatine foramen and runs in the anterior direction, parallel to the dental arch. The surface marking is midway between the free gingival margin and the midline of the palate. The palatal mucoperiosteal flap with greater palatine vessels is raised from its bed and rotated across the fistula with greater palatine foramen as the centre of rotation. When the flap is sutured, it rests on the normal buccal alveolar bone. Incision is made with B.P. blade No. 11 around the fistulous tract at least 2 mm away from the epithelialized surface. It is dissected out and removed. Care is taken to remove some of the mucoperiosteum on the buccal aspect of the fistula to ensure that the suture line moves more buccally, so that suture line rests on the normal bone. Through the fistula, maxillary sinus should be inspected to decide the need for Caldwell-Luc procedure. Now, flap design and the length of the flap are determined. Keeping in mind the direction of the greater palatine vessels, parallel incisions are made on either side of the vessel, one on the midline and the other, 5 mm away from the free gingival margin. Depending on the length of the flap, both these incisions are joined with a convex incision anteriorly. The mucoperiosteal flap is raised carefully since the survival of the flap entirely depends on the vascularity. The flap is rotated buccally with the greater palatine foramen as the centre of rotation to the extent needed to cover the fistula. Tip of the flap is anchored to the buccal and fistulous margin with mattress sutures. The portion of the donor area is covered with ribbon gauze soaked in whitehead varnish so that the denuded area of bone granulates in due course of time. This procedure is technically more difficult than Rehrmann's operation. It leaves a depression deformity at the donor area for a few months. It is successful at the hands of experienced operators.

(c) Combination procedure

A combination procedure has been described wherein alveolar bone-based buccal flap is reversed and sutured with palatal margin. This replaces the lining part of the wound. The palatal flap is rotated and placed in the usual manner. Thus, raw surfaces of both the flaps are placed against each other. This is a two-layered closure.

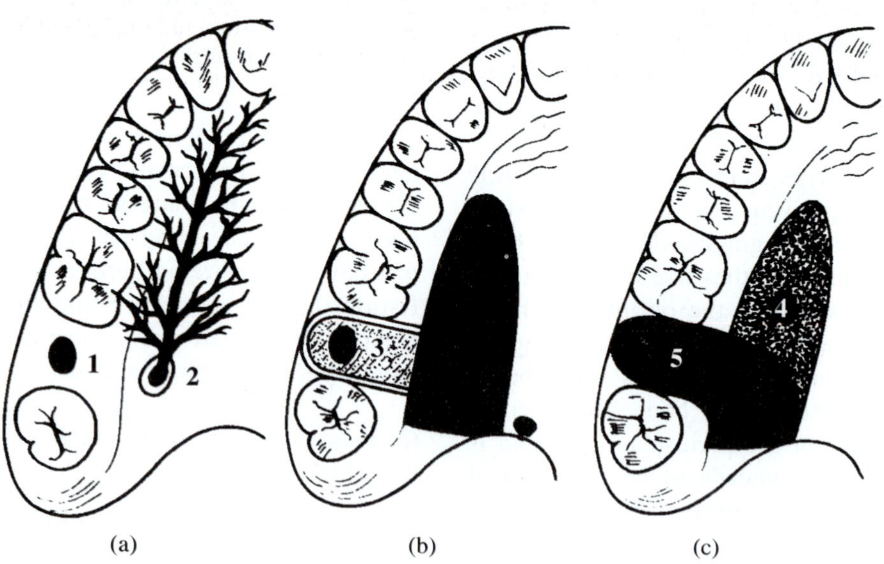

Fig. 14.5 Palatal pedicle flap: 1- Oroantral fistula (OAF). 2- Greater palatine foramen with vessels coming out. 3- The recipient area and oroantral fistulous tract is deepithelialized. 4- Outline of the palatal flap based on greater palatine vessels. 5- Palatal flap transpositioned to cover the raw area and fistula, leaving the palatal area to granulate.

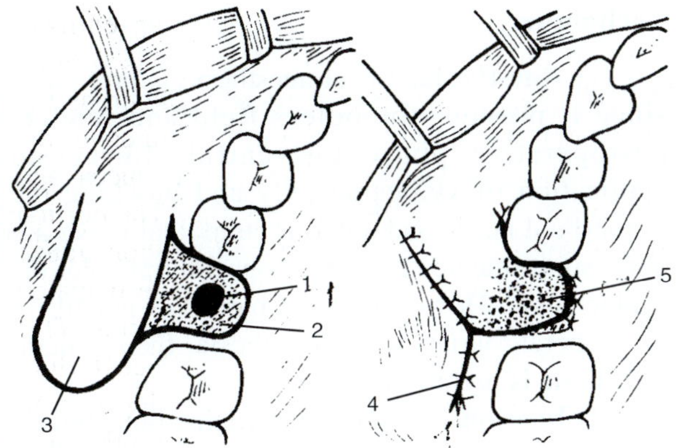

Fig. 14.6 Buccal flap modification: 1- Oroantral fistula. 2-Raw area over the alveolar margin. 3- Buccal flap raised in an anteroposterior direction. 4- Donor area of the buccal flap sutured by primary closure. 5- Raw area of the fistular region covered with buccal flap.

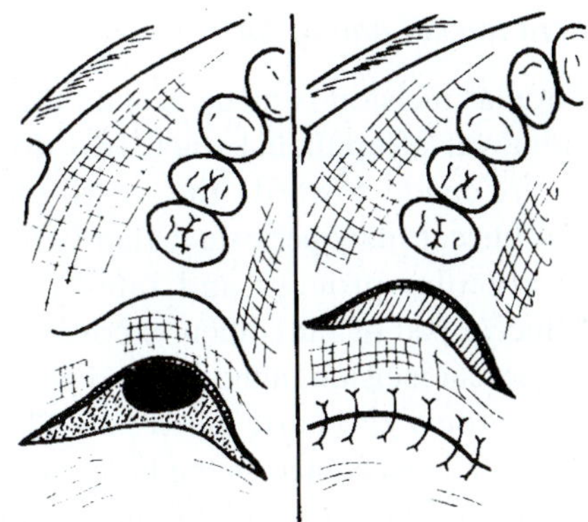

Fig. 14.7 Bipedicled flap from buccal to palatal region is used to cover the fistula, leaving the raw area to granulate.

(d) Modified surgical closure with a double flap repair

Incision is placed on the mucosa surrounding the oroantral fistula and mobilized in a funnel shape. The mucoperiosteal flap around the fistula is raised sufficiently for the formation of the lining layer. Then, the palatal flap is raised in the usual manner. The remaining epithelial bridge between the bed of the first phase and the palatal flap is removed. Now the palatal flap is positioned over the raw area and anchored with mattress sutures. The donor area of the palatal flap heals by secondary intention following the application of gauze with Whitehead's varnish on the raw area of the bone. The modified buccal flap is illustrated in Fig. 14.6 and bipedicled flap in Fig 14.7.

Whitehead's varnish

Benzoin	10 parts (44g)
Storax	7.5 parts (33g)
Balsam of tolu	5 parts (22g)
Iodoform	10 parts (44g)

Solvent ether to 1 fl oz or 100 parts.

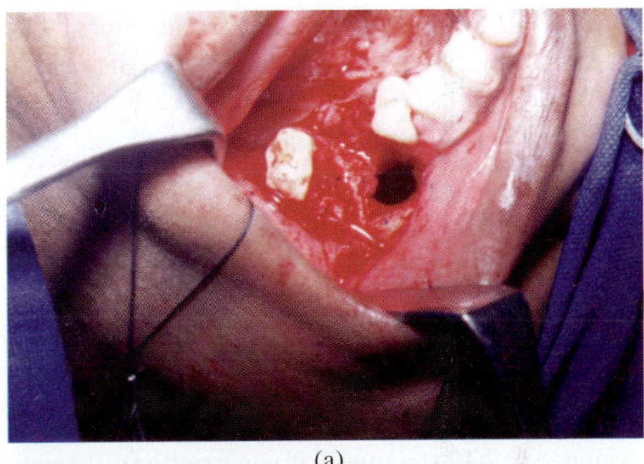

(a)

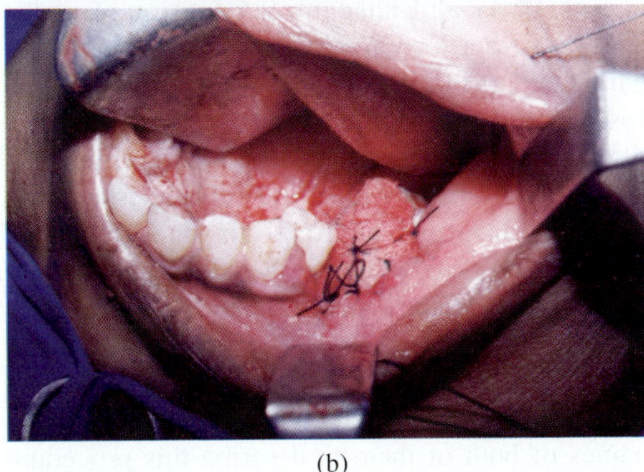

(b)

Fig. 14.8 (a) Chronic oroantral fistula–clinical photograph, **(b)** Postoperative appearance.

(e) Pedicled buccal pad of fat

After a circular incision is made around the fistula and the removal of epithelial tract, two divergent incisions are made towards the vestibule. The trapezoidal buccal mucoperiosteal flap is reflected from the alveolar process and lateral wall of maxilla. Buccal pad of fat is then exposed through 1cm long vertical incision in the reflcted periosteum posterior to the zygomatic buttress. Then the pedicled fat is advanced across the bony defect and secured to the palatal mucosa without tension. The blood supply to the buccal pad of fat is derived from buccal and deep temporal branches of the maxillary artery and small contributing branches from superficial temporal artery and facial artery. The buccal advancement flap is then replaced in position and sutured. This procedure is highly recommended in cases where other methods have failed.

CALDWELL-LUC OPERATION

Introduction

The earliest surgery for the relief of infection of maxillary sinus was performed through the extracted tooth socket. John Hunter considered the drainage to be effective if it is carried out through canine fossa and nasoantral partition. George Caldwell from New York reported his method of gaining entry into the maxillary antrum via canine fossa with a nasal counter opening for effective drainage of the antrum. By about the same time, Henri Luc from Paris independently described it in French literature as his own method. The description was exactly the same as that of Caldwell's procedure. In fact, he did not even know how to read or speak English. It is believed that an Englishmen heard both the descriptions. Hence, by way of compromise, interestingly, he fused the names of both of them to describe this procedure as "Caldwell-Luc operation" which stood the test of time.

Technique

(1) **Anesthesia.** Local anesthesia is preferable since it provides bloodless field and renders postoperative phase uneventful. Intranasal application of xylocaine jelly and blocking the infraorbital nerve and anterior ethmoidal nerve are done, supplemented by submucous infiltration of the canine fossa. However, if the patient is not likely to cooperate under local anesthesia, then general anesthesia is preferred.

(2) **Incision** is made at the canine mucobuccal fold, and the mucoperiosteal flap is gently raised upwards to the point of emergence of the infraorbital nerve. Chisel or a round bur of convenient size is used to create a window at the anterior wall of the sinus. The opening is enlarged carefully in all directions with Rongeur's forceps. It may not be wise to proceed too far laterally because of the possibility of damage of anterolateral terminal branch of sphenopalatine artery. The sinus is exposed and the secretion of the sinus is cleaned out with suction. If the bleeding is profuse, the bony cavity is packed with ribbon gauze soaked in epinephrine 1 in 1,00,000 for a minute. The next step is to elevate the mucosal lining with Howarth periosteal elevator. Special attention must be paid to the floor, inferolateral angle and root of the maxillary sinus. Even if lining is apparently healthy, it is preferable to remove the entire lining since in such cases, one finds submucosal encysted pus. The wound is closed with interrupted sutures. Some ENT surgeons advocate conservative approach.

Postoperative care

(1) Antibiotic therapy for 5 days.
(2) Tr. Benzoin inhalations.
(3) Frequent mouth washes.
(4) The patient is instructed not to blow the nose for a week.

Postoperative complications

(1) Pain is taken care of with analgesics.

(2) Paresthesia of upper lip, gum and teeth are due to the pressure effect on the infraorbital nerve. Usually, it wears off in a few weeks or months by itself.

(3) Devitalization of upper teeth have also been reported.

(4) Postoperative hemorrhage occasionally occurs from the branch of sphenopalatine artery. Nasal pack may be useful.

RADIOLOGICAL CONSIDERATIONS

Radiographic examination of the maxillary sinus is one of the important investigations in clinical practice. The structures are more difficult to interpret radiographically due to the superimposition. To avoid this, Waters described 30 degrees occipitomental view, popularly known as *Waters' view*. It aids in evaluating the relative radiolucency and radioopacity of the antral pathology. When x-rays are allowed to pass through the middle third of the face with a 30 degree tilt of the head, the resultant radiograph presents a shadow of the bony margins of the antrum, mucosal lining and fluid collection as radioopacities. Air cavity is seen as radiolucency. The sinuses are seen as roughly triangular with well circumscribed and defined margins and radiolucent throughout. When infection occurs, mucosa is thickened encroaching the air space, thereby the normal radiolucency is replaced by radioopacity.

The accuracy of this view can be verified by observing the following anatomical factors:

(1) Coronoid processes are equidistant on either side from the zygomatic bones.

(2) Petrous part of the temporal bone appears below the sinus. If it is not so, it only indicates that backward tilt of the head is not correct.

(3) Odontoid process of axis is in the midline.

(4) Angle of the mandible is equidistant from the edge of the skull.

Normal antrum is radiolucent since it is an air chamber. But the radiographic interpretation of radioopacities could be nonspecific since inflammatory exudates or blood will produce similar shadows. To determine the change in the fluid level, another x-ray with the head tilted to the affected side will be useful.

Interpretation of varying thickness of mucosal lining is equally significant. For example, incomplete radioopacity will have a central residual radiolucency while gross thickening completely obliterates the sinus so that it is completely radioopaque. In fractures of midface, bleeding into the antrum can be identified.

"Cyst like" lesions appear as convex radioopaque line with a portion of the sinus appearing radiolucent. Solid masses like sialolith, osteoma and fibroosseous lesions will appear as varying dense radioopacities. Irregular margins due to erosion of walls of the sinus are significant to diagnose malignancy. Since the other paranasal sinuses open at the lateral wall of the nose, condition of the other sinuses, particularly that of frontal sinus, should also be visualized.

Waters' view is supplemented with submentovertex view, lateral view and orthopantomograms. Three-dimensional study is possible with tomograms. However, intraoral periapical radiograph is absolutely essential to study the status of the alveolar bone.

Computed tomography

This has more or less replaced conventional radiographs. For the diagnosis of the pathology of paranasal sinuses, coronary projection is best suited.

Endoscopy

With the development of rigid and flexible endoscopes, the diagnosis can be made accurately since endoscopes permit excellent internal view of the middle meatus. Sinus scopy can be made through canine fossa. It can also be used for performing sinus surgery.

CHAPTER 15 Surgical Considerations of Oral Neoplasms

INTRODUCTION

The oral cavity can be the site of a variety of neoplasms found elsewhere in the body. An additional group of tumors may arise from odontogenic tissues. Hence, oral tumors are broadly classified into three categories:

(1) *Odontogenic tumors.*
(2) *Non-odontogenic tumors.*
(3) *Tumor-like lesions.*

In general, behavior of all these lesions depends on whether they are benign or malignant. The individual tumor is named after the cell of its origin. On these guidelines, the classification of oral tumors provides a comprehensive view about them. A general outline of the guidelines involved in the management of oral tumors has been provided so that depending on the lesion, the practitioner can take a suitable decision regarding the nature of the management of the tumors, commonly encountered in the oral cavity.

ODONTOGENIC TUMORS

(1) Tumors of ectodermal origin
 (a) Benign
  (i) Ameloblastoma
  (ii) Adenoameloblastoma
  (iii) Calcifying epithelial odontogenic tumor
  (iv) Ameloblastic fibroma
  (v) Odontogenic fibroma
  (vi) Odontogenic myxoma
  (vii) Cementoma
  (viii) Odontomes.
 (b) Malignant
  (i) Intraalveolar carcinoma.
  (ii) Squamous cell carcinoma from the cyst-lining.
(2) Tumors of mesodermal origin
 (a) Benign
  (i) Odontogenic myxoma
  (ii) Odontogenic fibroma
  (iii) Cementifying fibroma
 (b) Malignant
  Odontogenic sarcoma
(3) Tumors of ectodermal and mesodermal

origin (mixed)
- (a) Benign
  - (i) Ameloblastic fibroma
  - (ii) Ameloblastic fibroodontoma (odontoameloblastoma)
- (b) Malignant
  Ameloblastic fibrosarcoma

The other lesions like odontomes have been described in the literature as odontogenic tumors. They are of odontogenic origin, but they do not fulfil the criteria of a neoplasm. They are called *hamartomas.*

Clinical behavior of odontogenic tumors

In general, true odontogenic tumors are highly unpredictable. For example, very few are truly malignant, a few others are locally invasive while many others are benign. Many clinicians consider hamartomas as benign lesions. Since hamartomas do not fulfil the criteria of a neoplasm, they are dealt with separately under the category of *"tumor-like lesions"*. On this basis, it is quite evident that (a) intraalveolar carcinomas and squamous cell carcinoma arising from the odontogenic cyst lining of ectodermal origin and (b) ameloblastic fibrosarcoma of mixed origin are malignant. Ameloblastomas, calcifying epithelial odontogenic tumor of epithelial origin and ameloblastic fibroma and myxoma of mixed origin are locally invasive. They frequently recur. The variations of cementomas are benign. Odontomes are benign in nature but they do not possess any neoplastic features. If different stages of the normal odontogenesis are compared with oncogenesis, one can draw parallel between them so that some basic consideration of its origin, development and clinical behavior can be reasonably understood. If a tumor or hamartoma arises from the primordial cells, they have the potential for invasiveness and recurrence. If it develops during the late stage of the tooth development, chances of aggressive growth and recurrence are reduced considerably. The hamartomas lack only the morphodifferentiation of the odontogenic tissues. Hence, they can be considered only as a morphological variation and not a neoplasm.

During normal odontogenesis, enamel organ interacts with the underlying connective tissue. Such an induction is considered very important for tooth development. Similar interactions between ectodermal and mesodermal tissues are noticed in salivary, lacrimal and mammary glands and hair follicles. The importance lies in that the mesenchyme is important for the proper development of ectodermal derivatives. It is interesting to note that in ameloblastomas, marked resemblance to different stages of tooth development exists. Similarity of tumor cells to those of normal dental lamina and enamel organ have been confirmed even by histochemical studies. Hence, origin of the dental tumors offers valuable clue with reference to the clinical behavior and possibilities of recurrence. In other words, as is with any other tumors, the more the differentiation of the tissues the less is the chance for its recurrence and invasion.

Radiographically, many lesions present themselves as multilocular radiolucencies. Following are some of them:

- (1) Odontogenic keratocyst
- (2) Multilocular cyst
- (3) Cherubism
- (4) Central giant cell granuloma
- (5) Aneurysmal bone cyst
- (6) Hyperparathyroidism
- (7) Ameloblastoma
- (8) Myxoma
- (9) Odontogenic fibroma
- (10) Fibrous dysplasia.

GENERAL GUIDELINES FOR THE TREATMENT OF ORAL TUMORS

The clinical behavior and treatment response of a few oral tumors are known to be similar. Hence, lesions of similar nature can be treated in a similar way. The classification of oral neoplasms reveals that, numerically, a number of possibilities exist in their clinical presentation. Due to the similarity in their clinical behavior, it is easy to consider them as a group conveniently in terms of management. An account of them is expected to form general guidelines for the management of these lesions. Only lesions which deserve special mention are described separately because of their characteristic features. A few surgical modalities found to be useful in the management of oral neoplasms are described here:

(1) Excision biopsy.
(2) Enucleation with or without curettage.
(3) Peripheral osteotomy.
(4) Segmental resection with or without bone grafting.
(5) Radical resection of the bone.
(6) Composite resection with or without reconstruction.
(7) Composite resection with treatment of the host tissue.

Suitable decision to perform the type of the surgical procedure is to be taken depending on many variable factors. The following are some of the important factors which need careful consideration:

(a) Size and location of the tumor

The size of the tumor dictates the extent of surgery. If it is very small, excision biopsy becomes an investigating as well as a therapeutic procedure. As the size of lesion increases, the procedure becomes radical. Anatomical location of the tumor has an important role to play in terms of postoperative morbidity. Hence, anatomy of the involved region influences the need for immediate reconstruction. The difficulties in diagnosis and management of the tumors arising from inaccessible areas depend on the location of the tumor. Inaccessibility may be responsible for inadequate surgical clearance of the tumor. Proximity to important anatomical structures

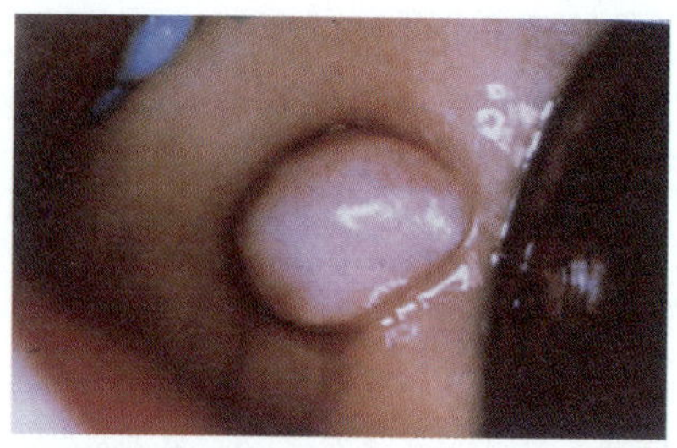

(a)

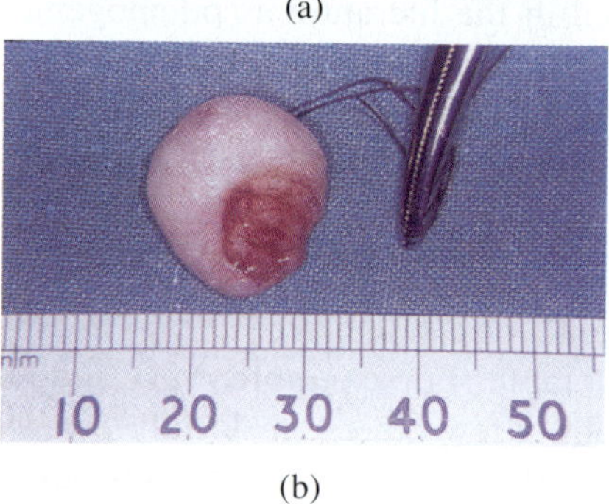

(b)

Fig. 15.1 (a) Fibroma - Cheek **(b)** Excised lesion

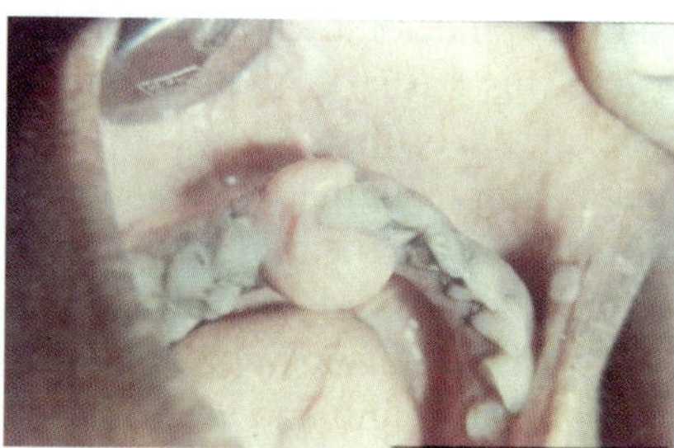

Fig. 15.1 (c) Epulis.

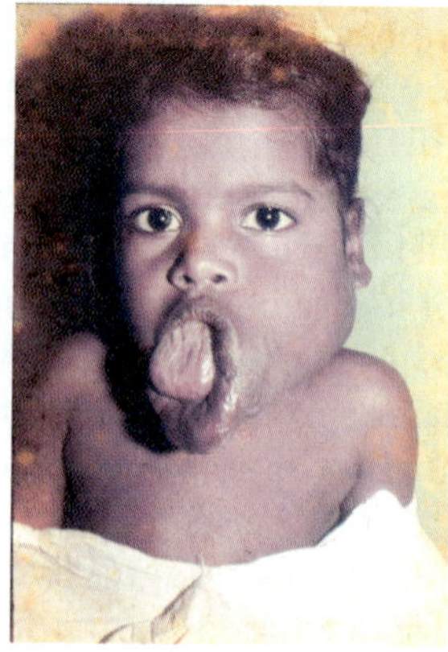

Fig. 15.1 (d) Hemangioma.

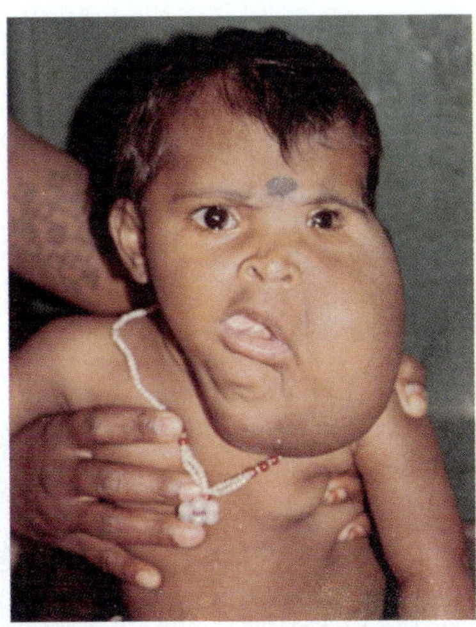

Fig. 15.1 (e) Lymphangioma.

may impose restrictions on the surgeon and the technique of surgery. Because of all these factors, anatomy and location need careful consideration.

(b) Duration

It is necessary to carefully elicit from the patient's history as to when the tumor was noticed by the patient or by the relatives. If it is fastly growing in short duration, immediate treatment must be instituted. Prognosis depends on the rate of growth of the tumor. Fast growing tumors indicate the malignant state. If it is slowly growing, treatment is more elective. Fastly growing tumors need immediate investigation and specialist's treatment.

(c) Benign vs malignant

All the benign tumors are treated conservatively. However, some benign tumors may behave aggressively. Such tumors need more radical surgery. The *excision* should include adequate margin alround. Failure to do so will result in the recurrence of the tumor. If the neoplasm is benign and small involving the bone, then it is *enucleated* or shelled out along the plane of cleavage. If it is not feasible and if the tumor extends into the surrounding bone in different directions, it is safer to *curette* the cavity alround until normal bone is encountered. If the infiltration is extensive, then it is preferable to make the *osteotomy* cut in the normal bone, leaving a safe margin alround so that there is no possibility of its recurrence. Without any break in continuity of bone, if this procedure is done, it is called *peripheral osteotomy*. If the lesion involves full thickness of bone, a *segmental resection* is done. It results in break in continuity of the bone. Such break in continuity can be treated by the transplantation of bone or with alloplastic materials. This way, function is restored. Otherwise, it will be difficult to prevent contraction and distortion of the soft tissues. Therefore, resection of these neoplasms ranges from peripheral osteotomy to segmental resection with or without immediate reconstruction.

If the lesion is very extensive, *radical resection* of the involved bone with or without *immediate reconstruction* is the treatment of choice. As far as possible, immediate reconstruction must be planned to restore the function and esthetics.

The lesions which exhibit malignancy need different modes of treatment. Surgery alone may not be enough. Many surgical and non-surgical modalities are available for the clinician. Usually, an oncology team consists of a surgeon, radiotherapist and chemotherapist who jointly plan the treatment. It may even involve composite resection of bone along with adjacent soft tissues and the associated lymphatic system called *block dissection*. The nature of the ablative surgery is directly related to the staging of malignancy. In extremes of cases, the residual host tissues will have to be treated by *radiotherapy* with or without *chemotherapy*.

Therefore, aggressiveness and staging of the malignant tumors must be taken into consideration to decide the nature and range of radical surgery and other modalities. Staging of the neoplasms depends on the tumor size, regional node involvement, presence or absence of distant metastasis, site and histopathology of the tumor. Proper evaluation of these factors forms one of the important guidelines for deciding the suitable modalities of treatment and prognosis.

(d) Invasion into the bone

The extent of the radical excision depends on this factor. If the lesion is extraosseous and benign, simple excision is adequate. But, if the tumor exhibits malignant features and the periosteal barrier is breached, the lesion is said to be intraosseous. In its initial stage, the cortical bone resists the invasion. Hence, the tumor takes longer time to invade through the cortical bone. Once it reaches the cancellous bone, irrespective of the nature of the tumor, it invades the cancellous and medullary portions faster. Radiologically, the extent of bony invasion can be identified by the abnormal radiolucency. When it encounters the neurovascular canal, the spread is quick which will ultimately need osteotomy or bone resection to a larger extent.

(e) Diagnosis

Whatever be the factors to be considered to decide the nature of management, ultimately it is the clinicians' responsibility to confirm the diagnosis so that a logical sequence of treatment can be instituted. The diagnosis is based on various clinical features including the histopathology of the tumor. If the histopathological evidences are not conclusive, benefit should be given to the patient. Radical nature of the surgical treatment can be justified only on the basis of confirmative diagnosis of the lesion. If the clinical features indicate the possibility of malignancy, the patient must be forewarned and referred to an appropriate and competent specialist for further management.

AMELOBLASTOMA (Figs 15.2 - 15.4)

These epithelial odontogenic tumors are locally invasive in character. They are not encapsulated.

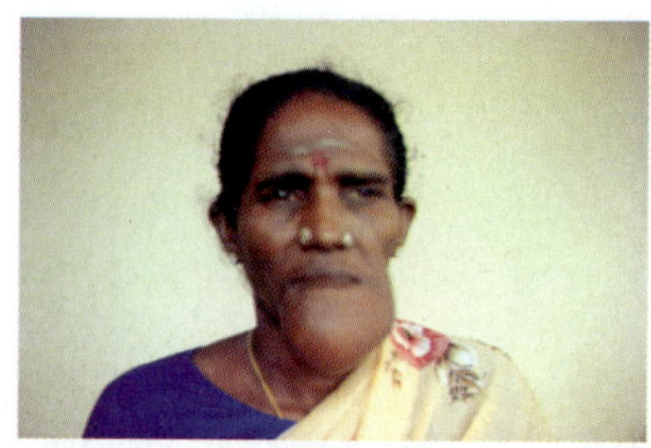

Fig. 15.2 Clinical photograph showing a large ameloblastoma of the left mandible extending along the symphysis on to the right side.

They grow and invade into the neighboring tissues by replacing them rather than pushing the adjacent tissue (like cysts). Microscopically, they extend through the finger-like extensions into the adjacent tissues. Hence, these locally invasive tumors require a resection which will ensure that tumor cells do not reach beyond the limits of the tumor permeation. These invasive tumors of epithelial origin contain collagenolytic substances in high levels which are responsible for osteolysis and the consequent invasiveness. The epithelial components retain their capacity to penetrate the mesenchyme as found in odontogenesis.

The question of the possibility of malignancy of the epithelial or mesenchymal cells of the tumor cannot be ruled out although it is rare. In reality, it has been seen that its clinical behavior is very similar to basal cell carcinoma. Hence, it is known to be locally malignant, locally destructive and locally invasive. 80% of them occur in the mandible while the remainder involve maxilla. In the mandible, 70% of them are seen in the molar region, 20% in the premolar region and 10% in the anterior region.

Histopathologically, these tumor cells bear a striking resemblance to ameloblasts. Hence, the term *ameloblastoma* was coined. The term adamantinoma is not correct since, they do not form enamel. A variety of histological variations have been identified. The most commonly recognized type of ameloblastoma contains islands of epithelial

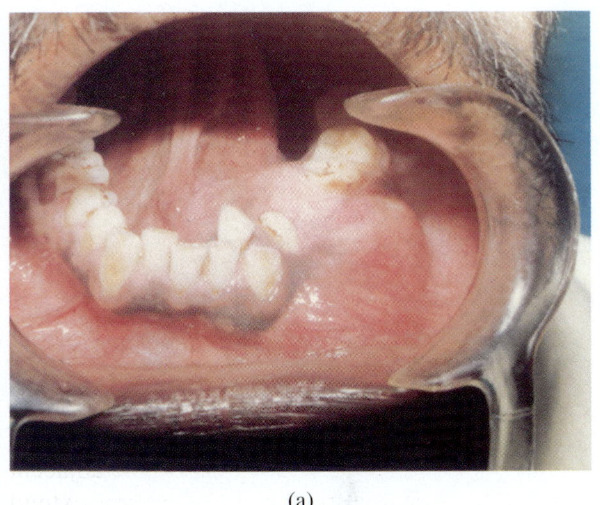

(a)

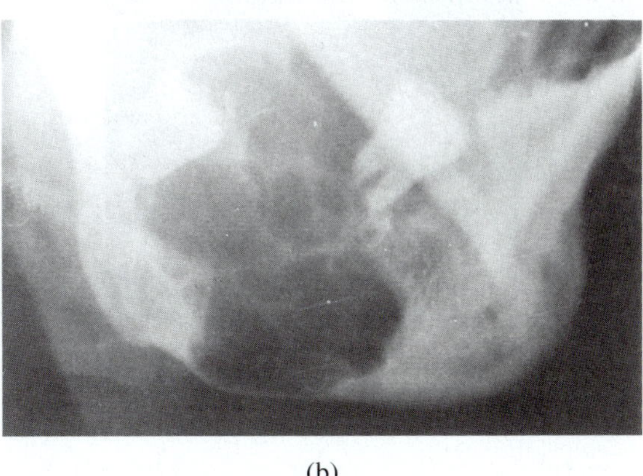

(b)

Fig. 15.3 (a) Orthopantomograph showing large well circumscribed radiolucent lesion involving the entire ramus. Unerupted mandibular III molar is seen near the sigmoid notch partly protruding into the lesion, **(b)** Resected mandibles with multilocular cystic lesion and III molar.

cells in a connective tissue stroma. The lining of these cysts contain flattened cells like a non-neoplastic cyst. Some tumors may not show any well-defined pattern. They vary considerably and the following variants have been described in the literature.

(i) **Follicular:** The tumor epithelium is in the form of more or less discrete islands. They contain a central mass of polyhedral cells resembling stellate reticulum, surrounded by a layer of cuboid or columnar cells resembling inner enamel epithelium. Cyst formation within these islands is common.

(ii) **Plexiform:** The tumor epithelium is arranged in irregular masses or as a network of strands. Each mass is bounded by a layer of columnar cells and includes cells resembling stellate reticulum. But they are less than in follicular type. Cyst formation is usually due to stromal degeneration rather than a cystic change.

(iii) **Acanthomatous type:** When there is extensive squamous metaplasia, this term is applied. Within the islands of tumor tissue, the general pattern of the tumor is similar to the follicular type.

(iv) **Basal cell type:** These tumors arising within the jaw bone or from the surface epithelium in the tooth-bearing area, resemble the basal cell carcinomas. Since the odontogenic epithelium is the special adnexal epithelium of the oral cavity, this is regarded as a histological counterpart of basal cell carcinoma.

(v) **Granular cell type:** Some of these tumors show a granular transformation of the epithelial cells. The cells are large and may be cuboidal, columnar or rounded. Their bulky cytoplasm is filled with acidophilic granules and hence the name.

(vi) **Other variants:** If they contain large blood-filled spaces, it is considered as hemangio-ameloblastoma. Rarely, it may be associated with neuroma.

Most ameloblastomas occur as intraosseus growth. But, a small number appear to arise directly from the surface epithelium or from the residue of the dental lamina lying outside the bone. Such an extraosseous lesion with proliferation of odontogenic epithelium may pose a problem of differential diagnosis.

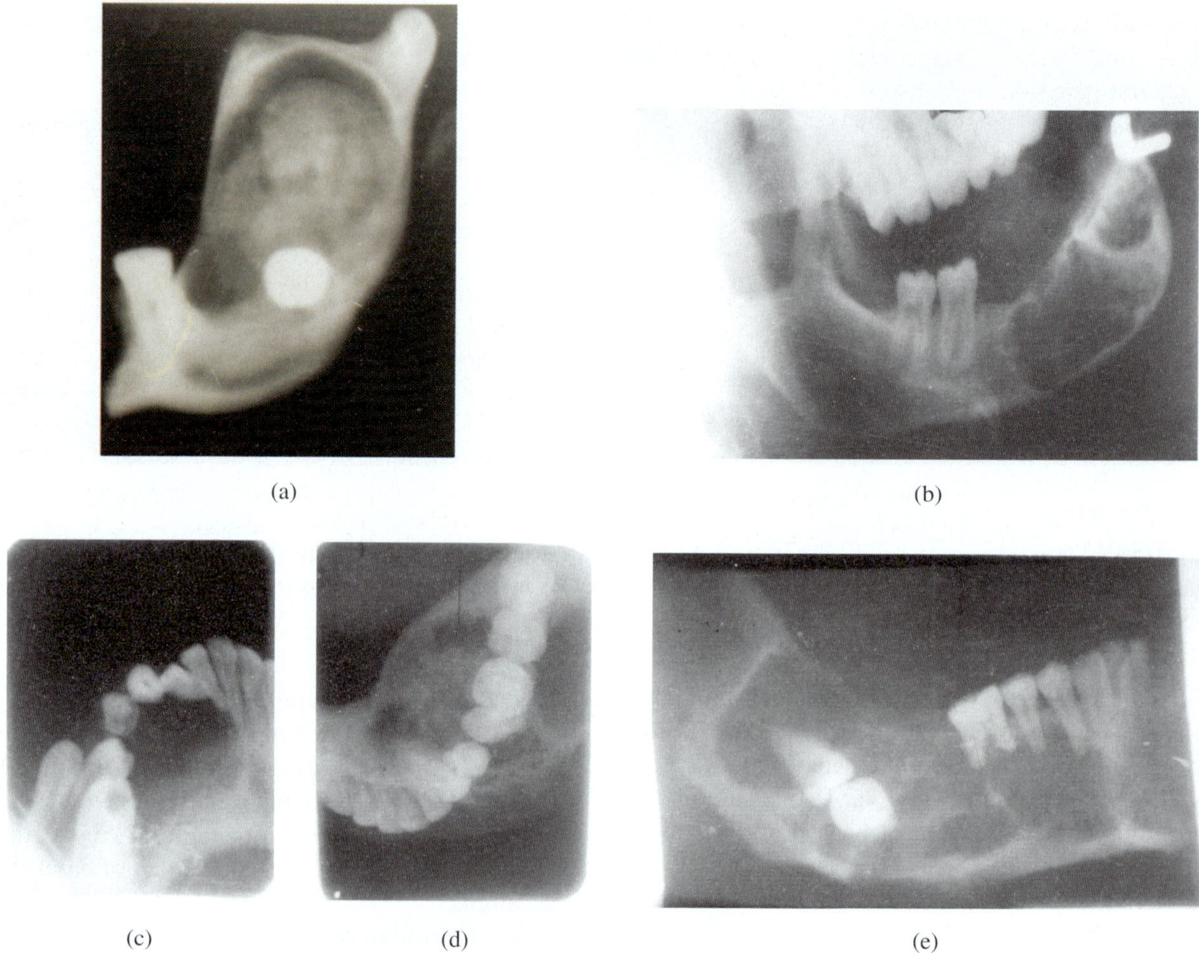

(a) (b) (c) (d) (e)

Fig. 15.4 (a) Lateral oblique view of mandible showing multilocular lesion, **(b)** Orthopantomogram showing a large radiolucent lesion involving the ramus with an unerupted third molar tooth, **(c)** & **(d)** Radiographs showing ameloblastoma, **(e)** Resected mandible - multilocular lesion with 2 unerupted molars.

Ameloblastomas are known to arise from the lining of odontogenic cyst.

Although these histological variants have been identified, there appear to be no consistent variations in their clinical behavior. Likewise, different parts of the same lesion may show different patterns.

Radiologically, they resemble unilocular or multilocular well-circumscribed *"cystic"* radiolucent lesions. Multilocular cysts are described as honey-comb pattern. Hence, it is difficult to differentiate from cysts of the jaws or hyperparathyroidism radiologically.

Management

Once diagnosis is histopathologically confirmed, the treatment consists of total excision of the tumor along with a safe margin of the normal tissue alround. Hence, depending on the size and its extension, various procedures described under "general guidelines" will apply. It may range from local excision to wide resection of the jaw bone. Since regional lymph node metastasis does not occur, there is no need for the removal of lymphatics.

Depending on the need for radical surgery, the various surgical procedures have been advocated.

(1) Excision.
(2) Peripheral osteotomy.
(3) Segmental resection.
(4) Wide resection of the bone with or without reconstruction.

The patient must be warned about the high rate of recurrence. Considering the volume of literature on this aspect, treatment continues to be controversial. The advocates of conservative management recommend enucleation or curettage. Because of the potential for recurrence, conservative management is not generally practiced. At the most, it can be considered as a form of excision biopsy. One may miss the diagnosis unless, histo-pathological examination of the tissue is done from various areas of the lining. Some have tried the conservative management with *cryotherapy*. Pathological fracture is a known risk when cryotherapy is applied to the mandible. Therefore, it is more appropriate to treat this lesion with more radical procedures followed by delayed reconstruction of the bone.

On the basis of the experience, one can develop a protocol for their management.

(1) Preoperative CT scans are preferred for better and adequate preoperative planning. It has been observed that lesions of less than 1 cm on plain radiographs are unlikely to have perforated the cortex. Therefore, lesions larger than 1 cm definitely require CT scans after the biopsy has been performed.

(2) The size of the lesion identified in a plain radiograph will serve as a guide as to whether incisional or excisional biopsy is to be performed. Unilocular lesions of 1 to 2cm size may be enucleated (excision biopsy) under local anesthesia.

(3) Multilocular lesions, those with difficult access and larger lesions are best diagnosed by incisional biopsy. To study the nature and extent of infiltration, CT scan is better.

(4) There is no role for marsupialization in the management of ameloblastomas.

(5) It is preferable to eradicate the lesion before any reconstruction is attempted. A safe period of 6 to 9 months follow up is a safe procedure, before reconstruction.

(6) Even if the lesion is extensive, age of the patient could be taken into consideration before deciding the nature of management - whether to manage with conservative or radical procedures.

(7) Prognosis depends on (a) the infiltration of cancellous/cortical bone, (b) location and size of the tumor, (c) unicystic or multicystic, (d) involvement of soft tissue (peripheral ameloblastoma), (e) microscopic criteria for the diagnosis of the lesion (Hyperchromatism of the nuclei of the basal cells of the epithelium, palisading of these basal cells and polarization of their nuclei to the distal ends of the cells called reverse polarization, vacuolation of the cytoplasm of the basal cells.) and (f) histological criteria for malignancy.

(8) Ameloblastomas are described as radioresistant, atleast from the therapeutic irradiation point of view. This modality is not recommended for the fear of the possibility of radionecrosis of the bone and the risk of inducing malignancy (carcinomas or sarcomas).

ADENOAMELOBLASTOMA

This is an intraosseous odontogenic neoplasm most commonly found in the maxillary cuspid region. This has a few characteristic clinical and pathological features.

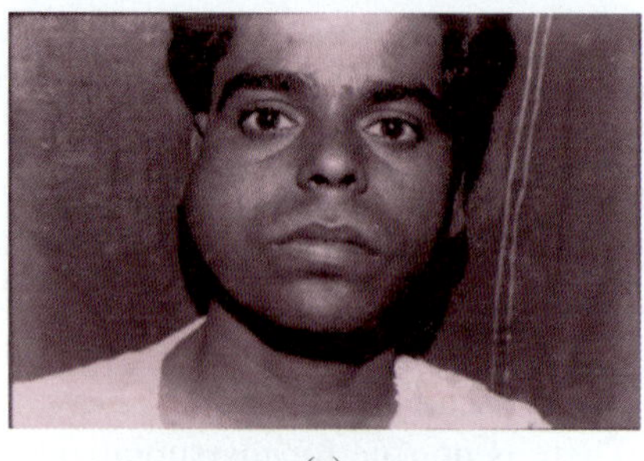

(a)

(b)

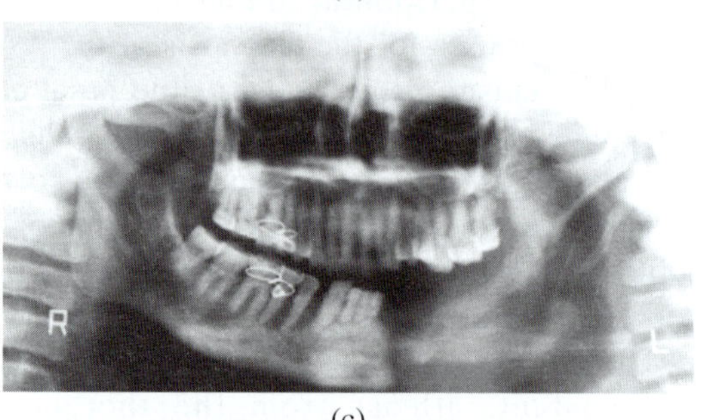

(c)

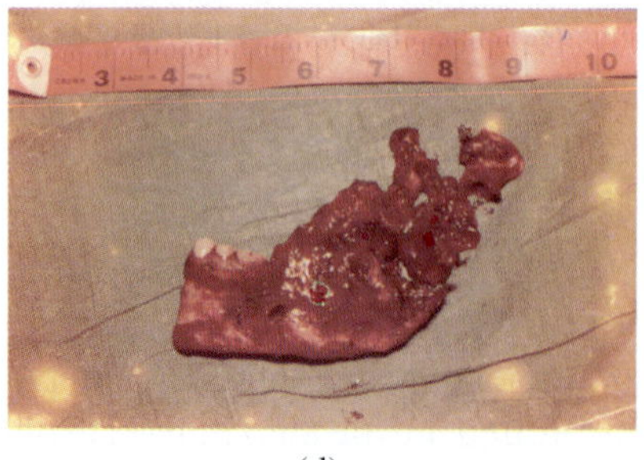

(d)

Fig. 15.5 (a) Ameloblastoma - left mandible (Preoperative), **(b)** Postoperative, **(c)** Ameloblastoma, **(d)** Excised mandible.

Pathogenesis

(1) The cell of origin of this tumor still remains obscure. Since it is commonly associated with an unerupted tooth and resembles a dentigerous cyst, it is believed to arise from the enamel organ or its remnants.

(2) It is also possible that it may arise from the wall of the dentigerous cyst.

Clinical features

(1) Common in the younger age group during the second decade of life. It is more common in females.

(2) Most common site is the interdental space between maxillary lateral incisor and cuspid.

(3) Many of them are associated with unerupted teeth. Hence, may closely simulate dentigerous cyst radiographically.

(4) Usually asymptomatic, small in size with a well-defined capsule. It is a very slowly growing lesion.

(5) Intraoperatively, in some cases, a calcified material may be encountered within the tumor.

Radiological features

It closely resembles a dentigerous cyst when it is associated with the crown of the unerupted tooth. If it does not involve an unerupted tooth, it gives the appearance of monocystic type of radiolucency. But aspiration test will prove negative.

Treatment

Conservative excision of the tumor in the form of enucleation of the lesion is indicated. Since it does not recur, radical surgery is unwarranted. The tumor tissue exhibits, in a cut section, small areas of hemorrhage in a greyish-white tissue. Cystic spaces of various sizes containing gelatinous material can be seen.

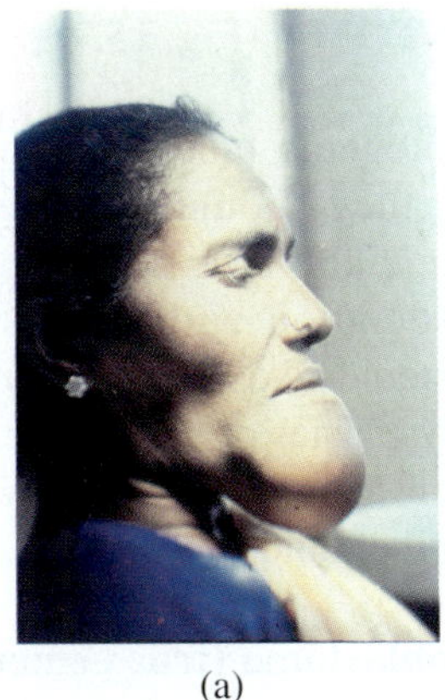
(a)

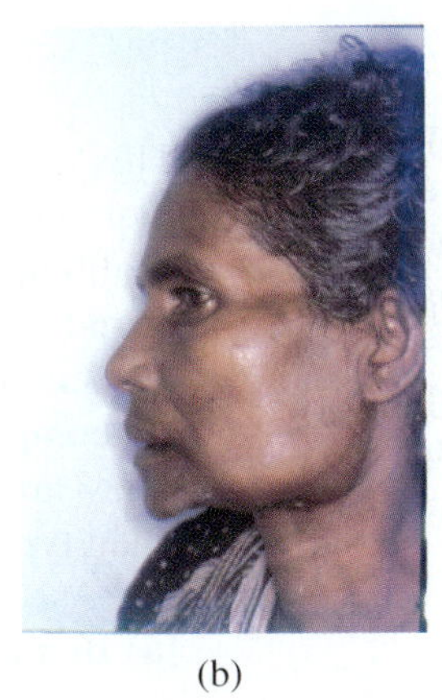
(b)

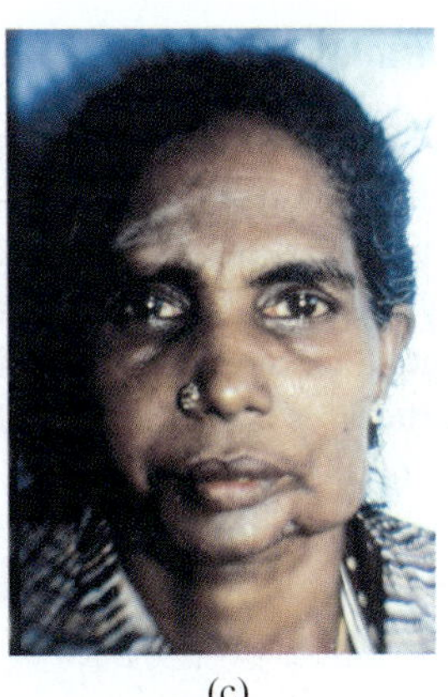
(c)

Fig. 15.6 (a) Tumor involving anterior mandible - Preoperative (side view), **(b)** Postoperative (side view), **(c)** Postoperative (front view).

Histopathology

The tumor tissue is composed of strands of epithelial cells. The cells are columnar resembling ameloblasts. They form duct-like spaces resembling glandular tissue and connective tissue stroma. Small foci of calcification may also be scattered all around the tumor tissue. Since the cells resemble ameloblasts and the microscopic appearance resembles glandular tissue, the tumor was termed as adenoameloblastoma.

Prognosis

This is benign in character and has no tendency to recur. Even with conservative treatment, the lesion is totally curable. Prognosis is excellent. In this aspect, it widely differs from a classical ameloblastoma.

CALCIFYING EPITHELIAL ODONTOGENIC TUMOR

This is also known as *Pindborg's tumor*, named after the person who identified it as a separate entity. It is rare but needs special mention because of (a) its probable odontogenic origin, (b) its usual structure commonly being mistaken as a poorly differentiated carcinoma. Although it appears well-circumscribed, it is not capsulated. It possesses all the characteristic features of local invasiveness. Some exhibit tendency to recur and some do not. The cellular pleomorphism and an alarming resemblance to a poorly differentiated carcinoma are the variable factors from one lesion to the other. Rarely, large giant cells with irregular hyperchromic multinuclei appear to be malignant to a pathologist who is not familiar about the Pindborg's tumor. However, it is not known to metastasize.

Clinical features

It is common during the third and fourth decades of life, involving the premolar-molar region of the mandible. It is usually symptomatic. Radiologically, the lesion is radiolucent with an ill-defined margin. Depending on the stage of maturity of the lesion, areas of radioopacity represents the amount of calcification.

Radiographic appearance is of an irregular radiolucent area containing radioopaque masses of varying size. They tend to be located close to the crown of the unerupted tooth. At the periphery of the lesion, there is often a radiolucent zone, which may or may not be clearly demarcated from the normal bone.

Histopathology

It has sheets of epithelial cells in a connective tissue stroma. In the tumor tissue, a few homogenous hyaline areas (similar to amyloid) are seen with a tendency for calcification around epithelial cells in a concentric fashion. Very rarely, dentine and other dental structures are present in the calcified material. Because of the rarity, nothing is definitely known about the histogenesis. However, due to the presence of identifiable dental tissues, it is described to be of odontogenic origin.

Management

It is very similar to ameloblastoma. However, its histopathological appearance seems to be the guiding factor to indicate its locally invasive character. As already pointed out, the clinician must be careful not to misdiagnose the condition as a poorly differentiated carcinoma.

Odontogenic fibroma

This is a neoplasm, composed of proliferating odontogenic epithelium embedded in a cellular mesodermal tissue that resembles dental papilla, but without the formation of odontoblasts. It is common in younger age group. The usual location is premolar-molar region of the mandible. Radiographically, it shows well-developed and well circumscribed radiolucency. The epithelial component is in the form of strands and islands, consisting of a peripheral layer of cuboidal or columnar cells resembling stellate reticulum. It usually occurs in children.

Odontogenic myxoma

This is a locally invasive neoplasm consisting of rounded and angular cells lying in an abundant mucoid stroma. Radiographically, myxoma shows multiple radiolucent areas of varying sizes seperated by straight or curved bony septa. It is described as "soap-bubble" appearance. It is non-capsulated. Growth may be quite rapid. It is very similar to ameloblastoma.

CEMENTOMA (Fig. 15.7)

This group of odontogenic tumors are benign in their behavior. So, they should not present any problem to the clinician. True cementomas are found in close association with roots of teeth. Cementum being osteoid-like tissue, the variations are comparable to dysplasias or neoplasms of bone. They are uncommon lesions. The following four main types are described under this group.

(a) Benign cementoblastoma (true cementoma)

This is a true neoplasm characterized by the formation of sheets of cement-like tissue, which may contain a very large number of reversal lines and be unmineralized at the periphery of the mass or in the active growth area. This lesion is usually found around the root of mandibular premolar-molar tooth. The lesion is benign and therefore can be readily enucleated.

(b) Cementifying fibroma

This lesion usually occurs in the mandible of elderly persons. There is initial bone destruction with the development of a radiolucent area. As the cementum-like tissue is laid down, this area gradually becomes radioopaque. Once the dense mass is formed, probably, little growth occurs.

(c) Cemental dysplasia (periapical fibrous dysplasia)

This lesion is similar in structure to the cementifying fibroma. It is fibroblastic in its early stages and contains increasing amounts of cementum-like tissue which occasionally interspersed with trabeculae of woven bone. This lesion is common in the mandibular incisor region, often involving several teeth. Radiologically, there may be an ill-defined radiolucent area in relation to root apices, resembling inflammatory rarefaction. Later, masses of increasing radioopacity are laid down.

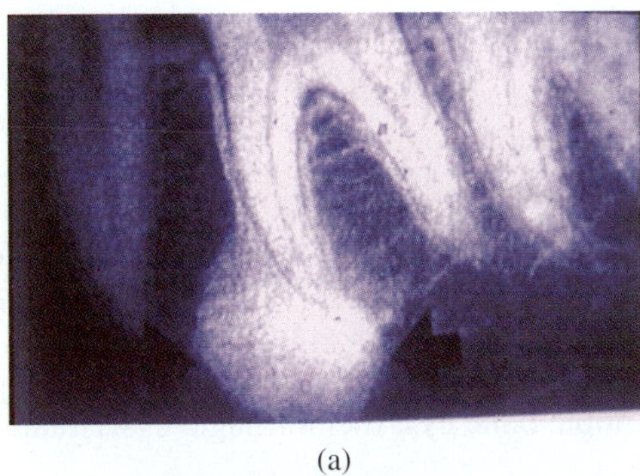

(a)

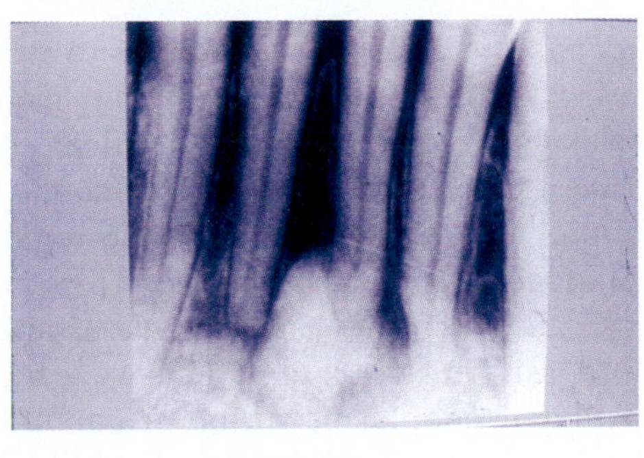

(b)

Fig. 15.7 (a) and **(b)** Cementoma.

(d) Gigantiform cementoma (familial multiple cementomas)

This is a lobulated mass of dense, highly calcified, acellular cementum occuring in several parts of the jaws. Radiologically, they are dense, radioopaque masses. Sometimes, they may attain a considerable size and cause expansion of the jaw.

ODONTOMES (Fig. 15.8)

Originally, this term was coined to include all the odontogenic neoplasms and hamartomas. Pindborg, in W.H.O. classification of odontogenic tumors, cautioned that this term should be reserved only to odontogenic malformations with complete histo-differentiation but lack morphodifferentiation. They are broadly divided into 3 groups.

(1) Complex odontomas.
(2) Compound odontomas.
(3) Ameloblastic odontomas.

They are generally asymptomatic. They may cause disturbances in position and eruption of teeth. Therefore, usually, odontomes are discovered while investigating the underlying cause for retained deciduous teeth or disturbance to the eruption of permanent teeth. Radiological and histopathological findings are useful to confirm the diagnosis.

Complex odontomas form an irregular mass of all dental calcified tissues bearing no morphological similarity to a tooth (histodifferentiation without morphodifferentiation). This is common in the premolar-molar region of the mandible. The active growth phase is during the formation of dentition. Radiographically, the lesion commences as a well-developed radiolucency in which there is progressive deposition of radioopaque material of a nodular nature. During its development, the complex odontome may be difficult to distinguish from ameloblastic fibroma or fibroodontoma. The growth is self limiting.

Compound odontomas are composed of all the odontogenic tissues arranged in an orderly pattern. But they also have no morphological similarity to a tooth although there is some orderly pattern in complex odontome. Therefore, the lesion consists of many tooth-like structures with all dental tissues arranged as in the normal tooth (denticles).

The distinction between compound and

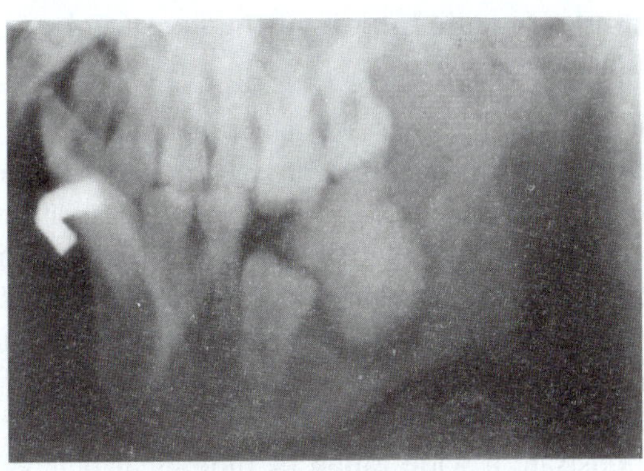

Fig. 15.8 Odontome.

complex odontomes is arbitrary. It is based on the presence of well-organized denticles or disorganized dental tissues rather than any absolute difference.

Ameloblastic odontomes contain varying amount of calcified odontogenic tissues with dental papilla-like tissue. The connective tissue stroma has a striking resemblance to ameloblastic fibroma. However, fibroodontomes are regarded as precursor of complex odontomas. This group of dental malformations are classified as follows:

(1) *Epithelial hamartoma*
    e.g. Enameloma (enamel pearl)
(2) Connective tissue hamartoma
    (a) Dentinoma
    (b) Cementoma
(3) Composite odontomes
    (a) Complex odontomes
    (b) Compound odontomes
    (c) Ameloblastic odontomes
    (d) Dilated odontomes
        (i) Coronal
        (ii) Radicular

Management

In general, treatment is conservative and form simple excision. Dilated odontomes predispose to apical pathology. If no conservative endodontic treatment is possible, extraction of the tooth is indicated.

Non-odontogenic tumors of the jaws (and related lesions)

This group of lesions are generally referred to as "Fibroosseous lesions".This term is a generic designation of a group of jaw disorders ranging from inflammatory to neoplastic lesions that microscopically exhibit a connective tissue matrix with islands of trabeculae of bone. Even though, the histologic, clinical and radiographic features may be similar for this group of lesions, they tend to demonstrate a wide range of biological behavior. Hence the treatment also varies.

Osteogenic neoplasms:
Ossifying fibroma.

Non-neoplastic bone lesions:
Fibrous dysplasia
Cherubism
Giant cell reparative granuloma
Aneurysmal bone cyst
Simple bone cyst (hemorrhagic cyst, traumatic cyst.)

Because of the overlapping microscopic features, diagnosis of individual lesions included under this group of lesions may be difficult. All of them have a fibroblastic matrix and new tumor bone formation. To understand these bone tumors, a general account is provided based on which proper diagnosis and treatment planning could be made.

(a) **Ossifying fibroma.** This is a benign encapsulated neoplasm, which is common in females in the second or third decade of life. Most of them occur in the mandible. It contains varying amounts of metaplastic bone and mineralized masses that have rounded outlines and a few entrapped cells. It may be indistinguishable from fibrous dysplasia, but it has a typical encapsulated growth that behaves as a benign neoplasm. Rarely, it may resemble cementifying fibroma or periapical cemental dysplasia. Radiographically, it is well defined, containing a variable amount of radioopaque material.

(b) **Fibrous dysplasia.** This is a benign self-limiting, non-encapsulated lesion occuring mainly in young persons. It commonly occurs in maxilla. The normal bone is replaced by a cellular fibrous tissue containing islands of metaplastic bone. Radiographically, the appearance depends on the stage of the lesion. In the osteolytic stage, there is an ill-defined radiolucency. In later stages, progressive deposition of lesional bone results in the ground-glass appearance. No sharp line of demarcation exists between the lesion and the normal tissue. The histological appearance varies with its age and the stage of development. There may be cyst formation. At some stages, osteoclasts may be numerous but it is unusual to see collections of multinuclear giant cells. Some cementum-like tissue may be deposited but cartilage is rarely seen.

(c) **Cherubism (familial multilocular cystic disease of the jaws).** It is a benign, self-limiting condition in which lesional tissue, consisting of a vascular fibrous tissue, containing varying numbers of multinuclear giant cells, arranged diffusely. They are commonly seen in children showing familial tendency. They affect more than one quadrants forming radiolucent cyst-like areas. The lesion is usually active in the younger age group. After the age of 12 years, activity diminishes and finally become "inactive." This explains the variation of the histological findings. More active lesions can be identified from the presence of many giant cells, containing multiple foci of extravasated blood. As the activity diminishes, the lesion becomes more fibrous with less number of giant cells and more bone formation.

(d) **Giant cell reparative granuloma.** If it occurs as an intraosseous lesion, it is termed as central giant cell reparative granuloma while, if it is extraosseous, it is called peripheral giant cell reparative granuloma.

The central lesion consists of cellular fibrous tissue containing multiple foci of hemorrhage, aggregation of multinucleated giant cells and sometimes, trabeculae of woven bone forming within the septa of more mature fibrous tissue that may traverse the lesion. It may occur in both the jaws at any age. It is most commonly seen in the tooth-bearing area of the jaws. Radiographically, there is an area of bone destruction with smooth or lobulated outline which may be traversed by slender bony septa. This is responsible for the similarity in the histological appearance of ameloblastoma. In some lesions, focal aggregation of giant cells are clear with trabeculae of bone extending between the foci of giant cell. In other lesions, it is loose textured and edematous.The giant cells may show little evidence of focal arrangement. Fresh hemorrhage may be a frequent feature. The lesion may expand and can penetrate the cortex and appear as gingival swelling. Such swelling is encapsulated. These lesions may present problems to distinguish histologically between giant cell granuloma, cheribism and brown tumor of hyper-parathyroidism. It is treated by surgical excision. Sometimes, they recur.

(e) **Aneurysmal bone cyst.** This is a benign intraosseous lesion, characterized by blood-filled spaces of varying size. It may also be associated with a fibroblastic tissue containing multinuclear giant cells and osteoid. It usually occurs in young persons and found more common in the mandible. Radiographically, this is a multiloculated radiolucent lesion which balloons the cortex. Histological examinations reveal the presence of many large and small cavernous spaces filled with erythrocytes. These spaces are contained within a cellular connective tissue and fresh/old hemorrhages which show organization with multinucleated giant cells and slender trabeculae of osteoid.

(f) **Hemorrhagic cyst (traumatic, simple bone cyst).** This is seen during first and second decades of life. The common site is the body of the mandible in the canine-angle region of the mandible. The details are described in the chapter on "cysts".

Surgical procedures

In general, many terms have been used to describe the various surgical procedures. An outline is provided on standardized surgical terminology for the excision of the lesions in bone.

(i) **Enucleation.** This term can be used for the seperation of a lesion from bone with preservation of continuity of bone. This is possible only when the lesion is restricted and defined by a capsule, a connective tissue envelop, derived from the lesion or surrounding bone. The term signifies the ability to separate the lesion from the surrounding bone along a cleavage plane between the lesion and bone.

(ii) **Curettage.** This term denotes the removal of a lesion from bone with preservation of bone continuity, by scraping. This may be necessary because of the friability of the lesion or the absence of a well-defined capsule. It signifies the inability to seperate the lesion from the bone along a distinct tissue cleavage plane between the lesion and bone. It does not ensure complete removal. It only conveys a sense of its physical state. If a measurable margin of bone has to be removed, then it should be termed as "resection without continuity defect". Curettage can be achieved mechanically or with physical/chemical agents.

(iii) **Marsupialization.** This procedure is carried out by creating a window and its removal which contains a part of the lesion. This results in decompression and exposes the interior of the bony cavity. It implies that multilocular lesion is rendered monolocular. It can be considered as a form of incisional biopsy. It should not be considered as a therapeutic procedure.

(iv) **Resection without continuity defect.** This means excision of the lesion along with a measurable surrounding bone, without interruption of bony continuity. While doing so, anatomic relationship of the lesion is taken into consideration to determine the extent of surrounding bone and soft tissue to be removed. Because of this, the surgeon may compromise the extent of the surgical excision to preserve important anatomical structures like inferior dental neurovascular bundle or to avoid fracture of the bone although, growth characteristics of the lesion may need wider excision. This problem can be overcome by an appropriate preoperative planning through imaging modalities, biochemical and histopathological evaluations.

(v) **Resection with continuity defect.** This term refers to the excision of the lesion along with a measurable surrounding bone resulting in continuity defect of bone. Bone excision with a safe margin is advocated to eliminate the possible extension of the lesion along the surrounding structures. While doing so, anatomic relationship of the lesion, size and extent of the lesion is properly studied through the imaging procedures before deciding the extent of surgery. In this way planning is done to assess the possible postoperative morbidity and the reconstruction of such a defect.

(vi) **Disarticulation.** This refers to the modification of resection with continuity, wherein the defect involves the temporomandibular joint. This is distinguished so that it helps in the reconstruction of the defect. This must be properly documented.

(vii) **Recontouring** (Fig. 15.9). This term refers to the surgical reduction of the size and shape of the surface of the bone. This is designed to reshape the surface of a bony lesion to conform to the normal bone surface. This is only a camouflaging procedure without totally excising the lesion. This is best performed by using rotatory instrument.

The above account is meant only to serve as a guideline for the clinician to differentiate between the various surgical procedures performed on the bony lesions.

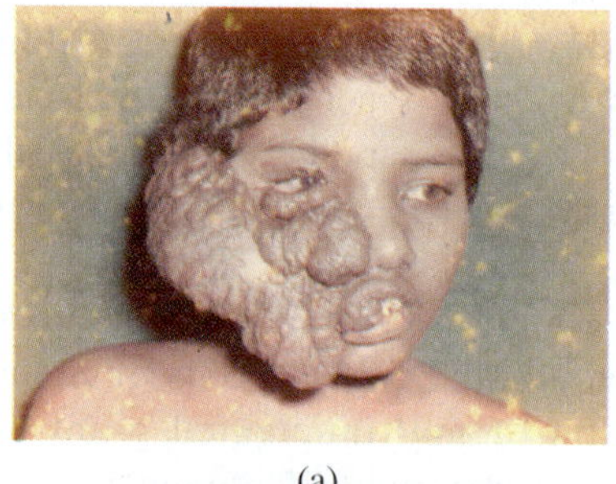

(a)

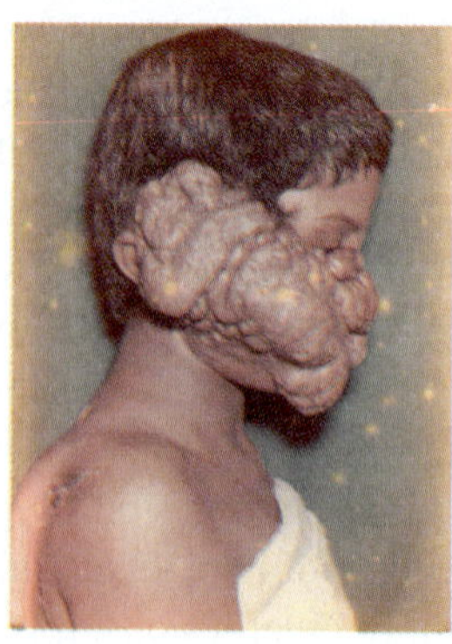

(b)

Fig. 15.9 Neurofibroma **(a)** Front view, **(b)** Side view.

ORAL MALIGNANCY

Oral oncology has become a highly specialized field. Theoretically, every known tumor occuring elsewhere in the body can also occur in the oral cavity. Hence, it is essential to keep in mind the possibility of development of various tumors depending on the histology of the oral tissues. The prognosis depends on the nature of the tumor and the histological variants. It becomes the responsibility of the clinician to identify and diagnose these tumors and their clinical behavior so that management of these tumors could be planned accordingly. Several benign tumors occur in the maxillofacial region. Although prognosis of benign tumors are excellent, the possibility of their malignant transformation cannot be ruled out. Therefore, it is a safe practice to carryout histopathological examination of any lesion. Documentation of these lesions is equally significant.

Once the tumor is diagnosed as oral malignant neoplasm, their management essentially involves a team work of a surgeon and/or an oral surgeon, radiotherapist and chemotherapist. In advanced cases, diagnosis of these lesions are quite obvious and may not present any problem. In such cases, instead of doing a biopsy, dental surgeon should preferably refer the patient to one of the members of the oncology team. It is an established practice that once biopsy conclusively establishes the diagnosis, treatment should be started immediately due to the possible risk of dissemination of the neoplastic cells along the lymphatic system. Moreover, an oncologist would prefer to examine the lesion before biopsy is done.

Anybody can face many of the common illnesses with the hope that modern medicine can cure the conditions. But the moment any suspicious lesion is confirmed as a malignant condition, the picture changes completely. Perhaps, no other lesion evokes so much of emotional disturbance in the minds of all concerned. Since prognosis of an early lesion is good, it is the responsibility of the dental surgeon to examine the oral cavity properly in every patient and advice accordingly.

Although different types of malignant lesions may affect the head and neck, squamous cell carcinoma is the most common type. Smokeless tobacco continues to be the specific etiologic agent for the oral cancers in India. Since they are preventable habits, all efforts must be directed to educate the population about the evil effects of tobacco in any form.

In general, malignant tumors are classified in terms of prognosis into 3 groups:

(a) preventable (b) treatable (c) untreatable.

Oral cancers are grouped as preventable and established cases are treatable. Since most of these lesions (precancerous and cancerous) are usually missed by the dental practitioner because of their varied clinical presentations, all the dental surgeons must be trained to diagnose these lesions. If the lesions are identified in the premalignant stage, it will be ideal. Unfortunately, patients do not seek treatment for early lesions. Therefore, all the health professionals need to be vigilant as prevention or early detection may be the only effective measure left to change the mortality of this condition. In the initial stages, it starts as an indolent crack with a superficial patch. Any such non-healing unexplained lesion must arouse high degree of suspicion. It is in these cases, dental surgeon can do biopsy under local anesthesia as an office procedure. As already described, the biopsy of any lesion should be of sufficient dimension. It should be accompanied by the following details:

(1) Full history.
(2) Proper description of the lesion.
(3) Diagrammatic orientation of the specimen.
(4) Relevant radiographs or at least radiographic findings.
(5) Previous laboratory reports, if any.
(6) Provisional diagnosis.

PREMALIGNANT LESIONS

The premalignant lesions of the oral cavity are of very great clinical importance since most of the oral malignant lesions can be identified even before the lesions undergo malignant transformation. WHO described the premalignant lesion as a morphologically altered tissue in which cancer is more likely to occur than with its apparently normal counterpart and in which its generalized state is associated with significant increased risk of cancer.

Leukoplakia

The white lesions of the oral cavity appear white because of any of the following reasons:

(a) If one or more epithelial layers are thickened,

(b) If an extrinsic or intrinsic membrane is adherent to the oral mucosa.

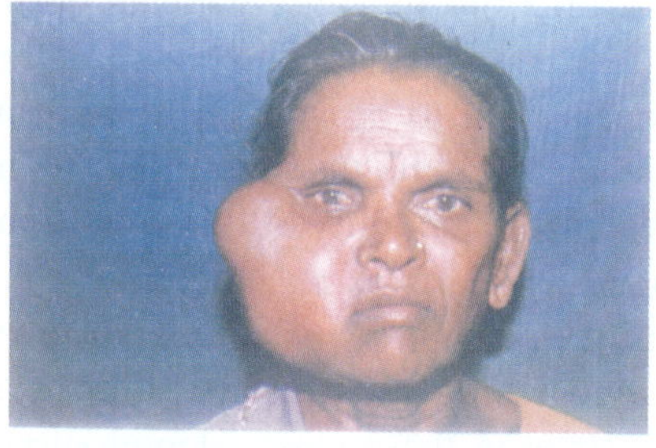

Fig. 15.10 Pleomorphic adenoma - Parotid.

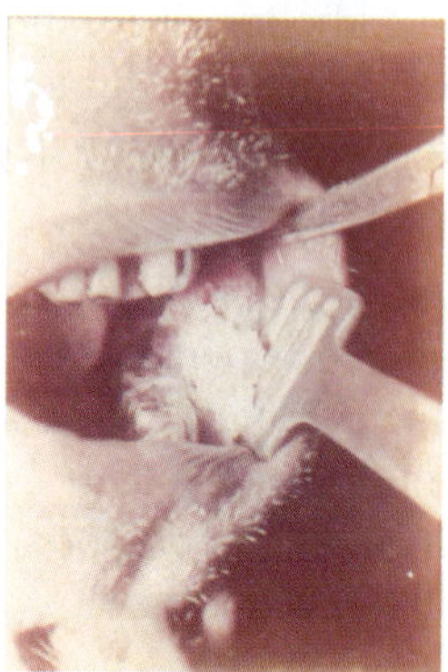

Fig. 15.11 Leukoplakia - Cheek.

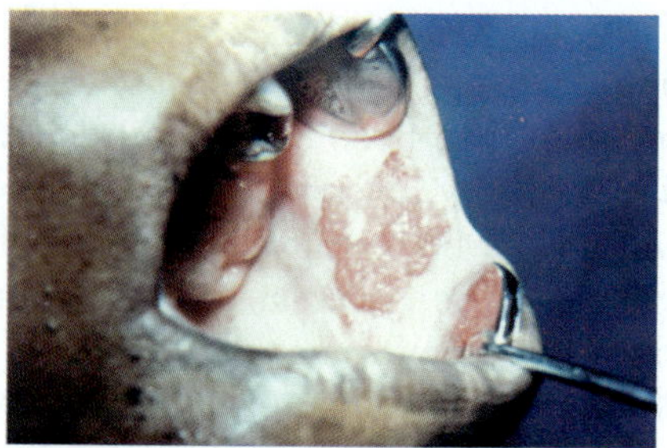

Fig. 15.12 (a) Carcinoma - Cheek.

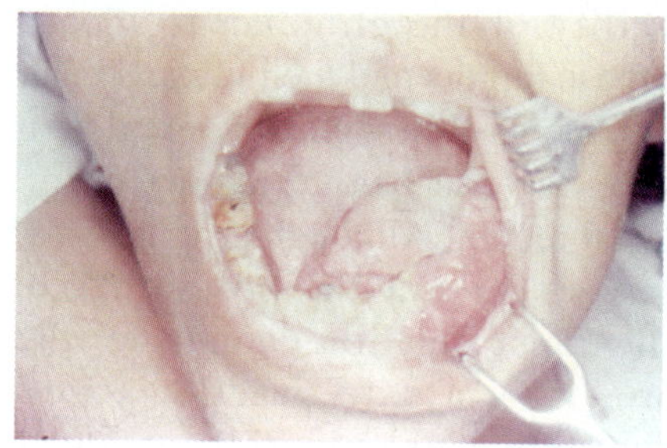

Fig. 15.12 (b) Carcinoma - Floor of the mouth.

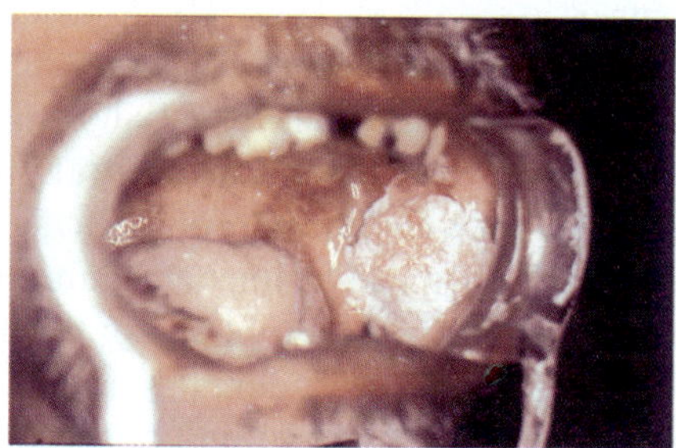

Fig. 15.12 (c) Carcinoma - Cheek extending over the retromolar region.

In general, they can be classified under various groups like keratoses, leukoplakia, dermatoses and inflammatory lesions.

Leukoplakia (Eg., Frictional leukoplakia, Tobacco-associated leukoplakia, Dysplasias, Leukoplakia) is defined as a white patch that can not be characterized clinically or pathologically as any other disease. This definition does not refer to any histological changes. Histologically, the white patches have three features. They are - (a) abnormal keratinization, (b) epithelial hyperplasia or hypoplasia and (c) variable maturation of the epithelial cells.

Keratinization is responsible for the white color. *Hyperkeratosis* means overproduction of mature keratin with the granular layer containing prekeratin granules. The term *Parakeratosis* means persistence of degenerating nuclei in the surface layer of cells without any sharp dividing line between the prickle cell layer and parakeratosis layer. Distinct granular cell layer is absent since nuclei mature and progressively become insignificant.

If the prickle cell layer is hyperplastic, then it is termed as *Acanthosis*. The thickness of the prickle cell layer has no correlation with the degree of keratinization. For example, hyperkeratosis may be associated with hypoplasia of the underlying epithelium. Likewise, the degree of hyperplasia has no relationship with premalignancy.

During the maturation process, the basal cell layer of cells progressively pass through the prickle cell stage and reach the surface before the matured cells lose nuclei and are shed away. The sequence of these events can be considered as normal in hyperkeratinization. Only when it is disordered to any degree, it is called *Dyskeratosis* (Dysplasia). It is the dysplastic change that must be considered as premalignant.

Differential diagnosis

(a) White spongy nevus.
(b) Smoker's keratosis.
(c) Frictional keratosis.
(d) Candidosis.
(e) Leukoplakia
(f) Lichen planus.
(g) Submucous fibrosis.
(h) Chemical burns.

The *white spongy nevus* is a well-defined, inherited, familial disorder. It is characterized by widespread soft, uneven thickening of the superficial layers of the epithelium. The epithelium is hyperplastic with gross intraepithelial edema. Entire oral cavity may be involved including sulci dorsum of the tongue and inner aspect of the lips. The lesion may not have definite boundary. It may gradually merge with the normal mucosa. No treatment is advocated for this condition. The patient needs reassurance.

In *Smoker's Keratosis*, the lesion is seen in the palate, cheek mucosa and floor of the mouth. This lesion develops due to the irritation by heat and the chemical components of the smoke. In this condition, hyperkeratinization is a distinct feature. Overproduction of keratin with consequent inflammation and swelling may cause blockage of the ducts of minor palatal salivary glands. There are varying degrees of keratosis, parakeratosis or acanthosis. Clinically, smoker's keratosis is readily recognizable as a white thickening of the palate and multiple glandular swellings. The white component of the lesion may be variable. If the patient stops smoking, these changes are reversible. Otherwise, this must serve as a warning to the patient about the possibility of its transforming into a malignant lesion.

Frictional Keratosis develops due to constant friction (abrasion) of the oral mucosa by any of the irritants like sharp teeth, denture irritation or frequent cheek biting. In the early stages, these lesions appear pale and translucent than white. But later, they become white and dense with a rough surface. Epithelium is hyperkeratotic with prominent granular cell layer. Removal of the irritant reverses the lesion into normal mucosa.

Even though majority of the white lesions may undergo premalignant changes, one should not hastily come to a conclusion that all leukoplakias are premalignant or all premalignant lesions are white patches. Since the term leukoplakia has been liberally used to all white lesions, at present, the term leukoplakia is to be restricted to premalignant lesions and NOT to all white lesions.

The red lesions are called *Erythroplakia* which usually have greater precancerous potential. Most of them are histologically *carcinoma-in-situ*. (intraepithelial carcinoma).

Dyskeratosis (Dysplasia) is a histological term. Usually, they appear as red and atrophic lesions in combination with white colored and speckled surface. The terms - atypia, dyskeratosis and dysplasia - denote disordered proliferation and maturation of the epithelial cells. Because of the malignant transformation of many of these lesions, great care is warranted while dealing with them.

Keratinization is usually incomplete in the form of parakeratosis. Nuclei of these epithelial cells may be characterized by any of the following changes:

(a) Hyperchromatism: Nuclei stain dark due to increased nucleic acid content.

(b) Pleomorphism: Altered nucleus : Cytoplasm ratio is striking. The nuclei appear large because of the disproportionately lesser amount of cytoplasm.

(c) Loss of polarity: Basal cells may appear at angles to one another. In the normal tissues, nuclei are arranged close to the basement membrane in an orderly fashion.

(d) Deep cell keratinization: The cells may start to degenerate even before they reach the surface. Therefore, the term is more appropriate to this abnormal keratinization.

(e) Loss of intercellular adherence: Boundaries of the cells may appear separate.

(f) Differentiation: No clearly differentiated basal cell and prickle cell layers can be differentiated.

The ultimate degree of dysplasia with all the cellular abnormalities of malignancy may be identified in case of carcinoma-in-situ. The only differentiating feature is the intact basement membrane. It means the absence of its invasion into the connective tissue. This is uncommon in the oral cavity.

The term *speckled leukoplakia* is used to denote the white lesions on an atrophic erythematous base. This is considered as the combination of erythroplasia and leukoplakia.

Management

Due to their unpredictable nature of the behavior, satisfactory method is yet to be formed. However, there is a general agreement on their management depending on their size. For example, if the lesion is small, excision of the lesion along with a margin of normal tissue is the accepted form of treatment. If the lesion is large, incision biopsy with a margin of normal tissue is a diagnostic procedure. The treatment depends on the histopathology of the lesion. It is better to treat carcinoma-in-situ as an invasive carcinoma. All the cases with dysplasia must be reviewed atleast for a year at two-monthly intervals. Therefore, Leukoplakia is the term, reserved to represent the possible dysplastic epithelium and must not be used for all white lesions. Throughout the world, the incidence varies widely. The frequency of malignant transformation in leukoplakia has been reported in the literature in the range of 1.5% to 6%. In India, tobacco chewing has been the main causative factor and malignancy develops in nearly 25% of the leukoplakia (Kramer).

Oral lichen planus

This is an oral manifestation of dermatological disorder. This is a chronic inflammatory immunological reaction in which epidermal or epithelial basal cell damage produces mucocutaneous lesions of various types. Often it does not respond to treatment. Complete remission is infrequent in cases of erosive lesions. Some of these patients develop *cancer phobia*. There are differing views about the malignant potential of these lesions. The risk is estimated as 0.5% to 2.5%. Some hold an opposing view that it is non-malignant.

Lichenoid dysplasia is frequently misdiagnosed as lichen planus that has the malignant potential. Molecular biological techniques suggest that oral lichen planus may not be premalignant but malignant transformation may be associated with "coincidental" development of dysplasia in these lesions. Present reports have suggested that atrophic, erosive, ulcerative or desquamative clinical variants must be viewed with caution for any malignant transformation. Under these circumstances, this lesion must be managed.

Management

The mainstay of the management remains corticosteroids - topical, intralesional and systemic. It may be applied topically as ointments, pastes, lozenges or mouthwashes. Betamethasone valerate pellets (0.1 mg) is found to be most effective. Triamcinolone acetonide is useful as a long-acting lozenge. Topical fluorinated corticosteroids are now being used as the first line of treatment. Unfortunately, prolonged topical application may lead to the development of oral candida infection. A 5% mixture of local anesthetics intralesionally will lessen the pain. Systemic steroid therapy must be reserved for acute exacerbations only.

Apart from steroids, many other drugs have been tried.

(i) Griseofulvin has been tried orally or parentally. The earliest studies were encouraging but subsequently, it has not been so. The mechanism of action is not known. But it has been postulated that when given parenterally, it is distributed throughout the body and gets deposited in the basal cell. As the basal cell gets matured progressively, it reaches the superficial strata of cells. It is contraindicated in pregnancy.

(ii) Cyclosporin is a non-myelotoxic immuno-suppressive agent. It inhibits the release of interleukin 1 from monocytes and interleukin 2 from T-cells. This drug has been found to be beneficial in cutaneous lesions but renal toxicity is well known. It is prohibitively expensive. Its efficacy is also questionable.

(iii) Vitamin A analogues and Retinoids have also been tried successfully in cases of asymptomatic white reticulated lesions.

(iv) Dapsone has been used to treat various inflammatory and infectious dermatoses. They have been successfully used in patients with bullous and erosive forms of cutaneous lichen planus.

There have been a number of reports of cryosurgery in oral lichen planus. It destroys the tissue and may even cause erosions to enlarge. Surgical excision and carbon dioxide lasers have been tried to treat erosive lesions. However, surgical excision should never be the primary mode of treatment. Surgical trauma may induce the formation of new lesions.

PROTOCOL FOR THE MANAGEMENT OF ORAL LICHEN PLANUS
(Ref: Third European Congress of Oral Medicine - 1996)

1. Asymptomatic disease:
   (a) No active treatment.
   (b) Six-monthly review for two years.
   (c) Subsequently, twelve-monthly review by the dental surgeon.
2. Symptomatic cases:
   (a) Try antifungal preperations for all lesions.
   (b) Maintenance of good oral hygiene desirable.
   (c) Relieve local irritants.
   (d) Restricted lesions: Topical steroids twice a day for 2 weeks and once a day for further 2 weeks.
   (e) Widespread lesions: Steroids as mouth wash - 0.5 mg dissolved in 10 ml warm water- for 5 minutes, four times a day. Patient must be adviced not to swallow the mouth wash material.
   (f) Erosions that reduce to small lesions after initial steroids: Intralesional injections of steroids like triamcinolone acetonide 10 mg/ml repeated once or twice as necessary.
   (g) Intractable lesions: Systemic steroids combined with topical steroids. Monitor for systemic side effects.
   (h) Follow-up: After remission, review after 3 months and after 6 months. Follow-up the persistent cases 3 to 6 monthly.

Oral submucous fibrosis (OSMF) (Fig 15.13)

Oral Submucous Fibrosis is a chronic disease of the oral mucosa. It occurs predominantly in Indians and people of south-east Asian origin. It is characterized by inflammation and progressive fibrosis of lamina propria. Major presenting complaint is progessive inability to open the mouth due to the extraarticular restricting influence of the jaw movement by the accumulation of inelastic fibrous bands in the cheek mucosa with concomitant muscle degeneration. Patients will complain about a gradual onset of burning sensation while eating spicy food that did not cause any distress. With passage of time, onset of fibrosis of the cheek mucosa may lead to difficulty in mastication, speech and swallowing. Due to the stenosis of the opening of the eustachian tube, patient may develop a relative loss of auditory acuity. In advanced cases, trismus may be very severe and because the inelastic mucosa is forced against the teeth, patient may develop chronic ulceration and subsequent infection. The cheek mucosa will present a marble-like mosaic appearance with normal reddish mucosa intermingling with depigmented diseased mucosa. The floor may become pale and thickened. In extreme cases, fibrosis may extend down to the esophagus resulting in progressive dysphagia.

Histologically, it is characterized by juxta-epithelial fibrosis, atrophy or hypoplasia of the overlying epithelium, keratinizing metaplasia and accumulation of hyalinized collagen below the basement membrane with progressive compromised vascularity.

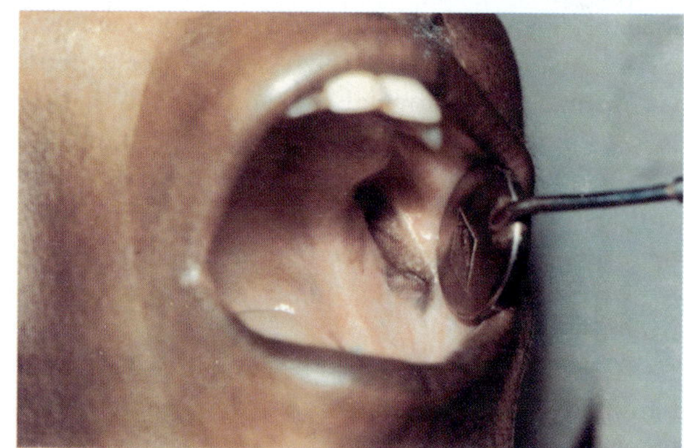

Fig. 15.13(a) Submucous fibrosis-cheek.

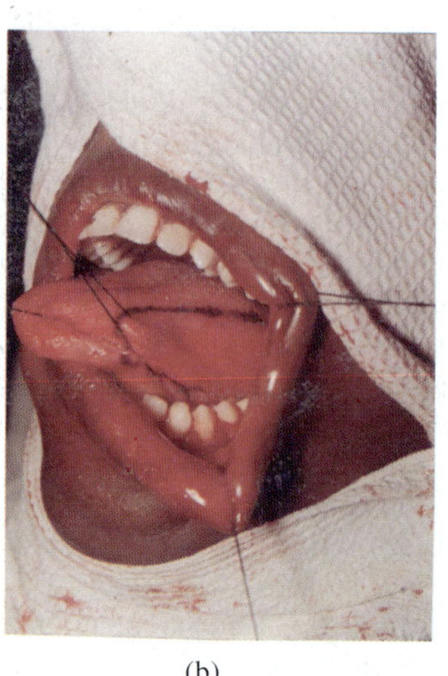

(b)

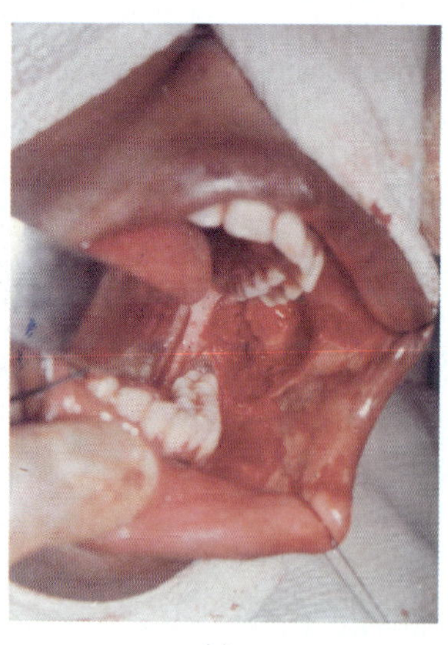

(c)

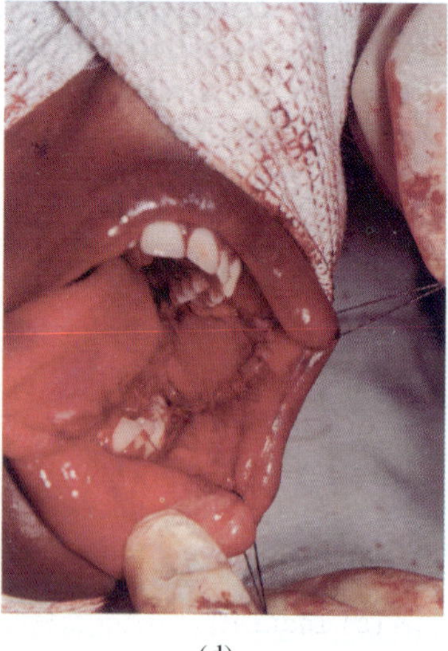

(d)

Fig. 15.13 Submucous fibrosis corrected with posteriorly based tongue flap: **(b)** Tongue flap outline, **(c)** Mucosal defect after excision of fibrotic bands, **(d)** Defect covered with tongue flap.

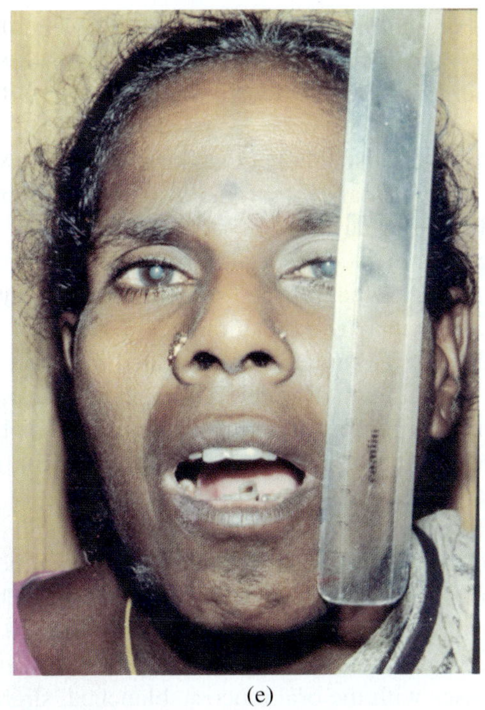

(e)

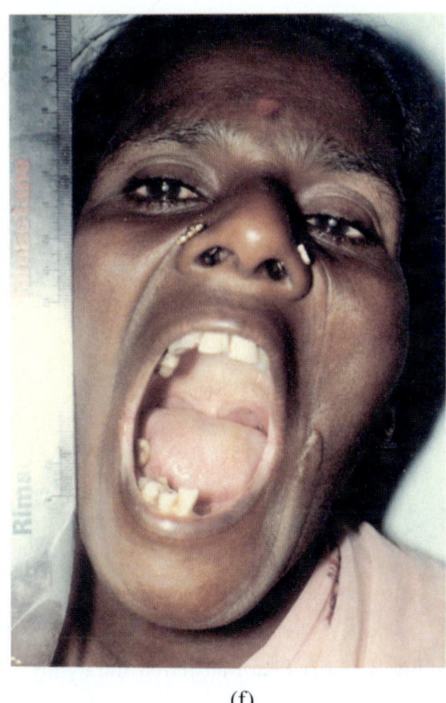

(f)

Fig. 15.13 OSMF corrected with nasolabial flap: **(e)** Preoperative mouth opening, **(f)** Postoperative mouth opening.

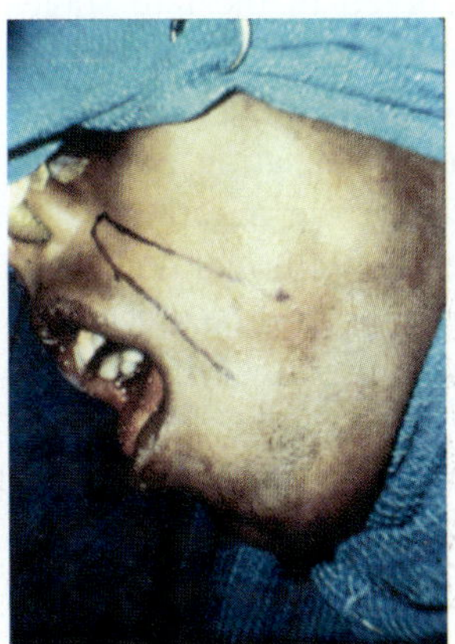

Fig. 15.13(g) Flap outline.

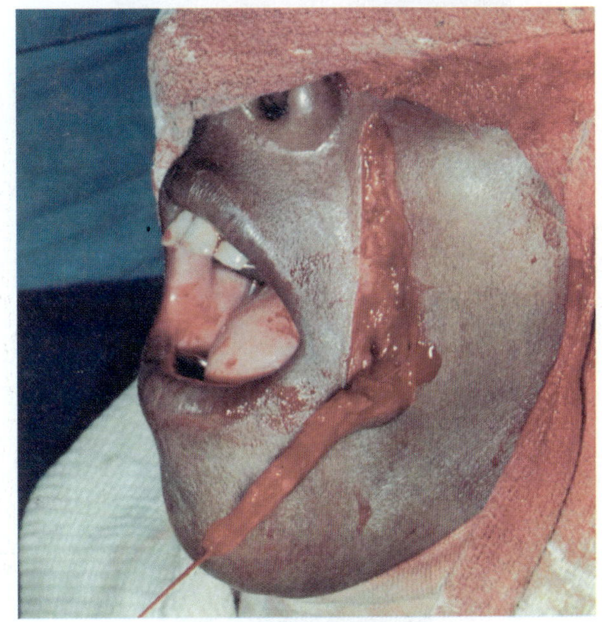

Fig. 15.13(h) Flap raised.

Pathogenesis

(a) Inability to tolerate food seasoned with chillies (capsicum) in patients with oral submucous fibrosis led to the hypothesis that this condition is due to some form of hypersensitivity to capsaicin, the

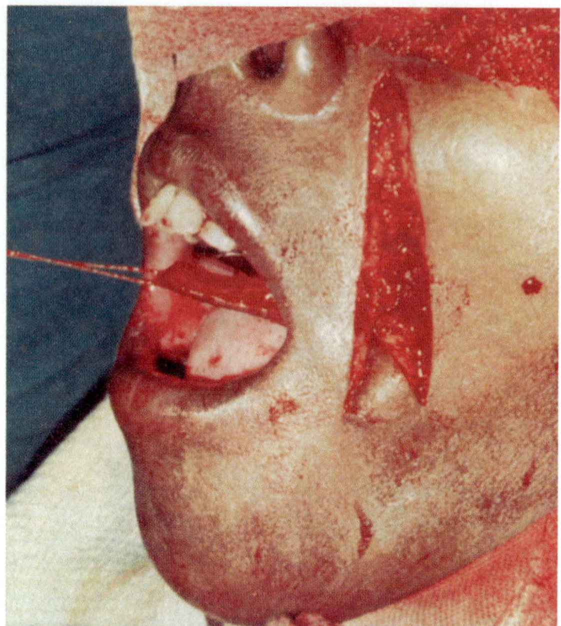

Fig. 15.13(i) Flap transferred intraorally.

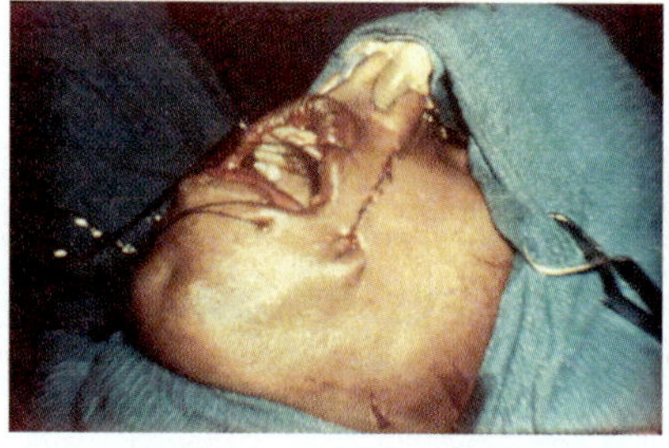

Fig. 15.13(j) Skin closure of labial donor area.

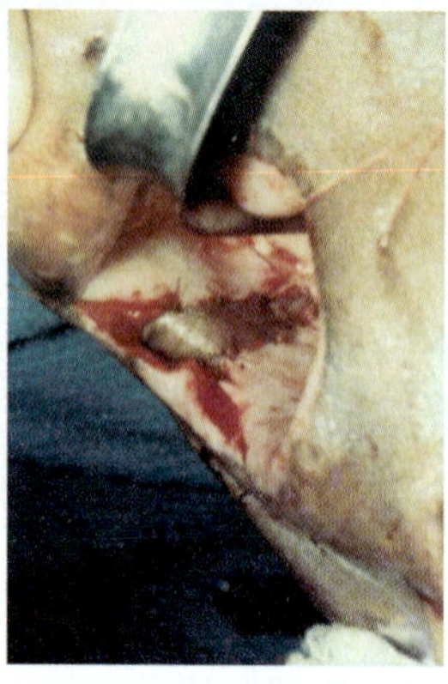

Fig. 15.13(k) Flap covering the intraoral defect.

irritant present in chillies. But a major objection to this hypothesis is the relative absence of this lesion in other parts of the world like Mexico, South America and Far East.

(b) It was also thought that the mucosal changes could be secondary to chronic iron and Vitamin B complex deficiency.

(c) Majority of the authors confirm through various studies that tobacco smoking or chewing of areca nut (supari) are the etiological factors.

(d) Several studies have revealed that it could be an autoimmune disorder. Although the nature of the immunological defect is not known in this condition, there is an evidence of an impaired cellular immune response.

The onset of this condition is insidious and it is of long duration. Initiation of this lesion may be in the form of vesicles. They are very painful. They soon rupture leaving behind small superficial ulcerations. With passage of time, the disease progresses with the oral mucosa, blanched, slightly opaque, white and fibrosed. The fibrous bands run in the mucosa in the vertical direction. Uvula is markedly involved in the late stages.The clinical condition can be classified into four stages.

(a) **Very early stage.** Patient's complaint includes burning sensation or ulcerations without difficulty to open the mouth. Histologically, it is distinct by the finely fibrillar collagen dispersed with edema. Polymorphs may be present.

(b) **Early stage.** In addition, patients complain of slight difficulty in opening the mouth. The juxtaepithelial area reveals the early hyalinization with thickened collagen bundles. The inflammatory cells like monocytes, lymphocytes and eosinophils are seen.

(c) **Moderately advanced stage.** Trismus is marked to such an account that patient's trismus is disturbing. Hence the patient will develop difficulties in mastication. Collagen is moderately hyalinized. Fibroblastic response is less marked. The inflammatory cells present include lymphocytes and plasma cells with occasional eosinophil.

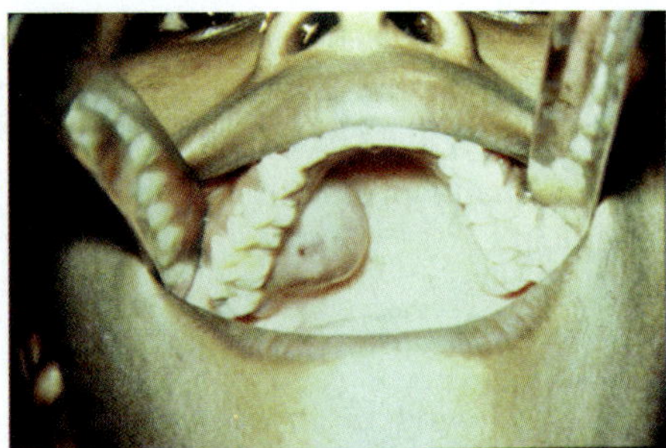

Fig. 15.14(a) Carcinoma - Palate.

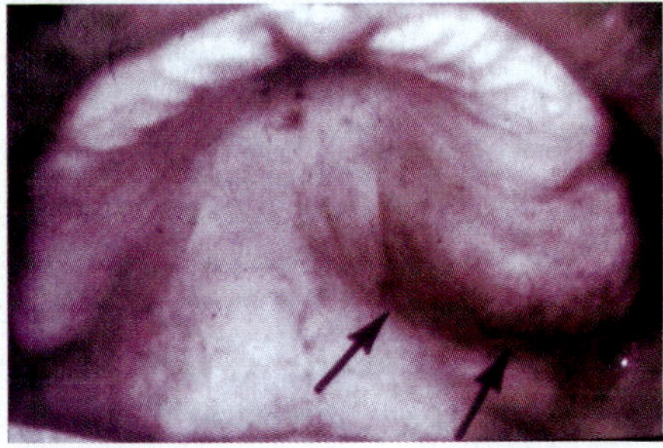

Fig. 15.14(b) Carcinoma - Palate involving alveolus.

(d) **Advanced stage.** Patient is undernourished, anemic with marked degree of trismus. Collagen is completely hyalinized and seen as smooth sheet. The blood vessels are totally obliterated. Inflammatory cells include lymphocytes and plasma cells. Melanin containing cells in the lamina propria are surrounded by dense collagen, resulting in the loss of pigment. 90% of the oral epithelium are involved in atrophic changes.

Treatment

At present no standard curative treatment-protocol is available to the clinician. Therefore, many methods have been tried either to provide symptomatic relief to the patient or to retard the progress of the lesion. Following are some of them:

(a) **Restriction of the habits.** Since the active ingredients-arecoline in the betel nut and capsaicin in the spices and chillies are considered to be the main causative factors of oral submucous fibrosis, it is considered safe to restrict betel nut chewing and to avoid spicy food. However, the exact role of these habits in the causation of this condition has not clearly been demonstrated.

(b) **Nutritional support.** Large doses of Vitamin B complex and iron therapy have been found to be effective as a supportive therapy. Recently, long-term therapy with antioxidants have been advised.

(c) **Intralesional injection.** Injection of steroids, intralesionally, has been very popular among the clinicians. This is aimed as an antifibrinolytic and antiinflammatory therapy. This offers temporary symptomatic relief to the patient. The treatment is started with intralesional injection of 1 ml suspension containing hydrocortisone along with 1 ml of lignocaine hydrochloride once a week. It may be increased to twice a week depending on the severity of the disease. Recurrence of the symptoms are noticed soon after the stoppage of the therapy.

Recently, instead of hydrocortisone, clinicians have found placenterex extract to be more effective. The action of placental extract is essentially biogenic stimulation and its use is based on tissue therapy method.

(d) **Medications.** Antioxidants like retinoid and B-carotine and Vitamin E prevent the formation of toxic substances and enhance the indigenous concentration of Vitamin A. The functional and structural ingredients of epithelial cells are dependent on adequate concentration of Vitamin A. It plays a major role in the induction and control of epithelial differentiation. The basal cells are stimulated to produce mucous and inhibition of keratinization. In the presence of Vitamin A, in adequate concentration, progress of premalignant cells to cells with invasive malignant potential is retarded, arrested or even reversed.

(e) **Surgery.** Surgical excision of the fibrotic bands definitely leads to the improvement in mouth opening. But as the wound heals, there is a tendency for the reappearance of trismus of varying degrees. To overcome this problem, many methods have been tried to resurface the raw area. Provision of skin graft has been unsuccessfully tried, although, it gives better result in smaller lesions. Coverage of the raw area with full thickness flaps like nasolabial, tongue and palatal flaps have provided better long-term relief. The main objection to the nasolabial flaps is the facial scar formation. In the case of tongue flaps, it is argued that once oral mucosa is susceptible to this condition, no useful purpose may be served by the use of intraoral tongue mucosa for the reconstruction. Moreover, both are major surgical procedures. Palatal flap has the restriction of the size of the flap. This may be helpful to cover the raw area in the retromolar area only.

Since it has been found that the conventional surgical excision with blade and knife results in scar formation, laser has been tried in an attempt to reduce scar formation.

ORAL CANCER (FIG. 15.14 - 15.17)

The most effective method of combating oral cancer is early detection, diagnosis and eradication of early stage lesions. Since the oral cavity can easily be accessible for visual examination, dental specialists should perform routine examinations of the entire oral cavity. Identification of warning signs of oral cancer and recognition of the hazards associated with tobacco use help a great deal to reverse the high mortality rate associated with this condition. Curative therapies are most effective in precancerous and cancerous lesions. Most of these lesions are well-differentiated squamous cell carcinomas with keratin formation (cell nests). A few may exhibit high degree of nuclear and cytoplasmic aberrations. This is particularly significant since correlation exists between the degree of differentiation and prognosis. Induration of the surrounding tissue indicates neoplastic infiltration. Regional spread occurs along the lymphatics and neurovascular canal of the mandible. Such bony involvement can be identified by the presence of radiological changes. Usually, advanced cases present many problems and hence involve more specialists.

Staging

Staging of the lesion is an effective prognostic indicator. This is also necessary to accurately describe the tumor objectively at any point of time. Since multiple modalities of treatment are available, every patient with oral malignancy must be properly evaluated so that appropriate treatment could be provided to the patient depending on the staging of the lesion. The widely used method is TNM system. It offers standardized parameters to (a) categorize the description of the lesion, (b) facilitate treatment planning, (c) compare the various modalities of treatments and (d) reasonably predict the prognosis on the basis of staging.

TNM Classification

T	**-**	**TUMOR**
T_0	-	Carcinoma-in-situ
T_1	-	2 cm or less in its greatest dimension
T_2	-	More than 2 cm but less than 4 cm in its greatest dimension
T_3	-	More than 4 cm in diameter
N	**-**	**NODE INVOLVEMENT**
N_0	-	No regional lymph node enlargement
N_1	-	Enlargement of single ipsilateral node
N_2	-	Enlargement of multiple ipsilateral nodes
N_3	-	Enlargement of contralateral/bilateral nodes
M	**-**	**DISTANT METASTASIS**
M_0	-	No distant metastasis
M_1	-	Distant metastasis present

Depending on these clinical features, the lesions are grouped under stage I, II, III, IV. This scale indicates the advanced stage relatively from stage I to IV.

Staging of cancer of the paranasal sinuses

Formerly, the classification was based on an imaginary line joining the medial canthus of the eye to the angle of the mandible. This plane of malignancy seperates unresectable posterior superior tumors from the resectable anterior inferior tumors. Since nasal cavity and paranasal sinuses form one anatomic unit, recognition of the morphogenetic and functional unit is indispensable to have a useful classification. Therefore the classification was modified to include the ethmoid sinuses and the nasal cavity in the classification. The maxilla is divided into supra-, mesio-, and infra structure by means of parallel lines on each side of the nose through the floor of the orbit and the floor of the maxillary sinus.

Prognostic indicators

The widely practiced method of staging by TNM classification is based on

(a) Size of the tumor,
(b) Regional lymph node enlargement,
(c) Distant metastasis.

It is found that more anteriorly placed neoplasms and slowly growing tumors have better prognosis. Hence, to evaluate the prognostic indicators, TNM classification was extended to STNMP wherein, S indicates the site of the lesion and P refers to histopathology. In order to objectively stage the lesion, STNMP system was utilized wherein, a relative numerical score was ascribed to all these five components in various stages which indicate the relative progress.

Principles of management

Following are the different modalities available to the oncologist.

(1) Surgery
(2) Radiotherapy
(3) Chemotherapy
(4) Hormone therapy
(5) Chemoradiotherapy
(6) Predictive assays
(7) Multidisciplinary approach
(8) Cryosurgery
(9) Palliative therapy
(10) Any combination of these methods.

The ultimate choice of the appropriate method of treatment is dictated by the following factors:

(1) Site of the lesion with reference to the anteroposterior axis
(2) Involvement of bone
(3) Extension/infiltration into the underlying tissues including muscles of mastication
(4) Status of the dentition
(5) Histopathology and staging
(6) Previous treatment, if any
(7) Availability of expertise and facilities
(8) General health of the patient.

Involvement of bone

Oral squamous cell carcinoma adjacent to the mandible have the ability to invade bone by direct expansion. The pattern of tumor invasion of the mandible depends on the extent of invasion. The knowledge of the pathway of entry of the tumor into the bone and the pattern of spread is essential to adopt a logical approach to oral cancer surgery. In the invasive pattern, projection of tumor advances into the cancellous bone with very little osteoclastic activity. In the erosive pattern, tumor advances on a broad front with a connective tissue layer and active osteoclasts seperating the tumor from the bone. The three possible routes of tumor entry are as follows:

(a) From the oral cavity through the surface of the mandible.

(b) From the surface into the bone through the mental foramen.

(c) Secondary tumors in the neck below the lower border of the mandible.

The functional and cosmetic morbidity after resection of bone and reconstruction of a section of mandible depends on the maintenance of the continuity. Extent of preservation and resection of bone depends on the tumor extension. But the pattern of spread inside the mandible has been found to be haphazard. The involvement of inferior dental canal influences the possibility of a limited surgical approach. Several imaging techniques like conventional radiography, ultrasonography, computer tomography, isotope scanning and MRI have all been used to evaluate the spread of the tumor cells. Orthopantomograms provide an excellent survey of the entire mandible. Bone scintigraphy using radioactive labelled phosphate compounds along with OPG improves the accuracy of the preoperative assessment. CT is the standard technique for staging the tumor. MRI is the superior modality in assessing the tumor invasion. Several studies have been reported in the literature on this aspect. A summary of the findings is as follows:

(a) The site of entry of the tumor into the mandible is mainly through the alveolar crest with additional entry through the lingual cortex.

(b) CT is useful to demonstrate the bony invasion, especially in edentulous bone.

(c) The pattern of invasion may vary along the bone-tumor interface.

(d) The periodontal space is considered to play a vital role in allowing the tumor spread into mandible.

(e) The inferior dental nerve involvement by tumor most often occurs by encroachment of the tumor onto the nerve rather than by perineural spread.

If irradiaton is used for the management of these conditions, preradiation dental screening is advocated. An evidence-based clinical guidelines have been proposed. The decision to extract depends on (a) periodontal and dental condition, (b) radiation dose, (c) tooth functionality. Earlier, it was a routine to do dental extraction of both the quandrants of the side of the oral cavity. This philosophy was based on the fact that healing will be delayed during the postradiation phase. Now there is a change in thinking towards a conservative approach. As far as possible, the teeth in the involved region must be treated so that they may not require any dental treatment during the irradiation period.

Conventionally, surgery and irradiation are the most frequently used modes of treatment. Any one method is considered adequate for early lesions while combination therapy is advocated for advanced lesions. Chemotherapy is used as a supplementary method, mainly to effect tumour regression. Its curative potential is extremely limited if it is used as the single mode of treatment. Toxicity of these drugs and cost of the treatment are considerably high. However, the modalities of cancer therapy are as follows:

(1) Surgery.
(2) Radiotherapy.
(3) Chemotherapy.

Biological therapy

Surgery and radiotherapy have the curative potential while, chemotherapy is curative only in certain lesions like lymphomas and osteosarcomas when used along with surgery and radiotherapy. In general, regional control of these lesions is of great importance. Preoperative or postoperative radiotherapy and adjuvant chemotherapy has the biological basis for their use in the management of these tumors. Radiotherapy alone can be effective in early cases. In cases of failure, they are salvageable with aggressive surgery since they are of localized nature. Wherever, this mode can cure completely, it is used as a preoperative therapy in T_3 and T_4 carcinomas. The following are responsible for the increased overall survival and quality of the surviving patients.

(1) Advances in imaging techniques.
(2) Predictive assays.
(3) Multidisciplinary approach.
(4) Improved methods of pre- and post-operative radiotherapy.
(5) Neoadjuvant chemotherapy.

(6) Brachytherapy.
(7) Use of laser for surgery.
(8) Advances in surgery and reconstructive methods.
(9) Better methods of palliative therapy during the terminal phase.

1. **Advances in imaging techniques.** *CT scan, Magnetic Resonance Imaging* (MRI) and *Digital Subtraction Angiography* have been instrumental in defining the extent of the tumor to facilitate better staging of the lesion. The reconstruction of the images in various planes helps in treatment planning with accuracy. This also helps in planning surgery for adequate tumor clearance.

Metastasis to the cervical lymph nodes is a very important factor to determine the prognosis and to select the strategy of treatment in patients with head and neck cancer. Usually, it is diagnosed by palpation, CT scan, MRI and ultrasonography. Out of them, palpation is most unreliable due to low accuracy rate. CT and MRI are superior in detecting clinically non-palpable lymph nodes and in permitting the detection of occult lymph nodes metastases.The disadvantage is its expense. In this respect, ultrasonography is less expensive and can detect small nodes involvement.

2. **Predictive assays.** These assays like immunocytochemistry are helpful in assessing the true nature of the biology of the tumor well in advance. They are also helpful in predicting the response to radiotherapy and chemotherapy.

3. **Multidisciplinary approach.** A team of various specialists examine the patient prior to starting the treatment. This helps in appropriate timing of each modality and also to produce synergistic effects by considering the strength and weakness of each modality of treatment.

4. **Chemotherapy.** Utilization of new effective drugs like Platinum analogues-either alone or in combination- has dramatically improved the response rate in these tumors. Sometimes, concurrent use of chemotherapy and radiotherapy is helpful in improving the local control. The biological therapy with drugs can be given in infusional form for better efficacy of radiotherapy.

The most active chemotherapy agents are cisplatinum, bleomycin, 5-fluouracil and methotrexate. They may be given in addition to surgical or radiation treatment (as an adjuvant) or before the other modes of treatment (nonadjuvant).

5. **Brachytherapy.** In this modality, radioactive source is placed either into the substance of the tumor or atleast close to the tumor.

6. **Surgical therapy.** The ultimate goal is the complete removal of the primary tumor with adequate margin along with regional lymph nodes depending on their involvement. Usually, squamous cell carcinoma of the oral cavity is slow growing and well-differentiated. Hence, surgery has been the primary mode of treatment. If the bone is involved, surgery is the treatment of choice. However, depending on staging, it can be supplemented with radiotherapy and/or chemotherapy. Their role is mainly as additional adjuvant therapy. The incidence of local recurrence seems to be significantly high.

(a) *Surgery in relation to various sites.* The primary site of the lesion, in relation to the line of occlusion, is an important consideration. Involvement of buccal mucosa alone limits the extent of surgery. Extension to the sulcus and the skin involves extensive surgery. Mucoperiosteum serves as a temporary barrier to bone invasion. The retromolar trigone is the triangular area of mucosa at the anterior border of the ramus. It extends from maxillary tuberosity to mandibular III molar region. The overlying mucosa blends into the surrounding buccal mucosa and soft palate. Extension of the lesion gives rise to varied spectrum of clinical presentation. If the lesion involves floor of the mouth, the lesion is ill-defined and usually multifocal. Surgery involves a three-dimensional excision with adequate margin. If mandible is involved, it has to be resected. Very high recurrence rate, as high as 70%, has been reported. Probably, this may be due to rich and compound lymphatic

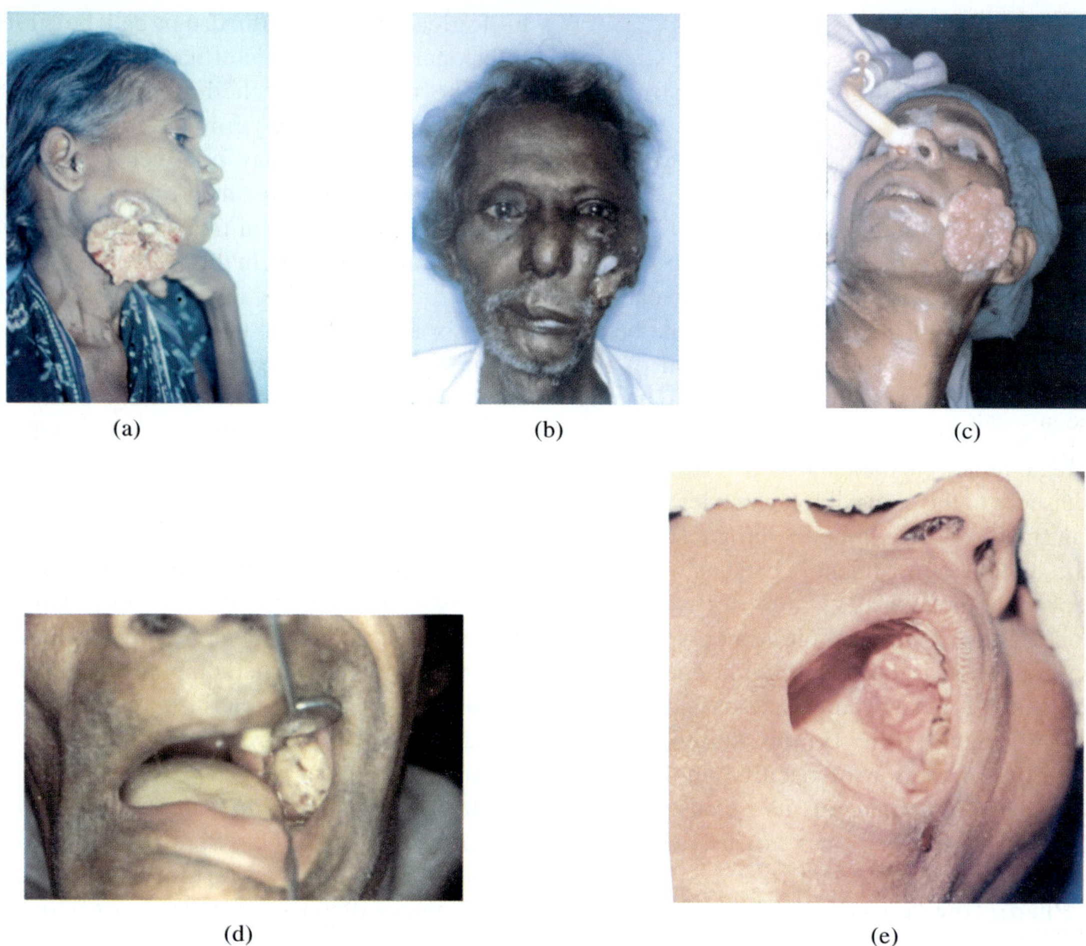

(a) (b) (c)

(d) (e)

Fig. 15.15 a, b, c Clinical photographs of oral malignancy: Carcinomatous growth eroding the full thickness of the neck. **(d)** Malignancy involving left retromandibular region, **(e)** Malignancy involving the palate extensively.

drainage with profuse blood supply. Low survival rate, in cases of mandibular carcinomas, deserves special emphasis. Radiologically, bone involvement may not be readily identifiable in its early phase. Only in advanced stages, bone destruction can be seen in the radiograph. Bone scanning has been suggested for evaluating mandibular bone extension.

Surgery, in case of malignancies involving paranasal sinuses, is based on two principles:

(i) Complete excision of the neoplasm with a safe margin.
(ii) Removal of a single block incorporating both tumor and the involved lymph nodes called "box resection" has advanced our ability to cure this lesion.

(b) *Neck dissection.* The importance of enlargements of regional lymph nodes is a well-recognized fact in terms of prognosis. Isolated nodes

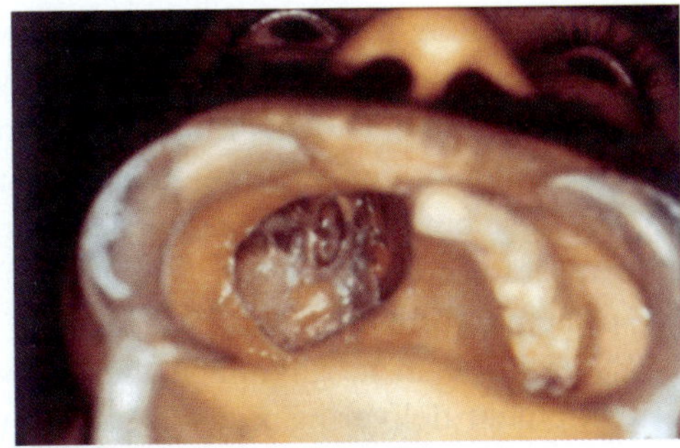

Fig. 15.16 Post-maxillectomy defect (intraoral view).

have been treated by irradiation. However, neck dissection is usually indicated if the nodes are extensively involved - either separately or as a composite resection along with the primary tumor. The lymph nodes in the neck are identified from level I to V for the purpose of neck dissection. Neck dissection at level V is called radical block dissection which results in extensive morbidity. On the other extreme, suprahyoid neck dissection involves the nodes at level I which includes the contents of submandibular triangle. By contrast, suprahyoid dissection consists of selective enbloc removal of only the lymph node groups, most likely to contain metastasis, namely submental and submandibular group (Level I). Dissection of jugulodigastric and juguloomohyoid group of nodes anterior to cutaneous branches of cervical plexus above the mylohyoid muscle form levels II and III, preserving sternomastoid muscle, spinal accessory nerve and internal jugular vein. Extended omohyoid neck dissections is level IV wherein omohyoid is divided and lymph nodes anterior to scalenus muscle and brachial plexus are removed. Thus, depending on the nodes involvement, neck dissection is done.

(c) *Reconstruction.* Considering the complexities of surgical resections, immediate reconstruction of bone and soft tissue morbidity play an important role in rehabilitating these patients. This can also be undertaken as a separate elective procedure. If lining or cover is lost while removing the tumor, the defect can be covered by a skin graft or by a mucosal graft. If full thickness of the cheek is lost, lining and cover will have to be provided. The flaps commonly used are forehead flap, based on the anterior branch of the superficial temporal artery or Deltopectoral flap based on the anterior perforators in the intercostal spaces or

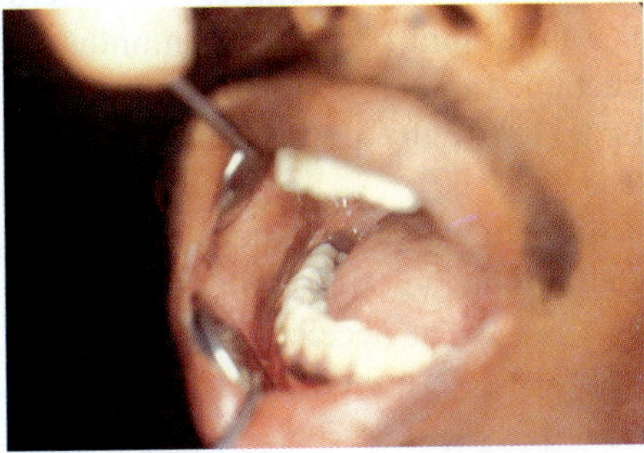

Fig. 15.17(a) Carcinoma-cheek extending to the vestibule.

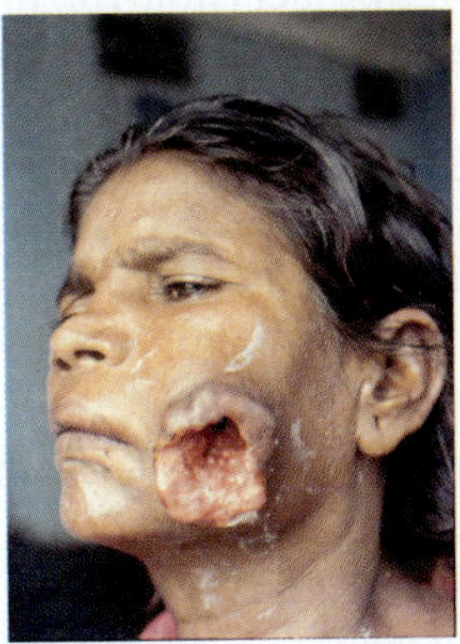

Fig. 15.17(b) Carcinoma-cheek involving full thickness of the cheek.

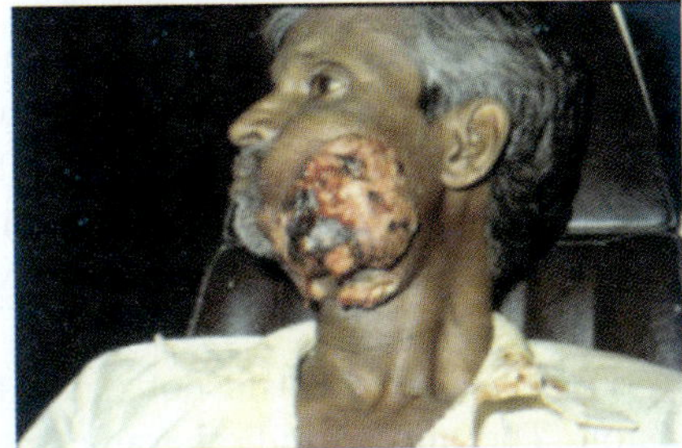

Fig. 15.17(c) Carcinoma-destroying the mandible cheek-advanced stage.

Pectoralis Major/Lattismus Dorsi myocutaneous flaps. It is preferable to use local flaps than distant flaps. Presently, microvascular tissue transfer has become popular.

In cases of bone reconstruction, free bone graft like rib, iliac crest or vascularized or free pectoralis with rib myocutaneous flap are used. In larger lesions or in cases of recurrence or lesions resistent to radiation or/and chemotherapy, it is preferable to wait for a minimum period of 6 months prior to reconstruction. In aged and debilitated patients, it is better to leave the defect until the health is improved.

7. **Radiotherapy.** Advances in imaging has revolutionized the radiotherapy by utilizing modern simulators and linear accelerators so that delivery of radiation is determined precisely to the target volume.

Once a decision is taken to utilize radiotherapy, the preirradiation decision for the purpose of identifying and eliminating the risk factors for the oral complications of cancer therapy is often challenging. The risk factors could be dental-related or /and radiotherapy-related which can influence the clinician's decision. The decision for preradiation dental extraction can be affected by the following factors:

(i) Condition of the teeth - moderate to gross dental pathology.
(ii) Function of the teeth - strategic / nonstrategic.
(iii) Location of teeth - upper or lower jaw.
(iv) Radiation dose on the teeth.

Radiotherapy destroys the cells by inducing ionization which causes chemical alteration and damage to nuclear DNA cells and die during or soon after mitosis. Resting cells are left unaffected until cell division starts. Lymphocytes are exceptions since they are destroyed at lower radiation dose by a mechanism not dependent on cell division. The aim of radiotherapy is to give maximum dose that normal tissues can tolerate so that chances of killing malignant cells are more. If successful, patient is said to have been cured with minimum of morbidity. The main limiting factor in the success is the tumor-volume. Bigger tumor needs higher dose but radiation tolerance of normal tissues decreases correspondingly.

Two principal forms are

(a) External beam megavoltage therapy with equipment delivering x-rays, gamma rays and electrons.
(b) Interstitial techniques where radioactive solid isotopes are implanted directly into the tumor tissue and the intermediate surrounding tissue. External beam radiation is given in divided doses for several weeks. The reason for dividing radiation dose into fractions is to increase the differential effect of radiation on tumor and normal tissue and to improve the therapeutic ratio. However, the effect of fractionalization is not well understood. Hypoxic cells are less susceptible to irradiation since tumor cells are generally thought to be less oxygenated than normal tissue. Probably, this has been thought to be the reason for the failure of radiotherapy. Treating the patients in hyperbaric oxygen chamber has been shown to improve local tumor control, but the procedure has proved to be hazardous, complex and time consuming. Hence, it is not widely practiced.

Complications of therapy. Ionizing radiation, delivered in doses that will kill malignant cells, induces unavoidable changes in the surrounding normal tissues causing compromises in function and host defenses.

Mucocutaneous changes. Most patients develop erythema and moderate tanning of the skin. Since hair follicles are radiosensitive, hair will cease to grow and will fallout.

Acute oral mucosal reaction (*mucositis*) is secondary to radiation-induced mitotic death of the basal cells in the mucosa. Oral microorganisms play a role in aggravating the impaired epithelium. Post-irradiation induced atrophy and telangiectasis of the mucosa often increase the risk of pain and necrosis. A short course of systemic prednisone 40 to 80 mg daily for not more than one week has been found to be helpful in reducing inflammation and discomfort.

Loss of taste occurs, since the taste buds - circumvalate and fungiform papillae are radio-sensitive. However, they regenerate within 4 to 5 weeks, although the period of impairment vary from patient to patient.

Salivary function is disturbed since radiation induces fibrosis, fatty degeneration, acinar atrophy and cellular necrosis within the salivary glands. Due to these changes, glandular secretions are usually diminished, thick and sticky in nature. It may even take 12 months for the patient to recover from xerostomia. Frequent sips of water are essential to overcome this problem. Pilocarpine hydrochloride 5 mg 3 to 4 times a day has been found to be effective in stimulating salivary secretion. Side effects include sweating and stomach discomfort.

Radiosensitizing drugs, which selectively sensitize hypoxic cells to radiation, have also been tried. Since they are neurotoxic, they have not been put into use. Patients treated with external beam radiation can be treated as outpatients. Treatment planning and the dose may be calculated using CT scan technology and computer planning. An acrylic mould of the head and neck is made which allows accurate positioning of the patient in each treatment session. Precise beaming devices ensure that the planned dose is correctly given. Treatment is painless, but associated with mucositis due to radiation effects on dividing epithelial cells, appearing two weeks after treatment. Hence, such patients need careful attention to oral hygiene, diet and antifungal therapy for candida infection in the area of the irradiation field. If teeth are present, radiation-induced cervical dental caries develop. Loss of taste is usually temporary. The late effects are skin pigmentation, atrophy, subcutaneous fibrosis and osteoradionecrosis. Some of them can be minimized by using shielding methods.

8. **Immunotherapy.** Animal studies have shown that inhibition of tumor cell growth can occur by attaching a specific monoclonal antibody to a suitable white cell. Antibodies on the tumor-specific killer cells thus produced react with the target tumor cell antigens, destroying the tumor cell. This is in its early stage of development. More research is necessary before clinically using it on cancer patients by using antibodies as "magic bullets".

Radical radiotherapy is given with the aim of curing cancer. The term radical is specifically used to describe the operation that ablates the tumor with a safe margin of healthy tissue. Radiotherapy can be given pre or postoperatively called combined therapy. But there is no overall agreement as to which of any of these different approaches are the best. Although age, sex, occupation, general health, ability to attend the follow-up regularly may influence the treatment policy, the most important factor is the disease itself.

Although chemotherapy was thought to be useful for palliation, its value in presurgical induction therapy is being explored. Recent studies suggest that chemotherapy combined with simultaneous irradiation may have greater value as induction treatment. It is also found that combination of surgery, irradiation and chemotherapy as a combined modality therapy has emerged as effective means of treating malignancies of head and neck.

9. **Palliative care.** Radiotherapy, chemotherapy and brachytherapy in combination have the potential to produce excellent palliation in cases of inoperable and recurrent tumors.

10. **Management of pain.** Continuous release of oral morphine, potent analgesics, nerve blocks, analgesia and multidisciplinary pain clinics have revolutionized pain management as part of terminal care. In the terminal stages of the disease, this is equally important since most of them suffer from intractable pain. Ultimately, the choice is shifted

from "curing" the lesion to "caring" the patient who is suffering from a state of escalating physical endurance and increased suffering. *"Where there is life, there exists hope. With loss of hope, suffering increases."* In such circumstances, "scavenging and palliative" surgery may be necessary although cancer clearance may not be possible.

Summary

Oral cancer remains a challenge and a frustration to the clinician. Results of treatment of early and moderately sized oral malignancies are satisfactory and gratifying with minimal cosmetic and functional disability in contrast to the results following treatment of massive oral cancers. Clearly, the importance of early detection and appropriate treatment while the lesion is still in the early stage need not be over emphasized. Increased knowledge of intricacies of chemotherapy and immunotherapy of their use as definitive treatment combined with advances in radiation therapy has improved the overall outlook. However, surgery remains a mainstay in the management of many of these patients. Main emphasis is on the importance of early diagnosis. Prevention is the ultimate goal but yet motivation and energies are not directed on these lines.

Prevention of oral cancer

In general, malignancies can be preventible or curable if diagnosed early. Management becomes difficult if lesions are treated in the advanced stage. Hence, strategies for prevention should be directed to reduce or eliminate the exposure to the known carcinogen in any form, apart from early detection of these lesions.

There is general agreement on oncogenic validity and significance of three principles: *summation, syncarcinogenesis* and *co-carcinogenesis*. Summation is due to chronic effect of the specific carcinogen. Irreversible individual effects can accumulate and lead to threshold dose which can finally initiate neoplasia. Thus, in the context of summation effect and syncarcinogenesis, the effect of bolstered tobacco consumptions in terms of quantity and duration must be appreciated. On this basis, the following should be the strategy for the prevention of oral cancer:

(1) *Abuse of tobacco* in all forms (smoking, chewing or snuff), betel nuts, hot food, alcohol, sharp teeth, ill-fitting dentures with repeated trauma are to be avoided.

(2) Whenever any ulcer, wound or swelling in the oral cavity does not respond within 2-3 weeks, its nature and etiology must be fully investigated and preferably biopsy should be done.

(3) Population must be motivated that chewing of paan with various combination are injurious. Unfortunately, these habits enjoy deep-rooted social and cultural acceptance. Awakening about these injurious habits is an urgent need.

(4) *Mass screening* of the population-at-risk to identify such patients and to advice treatment must be undertaken.

(5) Standard screening procedure for oral cancer is in the following sequence:

   (a) Raise the upper lip (with teeth in occlusion) and carefully examine maxillary labial mucosa, attached gingival tissues, alveolar gingival mucosa and maxillary vestibule.

   (b) Evert the lower lip (with teeth in occlusion) and examine mandibular labial mucosa, attached gingival mucosa, alveolar gingival mucosa and mandibular mucosa.

   (c) Retract the cheek intraorally and examine the cheek mucosa bilaterally.

   (d) Open the mouth widely and examine the hard palate, soft palate and pharyngeal area.

   (e) With the tongue in extended position, examine the dorsal, right and left lateral and ventral surfaces of the tongue.

(f) With the tongue touching the palate, examine the floor of the mouth .

(6) All premalignant white lesions exhibiting epithelial dysplasia, any non-healing ulcer with everted margins and induration, any lesion fixed to the surrounding tissues with lymphadenopathy must be subjected to histopathological examination. If the biopsy is negative, but the lesion appears to be suspicious, repeat the biopsy to confirm the diagnosis.

CHAPTER 16 Temporomandibular Joint Disorders

APPLIED ANATOMY

Temporomandibular joint (TMJ) is a highly specialized synovial joint. The characteristic features are:

(1) Diarthrodal, non-weightbearing joint.
(2) Both the joints are interdependent.
(3) Both the joints are interdependent on dentition.

Mandible is a single bone with the joints situated on its terminal portions and carry teeth which occlude with maxillary teeth. Hence, dentition has an important role to play in the pathology of temporomandibular joint.

(a) **Bony component** (Fig. 16.1) includes mandibular condyle and articular surface of the temporal bone consisting of glenoid fossa and articular eminence.

(b) **Soft tissue components** (Fig 16.2)

(i) *Disc* is a fibrocartilaginous, avascular structure situated between the bony components separating the joint space into two cavities: upper and lower joint cavities. The disc has three regions. Central zone is thin and thicker along the periphery. Anterior zone is 2 mm thick. The posterior zone is

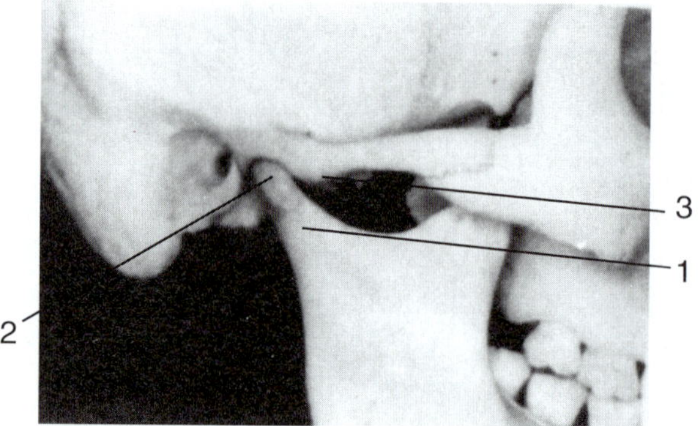

Fig. 16.1 (a) Bony components of the temporomandibular joint. 1. Mandibular condyle, 2. Glenoid fossa, 3. Articular eminence.

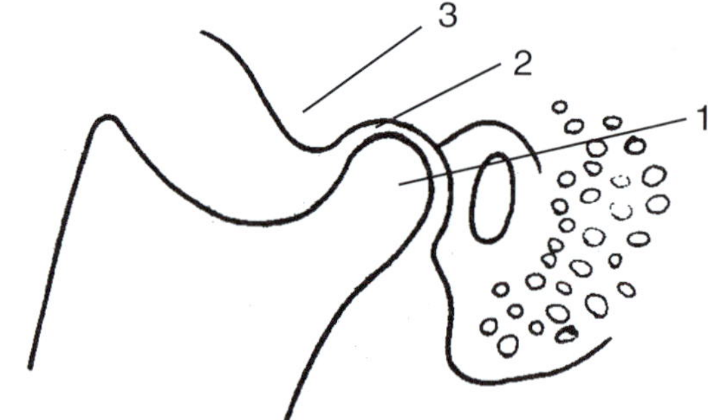

Fig. 16.1 (b) Cross-section of the bony components of the TM joint.

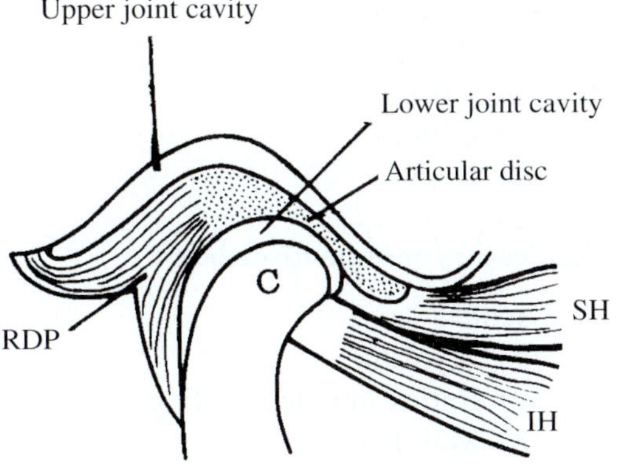

Fig. 16.2 Soft-tissue components of the TM joint. SH - Superior head of lateral pterygoid. IH - Inferior head of lateral pterygoid. C-Mandibular condyle. RDP-Retrodiscal pad.

3 mm thick and bilaminar. Both the laminae are separated by loose areolar tissue. It is richly innervated by auriculotemporal nerve. Superior surface is concavo-convex while inferior surface is concave. The disc is firmly attached to the medial and lateral poles of the head of the condyle.

(ii) *Both the joint cavities* are lined by synovial membrane. The joint cavities contain synovial fluid. Articular surfaces are covered by dense fibrous tissue.

(iii) *Lateral pterygoid muscle* has two heads. Upper head gains attachment to the disc (intra-articular) and lower head to the fovea of the condyle (extraarticular).

(iv) *Capsule* is the limiting factor of the joint space. It is attached below to the articular margins of the head of the condyle and above to the margins of glenoid fossa and articular eminence.

(v) *Ligaments*. At the sides, capsule is reinforced by collateral ligaments. Temporo-mandibular (lateral) ligament is the strongest. The accessory ligaments are stylomandibular and sphenomandibular ligaments.

(vi) *Nerve and blood supply*. Sensory nerve supply is derived from auriculotemporal nerve. The rich vascular network of the joint is derived from superficial temporal artery, a branch of external carotid artery.

APPLIED PHYSIOLOGY (Fig. 16.3)

In the upper joint cavity, gliding movements and in the lower joint cavity, hinge movements take place. The movements of the mandible are produced by the bilateral muscles of mastication, acting on both the joints. Muscles which help in the mastication are called muscles of mastication. The range of movements are protrusion, retrusion, opening, closing and side to side. The biting force is more in the molar region while it diminishes towards anterior teeth. The limits to the biting force between the teeth are determined by the power of the masticatory muscles and the sensitivity of periodontal tissues to pain.

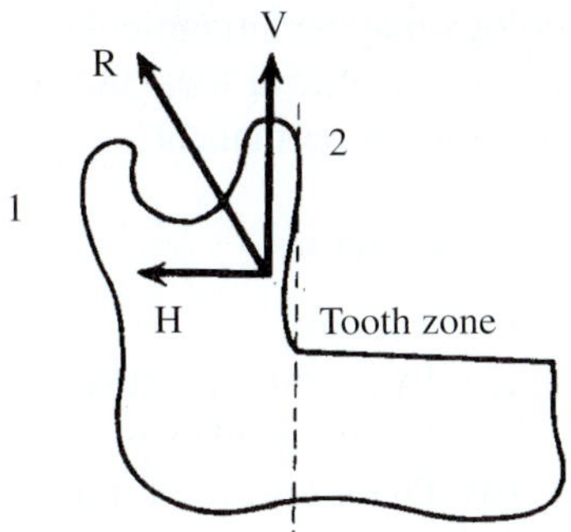

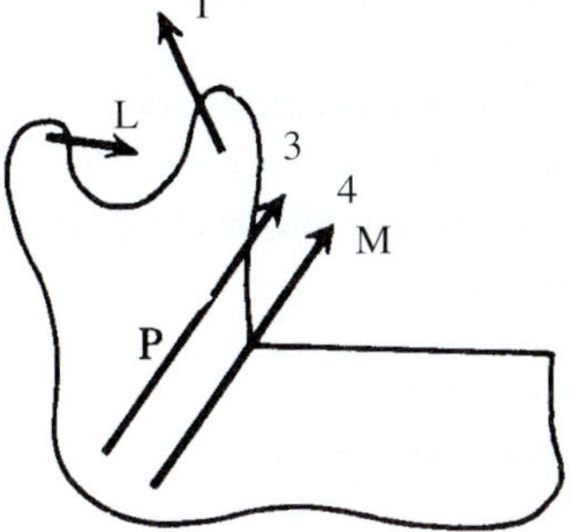

Fig. 16.3 Biomechanics of TM joint. Direction of the pull of the muscles of mastication and the resultant forces. 1 - Condyle. 2 - Coronoid. 3 - Masseter. 4 - Medial pterygoid. V-Vertical, H-Horizontal, R-Retraction force, L-Lateral pterygoid, T-Temporalis.

The nervous control of mastication is derived from:

(a) Temporomandibular joint,
(b) Masticatory muscles,
(c) Periodontal tissues,
(d) Oral mucous membrane.

Masticatory cycle is divided into three phases:

(a) Opening phase.
(b) Closing phase.
(c) Occlusal phase.

In the opening and closing phases, the concerned muscles show isotonic contraction or relaxation. In the occlusal phase, elevator muscles show isometric contraction. The feedback through the nervous control decides the masticatory efficiency.

DISEASES OF THE TEMPOROMANDIBULAR JOINT

The American Academy of Orofacial Pain has published a TMD (Temporomandibular disorders) classification system with an existing medical diagnosis classification.

I. Joint Disorders

- A. Deviation in form:
  - (1) Articular surface defects
  - (2) Disc thinning and perforation
- B. Disc displacements:
  - (1) Disc displacement with reduction
  - (2) Disc displacement without reduction
- C. Displacement of the disc-condyle complex:
  - (1) Hypermobility
  - (2) Dislocation
- D. Inflammatory conditions:
  - (1) Capsulitis and synovitis
  - (2) Retrodiscitis
- E. Degenerative disease
  - (1) Osteoarthrosis
  - (2) Osteoarthritis
  - (3) Polyarthritis
- F. Ankylosis:
  - (1) Fibrous
  - (2) Bony

II. Masticatory muscle disorders

- A. Acute
  - (1) Myositis
  - (2) Reflex muscle splinting
  - (3) Muscle spasm
- B. Chronic
  - (1) Myofacial pain
  - (2) Muscle contracture
  - (3) Hypertrophy
  - (4) Myalgia secondary to systemic disease.

III. Congenital and developmental disorders

- A. Condylar hyperplasia
- B. Condylar hypoplasia
- C. Aplasia
- D. Neoplasms
- E. Fractures.

The joint disorders may cause
(a) Hypomobility (limitation of movement) or,
(b) Hypermobility.

Hypomobility

Inability to open the mouth is referred to as trismus. Etiology may be intraarticular or extraarticular. They may be systemic or local factors. They may be either temporary or permanent.

Systemic factors

(1) Tetanus.
(2) Intracranial causes like extrapyramidal lesions, epilepsy.
(3) Drug-induced factors like strychnine poisoning.
(4) Psychogenic, e.g. hysteria.

Local factors

(1) Infection: Intraarticular e.g. arthritis. Extra-articular e.g. pericoronitis.
(2) Trauma: Fractures of the mandible. Faulty inferior dental nerve block anesthesia, impaction painful oral conditions.
(3) Temporomandibular joint dysfunction syndrome.
(4) Ankylosis.
(5) Oral submucous fibrosis.
(6) Postirradiation fibrosis.
(7) Neoplasms infiltrating the masticator muscles.

Detailed descriptions are provided here to the following conditions which are of clinical significance in everyday practice.

(1) Ankylosis
(2) Temporomandibular joint dysfunction syndrome.
(3) Dislocation
 (a) Acute.
 (b) Chronic (recurrent, known as subluxation).

ANKYLOSIS OF THE TEMPOROMANDIBULAR JOINT

Ankylosis is a Greek word, meaning *"stiff joint"*. It also denotes abnormal immobility and consolidation of the joint. Functionally and esthetically, this is a distressing condition, commonly encountered in children. Even though many conflicting and controversial opinions have been expressed, all converge ultimately towards identical anatomical and physiological observations. Since 1850, there has been a gradual evolution on the knowledge of this problem. But very little progress has taken place after the initial outbursts of enthusiasm.

Etiology and pathogenesis

(1) **Trauma.** In young condyles, rich anastomosis of capillaries penetrates the articular layer of the condylar cartilage and are found lying just under the thin cortex. Hence, they are vulnerable to injury. Since neck is broad, condylar neck in children do not fracture that readily. Even trivial trauma results in hemarthrosis. Subsequent increase in carbon dioxide tension appears to stimulate bone deposition and sclerosis. Thus, it is predisposed to the onset of ankylosis from an apparently insignificant injury that might have been overlooked by the patient's guardians. This seems to be the most common etiology of ankylosis. It is called true ankylosis. Such hemarthrosis can also occur due to injury at the symphysis so that the force is transmitted to the condyles.

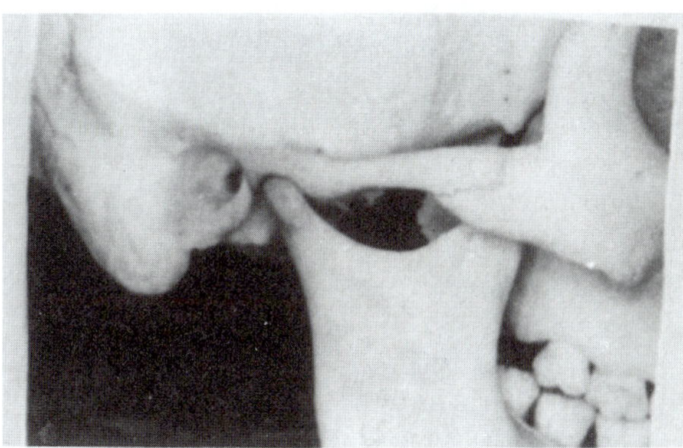

Fig. 16.4 Normal T.M. joint.

(2) **Infection** from middle ear, necrotic osteitis of exanthemas or of hematogenous origin may result in septic arthritis. This was considered to be the main etiological factor. With improved antibiotic therapy, infection is not so common.

(3) **Degenerative arthritis** as an aging process may lead to bony ankylosis of the temporomandibular joint in elderly persons. Spondylitis, rheumatoid arthritis, etc. are also known to be responsible.

Of these three factors, trauma in children and less frequently infection are the major etiological factors.

Classification

In 1938, on the basis of location, Kazanjian classified ankylosis as true and false. True ankylosis has fibrous or bony adhesion between articular surfaces of the joint. False ankylosis results from pathology outside the joint resulting in limitation of the mandibular mobility. They are also classified as fibrous, fibroosseous and bony ankylosis, depending on the type of tissue involved.

Pathology

Early pathologic findings are generally vague. Atrophic changes are seen in the cartilaginous components of the joint with the loss of meniscus. Progressive destruction of the joint tissues with narrowing of the joint space are noticed. Normal soft tissues are replaced by thick fibrous bands. Bony changes are characterized by overall flattening of the articulation. Glenoid fossa and articular eminence become less pronounced. The condyle

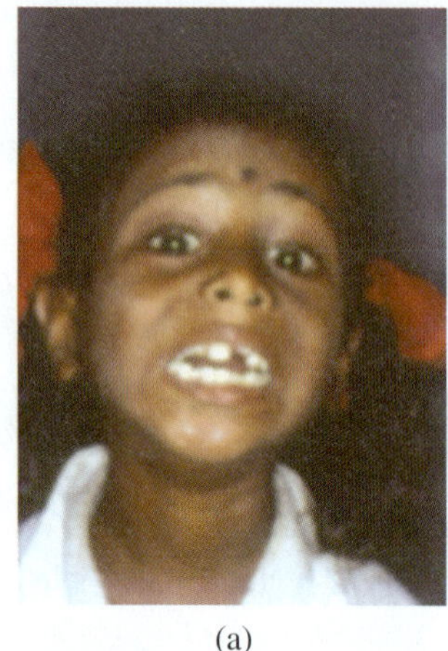

(a)

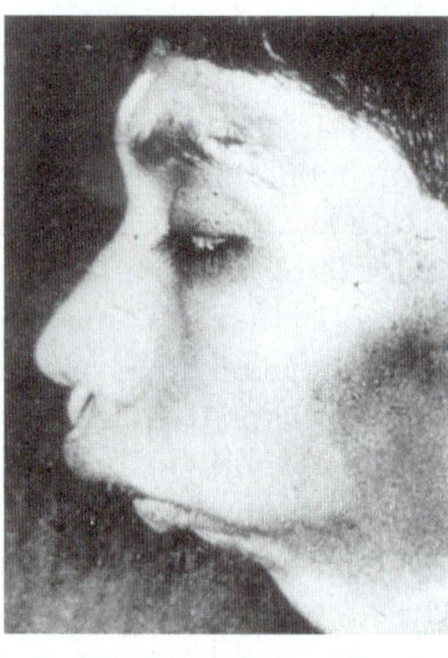

(b)

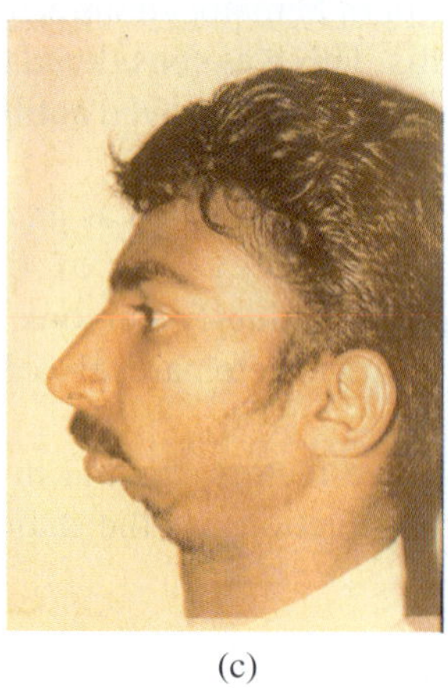

(c)

Fig. 16.5 (a) Clinical photograph - Ankylosis with micrognathism, **(b)** & **(c)** Ankylosis of T.M. joint with severe micrognathia.

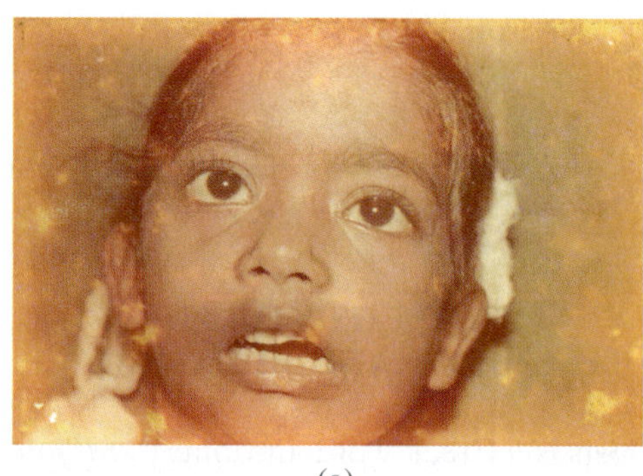

(a)

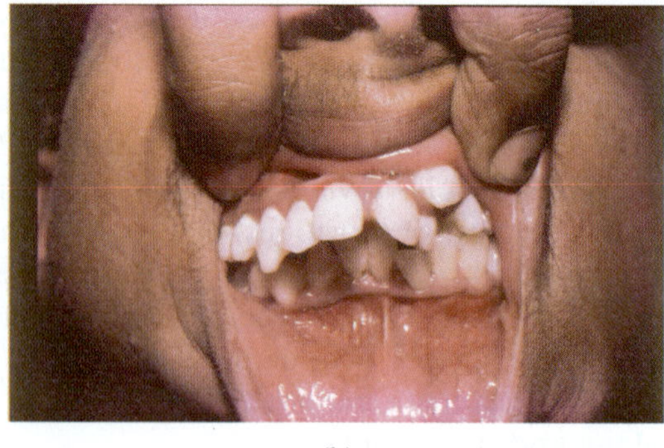

(b)

Fig. 16.6 (a) Ankylosis-early case with restricted mouth opening, **(b)** Severe malocclusion following the arrest of mandibular growth.

becomes enlarged, composed of dense sclerotic bone. Ultimately, bony fusion takes place between the articular surfaces. The normal anatomical features are obscured by dense bone and the joint space gets obliterated.

Clinical features

(1) Even though mouth cannot be opened, these patients often seek the dental consultation because of toothache.

(2) The most obvious finding is the associated facial deformity. It is directly related to the duration of ankylosis. In unilateral cases, face is asymmetrical with fullness on the affected side of the mandible and relative flattening on the unaffected side. In bilateral ankylosis, mandible is symmetrical but micrognathic. The patient develops a bird-like face with retruded chin.

(3) Clinical examination may reveal the presence of a scar on the chin (possibly due to trauma).

(4) Mandibular mobility. If interincisal distance is less than 5 mm, it is indicative of bony ankylosis. In unilateral cases, slight gliding movement towards the affected side is best visualized in the posterior occlusion.

(5) Palpation may disclose movement of the unaffected condyle. In bilateral ankylosis, there is no gliding movement. Neither protrusive nor lateral movement is possible.

(6) Intraoral examination may be difficult. Findings are proportional to the time of onset and duration of ankylosis.

(7) Malocclusion may be marked. In unilateral cases of early onset, there will be cross-bite. In bilateral cases, class II malocclusion can be noticed. Incisors are often protrusive with anterior open-bite as a result of unopposed tongue action. Open-bite may be due to the patient's attempt to force the food through the anterior space.

(8) Acute antegonial notch on the affected side is obvious. It is caused by the continuous appositional bone growth in association with the masseteric sling and poorly developed body of the mandible. Growth of the alveolus is influenced by the soft tissue progressively.

(9) Ramus on the affected side is short and wide with a relatively long coronoid process and obliteration of the sigmoid notch.

Radiological features

Radiological changes are indispensable for diagnosis. In the fibrous variety, evidence of destructive and more often proliferative changes are seen in the bony components of the temporomandibular joint associated with narrowing of the joint space. In bony ankylosis, there is an overall obliteration of the joint space with dense sclerotic bone.

For proper evaluation, several radiographic views are useful.

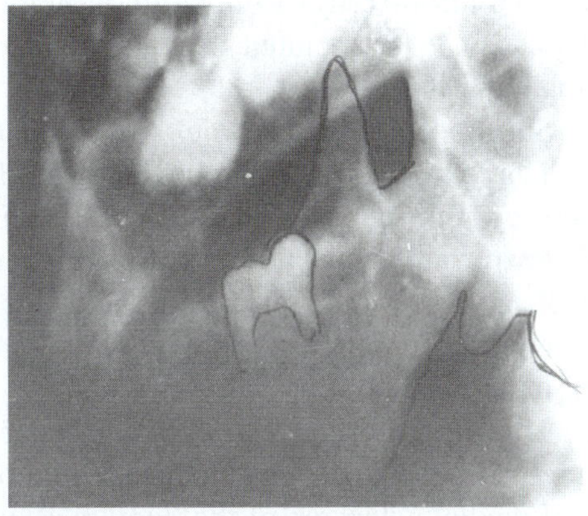

Fig. 16.7 (a) Orthopantomogram showing ankylosis and elongated coronoid process.

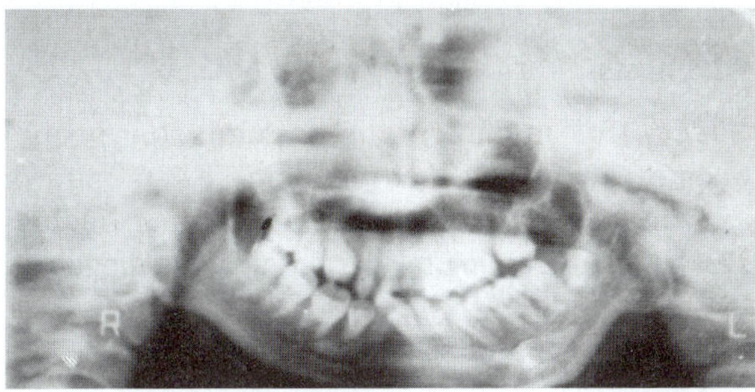

Fig. 16.7 (b) Orthopantomogram demonstrating ankylosis.

Fig. 16.8 OPG radiograph of ankylosis.

(1) **Lateral oblique view or panoramic view** (Fig. 16.7) will present the anteroposterior dimension of the condylar mass. Antegonial notch is characteristically seen at the lower border of the mandible. This develops secondary to the isotonic contraction of the depressor muscles at the attachment of masseter muscle. Panoramic x-ray may also present an overall assessment of carious and periodontal lesions.

(2) **Cephalometric radiograph** is helpful in the evaluation of associated mandibular skeletal abnormalities.

(3) **Submentovertex view** helps to evaluate the involvement of the coronoid process and an idea of the diameter of the condylar mass.

(4) **Posteroanterior radiograph** will reveal the extent of mediolateral extent of the bony mass. It also provides a graphic record of any asymmetry present in the mandible.

(5) **Tomogram** of the temporomandibular joint region provides the most valuable data regarding the extent of medial extension of the bony mass which is essential to plan the corrective treatment of the ankylosed joint.

Diagnosis

Successful management depends on proper diagnosis as to whether pathology exists intra or extraarticularly. Clinical and radiological findings are the major guiding factors for accurate diagnosis.

Objectives of management

Surgeon is more often guided by the understanding of facial growth and development for the selection of the mode of treatment.

(1) Meticulous and radical removal of the ankylosed bone to mobilize the frozen joint (ostectomy).
(2) Reconstruction and restoration of a physiological joint.
(3) Prevention from recurrence.
(4) Restoration of occlusion.
(5) To correct and restore the secondary facial deformities.

From the mechanical point of view, these objectives can be achieved by operating at the level of the glenoid fossa. The physical principle involved is lever of order III with condyle as the fulcrum, elevator muscles as the working force and food bolus as the resisting force. If the joint is not reconstructed at this level but at a lower level, then it is converted into an unstable lever of I order with III molar as the fulcrum, lying anterior to the working force.

Management-suggested protocol

(1) Aggressive resection of ankylosed tissue is considered to be crucial. Incomplete removal, particularly at the medial aspect, results in recurrence.

(2) Dissection and stripping of muscles of mastication from the ramus and ipsilateral coronoidectomy are essential. Interincisal opening should be critically evaluated to ensure that it should be more than 35 mm.

(3) If this could not be achieved without force intraorally, contralateral coronoidectomy must be done. Preoperative radiograph of the opposite side is taken to find out whether there is any evidence of decreased joint space. If it is present, opposite joint must be surgically explored.

(4) A suitable interpositional material must be placed to avoid the risk of reankylosis.

(5) Reconstruction of the joint with costochondral graft helps to maintain the ramus

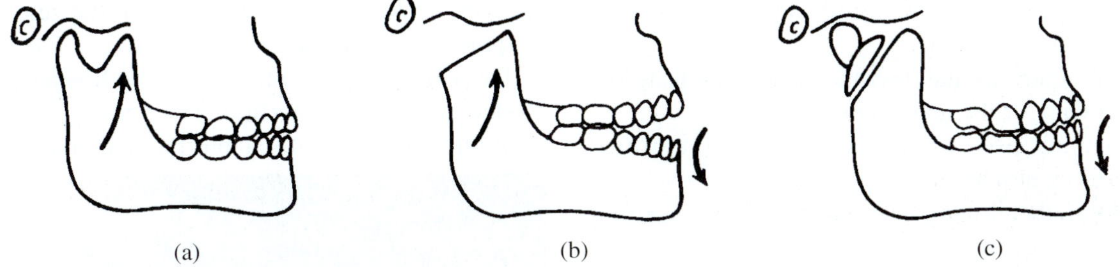

Fig. 16.9 Biomechanics of TM joint: **(a)** Normal joint, **(b)** Gap arthroplasty resulting in anterior open-bite, **(c)** Interposing materials are used to restore the height of the ramus. Arrows indicate the mobility of the mandible.

height. Failure to do so will result in converting the unstable new joint to be lever of I order.

(6) Rigid fixation of the graft with ramus is necessary for early mobilization of the joint.

(7) Early mobilization and active physiotherapy are necessary to prevent soft tissue contraction. After 6-8 weeks of physiotherapy, signs of increased mouth opening can be noticed.

(8) If no further improvement is noticed postoperatively, joint is stretched under general anesthesia. Unfortunately, a good surgical reconstruction should not be spoiled by poor postoperative physiotherapy.

(9) Later on, if needed, excessive growth of the costochondral graft may have to be recontoured so that no disturbance in occlusion and jaw relationship develop.

Recurrence (Fig. 16.10)

(1) Inadequate exposure of the joint region and incomplete surgical excision of callus at the ankylosed joint (particularly the medial extension) are the main causes for recurrence. Technically, this is difficult due to the proximity of (a) facial nerve, (b) carotid, jugular and maxillary vessels. Disturbance will result in facial nerve palsy and intraoperative hemorrhage respectively. Medial extension of the callus along the skull base up to carotid-jugular vessels may be responsible following insufficient excision.

(2) Long-standing ankylosis may lead to fibrosis of the temporalis muscle and relative lengthening of the coronoid. If the mouth opening during surgery is less than 35 mm and if coronoid process is not excised, recurrence develops.

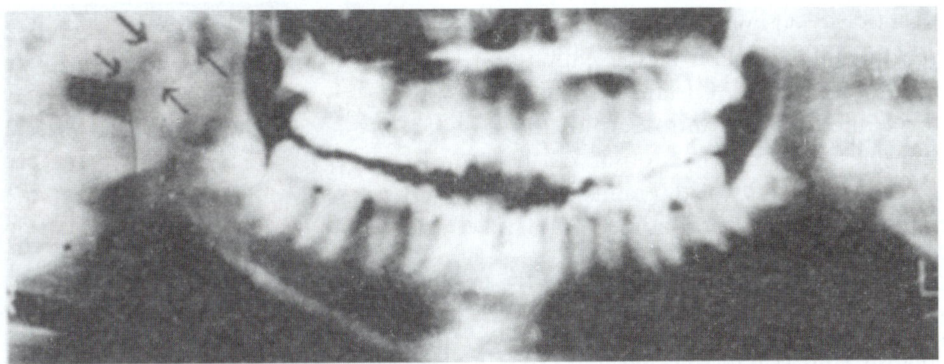

Fig. 16.10 Orthopantomograph showing recurrence of ankylosis after gap arthroplasty.

(3) Insufficient and unsatisfactory physiotherapy.

(4) Failure to maintain the ramus height leads to narrowing of the interfragmentary gap.

(5) Failure to provide a satisfactory interpositional material.

(6) Higher osteogenic and periosteal reaction may be responsible for high rate of recurrence in children.

Surgical technique (surgical approach)

(a) *Preauricular approach* is a widely accepted procedure to expose the condylar head. Incision is in an inconspicuous location and hence scar is acceptable.

(b) *Risdon's submandibular approach* is good for exposing the ramus and also for the fixation of the costochondral graft.

Other methods like *postauricular approach, endaural approach* and *retromandibular (postramus) approach* are not found suitable for the surgical management of ankylosed joints.

(c) *Temporal approach:* It is best to approach the joint through a curvilinear preauricular incision, extending 3 cm long into the temporal region for the exposure of the temporal fascia. Then, dissection of the soft tissue is proceeded up to zygomatic arch. The capsule of the joint is opened with a T-shaped incision of the fascia.

Once the joint region is exposed and ankylosed site is identified, aggressive excision of the fibrous and bony mass are carried out. Special attention is directed to the medial extension of the callus to ensure adequate excision. Glenoid fossa is recontoured as needed. Coronoidectomy and stripping of muscles are done. It is observed that nearly one-third of the height of the ramus is lost following condylectomy and coronoidectomy. If interincisal distance is less than 35 mm, contralateral coronoidectomy through intraoral approach is indicated.

Costochondral graft is removed through inframammary incision. Through submandibular approach, ramus is exposed. Masseter and temporalis are stripped from the ramus. Then the surfaces of the graft and ramus are freshened to produce good bony interface. The graft is placed in position and fixed with stable internal fixation so

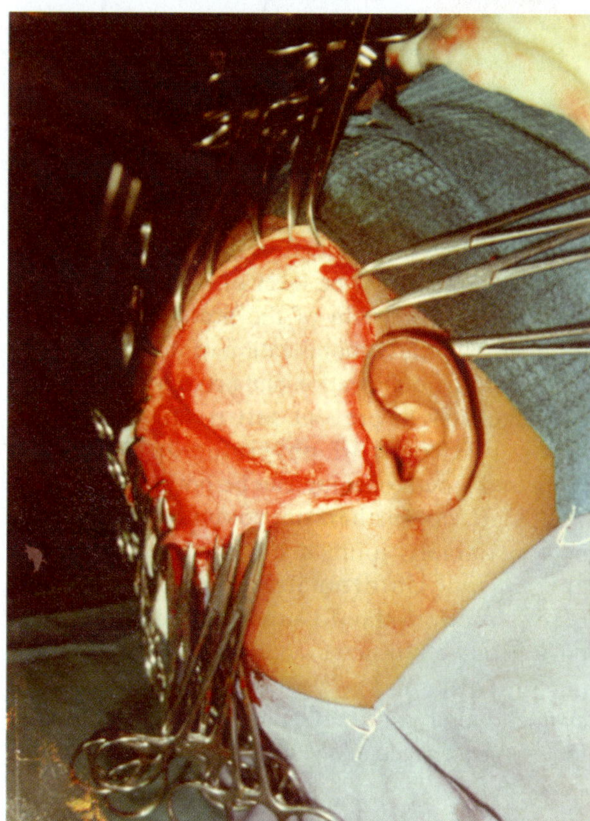

Fig. 16.11 (a) Temporal approach to T.M. joint.

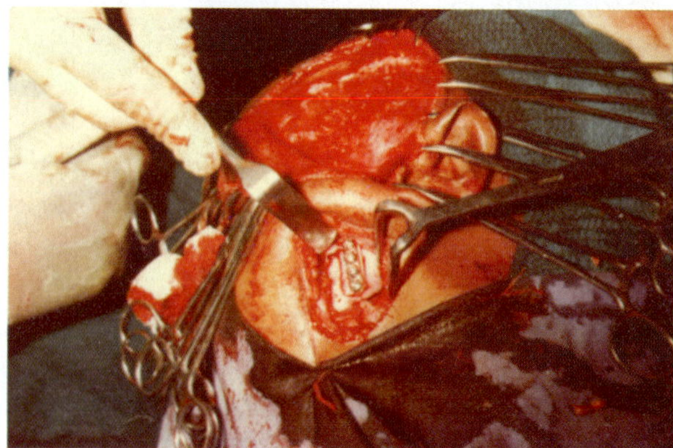

Fig. 16.11 (b) Joint replacement with costochondral graft.

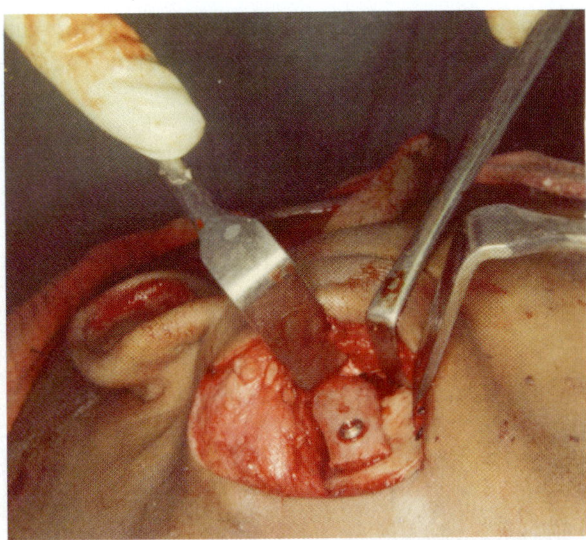

Fig. 16.11 (c) Graft with lag screw fixation.

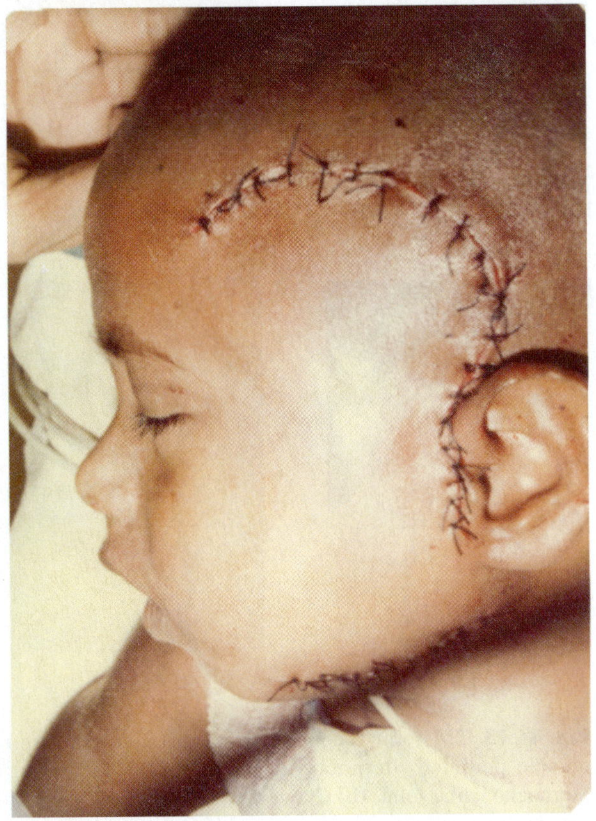

Fig. 16.11 (d) Surgical closure.

that 2 mm of posterior open bite is created to compensate for remodeling of the costochondral graft. The length of the graft is determined by the ramus height discrepancy and the facial asymmetry to be corrected. A drain is placed and the wounds are closed in layers. After intermaxillary fixation for a few days, jaw is mobilized vigorously and physiotherapy is continued. If there is no sign of satisfactory improvement, tissues are stretched under general anesthesia. A few aspects of this problem need further evaluation.

Discussion

(1) *Early vs. delayed surgery*. High rate of recurrence in young children and the supposed interference with condylar growth centre are responsible for delayed surgery. On the contrary, any delay results in severe shortening of the ramus, pronounced antegonial notch and micrognathia. Hence, early surgery is preferable even if the child may not cooperate for physiotherapy. Even if condyle is considered as a growth centre, ankylosis would have destroyed the condyle. Since it is a well-established fact that mandibular growth is primarily a response to functional stimulation, early surgery with costochondral grafting is preferable.

(2) *Site of surgery*. It is a matter of personal preference based on one's own knowledge of facial growth. However, as far as possible, surgery near the joint region is preferable.

The various procedures practiced are:

(a) Esmarch's method at the mandibular molar region.
(b) Ramus, close to the level of lingula with an interpositional material.
(c) Subcondylar osteotomy without the surgery on the callus.
(d) Condylar head region where the bone is medially extended and the callus is sclerotic.

Surgery as close to the joint region as possible is preferred since as already described, lever of III

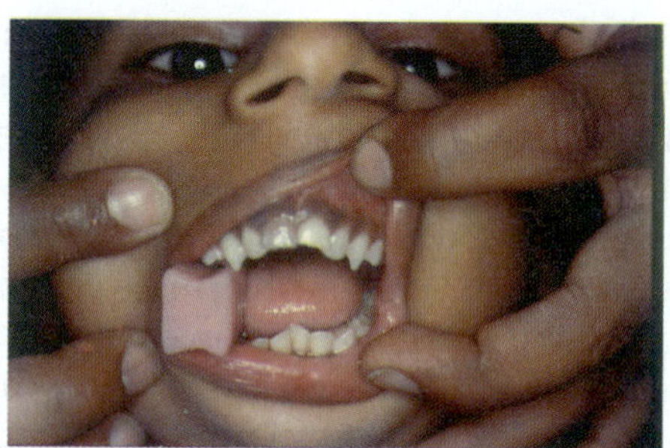

Fig. 16.12 (a) Postoperative intraoral view showing mouth opening.

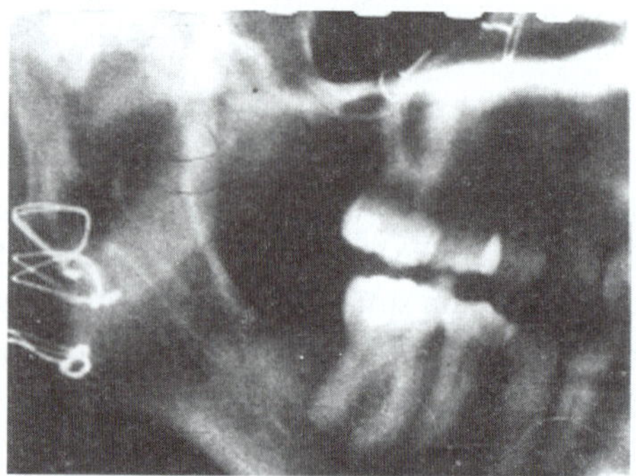

Fig. 16.12 (b) Radiograph showing costochondral graft with wire fixation.

order is stable while lever of I order is unstable.

(3) *Interposition material: Gap arthroplasty* (with or without inter-positional medium) (Fig.16.9, 16.10). This aims at maintaining the ramus height and also to prevent reankylosis. Many biological and alloplastic materials are used for obliterating the gap.

Biological - e.g. Dermis, Fascia lata, bone and cartilage (costochondral).

Alloplastic - e.g. Vitallium, tantalum, silastic and acrylic. (Fig. 16.11).

(4) *Most effective technique of removal of bone*. It is based on density of bone and the location of resection. If condyle is relatively soft as in children, sharp tap with osteotome is sufficient. If the bone is dense and hard as in adult, use of large, round or flame-shaped bur may have to be used to remove the callus.

(5) *Success rate*. It depends on (a) creation of the gap with at least 1.5 cm width, (b) appropriate interpositional medium to prevent recurrence and (c) jaw exercise.

(6) *Complications*.

- (a) Damage to the facial nerve.
- (b) Accidental entry into external auditory canal.
- (c) Hemorrhage following damage to maxillary artery and pterygoid plexus of veins.
- (d) Perforation of glenoid fossa.

(7) *Joint reconstruction*. It can be carried out

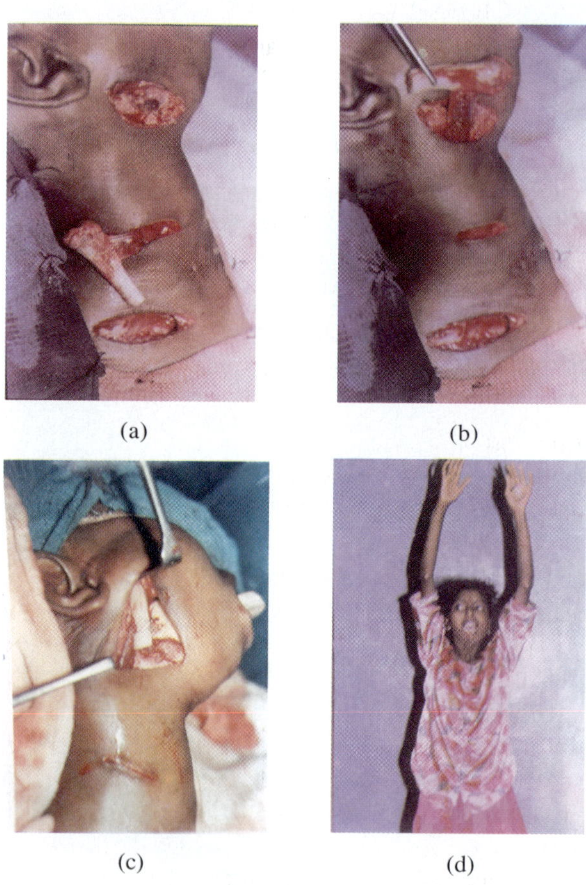

(a) (b) (c) (d)

Fig. 16.13 TM joint reconstruction with sternomastoid muscle pedicled Sternoclavicular joint. **(a)** Migrating Sternoclavicular joint, **(b)** Clavicle reaching the mandibular region, **(c)** Graft fixed in position, **(d)** Demonstrating that function of the limbs is not affected.

with costochondral graft, sternoclavicular joint and metatarsal head. Costochondral graft is very popular because of the biological acceptability and the possibility of remodeling by appositional growth in children.

Management (summary)

(a) Prior to 1851, it was considered to be *incurable*.
(b) Brisement force (forceful opening under GA) was tried without success.
(c) Esmarch suggested wedge resection of the body of the mandible.
(d) Condylectomy in early cases.
(e) Gap arthroplasty led to recurrence.
(f) Osteoarthrotomy (gap and interpositional arthroplasty) improved the prognosis.
(g) Excision of callus and joint reconstruction become the treatment of choice.

INTERNAL DERANGEMENT OF THE TEMPOROMANDIBULAR JOINT

Introduction

Internal derangements are defined as the malrelationship of the meniscus to the condylar head and the articular eminence. These alterations allow the meniscus to assume an abnormal position. The degenerative joint disease represents changes associated with the breakdown of the articular surface layer. Often, it is associated with the disc derangements and hence considered to be a component of internal derangement. Such derangement produces changes in the smooth functioning of the joint, often associated with production of sound (clicking) and orofacial pain. This is termed as meniscus displacement or dislocation. Most commonly, it is dislocated in the anteromedial direction.

Etiology

It is only speculative in nature.

(1) *Macrotrauma* to the mandible or microtrauma to the joint resulting from the loss of posterior teeth lead to posterior displacement of the condyle.

(2) *Myofacial pain*, (dysfunction due to bruxism). Depending on the need for radical surgery, the various surgical procedures have been advocated. Occlusal disharmony and alterations in the form of articular components are related to biomechanical loading of the joint and ultimately dental occlusion. Occlusal disharmony is observed to increase the susceptibility to changes in the functional loading of the joint resulting in arthrosis.

Pathophysiology

Molecular biology of the TMJ:

Three mechanisms of injury have been suggested.

(a) Direct mechanical injury.
(b) Hypoxia - perfusion injury.
(c) Neurogenic inflammation.

(a) **Direct mechanical injury:** Excessive mechanical loading of articular tissues can limit cellular functions, impair fluid transport and produce free radicals in the affected tissues, leading to pathological state.

(b) **Hypoxia (perfusion injury):** When the intracapsular hydrostatic pressure exceeds the end capillary perfusion pressure, blood flow is transiently disrupted resulting in tissue hypoxia with repeated episodes of hypoxia which is responsible for heightened muscular tension and bruxism. This leads to altered metabolic response of the affected tissues.

(c) **Neurogenic inflammation:** Substance-P, Calcitonin and substance-Y found in the TMJ spaces released from the peripheral nerve terminals are responsible for a proinflammatory response in the articular spaces producing pain.

All these three mechanisms are involved in the degenerative process of TMJ. In the normal joint, the disc fits over the head of the condyle. The thin central portion is related to the anterosuperior aspect of the condyle when the teeth are in occlusion. The complex sequence of rotational and transitional movements take place in the lower and upper joint cavities respectively during mouth opening. During closing, the reverse sequence takes place. All these movements are initiated and controlled by the muscles of mastication. Anatomical differences exist between the two heads of lateral pterygoid muscle. Inferior head is larger and gains attachment to the anterior aspect of the condyle. It helps in opening by drawing the condyle forward. The superior head is smaller and it is attached to the joint capsule and the anterior edge of the meniscus. Since the disc is firmly attached to the lateral and medial poles of the head of the condyle, disc moves along with the head of the condyle. During the movements, upper smaller head is active during the final phase of closing as in chewing or swallowing. It has been suggested that the superior head of the lateral pterygoid muscle helps to trace the meniscus and the head of the condyle against the posterior slope of the articular eminence and also to distribute and absorb the pressures generated during the masticatory movements.

In myofascial pain dysfunction syndrome, increased persistent tone has been found in the superior head. Hence, it tends to pull the meniscus, anteromedial to the head of the condyle. This pull is generally resisted by the attachment of the disc to the two poles of the head of the condyle. It is also counteracted by elastic tension created in the bilaminar zone posteriorly.

If the disc has moved anterior to the condylar head, a clicking sound is heard in the early opening as the condyle reseats into the thin central portion of the disc. This sound is reversible by physiotherapy that relieves spasm of the masticatory muscles. If the sound is not eliminated at this stage, constant stretching and degeneration result in separation of the meniscus and becomes still more mobile. It starts moving independently with reference to condylar movements. If the meniscus is pushed ahead of the condylar head during the contraction of lateral pterygoid, it gets trapped between the articular eminence and the condyle during mouth opening. This results in mechanical impediment that prevents full mouth opening. Hence, head impinges on the bilaminar zone of the disc which contains rich sensory innervation. Further, degenerative changes lead to morphological changes in the meniscus, its attachments and the bony components of the joint. The disc snaps behind faster ahead of the condyle, which also gives rise to clicking sound during the closing movement.

Thus, it is clear that intervention that relieves muscular spasm of muscles of mastication, relocation of the displaced disc and reversal of the predisposing factors resolve most of the internal derangements. Surgery is indicated only in patients with irreversible degenerative soft tissue changes in the joint.

Clinical diagnosis

The clinical diagnosis depends on recording of

(a) Detailed history.
(b) Clinical findings.
(c) Accuracy of the interpretation of the non-invasive and invasive investigations carried out on the patient.

History

(1) Pain.
(2) Joint sound.
(3) Occlusal disharmony.
(4) History of any previous treatment.
(5) Any other relevant information.
(6) Psychological background of the patient.

Clinical examination

(1) Confirming the history.
(2) Occlusal disharmonies.
(3) Interincisal distance during mouth opening.
(4) Range of mandibular movements present.
(5) Midline deviation.
(6) Correlation of clicking with pain and

mouth opening confirmed by auscultation.

(7) Palpation of the joint region and muscles of mastication.

Special investigations

(1) Plain radiographs of the joint in closed and open position (Fig. 16.3a).
(2) Arthrography.
(3) Computerized tomography (CT scan).
(4) Magnetic resonance imaging (MRI).
(5) Temporomandibular joint arthroscopy.
(6) Acoustic evaluation.

Clinically, *internal derangements* can be distinguished into three stages.

(a) *Initial stage*. Anterior displacement of the disc with reduction.
(b) *Intermediate stage*. Anterior displacement of the disc without reduction.
(c) *Terminal stage*. Anterior displacement of the disc with perforation of the disc.

(a) *Anterior displacement* with reduction that reduces to its normal position during mouth opening. Clinically, clicking occurs during opening and closing movements termed as *reciprocal clicking*. These patients give the history that mouth opening occurs only up to a certain point. Any attempt to open the mouth further reduces pain in the joint with a clicking noise. On examination, physical findings confirm the history with the cycle of hinge opening – lock–pain–deviation away from the painful side–clicking–return to midline–full translatory mouth opening–clicking–translatory mouth closing. The definite mechanical locking by the disc must be different from the trismus due to muscle spasm. Thus, the diagnosis can be demonstrated clinically by the release of the lock by the clicking sound. The direction of the pull of lateral pterygoid is anteromedial. Hence, to reduce the dislocation, the patient needs to move the condylar head in the direction taken by the meniscus under the influence of the lateral pterygoid muscle. This clearly correlates with the clinical findings. Once the normal anatomical relationship is established, full mouth opening is possible. At this stage, disc is morphologically normal. Only the laxity of the attachments allows considerable mobility. The marked degree of redundancy of the posterior bilaminar zone secondary to stretching results in distortion and hypertrophy of the soft tissues. The elasticity of the bilaminar zone is lost. This ultimately leads to loss of spontaneous reduction if this stage continues for a long period.

(b) *Anterior displacement without reduction* can be diagnosed if the history is characteristic with patients who are not able to open the mouth fully. To increase the range of mouth opening, if the patient attempts to open the mouth further, pain in the joint and deviation to the painful side is characteristic. The cycle will include hinge movement–pain–deviation towards the painful side–pain–painful side remains locked–translatory opening of the opposite side. The clinical examination confirms the history. The affected joint is tender. The meniscus is displaced ahead of the condyle and continues to remain in the same relationship to the condylar head so that forward translation is markedly restricted. If this continues, pressure effects may lead to even perforation of the disc resulting in bone-to-bone contact between the bony components of the joint and consequently osteoarthritic changes in the joint. The above progression of the joint disease is usually a chronic process.

(c) *Anterior displacement with perforation of disc* ultimately results if the joint disorder becomes a chronic process. Although one may progress from one stage to the other, it is impossible to predict the future changes. As the disorder progresses, pain becomes a chronic process. Although one may progress from one stage to the other, it is impossible to predict the future changes. As the disorder progresses, pain becomes the predominant feature around the preauricular joint region. The patient may also develop referred pain to the ear, tinnitus and headache. The sound from the joint is in the form of clicking and crepitus with diffuse muscle tenderness. Usually, joint sound is audible. But it is advisable to identify the sound with the aid of a stethoscope and correlate the sound with the cyclic jaw movements.

(1) **Plain temporomandibular joint radiography (open and close position)** reveals that the joint may be normal or with osteoarthritic changes. Attempts have been made for the joint space analysis with transcranial radiographs or tomograms to demonstrate the relative posterior positioning of the condyle but the diagnosis is confirmed more as a clinical diagnosis. The joint space analysis continues to be inconclusive.

(2) **Temporomandibular joint arthrography** is an imaging technique to visualize the soft tissue components of the joint. It involves the injection of contrast material into the joint cavities prior to radiography. Such a contrast study is expected to demonstrate the morphology and the position of the meniscus. Hence, it will be helpful to confirm the presence of perforation and adhesions of the meniscus. Unfortunately, it has been clearly pointed out that over-reliance on the sophisticated investigations and imaging techniques should not result in the deterioration of the clinical diagnostic skills. Hence, this must be utilized only in difficult cases rather than a routine modality for diagnosis.

The spasm of lateral pterygoid muscle, anterior displacement of the disc with or without reduction and perforation of the disc with or without osteoarthritic changes in the joint may form part of the same clinical entity in its different stages. But the degree of degenerative changes in the meniscus and bony components of the joint and the clinical features help to differentiate various stages of this clinical condition. Since one joint depends on the other for its integrity, it is interesting to note that the disorders of one joint may lead to the other joint.

(3) **Computerized tomography** has been tried as an alternative to arthrography. But it has been demonstrated that it is less accurate and it does not permit a dynamic study of the joint structures.

(4) **Magnetic resonance imaging (MRI)** is yet another method of a non-invasive technique to image the soft tissue components of the joint. The results so far obtained have been encouraging. By this technique, disc and its attachments, joint spaces, disc perforations and anterior disc displacements can be demonstrated.

(5) **Temporomandibular joint arthroscopy** is the latest and the least invasive method. This permits direct visualization of the interior of the joint with the help of a small telescope. This technique is utilized as a diagnostic and therapeutic modality. For example, it has been used for the lavage of the upper joint cavity, intraarticular injection of steroids and lysis of adhesions. Recently, reports have appeared in the literature claiming that *diagnostic arthroscopy* has yielded therapeutic effects in some of the joint disorders. Hence, as is the case with any new sophisticated methods, a bout of enthusiasm has been generated but results seem to be very unpredictable. Recently, it has become a popular method to approach the joint through a preauricular incision for disc repositioning and plication without damaging important adjoining structures like facial nerve. If gross osteoarthrosis is present, attempts have been made to contour the surfaces of the bony components of the joint.

(6) **Acoustic evaluation.** Special instrumentation is utilized to analyze the sound from the joint during the jaw movements. It is useful to measure the intensity and character of the clicking sound. The internal derangements are characterized by the identified reciprocal clicks. When the amplitude of the sound is successfully measured, there is an objective increase with the severity of joint internal derangement. This method of non-invasive technique is known as *temporomandibular joint sonography*.

Management

The literature is voluminous, ranging from conservative to most radical methods. On a "trial and error" basis, every known modality has been tried with varying success. At the initial stage, clicking is the main symptom. This is probably the only phase that is reversible. No radiographic alteration can be seen. At the intermediate stage, locking, restriction of movement and pain are the main symptoms. Locking is caused by a permanent disc displacement without reduction. Radiographic alterations are progressively evident, leading to flattening of the condyle. In the terminal stage, symptoms are mild or absent. There are clear alterations in the radiographs but not progressive.

The clinical importance of distinguishing these three stages is that diagnostic techniques and methods of management are different in each stage. In the initial and intermediate stage, bony changes can be detected radiologically. These changes are progressive. In the terminal stage, disc position and form are to be determined to confirm the diagnosis.

(1) *Initial treatment.* This must aim to bring the joint back to its healthy normal position although this may or may not be possible. Management is primarily symptom directed.

(a) Primarily, the most simple form of management starts with offering explanation to the patient about the nature and prognosis of the disorder. It is aimed at relieving the joint from any trauma by changing the diet to soft and smaller food, avoidance of empty chewing, like chewing gum, bruxism and providing exercises.

(b) Motivation of the patient seems to be an important factor in understanding the nature of the disorder and its prognosis.

(c) Medications are helpful since inflammation is one of the components of dysfunction. A nonsteroidal antiinflammatory agent with analgesic effect is found to be effective.

(d) Muscle spasm is another component. Muscle relaxants or tranquilizers are useful, e.g. Diazepam. It has been found that reducing the anxiety of the patient and steps to prevent the recurrence of the symptoms are essential in the conservative management of this condition.

(e) Great care must be taken in using methods causing irreversible changes to dentition of the joint. In other words, surgery must be reserved for patients with terminal stages of this condition. The main philosophy of the conservative management should be directed to the (i) elimination of clicking and instability, (ii) improvement of mobility and function, (iii) control of pain and (iv) counseling of the patient. Application of physical agents like heat, cold or short wave diathermy provides rapid relief. The patient should be advised to limit the mouth opening.

(f) Intraarticular injection of triamcinolone, placenteral extract or hydrocortisone provides quick relief. This disorder has a natural course. The real cause and exact relationship between internal derangement and osteoarthritic changes are not definitely known. Hence, in nearly 85% of the patients, symptoms disappear with conservative management in due course of time. Only the remaining 15% of patients may need special diagnostic procedures and more extensive treatment.

(2) *Supportive therapy.* Even though there is an appreciable reduction of symptoms following conservative initial treatment, some cases need additional supportive treatment modalities. The following are some of them:

- (a) Appliances (splints)
  - (i) Stabilization splint.
  - (ii) Repositioning splint.
- (b) Physiotherapy
  - (i) Joint mobilization.
  - (ii) Movement education.

(a) Appliances

An occlusal splint is a bio-mechanical method of management. It is placed interocclusally either to stabilize the occlusal position or to influence the anatomical relationship by anterior repositioning of the mandible. To avoid any orthodontic side effects on dentition, full coverage of teeth with adequate occlusal matrix is provided. The patient should be evaluated periodically to check the occlusion. Likewise, the hard palate should be covered to increase the retention of the splint. Once the patient starts wearing the appliances, advice is given regarding the care of the appliance and oral hygiene.

(i) **Stabilization splint.** This reduces the masticatory load on the bilaminar zone of the articular disc so that the pain is reduced considerably. Reflex responses of the muscles and occlusal interferences are also eliminated. This provides muscular relaxation and corrects the habits like bruxism. It also protects the occlusal surfaces of teeth from further abrasive damage. It neutralizes alteration of occlusion which are induced by muscular or joint problems.

(ii) **Anterior repositioning splint.** This is mainly to eliminate the disc displacement and reciprocal click. This should be restricted to the phase of beginning of translatory movement of the condylar head and also if closing click occurs before reaching maximal occlusion. The main objective is to reposition the mandible into the occlusal position to prevent displacement of the disc during closing movement. To be effective, the patient must be advised to wear this splint always. Once the patient is relieved of the symptoms at least for 3-4 months, the splint should be adjusted once in 2-3 weeks so that the joint gradually adapts to a new position without relapse of the clicking sound. However, if this does not provide adequate relief, permanent alteration of occlusion or surgery is indicated.

There are six cardinal features common to all these devices which decrease muscle activity and symptoms.

(a) Alteration of the occlusion position.
(b) Increased vertical dimension.
(c) Alteration of the condylar position.
(d) Cognitive awareness.
(e) Increased peripheral input to the CVS.
(f) Placebo effect.

(b) Physiotherapy

(i) **Joint mobilization.** The patient's head is firmly supported. To mobilize the left joint, this joint is palpated with left index finger. The right hand thumb is placed on the occlusal surface of left posterior teeth while the other fingers of the right hand are placed extraorally around the lower border of the mandible and chin. Pressure directed on the posterior teeth with upward pressure against the chin results in downward distraction of the joint capsule. This technique is useful when disc is permanently displaced in the intermediate phase. Several sessions may be necessary. In any synovial joint, small passive movements are possible in addition to voluntary movements. Such small movements are known as "joint play" movements. The technique that utilizes joint play movements to improve the active range of movements is known as mobilization. By doing so, it does not affect the passive performance of voluntary movements.

(ii) **Movement education.** The ultimate goals of therapeutic exercises include increase or maintenance of (a) range of movement, (b) coordination, (c) strength, and (d) endurance. Hence, motivation of the patient is very important. The patient must be made aware of that if exercise causes pain, it should be stopped. It only indicates that the limit of endurance has been crossed or the exercise is performed wrongly or too vigorously. If tension interferes with the desired effect of physiotherapy, active relaxation should be advocated. The exercise therapy should include techniques (a) to improve coordination, (b) to improve and maintain joint mobility through mobilizing exercise and (c) to improve the strength and endurance through resisted exercises. If all these techniques fail to produce the desired result, the patient should be referred to a consultant for further management.

Occlusal rehabilitation. This method should not be used indiscriminately. It includes selective grinding, relief of traumatic occlusion by restorative or orthodontic methods and if necessary, removal of teeth selectively. The main objective is to establish a stabilized occlusion. If this is not done properly, instead of relieving, new occlusal disturbances appear. Hence, this is to be done with great caution.

Surgical management

If any of the conservative modes of management fail to restore normalcy, surgical intervention may be necessary.

Surgical access

The preauricular approach provides adequate exposure of the joint, irrespective of the surgical procedure. The advantages are (a) esthetically acceptable scar, (b) relatively complication free and (c) provides direct exposure. Many variations to the standard incisions like releasing incision in superior or anterior oblique direction or curvilinear modification have been advocated. The choice of these modifications are mostly left to the operator's choice. Whenever additional exposure is required, submandibular Risdon's approach is combined with preauricular approach. The anatomical consideration of the surgical exposure of the TM joint are (a) parotid gland, (b) superficial temporal vessels, (c) facial nerve, and (d) external auditory meatus.

Procedures

(i) **Meniscectomy.** Since disturbance occurs mainly around the disc, removal of the disc has logically been the procedure of choice. Anatomically, meniscus (disc) is a fibrocartilaginous, separating medium between the two bony components of the joint. Its anterior portion acts as a buffer. The synovial fluid in the joint cavities acts as a hydrocushion. The main problem is in the altered pathophysiology of the disc and its structural damage-like perforation or thinning. Functionally, most of the features are due to (a) severance of the disc anteriorly due to trauma, (b) incoordination in its movement with reference to the head of the condyle, (c) tearing or thinning of the disc resulting in the functional disturbance and (d) consequent impingement on the meniscus and synovial membrane at the anterior periphery. Hence, excision of meniscus (meniscectomy) became a popular surgical method in the 1950s with the hope that its complete removal eliminates the painful symptoms. But, unfortunately, it has proved to be theoretically sound but unsuccessful in its execution because of the technical difficulties encountered in the total excision of the disc. In practice, remnant of the disc remains inaccessible in a few areas. Hence, this procedure has definite limitations. In order to excise the disc completely, surgeons modified the procedure by removing the associated portion of the head of the condyle called high condylectomy with meniscectomy.

(ii) **High condylectomy.** This involves the removal of the anterior aspect of the head of the condyle. This was performed along with meniscectomy. Since excision of the disc disturbs the fibrous attachment of the disc, the procedure of meniscectomy was gradually discarded. In due course of time, techniques were evolved to suture the torn disc so that attachment of the lateral pterygoid muscle is restored.

(iii) **Condylectomy.** Over the course of time, excision of the condyle became the treatment of choice, irrespective of the stage of the dysfunction. Although this procedure eliminates the joint, certain unfortunate functional postsurgical impairment develops. This ranges from deviation and occlusal disharmony in unilateral condylectomy to gross non-occlusion and open bite following bilateral condylectomy. This is due to shortening of the height of the ramus by the contractions of elevator group of muscles and the loss of attachments of lateral pterygoid muscle. To overcome this significant morbidity, attempts were made for immediate reconstruction so that ramus height is restored. Because of the technical difficulties with immediate reconstruction, this procedure is not widely practiced. Total joint reconstruction has been attempted with cast vitallium prosthesis or autotransplantation of the digits or costochondral grafts.

(iv) **Condylotomy.** It was an incidental finding that when condylar fractures were conservatively treated in patients with temporomandibular joint dysfunction, the joint pain disappeared. This observation led to the concept that condylar repositioning can relieve the pressure on the anterior periphery of the disc and the pain. The concept consolidated the role of condylotomy in these patients.

This procedure was originally described by Ward (1961) who advocated a closed surgical division of the neck of the condyle when all the conservative measures fail. By doing so, condyle takes up a new position with increased radiographic joint space. It will also indirectly shorten the lateral pterygoid muscle, thus eliminating its pulling power of the condyle. Following condylotomy, condylar head usually moves slightly forwards and medially. This has also been found very useful in recurrent dislocation or luxation of the condyle. Since it is a closed procedure, care must be taken to avoid damage to facial nerve and maxillary artery.

(v) **Eminectomy.** Injury to the anterior aspect of the disc may lead to pain when the condyle rests on the posterior slope of the articular eminence. Hence, it was thought that removal of the articular eminence relieves the pain and clicking sound. The glenoid fossa is exposed by the preauricular approach. The periosteum is incised and elevated and the articular eminence is removed to the desired extent from lateral to the medial aspect. The rationale is to encourage self reduction spontaneously. This is indicated in (a) intractable temporomandibular joint pain, (b) chronic hypermobility and recurrent dislocation. This method also leads to the increase of the functional joint space since steeply angulated eminence is associated with displacement of the disc. This is also a relatively simple procedure.

(vi) **Zygomectomy.** In recurrent dislocations, a vertical cut is extended through the ascending slope of the articular eminence and the distal portion of zygoma is fractured through frontozygomatic suture line. The fractured bone is placed downwards and held in position. This method prevents the condyle from subluxating.

(vii) **Shortening of the temporalis tendon.** In patients with temporomandibular joint syndromes associated with pain and hypermobility, this procedure is carried out. Under general anesthesia, anterior border of the coronoid and mandible are exposed through a vertical incision from coronoid to the retromolar region, along the anterior border of the mandible. Temporalis tendon and the underlying periosteum are divided and elevated. Masseter muscle is also partly elevated from the lateral surface of the mandible. By suturing all the layers of the wound together from above downwards, the vertical wound is transformed into a tight horizontal scar, this operation is followed by intense facial swelling. The interincisal opening gradually decreases and hence found useful in hypermobility and recurrent dislocation.

(viii) **Temporal fascia sling.** This procedure can be performed under local anesthesia. An extended preauricular incision towards the temporal space is made to expose the temporal facia and temporomandibular joint region. An inferiorly-based temporal facial sling is raised and passed through a hole drilled in the condyle and attaching it deep to the temporalis muscle. The vertical dimension of the ramus remains unaltered. The temporal sling counteracts the hypermobility of the condyle anteriorly. Postoperatively, jaws are immobilized in occlusion. This method is mainly indicated in subluxation or chronic recurrent dislocation of the condyle.

(ix) **Plication of the capsule.** The orthopedic surgeons perform this procedure for the hypermobility of the shoulder joint. Likewise, in temporomandibular joint disorders, hypermobility is being corrected by plication (folding) of the capsule of the TM joint. Although immediate postoperative success is good, the long term follow-up has revealed that the success of this method is only for a short duration. This is mainly aimed at eliminating redundant capsule.

Dislocation of the TM joint

When mandibular condyle is displaced anteriorly

beyond the articular eminence, it is known as dislocation. This term is being used liberally by the clinicians. For example, if the condyle moves out of the glenoid fossa anterosuperior to the articular eminence but unable to return back to the glenoid fossa, it is termed as acute or complete dislocation which is not self-reducible. Whatever be the underlying cause, with each episode of dislocation, further episodes tend to occur more easily. Then it becomes self-reducible and is referred to as chronic, habitual or recurrent dislocation or subluxation.

Precipitating factors of subluxation:

Abnormalities in the stability factors of the TM joint may be associated with dislocation. Stability of any joint depends on 3 factors:

(1) Integrity of the ligaments associated with the joint.
(2) Bony architecture of the joint surfaces.
(3) Activity of the musculature acting on the joint.

For example, deep overbite seems to be frequently associated with deep glenoid fossa and steep articular eminence which is conducive to dislocation. Some have postulated that chronic stretching of the capsule and lateral ligaments also predispose to dislocation. Likewise, neuromuscular mechanism controlling muscles of mastication [neuromuscular incoordination] also may predispose to this condition.

Clinical features of dislocation:

(1) Inability to close the mouth.
(2) Preauricular depression.
(3) Tense, spasmatic muscles of mastication.
(4) Excessive salivation.
(5) Severe pain of the joint.

Treatment

In acute dislocation, TM joint gets fixed in the open position. Condyle is positioned anterior to the articular eminence with the elevators of the mandible in a fully contracted stage. This is due to the forcible or prolonged opening of the mouth like dental extraction under general anesthesia. If dental treatment is prolonged for an extended period, as in the removal of impactions, elevators of the mandible get into a fatigued stage and therefore unable to relax when required.

This condition is of short duration. Well padded thumb of both hands are placed at the mandibular III molar region and with the rest of the fingers, mandible is held firmly and pulled downwards to counteract the contraction of the elevator muscles. By this act, condyle is guided to overcome the articular eminence so that, mandible snaps back to its rests position. Thumbs are well-padded to avoid injury due to sudden snapping of the lower jaw. One should not overlook the fact that periarticular soft tissues are stretched. To avoid the consequence of this stretching, patient should be adviced to give rest to the jaws by taking only liquid diet for a few days. Some clinicians prefer even intermaxillary fixation for a few days for the periarticular tissues to settle down. If this is not avoided, laxed capsule and tendons may lead to chronic dislocation of the joint.

If the joint becomes hypermobile or fixed in the dislocated position, then treatment may have to be initiated to avoid recurrent dislocation of the condyle. This is based on the alteration of the (a) ligaments, (b) associated musculature and (c) bony anatomy.

(a) Ligament function is affected by the introduction of sclerosing agent into the capsular space of the joint. This causes fibrosis with resultant tightening of the capsule. This prevents or limits hypermobility of the condyle.

Eg., Alcohol, 5% sodium psylliate, sodium morrhuate.

However, administration of sclerosing agent may be associated with side effects like pain, muscle tenderness, occlusal disharmony, temorary paresis and excessive salivation. As an adjunctive treatment to sclerosing agents or as a sole therapy, maxillomandibular fixation for a period of 3 to 6 weeks will facilitate the development of a mature fibrosis, within the joint capsule. Attempts to strengthen the capsular ligament achieved by surgically exposing the fascia of the temporal muscle and suturing a flap of fascia onto the capsular ligament. Plication of the capsule also helps in strengthening the capsule.

(b) For the alteration of the musculature, active physiotherapy has been tried. Recently, type A botulinum toxin (BTA), derived from the anaerobic, gram positive rod clostridium botulinum is injected through preauricular transcutaneous approach, (very similar to injecting the sclerosing solutions) 1 cm anterior to the condyle in a slightly open-mouth position. The fluid is directed towards the lateral pterygoid muscle. After ensuring that the tip of the needle has not penetrated the blood vessel, upto 500 MU (mouse units) of BTA is injected. This is to weaken the lateral pterygoid muscle to prevent dislocation. It takes nearly 5 to 6 days for the onset of relief to the patient. Multiple injections of 100 MU may be necessary once in 2 to 4 months to achieve long-term relief. Some patients develop transient dysphagia.

Closed condylotomy has also been tried to affect the lateral pterygoid muscle following the displacement of the condyle in an anteromedial direction. Although this procedure is said to have provided relief in about 80 % of the patients, potential bleeding from internal maxillary artery should be borne in mind.

In contrast to this, the bilateral release of lateral pterygoid muscle results in the alteration of the musculature directly. Nothing prevents the reattachment of the insertion of the muscle. Attempts have been made to interfere with the function of temporal muscle.

(c) Bony alteration: Initially, condylectomy was performed to limit the mandibular motion.

Mayer (1933) was the first to describe the procedure of displacement of the zygomatic arch to augment the articular eminence so that path of the translating condyle is obstructed. Later, Dautrey modified the procedure. Through preauricular incision, zygomatic arch and capsular ligament are exposed and periosteum is reflected from the arch. An oblique osteotomy is performed on the arch to produce greenstick fracture occuring at the zygomaticotemporal suture. It provides the segment some rebound elasticity to provide stability in its altered position. Since this procedure does not violate the joint space and allows immediete anterior movement with no limitation in maximal opening, it is popular among the oral surgeons. This can easily be performed under local anesthesia. Since with increasing age, bone becomes brittle, it is safe in individuals under 40 years of age. If the segment fractures completely, use of wire or bone plate does not present any problem. Sometimes, resorption of the distal or the down-fractured segment during the healing phase may become a problem. High success rate has been reported in the literature.

Iliac crest or calvarial bone grafts have been tried to augment the articular eminence, but variable degree of bone resorption is inevitable. To avoid this problem, use of bovine grafts have been advocated.

Use of L-shaped pins, vitallium mesh implants miniplates and silicone blocks have also been tried.

In contrast to augmentation, reduction of the articular eminence known as eminectomy has also been tried. This procedure has been rationalized by suggesting that obstruction is eliminated. Care is taken not to violate the intracapsular space. In some patients, pneumatization of the eminence may lead to dural tear. Difficult access to the medial portion of the articular eminence may also result in incomplete reduction of the eminence.

In most cases, conservative methods provide relief. But recurrence is common. In general, surgical therapy provides long-term relief. Therefore, surgical intervention remains as the mainstay in the management of this clinical entity.

Control of Orofacial Pain and Anesthesia

INTRODUCTION

The pain could be defined *subjectively* as "an unpleasant sensory and emotional experience associated with actual and potential tissue damage or described in terms of such damage." *Objectively*, it is defined as "an unpleasant emotional experience usually initiated by a noxious stimulus and transmitted over a specialized neural network to the central nervous system where it is interpreted as pain." Pain should not be considered as a neurophysiological signal alone. It can be modified by psychological, ethnic, social and environmental factors. One of the major concerns of any branch of health sciences is pain and its control. While it attracts the maximum attention, equal amount of confusion exists because of the neuroanatomical complexity and the absence of the standard objective method of measuring pain. The orofacial pain denotes the pain arising from the area of the distribution of trigeminal nerve.

On the basis of differential diagnosis, the orofacial pain has been classified broadly into four groups.

CLASSIFICATION

I. **Typical facial pain.** Pain of extracranial origin, e.g. dental, ocular, ear-nose-throat, salivary gland, temporomandibular joint, anginal pain, etc.

II. **Primary neuralgias.** Trigeminal, glossopharyngeal, geniculate and post-herpetic neuralgias.

III. **Secondary neuralgias.**

IV. **Atypical neuralgias.** Pain of vascular origin.

HISTORY OF PAIN EVALUATION

The patient's history of pain is very important for proper diagnosis in the absence of any other associated symptoms or detectable physical signs. If empirical treatment is instituted, it is likely to complicate the diagnostic process. Hence, efforts must be directed towards a systematic analysis of pain as a symptom on the following aspects:

1. Total duration of pain —How long?
2. Details of onset of pain
   (a) When, how, and where?
   (b) Any predisposing factors?
   (c) Any relieving factors?
   (d) Any associated clinical features?
3. Characteristics of pain
   (a) Quality.
   (b) Severity.
   (c) Type of pain.
   (d) Localized or radiating.
   (e) Time factor.
4. Other relevant data
   (a) Family history.
   (b) Medical history.
   (c) Any drug therapy.
5. Source of pain
6. Course and progress of the symptom.
   (a) Unchanged, better or worse.
   (b) Effect of therapy on pain.

Objective measurement of pain

Unfortunately, pain as an indicator of disease is notoriously unreliable. It is important not only to identify the source of pain but also its severity. More often, history of pain is unreliable as a diagnostic aid for the differential diagnosis of the orofacial pain.

EXPERIENCE OF PAIN

Pain is a complex experience. It includes not only the sensation experienced but also the accompanying reactions or the response evoked by such stimulus. These reactions may be emotional and hence may vary from person to person, depending on the circumstances under which stimulus was given. Such stimulus may or may not be damaging to the body. Hence, it is important to understand the puzzling and multifactorial nature of pain.

Referred pain is a poorly understood phenomenon, since the pain is referred from the site of the lesion to another distant site, not involved by any pathological process. This phenomenon can only be explained on the basis of neuroanatomy alone.

All types of pains are readily modifiable. For example, trigeminal neuralgic pain is usually triggered not by any painful stimulus to orofacial region but even by touch. The patient may even be unwilling to shave, brush the teeth or to eat for the fear of triggering the neuralgic pain.

Thus, the clinician does not deal with a simple sensory phenomenon, but with the interaction of events with the central nervous system of the patient which includes powerful influences of memory, self image, ethnic background, past experience, personality and motivation of the person. This is all the more complicated since, there is no satisfactory method of measuring the pain objectively.

MEASUREMENT OF PAIN

An objective method of measurement will assist the clinician to make a diagnosis, to monitor the response of pain to treatment and to assess the efficacy of the treatment.

(1) **Verbal rating scale (VRS)** grades the pain as (a) no pain, (b) mild, (c) moderate and (d) severe, analogous to four degrees of expression of the patient.

(2) **Visual analogue scale (VAS)** presents a pictorial representation of pain as a 10-point scale. Both the ends of the scale correspond to "unbearable pain" and "no pain" respectively. This numerical rating scale helps to record the efficiency of pain relief. The difference is more significant in this 10-point scale than the 4-point scale of verbal rating scale. But the disadvantage of this scale is that it is sensitive to the contrast effects. The rapid changes tend to be exaggerated. Many patients find

that both the scales, VRS and VAS, are difficult to use in the daily clinical practice.

(3) **McGill pain questionnaire (MPQ)** attempts to overcome the problem of difficulty in expressing the complexity of pain and its emotional component by asking the patient to specify pain in terms of sensory and evaluative descriptors. These terms relate to pain as it is localized in the body. Some terms communicate somatic sensations like aches, throbbing, dull pain etc, while other terms communicate sensations in terms of objective stimuli that might produce the pain, e.g., shooting, cutting or stabbing type of pain. A few others describe the feelings of the patient as "frightful" etc. All these terms are broadly grouped under three categories: sensory, affective, and evaluative. The sensory group represents qualities of pain like space, time and temperature. Affective group represents the phenomena like fear, tension, etc. Evaluative groups deal with descriptive terms like unbearable and agonizing, indicating the intensity of pain. Total of 78 descriptive terms are arranged in 20 groups of which 1-10 are sensory, 11-15 are affective and 16 are evaluative. The remaining groups are miscellaneous. In each group, words are arranged in the order of intensity. The patient is requested to choose the most descriptive term to describe the experience of pain. Unfortunately, the reaction reflects the personality of the affected person.

The **pain rating index (PRI)** is obtained on the scale values of each word and calculated as a total score. With this questionnaire, it is possible to distinguish between different types of pain. Regular use of McGill pain questionnaire (MPQ) during treatment helps to accurately assess the patient's progress.

McGill Pain Questionnaire

Name: Date: Registration No.

1. *Circle the word that describes how your pain feels right now.*
   a. Nil
   b. Mild
   c. Moderate
   d. Severe
   e. Most severe.
2. *Circle the word that describes how your pain usually is.*
   a. Nil
   b. Mild
   c. Moderate
   d. Severe
   e. Most severe.
3. *Circle the words below that best describe your pain. Use only one word in each group. Leave out any group if the words are unsuitable.*

1	2	3
a. Flickering	a. Jumping	a. Pricking
b. Quivering	b. Flashing	b. Boring
c. Pulsating	c. Shooting	c. Drilling
d. Throbbing		d. Stabbing
e. Beating		e. Lancinating
4	**5**	**6**
a. Sharp	a. Pinching	a. Tugging
b. Cutting	b. Pressing	b. Pulling
c. Lacerating	c. Gnawing	c. Wrenching
	d. Cramping	
	e. Crushing	
7	**8**	**9**
a. Hot	a. Tingling	a. Dull
b. Burning	b. Itchy	b. Sore
c. Scalding	c. Smarting	c. Hurting
d. Searing	d. Stinging	d. Aching
		e. Heavy
10	**11**	**12**
a. Tender	a. Tiring	a. Sickening
b. Taut	b. Exhausting	b. Suffocating
c. Rasping		
d. Splitting		
13	**14**	**15**
a. Fearful	a. Punishing	a. Wretched
b. Frightful	b. Gruelling	b. Binding
c. Terrifying	c. Cruel	
	d. Vicious	
	e. Killing	
16	**17**	**18**
a. Annoying	a. Spreading	a. Tight
b. Troublesome	b. Radiating	b. Numb
c. Miserable	c. Penetrating	c. Drawing
d. Intense	d. Piercing	d. Squeezing
e. Unbearable		e. Tearing

19	20
a. Cool	a. Nagging
b. Cold	b. Nauseating
c. Freezing	c. Agonizing
	d. Dreadful
	e. Torturing

(4) **Hospital anxiety and depression (HAD) scale.** Measurement of pain has been found to be unsatisfactory. There has been an increasing awareness to incorporate the patient's perspectives into the clinical assessment. This has led to the development of measures, which assess the quality of life. It is an accepted fact that there is a relationship between pain, depression and anxiety, although, it is very difficult to evaluate the exact relationship. Probably, removal of pain results in some changes in anxiety and depression. Many scales have been used to measure depression like weight loss, insomnia, nausea, etc. which may also be due to many physical illnesses. Hence, to overcome this problem, Hospital Anxiety and Depression (HAD) Scale has been developed; specifically it is used for nonpsychiatric patients to assess the impact of physical illness on their psychological well-being. Some of the main characteristics are as follows:

(a) Concept of anxiety and depression are separated.
(b) Concept of depression is focussed on a lowered ability to experience the pleasure state.
(c) The scale aims to detect the presence of relatively mild degree of mood disorders.
(d) The scale is brief and comprehensible.

There are seven items for depression and seven for anxiety. Each item is followed by four possible responses, scored as 0, 1, 2, and 3. Scores of 0 to 7 indicate no depression or anxiety, while scores of 8 to 10 indicate mild depression or anxiety. Any score of 11 and above indicate frank anxiety or depression.

HAD score has been used in patients with atypical facial pain and trigeminal neuralgias and found to be effective in assessing the effect of pain on the well-being of the patient.

HAD Scale

Name:........................ Date:.....................

This questionnaire is designed to help the doctor to know how the patient feels about pain. Each item must be read before ticking opposite the reply which comes closest. Patient should not take too long to reply, since immediate reaction to each item will probably be more accurate than a long thought out response.

Tick only one in each section

1. *I feel tense or "wound up"*
   (a) Most of the time
   (b) A lot of time
   (c) Occasionally
   (d) Not at all
2. *I feel as if I am slowed down*
   (a) Nearly all the time
   (b) Very often
   (c) Sometimes
   (d) Not at all
3. *I still enjoy the things I used to enjoy*
   (a) Definitely as much
   (b) Not quite so much
   (c) Only a little
   (d) Hardly at all
4. *I get a sort of frightened feeling like 'butterflies' in the stomach.*
   (a) Not at all
   (b) Occasionally
   (c) Quite often
   (d) Very often
5. *I get a sort of frightened feeling as if something awful is about to happen*
   (a) Very definitely
   (b) Yes, but not too badly
   (c) A little, but it doesn't worry me
   (d) Not at all
6. *I have lost interest in my appearance*
   (a) Definitely
   (b) I don't take as much as I should
   (c) I may not take quite as much care
   (d) I take just as much care as ever
7. *I can laugh and see the funny side of things*
   (a) As much as I always could
   (b) Not quite so much now
   (c) Definitely not so much now
   (d) Not at all

8. *I feel restless as if I have to be on the move*
   (a) Very much indeed
   (b) Quite a lot
   (c) Not very much
   (d) Not at all
9. *Worrying thoughts go through my mind*
   (a) A great deal of time
   (b) A lot of time
   (c) From time to time but not too often
   (d) Only occasionally
10. *I look forward with enjoyment to things*
   (a) As much as ever I did
   (b) Rather less than I used to
   (c) Definitely less than I used to
   (d) Hardly at all
11. *I feel cheerful*
   (a) Not at all
   (b) Not often
   (c) Sometimes
   (d) Most of the time
12. *I get sudden feelings of panic*
   (a) Very often indeed
   (b) Quite often
   (c) Not very often
   (d) Not at all
13. *I can sit at ease and feel relaxed*
   (a) Definitely
   (b) Usually
   (c) Not often
   (d) Not at all
14. *I can enjoy a good book or radio or TV programme*
   (a) Often
   (b) Sometimes
   (c) Not often
   (d) Very seldom

PAIN MECHANISM

(1) **Specificity theory.** This maintains that pain is a specific sensation involving anatomical framework of receptors, nerves, tracts and relays in the brain. The receptors respond only to noxious stimulations and not to sensations like cold, warmth or touch. All the nerve tracts and brain centres deal exclusively with neural information resulting from noxious stimuli. The nerve endings in the facial skin, oral mucosa, temporomandibular joint and other structures in relation to trigeminal nerve generate nerve impulses that travel along the nerve fibres of the trigeminal nerve through the semilunar ganglion into the brain stem. These nerve fibres have their first relay on cells in the spinal tract nucleus, situated approximately at the junction of the brain stem and the spinal cord. From here, the neural path related to orofacial tissues relay through thalamus and then to the cerebral cortex. The various inadequacies of the specificity theory has led to many theories, viz.:

(2) **Intensive or summation theory:** Overstimulation of other sensory process.

(3) **Pattern theory:** Pattern of neural impulses by noxious stimuli.

(4) **Gate-control theory** of pain attempts to explain the complexity, components and puzzles of pain. This theory postulates that noxious stimulus excites "central transmission" or "T" cells in the spinal cord that activate ascending neural path. The output of these cells is controlled by nerve impulses entering central nervous system. This control of cells is provided by largely undefined gating mechanism. When excitation is sufficient, "the gate is opened" to reflex, higher brain centres and pain may ensure. Thus according to this theory, the brain is influenced by injury messages, other afferent impulses and the descending control.

ODONTALGIA

The pain impulses are conducted, in general, by two types of nerves depending on the size of the nerve fibre and speed with which impulses are conducted.

(1) **A (delta) fibres** are large myelinated nerves, which conduct the pain impulses fast.

(2) **B fibres** are preganglionic autonomic fibers, which transmit the impulses in lesser speed. They have no afferent function.

(3) **C fibres** are small unmyelinated fibres that conduct the pain very slowly.

The **gate-control theory** postulates that an action system exists as a complex interconnection of higher nerve centres. Such an action system is closely involved with cortical and subcortical areas of brain including thalamus and hypothalamus. The spinothalamic system provides the neural pathways for the various components of pain. If the pain does not evoke the usual responses like fear or anxiety, the person's threshold of pain (ability to tolerate pain) is considered to be high. Another important aspect of the gate-control theory is the ability of the nervous system centres to facilitate or inhibit the neural transmission, at the first synapse. Such descending control explains one's ability to tolerate pain. The role of chemical mediators of pain is too well known, in the initiation, transmission, modulation and modification of any painful impulses.

Irrespective of various theories of pain, there is general agreement on the dual nature of pain: *pain perception and pain reaction*. The pain perception is a physioanatomical process of generating the pain impulse. This aspect of pain is remarkably similar in all the persons under similar circumstances. But the pain reaction is a psychophysiological phenomenon, representing the individual's manifestation of unpleasant reaction. Hence, this involves complex neuroanatomical and psychological factors. The pain reaction, therefore, varies from one person to the other, depending on the pain-threshold. These factors explain the relative role of both the aspects of pain.

Pain pathways. Trigeminal nerve is the principal afferent nerve of the orofacial region. Any stimulus received by myelinated and unmyelinated nerve fibres in this region is first received by the gasserian ganglion. Then, the impulses are transmitted along the sensory root of the nerve into the pons. At this place, the sensory root terminates either into the main sensory nucleus or bifurcates into ascending and descending fibres. The ascending fibres transmit general sensations while descending fibres convey pain and temperature through medulla, down to the level of the second cervical segment. Then axons of the secondary neurons start from the spinal tract nucleus across the midline and ascend to join with fibres of mesencephalic nucleus to form the spinothalamic tract of the trigeminal nerve. This terminates in posteroventral nucleus of the thalamus. Here the pain impulses are mediated by secondary connecting neurons that project to postcentral gyrus of the cerebral cortex.

Apart from fifth, ninth and tenth cranial nerves, second and third cervical nerves also take part in the transmission of pain impulses from the orofacial region.

Control of pain. The following methods have been utilized for the control of pain:

(1) Elimination of etiological factors.
(2) Raising the threshold of pain of the individual.
(3) Blocking the pathway of painful impulses.
(4) Controlling the pain reaction by cortical depression.
(5) Utilizing psychosomatic methods.

As already described, the two important factors to be considered in relation to pain are pain perception and pain reaction. Elimination of the causative factors and raising the pain threshold involve the pain perception while cortical depression and use of psychosomatic methods affect in the pain reaction. Both the factors are involved in blocking the pathway by anesthesia.

The differential diagnosis of dental pain is based on parameters like radiographic appearance, pulp vitality, periodontal pocket, etc. Analysis of patients with dental pain has revealed that in nearly 50% of the patients, pain originate from the exposed vital dental pulp and 25% of patients had pain with periodontal disturbances. It is important to identify the source, type and severity of pain.

Diagnosis

An accurate diagnosis of dental pain can be made on the basis of the following clinical features:

(1) **Pain of pulpal origin (pulpitis).** Mechanical, thermal, chemical or electrical

stimulation of pulp tissue results in the inflammation of dental pulp. Since pulp is encased in the hard tissue, the inflammation creates increase in fluid volume within a restricted space, resulting in sharp and severe pain. The pain is precipitated by intraoral thermal and osmotic changes and is relieved by the withdrawal of the stimulus and with analgesics. Marked tenderness to temperature changes indicates pulpitis.

Dentine is unique since it is vital but without any blood vascular system and sensory innervation. Exposed dentinal tubules can transmit sensory stimuli to pulp. Painful pulpitis is due to caries or traumatic exposure of the pulp.

(2) **Pain from periapical lesions.** Clinically, three common forms of pathosis can develop—abscess, granuloma and cyst. Usually, granuloma and cyst are painless. But the granuloma may precede or follow the abscess. In periodontitis, the pain will be dull initially. Later, acute exacerbation may develop due to occlusal pressure. The affected tooth can be identified. The patient gets relief with analgesics but pain gets worse during meals. In abscess formation, the pain is dull and throbbing. Later, it tends to become severe so as to disturb sleep.

(3) **Pain from pericoronitis.** The tissue flap covering the incompletely erupted tooth is inflamed with or without abscess formation. The pain is localized, dull and continuous. It aggravates with traumatic occlusion. The pain may have systemic features like pyrexia, trismus, halitosis and regional lymphadenopathy.

(4) **Dry socket.** In alveolitis, the pain develops from third to tenth post extraction day. The pain is dull, throbbing and sometimes it becomes unbearable. It gets aggravated on touching the affected area. The patient gets relief with thermal change and a course of analgesics. The pain disturbs the patient even during sleep.

Time factor in "toothache". It is of great significance to diagnose the nature of pain. The following factors help in proper assessment:

(1) Acute or chronic pain.
(2) After the anesthetic effect passes off, whether pain reappears.
(3) Pain of pulpal origin. Eg., when two dissimilar metallic dental restorations come in contact as in Galvanic shock.
(4) Pain developing two or more days after dental extraction as in dry socket.
(5) Time between the onset of pain and seeking treatment as a measure of severity of pain.
(6) Pain in relation to thermal changes.
(7) Period for which pain lasts
 (a) one or two seconds (spontaneous),
 (b) several seconds,
 (c) minutes to hours (continuous).
(8) Pain during sleep, day or night.
(9) Frequency of occurrence (increasing or decreasing pain episode).
(10) Reaction time.
(11) Time needed for the relief of pain.

Differential diagnosis

Several symptoms and signs are taken into consideration. The computers tackling the problem of differential diagnosis in an objective way. Careful history-taking, thorough and systematic clinical examination are helpful in the correct diagnosis.

Treatment

It depends on the causative factor, responsible for pain. Toothache, in the absence of the appropriate clinical features, must be investigated thoroughly. Until then, only symptomatic treatment must be instituted.

TEMPOROMANDIBULAR JOINT PAIN - DYSFUNCTION SYNDROME

More detailed account is given in the chapter on the disorders of temporomandibular joint. This aspect of pain is dealt with briefly here.

The patient experiences discomfort in the temporomandibular joint region. The pain is of chronic nature, distributed over one side of the face, particularly around temporalis and masseter muscles. It may or may not be associated with clicking of the joint and trismus. It is said that if any condition is not well understood with history of different treatment modalities, the clinician must realize that etiology is equally unclear and the specific therapy is not known. This is very true with reference to temporomandibular joint pain dysfunction syndrome. Usually the treatment starts with conservative non-surgical methods. With varying success, it ranges up to heroic and radical treatment like surgery of the joint. Much emphasis has been placed on traumatic occlusion as the important etiological factor, in spite of the fact that occlusal equilibrium has not been found to be the specific cure of this condition. Before instituting any specific treatment, the following methods may be adopted:

(1) Elimination of all the probable dental etiological factors.
(2) Appreciation of the underlying stress factor and reassurance to the patient.
(3) Tricyclic antidepressants have been used up to a maximum tolerated level for its centrally acting muscle relaxant analgesic effect and not as antidepressants.
(4) Occlusal equilibration and bite-raising appliances have been found to be useful in many cases.
(5) Severely disturbed patients benefit from psychiatric consultations.
(6) Role of radical surgery remains controversial. Hence, they must be reserved for extreme cases, where all the other measures have failed.
(7) The vulnerability of recurrent pain persists throughout life. Even if the patient gets relief, relapse is possible. Hence, periodical review of such patients is necessary.

PRIMARY NEURALGIA

Neuralgia is a paroxysmal, intermittent, excruciating pain, confining to a specific nerve distribution. The most common type of neuralgia involving orofacial region arise in relation to trigeminal nerve. The other nerves involved are glossopharyngeal nerve and superior laryngeal branch of vagus nerve. Etiology is not definitely known. The following probable causes have been attributed:

(1) Viral lesions of the ganglion.
(2) Loss of a portion of myelination which insulates the sensory axons from each other (demyelination).
(3) Dural bands or narrowing of the nerve foramina.
(4) Ill-defined foci of chronic osteitis of the jaws.
(5) Idiopathic.

Neuralgia must be differentiated from neuritis, which is an acute, reversible inflammation of the nerve resulting in pain due to specific clinical entities like pulpitis, periodontitis, sialadenitis, osteitis, etc.

The most common form of orofacial neuralgias involve maxillary or mandibular branch of trigeminal nerve called *trigeminal neuralgia.* This clinical condition is characterized by the following features:

(a) Usually affects persons beyond 40 years of age.

(b) Excruciating pain, described by the patient as "severe", "stabbing", "burning" or "shocking". It lasts for several seconds. The problem is general cyclic in nature. The pain is associated with lacrimation, flush and salivation.

(c) Pain is initiated if the *"trigger zone"* is stimulated like chewing, shaving, brushing of teeth, etc. Hence, trigger zones must be demonstrated for confirming the diagnosis of neuralgia. The most common sites involved are mental foramen and maxillary canine regions.

(d) Pain radiates along the distribution of the nerve. It does not cross the midline.

(e) Usually, such paroxysmal attacks do not disturb the patient during sleep.

(f) As the clinical condition becomes chronic, the number of attacks per day may increase so that intervals between the attacks decrease. Perhaps, this leads to constant fear in the patient's mind. So, one may not even be willing to shave, brush the teeth or wash the face, as a measure of exaggerated precautions.

(g) Clinical examination of the affected region of the face is usually hyperkeratinized, due to vigorous rubbing of the facial skin by the patient during the neuralgic attack.

(h) Periods of remission are common. This should not be confused with successful treatment. Potentially, this condition may recur at any time.

(i) This condition is not associated with any objective sensory or motor nerve deficit in the involved region.

(j) Thus, the patient becomes justifiably depressed.

(k) Such pain may be an early manifestation of clinical conditions like disseminated sclerosis or intracranial neoplasms.

Diagnosis

The diagnosis is mainly based on the clinical features as mentioned above. The diagnosis is usually made only when no etiology can be demonstrated but trigger zone can be identified. However, diagnosis is confirmed by performing the following confirmatory test.

Diagnostic test block. 0.5 ml of normal saline is injected around the trigger zone. After 5 minutes, if the patient says that pain is relieved, the diagnosis is psychogenic pain. If pain persists, injection is repeated in the same area with 0.5 ml of 2% Xylocaine hydrochloride solution. If pain is relieved, the diagnosis is confirmed as paroxysmal trigeminal neuralgia. It can be reconfirmed by the usual methods of stimulating the trigger zone to ensure that the typical neuralgic type of pain does not develop.

Treatment

(1) Anticonvulsant carbamazepine (Tegretol) 100 mg tablets one to three times a day is the treatment of choice depending on the severity and frequency of attacks. It has been observed that the patient has relief from pain, so long as the patient continues to be on this medication. The dose may have to be increased depending on the need.

Toxicity:

(a) It is essential to gradually increase the dose to avoid nausea, drowsiness and gastric irritation. Usually, as the time passes by, these symptoms tend to decrease.

(b) In some patients, allergic dermatitis has been noticed.

(c) It is known to suppress the bone marrow. Hence, the patient should be monitored constantly to avoid agranulocytosis.

(2) As an alternative, phenytoin 200-400 mg has been tried with varying success.

(3) When medications do not provide complete relief, injection of one ml of 60-90% alcohol around the nerve trunk or ganglion has been tried. Care must be taken to ensure that intravascular injection is avoided by aspiration before injecting alcohol. This provides immediate relief which may last for 9-12 months.

(4) *Peripheral neurectomy* or cryotherapy of the concerned branch eliminates the peripheral trigger effects. But the result lasts only for 12 to 18 months. Following cryotherapy, the appearances of sensation precede recurrence. Hence, this serves as a warning before the recurrence of pain.

(5) *Intracranial preganglionic selective section of the sensory root* has yielded better and long-lasting result. But this procedure must be reserved where all the other measures have failed.

(6) *Tractotomy of the spinal tract nucleus of the trigeminal nerve* was tried but now, it is abandoned because of high incidence of mortality.

(7) Recently, two procedures - peripheral radiofrequency *thermoneurolysis* and radiofrequency *thermogangliolysis* - have shown promising results but long-term evaluation is awaited.

(8) More recently, a microvascular nerve root decompression procedure has been successfully tried. It is a neurosurgical procedure involving the division or lifting of the intracranial vascular loops of superior cerebellar artery that is believed to compress the trigeminal nerve root. This procedure relieves pain without altering the sensation as in all the other surgical procedures. The long-term evaluation of this procedure is also awaited.

Secondary neuralgia

These neuralgias are due to irritation of the nerves by some demonstrable lesion and may mimic the primary paroxysmal pain.

(1) **Mental nerve neuralgia.** The lower denture flange may compress the mental nerve, if the nerve is superficially placed due to the resorption of alveolar bone. By digital compression, similar pain can be elicited. Radiologically, the mental foramen can be located at the surface of the alveolar ridge. Shifting the foramen lower down is the treatment of choice.

Sometimes, narrowing of the mental foramen may initiate a paroxysmal type of pain. Radiologically, this can be confirmed. Decompression of the mental nerve by carefully enlarging the mental foramen without the nerve damage is the treatment of choice.

(2) **Causalgia.** This is a very rare type of neuralgic pain arising at the site of nerve injury. The pain is a well localized, burning or throbbing type of pain originating from the mandibular third molar region. This is attributed to traumatic neuromas. This is one of the difficult conditions to treat. Relief can be obtained by the blockage of the sensory pathways. Cryotherapy has been tried successfully. Nerve avulsion is preferable rather than intracranial procedures like division of the sensory root.

(3) **Auriculotemporal nerve syndrome (Frey's syndrome).** This condition is known to develop in the following conditions:

(a) Diabetic neuropathy.
(b) After parotid and temporomandibular joint surgery and cervical sympathectomy.
(c) Following trauma to the parotid region.

Clinical features:

(a) Burning sensation at the temporal and facial region.
(b) Flushing and profuse sweating in the region during eating.
(c) Occasional hyperalgesia between the attacks.

Pathogenesis:

(a) In diabetic neuropathy, it may be due to lack of inhibitory sympathetic tone.
(b) In the postsurgical and posttraumatic group, it may be due to parasympathetic secretomotor fibre reinnervation of the cut ends of sympathetic vasomotor fibres.

Treatment:

(a) Conservatively treated by parasympathomimetic blockade. Unfortunately, it may produce xerostomia and constipation.
(b) Topical application of anticholinergic cream (2% hyoscine) may provide relief for a few days.
(c) Surgical avulsion of auriculotemporal nerve is not helpful.

(4) **Postherpetic neuralgia.** This type of neuralgia develops with untreated herpes zoster. It is seen as a persistent burning pain in an area of diminished sensation. It is considered to be due to the damage of large myelinated sensory fibres by the Herpes virus. The pain gradually disappears in 12-24 months time. It can be treated with analgesics supplemented with tricyclic antidepressant drug.

(5) **Disseminated sclerosis.** This condition may be indistinguishable from idiopathic form of trigeminal neuralgia. The associated neurological features are disturbances to sensations of the face, loss of taste and many other neurological deficits. These symptoms characteristically disseminate in

varied anatomical sites. No specific treatment is known. The treatment is similar to the one advocated for the primary neuralgias.

(6) **Eagle's syndrome:** *Orofacial pain* associated with elongation of styloid process of temporal bone was first described by Eagle in 1937. He later described two distinct categories - classical Eagle's syndrome and carotid artery syndrome—2 to 4% of the general population present with evidence of ossification of the stylohyoid. Majority of them are asymptomatic. The symptomatic patients are over 40 years of age. Four typical symptoms of this syndrome are: facial pain, tinnitus, problems with swallowing and pain on turning the head. Steinman has proposed three theories to explain the "elongation" of the styloid process.

(a) *Theory of reactive hyperplasia:* If the styloid process is stimulated, e.g., trauma, ossification may occur.
(b) *Theory of reactive metaplasia:* It involves a traumatic stimulus so as to induce the ligament to undergo metaplastic changes in the form of ossification.
(c) *Theory of anatomic variance:* Radiographic evidence of ossification in children and young adolescents without any history of cervicopharyngeal trauma.

Based on the radiographic appearance of the elongated styloid process and mineralized styloid ligament, they have been classified into three types: Type I is elongated, type II is pseudoarticulated and type III is segmented.

Normal styloid process is a thin, narrow bony process, around 25 mm long. Tip of the process is positioned between internal and external carotid arteries, lying lateral to the pharyngeal wall and posterior to tonsillar fossa. Its base is located near the stylomastoid foramen. The three muscles attached are styloglossus to the tip, stylohyoid to the middle portion and stylopharyngeus to the base. Two ligaments attached are stylohyoid and stylomandibular ligaments.

Clinical features: The classical syndrome may develop following tonsillectomy. The patient develops a sensation of foreign body in the pharynx, referred pain over the ear, dysphagia and persitent sore throat. Pain is attributed to the stimulation of V, VII, IX and X cranial nerves.

In carotid artery syndrome, symptoms are related to stimulation of sympathetic nerves around the walls of the carotid artery. If the internal carotid artery is impinged, pain radiates over the entire head from the ophthalmic region to the occiput. If the external carotid is impinged, pain is felt in the neck or radiating to the eye.

Diagnosis: This is based on history of the presenting illness and thorough review of T.M. joint. The pain is precipitated by the palpation over the styloid process. Tomographic radiography with mouth open position will reveal the degree of impingement of the styloid process on the related structures.

Treatment: (a) nonsurgical (b) surgical.

Nonsurgical: A transpharyngeal injection of steroids and lignocaine may provide relief temporarily. Under local anesthesia, through transpharyngeal manipulation, manual fracturing of of the elongated styloid process has been tried.

Surgical: Transpharyngeal approach to the styloid process is used. After palpation, by using styloid process in the tonsillar fossa as a landmark, a 1 cm long incision is made over the mucosa. After the exposure, tip can be removed with rongeur forceps and the edges are smoothened.

Through an extra oral approach also, it can be exposed. The disadvantage is the length of surgical time, morbidity and disturbance to the adjacent vital structures.

PAIN AROUND NEARBY REGIONS

(1) **Maxillary sinus.** In acute maxillary sinusitis, the pain is dull and sometimes severe. It gets aggravated with upright posture. The pain may radiate along the maxillary premolar and molar teeth. The patient gives history of recent upper

respiratory tract infection and nasal discharge. Radiologically, sinus will be radio-opaque.

In chronic sinusitis, nasal obstruction with persistent pain is present. Radiologically, sinus will be radioopaque due to mucosal thickening and polyp formation. This condition is readily identifiable.

(2) **Tongue.** Pain over the tongue may be sharp, burning and referred to the ear. It is provoked by spicy or hot food. They may be due to aphthous ulcers, erosive lichen planus or atrophic glossitis due to iron deficiency. Pain may be the first symptom in carcinomatous ulcers of the tongue. When in doubt, biopsy is necessary to confirm the nature of the ulcer.

(3) **Angina pectoris.** Sometimes, pain in angina pectoris manifests itself as pain at the left angle of the mandible, over the area of distribution of great auricular nerve from the cervical plexus. Pain is felt on effort. ECG will reveal the features of ischemic heart disease. If this phenomenon is not borne in mind, a dental extraction in such patients will definitely lead to very serious consequences.

(4) **Burning mouth.** This is often considered to be of psychological origin. The organic disease entities suspected by being etiologic or contributory are as follows:

(a) Hyperglycemia (diabetes mellitus)
(b) Pernicious anemia
(c) Moniliasis
(d) Physical trauma
(e) Geographic tongue.

The following diagnostic protocol has been suggested when a patient presents with a complaint of "burning mouth".

(a) Complete oral examination must be carried out. The clinical investigations with special emphasis on detecting lesions, which might be associated with anemia, diabetes, moniliasis, geographic tongue, malnutrition, local irritation and trauma.

(b) History should be taken with emphasis on psychiatric disorders and the associated systemic diseases like peptic ulcer, spastic colon, ulcerative colitis, administration of medications, anxiety, worry, fear, stress and depression.

(c) Investigations. Complete hemogram, blood glucose level, cultures for candida albicans and if necessary, histopathological diagnosis, salivary analysis and radiographic examination should be performed.

LOCAL ANESTHESIA

General considerations

The field of local anesthesia has proved to be one of the safe, accepted modalities of pain control in dental practice. With advances in medications and techniques, clinical dentistry has been elevated from its image as a "painful experience" to a clinical "painless service". In this direction, local anesthesia can even be considered as a "back bone" to contemporary dental and oral surgery practice. Till date, many methods have been known to produce regional anesthesia.

(1) Trauma to the sensory nerve.
   (a) Mechanical
   (b) Chemical irritants as neurolytic agents, e.g., alcohol, phenol.
(2) Hypothermia (lowering the temperature)
(3) Anoxia (local or regional)
(4) Chemicals, e.g., local anesthesia agents.

Historically, cocaine was the first drug tried to produce surface anesthesia. In an attempt to retard the absorption of the drug, cool spray was used to produce vasoconstriction. Incidentally, hypothermia was found to produce transient local anesthesia effect. Soon, procaine was widely used but it was found to produce systemic toxic effects. The introduction of xylocaine, development of newer anesthetic techniques and better understanding of the mechanism of pain were responsible for giving a new dimension to the field of local anesthesia and pain control. Therefore, it is very essential for every dental practitioner to possess adequate knowledge on all the important aspects of this fascinating field.

Neurophysiology

The understanding of the mechanism of generation and transmission of the pain impulses are necessary to learn the concept of pain control through the use of local anesthetics. Basically, the conduction of an impulse by a sensory nerve depends on the electric potential that is present across the cell membrane and the transmission of the impulses along its length by the flow of current across the cell membrane from the resting to the active state. The local anesthetic drug is the chemical that blocks the passage of the impulses. In other words, it creates a reversible blockage between the source of impulses and the brain at the site of local anesthesia. Many theories have been proposed to explain the phenomenon of mode of action of the local anesthetic drugs. Neuron is an architectural unit of the nervous system, mainly concerned with the transmission of messages from different parts of the body to the brain. The sensory neuron is composed of three parts.

(1) Dendrite is the most distal segment, containing arborization of free nerve endings.

(2) Axon is a thin, long, cable-like structure. At its central end, the arborization is very similar to dendrite zone.

(3) The cell body is located away from the axon. Hence, it is not involved in the transmission of impulses. Its function is to provide metabolic support for the entire neuron.

The **neural cytoplasm (axoplasm)** is encased in a sheath called neurilemma. The axoplasm is a gelatinous substance, which is separated from the extracellular fluids by the nerve membrane. The nerve cell-membrane is a thin, elastic covering composed of a layer of lipid between the two layers of protein. The membrane is believed to contain many pores through which ions can diffuse. In the resting state, electrolytic solution containing equal concentrations of cations and anions are present on both the sides of the membranes. The process of excitability of sensory nerve and conduction of the impulses are considered to be due to changes that develop within the cell membrane. The resting nerve membrane has an electric resistance, nearly 50 times more than that of intracellular and extracellular fluids, thereby preventing the passage of ions. When the nerve is at rest, a number of negative anions (potassium) are present inside the cell membrane, while, equal number of positive cations (sodium and chloride) are present outside the cell membrane. The difference in the concentration of the respective ions across the membrane creates a potential electrical difference between positive on the outside and negative on the inside. The ionic imbalance can develop by the active diffusion of the ions from either side across the membrane. The nerve at rest is believed to have the resting potential during which, membrane is polarized and thus there is a potential source of energy. The polarization of the membrane continues until the nerve is in the resting state. When the impulses pass along the nerve, electric conductivity of the nerve membrane increases many fold. This readily permits sodium and potassium ions to diffuse through the membrane. Movement of these ions readily provide a source of energy for the conduction of the impulses along the nerve. The impulse produces an initial phase of slow depolarization. The membrane is activated by the alteration in its permeability which emits sodium to diffuse through the membrane into the cell is followed by the passage of potassium out of the cell. This abolishes the resting potential, thereby depolarizing the membrane. It will be more appropriate to call it as reversal of polarity rather than depolarization. When the electric potential reaches a critical level, a rapid phase of reversal of polarity results, known as threshold potential. All these changes depend on the selective permeability of the nerve membrane to sodium and potassium ions and the electrolytes concentration in the nerve cell. The negative potassium ions, present within the axoplasm, restrain the positive sodium ions by electrostatic attraction. Positively charged chloride ions continue to remain outside the membrane.

In myelinated nerves, stimulation takes place only at the nodes of Ranvier. The impulse is conducted along the nerve from one node to the other. Such jumping of the impulse from one node to another through the interstitial tissues are known as saltatory conduction. Following the reversal of polarity (*depolarization*), the permeability of membrane gradually decreases. This results in the reversal of electric potential and restoration of equilibrium and resting potential. This is known as *repolarization*. The spread of impulses is a relatively slow forward creeping process in unmyelinated nerve fibres.

Desirable properties of an ideal local anesthetic drug

(1) The drug must have the specific action on the nerves.
(2) Action of the drug on the nerve must be reversible. It must be capable of inducing a temporary interference to the nerve conduction.
(3) Should not be injurious to the tissues.
(4) Should have low or no systemic toxicity.
(5) Onset of anesthesia must be rapid and the effect must be of sufficient duration but not too prolonged.
(6) The drug when injected, must be able to readily undergo biotransformation.
(7) Should be stable in solution form with adequate shelf-life.
(8) The drug must be sterilizable without losing its potency.
(9) The drug should possess adequate safety margin.
(10) It must be economical.

No drug fulfills all these criteria. The systemic toxicity is directly proportional to the potency.

Mode of action of local anesthesia

There are many theories to explain the mechanism of local anesthesia. However, general agreement exists on the following aspects:

(1) The primary site of action is the nerve membrane, the outer bimolecular lipoprotein layer.

(2) The primary effect of the local anesthetic drug is to decrease the permeability of the nerve membrane to sodium ions. Permeability to potassium ions is relatively insignificant.

(3) The calcium ions, present in bound form within the cell membrane, exert a regulatory role on the movement of sodium ions across the cell membrane.

(4) Binding of the local anesthesia molecule in the receptor site and blockade of sodium channel are to stabilize the nerve membrane in the polarized state so that the nerve conduction is blocked.

(5) While all the neurolytic materials like phenol and alcohol also possess the ability to block the nerve conduction, the action of local anesthetics on the nerve is reversible in contrast to the neurolytic chemicals.

(6) The local anesthetics alter the mechanism of initiating action potential due to sodium ions gaining entry into the cell. Since electric potential remains unchanged, local currents do not occur. Thus, transmission of impulses are interfered with. When the impulses reach the blocked nerve segment, it is prevented to pass beyond this site. Such a blockade produced by local anesthetics is called non-depolarizing nerve block. It progressively lowers the amplitude of the action potential and retards the velocity of impulse conduction until the nerve is rendered blocked. However, the exact site of action is still not clear. It is possible that these drugs interfere with excitation process of the nerve membrane in any of the following ways:

(a) By altering the basic resting potential of the cell membrane or the threshold potential.
(b) By retarding the depolarization.
(c) By prolonging the repolarization phase.

The following theories have been suggested to explain the phenomenon of mode of action.

(i) Acetylcholine theory.
(ii) Calcium displacement theory.
(iii) Surface charge theory.
(iv) Membrane expansion theory.
(v) Specific receptor hypothesis.

(i) ***Acetylcholine theory.*** This theory is involved in the nerve conduction, in addition to its role as a neurotransmitter at the nerve synapse. No evidence is available to prove this hypothesis.

(ii) ***Calcium displacement theory.*** Anesthesia is produced by the displacement of calcium from the membrane site that controls permeability to sodium. But varying the concentration of calcium ions around the nerve has no effect on the potency of local anesthetic. Although it was popular, now its credibility has decreased.

(iii) ***Surface charge theory.*** Local anesthetics act by binding the molecules to the nerve membrane and changing the electric potential at the surface of the membrane. The resting potential of the nerve membrane is not altered by local anesthetics. They do not become hyperpolarized. This theory does not explain the activity of uncharged anesthetic molecules.

(iv) ***Membrane expansion theory.*** This theory postulates that the local anesthetic molecules diffuse to hydrophilic regions of excitable membranes thereby expanding a few critical regions in the membrane. An increased pressure within the nerve produces constriction of the pores through which, sodium ions pass during depolarization. This is considered to prevent the permeability of sodium ions. By virtue of these agents being lipid soluble, they produce changes in the lipoprotein matrix of the cell membrane, sodium influx and neural excitation. However, there is no direct evidence that nerve conduction is blocked by membrane expansion.

(v) ***Specific receptor hypothesis.*** This is the most popular and widely accepted theory which explains by the attachment of the drug to the specific receptor site in the nerve membrane. This hypothesis postulates that, biochemical and electrophysiological evidence indicate the existence of specific receptor site - either at or near the sodium channel in the nerve membrane. The external receptor site is on the external surface or on the internal axoplasmic surface of the sodium channel. Once the local anesthetic molecule gains access to the receptor, sodium ion permeability decreases and hence, nerve conduction is interrupted.

General features of local anesthetics

(1) None of these theories can be considered to be conclusive. Local anesthetics differ from most of the other drugs. Irrespective of the route of administration, they ultimately circulate in the blood stream in sufficient concentration to exert the clinical effect, once they are absorbed into the blood stream from the site of administration.

(2) Many of these drugs have the pharmacological action of vasodilatation.

(3) Most of the injectable local anesthetics are tertiary amines. Structurally, a typical local anesthetic has a large lipophilic part (an aromatic derived from benzoic acid or aniline), a hydrophilic part (an amino derivative of ethyl alcohol or acetic acid) and an intermediate hydrocarbon chain containing ester or amide linkage. Based on chemical linkage, this group of drugs can be divided into two groups: (a) Ester compounds and (b) amide type of compounds. It is the nature of linkage which decides the properties and mode of biotransformation. The drug which lack the hydraulic part is suitable only as a topical anesthetic and not for injection. Other chemicals like anticholinergic and antihistamines which share their basic structures exhibit weak local anesthetic properties.

The ester-linked local anesthetics like Procaine are hydrolyzed in aqueous solution. But amide-linked drugs like Lidocaine are relatively resistant to hydrolysis. It has been found that most of the amide-linked drugs are excreted in the unchanged form in the urine. The injectable local anesthetics are dispensed as hydrochloride salts, dissolved in saline or sterile water, since they are soluble in water and comparatively stable.

(4) All are synthetic chemicals.

(5) All of them are compatible with epinephrine and allied drugs.

(6) All of them produce systemic toxic effects in higher plasma concentrations.

(7) They are incompatible with metals like mercury, silver, etc.

(8) They undergo biotransformation in liver or hydrolyzed by plasma cholinesterase.

(9) These drugs have effect on central nervous system.

(10) They also inhibit the contractility of the heart muscle.

(11) In general, potency depends on its chemical structure, while duration of anesthetics is influenced by the molecular configuration which can be altered by adding the vasoconstrictor.

The following are the drugs, commonly used in dentistry:

	Ester group	*Non-ester group*
(a)	Benzoic acid esters e.g., cocaine and benzocaine as topical (Carbocaine) anesthesia	e.g., lidocaine (Xylocaine), bupivacaine and mepivacaine
(b)	Para-amino-benzoic-acid esters e.g., procaine and tetracaine.	

Effectiveness of the local anesthesia

Many factors play important roles in modifying the action of the local anesthetics. Hence, every practitioner must be aware of the relative roles of these factors.

(1) **pH of the local anesthetic.** They are weak alkaloid bases combined with hydrochloric acid to form water soluble salts. The salt exists in two molecular forms simultaneously: (a) uncharged molecules called base and (b) positively charged molecules called cation in equilibirium with each other. The relative proportion of each form depends on pH of the solution or the local tissues. The anesthetic solution exits in cationic form in low pH. When pH and pKa (dissociation constant) are the same, exactly half the drug exists in cationic form and the rest as free base. When a hydrogen ion concentration decreases, as in higher pH, equilibrium shifts towards the free-base form. It is found that, lower pka possesses more rapid onset of anesthesia. pKa for the popular local anesthetic drugs are as follows:

Mepivacaine	7.6
Lidocaine	7.9
Prilocaine	7.9
Bupivacaine	8.1
Procaine	9.1

Acidification of the tissues at the site of injection decreases the action of the drug. For example, the infected and inflamed areas are acidic with a pH of 5 to 6, while pH of the normal tissues is 7.4. Hence, low tissue pH interferes with the development of anesthesia by preventing depolarization of free base.

During the manufacturing phase, the local anesthetics containing epinephrine are acidified to inhibit the oxidation of epinephrine. Hence, pH of the drug without epinephrine is 5.5 to 7.00 while with epinephrine, it is around 5. When this is injected into the tissue, the buffering capacity of the tissue fluids raise the pH back to 7.4.

Retardation of oxidation to increase the shelf-life is achieved by the addition of antioxidants like sodium bisulfite in 0.05 to 0.1% concentration. By the addition of the antioxidant, 2% Xylocaine with a pH of 7.4 is lowered to 4.2. The buffering capacity of the normal tissue restores the pH of the solution from 4.2 to 7.4 but it takes time. Hence, the onset of action of the drug is slow when compared to the drug without epinephrine.

(2) **Type and size of the nerve.** Adequate amount of the drug should penetrate the nerve before the conduction of the impulses could be blocked. Hence, the type and size of the nerve are important factors in the production of satisfactory anesthesia.

(a) Myelinated fibres required greater concentration of the drug and more time for the onset of anesthesia, because of the insulating barrier, (myelin sheath).

(b) The larger the diameter of the nerve, the greater the concentration of the drug required for blocking the conduction of impulses.

(3) **Barrier to the solution.**

(a) The anesthetic drug is effective on axons and the nerve endings. But, it is unable to penetrate the intact skin. Hence, the drug cannot anesthetize the skin. However, it can cross the injured skin and intact mucous membrane.

(b) The peripheral nerves have numerous tightly packed axons, which are protected, well supported and nourished by layers of fibrous and elastic tissues. The axons are insulated by endoneurium. The perineurium binds the nerve fibres into bundles called fasciculi. The thicker the perineurium the slower the diffusion of the drug. The innermost layer of the perineurium is ***perilemma*** which is the main barrier for the drug to diffuse into the nerve, although diffusion through epineurium is fast due to its loose consistency. Some amount of drug enters the nutrient blood vessels and lymphatics. However, epineural sheath does not constitute a barrier for the local anesthetic drug to diffuse into the nerve.

(4) **Induction of local anesthesia.** When the drug is deposited into the soft tissues around the nerve, the local anesthetic molecules move according to the concentration-gradient. During the induction phase, the drug molecules move from the extra neural site towards the nerve known as ***diffusion***. It refers to the migration of ions through the fluid medium under the influence of the concentration-gradient. Penetration refers to the diffusion of the drug through the anatomical barrier which tend to restrict free molecular movement. The rate of diffusion of the drug depends on the concentration gradient. If the initial concentration of the drug is greater, diffusion of the molecules is more, resulting in rapid onset of anesthesia.

The fasciculi near the surface are called ***mantle bundles***. They are exposed to higher concentration of drugs earlier. The bundles near the centre are known as ***core bundle***. They come under the influence of the drug later. By the time the drug reaches the core bundles, it becomes increasingly diluted. The core fibres innervate molars and premolars while the mantle bundles innervate the anterior teeth. This explains the reason for occasional inadequate pulpal anesthesia in posterior teeth. When the local anesthetic drug is injected around the nerve, it tends to diffuse in different directions. Hence, only a portion of the drug diffuses towards the nerve. Some amount of the drug is absorbed by neural tissues like muscle, fat etc. The interstitial fluid dilutes the drug, some absorbed by vessels and ester group of drugs are hydrolyzed. Therefore, only a portion of the drug diffuses into the nerve, until the equilibrium of the drug concentration takes place inside and outside the nerve.

The induction time refers to the time taken after the deposition of the anesthetic solution for effecting the blockade. It is seen that (a) concentration of the drug, (b) pH of the solution (which are under the operator's control, (c) the diffusion constant for the anesthetic agent and (d) the anatomical diffusion barriers ultimately decide the induction of local anesthesia.

(5) **Potency of the drug.** The lipid solubility of the drug seems to be closely related to the intrinsic potency of the drug. The penetration of the drug is directly proportional to increased lipid solubility since the nerve membrane contains nearly 90% of lipid. After the drug penetrates the nerve sheath, equilibrium occurs between the base and cationic form. The charged cationic form binds itself to the protein receptor site. It is seen that the degree of protein binding of the anesthetic molecules is responsible for the duration of anesthesia.

(6) **Duration of anesthesia** (Table 17.1).

(a) As the anesthetic effect passes off, the function of the nerve recovers rapidly to start with but later, it gradually slows down. Therefore the onset of anesthesia is rapid but the recovery is slow. The long-acting local anesthetics like bupivacaine and tetracaine are bound to the nerve sheath more firmly than drugs like procaine and lidocaine. Therefore, the drug is released slowly, thereby duration of anesthesia is also prolonged.

Table 17.1 Duration of anesthetic effect

Agent	Approximate lipid	Percentage of the effective concentration	Approximate protein binding	Approximate duration of action in minutes
1. Procaine	0.02	2%	6	60-90
2. Lidocaine	2.90	2%	65	90-200
3. Mepivacaine	0.8	1-3%	5	120-240
4. Bupivacaine	27.5	0.5-0.75%	95	180-600
5. Prilocaine	0.9	4%	55	100-240
6. Tetracaine	0.14	0.25%	75	180-600

(b) The duration of anesthesia is increased in the areas of decreased vascularity. This observation has led to the addition of vasoconstrictor with the local anesthetic drug to prolong the duration of anesthesia. If the drug does not contain any vasoconstrictor, the relative vasodilator property of the anesthetic drug results in increased blood flow. This may lead to any of the following:

(i) The drug may be removed from the site quickly resulting in decreased duration of anesthesia.

(ii) Increased rate of absorption runs the risk of increased systemic toxicity.

(iii) Due to the vasodilating effect, the increased blood flow at the site of administration may lead to increased bleeding.

To overcome all these problems, vasoconstrictors are added (a) to control the tissue perfusion of the drug, (b) to decrease the toxicity of the drug, (c) to increase the drug to come in contact with the nerve for more time to prolong the duration of anesthesia and (d) to decrease the blood flow at the site of injection.

When vasoconstrictors are used (adrenaline or nor-adrenaline) along with the local anesthetic drug, the effect of vasoconstrictor is chemically identical to the mediators of sympathetic nervous system. In other words, the action is sympathomimetic.

Pharmacologically, there are three possibilities of mode of action of sympathomimetic amines.

(a) *Direct action.* The vasoconstrictor can exert its action directly on the adrenergic receptors. Activation of alpha receptor produces constriction of smooth muscle in blood vessels. Activation of beta receptors relaxes the smooth muscles producing vasodilatation and bronchodilatation.

The drugs acting on adrenergic receptors are epinephrine, nor-adrenaline, levonordefrin, isoproterofrol, dopamine, methoxamine.

(b) *Indirect action,* e.g., amphetamine, tyramine. These drugs act by releasing nor-epinephrine from the adrenergic nerve terminal.

(c) *Mixed action,* e.g., ephedrine. This drug possess both direct and indirect action.

Epinephrine is highly water-soluble acid salt. Weak acid solution is relatively stable. The deterioration by oxidation can be hastened by heat and light. Sodium bisulfite is used to delay its deterioration through oxidation thereby increasing the shelf life of the local anesthetic solution containing adrenaline. Lidocaine with adrenaline in the concentration of 1:2,00,000 is being used in clinical dental practice. Usually, physicians request the dental surgeons not to use the local anesthetics with adrenaline in cardiac and hypertensive patients. To avoid or minimize the systemic complications in such patient, the following precautions can be taken:

(i) Its use must be restricted to the minimum possible.

(ii) In hypertensive patients with more than 200

mm of Hg systolic and 120 mm of Hg diastolic pressure, it is preferably avoided.

(iii) It must be used with great caution in patients with uncontrolled hyperthyroidism.

(iv) In cardiac patients, cardiologist's advice must be obtained regarding the use of local anesthetics with adrenaline.

(v) In patients under general anesthesia with halogenated agents, adrenaline is not to be used.

As per ASA-classification of patients-at-risk, local anesthetics with vasoconstrictor should be used with great caution.

Levarterenol (non-epinephrine) is relatively stable in acid solutions. It has a shelf-life of about 18 months. Acetone sodium bisulfite is added by the manufacturers to retard its deterioration. It is about 25% as potent as epinephrine. In risk patients, it is preferred as an alternative to epinephrine. It acts on alfa receptors.

Levonordefrin is freely soluble in dilute acidic solution. Sodium bisulfite is added by the manufacturers to retard its deterioration. Its shelf-life is around 18 months. It also acts through alpha-receptors. It is about 15% as potent as epinephrine.

The choice of the vasoconstrictors depends on the following factors:

(a) *Medical status of the patient.* Whether the patient is medially compromised or not.

(b) *Duration of anesthesia.* Prolongation of duration of anesthesia is effective in the above order (more in epinephrine). (Table 17.1)

(c) *Need for hemostasis.* All these vasoconstrictors produce hemostasis at the site of injection. But it has a rebound beta effect after the alfa-induced vasoconstrictor effect passes off, resulting in the increased blood loss.

In general, it is found that the vasoconstrictors (i) improve the quality of pain control of the local anesthetic drug, (ii) prolong the duration of anesthesia and (iii) decrease the toxicity of the drug. Unless it is contraindicated, it must be added. Care must always be taken to avoid intravascular injection by aspiration and also by slow administration of the local anesthetic drugs.

(7) **Recovery from anesthetic effect.** The recovery from the local anesthesia follows the same pattern of diffusion of the drug but in the reverse order. The concentration of the drug is extra neurally depleted faster but the intraneural concentration remains relatively stable. The reversal of concentration gradient and the higher concentration of the drug intraneurally result in the diffusion of the drug out of the nerve. The mantle fibres lose the drug more than the core fibres. This is responsible for the earlier recovery from anesthesia in anteriors when compared to the posterior teeth. But generally, recovery is a slow process when compared to the induction phase. The local anesthetic drug is always found to be released slowly when compared to its absorption.

(8) **Tachyphylaxis.** It refers to the increasing tolerance to a drug if given repeatedly. For example, if the pain sensation returns back before the reinjection, the duration, intensity and the depth of anesthesia are reduced. The factors considered to be responsible for such a phenomenon are edema, localized bleeding, clot-formation, hypernatremia and decreased pH of the tissues at the injection site. Most of these factors prevent the drug to come in contact with the nerve. But hypernatremia raises the sodium ion gradient. The change in pH into acidic state renders the drug ineffective.

(9) **Lipid solubility.** The lipid solubility of the anesthetic agent is related to its potency. Increased lipid solubility results in better penetration of the drug through the membrane since it contains lipid. Greater lipid solubility leads to effective conduction blockage at lower concentration of the drug. Likewise, higher degree of protein binding of the local anesthetic drug molecule results in longer duration of the anesthesia.

(10) **Biotransformation of the drug.** It depends on the nature of the intermediate chain, ester or amide linkage. If it is of ester group, the drug is inactivated by hydrolysis (water molecule added to the ester

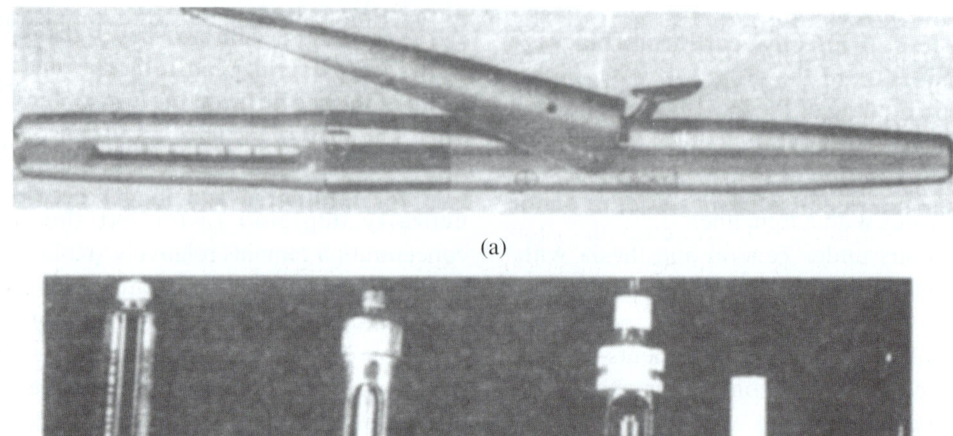

(a)

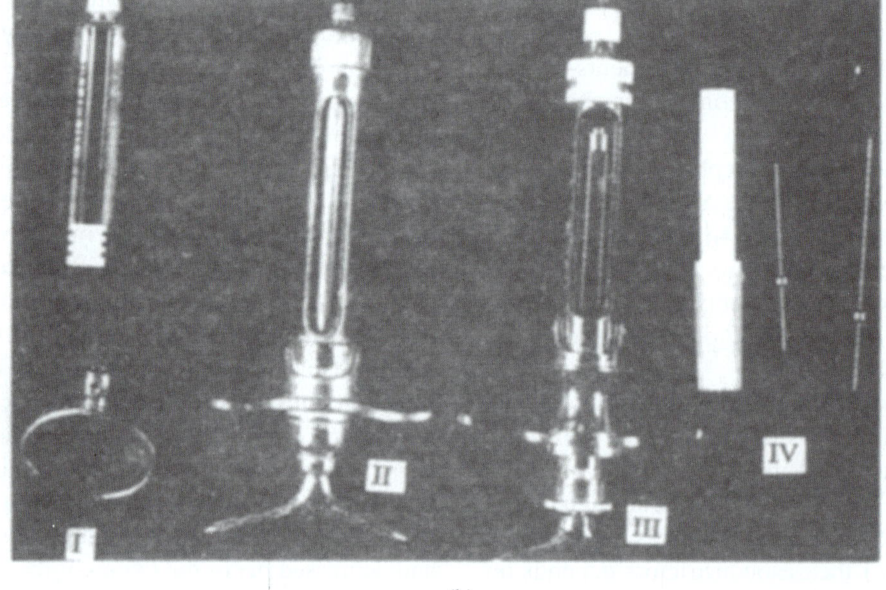

(b)

Fig. 17.1 Anesthesia and control of orofacial pain: **(a)** Syringe for intraligamental injection, **(b)** Cartridge syringe: (i) cartridge and handle, (ii) cartridge syringe, (iii) cartridge syringe with aspiration device and (iv) disposable needles - short and long.

linkage). It occurs in plasma by the enzyme plasma cholinesterase. It may also occur in liver. Depending on the structural formula, the drug is metabolized. If it is amide type, it undergoes biotransformation in the liver. Subsequently, it is by hydrolysis. The end-products of the reaction are excreted by kidney.

A small fraction (10% of amides) may appear in urine unchanged. Cocaine is excreted completely in altered form by the kidneys. Some believe that hepatic or renal disturbances are the relative contraindications. But it can be used with caution.

General guidelines for local anesthesia

Syringe (Fig 17.1 a, b). There are many options open for the dental surgeon in the choice of the syringe. They are:

(1) Disposable plastic syringe.

(2) Cartridge syringe.

  (a) Breach-loading, non-aspiration type.

  (b) Breach-loading, aspiration type.

  (c) Special type, e.g., syringe for intraligamental anesthesia.

If cartridges are not available, disposable plastic

2 ml syringes can be used. It is better to avoid using glass syringes since, asepsis is not under the control of the operator, if they are used after resterilization. Moreover, the patient may accidentally bite the glass syringe during the injection procedure. The metallic cartridge syringe has a barrel to hold the cartridge on one end and needle adapter with piston on the other side. It pushes the rubber plunger of the cartridge towards the inner end of the needle so that solution is driven out of the cartridge. The barrel has a convenient finger bar.

Needle. This only pierces the tissues to convey the drug. Stainless-steel needles are recommended. Presterilized disposable cartridge needles are available in the market for ready use.

The cartridge needle has a bevel, shank, hub and the shorter pointed syringe end. In the conventional needles, the tip of the needle lies at the lower edge of the needle shaft. The shaft of the needle varies depending on the needle gauge (lumen) and length. Shorter needles are used for infiltration and longer needles for block anesthesia.

The end of the needle towards the barrel is relatively shorter and pointed to facilitate the tip of the needle to pierce the rubber diaphragm of the cartridge. Hence, this portion of the needle will be inside the cartridge during the injection technique. The syringe adapter is metallic, while it is plastic in disposable cartridge syringes. It has been observed that during the injection procedures, the needle deflects to the side inside the tissues, depending on the gauge of the needle. The length is 40 mm (15/8 inches) for long needles while 25 mm (I inch) for shorter needles. Irrespective of the technique and length of the needle, at least one-third of the needle must always be outside the tissues. Injection with disposable needles are painless. If the needles are repeatedly sterilized and reused, tip of the bevel bends and the blunt tip forms a hook so that, it can lacerate the soft tissues during withdrawal and hence can be very painful. The needle should never be forced against any resistance during injection.

Dental cartridge. It is a glass cylinder. It is manufactured to contain 1.8 ml, 2 ml, or 2.2 ml of the drug. The cylindrical glass tube has rubber diaphragm with aluminium cap on one end and a mobile rubber stopper at the other end of the fluid column.

Basic principles

It is ironical that the very act of local anesthetic injection is intended for the control of pain, but the injection of pain-relieving drug itself produces high level of anxiety of pain. In order to administer the local anesthetic drug in a non-painful, atraumatic manner, care must be directed to important components of such atraumatic injection technique. They are (a) technical aspect, (b) communicative aspect. Both are equally important for achieving painless injection.

Covering both these aspects, the following are some of the important guidelines to be followed routinely:

(1) Sterilized or presterilized sharp needle must be selected. If the needle has already been used, tip of the needle must be checked to ensure that it is sharp. Insertion will be painful if it is blunt. Withdrawal is also painful because, hook tears the tissue. The gauge and length have no relevance to pain. It depends on the technique.

(2) Free flow of the local anesthetic solution should be ensured prior to use. By this way, air-bubbles, if any, are also eliminated.

(3) The patient is positioned comfortably. In the presence of anxiety, blood flow is selectively increased towards the muscles. Vasodepressor syncope may develop because of the inability of the heart to supply the brain with an adequate volume of oxygenated blood. Due to the upright posture, pressure falls in the cerebral arteries. Slight decrease in cerebral blood flow leads to syncope. That is why, the posture of the patient is very important to avoid this complication.

(4) After clearing the site of injection to remove the debris, surface anesthetic jelly is applied to

anesthetize the mucous membrane. It must be allowed to be in contact at least for one minute.

(5) Since the patient is anxious about painful injection, the operator must communicate with the patient about the purpose of application of the topical anesthetic. Care must be taken to avoid using words like "injection" or "pain". The word "discomfort" seems to be more appropriate instead of the word "pain".

(6) After establishing a firm hand support, the tissue is penetrated with the needle accurately. To a great extent, this will resist the undesirable movement of the arms of the apprehensive patients during the anesthetic administration. Simultaneously, the tissues at the injection site should be stretched before the injection, so that the needle pierces the tissues with minimum of resistance. Loose tissues produce more discomfort. During the injection procedure, as far as possible, the needle must be kept out of sight of the patient for better cooperation, irrespective of the age.

(7) As the needle is inserted into tissues, the patient's reaction is carefully watched. To distract the attention, it is essential to communicate constantly.

(8) The patient's general reaction, level of consciousness, color of the skin and mucous membrane and pupillary reactions must be carefully observed at the time of injecting the drug slowly. Simultaneously, the needle is advanced towards the target.

(9) Before injecting the drug, it is always better to aspirate, to ensure that injection is not intravascular.

(10) During the deposition of the solution and slow withdrawal of the syringe, the operator must continue to communicate with the patient. At no stage, patient should be left unattended, after administering the local anesthetic drug.

Techniques of local anesthesia

(A) Surface anesthesia

(B) Infiltration anesthesia

- (a) Submucosal
- (b) Supraperiosteal
- (c) Subperiosteal
- (d) Intraosseus
- (e) Pericemental
- (f) Intrapulpal

(C) Block (conduction) anesthesia

- (a) Inferior alveolar (dental)
- (b) Mental
- (c) Infraorbital
- (d) Posterior superior alveolar

(A) Surface anesthesia

This is effective only on the mucous membrane surfaces. Surface anesthesia can be achieved by cool spray or by the application of the local anesthetic drug in higher concentration (4% Xylocaine). Immediately, the mucous membrane becomes insensitive. This method is indicated in the following clinical situations:

- (a) Site of injection.
- (b) Incision and drainage of abscess.
- (c) Prior to periodontal treatment.
- (d) To relieve pain from painful ulcers of the mucosa.
- (e) To avoid troublesome gagging during the impression techniques in hypertensive patients.

The onset of anesthesia is immediate but it is of short duration. No injection is involved in this technique. Therefore, this is a helpful adjunct in local anesthetic practice.

(B) Infiltration anesthesia

The practitioner must carefully assess before choosing the type of anesthesia (whether infiltration or block). The following factors are to be considered if infiltration anesthesia is chosen:

- (a) Bone is cancellous.
- (b) Duration of anesthesia is less.
- (c) The field of anesthesia is small.
- (d) If bloodless operative field is needed,

infiltration of local anesthetic drug with vasoconstrictor is preferable.

The following are the contraindications for infiltration anesthesia:

(a) If the bone is cortical;

(b) If anesthesia required is for longer duration;

(c) If wider field of anesthesia is required;

(d) In acutely inflamed and infected regions, infiltration is contraindicated, since local anesthetic is not effective in the acidic medium. Moreover, injection into the infected area may result in spread of infection along the injection stream to the neighboring areas. Increased tension in such areas will make the injection very painful.

The foregoing discussion reveals that infiltration anesthesia is indicated for the routine oral surgery concerning all the maxillary teeth and mandibular anterior teeth.

Infiltration for maxillary teeth. The most commonly employed method is *supraperiosteal* injection for anesthetizing anterior superior dental plexus formed by superior dental nerves and *subperiosteal* injection for the inner superior dental plexus formed by greater palatine and incisive nerves. If infiltration is contraindicated, infraorbital and posterior superior alveolar blocks are useful.

Buccal-labial anesthesia (Supraperiosteal)

(1) Bevel of the needle must face the bone. After cleaning the surface, topical anesthetic is applied around the mucobuccal fold to make the injection painless.

(2) Syringe is held parallel to the long axis of the tooth or at an angle of 45° to the alveolus. The needle is inserted at the depth of the mucobuccal fold. As the needle is advanced further, its tip is positioned as close to the bone as possible, at the level of the root apex.

(3) After aspirating, a few drops of the solution are deposited.

(4) The anesthetic solution is deposited opposite the roots of the corresponding teeth supraperiosteally, so that the corresponding nerve terminals are anesthetized.

(5) Then the needle is slowly withdrawn.

(6) After waiting for a sufficient period, anesthesia is tested for numbness of the gingiva.

Palatal anesthesia

(Subperiosteal) Palatal injection is a very traumatic experience to most of the patients. More often, the patient is forewarned that injection is liable to be slightly unpleasant so that the patient is psychologically prepared. However, the operator must take all efforts to inject painlessly.

(1) Topical anesthetic jelly is applied over the site of the injection.

(2) Finger pressure is applied firmly, adjacent to the injection site. The aim is to produce ischemia of the soft tissues so that anesthesia lasts for 30 seconds. Continuous pressure is maintained during the injection procedure.

(3) The needle is inserted at right angles to the surface of the bone and advanced until its tip pierces the periosteum and rests on the bone.

(4) The injection must be carried out very slowly with a firm hand rest. Slow deposition of the solution is of very great importance. The palatal tissue is a dense mucoperiosteum. If the drug is injected rapidly, increased pressure forcibly raises the mucoperiosteum, leading to pain. It also leads to stretching and damage of the subperiosteal blood vessels resulting in hematoma. It takes a very long time to resolve.

(5) Considering the supraperiosteal injection, less quantity of the drug has to be injected for the subperiosteal technique.

Intraligamental anesthesia

In the recent past, this old technique has been popularized with improved instrumentation. Originally, it was described in 1912 as a periodontal injection. Although, it was abandoned, some practitioners used this method to supplement where, inferior dental nerve anesthesia fail to produce adequate depth of anesthesia. By injecting a few drops forcibly into the periodontal space, it provides better pain control. In the early 1980s, intraligamental injection technique gained popularity with the introduction of a special type of a syringe which provides mechanical advantage. The greatest potential benefit lies in that, it permits soft tissue and pulpal anesthesia in a localized area, without providing extensive soft tissue anesthesia (Fig. 17.1a).

Indications:

(1) Selective anesthesia for one to two teeth segments.

(2) In children, it is useful to prevent extensive numbness of lip and consequent trauma by subconscious biting of the lower lip.

(3) If anesthesia of different tooth segments in several quadrants are needed simultaneously in the same appointment, this technique is indicated, e.g., extraction of premolars for orthodontic purposes.

(4) For treating infected root canals.

(5) Periodontal interventions like deep curettage.

(6) Medically compromised patients in whom potential toxicity of the anesthetic drug needs to be reduced by injecting less quantity, e.g., cardiovascular patients, hemophiliacs.

Advantages:

(1) Anesthesia of wide areas like lip and tongue are avoided.

(2) Only fractional amount of anesthetic drug is utilized. Hence, toxicity is reduced considerably.

(3) Onset of anesthesia is quick.

(4) Depth of anesthesia is good.

(5) Less painful injection.

(6) Intravascular injection is avoided.

This is contraindicated in inflamed site and in patients who feel apprehensive because of the absence of numbness.

Disadvantages:

(a) Special type of syringe is required.

(b) Multiple injections are required for wide areas of anesthesia.

Mechanism: The anesthetic solution diffuses into the periodontal, periapical tissues and marrow spaces surrounding the teeth. Hence, it is very similar to intraseptal and intraosseous injections. Too rapid injection of excessive amount of the solution produces postinjection discomfort. This is possible only by using the conventional local anesthetic syringe. On the contrary, by using the special syringe, e.g., citojet, pressure and quantity of the solution are under control and predetermined.

Technique:

(1) The needle is inserted at the depth of the gingival sulcus, parallel to the long axis of the tooth at the interproximal region. The angled nostle facilitates the introduction of the needle into the sulcus.

(2) The needle must be in contact with the tooth, about 2 mm deep into the gingival sulcus.

(3) Bevel of the needle must face the root surface to permit easy advancement of the needle.

(4) With the special syringe marketed for the purpose, each squeeze of the trigger delivers 0.2 ml of the anesthetic solution. When correctly applied, a definite resistance is noticeable during the injection procedure. The resistance must be overcome by uninterrupted pressure.

(5) If the tooth is multirooted, the needle is removed and reinserted around the other roots.

(6) Since anesthesia is circumscribed, no specific signs and symptoms are identifiable.

(7) The duration of anesthesia is extremely variable ranging from 5 to 60 minutes. Hence if necessary, the injection has to be repeated.

(C) Block (conduction) anesthesia

(1) **Infraorbital nerve block.** This is a frequently used technique in daily practice. The nerves anesthetized by this method are infraorbital nerve and its branches [superior labial, lateral nasal and inferior palpable nerves, anterior superior alveolar (dental) nerve and middle superior alveolar (dental) nerve, if present].

Indications:

(a) Procedures involving more than two maxillary anterior teeth.

(b) In cases of infection which is a contraindication for infiltration.

(c) In surgical interventions requiring longer duration of anesthesia.

This is comparatively an easy technique.

Technique:

(a) A 25-gauge long needle is used. The site of insertion of the needle is at the height of mucobuccal fold over the first premolar. It provides the shortest route to the infraorbital foramen, as the target area.

(b) The bevel of the needle should face the bone.

(c) Landmark: The infraorbital foramen can be located by feeling the infraorbital notch, since the foramen is located just below the infraorbital notch. By applying pressure over this region, the patient will feel the sensation.

(d) Left index finger is used for locating the foramen. Left thumb is used to retract the upper lip and also to stretch the mucobuccal fold.

(e) The needle is directed towards the infraorbital foramen keeping it parallel to the long axis of the tooth. The needle faces the bony resistance around the upper rim of the infraorbital foramen. The needle must have penetrated approximately a depth of 16-20 mm. After depositing 1 to 1.5 ml of the solution, the area is massaged towards the foramen to enable the solution to diffuse towards the infraorbital foramen.

(f) Signs and symptoms are very appreciable by the patient since the numbness is very pronounced in the upper lip and the surrounding region.

(2) **Posterior superior alveolar nerve block (tuberosity block).** Even though it is a highly successful technique, a few factors are responsible for not using this method routinely.

(a) Potential hematoma in the pterygomaxillary region.

(b) Mesiobuccal root needs separate supra-periosteal injection.

(c) Palatal anesthesia needs another sub-periosteal injection to anesthetize greater palatine nerve.

(d) Duration of anesthesia is similar to infiltration and not like conduction anesthesia since the cross-section of the nerve is less.

(e) Due to the technique, longer needle is required.

(f) Because of the shifting of the syringe posteriorly, the needle is liable to bend, damage or break.

(g) Chances of inadvertent intravascular injection is high.

(h) It carries high risk of infection of inaccessible areas.

Hence in routine practice, infiltration is routinely preferred for anesthetizing maxillary molars.

Technique:

(a) The target of the tip of the needle is the posterior border of maxilla.

(b) Bevel should be facing towards the bone during injection.

(c) The patient is directed to open the mouth partially with the mandible shifted towards the side of injection to provide more space for the insertion of the needle.

(d) After the application of the topical anesthetic, the needle is inserted at the height of mucobuccal fold, above the maxillary second molar.

(e) The needle is advanced slowly through the soft tissues (i) in an upward direction at an angle of 45° to occlusal plane, (ii) posteriorly at an angle of 45° to the long axis of the maxillary second molar, and (iii) medially at an angle of 45° to the long axis of the second molar tooth. On an average, 16-20 mm of penetration will result in the needle tip reaching the vicinity of the posterior superior alveolar foramina.

(f) Usually, the patient does not appreciate any altered sensation in such inaccessible areas and the extent of anesthesia.

(3) **Inferior alveolar (dental) nerve block.** This is the most frequently employed technique in clinical dentistry. However, it has been proved to

be frustrating in nearly 15% of the cases due to the anatomical variations of the mandibular nerve. One such technique is called Fischer 1-2-3 indirect technique.

(a) Inferior alveolar (dental), lingual and long buccal nerves are anesthetized by this technique.

(b) Applied anatomy: All the three nerves are to be anesthetized by the injection of 2 ml of 2% anesthetic solution containing epinephrine (1:2,00,000) into the pterygomandibular space. It is a potential space bounded laterally by the medial surface of the ramus, medioobliquely by the lateral surface of medial pterygoid muscle, superoobliquely by the inferior surface of the lateral pterygoid muscle. Anteriorly, it is crossed by pterygomandibular raphe with buccinator (anteriorly) and superior constrictor (posteromedially) on either side of the raphe.

Posteriorly, it is open to a space occupied by the deeper lobe of the parotid gland. The pterygomandibular space is filled with loose areolar tissue containing mandibular nerve and its branches. Five important landmarks must be identified buccolingually prior to the injection. They are as follows:

(i) Anterior border of the masseter muscle.
(ii) External oblique ridge.
(iii) Retromolar fossa.
(iv) Internal oblique ridge.
(v) Anterior border of the medial pterygoid muscle.

(c) The patient is comfortably positioned in the dental chair in a *semireclined position.*

(d) When the patient opens the mouth widely, the head is adjusted in such a way that the mandibular occlusal plane is parallel to the ground and maxillary occlusal plane is at an angle of 45° to the mandibular occlusal plane.

(e) The operator is positioned in front and to the right of the patient. The surface anesthetic jelly is applied over the site of injection. Then the left index finger is placed in the retromolar region.

(f) In the fully open position, muscles will be stretched so that they resemble the bony oblique ridges. To differentiate the muscle borders from the bone, the patient is asked to open and close the mouth alternatively. By this way muscle and bony landmarks can be differentiated.

(g) The tip of the finger is then placed in the retromolar fossa. The soft tissue is retracted so that the nail corresponds to the internal oblique ridge. Now the thumb surface of the index finger must rest on the occlusal surface of the mandibular teeth and the pulp of the finger must rest on the retromandibular fossa.

(h) The tip of the needle must penetrate the mucous membrane, at the mid-point of the nail with the barrel of the syringe resting on the occlusal surface of premolar teeth from the opposite side. A 25-gauge long needle is used for this technique. The target area of the needle tip can be defined by an imaginary line drawn at the mid-point of the nail, parallel to the occlusal plane of the mandibular teeth. It will cross the medial surface of the ramus, above the inferior dental foramen and lingula. This is approximately 5 mm above the mandibular occlusal plane. The needle penetrates the mucous membrane and pterygomandibular raphe (or buccinator/superior constrictor muscle) before entering the pterygomandibular space between the internal oblique ridge and medial pterygoid muscle.

(i) *Indirect technique* can be carried out in three phases.

Phase I. In the first position, the barrel of the syringe rests on the occlusal surface of the opposite premolars. The tip of the needle rests on the internal oblique ridge at the mid-point of the nail when 6 mm of the needle would have penetrated the tissue. The needle is slightly withdrawn. After aspiration, a few drops of solution are deposited. This is intended to anesthetize the *long buccal nerve.* It is notorious for its anatomical variation. Hence, in nearly 50% of patients, long buccal nerve may not be anesthetized in position-I.

Phase II. The syringe is withdrawn slightly and shifted to the same side so that the needle glides over the temporalis tendon on the internal oblique ridge. By keeping the barrel of the syringe parallel to the mandibular occlusal plane, the needle is further advanced for a distance of 6-9 mm. In this position, the needle is parallel to (with bevel facing) the medial surface of the ramus. 0.5 ml of the drug is injected to anesthetize the *lingual nerve*.

Phase III. Now, the syringe is returned to the opposite side, near the I premolar and the needle is advanced further for a distance of 12-15 mm until the bony resistance (around lingula) is felt by the tip of the needle. After slightly withdrawing the needle and aspirating to ensure that the needle is not inside the vessel, 1 ml of the drug is injected slowly. This is intended to anesthetize the *inferior dental nerve*. Thus, the needle would have penetrated not more than 24-30 mm into the tissue with still one-third of the needle remaining outside. After 5 to 7 minutes, the patient is tested for the sign and symptoms of anesthesia.

Symptoms. The patient feels the tingling and numbness of the corresponding half of the lower lip and the half of the tongue. Although, it is an indication of the onset of anesthesia, it is not a reliable indicator for the depth of anesthesia.

Signs. Objectively, it is better to confirm the depth of anesthesia by selectively pricking the following three selected spots with a pointed probe.

(a) Buccal gingiva near mandibular canine (anterior to the mental foramen).
(b) Lingual gingiva near the area of surgery.
(c) Buccal gingiva near the molar tooth.

If there is no painful response in all the three spots, it is an indication that inferior dental, lingual and long buccal nerves are anesthetized. In nearly 50% of the patients, long buccal nerve anesthesia may not be successful. In such an eventuality, long buccal nerve is anesthetized by injecting a few drops at the buccal mucobuccal fold opposite the II molar. It is better to confirm the painful response objectively by observing the pupillary reaction rather than the patient's subjective response while testing the block anesthesia.

Direct technique differs from the indirect technique on the following aspects:

(a) To start with, it is similar to the third position of the indirect technique.

(b) After depositing about one ml of the solution, the rest of the solution is slowly released as the syringe is gradually withdrawn.

(c) Hence, the nerves are anesthetized in the reverse order—inferior dental, lingual and lastly long buccal nerves.

(d) Because of this, the onset of anesthesia seems to be faster in this technique, when compared to the indirect technique.

(e) Because of the variation in the anatomy of long buccal nerve, separate injection is necessary for long buccal nerve anesthesia.

(f) Since the syringe is not shifted throughout the procedure, chance of needle breakage is less in this technique.

However, to start with, 1-2-3 indirect technique should be practised and mastered by the inexperienced persons before attempting the direct

Table 17.2 Phases of the inferior alveolar nerve block

	Factors	*Position I*	*Position II*	*Position III*
1.	Nerve anesthetized	Long buccal nerve	Lingual nerve	Inferior dental nerve
2.	Anesthetic effect	Sometimes	Always	Always
3.	Needle penetration	6 mm	6 to 9 mm more [12 to 15 mm]	12 to 15 mm more [24 to 30 mm]
4.	Bony resistance	Internal oblique ridge	No bony resistance	Lingula
5.	Quantity of the solution	A few drops	0.5 ml	1ml
6.	Side from where injected	Opposite side	Same side	Opposite side

technique.

(4) **Mandibular nerve block (Gow-Gates technique).** In practice, it is found that in nearly 20-25% cases, it is difficult to obtain satisfactory depth of anesthesia of mandibular teeth with the conventional inferior dental nerve block technique. This may be due to any of the following factors:

(a) Anatomical variations of the mandibular nerve.

(b) Depth of soft-tissue penetration by the anesthetic drug.

(c) Accessory source of neural pathways from the mandibular region.

In 1973, George Gow-Gates described a technique, claiming high success rate (over 95%). This is considered to be a true mandibular nerve block anesthetizing inferior dental, lingual, long buccal, mylohyoid and auriculotemporal nerves. Thus, the problems of accessory sensory innervation of mandibular teeth can be overcome.

Indications:

(1) Multiple procedures on mandibular teeth.

(2) When the conventional technique has not been successful.

Technique:

(1) A 25-gauge long needle is used. The point of entry of the needle is distal to the maxillary II molar, where the line of joining intertragic notch to the corner of the mouth crosses the medial border of the mandibular ramus.

(2) Medial region of the neck of the condyle, below the insertion of the lateral pterygoid muscle is the *target area*.

(3) Intraorally, the height of the needle prick is established below the mesiopalatal cusp of the maxillary II molar tooth. The needle penetrates the tissues distal to the II molar. Wherever III molar is present, the point of entry is behind maxillary III molar tooth.

(4) *Semisupine or supine position* of the patient is recommended. The patient is requested to widely open the mouth, when condyle lies closer to the mandibular nerve trunk.

(5) After the overlying mucous membrane is applied with topical anesthetic, the left index finger is placed on the coronoid process.

(6) The syringe is directed from the opposite side (corner of the mouth), towards the site of injections. The needle is gently inserted, distal to the maxillary II molar, (or III molar) below the mesiopalatal cusp.

(7) The long axis of the needle is aligned to the plane extending from the corner of the mouth of the *intertragic* notch. Now, the syringe is advanced towards the target area. It is found that, syringe lies over the corner of the mouth, but crossing any of the mandibular tooth depends on the divergence of the ramus.

(8) The height of the injection site is above the mandibular plane, nearly 5-10 mm above the occlusal plane.

(9) The needle is slowly advanced, until the tip of the needle touches the condylar neck. The average depth is around 25 mm similar to the conventional inferior alveolar nerve block technique.

(10) If bone is not contacted, then the needle is slightly withdrawn and readvanced after the syringe is moved distally so that the tip is angulated anteriorly. Medial deflection of the needle is the common cause of its failure to touch the bone. After the bony resistance is felt by the tip of the needle, it is slightly withdrawn. After aspiration, anesthetic solution (1.8 ml) is slowly deposited.

(11) The needle is slowly withdrawn.

(12) The patient is requested to keep the mouth open for 30-40 seconds, to enable the solution to diffuse over the target area.

(13) After waiting for 5-7 minutes, the patient is ready for the surgical procedure. The onset of anesthesia is delayed than in the conventional technique.

(14) Anesthesia is tested subjectively for the presence of symptoms like numbness over the distribution of the nerves mentioned above.

(15) In this technique, aspirations ensure that the injection is not given intravascularly since, the needle is very close to internal maxillary artery.

(16) Failure of anesthesia is very rare in this

technique.

Akinosi's closed mouth technique. In 1977 Joseph Akinosi described a closed mouth technique for mandibular nerve anesthesia, as another alternative method. This method is indicated in patients with restricted mouth opening. The nerves anesthetized in this method are inferior dental, lingual and mylohyoid nerves. Unlike the other techniques, no bony resistance will be felt. Hence, the depth of penetration of the needle is arbitrary. But, in patients with trismus, this method is a reasonable alternative.

(1) The topical anesthetic is applied over the injection site.

(2) The index finger is placed on the coronoid and the tissues are reflected laterally.

(3) A 25-gauge long needle is used. Bevel of the needle must face the bone. The point of insertion is the mucous membrane, over the medial border of the ramus, adjacent to maxillary tuberosity at the mucogingiva junction of the maxillary III molar.

(4) The point of injection is below that of Gow-Gates technique but above the conventional inferior dental nerve block technique.

(5) The target area is on the medial aspect of the ramus, where inferior dental, lingual, and mylohyoid nerves descend from the foramen ovale downwards.

(6) The barrel of the syringe is kept parallel to the ramus and the occlusal plane. Now, the syringe is directed posteriorly and slightly laterally.

(7) As the needle crosses a distance of 25-30 mm, the tip of the needle is positioned in the mid-portion of pterygomandibular space.

(8) After the aspiration, 1.5 to 2.0 ml of the anesthetic solution is injected slowly. Injection is completed as the needle is withdrawn gradually.

(9) The surgical procedure can be started after a period of 5 minutes, when the depth of anesthesia could be confirmed.

(10) If the needle is deflected towards the medial direction, the solution is likely to be deposited far away from the nerves. If the needle is inserted too low, failure of anesthesia is a possibility.

(11) If the injection is too posterior, transient Bell's palsy occurs.

COMPLICATIONS OF ANESTHESIA

(1) General considerations

(2) Systemic complications

- (a) Acute circulatory insufficiency (Orthostatic cardiovascular) collapse
- (b) Toxic reactions
- (c) Intoxication by vasoconstrictor
- (d) Allergic manifestations
- (e) Complications due to predisposing systemic conditions
- (f) Hyperventilation tetany.

(3) Local complications

- (a) *Immediate complications (during injection)*
  - (i) Pain at the site of injection
  - (ii) Blanching of the tissues
  - (iii) Needle breakage
  - (iv) Burning sensation during injection
  - (v) Hematoma formation
  - (vi) Aspiration of foreign bodies like needles
  - (vii) Double vision
  - (viii) Temporary blindness
  - (ix) Transient Bell's palsy
- (b) *Late complications (delayed)*
  - (i) Necrosis of the mucosa
  - (ii) Infection
  - (iii) Trismus
  - (iv) Dry socket
  - (v) Prolonged anesthesia (paresthesia)
  - (vii) Postinjection herpes

(1) General considerations

Local anesthetics which are routinely used in dental practice are considered to be very safe agents. Unfortunately, due to such highly commendable safety records, the dental practitioners sometimes face difficulties because of the relaxed attitude during the administration of the local anesthetics. One should not forget that serious complications can develop. On such circumstances, usually the responsibility of the patients are passed on to the physicians. Early recognition improves the prognosis. However, a large number of less serious complications can cause considerable difficulties to the patients. Fortunately most of them are preventable. Hence, the dental practitioner must know to prevent them apart from diagnosis and management. In general, the complications are classified as systemic and local complications. They may be related to:

(a) Local anesthetic drug
(b) Vasoconstrictors
(c) Preservatives in the solution
(d) Psychomotor reactions
(e) Wrong techniques.

The systemic reactions are more serious than the local complications.

(2) Systemic complications

(a) Acute circulatory insufficiency (orthostatic cardiovascular collapse)

It involves the sudden dilatation of the peripheral vessels due to the reflex action of vasomotor centre. Consequently, pooling of blood in the peripheral and splanchnic vessels lead to diminished venous return. This is markedly evident in patients seated in the dental chair. This is soon followed by deficient blood circulation to brain and rapid loss of consciousness. This is termed as orthostatic cardiovascular collapse. This may occur due to any of the following reasons:

(i) Psychosomatic factors like anxiety, fear of pain, repulsive attitude to the very sight of blood and needle, autonomic instability and the smell of the disinfectants.

(ii) Environment with lack of oxygen as in poorly ventilated room with superadded dehydration.

(iii) Hormonal disturbances as in pregnancy, menstruation, menopause.

(iv) Epinephrine sensitivity, usually common in hypotensive patients. It is more pronounced in patients seated in the dental chair (orthostatic). In such patients, initial vasoconstriction is followed by excessive compensatory vasodilation and hypotension.

Early recognition is of paramount importance. It is characterized by the onset of perspiration, cold, and clammy skin, weak pulse, dizziness, and shallow respiration. As a result, loss of consciousness develops due to ischemia of cerebral cortex. If the condition is not recognized for more than three minutes in the orthostatic posture irreversible damage to the cerebral cortex is likely to set in. Therefore, essential treatment consists of (a) placing the patient in horizontal position, (b) elevation of the legs to promote increased blood supply to cerebral cortex, (c) extension of the neck to ensure free airway, (d) oxygen to counteract hypoxia of brain and (e) if necessary, administration of vasopressor drugs to improve the venous return. If the patient does not recover within a reasonable period, the physician's help must be sought without any delay.

Anaphylactic shock after the administration of Xylocaine is one of the uncommon systemic causes for acute circulatory insufficiency. But, when it occurs, it is accompanied by severe circulatory and respiratory collapse, urticaria, laryngeal edema, steep fall in BP, weak pulse, bronchospasm and loss of consciousness. Syncope (vasovagal attack) is reversible but anaphylaxis is irreversible. Hence, the treatment must be provided as an emergency to improve the prognosis. Otherwise, it can be fatal. Immediate emergency treatment includes the following:

— Injection epinephrine 1:1000, 0.5 to 1.0 ml subcutaneously.
— Maintenance of ventilation with oxygen under pressure.

— If severe bronchospasm develops, 250 to 500 mg of aminophylline intravenously.
— Resuscitation methods like cardiac massage, mouth to mouth breathing, if necessary.
— Without any delay, immediate medical consultation and hospitalization must be arranged to save the life of the patient. Mild anaphylaxis may even be due to the preservatives added in the local anesthetics.

(b) Toxic reaction

Whenever a local anesthetic is administered, two types of actions are possible:

- Desirable drug reactions.
- Undesirable (harmful) drug reactions.

The harmful effects may range from those effects which are reversible to certain effects which are uncomfortable to the patient and may even be fatal.

Every clinician should be aware of a few general principles in the administration of these drugs:

(i) Even in the minimum therapeutic dosage, no drug is said to be devoid of toxicity.

(ii) However, the potential toxicity rests in the hands of the operator.

(iii) Every drug is capable of exerting multiple actions.

(iv) The toxicity of the drug also depends on the idiosyncracy of the individual patient since patients vary in their reactions to drug. Thus, no local anesthetic drug is absolutely safe or completely harmful, if it is not used properly. Likewise, complications can be minimal if adequate precautions are taken. The adverse reactions are directly related to:

(a) Overdosage of the drug.
(b) Accelerated absorption of the drug.
(c) Accidental intravascular injection.

Overdosage of local anesthetics. This is essentially related to the blood level of the local anesthetic agents and not entirely in terms of quantity of the drug administered. The predisposing factors for the development of overdose reaction may be related to the patient or the drug.

Patient factors include: (a) age, (b) sex, (c) weight, (d) presence of the predisposing systemic diseases, and (e) mental attitude.

The drug factors are: (a) dose, (b) concentration of the drug, (c) route of administration, (d) vascularity of the injection site, (e) rate of injection, and (f) the presence or absence of the vasoconstrictors in the local anesthetics drug.

The blood-level of the local anesthetic drug is elevated, if:

(a) The drug administered is in excess quantity.
(b) The drug is injected intravenously.
(c) The rate of absorption is rapid.
(d) The biotransformation and metabolism are retarded.
(e) Excreted by the kidneys slowly.

Biotransformation and excretion of the ester-type of local anesthetics are rapid in the liver and blood. Amid-type of local anesthetics undergo biotransformation in the liver, slowly broken down by hydrolysis and metabolized in liver. Therefore, patients with advanced liver disorders are potential contraindications for local anesthesia. Even normal dosage may exhibit toxicity. Hence, minimum quantity should be employed. In patients with renal dysfunction, degradation products are not excreted by kidneys properly. Hence, metabolic byproducts accumulate and it may lead to a gradual increase in the blood level of the local anesthetics. As with any drug, maximum dosage of the local anesthetics must be determined in terms of age, body weight and physical status. At no time, the dental practitioner shall ever administer maximum therapeutic dose. It is not the precise dose of the drug that is important. With increase in the concentration of the drug, toxicity increases. Rate of absorption is high where vascularity is relatively high. That is why, vasoconstrictor is added in the local anesthesia to reduce the rate of absorption.

Rate of absorption. It depends on the vascularity of the site of injection. It is higher in the following circumstances:

(a) Oral cavity is more vascular than the other areas.

(b) Inflamed areas are hyperemic.

(c) Local anesthetic, without adrenaline, is absorbed faster.

(d) Rate of absorption is high with higher concentration of the drugs.

(e) If the drug is injected faster or intravascularly.

To reduce the rate of absorption, local anesthetics with adrenaline is injected slowly. Injection in the inflamed region or into the blood vessels must be avoided. Perhaps, routine aspiration before injection is a safe procedure.

Symptomatology. In general, the initial excitatory phase is followed by transition of a state of depression. The features could, therefore, be summarized under both the phases, involving central nervous system, autonomous nervous system and cardiovascular system.

Management. Prompt symptomatic treatment is essential.

(i) To combat hypoxia of the vital centres of the brain and to compensate for the increased oxygen consumption due to spasm of the muscles, oxygen therapy must be started. This will also counteract the respiratory depression.

(ii) Early recognition improves the prognosis. During the early phase, the medical aid and hospitalization (if necessary) must be arranged.

(iii) These complications can be prevented by the strict adherence of all the precautionary measures like (a) slow injection, (b) use of local anesthetic drug with adrenaline, (c) avoidance of intravascular injection of local anesthetics in the inflamed and hyperemic region. The patient must be advised not to drive the vehicle independently, since local anesthetics have a sedative effect which restricts the ability to independently drive the vehicle.

(c) Intoxication by vasoconstrictors

Since vasoconstrictor is used in negligible quantity, its toxic effect is rare. Toxic effect of non-adrenaline is still more rare. If it occurs, it must be recognized and oxygen therapy must be started to avoid hypoxia of the cardiac muscle. Vasodilators like sublingual nitroglycerine or inhalation of amylnitrite will relieve the problem.

(d) Allergic manifestation

Very similar to the reactions of antibiotics, allergy ranges from mild urticaria and rashes to life-threatening acute reactions. The administered local anesthetics are the antigens. As a result of the reactions, antibodies are formed in the body. In the course of the antigen-antibody reaction, histamine is liberated which is responsible for triggering the allergic reactions which can be rapidly progressing: the most dangerous form of anaphylaxis. It can result in acute circulatory insufficiency. The patient becomes restless and develops urticaria, rashes, peripheral cyanosis and vomiting with dyspnea. Later, there is a steep fall in B.P., increased pulse rate, and unconsciousness. Ultimately, the condition terminates with cardiovascular arrest and death.

(e) Complications due to predisposing systemic conditions

(i) **Hypotension.** Patients with hypotension have low functional capacity and cerebral ischemia. They also exhibit signs of emotional and autonomic instability. Hence, any known hypotensive patient must not be administered local anesthetic with the patient seated in the conventional sitting posture. Such patients are also known to react adversely with epinephrine. To avoid cardiovascular collapse, it is preferable to inject slowly with sedatives in patient in the lying posture.

(ii) **Cardiac insufficiency.** This is characterized by dyspnea, cyanosis, and edema of the lower limbs. Any psychic trauma and stress may lead to the discharge of endogenous adrenaline into the systemic circulation. Injection of local anesthetics and any oral treatment can lead to considerable strain to the cardiovascular system resulting in a dangerous state of decompensation. Hence, cardiologists must be consulted prior to undertaking any treatment in such patients under local anesthesia. Before the patient is taken up under local anesthesia, care should be taken not to use the drug with adrenaline. It is better to hospitalize such patients prior to treatment.

(iii) **Angina pectoris.** This is characterized by the sudden onset of acute pain radiating from the cardiac region along the left shoulder region and left arm. This results as a consequence of coronary sclerosis although left ventricle is functioning normally. Attacks are precipitated by physical exertion and emotional excitement. The cardiac muscle needs more blood under stressful conditions but not sufficiently available because of the spasm of the coronary system. Hence, myocardial ischemia is responsible for the characteristic anginal pain. The patient with history of previous anginal attack must be premedicated with sedatives. The local anesthetics without adrenaline may be used.

(iv) **Cardiac infarct.** This develops as a result of thrombosis involving one of the coronary vessels. It resembles angina but varies in its increasing severity. Pain becomes more intense which cannot be relieved with coronary vasodilators like sublingual nitroglycerin. Preoperatively, the patient must be sedated and the treatment must be undertaken after hospitalization, under physician's supervision.

(v) **Cardiac asthma.** This is characterized by an attack of increasing dyspnea. In such patients, acute decompensation of the left side of the heart occurs while, right side functions normally. Hence, any physical exertion and emotional excitement involves the cardiovascular system. But the pathologically overloaded left ventricle is unable to handle the situation while, right side of the heart can. Therefore, pulmonary circulation becomes congested resulting in acute pulmonary edema. This condition is manifested by marked dyspnea, wheezing and red colored sputum. It may even be fatal. Injection of local anesthetics accompanied by pain and psychic excitement are sufficient enough to precipitate such a crisis. Hence, such patients must be taken up for treatment under strict medical supervision and should not be treated lightly.

(vi) **Hypoglycemic shock.** In diabetic patients, overdose of insulin or omission of a meal with normal insulin administration may lead to hypoglycemia. It is characterized by restlessness, fatigue, hunger, and even unconsciousness. Hence as a prophylaxis, one must ensure that diabetic patients do not miss the meal prior to the procedure under local anesthesia.

Table 17.3 Systemic complications of local anesthesia

System	Excitatory phase	Depression phase
1. Central nervous system	Restlessness and convulsions	Loss of consciousness followed by coma and paralysis
2. Autonomic nervous system	(a) Nausea, vomiting and perspiration (b) Pale face, cold and clammy extremities	Profuse perspiration followed by loss of bladder control
3. Cardio-vascular system	Elevation of BP and tachycardia	Fall in BP and tachycardia, later cardiac arrest with fatal outcome

(f) Hyperventilation tetany

This may occur during the fear reaction of the patient, in connection with local anesthetic administration. Some of these fearful and nervous patients try to calm themselves by increasing the respiratory rate. This leads to lowered CO_2 level in blood. Calcium ions inhibit neuromuscular excitability at the motor terminal plates. With the decreased calcium ion level, such inhibitory effect is correspondingly lessened. Therefore increased muscle contractions lead to tetanic spasm, preceded by the paresthesia of the finger tips. Such patients must be identified sufficiently early so that they can be adviced to breathe normally. If the attempt is unsuccessful, the only other alternate method is the intravenous injection of calcium gluconate (10 ml). This alone will relieve the spasm of the muscles.

The general rule to be observed in these groups of patients is "prevention is better than cure".

Local (regional) complications

For the purpose of convenience, regional complications can be broadly grouped as immediate and late (delayed) complications.

Painful injections. This can be prevented or reduced to the minimum by carefully avoiding the following during injections :

(i) Careless injection.
(ii) Use of blunt needles.
(iii) Rapid injections.
(iv) Impurities in the anesthetic solution.

Pain at the injection site increases anxiety. The unexpected movement of the patient may predispose to breakage of the needle. (a) Slow injection, (b) use of sharp needle, (c) use of topical anesthetic prior to injection, (d) injection of sterile local anesthetics and (e) reduction of anxiety through premedications are some of the methods of preventing painful injections.

Needle breakage. With the introduction of disposable needles, incidence of needle breakage has become very rare. However, the operator must bear in mind the various causes for the needle breakage during inferior dental block anesthesia so that, it will help in the prevention of such a complication. They can be considered under three aspects—due to the (a) operator, (b) patient and (c) manufacturer.

(i) *Faulty injection technique.* Wrong technique may result in the needle piercing the muscle or tendon. When the needle is driven against such a resistance or too deep into the tissue, any manipulation may result in breakage.

(ii) *Repeated sterilization of the needle* may result in the weakening of the metal. Due to water sterilization, the needle may get rusty at the junction with the hub.

(iii) Sudden and unexpected jerky movement by the patient out of fear or pain during the injection procedure.

(iv) The thinner the gauge of the needle, the greater the chances of breakage.

Management

(1) If the injection technique is faulty, very little portion of the needle is available outside the tissues. Then, it will be difficult to grasp the needle with a pair of artery forceps. Surgical intervention may be necessary in such cases.

(2) If it cannot be located clinically, the operator must reassure the patient without getting panicky. Appropriate decision must be taken whether :

(a) to leave it alone,
(b) to remove it immediately or
(c) to refer the patient to a specialist.

(3) If a decision is taken to retrieve the needle immediately, efforts must be directed to localize the fractured needle by any practical method.

(a) Any attempt made by palpation which may lead to the displacement or the needle into the tissues will render the procedure more difficult.

(b) Lateral oblique view of orthopantomogram of the mandible helps to locate the needle two dimensionally-anteroposteriorly and supero-inferiorly.

(c) To locate it in the third dimension, lateral oblique view or orthopantomogram is repeated with another syringe and the needle in the correct position of the block technique. By comparing both, it is easy to locate the broken needle with reference to the needle in the correct position.

(d) With the needle in position as a known landmark, a vertical incision is placed from above downwards along the anterior border of the ramus. The needle is located and removed. The wound is closed with interrupted sutures. Some have tried to use a magnet for the removal of the needle fragment.

Prevention

(1) Disposable needle of at least 25 gauge with 40 mm (1.25 inch) length is used.

(2) At any position, not more than two-thirds of the needle should be inserted into the tissues.

(3) The needle should always be withdrawn slightly before changing the direction to advance the needle into the tissues.

(4) If by chance, the needle is broken and could not be recovered immediately, the patient must be evaluated properly before attempting to remove it surgically.

Bacterial contamination. Inadvertently, if the needle touches any contamination or if the needle is not properly sterilized, it leads to varying grades of infection depending on the bacterial contamination, virulence and resistance of the patient. These factors are responsible for inflammation and pain. In some instances, failure to adhere to the principles of injection may result in post injection neuritis and paresthesia probably due to nerve damage. The infection or trauma involving any muscles of mastication may lead to reflex spasm of the consequent trismus.

Lip-chewing. This is one of the most unpleasant postinjection complications in children. It is better to use short-acting anesthetics in children. Accompanying persons must be warned about the possibility of the child chewing the lip, until the anesthetic effect lasts. Failure to do so will result in edema and ulceration of the half of the lower lip. Analgesics, antibodies, lukewarm saline rinses and application of petrolatum jelly are useful to relieve the pain.

Transient facial paralysis. If the needle has penetrated deeply and superiorly, anesthetic solution is deposited around the facial nerve trunk causing Bell's palsy. The patient recovers once the anesthetic effect passes away. If this complication arises, it means that the injection technique is wrong.

Hematoma. During the injection procedure (infiltration or block anesthesia) if the blood vessel is accidentally damaged, bleeding inside the tissues may lead to the formation of hematoma.

Prolonged bleeding. It occurs in patients who are on anticoagulant therapy, hemophiliacs and other blood dyscrasias. That is why, in these groups of patients, local anesthesia is contraindicated.

Postanesthetic intraoral lesions. 2-3 days after the injection, some patients may develop ulcerations around the site of injection. Recurrent apthous stomatitis and herpes simplex can develop intraorally. They are very painful. Primary management is symptomatic. If pain is not severe, it can be left alone. If it is very painful, the ulcerated painful areas are anesthetized to relieve the pain. Lidocaine topical anesthetics can be applied over the painful areas. Corticosteroid application increases the risk of bacterial or viral involvement. The period of such ulcerations ranges from 7 to 10 days.

Reasons for local anesthesia failures

Proper local anesthetic practice not only permits comfortable and painless treatment but also increases the patients' confidence. These techniques are based on anatomic norms and statistical averages of bone structure and nerve pathways. They are designed for the normal healthy physiological and biochemical environment at the injection site. In practice, nearly 50% of the injections are inferior dental block and an estimated 5 to 15 % cases form the failure rate. A few common reasons are analysed briefly.

(1) **Infiltration technique:** As long as the needle is placed correctly near the operative field, the volume of solution diffuses from the injection site and anesthetize the nerve fibres as planned. However, bone density may alter the diffusion of the solution. The other factors include the presence of infection, quantity and concentration of the solution

(2) **Inferior alveolar block anesthesia:**

(a) Anatomical variations like wide flaring mandible, wide ramus of the mandible in the antero-posterior direction, long ramus of the mandible in the superiorinferior direction, bulky musculature and excess of adipose tissue. Occasionally, a bifid mandibular nerve may be responsible.

(b) Technical errors of injection technique - too low or too deep(posteriorly), too superficial, too high and intravascular injection.

(c) Highly anxious patients.

(d) Inflammation and infection - acidic nature may render the local anesthetic solution ineffective.

(e) Defective solutions.

SEDATION AND ANESTHESIA

Local anesthesia refers to the elimination of painful sensations in a part of the body in a conscious patient.

General anesthesia deals with the controlled state of unconsciousness accompanied by partial or complete loss of (a) protective reflexes including the ability to maintain the airway independently and (b) response to the verbal commands and physical simulations. The concepts of sedation seem to lie in the grey zone between local and general anesthesia. It refers to the induction of the controlled depressed level of consciousness with the ability to maintain the airway independently and also to respond to the verbal commands and physical stimulation.

Conscious sedation refers to a minimally depressed level of consciousness without disturbance to the protective reflex.

Deep sedation refers to a controlled state of depressed consciousness with partial loss of protective reflexes including the ability to respond purposefully to verbal commands.

Relative analgesia is considered to be one of the efficient and safe methods of pain control used judiciously by combining nitrous oxide-oxygen or premedications to supplement local anesthesia. The modern concepts of pain control are not limited to any one particular technique, drug or route of administration. The very diversity of techniques, drugs employed and the psychological make-up of the patient as well as the practitioner make the subject of pain control one of the unending progress and interest.

One end of the spectrum of pain control is the unmedicated, awake patient while at the other end, the patient is unconscious due to general anesthesia. The understanding of the pain mechanism has revealed the existence of the grey area between both the ends of the spectrum. This has led to the control of pain perception and pain reaction with patient remaining conscious.

Pain-perception indicates the physioanatomical process by which pain is perceived and transmitted by the neural structures by the central nervous system. The stimulus that is applied must be of minimum intensity and period so as to initiate the nerve impulses. This is called pain perception threshold.

Pain-reaction embraces an extremely complex neuroanatomical and physiopsychological factors involving the higher centres of the nervous system. This differs from person to person depending on the reaction of the individual to the unpleasant experiences. Once modulated with the nervous system, the impulse triggers a sequence of responses. Similar to pain perception, pain reaction also has a threshold. This is inversely proportional to the pain reaction. Therefore, the patient who has high pain reaction threshold reacts less, while a patient with low pain threshold is hyperreactive. Consequently, the patient's pain reaction threshold indicates the conscious reaction to a specific unpleasant sensory experience. Both pain reaction and perception threshold are quite labile within the individuals. That is why, emotionally unstable, fearful or apprehensive persons in a state of fatigue develop low pain reaction threshold. If one were to adequately control the total pain experience, both the phases–pain perception and pain reaction-must be duly considered.

In oral surgery practice, control of pain can be routinely accomplished by blocking the pain pathway with regional anesthesia to prevent pain perception. But in many situations, certain additional measures may have to be taken. An apprehensive patient is likely to misinterpret subconsciously other modalities of sensation like touch, pressure, etc. as being painful. In such patients, it is necessary to allay the fear, alter the mood or to elevate the pain reaction -threshold as adjuncts to regional analgesia. It is in this direction, conscious sedation can be used as a technique to combine the control of pain reaction with control of perception. In this context, the term "conscious" means that the patient is capable of rational response to commands with all the protective reflexes intact including the entire philosophy of conscious sedation. Whenever the operator fails to exercise reasonable skill and care, any of these techniques tend to become dangerous and unpredictable with profound differences in the reaction of the patient including level of consciousness. Hence, one must be aware of the inherent potential dangers and the necessity to possess the adequate knowledge of the emergency resuscitation equipment and techniques. The problem seems to be more complicated by the use of multi-drug therapy in the medically compromised patients. With sedation combined with local anesthesia, the professional is looking for a new dimension in the management of patients with less complications. Ideally, general anesthesia should be reserved for the ideal situations like operation theatres with the service of a qualified anesthetist. However, there can be no rigid distinction between sedation and anesthesia. Technically, both are capable of producing similar systemic effects and complications. Hypothetically, a well-sedated patient must remain unconscious during the procedure while an anesthetized patient becomes unconscious for a specific period. Ironically, sedation not provided with skill and due care induces anesthesia. Likewise, an improperly administered anesthetic agent may not produce satisfactory anesthesia. Instead, it may even result in complications.

Recent advances in the technology and pharmacology have provided the profession with facility to eliminate pain and awareness during oral surgery without compromising high degree of safety and effectiveness. Hence, the practitioner must acquire the professional competence, knowledge and technical training to use the techniques of relative analgesia and intravenous sedation.

Spectrum of the patient's management

Minor oral surgery like dental extraction requires local anesthesia. In case of difficult procedures like removal of impacted teeth, cyst enucleation and other techniques, the patients will desire to overcome the discomfort and fear while being conscious. If they are performed under general anesthesia the patient's main concern will be about the cost involved in addition to the associated risks. These factors have led to the development of alternate methods like sedation to enable the patients to undergo the surgery with ease.

Relative analgesia

This term refers to inhalation sedation with oxygen and nitrous oxide. This technique aims to alleviate pain and fear and also to improve the patient's cooperation. It is achieved by a triad of interrelated factors.

(a) Administration of oxygen and nitrous oxide.

(b) Utilization of an equipment to administer more than 30% of oxygen with a safety mechanism, to cut off the flow of nitrous oxide, if oxygen flow is less than 30%.

(c) Reassurance to the patient.

There seems to be no clear cut demarcation of different phases of sedation and general anesthesia. They overlap to a considerable degree. Hence, it is essential to review the various stages of anesthesia to evaluate the relative position of sedation in terms of general anesthesia.

Stage I *(analgesia)* is characterized by (a) elevation of the threshold of pain, (b) loss of intellect and sense of time, (c) disorientation and (d) consciousness.

Stage II *(excitement)* is characterized by (a)

irregular breathing, (b) violent reaction and (c) vomiting due to the depression of the laryngeal reflex. Hence, there is a possibility of aspiration of foreign body including blood, vomitus and gastric contents.

Stage III *(surgical anesthesia)* is characterized by four planes. For oral surgery, plane I is ideal. The higher planes are associated with risk, ranging from altered respiratory pattern to cessation of respiration.

Stage IV is characterized by the onset of diaphragmatic paralysis, apnea and may even prove fatal. This is not a clinically useful stage.

Hence, it is evident that stage III is mainly concerned with general anesthesia, while stage I is concerned with sedation. Sedation can be differentiated into (a) light (conscious) sedation and analgesia (b) dissociation sedation and analgesia. Light sedation is produced by 5 to 25% of nitrous oxide with 75 to 95% of oxygen in plane I. Dissociation sedation is produced by 20 to 55% of the nitrous oxide with 80 to 45% of oxygen in plane II. Plane III act as a buffer, after the patient passes from stage I to excitement (stage II). It is reduced by 50 to 70% of nitrous oxide, with 50-30% of oxygen. In all the three planes, local anesthesia is necessary to produce analgesia.

Objectives of conscious sedation

(1) The patient's mood is altered/elevated so that the procedures that would ordinarily affect the person are now well tolerated. The goal is to eliminate fear and apprehension as an aid in the control of pain reaction.

(2) Pain-threshold must be elevated without central depression.

(3) The patient must remain cooperative during the treatment phase.

(4) There shall be only minor deviations in the vital signs of the patient. The patient's physiology is not altered to the extent seen in an unconscious

Flowchart showing different stages of inhalation anesthesia

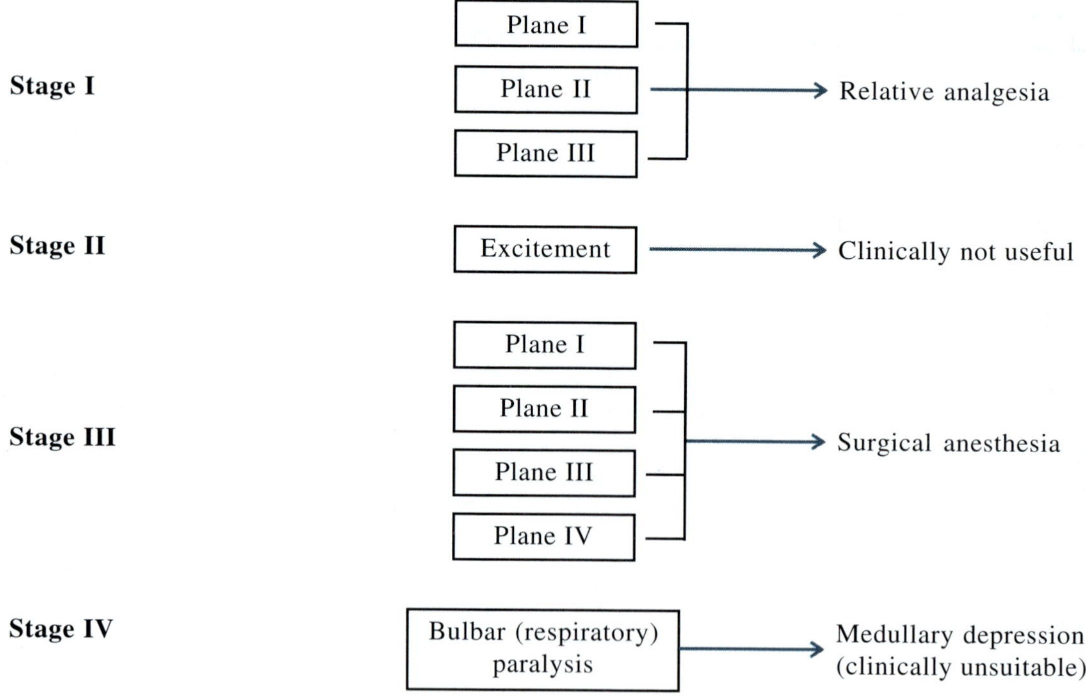

patient. Perhaps, that is why, it is essential to modulate the dosage and rate of administration of the drug so that minor changes in vital signs occur within limits.

(5) Certain degree of amnesia is desirable since, it reduces postoperative trauma. The patient is also motivated to undergo the treatment without fear and apprehension. However, for the sake of amnesia, patient should not be rendered unconscious.

(6) Throughout the procedure, the patient must retain the protective reflexes so that no parasympathomimetic stimulation occurs like laryngospasm etc.

Philosophy of conscious sedation

Many patients with fear, anxiety and apprehension are psychologically unable to withstand the procedures under local anesthesia. It is the fear that is responsible for the patient to become uncooperative. The gradation varies between mild, moderate and very apprehensive patient to produce the desired level of awareness.

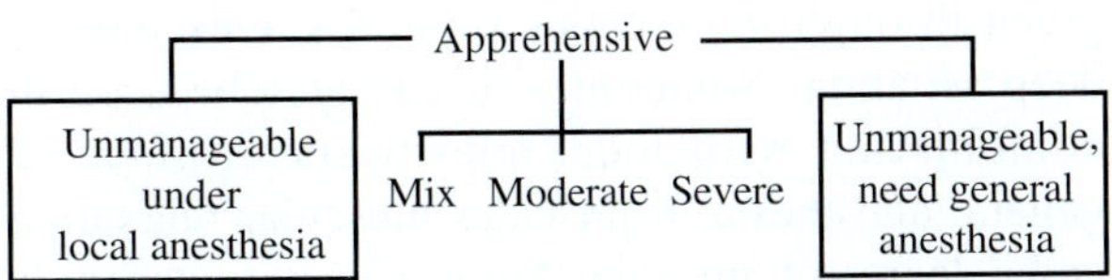

Thus, it is seen that control of pain is not the objective of conscious sedation. Such a state can be achieved when sedatives are combined with adequate control of pain perception. If this aspect is not realized, one is liable to compensate for a poor regional analgesia technique by increasing the dosage of the drug resulting in crossing the realm of conscious sedation. This must be avoided.

The term premedication is used to denote the administration of certain specific drugs to facilitate the main sedation procedure and to establish the proper mood of acceptance.

Routes of administration

(1) *Inhalation route* is dependable and convenient. The onset is rapid and recovery is short. The pharmacological effect can easily be reversed at will than in any other route. For example, nitrous oxide-oxygen can be used judiciously in proper ratio. By increasing the ratio of oxygen, the patient will recover quickly. However, the "inherent" disadvantage is that the agent used for this route is the weakest. To accurately meter the gas concentrations and to regulate it, special equipment including regulators and flow meters are required.

(2) Out of the parental routes (e.g. intramuscular, subcutaneous and intravenous) intravenous route is preferable. It is most effective, predictable and reliablc. Because of the rapid effect, it can be accurately controlled. A drug injected into the circulatory system can be measured correctly and its absorption can be predicted accurately.

Plane I - Conscious sedation

Clinical features

(a) The patient starts feeling relaxed.
(b) Fear is decreased.
(c) The patient is almost normal except that one begins to be indifferent to the surroundings.

Objective

(a) The patient is awake.
(b) Lessened reaction to painful stimuli.
(c) Heart rate, blood pressure and pulse rate normal.
(d) Mouth can be easily maintained in open position.

Plane II - Dissociation deep sedation

Subjective

(a) The patient begins to feel psychological dissociation from the environment.
(b) The patient may complain of abnormal sense of hearing, taste and visual disturbances.
(c) Apparent loss of memory (amnesia).
(d) Indifference to passage of time.

(e) Tendency to dream.
(f) Marked proprioceptive changes which are responsible for the "floating" sensation of the patient.
(g) Widespread paresthesia, particularly in the fingers, toes, lip, and tongue.
(h) Some patients may complain of nausea.

Objective

(a) The patient is awake but response is delayed.
(b) Develops a relaxed feeling.
(c) The patient is awake by delayed sedation.
(d) Heart rate, respiratory rate, BP and laryngeal reflex are normal. Mouth opening is good.
(e) May appear sleepy.

Plane III - Total analgesia (buffer zone)

Clinical features

Subjective. Sedation deepens. Hence patient exhibits closure of eyes, loss of verbal contact, sleepiness and patient becomes almost unresponsive to painful stimulus.

Objective.

(a) Analgesia nearly complete but not sufficient enough to perform surgery.

(b) Reduction in the gag-reflex and laryngeal reflex but functions normally.

(c) The patient begins to lose verbal contact.

(d) The patient exhibits staring of the eyes.

(e) In the deeper phase of plane III, the patient may find it difficult to keep the mouth wide open at will. Hence, this is the important sign to differentiate between phase II and III. That is why, practitioner is adviced not to keep the mouth prop to maintain the mouth opening by the patient consciously.

Clinical application. During effective conscious sedation, the patient cooperates in the conscious state. The drugs used are inhalants and injectables. The most suitable injectable may be grouped under three categories: (a) psychosedatives, (b) narcotics and (c) barbiturates. *Psychosedatives* produce a calming effect through their action on subcortical centers. The effect is psychosedative rather than sleep. Action of *narcotics* and *barbiturates* can be potentiated by psychosedatives when they are used in combination with proper doses. In addition to elevating the pain threshold, they may also produce a degree of euphoria, freedom from fear and general sense of well-being. Barbiturates are generally depressants of the central nervous system. However, by varying the dose, they can be used as sedatives, hypnotics or general anesthetics. It is considered that the primary site of action is cerebral cortex and reticular formation. They are not effective for pain control. In the presence of pain, if they are administered alone, they produce excitation rather than sedation. But if they are used with analgesics or narcotics, barbiturates potentiate their action. Of the many available agents, it is found that the use of Diazepam with or without nitrous oxide and Xylocaine meet the requirements for a safe, effective, versatile technique of conscious sedation.

Diazepam when given orally is one of the readily acceptable tranquilizing drugs. It can be given through intravenous route for conscious or deep sedation. Sometimes, it can also be used in combination with local anesthesia in place of general anesthesia. It provides muscular relaxation and a degree of amnesia. Amnesia is not retrograde in type. It is not an analgesic. Hence adequate local anesthesia is required. If necessary, narcotics can also be added. Physostigmine 1-4 mg is used to reverse respiratory depression caused by the administration of Diazepam. Cardiovascular system is not significantly affected. The patient may exhibit dizziness and light-headedness. It should be avoided in patients during early pregnancy. Alcohol must be avoided.

Minimum dosage: In normal adults, 10 mg.

In children 5 to 7.5 mg depending on the age group.

For intravenous route, 2 ml with 5 mg of Diazepam in each ml is available in amber colored ampoule. It is better to avoid small veins. An initial dose of 2.5 mg (.5 ml) is injected slowly, followed by observation period of one minute. If there is no unusual response, additional increments are injected at the rate of 1 ml/min. It can also be administered along with I.V. infusion of 5% dextrose of Ringer's lactate solution. Not more than 20 mg (4 ml) should be administered. When the quality of response changes, the local anesthetics is injected. After waiting for the local anesthetics to act, surgery can be started. Rapid injection of Diazepam may cause apnea and fall in BP. Some patients tend to become talkative with postoperative euphoria. Recovery from the effect of sedation may be slow. The patient may be unsteady and develop mild postural hypotension. Therefore the patient must lie down at least for 1 or 2 hours. This drug is an irritant to the vessel walls. However, in experienced and competent hands, Diazepam is a safe agent even in poor risk patients. Rarely, narcotic analgesics like Pentazocaine is used to potentiate the sedative effect of Diazepam.

It is better to monitor the patient during this procedure so as to increase the safety. The routine application of minimal monitoring devices would detect even subtle physiological changes so that proper remedial measures can be instituted before the situation deteriorates into a catastrophe.

Positive factors.

(1) They improve the patient's care.
(2) They remind the practitioners about the patient's safety.
(3) Ensure quality of care and protect the practitioner against the possible crisis.

Negative factors.

(1) Possible resistance from the practitioners, due to economical factors by way of additional expenses.
(2) Erroneous interpretations of data possible.
(3) Possibilities of diversion of the attention.

Monitoring guidelines.

(1) *Qualified personnel.* Minimum of two technical persons including one anesthetist must be present. In case of deep sedation and anesthesia, one more person is preferable. During emergencies, number of persons depend on the need.

(2) *Oxygenation.* Objective is to ensure adequate and continuous oxygenation so that oxygen is provided to the tissues adequately. If the anesthetic machine delivers more than 80% of nitrous oxide, low-oxygen alarm and oxygen analyzer must be used. Blood oxygenation can be monitored from the color of skin, mucosa, or blood. Mechanical monitors are useful to supplement the clinical signs. Pulse oximeter is desirable, particularly in patients of extremes of age.

(3) *Body temperature.* Increase in body temperature causes hypermetabolic state and increased oxygen consumption. Low body temperature results in delay in the metabolism of drugs and patient's recovery.

(4) *Ventilation.* The object is to adequately maintain the exchange of oxygen and carbon dioxide adequately. During the sedation procedures and anesthesia, clinical signs to be observed include chest excursion, auscultation of breath sounds and the movements of the reservoir bag in the anesthesia machine.

(5) *Circulation.* The object is to maintain adequate perfusion of blood in the tissue. BP must be monitored before, during and after the procedure continuously. Electrocardiogram display on the monitor helps to observe the cardiac rhythm.

These guidelines are technically feasible and affordable in terms of efforts and expense. Early detection of potentially dangerous trends can be prevented. Human errors will continue to occur under different circumstances. The safety monitoring alone will prevent these errors from escalating the severe morbidity or even mortality.

Nitrous oxide analgesia

The administration of nitrous oxide-oxygen inhalation analgesia has undergone cyclic bouts of enthusiasm and disfavor. Recently, it has become popular again. The inhalation of nitrous oxide-oxygen is in the ratio of 80:20. It cannot induce general anesthetic state. The patient continues to remain conscious with intact protective reflexes. In terms of stages of anesthesia, the patient will remain in stage I. Analgesia will be increased as the lower extent of stage I is approached and will reach 85% of the depth of this stage. Deeper with stage I, amnesia also progresses from minimal to complete forgetfulness. One should however avoid the patient encroaching into stage II. Amnesia, analgesia and relaxation are achieved well in stage I itself. Sedative effects are rapid in onset. Sensory changes are evident in less than one minute. Recovery is usually rapid with full return to presedative psychomotor capacity. The level of sedation is ideally one of complete mental relaxation. Nitrous oxide should be stopped before the work is completed and only oxygen is given to assist full recovery. The patient remains conscious and fully cooperative. Hence, nitrous oxide-oxygen analgesia is very safe without any adverse hemodynamic or respiratory depressant effects.

Day care anesthesia

Short stay of the patient provides a cost-effective method of health delivery system. If it is to become an attractive proposition among the practitioners, anesthetist's effort must be diverted to provide rapid recovery from anesthesia with minimum adverse postoperative sequelae. For example, extraction of the impact III molars under general anesthesia is one of the most commonly performed surgical procedures. Day care surgery can be potentially attractive both to the patient and to the practitioner. The criteria for determining such a proposition appears to be arbitrary and differ widely from place to place. The following are some of the important factors to be taken into consideration.

(1) *Postoperative morbidity:* Many of the patients with postoperative morbidity are unwilling to undergo surgery under local anesthesia again. Hence, it seems to be an acceptable alternative.

(2) *Rapid metabolism* of the induction agent and hence rapid recovery from anesthesia occurs. The recovery can be tested by the clinical features including the level of consciousness.

(3) *Development of postoperative symptoms:*
- (a) General myalgia
- (b) Nausea and vomiting
- (c) Pain and edema
- (d) Patient's acceptability.

Ketamine hydrochloride: It is a non-barbiturate, non-narcotic, short acting general anesthetic. It is devoid of sedative and hypnotic properties, but has profound analgesia and amnesic characteristics even in lower doses. When fully anesthetized, the patient is in a state with eyes open and retention of pharyngeal, laryngeal and corneal reflexes. Hence, airway remains patent. Endotracheal anesthesia is not necessary.

Contraindications

(1) Allergy or hypersensitive reactions.
(2) History of cerebrovascular accidents.
(3) Atherosclerotic heart disease.
(4) Severe cardiac decompensation.
(5) Severe hypertension.
(6) Increased intracranial pressure.
(7) Increased intraocular pressure (glaucoma).
(8) Patients with psychiatric disorders.
(9) Epileptics.

Dose: 5 mg/kg ketamine is considered to stimulate the higher brain centres involving sympathetic nervous system. The increase in BP may be due to the drug producing deprivation of the frequency of impulses on the baroreceptors in the carotid sinuses. When it is used without any premedication, it elicits intolerable emergence reactions, characterized by excitement, irrational behavior, confusion, frightening dreams, severe nausea, vomiting and long postoperative recovery period.

It has been found that low-dose ketamine can be considered as a reasonable alternative to the light general anesthesia. It is useful in pediatric anesthesia for oral surgery.

Physiological status

(1) *Blood pressure (BP):* Systolic and diastolic pressures are slightly elevated due to anxiety. Once local anesthetic is given, BP settles down, diastolic pressure fluctuates very marginally.

(2) *Pulse rate:* Very similar to BP elevation, it corresponds to heart rate.

(3) *Respiratory rate* also fluctuates by 2 or 3 times per minute. It has been found that in case of patients "at risk" due to cardiovascular problems, adrenaline and non-adrenaline are to be reduced during inhalation sedation technique. Hence nitrous oxide-oxygen inhalation has been found to be beneficial to such patients.

(4) *Psychomotor ability:* The patients' psychomotor ability seems to be directly proportional to the oxygen content.

(5) *Laryngeal competence:* The gag reflex and laryngeal reflex are depressed if oxygen is below the critical level - 30%.

(6) *Behavioral changes:* The patient's motivation to undergo the treatment is better. Perhaps, this helps in the completion of the treatment in less time.

Clinical status

The patient's level of consciousness can be determined by the following criteria:

(1) Ability to maintain the patient's airway independently can be tested by advicing the patient to flex the head forward and swallow. This is called *"head-flexion"* test.

(2) Ability to maintain the verbal contact.

(3) Ability to keep the mouth open voluntarily. This is called *"mouth open"* sign. To determine this ability, use of mouth prop is discouraged.

(4) Ability to keep the eyes open voluntarily.

(5) Ability to swallow voluntarily.

GENERAL ANESTHESIA

General anesthesia is a state of controlled unconsciousness from which the person cannot be roused by external stimuli. Most of the central depressants can produce unconsciousness. However, anesthetic agents are those drugs which rapidly produce unconsciousness without depressing respiratory and cardiovascular functions. Many of the anesthetic agents are fat-soluble which is related to the potency of the drug. The main objectives of general anesthesia are (i) analgesia, (ii) loss of consciousness, (iii) relaxation of muscles without depressing respiratory and cardiovascular functions.

Desirable properties of an ideal anesthetic agent:

(1) Capable of producing reversible and controllable levels of anesthesia.

(2) Must have wide safety margin.

(3) Should not have any cytotoxic effects.

(4) Induction of anesthesia must be smooth and pleasant.

(5) Recovery from anesthesia must be pleasant and rapid.

(6) Must be metabolized and excreted quickly.

(7) Should not have any undesirable interactions with drugs which are likely to be given before, during or after anesthesia.

(8) In oral surgery, it is desirable that anesthetic agent possess potent analgesic property even at the level of light anesthesia.

Anesthetic state: The depth of anesthesia is such that it absorbs the pain response while the patient is under controlled and reversible stage of unconsciousness. These drugs are safe, so long as they rapidly induce unconsciousness without significant depression of cardiovascular and respiratory functions, but the reflex movements must be abolished with complete muscular relaxation. There seems to be correlation between lipid solubility and its potency.

The techniques of general anesthesia are better practiced by the trained anesthetists. But the surgeon who performs oral surgery must possess the basic knowledge of the principles of general anesthesia.

Screening patients for general anesthesia: Although, this is the primary responsibility of the anesthetist, the dental practitioner must be able to grossly evaluate the patient, before referring to the anesthetist for screening. The anesthetist may certify regarding the fitness for general anesthesia. But it is the oral surgeon who must take a decision as to whether, there is a need for oral surgery for such patients. Since the oral surgeon must be familiar about the basic principles, one must be familiar with the useful classification based on health status of the patient provided by American Society for Anesthesiologists (ASA).

ASA classification

Class I An apparently healthy patient, on whom, nothing abnormal could be detected.

Class II Patients with mild risk factors.

Class III Patients with severe risk factors, but not serious enough to incapacitate the person.

Class IV Patients dangerously ill and not expected to survive.

The above classification is useful for the evaluation of the patient for fitness to undergo surgery under general anesthesia. Patients grouped under category I are risk-free. Patients under category II can be taken up for surgery, but evaluation is needed to diagnose and manage mild risk factors. Failure to provide the necessary medications under the physician's care and monitoring of the patient during surgery may lead to complications. Hence these patients are to be considered as *"calculated risks"*.

Patients with severe risk factors (category III) need careful evaluation and healthy care. These patients must be made to be fit for general anesthesia. Hence, they must be hospitalized for evaluation under expert guidance and for the management of systemic complications that might arise during surgery. It is preferable to avoid ambulatory oral surgery for such patients.

If they are grouped under category IV, they must be considered as *"risky"*. Hence the treatment must be restricted to the minimum and should be aimed at relieving the pain. Certainly, risks in such patients are avoidable, since no useful purpose will be served by performing oral surgery on such patients.

Therefore, it is reasonable to categorize all the patients, who are to undergo oral surgery under general anesthesia and to take all the necessary precautions to minimize the systemic complications.

Stages of general anesthesia

Stage I. **Analgesia.** The consciousness is progressively lost but the moment the patient loses consciousness, he passes on to the second stage.

Stage II. **Excitement.** The patient gradually becomes unconscious but all the reflexes are intact. Sometimes, patient may struggle violently and shout. Hence, efforts must be directed to restrain the patient to prevent any physical injuries. This problem can be through quick, skillful induction by the use of short acting barbiturate like Thiopentone intravenously. To avoid vagal stimulation during this stage, the patient is premedicated with atropine.

Stage III. **Surgical anesthesia.** For the purposes of anesthesia, this stage is further divided into four planes. This signifies increasing depth of anesthesia and progressive loss of reflex activity and muscle tone.

Usually, depth of anesthesia can be judged by testing the reflex responses like eyeball and pupillary movements, rate, depth, and rhythm of respiration. Usually for oral surgery, phase I or rarely II are sufficient.

Stage IV. **Medullary / bulbar paralysis.** This is possible only by the overdosage of the anesthetic drugs.

Halothane. It is the most widely used general anesthetic agent. It is noninflammable and non-explosive. It is nonirritant. Usually, it is given with nitrous oxide and oxygen in concentration of 2% to 3% for induction. Then, anesthesia is maintained at 0.5% to 2%. Induction is pleasant and smooth with minimal excitement. Surgical anesthesia is achieved in 2-3 minutes. It provides good muscle relaxation.

Its dose can be reduced, if muscle relaxants are also used. Recovery is also rapid. Overdosage of halothane is likely to cause paralysis of vasomotor centres. Depending on the depth of anesthesia, blood pressure is lowered. It is of relevance to oral surgery that halothane sensitizes myocardium to adrenaline, resulting in dysarrhythmias. Beta-blocking agents help to prevent these arrhythmias. Repeated administration of halothane at short intervals should be avoided because of the hepatotoxicity. Otherwise, halothane has been found to be a safe and useful anesthetic agent in the field of oral surgery.

Thiopentone. It is the first intravenous barbiturate used for the induction of anesthesia. It is administered intravenously as a 2.5% solution. Induction is rapid and pleasant without excitement. But it has no analgesic effect. Muscular relaxation is also poor. Deep anesthesia with thiopentone is followed by respiratory and cardiac depression. Once given, it cannot be withdrawn like inhalant anesthetics. Recovery depends on the dosage.

Responsibilities of an anesthetist

During anesthesia

(1) It is the anesthetist's responsibility to ensure that anesthetic equipment are in working order with sufficient quantity of anesthetic agents required for the surgical procedure before starting the procedure.

(2) Throat pack and suction apparatus are available.

(3) Endotracheal tubes, laryngoscope and resuscitation equipment are in proper condition.

(4) Enough assistants are available to help the anesthetist.

After anesthesia

(1) The patient must be positioned in such a way that saliva or blood does not drain into the larynx.
(2) To ensure that throat pack has been removed and pharynx has been cleared of all secretions and blood.
(3) If the patient is not yet conscious, tongue must be adequately controlled.
(4) No oral fluids to be given for 2 or 3 hours to avoid vomiting and aspiration of fluid into the respiratory system.
(5) To ensure that proper medications for the patient's general conditions are being continued, e.g. steroids, hypotensive and antidiabetic drugs.

Complications

(1) Intraarterial injection can have disastrous results. Pain in the hand/arm followed by spasm and consequent thrombosis may lead to blanching of fingers.
(2) Extravascular injection results in the irritation of the tissues with inflammation and pain. Injection with procaine and hyaluronidase help to disperse the drug.
(3) Overdose may lead to respiratory depression and cardiovascular collapse.
(4) Laryngeal spasm may occur during induction, probably due to overactive reflex response. Such a spasm, if occurs, is usually short-lived. Usually, spasm does not last long. However, if it persists, muscle relaxant must be administered and oxygen must be given under positive pressure.

To summarize, the risks of anesthesia depend on many factors. Mainly, it is proportional to the depth of anesthesia and duration of the procedure. If the surgery is of short duration, sedation with regional anesthesia will be sufficient. But in prolonged operative procedures in the oral cavity, the following factors must be taken into consideration.

Precautions prior to the administration of anesthesia

(1) Fitness for anesthesia must be evaluated.
(2) Any history of adverse reactions and drug interactions must be recorded.
(3) The patient should not be given anything to drink or eat at least 4 hours prior to

anesthesia.

(4) Informed consent from the patient must have been obtained from the patient or the guardian.
(5) It is a good idea to ensure that patient's bladder is emptied.
(6) All emergency drugs are available in the emergency tray.
(7) Premedication has been given as per the need.

The purposes of premedications are:

(a) To allay fear and anxiety.
(b) To minimize the oral and bronchial secretions.
(c) To appropriately modify the action of the anesthetic agents.
(d) To help smooth induction and recovery from anesthesia.
(e) To afford protection against some possible adverse effects of anesthesia.

CHAPTER 18

Salivary Gland Disorders

INTRODUCTION

The primary function of the salivary glands is production of saliva. Mastication, deglutition and speech are adversely affected without the lubricating effect of saliva. The salivary glands are divided into major and minor glands. Major glands are parotid, submandibular and sublingual. Minor glands are scattered in the palate, buccal mucosa and floor of the mouth. They secrete primarily mucus in small quantities. The three pairs of major and many minor salivary glands empty saliva into the oral cavity. They are developed from proliferating buds of ectoderm that differentiate to form glandular structures. Parotids develop during the fourth week of intrauterine life, while submandibular gland during the sixth week, sublingual glands during the eighth week and minor glands thereafter.

APPLIED ANATOMY AND PHYSIOLOGY

Parotid gland

It is a paired, bilobular serous gland situated laterally over the masseter muscle. Posteriorly, it lies above the posterior belly of the digastric muscle and inferiorly near the sternomastoid muscle. It wraps around the posterior border of the mandible. It is separated from the submandibular gland by the stylomandibular ligament. Medially, retro-mandibular extension is closely related to parapharyngeal space. Parotid has facial nerve growing through it. Lymphatic tissue is impregnated into the substance of the gland. The gland is surrounded by a fibrous capsule. Salivary secretions are serous in nature, discharged into the oral cavity through the Stenson's duct. The duct emerges out from the anterior aspect of the gland, crosses the masseter, pierces the buccinator muscle and opens opposite to the maxillary II molar.

Submandibular gland

It is a mixed gland. The lymphoid structures are incorporated inside the gland. Secretions are discharged sublingually into the oral cavity through the Wharton's duct. The gland is present in the submandibular triangle. It is related superiorly to mylohyoid muscle, anteriorly to body of mandible and inferiorly to digastric muscle. It lies on the hyoglossus muscle. The gland is covered by skin and platysma muscle. The duct passes from the gland at the posterior border of the mylohyoid muscle, turns upwards, entering into sublingual space and runs in an anterior direction. It opens into the oral mucosa. It is closely related to the lingual nerve at the third molar region.

Facial artery enters the posteromedial region of the gland. After making an S-shaped bend, it emerges out of the gland and enters the face at the anterior border of the masseter muscle. Two lymph nodes - pre and retrovascular nodes, can be identified at the inferior border of the mandible where facial artery enters the face. Marginal branch of mandibular nerve is present deeper and superior to the nodes. Anterior facial vein is present posterior to the lymph nodes. At this point, medial to the facial artery and at the posterior border of mylohyoid muscle, ganglionic connections from the lingual nerve can be noticed. Hypoglossal nerve and sublingual vein cross the lateral surface of the hyoglossus muscle.

Sublingual gland

It is present at the anterior lingual space on the surface of the mylohyoid muscle, parallel to the Wharton's duct. It secretes mainly mucus through multiple ridges in the floor of the mouth. The principal duct is called Bartholin's duct which occasionally communicates with submandibular duct.

Microscopic anatomy. They are all similar in structure. It is composed of serous and mucous acini. The relative number of serous or mucous acini depends on the gland. Parotid and submandibular ducts are composed of many small ducts which ultimately join to form a large duct. Cuboidal epithelium line the ducts. Minor glands and sublingual glands have simple epithelium-lined short excretory ducts.

Innervation. The innervation is mediated through autonomic nervous system. Physical and psychic stimuli are relayed along the medulla. Preganglionic parasympathetic fibres leave the inferior salivary nucleus with glossopharyngeal nerve and cross the tympanic cavity as the lesser superficial petrosal nerve and travels to the otic ganglion. After the synapse, postganglionic fibres pass to the parotid gland through the auriculotemporal nerve. Fibres to submandibular and sublingual glands leave the superior salivary nucleus at the nervus intermedius of facial nerve. These fibres leave the facial nerve through chorda tympani, crosses the tympanic cavity to join the lingual nerve which is a branch of mandibular nerve. The short postganglionic fibres reach the gland from submandibular ganglion that hangs down from the lingual nerve.

Saliva

Parotid secretion is serous and watery. Secretion from submandibular and sublingual glands contain mucin. Nearly 19% of the total volume of saliva is from parotid and submandibular glands in approximately equal quantities. The remaining 10% of saliva is from sublingual and minor salivary glands.

Salivary flow. The greatest quantity of saliva is secreted during the afternoon and negligible during sleep. The total salivary secretions on an average per day is around 1000 ml. Many factors are responsible for the reduction of salivary flow. Such a phenomenon is called *xerostomia*. The main salivary protein is amylase, electrolytes, enzymes, vitamins. Immunoglobulins are also present.

Functions of saliva.

(a) Mainly during mastication, speech and swallowing to keep the oral cavity moist to provide lubricating effect.
(b) Proper salivary flow is essential for the preservation of dentition.
(c) Neutralization of acids.
(d) Antibacterial and antiviral.
(e) To help in the mechanical removal of food.
(f) Digestion in the oral cavity.

Anatomically weak areas

(i) Ducts of sublingual and minor salivary glands are short. Hence, the glands react quickly to changes in the mucous membrane. Partial closure or rupture of the duct leads to mucous retention cysts while complete closure leads to atrophy.

(ii) In the parotid gland, the duct has a sharp bend at the anterior border of the masseter muscle. Its opening is smaller than the diameter of the duct. Hence, at these two sites, epithelial cells settle down with stasis of salivary flow.

(iii) The submandibular gland lies in a dependent position. Hence, saliva has to flow against the gravity. Unlike parotid, saliva is not totally serous. The diameter of the opening is smaller than the duct. Submandibular duct makes an acute bend at the posterior border of the mylohyoid muscle. These factors predispose to obstruction and stasis of salivary flow.

SALIVARY GLAND DISORDERS

Classification

(i) Developmental
(ii) Inflammation (sialadenitis)
  (a) Acute or chronic of bacterial origin.
  (b) Viral origin
(iii) Obstructive and traumatic lesions
  (a) Sialolithiasis
  (b) Retention cysts
  (c) Atrophy
(iv) Functional disorders
  (a) Xerostomia
  (b) Increased salivation
(v) Neoplastic lesions
  (a) Benign
  (b) Mixed tumors
  (c) Malignant
(vi) Autoimmune conditions
  (a) Sjögren's syndrome

Differential diagnosis

One of the main problems in treating the salivary gland disorders is to diagnose the lesion with proper understanding of the anatomy of the associated structures. Although many investigations have been suggested to establish the diagnosis, the validity of them depends on the accuracy of the techniques. Histopathology confirms the diagnosis but it involves surgery. Hence, the nonsurgical investigations must be utilized as far as possible before subjecting the patient to surgery. The clinical examination includes the following:

(i) *History*
  (a) Duration of the complaint
  (b) Nature of onset
  (c) Nature of the progress
(ii) *Investigation of the swelling in all its aspects.*

INVESTIGATION OF SALIVARY GLAND DISORDERS

Many of the disorders of salivary gland can be diagnosed on the basis of history and a thorough clinical examination. It has been found that laboratory investigations have a very limited role in the diagnosis of salivary gland diseases.

(a) WBC count is raised in infections of salivary glands.
(b) Erythrocyte sedimentation rate (ESR) is raised in Sjögren's syndrome.
(c) In purulent sialadenitis, the discharge can be sent for microbiologic culture and antibiotic sensitivity tests.

Specific non invasive investigations

(a) **Radiographs.** Plain radiographs of the salivary glands will reveal the presence of salivary calculi by its radioopacity.

(b) **Sialography.** Radiological evaluation of the salivary glands by injecting radioopaque dye is useful to detect and locate any obstructive lesions like salivary calculi. In case of salivary gland diseases, variation of acini pattern of filling defects can be noticed. It also helps to differentiate whether the mass is intraglandular or extraglandular.

(c) **Computed tomography (CT).** High resolution CT scanning is being used widely in the investigation of salivary diseases. CT scan reveals the mass better than sialography. It is very sensitive in detecting salivary gland tumors and in distinguishing extra glandular masses.

(d) **Ultrasound scanning.** The high frequency pulsed ultrasound has been widely utilized to image many internal organs. Sensitivity to detect the tumors may be almost cent percent. Experienced clinicians can distinguish them accurately from the scan appearances. Calculi with a diameter of more than 2 mm can be identified very accurately with ultrasound than with plain radiography.

(e) **Magnetic resonance imaging (MRI).** This is a new technique which is becoming popular and is widely used. In this technique ionizing radiation is used. It is possible to get image in multiple planes without changing the position of the patient. It provides better imaging of the soft tissues than CT scanning. MRI is considered to be superior to CT scan in distinguishing the parotid gland from the surrounding structures.

Minimally invasive investigation

Minimally invasive endoscopic techniques for the extraction of biliary and renal calculi and release of obstruction are well documented in the literature. The conventional diagnostic methods are indirect and provide partial information regarding the calculi and the glandular status. Therefore, success of endoscopic procedures in the general and urological surgical practice prompted the oral surgeons to use mini endoscope into the ductal system of major salivary glands. The indications include (a) removal of calculus, (b) screening the ductal system for any residual calculi after sialolithotomy and (c) to determine the status of the major duct lumen. Rigid endoscope provides better and clear view than the flexible endoscope. This is very useful to identify the radiolucent calculi particularly in the submandibular ductal system. Considering the reduced hospital stay and complications, endoscopy is offering financial and clinical advantages. It can be concluded that sialoendoscopy is yet another tool to be used in the diagnostic, removal and postoperative management of the salivary calculi.

Invasive investigations

(1) **Biopsy.** The imaging techniques provide information about the anatomic extent of the disease and the glandular function but may not provide specific information about the nature of the underlying pathological condition. Hence, diagnosis can be confirmed by histopathological examination.

(2) **Fine-needle aspiration cytology.** More recently, fine needle aspiration cytology (FNAC) examination has been introduced. It is yet to become popular because of the possible risk of seeding tumor cells along the needles track. Moreover, the laboratories are not yet familiar with this technique for the investigation. However, this is considered to be a rapid, safe and cost-effective diagnostic technique by some clinicians although it is still controversial. The investigation of salivary glands by this technique can yield considerable diagnostic information. It takes very little time to perform and cause minimal discomfort to the patient. Yet, there are a few disadvantages and limitations that must be appreciated by the pathologist and the surgeon. The basic indication is a localized palpable mass suspected to be a neoplasm of the salivary gland. It helps to identify whether the lump is of salivary gland origin and also to identify its nature. For this technique to be clinically efficient, close co-operation between the surgeon and the cytopathologist is essential. Only positive findings give useful information.

Developmental anomalies

Agenesis or aplasia means congenital absence (of the salivary glands). This is an uncommon condition. If any gland is absent, then it may lead to the development of xerostomia and the consequent characteristic high caries rate.

The term aberrant gland refers to the presence of salivary gland tissue at an abnormal location. For example, it may be found included in the body of the mandible during development.

Inflammatory lesions

Bacterial. Infection of the major salivary gland is manifested by painful swelling of the gland, alteration of the secretion rate and its character. The consistency of saliva changes and becomes thick and cloudy. Infection by direct spread is seen from the oral cavity, particularly as a postoperative complication due to bad oral hygiene. Retrograde infection from the oral cavity through the duct is responsible for such infection. Most often, staphylococcus aureus is one of the important causative organisms. On examination, the gland becomes tense and the pus can be seen at the orifice of the duct. Systemic features like pyrexia and blood picture will reflect the toxicity of infection.

Treatment.

(a) Medical treatment consists of a course of antibiotics and analgesics. If it does not respond, then the pus must be sent for culture and antibiotic sensitivity. Steps are taken to take the swab directly from the orifice rather than from saliva.

(b) If necessary, duct may be dilated to effect better drainage.

(c) In chronic sialadenitis, sialogram may be useful to assess the cause and extent of damage of the gland.

Sialadenitis of viral origin. The most common form of viral acute parotitis is called mumps. Usually, it occurs in children primarily involving parotid gland while submandibular gland may be involved later in a few cases. The incubation period is 12 to 21 days. Fever, malaise and swelling develop. Treatment consists of bed rest. Depending on the need, analgesics can be prescribed. Usually, treatment is supportive in nature. It resolves by itself. Testicular involvement in 25% of males and 5% of oophoritis in females are seen. Deafness may develop in children.

Sialolithiasis. Obstruction to salivary flow may be due to the formation of sialolith (salivary calculi) or mucous plug either at the duct orifice or in the duct. They are four times more common in submandibular glands than in parotid. The possible reasons are as follows:

(a) Secretion of the submandibular gland is more viscous because large number of mucous acini are present.

(b) Presence of anatomical weakness.

(c) Secretion is more alkaline with higher concentration of calcium and phosphate ions.

(d) Flow of saliva is in an unfavorable direction against the gravity. The duct is nearly 4 cm long and runs in an ascending direction. It has a tortuous bend at the posterior edge of the mylohyoid muscle. Hence, this is the most common site of sialolithiasis.

The salivary calculus contains inorganic calcium phosphate with other salts. The organic materials like mucous and cell debris are entrapped around which calculi enlarge in size.

Clinical features.

(a) Acute infection consequent to obstruction by sialolith has the same clinical features of acute sialadenitis like swelling, pain, pyrexia and tenderness of the affected gland. Pus may be noticed at the duct orifice.

(b) Salivary calculus may be palpable along the duct intraorally.

(c) The characteristic symptom is the painful enlargement of the involved gland due to the obstructive phenomenon particularly during meal time.

(d) Swelling reduces in size, but only to swell again during the subsequent meals time when salivary flow is stimulated.

(e) Recurrent obstruction with or without super added infection may lead to atrophy of the secretary cells and chronic sialadenitis. It may also lead to sialectasis (irregular dilatation of the duct system) resulting in stasis and further calculi formation.

(f) Most of the calculi are radioopaque and hence, plain radiograph is sufficient to demonstrate its presence.

(g) When radioopaque dye is injected into the duct, the duct system does not fill beyond the calculus.

Treatment.

(a) *Conservative.* Salivary stimulants and massage of the gland will help to wash the fine debris out and also to prevent further sialolithiasis.

(b) *Transoral sialolithotomy.* If the stone is in a favorable location, removal through the mouth is advocated. The calculus is located accurately by clinical examination and radiograph.

Transoral sialolithotomy of submandibular duct. This can be carried out as an office procedure under local anesthesia. A stay suture is placed below the duct, just posterior to the location of the calculus. This is to prevent the stone from slipping backwards during its manipulation. With a stay suture, tongue is kept retracted towards the opposite side to keep the floor of the mouth also in a desirable position without sagging downwards. The gland is palpated extraorally and pushed upwards to fix the floor of the mouth under tension. An attempt can be made to milk the calculus out of the duct. If that is not possible, then an incision is made along the long axis of the duct through the mucous membrane and the duct wall to expose the calculus. Care is taken not to damage the lingual nerve and sublingual gland. Posteriorly, lingual nerve is superior and lateral to the duct, near the III molar region. It crosses beneath the duct at the posterior end of the mylohyoid ridge. Hence, if the stone is posteriorly situated, incision must be shallow to prevent the damage of the lingual nerve. If the stone is anteriorly placed, the incision is made medial to the plica sublingualis and over the stone. Bleeding is seldom a problem. At the location of the calculus, the duct is identified and a longitudinal incision is made directly over the calculus. If the incision is made in a transverse direction, fistula may result. The stone is removed with a forceps. Then, a small cannula is passed into the duct towards the gland and the pus is aspirated along with mucous plugs and satellite stone particles, if any. The duct is left without suturing the duct wall. The mucosal incision is sutured with interrupted sutures. During healing, recanalization occurs.

Transoral lithotomy of parotid duct is a more difficult procedure than in the submandibular duct because of the anatomy of the parotid duct. Intraorally, the caruncle is situated opposite the maxillary second molar tooth. After a short course, the duct turns laterally around the anterior border of the masseter before proceeding towards the gland. If the stone is anterior to the anterior border of the masseter muscle, a direct transoral sialolithotomy is possible. If it is posteriorly placed, oral approach is not indicated.

Intraorally, a semilunar incision is made from above downwards in front of the caruncle. Then the flap is retracted medially while the cheek is retracted laterally. Through blunt dissection, calculus is delivered through the opening. If necessary, a longitudinal incision is made to expose the stone on the lateral side of the duct. Duct need not be sutured but the mucosal defect is sutured. During the healing process, recanalization occurs.

Submandibular gland excision

Due to the recurrent chronic infection and the location of the calculus in a disadvantageous position, excision of the gland may be necessary. Until all the conservative methods have failed, gland excision should not be undertaken as a routine.

Procedure. Extraorally, a semilunar submandibular incision is made parallel to the digastric muscle. The surface landmarks are mastoid eminence, lateral surface of hyoid and genial tubercle. Line joining these three landmarks represents the course of digastric muscle.

4-5 cm long incision is made over the skin, superficial fascia and platysma. Facial vein is identified, ligated and divided. In the region of deep fascia, cervical branch of the facial nerve where it communicates with cervical branch of the cervical plexus is encountered. Deep to the fascia, blunt dissection is continued around the pulley of the digastric muscle to free the anterior and inferior surface of the gland. Later, posteroinferior pole is also cleared. Superior and medial poles of the gland remain to be dissected. Facial artery, submandibular duct and lingual nerve are the three important structures to be identified at this stage of dissection. The facial artery runs over the superior aspect of the gland before emerging on the lateral aspect of the body of the mandible at the anterior border of masseter muscle. The pre and retrovascular lymph nodes are useful landmarks on either side of the artery. Since it is the major vessel to cause alarming bleeding, elective double ligation should be done before severing the artery - both above and below the gland. The gland is retracted posteriorly and detached from the ganglionic connections with the lingual nerve. The submandibular duct can be identified anteriorly and superiorly on the surface of the mylohyoid muscle. The muscle is retracted anteriorly and the duct is ligated and divided to prevent the escape of the infected material into the wound. Now, the gland is free and removed from its bed. To avoid accumulation of fluid in the dead space, it is preferable to place a drain. Wound is closed in layers - deep fascia and then platysma with catgut. Skin is closed with interrupted sutures with 3-0 silk. The drain is placed in such a way that one end of the drain emerges out of the surgical field at the most dependent part - posteroinferior aspect of the wound - through a separate stab incision. The surgical field is given a pressure dressing. Drain is removed after 48 hours and the sutures are removed on the 5th or 6th postoperative day.

Excision of the parotid gland is not within the scope of this text since it is a major procedure to be performed by a maxillofacial surgeon. It is not advisable to perform this procedure unless it is absolutely essential.

Xerostomia

The term "xerostomia" refers to the clinical condition in which salivary flow is less than normal without defining any boundary between abnormal and normal.

Etiology

(a) *Associated wide systemic conditions:* It may vary from transient decrease in flow as in psychogenic responses to severe and permanent alteration like Sjögren's syndrome. It is also found in many deficiency states like pernicious anemia and iron deficiency anemia, deficiency of Vitamin A and hormones but no definite cause-and-effect relationship has been demonstrated. Patients with diabetes mellitus have shown significant decrease in salivary flow. Decreased salivary flow is associated with sweating, hemorrhage, vomiting, diabetes insipidus, developmental abnormalities of

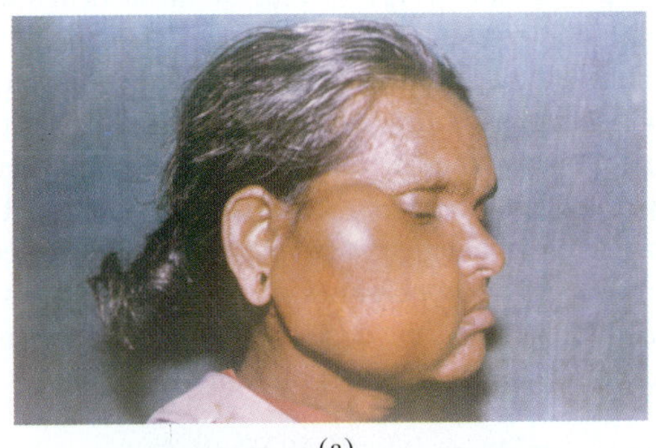

(a)

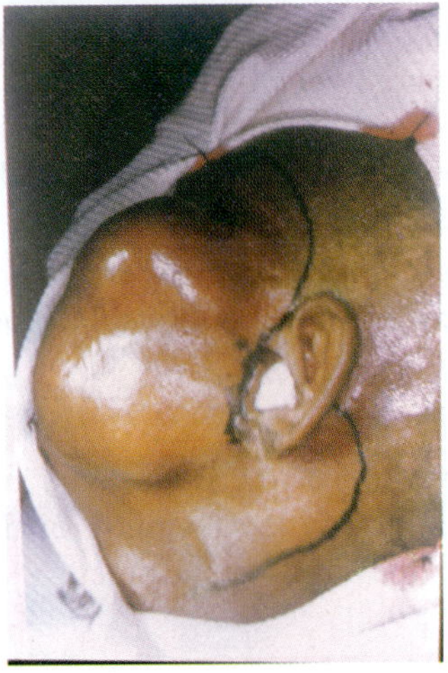

(b)

Fig. 18.1 (a) Swelling of parotid gland, **(b)** Incision line for parotidectomy.

salivary glands, infections and autoimmune states like Sjögren's syndrome. In mouth-breathing children and elderly persons, xerostomia can develop.

(b) *Radiation induced:* Ionized radiation of head and neck region involving the salivary gland region results in degeneration of acini and replacement by fibrous or fatty tissue. The extent of damage is directly proportional to the radiation dose.

(c) *Pharmacologically induced*: Since most of the dental patients are prescribed similar type of medication, one must keep in mind the groups of drugs which may have xerostomic side effect. In general, anticholinergic effect of these drugs and eventual interference with salivary secretion are not exclusive to the salivary glands. They may also produce itchy or dry eyes and constipation. It is debated as to whether long-term therapy may lead to irreversible changes in the salivary glands. The pharmacological agents with xerostomia side effects include anticonvulsants, antipyretics, anti-spasmodics, diuretics, decongestants, expectorants, muscle relaxants, CNS depression and sedatives.

Oral manifestations

The following are some of the main functions of saliva which are likely to be affected:

(i) The oral tissues are kept moist during chewing, deglutition and speech.
(ii) Neutralization of the acid.
(iii) Protection against disease.
(iv) The mechanical removal of food.

Symptoms

Burning sensation of the oral cavity, ulcerations, dryness, difficulty in the retention of the dentures and abnormalities of taste and smell.

Signs

Rampant caries, epithelial atrophy and infection of the salivary glands.

The oral mucosa is dry, smooth and shiny. Changes in the tongue vary from slight reddening and fissuring to severe lobulations. The glands are more prone to infections, prevalent with candidiasis. Dental caries develop in all the surfaces of teeth resulting in the amputation of the crown.

Investigations

Salivary gland imaging:

Sialography is useful to visualize the ductal structure radiographically. It defines sialoliths, strictures, infections and neoplasms.

MRI (magnetic resonance imaging) and *CT images* provide very good visualization of the glandular parenchyma. They also help to determine volumetric estimation of the gland.

Scintigraphy provides dynamic measures of the gland in function.

Serologic evaluation may be helpful in these cases. Serum amylase is elevated in cases of salivary gland dysfunctions.

Biopsy and FNAC (Fine Needle Aspiration biopsy) may provide clue to the true nature of changes.

Treatment

This include management of xerostomia and prevention of side effects due to lack of saliva.

(i) *Acid mouth-wash* increases the salivation, but prolonged use of citric acid results in the erosion of the enamel. If there is no response to stimulants, salivary substitutes may be necessary to relieve the soft tissue discomfort and to induce rehardening of softened tooth surface. It is preferable to avoid dry, spicy or acidic foods and carbonated beverages.

(ii) *Reversibility of xerostomia.* Etiology of mouth breathing should be eliminated. Patients on self medication are to be advised to abstain from such drugs, if possible.

(iii) *Reduction of medication.* Whenever it is not possible to reverse the process of xerostomia by stopping such drugs, reduction of medication provides some relief.

(iv) *Alternate therapy.* Patients on antidepressant medication with xerostomic effects should be advised to change over to drugs without the xerostomic effects. Wherever not possible, concurrent use of cholinergic drugs are helpful to minimize the anticholinergic effect. Bethanechol chloride is one such drug which does not interfere with antidepressant effect, but at the same time, relieving anticholinergic effect of tricyclic antidepressants. Sialogogues like pilocarpine can be prescribed to counter the anticholinergic effect of the drug.

(v) *Patient's motivation.* Dental procedures fail in the absence of strict adherence to prescribed home care. Even if all the teeth are extracted and dentures are provided, xerostomic patients suffer from increased denture sores and problems of denture retention.

(vi) *Long-term xerostomia* results in poor prognosis for the remaining dentition. Hence, every attempt must be made to eliminate xerostomia.

Cleft Lip and Cleft Palate

INTRODUCTION

Malformations are nothing but variations of natural development (embryogenesis). In general, many grades of the individual malformations can be seen in clinical practice. The clefts of the upper lip and palate are one of the common developmental anomalies found in everyday practice. The future of a person with cleft can influence the psychic development and be reflected in the personality. For social interaction, unacceptable appearance of the face, unclear language and even hearing loss could be a handicap. All of them can affect the self-confidence of the affected person.

Cleft lip and palate forms a small proportion of all the congenital malformations in the range of one in every 1000 live births (1:1000). This ratio may vary from country to country. Studies have revealed several interesting facts about these conditions.

(i) *Hereditary etiology* has been attributed to nearly 50% of children with cleft lip and palate and 20 to 25 % of children with cleft palate.

(ii) *Risk factor:*
  (a) If both the parents are *not* affected with cleft — 4% risk of the child developing cleft lip and palate, and 2% risk for cleft palate.
  (b) If any one parent is affected with cleft-9% risk for developing cleft lip and palate and — 1% risk for developing only cleft palate.
  (c) If both the parents are affected with cleft — 50 to 60 % risk of developing cleft.
  (d) If one child is affected with cleft — 15 to 20 % risk of the next child developing cleft.

(iii) The incidence of cleft lip and palate is 2 or 3 times more than the incidence of cleft palate.

(iv) In general, boys are more prone to cleft lip and palate while, cleft palate appears to be more common in girls.

(v) Submucous clefts form 5 to 10 % of all the clefts.

(vi) Unilateral clefts are more common than bilateral clefts, in the ratio of nearly 3:1, more commonly involving the left side of the face.

(vii) They frequently occur following consanguinous marriage. Since many of these cases have a positive family history, it is better to routinely chart the pedigree of the family at least for three generations.

(viii) Cleft children are born to young mothers and aged fathers.

CLASSIFICATION

GROUP I Cleft involving lip only - Unilateral (right or left) or bilateral. Complete or incomplete. (Fig. 19.1a) (Cleft of the primary palate).

GROUP I(a) Cleft involving lip and alveolus—Unilateral (right or left) or bilateral. (Cleft of the primary palate). (Fig. 19.1b)

GROUP II Cleft involving palate only (in various grades seen in the midline, in the order of severity)

— bifid uvula
— bifid uvula and soft palate
— bifid uvula, soft and hard palate
— submucous cleft of the soft palate.

(Cleft of the secondary palate).

GROUP III Cleft involving lip, alveolus and palate — Unilateral or bilateral. (Cleft of the primary and secondary palate). (Fig. 19.1c, d)

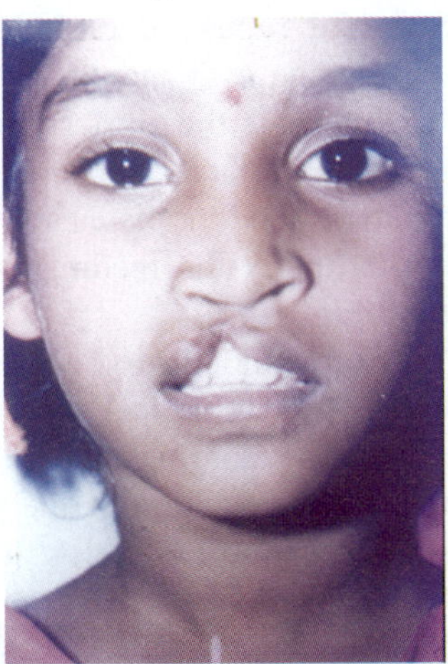

Fig. 19.1 (a) Unilateral incomplete cleft lip-left side.

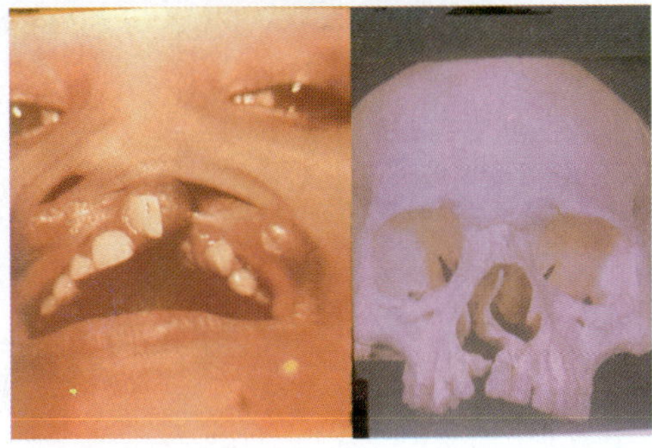

Fig. 19.1 (b) Unilateral incomplete cleft lip-right side. Small showing the bony defect.

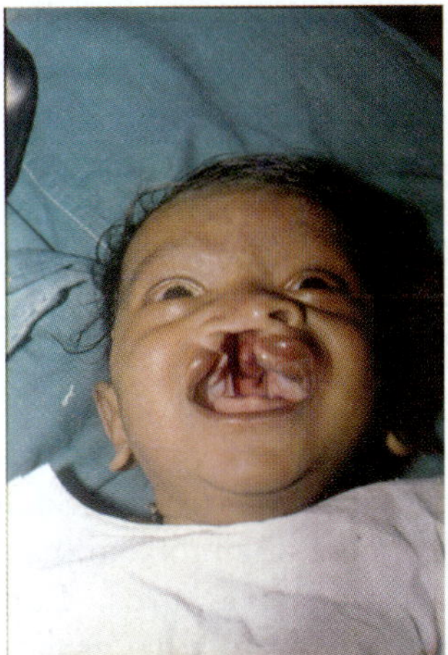

Fig. 19.1 (c) Group-III unilateral cleft.

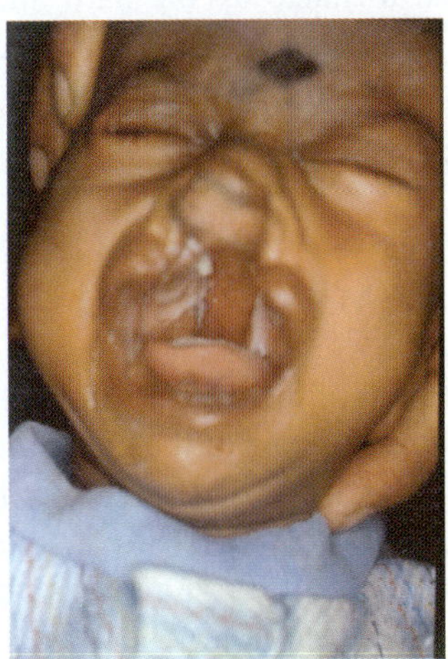

Fig. 19.1 (d) Group-III bilateral cleft with projecting premaxilla.

ANATOMY OF THE CLEFTS

Anatomically, the cleft is the discontinuity of the lip and/or dental alveolus and palatal shelf with the nasal lining continuous with intraoral palatal and labial mucosa. This will lead to the development of oronasal fistula of varying shapes and sizes.

(a) *Unilateral cleft lip (complete):* Functional abnormalities arise due to the lack of attachment of all the nasolabial muscles. The cleft is situated on one side of the midline, resulting in a larger two-thirds and a smaller one-third segment of the lip.

(b) *Unilateral incomplete cleft lip:* It varies from a small notch to almost complete cleft of the affected side of the lip.

(c) *Bilateral complete cleft lip:* The lip is divided into two lateral segments and one medial segment. Muscle is absent in the middle segment and it is attached to the premaxilla. Because of the absence of muscle control, premaxilla is placed anterior to the rest of the maxilla.

In these deformities, there is a deficiency of primary mesoectodermal tissues. Such absence of tissues creates more of a problem than the obvious seperation of the structures. Early surgical intervention interferes with the growth of maxilla. That is why mere surgical repair will not be enough. It is essential to make up the hard and soft tissue deficiency. Dental occlusion tends to be mutilated unless it is corrected during the growth period. Due to the deficiency of the oropharyngeal structures, speech will also be affected.

MANAGEMENT

The management of the cleft lip and palate does not stop with surgical repair of the clefts alone. It starts from the day of birth of the child till the facial growth is completed by 18 to 21 years of age. Ideally, these patients require structural and functional reconstruction. Therefore, the overall management is best undertaken by a team of professionals including plastic surgeons, orthodontists, oral and maxillofacial surgeons, ENT surgeons and speech therapists with any one of them to assume the primary responsibility of the child depending on the available professional services. Irrespective of whosoever takes the primary responsibility, the general principles of the objectives and sequence of treatment is determined by the facilities available, which may vary from country to country. However, the following protocol has been found to be effective in the majority of cleft lip and palate patients.

Sequence and objectives of treatment

The following sequence is suggested based on the dental criteria.

Phase I (Upto 6 months - *PREDENTITION PHASE*). Surgical repair of cleft lip is usually undertaken at the age of 3 months or even before. This is to reconstruct the oral sphincter and to restore the acceptable facial appearance. To avoid nasal regurgitation, feeding plates are utilized. Still better method is to fix the feeding plate with the feeding bottle. (Fig. 19.2).

Phase II (from 6 months to 6 years - *PRIMARY DENTITION PHASE*). Surgical repair of the cleft palate (soft and hard palate) is undertaken at the age of 12 months. Reconstruction of the palate before the child attempts to speak helps to reduce the

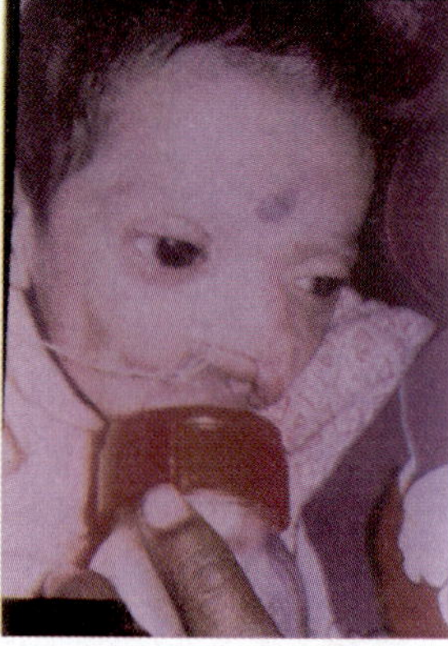

Fig. 19.2 Cleft child with the feeding bottle with acrylic plate in position.

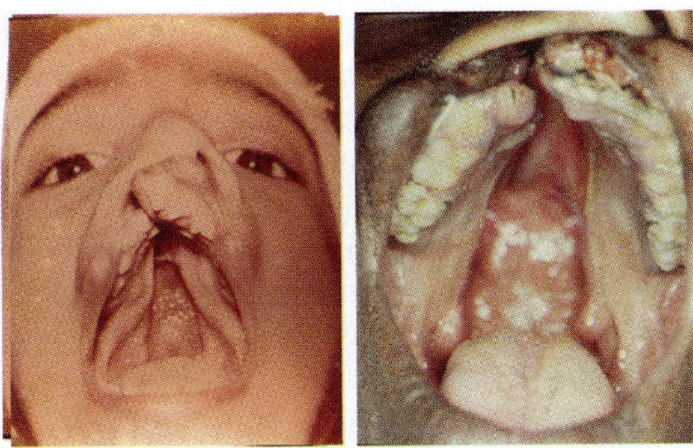

Fig. 19.3 Unilateral and bilateral group-III.

severity of the defective speech. Soon after the palate is repaired, the child must be evaluated by an ENT surgeon and a speech therapist. Dental surgeon should attend to the dental needs of the primary dentition. Mutilation of the dental arches needs correction, as shown in the photograph (Fig. 19.3)

Phase III (from 6 to 12 years. - *MIXED DENTITION PHASE*). During this phase, secondary repair of the lip and palate and correction of the cleft lip nose are undertaken. Simultaneously, it is the responsibility of the dental surgeon to provide preventive and restorative care of the deciduous and permanent dentition including prevention of malocclusion and maintenance of oral hygiene. Experience has taught us that the typical nose deformity in these children can be corrected by performing alveolar bone grafting to reconstruct the alveolar defect between the age of 8 and 11 years. This also helps the canine tooth to erupt properly. (Fig. 19.4)

Phase IV (from 12 to 18 years - *ADOLESCENT PHASE*). Active orthodontic treatment is undertaken during this phase. Growth disturbances in horizontal and /or vertical directions become obvious. Therefore, objective of orthodontic treatment is to correct these growth

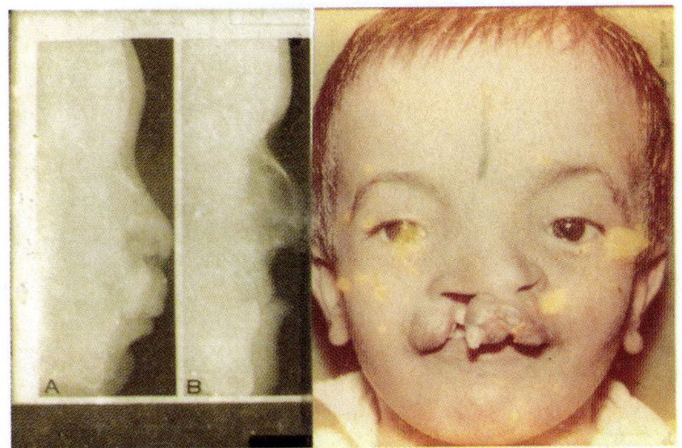

Fig. 19.4 (a) Facial deformity obvious during growth phase.

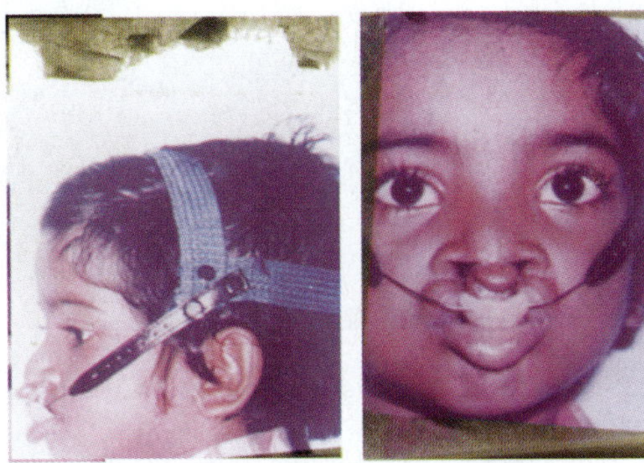

Fig. 19.4 (c) Dentofacial orthopedic appliance in position.

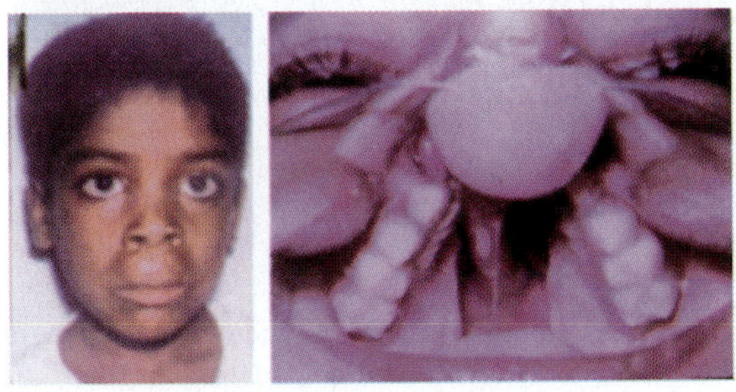

Fig. 19.4 (b) Prominent premaxilla.

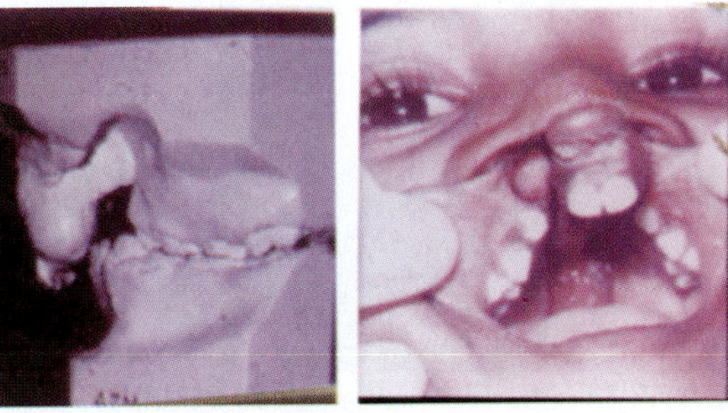

Fig. 19.4 (d) Projecting premaxilla.

disturbances to the extent possible. By 18 years of age, the residual deformities, if any, will need surgical correction. (Figs 19.5 to 19.8).

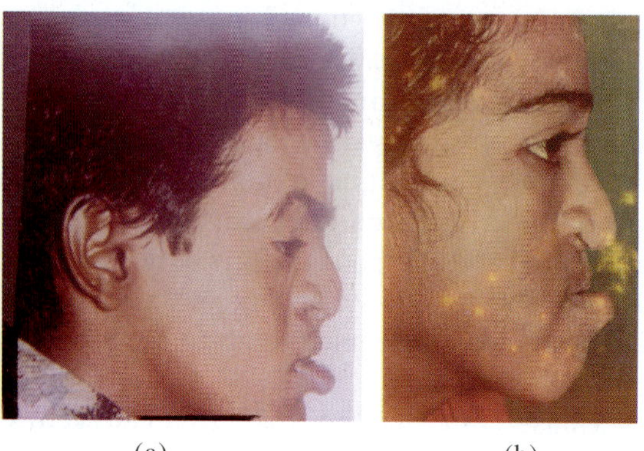

(a) (b)

Fig. 19.5 **(a)** Midface retrusion, **(b)** Retrusion more obvious when the patient grows.

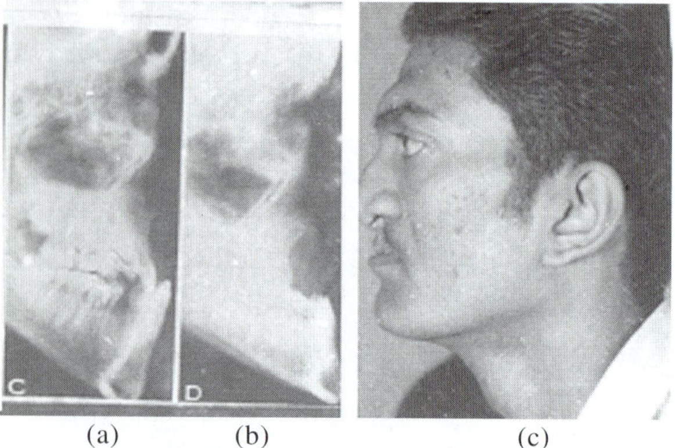

(a) (b) (c)

Fig. 19.6 Midface retrusion obvious with pseudo-prognathic mandible.

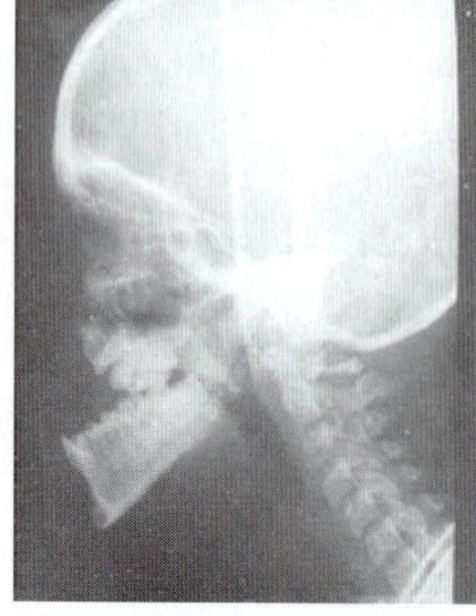

Fig. 19.7 Maxilla rudimentary due to multiple surgery of the palate. Mandible prognathic.

Phase V (above 18 years - ADULT PHASE). Orthognathic surgery can ideally be undertaken during this phase. Finally, a suitable protheses will restore the defective dental occlusion. (Figs 19.6, 19.7)

The above account will provide a general bird's eye view of the overall management of the cleft patients. This is to help the dental surgeon who is

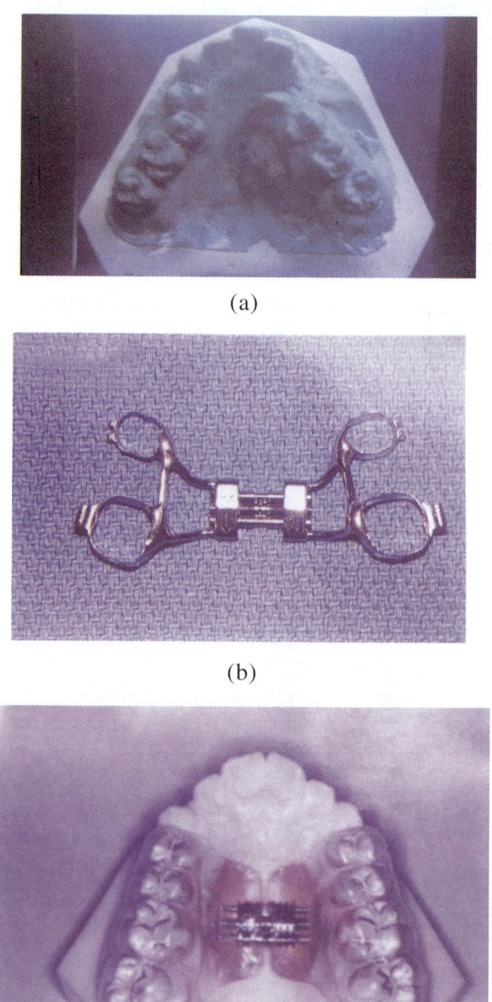

(a)

(b)

(c)

Fig. 19.8 **(a)** Collapsed lateral segment, **(b)** Expansion appliance to be bonded, **(c)** Expansion appliance in position-collapsed arch corrected.

willing to undertake the primary responsibility of the cleft child. From the dental specialist's point of view four aspects of the problem are illustrated below.

1. Teeth in relation to the alveolar clefts

Four possibilities exist:

(a) Cleft is seen between the central incisor and canine with the absence of lateral incisor tooth.

(b) Cleft is seen between lateral incisor and canine with malformed (conical) lateral incisor tooth.

(c) Cleft is seen between central incisor and canine tooth with a split lateral incisor tooth - one in the mesial segment and the other in the distal segment. Both are malformed.

(d) Very rarely, cleft is seen between central and lateral incisor tooth.

In all these cases, canine tooth may be malpositioned or may fail to erupt for want of bony base.

2. Morbidities associated with alveolar clefts

(a) *Oronasal fistula* results in the regurgitation of food materials and fluids through the nasal cavity. The nasal escape of air will produce faulty nasal speech.

(b) On the affected side, alar support is lost resulting in the typical cleft-lip nose deformity. (Fig. 19.4 (a))

(c) In bilateral cases, premaxilla may be mobile, attached to the nasal septum. In younger children, it may look protuberant but later, it will be retropositioned due to the deficient growth of the midface. (Fig. 19.4 (d))

(d) A three-dimensional collapse of the maxillary segment on the affected side leads to dental malocclusion. (Fig. 19.8 (a))

(e) Teeth in relation to the cleft show many variations, as described above. Some of them may erupt into the cleft.

3. Alveolar bone grafting

Aims and objectives:

(a) To provide the bony bridge in the cleft region to stabilize the maxillary alveolar segments.

(b) To provide the required bony base for the teeth in the cleft region to erupt properly.

(c) To provide the bony base for the nasal alar base - to avoid cleft nose deformity.

(d) To close the oronasal fistula so that the need for the prostheses can be eliminated.

(e) To avoid the development of malocclusion thereby providing a satisfactory complete dental arch.

Timing: Formerly, many have attempted unsuccessfully to perform primary bone grafting at the time of primary lip repair since this procedure was found to be responsible for severe disturbances of maxillary growth as the child grows. Now it is universally accepted all over the world to do secondary bone grafting during the mixed dentition phase, prior to the eruption of the permanent canine tooth between 8 and 11 years. This corresponds to the initiation of root formation. This means that earlier the bone graft (before 8 years) higher will be the risk for the maxillary growth disturbances.

4. Biomechanics of bone grafting

(a) The osteogenesis depends on the biological status and survival of new bone cell following grafting.

(b) Cancellous bone is the ideal grafting material since they form a network of bony trabeculae with bone marrow containing osteogenic cells. Therefore, invasion of bone marrow spaces by the new vessels from the recipient site becomes easier. On the contrary, very few cells survive from cortical bone grafts. Moreover, resorption of the cortical bone with the invasion of new blood vessels is a slow process.

(c) Donor sites: The common donor sites are (i) Iliac crest, (ii) Rib, (iii) Mandible, (iv) Calvarian bone and (v) Tibia. Iliac crest provides plenty of cancellous bone. Morbidity is low. Therefore, it is the most widely used bone graft donor site. Recently, other sites have been utilized to get intramembranous bone grafts. For example, mandibular symphysis after the eruption of incisors (after 8 years of age) provide an alternate donor site. Easy access through intraoral approach is the reason for utilizing this donor site. However, quantity of the graft may not be sufficient for reconstructing bilateral alveolar clefts. Outer table of the parietal bone provides unlimited amount of bone. Likewise, rib can also be another alternate site.

(d) In all the cases of alveolar bone grafting, marginal bone level on cleft-related teeth must be assessed on intraoral periapical radiographs and quantified.

Surgically assisted rapid palatal expansion (Fig. 19.8)

Orthodontic rapid palatal expansion [RPE] is an useful procedure in growing children exhibiting marked three-dimensional maxillary collapse. Determination of the need for surgery before orthodontic expansion of the maxillary arch requires differentiation between skeletal and occlusal discrepancies. In such selected cases, this procedure becomes an integral part of orthodontic surgery in cleft patients. The relative lack of complications and good stability are some of the important reasons for performing this procedure. Extensive studies have proved that midpalatal, zygomaticomaxillary and pterygomaxillary articulations are found to be the primary sites of resistance to expansion forces. Therefore, this forms the biomechanical rationale for the osteotomies in this procedure. (Fig. 19.8 a, b, c)

Orthognathic surgery (Fig. 19.9 a, b)

During the adolescent period, active orthodontic treatment will be very helpful to reduce the severity of the maxillary hypoplasia. Clinical, model and cephalometric analysis will reveal the residual three-dimentional deformities of the maxillofacial region. Efforts must be directed to assess whether maxillary hypoplasia is at the dentoalveolar level (Le Fort I level) or at the nasomaxillary level (Le Fort II).

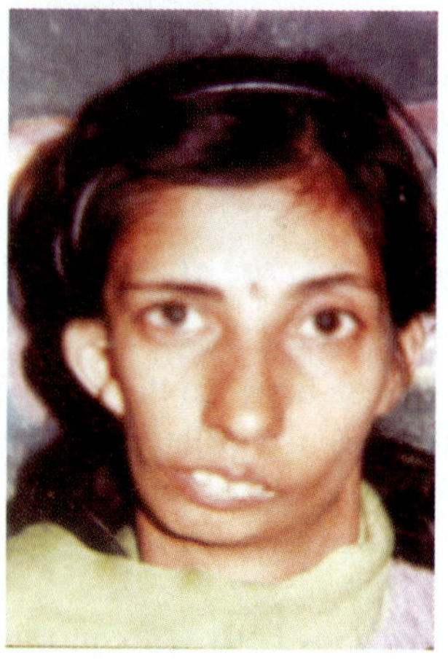

(a)

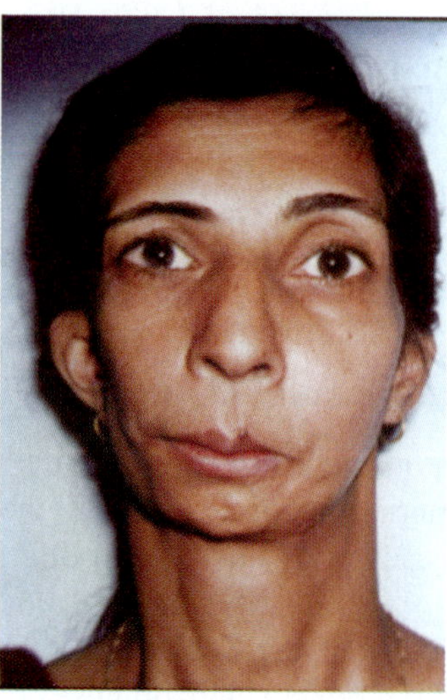

(b)

Fig. 19.9 Congenital defects of the mandible. **(a)** & **(b)** Pre and postoperative photographs, correcting the defect with orthognathic surgery.

Secondly, attention must be directed to the mandible. Various possibilities exist with regard to the maxillomandibular relationship.

(a) In case of hypoplasia of maxilla with normal

mandible, surgery of the maxilla is indicated. This is likely to be misdiagnosed as prognathic mandible. Correct diagnosis would be hypoplastic maxilla (Pseudoprognathic mandible). (Fig. 19.6 (b))

(b) Maxilla may be hypoplastic associated with prognathic mandible. In such cases, bimaxillary surgery will be the treatment of choice.

(c) In unilateral cleft cases, facial asymmetry will develop with unilateral cross bite. Le Fort osteotomies in cleft patients develop more morbidities than in non cleft patients. Some of them are vascular complications, avascular necrosis of the cleft segments and residual orofacial deformities. On the whole, the entire defect must be viewed as a single entity with many components.

Our aim and objective should be to achieve excellent results with regard to speech, esthetics, class I occlusion and perfect hearing. Therefore there must be a perfect coordination among various members of the team to achieve optimum results.

Emergencies and Complications in Oral Surgery

MEDICAL EMERGENCIES

General consideration

Emergency is defined as an unforeseen or unexpected situation requiring immediate attention. In oral surgery practice, there are two possibilities: (a) A dental surgeon may be required to manage dental emergencies which may not arise as a result of treatment and (b) Sometimes the patient may call upon the dental surgeon, seeking emergency treatment for the suffering. Therefore, urgent treatment may be required to treat a complication or to relieve the suffering of the patient.

Fortunately, medical emergencies are relatively rare in a dental clinic. However, the prestige and professional success depends on the way the emergency is managed without mortality or morbidity, irrespective of the type of emergency. No discussion on emergencies and complications will be complete unless the following aspects are considered:

(a) General guidelines on emergencies
(b) Recognition of the emergency
(c) Management
(d) Preventive measures
(e) Complications.

General guidelines

Awareness, judgement and *preparedness* are the three basic requirements in professional practice.

Awareness. Every dental surgeon who is engaged in oral surgery practice must be aware of the general nature of the common medical emergencies that may arise during professional practice.

Judgement. In case of any such emergency, the dental surgeon should keep the mind calm and cool. Sound judgement without getting panicky will ensure successful management.

Preparedness. Instead of looking for the necessary aids after the onset of emergency, it is wise to prepare oneself and be in readiness to face such eventuality as a precautionary measure.

(i) To ensure non-occurrence of the medical emergencies, a comprehensive medical history must be elicited from the ambulatory patients to identify the medically compromised patients. Prevention is better than cure.
(ii) The clinician must be watchful to recognize any emergency which may arise. In certain emergencies, the time factor is very

important. Quick, spontaneous identification of such problems and institution of the emergency measures will save the life of the patient.

(iii) Availability of emergency drugs and equipment must be periodically checked.

(iv) Clinician must be familiar with all the resuscitative measures necessary for such emergency situations.

In case of any life-threatening emergency, one must adopt the following measures before the patient is taken over by the physician for further management:

Step I- The patient is positioned in a comfortable lying posture.

Step II- Patency of the airway must be monitored constantly. If necessary, the patient should be ventilated with free flow of oxygen under positive pressure.

Step III- Minimum of medication must be given to the patient. An accurate record of all the drugs given to the patient must be maintained in the chronological order.

Step IV- All the vital signs of the patient must be monitored and properly recorded.

Step V- Based on sound judgement, if necessary, resuscitative measures can be taken.

Step VI- In the meantime, arrangement must be made to seek the help of a competent physician.

Step VII- If necessary, transport arrangements must be kept ready for the hospitalization of the patient.

A brief account of the commonly encountered emergencies with the pathophysiology, clinical manifestations and salient features of crisis management are provided below. It is important that a few conditions are differentiated depending on the clinical manifestation.

The problems normally encountered are (a) altered consciousness, (b) chest pain and discomfort, (c) respiratory disturbances, and (d) allergic manifestations/anaphylaxis.

Systemic emergencies

Altered consciousness

During oral surgery procedures in conscious patients, disturbance to the level of consciousness must be recognized and attention must be given to avoid further complications. Many conditions may be responsible for its occurrence. The disturbance may range from disorientation to total loss of consciousness.

Vasovagal attack

It is one of the common causes for the transient loss of consciousness. The predisposing factors are anxiety, fear, sight of blood, pain and exhaustion. Such emotional stress induces the release of increased amounts of catecholamines. Consequent decrease in peripheral resistance results in peripheral pooling of blood and fall in blood pressure. This leads to a series of compensatory mechanisms like tachycardia, rapid breathing, sweating and a feeling of warmth. This chain of reactions leads to vagally mediated reflex, bradycardia, hypotension, cerebral ischemia and loss of consciousness. The clinician must recognize these features sufficiently early so that further progress could be prevented by instituting the following measures:

(a) Termination of further dental treatment until the patient recovers.

(b) The patient should be placed in the supine position.

(c) Legs should be raised to promote venous return and also to prevent pooling of blood at the extremities.

(d) Loosening of the clothing.

(e) Monitoring the airway and vital signs.

(f) Administration of oxygen, if necessary.

(g) Respiratory stimulant like spiritus ammonia should be placed near the nostril.

(h) If fainting episode prolongs beyond 5 to 10 minutes, the patient should be monitored and evaluated to rule out the conditions like hypoglycemia, cardiac problems, cerebrovascular accident, shock. etc.

Postural hypotension

There are some ambulatory patients who have predisposition to such orthostatic hypotension. This is common in medically compromised patients who are on medications which produce intravascular depletion, e.g. diuretics, non-diuretic antihypertensive agents, psychiatric drugs and narcotics. If such patients complain of palpitations and generalized weakness, they should be put on reclining position so that they recover immediately.

Diabetes mellitus

If a diabetic becomes unconscious during the course of the oral surgical procedures, the treatment should be stopped forthwith. There are two possibilities for the unconsciousness: (a) Hypoglycemia or (b) Diabetic coma. Hypoglycemic coma is more common.

Pathophysiology: Any diabetic (particularly uncontrolled) runs the risk of lowered serum glucose level. In a diabetic patient, glucose level represents the delicate balance between the insulin level and the glucose utilization. Physical activity, increased administration of insulin, increased metabolic utilization like infection and emotional stress lead to hypoglycemia. Decreased intake of food or missing a meal prior to oral surgery further aggravates the situation. If insulin intake is not reduced, hypoglycemic condition gets worsened and the patient may develop symptoms. Depending on whether it is mild, moderate or severe, symptoms like tachycardia, headache, visual disturbances, confusion, disorientation, weakness and loss of consciousness may develop.

If mild, the patient will be disoriented but conscious. Glucose is the only source of energy to maintain the intracellular metabolism in the brain. Brain is very sensitive to lowering of the glucose level. It is unable to utilize the circulating fatty acids as the source of energy. Hence, early recognition of hypoglycemic features help the dental surgeon to reverse this condition by encouraging the patient to take glucose orally. The response is usually quick and rapid. If the patient becomes semiconscious or unconscious, dextrose solution must be administered parenterally. All the important vital signs must be monitored. If necessary, oxygen can be administered. Immediately, services of a physician must be requisitioned for further management. In practice, hypoglycemia is one of the common problems encountered in a diabetic patient. Hence, it can be avoided by undertaking the treatment in the mornings.

It is relatively uncommon for hyperglycemia to develop in an ambulant diabetic patient. Usually, diabetic coma develops in patients who are ill for a few days. The characteristic features are dry skin, hypotension and acetone breath. The onset is slow and pulse becomes weak. Such a patient is best managed by a physician for the correct diagnosis and prompt treatment.

Primary insufficiency due to pathology of adrenal cortex

It is very rare. But secondary insufficiency is relatively a common condition because corticosteroids are therapeutically administered for a variety of systemic conditions. If any such patient is physiologically or emotionally stressed, adrenal suppression due to steroid therapy may prevent the normal release of endogenous glucocorticoids needed to meet the increased metabolic demands.

The symptoms of secondary insufficiency are disorientation, fatigue, hypotension, nausea, abdominal pain and partial or complete loss of consciousness. The body is unable to manage the challenge of stresses like infection, surgery, pain and anxiety. This results in adrenal crisis in patients who are on 20 mg or more of steroid, at least for 2 to 3 weeks period. In such patients, coma is the prefatal condition. Therefore, they should be supplemented with additional steroids prior to any dental treatment. Early recognition of the clinical features is of great importance. Further dental treatment should be stopped. The patient is put on supine position with elevation of feet. All the vital signs must be carefully monitored. Oxygen therapy must be started immediately. Services of the physician must be requisitioned. In the meantime, intravenous fluids must be given to combat hypotension. Depending on the degree of crisis, intravenous steroid is the life-saving drug. Prevention of such crisis is preferable in such patients.

Epilepsy

This is a chronic and recurrent disturbance of the central nervous system with convulsions followed by loss of consciousness. Most of these patients are aware of their problem. They must be warned about the importance of medications. Hence, usually it is rare to have any emergency with this group of patients.

Sometimes, during the dental treatment, grand mal epileptic fits begin with a warning or premonition. Rarely, intravenous sedation may be necessary. But care is taken to ensure that airway is kept patent during the unconscious phase.

Chest pain and discomfort

Even though a variety of clinical conditions may be responsible for the chest pain, the clinician must be aware of the importance of early recognition of the heart disease and the conditions which can mimic the cardiac problems. Any patient above the middle age with family history of ischemic heart disease and who is a chronic smoker is at potential risk. Coronary heart disease may be due to decreased blood supply to the myocardium. Mild imbalance between the demand and supply of oxygen to myocardium results in angina pectoris while partial or complete depletion results in myocardial infarction referred to as "heart attack".

In angina, the patient describes it as chest discomfort. Such pain may range from mild to moderate intensity, originating from the substernal region, radiating across the chest, mandible, shoulder and other areas of the diaphragm over the left side. This may be precipitated by physical exertion and emotional stress. It lasts for a few minutes. It is usually relieved with sublingual nitroglycerine.

In myocardial infarction, the arterial insufficiency to the myocardium is more acute. Its clinical preservation is characterized by chest discomfort. The patient characteristically describes the discomfort as substernal squeezing, choking, crushing, sharp or lancinating type of pain. The pain typically radiates along the left shoulder, arm and the mandibular region. This is usually precipitated in patient-at-risk by exertion, anxiety or emotional stress. It is accompanied by nausea, dyspnea, palpitations, profuse sweating and hypotension. The pain is not relieved by rest or nitroglycerine.

(a) In either case, further dental treatment should be stopped and the patient is put on reclined position. Oxygen must be administered immediately. All the vital signs must be monitored carefully, 0.4 mg nitroglycerine tablet must be given to the patient.

(b) If it is anginal attack, improvement can be noticed. Within 3-4 minutes, if there is no improvement, the patient must be presumed to have suffered from heart attack. Immediately, services of a physician must be requested. Any delay during the immediate phase to impart the necessary resuscitative measures is likely to be hazardous.

(c) The oral surgeon must be aware of the possible differential diagnosis in case of such chest discomfort:

- (i) Gastrointestinal disturbances like dyspepsia.
- (ii) Muscular spasm of the intercostal muscles.
- (iii) Psychogenic hyperventilation.
- (iv) Cardiopulmonary arrest.

Respiratory emergencies

The following are some of the emergencies

involving respiratory system which may become life-threatening if resuscitative measures are not promptly provided:

(a) Foreign body aspiration
(b) Bronchial asthma
(c) Hyperventilation
(d) Cardiopulmonary arrest.

(a) **Foreign body aspiration.** Aspiration of a foreign body may be accidental during the oral surgery procedures. Airway obstruction may be partial or complete depending on the degree of blockage of the airway. If it happens to be small and partial, the patient is encouraged to cough out foreign bodies like inlay restorations, tooth, root canal instruments, etc. If the obstruction is complete due to objects like the denture blocking the airway completely, serious complications may arise, e.g. loss of consciousness and dyspnea. Laryngoscope, if available, is useful to visualize the object by a trained personnel. In emergency situations, airway can be restored by puncturing the cricothyroid membrane as a simple procedure. It may not be feasible to perform procedures like tracheostomy. Sooner the arrangements are made to get the physician's services and to hospitalize the patient for further management, the better for the patient.

(b) **Bronchial asthma.** The patient who gives history of bronchial asthma may develop acute attack triggered by emotional stress during the treatment procedures. Since most of them are familiar with the characteristic features of bronchospasm, they themselves provide relief through self-medication like bronchodilator inhalations. It is characterized by paroxysmal wheezing, dyspnea, cough and reversible bronchial smooth muscle spasm. The term *orthopnea* refers to difficulty in breathing in all the positions except in the upright posture. *Dyspnea* means difficulty in breathing. It is also air-hunger (on exertion or even at rest). *Wheezing* is forced respiration due to bronchial narrowing. In asthma, it is paroxysmal, while it is localized in bronchial obstructions. In asthmatic patients, inspiration is normal but bronchospasm produces labored expiration and wheezing. The patient may express desire to sit up, very much agitated and becomes restless. Rarely, the patient may also develop cyanosis. Asthma is of two types. Allergy may be the etiological factor in extrinsic type while due to emotional stress, anxiety, or as a response to infection, the patient may develop asthma of intrinsic type. Before he becomes unconscious, a series of relief measures must be provided.

Management.

(i) Reassurance to the patient.
(ii) The patient must be allowed to assume the erect or reclining posture.
(iii) Administration of bronchodilators in the form of inhalations or injection of ephedrine 0.3ml (1:1000 dilution) through intramuscular route.
(iv) Oxygen administration.
(v) Stress reduction with sedation.
(vi) Provision of medical assistance and arrangement of hospitalization.

(c) **Hyperventilation.** It is one of the common causes for the collapse of the patient in the dental chair. It is considered to be a hysteria anxiety component, manifested at the conscious level. It refers to ventilation in excess, more than what is required for the maintenance of optimum levels of oxygen and carbon dioxide. It results in respiratory alkalosis. One may notice increased respiratory rate and depth in such a condition. As the pH of the blood rises, calcium metabolism becomes altered. Such a decreased blood ionized calcium leads to paresthesia and numbness of extremities, perioral region, cramps and even convulsions. As in the case of fainting, prevention is preferable.

Management.

(i) It is aimed at early recognition.
(ii) Reduction of the anxiety level.
(iii) Correction of the respiratory problem can be achieved by advising the patient to hold the breath for sometime, just enough to reverse the respiratory alkalosis.

(iv) Reassurance of the patient and regulation of breathing.

(v) The patient is seated in the upright posture.

(vi) If these steps are not effective, the patient can be encouraged by rebreathing the exhaled air through a paper bag.

(vii) Hospitalization, if necessary.

(d) **Cardiopulmonary arrest.** This is a more serious emergency which should be recognized early and should be treated efficiently. This is a disorder involving the arrest of ventilation and circulation. This occurs usually in patients with pre-existing cardiovascular disease, anaphylaxis, asphyxia and overdose of drugs. Careful monitoring of vital signs is mandatory. The clinical presentation is characterized by lack of chest and abdominal movements, pulse, breath sounds and consciousness. Pupils are dilated.

Management.

(i) Early recognition and institution of urgent relief measures alone can save the life of the patient. Cardiopulmonary resuscitation must be started immediately. Delay of more than 4 minutes will result in irreversible brain damage.

(ii) The condition of the patient will deteriorate rapidly. A good teamwork is needed to save the life under such threatening circumstances.

(iii) Maintenance of patent airway is of paramount importance.

(iv) If breathing fails to resume spontaneously, there should not be any delay in requisitioning the services of a physician and hospitalization at the earliest possible opportunity.

(v) Depending on the available facilities, any of the accepted remedial measures must be provided. They include mouth-to-mouth breathing, closed cardiac massage, etc.

(vi) Further management should be left under the care of a competent physician since this complication may prove fatal.

Allergy and anaphylaxis

These terms refer to immunologically mediated response often called hypersensitivity. Even though it is uncommon in day-to-day practice, the dental surgeon must be familiar with this so that early recognition is possible. During the surgery practice, it develops as an emergency, sequel to administration of a few drugs. The drug responsible for such a reaction is called antigen. For anaphylaxis to develop, an initial exposure to an antigen is necessary. At that time, lymphocytes are stimulated by antigens, resulting in the release of specific antibodies. They attach themselves to the cell walls of the tissue mast cells and circulating basophils. On subsequent exposure, such sensitized antibodies are capable of initiating anaphylactic reactions. This results in degranulation of mast cells and basophils and the release of chemical mediators like histamine and prostaglandin. These chemical mediators are responsible for a series of reactions involving cardiovascular, respiratory, gastrointestinal and central nervous systems. The common drugs responsible for these reactions include ester type of local anesthetic agents like procaine or benzocaine and very rarely lidocaine. It may be in the form of urticaria, angioedema, generalized loss of vascular tone and hypotension. Histamine released during this reaction leads to capillary dilatation, increased capillary permeability, bronchospasm and stimulation of secretions like expectoration, rhinorrhea, etc. The histamine leads to pronounced circulatory failure.

Management.

(a) Stress reduction.

(b) The patient placed in supine position.

(c) Maintenance of the airway.

(d) Oxygen administration.

(e) Starting of I.V. infusion.

(f) If the circulatory response has resulted in blood pressure falling below 50 mm of mercury, epinephrine is administered intramuscularly. Administration of anti-histamine and injection of glucocorticoid are optional. Acute angioneurotic edema and dyspnea are also relieved by the injection of ephedrine.

(g) Convulsions may be treated symptomatically with Diazepam IV.

(h) Physician's services and hospitalization must be arranged without delay.

HEMORRHAGE IN ORAL SURGERY

(1) General considerations
(2) Normal patients
    (a) Intraoperative
        (i) Incisions
        (ii) Various hemostatic techniques
    (b) Postoperative
        (i) Primary
        (ii) Reactionary
        (iii) Secondary
    (c) Management of bleeding following dental extraction
(3) Bleeding disorders
    (a) Coagulation defects
    (b) Thrombocytopenia
    (c) Capillary abnormalities
(4) Transfusions
    (a) To set up a drip
    (b) Autotransfusion
    (c) Homologous transfusion
    (d) RBC (packed cells)
    (e) Platelet concentrates
    (f) Cryoprecipitate

General considerations

Hemostasis is a physiological process by which bleeding gets arrested from the traumatized vascular system. In a normal person, this process is usually under control. But anomalies of the bleeding process may occur due to many factors which may interfere with hemostasis. Prolonged bleeding in oral surgery practice is one of the common complications which can be annoying to the patient and the clinician. Physiologically, the intravascular factors are present in the blood platelets, calcium and the coagulation proteins. Extravascular factors are present in the organ systems and connective tissue. The vascular factors include the type, size and location of the blood vessels.

In oral surgery practice, one must take adequate precautions during the surgery to avoid this unpleasant complication. If it develops, one must be able to manage the patient effectively.

Thus, management of these patients is grouped as follows:

(1) Normal patients
    (a) Intraoperative
    (b) Postoperative
(2) Patients with bleeding as a complication
(3) Patients with preexisting bleeding disorders.

Intraoperative hemorrhage

It may occur in patients without the bleeding diathesis due to many reasons. All of them are concerned with the surgeon and surgical techniques. Adequate steps are required on the following aspects to keep the hemorrhage under control:

(a) Placement of incision in relation to the blood vessels.
(b) Adoption of various hemostatic techniques.
(i) Vasoconstrictors added in the local anesthetic agent.
(ii) Hypotensive general anesthesia.
(iii) Intraoperative measures for securing hemostasis.

Incisions. Incisions in oral surgery have been designed in such a way that the surgeon will not encounter or avoid any major blood vessels while placing the incisions. If at all necessary, it can be placed parallel to the long axis of the blood vessel. For example, greater palatine vessels run parallel to the dental arch. Hence, it is advantageous to place the incisions parallel to the dental arch, avoiding the location of the blood vessel. Similarly, incisions on the labial aspect of maxillary canines can injure superior labial vessels. Labial vestibular incisions around the mandibular molar region can damage the facial artery. One has to be careful about the anatomical limitations while making incisions. Similarly, incision for a mucoperiosteal flap must be made deep down to the bone since the blood vessels are situated supraperiosteally. If the flap is raised supraperiosteally, brisk and troublesome bleeding is encountered. It is also better to avoid placing incisions over any inflamed area which predisposes to bleeding. Incisions may be made with surgical diathermy knife to arrest hemorrhage during incision.

Hemostatic techniques and their importance. These are established facts for a relatively bloodless operating field. Failure to achieve adequate hemostasis will interfere with surgical procedures. Sometimes, it may even produce adverse systemic effects, including shock. To avoid such surgical complications, the surgeon has to institute various hemostatic measures.

(i) *Vasoconstrictors.* They are usually incorporated in the local anesthetic drugs to prolong the anesthetic effect. Incidentally, the surgeon gets an additional benefit of relative hemostasis by reducing capillary hemorrhage. However, this advantage is effective in infiltration and not possible in block anesthesia. Unfortunately, it has been noticed that once the effect of adrenaline passes off, the consequent reactive hyperemia produces bleeding after a few hours called *reactionary hemorrhage*. Adrenaline is also known to produce a few undesirable cardiac arrhythmias, if halogenated anesthetic agents are employed.

(ii) *Hypotensive general anesthesia.* It is one of the accepted methods adopted by the anesthetist to avoid intraoperative hemorrhage complications. By this technique, blood pressure is intentionally brought down by using certain hypotensive anesthetic agents like Arfonad and maintained during the surgical procedure. By doing so, bleeding is also controlled. On completion of surgery, BP of the patient is restored to the optimum level. Unfortunately, inexperienced surgeon fails to identify the bleeding spots during the hypotensive state and hence such obvious bleeding points may be overlooked. When the BP returns to the normal level, bleeding starts from these spots. In elderly patients, it is likely that there may be the risk of thrombosis. Hence, the surgeon must realize the advantages and limitations of hypotensive anesthesia.

Intraoperative measures to secure hemostasis are too well known to all the surgeons. The following are some of them:

(1) Application of pressure (mechanical).
(2) Elective ligation of the arteries.
(3) Hemostats used for catching the bleeding points.
(4) Application of thrombin or viper venom precipitates clot formation.
(5) Packing the bony cavities with gauze pack soaked in Tr. Benzoin or Whitehead's varnish.
(6) Packing with oxidized regenerated cellulose (surgical) or any absorbable hemostatic agent like gelfoam.
(7) Application of hemostatic agent like bone wax on the bone bleeding points.
(8) Care must be taken to cauterize the bleeding spots with chemical agents since they can burn the normal mucous membrane.

Postoperative hemorrhage

Postoperative hemorrhage may occur due to the following factors:

(i) Failure to secure hemostasis even after the completion of surgery (primary hemorrhage).
(ii) After a short period of arrest of bleeding, hemorrhage restarts after a few hours (reactionary hemorrhage).
(iii) Bleeding starts after a few days following the breakdown of the blood-clot due to infection (secondary hemorrhage).

Primary hemorrhage. This refers to persistent bleeding even after the completion of surgery. Failure to provide hemostasis may be due to any of the following reasons:

(a) The patient is hypertensive with or without emotional stress.
(b) Preexistence of local infection at the site of surgery. For example, extraction of teeth with advanced periodontal disturbances are known to be notorious for troublesome bleeding.
(c) Punctured wounds, involving blood vessels like superior labial, facial or greater palatine vessels.

Reactionary hemorrhage. This occurs due to the following reasons:

(i) Reactionary vasodilation of vessels which are contracted during surgery because of the use of vasoconstrictors with local anesthetic drugs.

(ii) The blood clots are yet to be matured and contracted, a few hours after extraction. The patient may disturb the clot

(a) by vigorously gargling with warm liquids,
(b) by the application of heat inducing local hyperemia,
(c) due to rise of *blood pressure* after surgery and
(d) due to violent exercise resulting in general peripheral vasodilation. Alcohol consumption may trigger the reactionary bleeding.

Secondary hemorrhage: This may occur 4-10 days after the surgical procedure. During the immediate postoperative period, if the blood clot gets infected by streptococci, the toxins like fibrinolysin dissolves the clot, thereby wound starts bleeding profusely. Sometimes, onset of acute Vincent's infection may also result in secondary hemorrhage. A course of appropriate antibiotics with hemostatic measures will arrest such a hemorrhage.

Management of bleeding following dental extraction

(1) Proper understanding of the various sources of bleeding and identification of the underlying causes are necessary.

(2) The patient must be made to relax comfortably.

(3) Mouth must be rinsed with cold water gently to wash out the adherent clot and also to locate the bleeding spots.

(4) Thumb and index fingers are placed on the buccal and lingual sides of the socket and compressed firmly so that bleeding is arrested or controlled.

(5) If the hemorrhage is under control, then placement of mattress sutures across the socket may provide hemostasis since such a suture will result in compression of the mucoperiosteal flap against the bone.

(6) If the bleeding does not stop with all these measures, it is quite obvious that the bleeding originates from the bony socket.

(7) If it is so, the tooth socket is packed with gelfoam or surgical or ribbon-gauze soaked with Tr. Benzoin. If the tooth socket is packed with gelfoam or any other absorbable hemostatic agent, the flap can be sutured across the socket.

(8) If the bleeding does not stop, attempts must be made to identify the bleeding points so that they can be cauterized with diathermy.

(9) In case of profuse, uncontrolled hemorrhage, emergency ligation of the regional blood vessel may be necessary to avoid hemorrhagic shock.

(10) In the meantime, blood from the oral cavity can be collected with a syringe and may be sent for further investigations like WBC -total and differential count, bleeding time, coagulation time etc. to evaluate the possibility of any hemorrhagic disorders. Such possibilitics include hemophilia, purpura, leukemia, liver disorders and Vitamin C deficiency etc.

For the natural hemostasis, there is an interplay of three factors: *coagulation, platelets* and *vascular factors*.

Hence, the disorders can be considered under the following three main groups:

(1) Coagulation defects

(2) Thrombocytopenia
(3) Capillary abnormalities.

Coagulation defects

The normal mechanism of coagulation of blood is essentially interlocking of factors brought about by contact with tissue factor. The coagulation pathways are intrinsic and extrinsic.

Intrinsic pathway is triggered by damage to the vascular endothelium. It activates factor XII, which in turn activates factor XI (PTA) and IX (Christmas factor). These factors together with platelets, factor VIII (AHG factor) and ionized calcium activate factor X and produce prothrombinase. By this, the phase I of coagulation is completed. It lasts for 5-10 minutes. When this phase is impaired, the blood clotting time is prolonged. This phase is intended for the intrinsic pathway to deal with intrinsic damage to the blood vessels.

In extrinsic pathway, blood comes in contact with factors present in the damaged tissue. It activates and competes with factor VIII and convert factor X into prothrombinase. Thus, in phase I, prothrombinase is produced while in phase II thrombus is formed from prothrombin. In phase III, thrombin converts fibrinogen into fibrin. One or more of the following factors may operate in a bleeding disorder:

(i) Failure to clot
(ii) Destruction of clot
(iii) Defective blood vessel
(iv) Defective platelets.

Any vascular trauma is followed by the aggregation of the platelets which acts as a hemostatic plug. It is reinforced by the vascular contraction to reduce the diameter of the larger blood vessels. The retraction of the clot and the associated vascular contraction are believed to occur due to any of the following factors:

(i) Trauma to the muscular wall
(ii) Release of substances by the platelets e.g. 5-hydroxy-tryptamine (5HT).

Aggregation of platelets is mainly due to adenosine diphosphate (a powerful platelet agglutinins) released by the damaged tissues and platelets. Usually, clotting mechanism is disrupted due to the deficiency of the clotting factors, characteristic to each disease. For example, hemophilia is due to the hereditary deficiency of factor VIII (AHG in plasma) and Christmas disease is due to the deficiency of factor IX.

Hemophilia. It is due to an inherited, X-linked recessive character, clinically manifests only in males. It is known to be transmitted through clinically normal female carriers. For example, if an affected male marries a normal female, then the daughters will become carriers while none of the sons will be affected. This is because the man transmits Y chromosomes and X-linked trait is never transmitted. If a woman carrying X-linked recessive trait marries a normal man, then half of her sons will be affected and half of her daughters will be carriers.

Hemophilia literally means "bleeding tendency", derived from the Greek word "haima" meaning blood and "philas" meaning "tendency towards". Thus, hemophilia is defined as a hereditary X-linked disorder of blood coagulation, characterized by the tendency to excessive bleeding and prolonged coagulation time. It is essentially a hypothromboplastinemia. Prothrombin time is normal while prothrombin consumption time is shortened. Fault seems to be in the production of plasma proteins called antihemophilic globulin factor (factor VIII). Some believed that AHG production is in normal range but it is neutralized by the production of enzyme inhibitors.

Diagnosis is based on the detailed personal and family history. As age advances, it seems to be less severe. By the time an adult hemophiliac comes to any practitioner, the diagnosis would have been confirmed due to the previous bleeding episodes following trivial injury. The patient may also give history of painful hemarthrosis, hematuria and hematemesis. In such patients, diagnosis is never in doubt.

If a child patient were to be diagnosed, it is usually by the characteristic history of frequent episodes of hemarthrosis. Hematological investigations like bleeding time, coagulation time and capillary fragility test help to differentiate this condition. Since they are only empirical, the patient must be referred to a hematologist for further investigations like, quantitative assay of factor VIII.

For clinical convenience, hemophilia can be categorized as classic, moderate, mild and sub hemophilia. This relates to the degree of sensitivity of partial thromboplastin time which is indirectly proportional to the factor VIII. If the factor VIII is around 30-50% in plasma, it is said to be subhemophilia with slight tendency to prolonged oozing. If it is mild, factor VIII is between 5-20% with severe bleeding. In moderate type, factor VIII is 1-5% with uncontrolled bleeding even after trivial injury. In classic type, it is 0%. Once hemophilia patient is investigated for the missing factor, the patient can be electively rendered fit by replacing the specific factor. The following are some of the sources of factor VIII:

(1) Fresh whole blood
(2) Fresh plasma
(3) Freeze dried human or animal AHG factor
(4) Cryoprecipitate from human plasma.

Thus, it has been found that the principles of management of these patients include identification of the deficient factor and its replacement. Fresh blood has relatively low concentration of factor VIII. It definitely helps to compensate the blood loss. But only a limited amount of AHG factor not exceeding 7% can be replaced without overloading the systemic circulation. Fresh plasma can replace 15-20% while the animal AHG replaces 60-100%. But animal AHG is antigenic and hence one has to be careful to avoid anaphylactic reaction. Half life of the injection of factor VIII is around 12 hours. After 24 hours, quarter of its injection level is reached. It is found that a level of 5% after 24 hours is usually adequate to manage minor trauma and single tooth extraction. Cryoprecipitate from human plasma and frozen plasma are used preoperatively with a syringe in the known hemophiliac. Frozen plasma has to be given through intravenous infusions. For multiple dental extractions, 40% of which falls down to 10% after 24 hours will be necessary. In case of major surgery, as in facial trauma, 100% of factor VIII may have to be replaced. Thus, it is seen that a comprehensive management of a hemophiliac implies a coordinated programme to restore and maintain physical, psychological and social well-being.

Epsilon Amino Caproic Acid (EACA) and Transamic Acid are inhibitors of plasminogen activator, thus acting as antifibrinolytic agent. This drug may be given orally or through intravenous route. EACA is found to protect and maintain the clot by preventing its premature dissolution by fibrinolysin present in blood. 24 gm of EACA is recommended for 24 hours in divided doses. It should be maintained at least for one day after suture removal. This drug must not be given for patients with hematuria.

Extraction preparation. Preoperatively, an impression is taken. After removal of the tooth on the plaster cast, an acrylic plate is constructed. This plate mainly provides support to the clot rather than controlling hemorrhage. In addition, it gives protection to the clot from being disturbed.

Anesthesia. Local anesthesia is preferable since during general anesthesia, pharyngeal trauma is possible. Similarly, mandibular block anesthesia may result in hemorrhage into the parapharyngeal space which may even be fatal. Hence, it is preferable to use intraligamental infiltration anesthesia.

Postoperative follow-up

(1) Hemophiliacs must not be given aspirin derivatives since they impair platelet function by inhibiting the enzyme cycle and prolong the bleeding time.
(2) It is preferable to nurse the patient in the reclining posture. Absolute rest must be

provided.

(3) To avoid disturbance to the clot, the acrylic plate is kept in-situ and the jaw movement is restricted with four-tailed bandage.

(4) Diet must be warm or cold but hot food should be avoided. Likewise, alcohol should be prohibited.

(5) It is better to restrict the visitors so that the patient will refrain from excessive talking. It is even better to sedate him.

(6) Booster dose of factor VIII must be administered at least for 5-7 days postoperatively.

Thrombocytopenia

(1) *Liver disorders*. Many of the coagulation factors are manufactured in liver. Hence, in liver disorders, hemostatic failure occurs. They can be classified under two heads:

(a) It may be due to lack of Vitamin K. The vitamin K dependent factors are prothrombin, factor VIII, IX and X.

(b) In liver diseases, in addition to the production of coagulation factor, the patient may suffer from consumption coagulopathy and consequent hemostatic failure.

(2) *Renal failures*. Normal hemostatic mechanism is disturbed due to depression of Vitamin K dependent factors and disturbed platelet function.

(3) *Obstructive jaundice*. It leads to Vitamin K deficiency.

(4) *Gram negative septicemia*.

(5) *Cyanotic congenital heart disease*. Due to shortage of clotting factors and tendency to fibrinolysis, bleeding tendency persists.

(6) Patients on *anticoagulant therapy*.

(7) In extreme cases of *malabsorption*.

(8) Patients suffering from *fatty diarrhea*.

(9) The following drugs may cause thrombocytopenia: cytotoxic drugs, tolbutamide, digitoxin, phenobarbitone, organic arsenicals and salicylates.

(10) In some diseases, platelets are normal in number but may become abnormal in function, e.g. von Willebrand's disease due to defective platelet adhesion.

Fibrinolysis in surgery. This refers to pathological fibrinolysis. The plasminogen-plasmin system (fibrinolytic enzyme system) has a physiological role in maintaining the intact vascular system. This is complementary to the coagulation system. Both are believed to be in a state of dynamic equilibrium. Through the coagulation system, fibrin plug seals the gap while fibrinolytic system removes the fibrin deposits after the endothelial repair is completed.

Plasminogen is an inert plasma globulin which is converted to plasmin by the activators. Plasmin is a proteolytic enzyme, capable of digesting proteins like fibrinogen, fibrin, factor V and AHG. The plasma and tissue activators are in high concentrations found in organs like thyroid, prostate and lungs. A few bacteria can also produce the plasminogen activators. Fear is also found to liberate plasminogen activators. The plasma inhibitors generally control the plasminogen found in tissues. Certain bacteria like cryophilic multiply in the chilled stored blood, leading to failure of hemostasis. EACA can rectify such a problem.

Leukemia. This clinical condition is characterized by the abnormal proliferation of leucopoietic tissue. According to the type of the affected WBC, it is classified as lymphatic, myeloid leukemia, etc. In leukemia, there is an associated low RBC and platelet counts. More often, prolonged post-extraction bleeding may be the presenting symptom. Hence, in all hemorrhagic disorders, this condition must be ruled out.

Capillary abnormalities

This is known as purpura. It can also be encountered in acute pyrexia, drug sensitivity due to heavy metals, salicylates, chlorpromazine and also in scurvy. *Capillary fragility test* is useful to confirm the diagnosis.

The following are some of the laboratory tests which can yield results quickly in cases of uncontrollable bleeding.

(1) Blood smear for platelet and RBC counts.
(2) Blood grouping and cross-matching.
(3) Estimation of prothrombin time.
(4) WBC - total and differential count.

If the bleeding is profuse, blood volume has to be restored by replacement therapy through transfusions.

Venepuncture

Every dental surgeon must be familiar with the technique of venepuncture. It is useful,

(i) to obtain sample of blood to carry out (a) hematological (blood grouping and cross matching) and (b) biochemical investigations.
(ii) for administration of drugs and fluids through intravenous route as life-saving measures.

General guidelines.

(i) Similar to biopsy procedure, a properly labelled container must be readily available to store blood before carrying out the investigations. The purpose and types of hematological evaluation will determine the quantity of blood to be drawn.
(ii) Applied anatomy: Any superficially placed vein can be used for the purpose. However, the usual site is the flexor side of the forearm because of the easy access and patient's comfort. The pattern of the veins here is one of the two types - V and H form. It is formed between inner basilic vein and the outer cephalic vein, joined by the median cubital vein.

Technique. The common site is basilic vein in the antecubital fossa. Once the appropriate site is chosen, tourniquet is applied with sphygmomanometer cuff above the elbow joint to obstruct the venous return. The pressure should be less than the arterial pressure. The continued pressure of the radial pulse is a simple test. Repeatedly tapping the vein may help in distending the vein, probably by the smooth muscle relaxation. Exercising the fist repeatedly is also an useful method. The operator may find it difficult to get a vein in emergency situations like cardiac arrest, acute blood loss, diabetic coma and convulsions. In case of poor venous access, "*cut-down*" method can be useful.

The needle insertion site needs to be carefully prepared to avoid thrombophlebitis. Visual location of vein is difficult if the stain of iodine-containing preparation is not removed before attempting the insertion of the needle. 70% alcohol with chlorhexidine is the commonly used antiseptic. The site can be infiltrated with 0.5% lignocaine hydrochloride solution so that multiple reinsertions of the needle for the drip are painless. It may also reduce reflex venous spasm.

Choice of cannula. Winged steel needles, e.g. butterfly, ported cannula range from 14 to 27 gauge. Butterfly patterns are widely used. Because of the sharpness, it requires a single manoeuvre for the insertion of the needle. It also has low incidence of sepsis. (presterilized)

Cannula insertion. After choosing the vein, the limb is held with one hand and the skin is extended over the vein. The cannula is advanced with a quick action through the skin away from the vein. The second quick movement of the needle into the vein results in "flashback" of blood into the needle hub indicating the successful venepuncture. The needle is still advanced further without counter puncture of the vein. Now, the tourniquet is released. Then, cannula is fixed appropriately with plaster strips. Specialized dressings are available to provide excellent anchorage and dressing.

Maintenance of patency of cannula. The minimum flow rate needed to maintain cannula patency is difficult to estimate. Stopping the infusion may allow the blood to track-back up the cannula. Care must be taken to avoid blocking of the cannula.

Transfusion

Autotransfusion. It is the safest form of blood transfusion. Autotransfusion refers to preoperative collection of blood for subsequent reinfusion into the donor's vascular system during elective surgery. This is ideally suited in healthy patients who are to undergo elective surgery. It is planned well in advance of the surgical procedure so that there is sufficient time left for hemopoietic regeneration of RBCs and restoration of hemoglobin level prior to surgery. The following are some of the advantages:

(1) It eliminates the risk of transmitting viral hepatitis.
(2) It avoids all transfusion reactions and blood incompatibility.
(3) It virtually ensures the availability of matched blood.

For autotransfusion, the donor must have minimum of 11% of hemoglobin and 34% of hematocrit value. Oral iron medications are useful to provide iron supplementation. It is not to correct the iron deficiency. The preexisting anemia precludes the person for autotransfusion. On an average, a patient, who requires one unit of whole blood intra or postoperatively, can donate 14-20 days preoperatively. For practical purposes, an amount of 450 ml of blood can be drawn from the donor for autotransfusion with the body weight of 110 pounds. As a safety measure, to prevent misidentification, compatibility testing of the autologous blood is advocated prior to transfusion.

Homologous transfusion. This is to correct hypovolemia or to increase hemoglobin content of the host's blood. To avoid any transfusion problems, the following tests are advocated:

(1) ABO blood grouping.
(2) Rh typing.

Prior to transfusion, cross-matching is absolutely essential. Replacement by homologous blood transfusion must be advised, only when necessary, especially due to the risk of hepatitis.

RBCs (packed cells) are given for the following reasons:

(1) Reduction in volume prevents circulatory overload. Posttransfusion hematocrit is greater when packed cells are transfused.
(2) Improved blood viscosity when RBCs are transfused to anemic patients who have low blood viscosity.
(3) Reduced sodium, reduced albumin and reduced phosphorus.

Platelet concentrate represents the most effective form of platelet transfusion. Cryoprecipitated antihemophilic factor contains factor VIII and fibrinogen. Hence, cryoprecipitate serves as the main source for replacement of fibrinogen.

ORAL SURGERY IN PREGNANCY

Pregnant mothers, their relatives and dental practitioners are always concerned with the safety of the patient during pregnancy. Hence, proper understanding of the physiology of pregnancy is a prerequisite to enable the practitioner to take appropriate steps to prevent any complications during the treatment. The physiological changes during pregnancy are responsible to make this group of patients unique. It is absolutely essential to make the patient feel relaxed since there is an exaggerated response to stress. The hormonal changes during the progressive growth of the fetus result in the increase of (a) blood volume and cardiac output, (b) decreased liver function, (c) glomerular filtration rate, (d) oxygen requirement, and (e) vital capacity. These changes are responsible for the altered response to stress. It is found that emotional and physical stress due to the treatment is detrimental than the treatment itself. As a result of the biochemical response to stress, large quantities of steroids and its derivatives are liberated into the bloodstream. The pituitary gland also secretes oxytocin which can stimulate uterine contraction. This may be responsible for the premature labor during the stressful phase. During the first trimester, the patient develops persistent vomiting, a serious form of morning sickness. Carbohydrate starvation, dehydration and subsequent ketosis may be responsible for the vomiting. It can be prevented by high carbohydrate feeding before the treatment.

During the third week of pregnancy, organogenesis begins and completes between 9-10 weeks of intrauterine life. Hence, from fourth to sixteenth week, the fetus is said to be sensitive and hence vulnerable to environmental and toxic influences. Therefore, the fetus is susceptible to the development of congenital malformations if the pregnant mother passes through emotional stress. That is why treatment must be avoided during this sensitive period. One has to be careful to prescribe any drug during the first trimester. If any necessity arises, the patient must be relieved of anxiety, emotional stress and painful experiences.

During the third trimester, the position of the patient during the treatment is very important. If the patient is semireclined or is in full-supine position, fetus will compress the inferior vena cava, thereby interfering with the venous return. This may result in *supine hypotensive syndrome*. By turning the patient to the left side either in the sitting or in the reclining posture, pressure on the vessels can be avoided.

Complications

While emergency is unavoidable, many of the complications are avoidable or preventable. By careful evaluation and comprehensive treatment planning, the practitioner can reasonably anticipate the occurrence of complications so that most of them could be prevented.

Complication can be defined as an event occurring intraoperatively or postoperatively. If it is left untreated or unrecognized, the patient may be adversely affected. From medicolegal point of view, if an emergency or complication arises in spite of due precautions, the practitioner cannot be accused of negligence. Perhaps, the best way to manage the complications is to prevent its occurrence through precautionary measures. On the contrary, if surgery is performed with unwarranted optimism without any consideration to one's own ability, obligation and medicolegal responsibility, the incidence of intraoperative and postoperative complications are bound to be exceptionally high.

Thus, emergencies and complications sequel to oral surgery can be classified under the following groups:

(1) *Intraoperative*
  (a) Local
  (b) Systemic
(2) *Postoperative*
  (a) Immediate
    (i) Local
    (ii) Systemic
  (b) Delayed
    (i) Local
    (ii) Systemic

Anesthetic complications and emergencies are discussed under "anesthesia" separately. Similarly, all the systemic complications have been described as medical emergencies. The local complications are discussed below:

Intraoperative complications

The following intraoperative complications are preventable:

(1) Primary hemorrhage
(2) Dislocation of the temporomandibular joint
(3) Fracture of the tooth or jaw bone
(4) Oroantral fistula
(5) Displacement of the tooth
(6) Damage to the soft tissues
(7) Damage to the neighboring dental structures
(8) Failure to complete the operation.

Postoperative complications

(1) Osteomyelitis
(2) Impairment of sensation
(3) Dry socket
(4) Reactionary or secondary hemorrhage
(5) Pain and swelling
(6) Trismus.

DRY SOCKET - AN AVOIDABLE COMPLICATION

Dry socket, the term coined by Crawford, represents a common, unpleasant, local complication following dental extractions and surgical removal of impacted teeth. Many other descriptive terms have been suggested like necrotic alveolar socket, alveolalgia, delayed extraction, wound healing, fibrinolytic alveolitis, alveolar osteitis and localized osteomyelitis. But the term "dry socket" has stood the test of time and still preferred by many. Studies have revealed that incidence following dental extraction is 1-3% while it may be even 12-30% after the surgical removal of mandibular impacted third molars. Even though it continues to be the most common local complication in oral surgical practice, etiology continues to be ill-understood.

Etiology

Etiology can be broadly considered as systemic and local factors.

Systemic factors

(1) *Age distribution.* The incidence seems to increase with age. It is most commonly seen in the age group of 20 to 40 years. Changes in bone and dental structures undoubtedly occur as the age advances which may render the removal of the tooth more difficult. Extraction of deeper and the more difficult impacted teeth in later years of life become more traumatic thereby predisposing to dry socket.

(2) *Sex distribution.* In general, female patients have lower threshold and tolerance of pain. Postextraction pain is more in females. Hence, it is wise to take into account the sex distribution in which pain is used as an indicator.

(3) *General factors.* The duration of this lesion is 2 to 10 days. Even though it is logical that decreased general resistance of the patient may be responsible for the occurrence of this condition, the importance of general factors can be confirmed only in a few cases as in diabetes.

Local factors

(1) *Distribution within the dental arches.* It is more common in the mandibular molar region but very rare in the anterior region. It is much more frequent after the removal of retained or unerupted teeth, probably due to the increased trauma during removal.

(2) *Insufficient blood supply to the alveolar socket.* Dry socket develops more often if the surgery is performed under local anesthesia with excess of vasoconstrictor-like adrenaline injected around dense, sclerosed bone in the mandibular molar region. In contrast, the incidence is found to be relatively less (a) under general anesthesia, (b) where bone is cancellous, as in maxilla and mandibular anterior region. The alveolar socket is considered to be one of the important determinants in the development of dry socket. Sclerotic bone changes caused by periapical infection can also result in decreased blood supply to the alveolus.

(3) *Preexisting infections* like pericoronitis and periapical infections are considered to be the predisposing factors of dry socket.

(4) *Trauma to the alveolar bone.* It is considered to be one of the main causes. Excessive trauma is known to result in delayed wound healing and osteitis of the alveolar socket. It has also been suggested that trauma results in weakening the local cellular defense mechanisms facilitating bacterial invasion. Trauma may lead to thrombosis of the vessels, reduction in the tissue resistance and the consequent wound infections. Smoking and oral contraceptives may also predispose to intravascular thrombosis. Wider stripping of periosteum and severance of the attachment of muscles and other trauma lead to liberation of tissue proactivators accounting for the increased local fibrinolysis.

(5) *Disturbance of the clot.* Once the clot formation is complete, energetic and repeated irrigation of the socket disturbs the clot and leaves the socket empty. Similarly, violent curettage might injure the alveolar bone.

(6) *Increased fibrinolytic activity.* The demonstration of the increased local fibrinolysis in dry

socket has resulted in better understanding of the pathogenesis of this clinical condition. Fibrinolysis is known to be a regulator of the coagulation process where and when clot formation is undesirable. Fibrinolysis can be traced in saliva and bacteria. It is an established fact that plasminogen is converted into plasmin in the presence of tissue or plasma proactivators. However, factors responsible for such conversion is not understood properly. Extensive studies have shown that fibrinolysis occurs locally but systemic effects are characteristically absent. Its level is directly proportional to the severity of the symptoms. Kinins present due to fibrinolytic mechanism in the alveolar socket is responsible for fibrinolysis, pain, trismus and swelling. Fibrinolysis is known to influence the integrity of the clot and its organization is important for the normal healing of the extracted socket. Fibrinolysis of the clot seems to be the most outstanding clinical feature of dry socket.

(7) *Microorganisms*. Fibrinolysis occurs due to the toxin-fibrinolysin released by *streptococcus viridans*. With the improvements in microbiological isolation techniques, the significance of anaerobic organisms as the etiological factors has attracted wide attention. A number of microorganisms other than streptococcus viridance are proved to have the fibrinolytic activity. It has been pointed out that the dry socket is not associated with clinical features of inflammation like redness, suppuration, swelling and pain. Metronidazole is found to reduce the incidence of dry socket.

Clear understanding of normal healing of the extracted socket is necessary to understand the pathogenesis and the role of various local etiological factors. In this connection, it is useful to review the relevant aspects of normal healing of an extracted socket. The main stages are (a) clot formation, (b) organization of blood clot, (c) replacement of connective tissue with woven bone and (d) replacement of woven bone with matured bone. The entire process takes around 2-3 months.

A few minutes after removal of the tooth, the socket is filled with blood. At the same time, the torn vessels in the periodontal and marrow spaces are blocked by intravascular clotting to arrest further hemorrhage. Now, clot formation takes place and soon fills the alveolar socket. Within the first 24 hours, the clot will be consolidated by the polymerization of the fibrin network. In this way, the clot shrinks and gets detached from the alveolar wall but the marginal gingiva folds over the extraction wound. The clot is infiltrated by polymorphonuclear leucocytes. Slight inflammatory reaction is seen in the adjacent marrow spaces. Within three days, inflammatory reaction is replaced by the proliferative phase in which the clot is organized and invaded by capillaries and young fibroblasts. Dry socket seems to be a disturbance during the first two stages of healing.

Pathogenesis

It is obvious that the dry socket results from the disturbed healing of an extracted socket. Etiology appears to be multifactoral in nature. Most of the factors merely act as aggravating or promoting agents.

Role of chemical mediators of inflammation: Apart from direct stimulation of the free nerve endings by the surgical instruments, the most immediate cause of pain is the release of histamine from mast cells. Kinins and prostaglandins possibly facilitate the action of histamine. Whatever be the cause, when the cells are damaged, all the three (a) prostaglandins, (b) kinin, (c) histamine are released into the tissue which are responsible for pain in dry socket.

Clinical features

(1) The patient usually complains of continuous, throbbing and excruciating pain, usually radiating to the ear.

(2) The site of pain can be clearly identified as the site of removal of the tooth, 48-72 hours earlier.

(3) The pain is such that it becomes worse during meals. It also disturbs the patient during sleep.

(4) The patient however has relief of pain with analgesics and local application of heat.

(5) The tooth socket appears dry and empty. It may also contain brownish foul smelling necrotic tissue. The bone is markedly tender.

(6) Halitosis is striking and marked.

(7) Usually, it resolves in a week or two. The healing may be hastened with the trusted local dressing like zinc oxide-eugenol impregnated cotton fibres.

Diagnosis

The clinical diagnosis is made on the basis of the following features:

(a) History of extraction a few days back.
(b) Empty alveolar socket, covered by greyish necrotic tissue.
(c) The surrounding gingiva exhibits mild inflammatory reactions.
(d) The patient complains of characteristic excruciating pain and halitosis.
(e) The patient complains of feeling of "unwell" due to lack of appetite and sleep.

Management

Dry socket is one of the well recognized complications following tooth removal due to a localized osteitis involving the condensed bone lining the socket. On the basis of etiology, pathogenesis and clinical features, a few preventive measures must be taken to avoid the incidence of this condition like scaling of teeth and treatment of inflammation of the gingiva prior to dental extraction. The technique must include the use of local anesthetic solution with minimum of vasoconstriction. Extraction technique must be as least traumatic as possible. Insertion of antibiotics or steroids after extraction or prophylactic parenteral antibiotic therapy into the socket are not found to be useful in reducing its incidence. In view of the gram negative organisms, metronidazole 600 to 800 mg per day appear to be effective. Incidence is high if the impacted tooth with preexisting pericoronitis is removed.

The main aim is to provide relief of pain and promote resolution of the condition. As a routine, if classical features are noticed, the "dry socket" should be irrigated with warm saline to eliminate the necrotic material from the socket. It is better to avoid surgical curettage. The time-honored popular remedy of loosely packed cotton impregnated with zinc oxide-eugenol is yet to be replaced by any other effective remedy. Usually, 2 or 3 dressings may be necessary depending on the relief of symptoms. Whitehead's varnish has also been tried but it is not so effective as zinc oxide-eugenol dressing. Perhaps, it can be left in-situ for a longer duration.

Inevitable postoperative complications

Trismus. Limitation of mouth opening during the immediate postoperative period is inevitable although the severity and duration vary depending on the surgical technique, operator and the patient's reaction to surgical trauma. It occurs due to the inhibition of the muscle function rather than any mechanical obstruction. If the mouth opening fails to restore to normal within a reasonable period, the patient must be investigated properly.

Mouth opening may be measured and recorded by any one of the following methods:

(1) The interincisal distance may be recorded with a scale or a bite gauge. It is better to use fixed landmarks than measuring the mouth opening between any points marked on the skin.

(2) Mouth opening varies from person to person. Hence, instead of expressing the distance in terms of millimetre, some prefer to record the interincisal distance preoperatively and record the postoperative restriction of the mouth opening in terms of percentage. This method overcomes the human inaccuracy during the measurement.

Swelling. Although swelling due to post-operative edema is inevitable, the size and duration depend on many factors. It may be of inflammatory or infective origin. The qualitative or subjective methods of describing the swelling ranges between "severe", "moderate", "slight" and "absent". Perhaps, the description is accurate if it is 2 point scales - "present" and "absent". Introduction of 2 more intermediate points of scales are exposed to the patient's bias.

Postoperative swelling is measured in terms of millimetre between any two known landmarks. This can be between mastoid and interincisal line. As is the case with trismus, the horizontal measurement of the cheek could be recorded preoperatively to compare it with postoperative measurement. When the swelling develops, comparison with the opposite side might help to describe the extent of facial asymmetry.

More accurate methods of evaluation like radiography and photogrammetry have been described in the literature. Just like cephalometry, a two-dimensional photography is useful with the head in a fixed relationship to the photographic film. van Goof's device has been developed for this purpose in which camera is in a fixed position and it is related to a sighting ring. A ring is fitted to the bite plate. The swelling in terms of the ring is recorded.

It is to be noted that swelling is obvious with the removal of third molar through buccal approach when compared to the lingual approach. Album (1977) advocated a method wherein a graph can be drawn in terms of actual measurement of the swelling recorded horizontally and subjective description vertically.

FOREIGN BODY ASPIRATION

A wide variety of aspirated foreign bodies have been reported in the literature. A number of factors can be identified in an oral and maxillofacial surgery setting as compared with the general dental environment. Careful analysis will reveal the existence of common situations, (a) common foreign bodies that are commonly aspirated, (b) patients at increased risk, (c) factors that may modify the risk factors, and (d) preventive techniques.

High risk patients

Dentally related objects are the second most common aspirated foreign bodies. It has been estimated that 90 to 92% objects enter the gastrointestinal tract. Children, between the ages of 1 and 3, form the high risk. Likewise, elderly, mentally handicapped, sedated and patients with facial injury - who have decreased gag reflex, swallowing incoordination and other protective airway mechanisms. In the clinical setting, the incidence increases by intravenous sedation, unexpected movement of the patient and inadequate lighting. In the hospital setting, this is prevented by throat pack.

Although anything placed inside the oral or nasal cavities can potentially be aspirated, some objects are more often aspirated than others. They include, natural or artificial teeth, root stumps, implant, root canal instruments and impression materials. Following road traffic accidents, commonly aspirated objects include tooth and bone fragments, dentures, crowns, dashboard components, etc.

Sequelae may range from relatively benign partial obstruction to life-threatening complete airway obstruction. Clinical features vary depending on the size and shape of the aspirated object, whether it is sharp or blunt. Early signs include cough, choking, gagging, paradoxical breathing, cyanosis and dullness on auscultation. Complete airway obstruction may lead to atelectasis. Long-term retention in the bronchial tree may lead to vocal cord paralysis, abscess, pneumothorax and even death. Sometimes, they may remain asymptomatic or may pass off in the motion.

In such eventualities, without wasting time, services of an ENT surgeon is mandatory. If the foreign bodies are lodged in the upper aspect of trachea or esophagus, they can be retrieved with simple instrumentation. Otherwise, procedures like bronchoscopy or endoscopy may have to be carried out. If they are non-retrievable, non-endoscopic surgical methods may be needed.

CHAPTER 21 Therapeutics in Oral Surgery

GENERAL CONSIDERATIONS

Whenever a patient attends the clinic for the first time, the dental surgeon must elicit the history carefully regarding the health status, past illness, medications and allergic episodes. More often, patients may not be aware of the significance of their medications and the possibility of interaction between the dental treatment and medications. One must take all precautions to prevent complex and undesirable reactions of the proposed therapy. The practitioner must be familiar with the basic range of drugs which are liable to be used routinely. In case of other drugs, it is worthwhile to maintain a checklist to determine the dosage, precautions to be taken, possible drug interactions and side effects. A brief account is provided on pain, infection control and other routine medications including certain basic facts regarding the medically compromised patients. Finally, a few details are provided concerning special considerations like antibiotic prophylaxis, drugs in pregnancy, drug allergy and drugs with reference to diet. Therapeutics being dynamic, the practitioner is advised to keep track of all medications which are likely to be used in oral surgery practice from time to time. Hence, applications of the knowledge of clinical pharmacology is indispensable. Drugs of varied combinations form invaluable tools in the armamentarium in oral surgery practice.

DRUGS AND PAIN CONTROL

General features

Skillful use of drugs is necessary for pain control. The sensation of pain may or may not truly reflect the extent of tissue damage. For a patient, it represents a protective reflex. For the practitioner, it represents a diagnostic symptom of the underlying pathology. Control of pain differs widely from all other types of therapy. The two components of pain are perception and reaction of the patient. Perception of pain is objective. But the patient's reaction differ subjectively depending on the emotional instability. Therefore, the basic formula for effective pain control must be a combination of

(a) Rational use of appropriate analgesics and sedation,
(b) Decreasing the emotional instability and
(c) Enhanced reassurance of the patient.

The great variations in the perception of pain in response to surgery may also depend on the release of endogenous "analgesic" substances in the central nervous system like enkephalin and endorphin which provide protection against pain. They are natural peptides present in the brain and hence properties mimic that of morphine. They react with specific receptors present in the brain. During pain episode, when they are released, pain threshold is raised. By stimulating the receptors, analgesic drugs not only raise the pain threshold but at the same time, feeling of relaxation and reduction of anxiety are also produced in varying degrees. In the analgesic therapy, if the response to analgesia is not satisfactory, then the surgeon must ensure that,

(a) the dose administered is adequate,
(b) the underlying pathology has been eliminated,
(c) the pain is not of psychogenic origin.

This type of pain does not respond to analgesics alone. Antidepressant drug therapy may be needed in such cases. On this basis, drugs which are effective for pain control, can be considered under the following groups:

I. *Non-narcotic, non-steroidal, anti-inflammatory analgesics*
   (1) Aspirin group, e.g. acetyl salicylic acid (aspirin)
   (2) Phenacetin group, e.g. acetaminophen (paracetamol)
   (3) Propionic acid group, e.g. ibuprofen
   (4) Phenylbutazone group, e.g. phenylbutazone (butazolidin)
   (5) Indomethacin group, e.g. Indomethacin (Indocid)
   (6) Piroxicam
II. *Narcotic analgesics*
   (1) Morphine
   (2) Codeine (methyl morphine)
   (3) Pethidine
   (4) Propylamines, e.g. propoxyphene
   (5) Benzomorphan, e.g. pentazocine.
III. *Steroids as antiinflammatory agents*
IV. *Antidepressant drugs*
V. *Anticonvulsant drugs, e.g. carbamazepine (Tegretol)*
VI. *Placebo*

(I) Non-narcotic analgesics

They relieve pain with minor alteration and consciousness. They are safer than narcotics (opioids) since they have fewer side effects. These analgesics principally act at the peripheral nerve endings which opioids act within the central nervous system. The non-narcotics inhibit the synthesis of prostaglandin at the site of tissue inflammation thereby, they produce antiinflammatory and analgesic effects peripherally and antipyretic effects centrally. Hence, if they are taken before the onset of pain and inflammation which is associated with prostaglandin synthesis, they are effective. Their long term use will not produce tolerance or addiction. The three classic examples which are used widely are salicylates, ibuprofen and acetaminophen. Salicylates and ibuprofen exhibit all the three effects - analgesic, antipyretic and anti-inflammatory actions - while acetaminophen has analgesic and antipyretic effects without anti-inflammatory action.

Acetyl salicylic acid (aspirin). When aspirin is taken through oral route, it is absorbed from gastrointestinal tract by diffusion. In stomach, greater part of it exists in non-ionized form. Therefore, the quicker the emptying of stomach, more the absorption. Plasma concentration reaches the higher level in 30 minutes after oral ingestion, but reaches its peak in 1½ hours. It is hydrolyzed to salicylic acid and the blood level is maintained for 4 hours. Its analgesic action is explained by synergism between prostaglandins and pain-producing substances like bradykinins released by the inflammatory process. The inhibition of prostaglandin synthesis leads to analgesia by raising the threshold of pain in the presence of pain producing substances. The antipyretic action results from inhibition of prostaglandin synthesis in hypothalamus. Antiinflammatory effects are also derived from their ability to inhibit prostaglandin synthesis. Since prostaglandins are potent vasodilator agents, aspirin provides symptomatic relief from inflammatory effects. Salicylates prolong prothrombin time so that it prevents intravascular clotting. Sensitive reactions may manifest as rashes, swelling, asthma and rarely anaphylaxis. Ingestion can promote nausea, vomiting, bronchospasm and gastrointestinal bleeding due to erosion of mucous membrane.

It is an effective analgesic for mild to moderate degrees of pain. It is also available in soluble form as (Disprin) buffered aspirin. Young children are highly susceptible to aspirin poisoning (therapeutic overdose).

Drug interactions

(a) Increased gastrointestinal bleeding with ethyl alcohol and anticoagulants.
(b) Enhanced hypoglycemia with antidiabetic drugs like tolbutamide, chlorpropamide.
(c) Reduced serum level of salicylates and gastric irritation with corticosteroids.
(d) When given with phenytoin, the effect of phenytoin is potentiated.
(e) Patients who take methotrexate must avoid aspirin to avoid fatal blood levels of methotrexate.

Ibuprofen. They are potent antiinflammatory agents and hence useful to relieve pain due to inflammation. The mechanism of action, pharmacological and adverse effects resemble aspirin. They inhibit the enzyme cyclooxygenase resulting in the reduction of the formation of prostaglandin precursors. The effect of food on its absorption is to reduce the rate of absorption of the drug. The drug is metabolized in liver and excreted by kidney. The antipyretic effect involves inhibition of prostaglandin synthesis in hypothalamus.

Due to vasodilatation, increased blood flow through skin and the consequent increased sweating result in loss of heat. Peripheral inhibition of prostaglandin synthesis and the local mediators of inflammatory response produce antiinflammatory action. The side effects include gastrointestinal irritation, pain and bleeding. These prostaglandin inhibitors may interfere with normal protective mechanisms in the stomach like production of cytoprotective mucous and reduction of gastric acid secretion. Because of the possibility of dizziness, headache and mental depression, the patient must be advised not to drive any automobile vehicle. Coagulopathics, peptic ulcer, asthma, cardiovascular diseases and ulcerative colitis are some of the contraindications.

This is a clinically tested drug as an effective analgesic and antiinflammatory agent. Hence, it has become a drug of choice in many painful oral conditions. It is marketed as 200 mg, 400 mg and 600 mg sugar coated tablets. The onset of action is slow but the duration of pain relief is longer than aspirin. It has been found that the administration of ibuprofen prior to the surgical procedure delays the onset of postoperative pain. The effective therapeutic dose is 600 mg every sixth hourly. It should not be taken on empty stomach to avoid gastric irritation. Simultaneous use of aspiring is to be avoided.

Acetaminophen. This is one of the widely used analgesics as an accepted alternative to aspirin. It is relatively a safe analgesic and antipyretic but it does not have any antiinflammatory action. Gastrointestinal irritation is less. Prolonged therapy may cause hepatic damage and nephrotoxicity. It is found to be useful in patients with aspirin hypersensitivity or aspirin-induced gastric irritation. It should not be administered to young children, less than 3-year-old for more than 10 days. Paracetamol has been widely accepted as the drug of choice for the relief of mild to moderate pain and for its antipyretic effect. It has very little antiinflammatory action.

Phenylbutazone and oxyphenbutazone. These drugs are potent antiinflammatory analgesics.

They are derivatives of pyrazolone group like amidopyrine. Hence, they are effective as antiinflammatory and analgesic agents but prove to cause agranulocytosis and leucopenia. They are known for the gastric irritation. Retention of sodium and water may aggravate hypertension and congestive cardiac failure. However, their judicious use is advocated for the pronounced anti-inflammatory effect.

Indomethacin is also a potent anti-inflammatory analgesic. The common side effects include headache, gastric irritation and rarely agranulocytosis.

(II) Narcotic analgesics

These are powerful analgesics. The other effects include cough, respiratory depression and inhibition of intestinal motility. Patients develop dependence and tolerance to these drugs. While they are most effective against severe pain, the accompanying emotional reaction to pain is also reduced. The tendency to cause addiction imposes the restriction of the liberal use of these drugs. Enkephalins and endorphins are natural peptides present in the brain. They are possibly released during pain. They react with specific receptors in the brain. When receptors are stimulated by these drugs, the pain threshold is raised and feeling of relaxation and reduction of anxiety are also produced.

Morphine. This is usually administered through parenteral route. Soon after the injection, there is a brief phase of excitement followed by sedation and sleep. Once the pain is relieved, the patient develops euphoria, feeling of self-confidence and relaxation. While sensation of pain is diminished, the emotional response to pain is suppressed. Because of its depressant action on respiratory centre and pupillary constriction, it should not be administered in head injuries and lung diseases. Morphine also releases histamine from the tissues, resulting in mucosal edema, bronchospasm and consequently difficulty in breathing. Due to the drug dependence, withdrawal symptoms begin with a sense of craving for this drug. Later, patient develops anxiety, agitation, restlessness followed by depression and restless sleep. Ultimately, the patient develops severe shock and may even die.

Codeine (methylmorphine). This is a natural alkaloid with all the pharmacological features of morphine. But it is a weak analgesic. It is not given independently because of many side effects, when injected in large doses.

Pethidine. This is a major synthetic analgesic. Its pharmacological actions are similar to morphine, but it also has some atropine-like properties. The size of the pupil is not affected. It is available as 100 mg of injectable solution. Unlike codeine, it can be injected in large doses. Respiration is not depressed. However, euphoria, addiction, dependence and sedation are similar to morphine. Monoamine oxidase inhibitors (MAOI) severely interact with pethidine.

Propoxyphene. This is a less potent analgesic. Side effects are similar to codeine. The abuse potential is less than pethidine. Another danger is self-poisoning.

Pentazocine. This is a potent analgesic which can be administered through oral or parenteral route. Its effectiveness is one-third of morphine. Unpleasant hallucinations and anxiety are produced. It is less prone to addiction.

(III) Corticosteroids

Trauma, surgery, infection and general anesthesia result in the release of ACTH (adrenocorticotrophic hormone) from anterior pituitary gland. ACTH stimulates adrenals to secrete large amount of adrenal glucocorticoids. It is determined by the release of ACTH through corticosteroid feedback mechanism. Failure of this response leads to fall in blood pressure. Glucocorticoids have the ability to decrease the inflammatory responses. However, the use of steroids to control the sequelae of inflammation and pain remains controversial. The exact mechanism is not known. But the possible mechanisms include (a) leucocyte suppressions,

(b) accumulation of macrophages at the site of inflammation and (c) prevention of prostaglandin release. In terms of antiinflammatory reaction, cortisone, hydrocortisone, prednisone and prednisolone are short acting. Triamcinolone is intermediate acting, while betamethasone and dexamethasone are long acting. Prednisone and prednisolone are nearly four times more potent as hydrocortisone. Triamcinolone is five times more potent while betamethasone and dexamethasone are nearly 25 times more potent. The onset, peak and duration of action depend on the route of administration, dosage and solubility of the drug.

Disease involving hypothalamus - anterior pituitary gland interfere with hypothalamic-pituitary-adrenal axis. Adrenals may be involved in conditions like tuberculosis or amyloidosis. Whatever be the reason, patients with less of endogenous steroid production are usually put on the maintenance dose of corticosteroids. In case of infection, trauma, stress or surgery, additional steroids will be required. In such patients, during major surgery under general anesthesia, the following therapies are advocated. 100 mg of hydrocortisone is given every sixth hourly, starting one hour preoperatively intravenously. This is followed by injection intramuscularly for 3 days from the time of premedication. For minor surgery under local anesthesia, single dose of 100 mg of hydrocortisone IM is given one hour preoperatively. Surgery for this group of patients is best carried out in the mornings so that they can be observed during the immediate postoperative period more effectively. BP must be monitored periodically.

In case of patients with suppressed adreno-cortical activity following steroid therapy, supplementary hydrocortisone should be given. If steroid is given to any patient for a long period, blood concentration of steroid passing through hypothalamus rises, resulting in decreased output of ACTH. This results in decreased function and atrophy of the adrenal cortex. Rapid withdrawal of hydrocortisone results in adrenal crisis. This may prove fatal in case of stressful conditions. For the routine activity, level of secretion may be sufficient. But adrenal cortex may be unable to secrete more to cope up when the demand is more in terms of stress. Even minor surgery may prove disastrous. Any patient requiring surgery or general anesthesia, who has been on prolonged steroid therapy, should be hospitalized. It is usual to supplement the dose of steroid during the period of stress. *The dose is doubled 2 days before the day of surgery and 2 days after surgery*. Later, gradually the *dose is tapered* during the following week. The patient's BP should be monitored during surgery and the postoperative period. If there is fall of BP, hydrocortisone hemi-succinate 100 mg (2 ml) can be given intravenously. If BP does not raise within 20 minutes, the dose is repeated. Atrophy of the adrenal cortex could be prevented or minimized by giving ACTH.

Many different regimens of glucocorticoid administration have been experimented to decrease postoperative sequelae of pain, trismus and edema following oral surgery procedures like removal of impacted third molars. A scientifically based recommendation of the optimal dosing regimen is yet to be formulated. While choosing a therapeutic regimen for glucocorticosteroid administration, a number of decisions must be made.

(1) *Type of steroid*. A steroid with minimal mineralocorticoid activity that maintains a therapeutic plasma level throughout the immediate postoperative period is used, e.g. methyl prednisolone, triamcinolone, betamethasone and dexamethasone.

(2) *Route of administration*. This is influenced by the operator-patient convenience and operator's experience. I.V. route offers instantaneous blood levels but requires expertise and additional armamentarium. I.M. route offers the advantage of negating the need for repetitive postoperative administration. The convenience of oral dosing has a general appeal but the patient's compliance has to be relied upon.

(3) *Dosage.*

(4) *Single vs. multiple dosing.*

(5) *Timing of administration* relative to the surgical procedure.

(6) *Side effects.*

One must carefully analyze these factors before using steroids for reducing postoperative swelling, pain and trismus in oral surgery practice. Several investigators have studied the effects of corticosteroids for the prevention of pain, edema and trismus associated with oral and maxillofacial surgery. In everyday practice, its use has attracted attention in case of III molar surgery. Based on various studies, the use of perioperative corticosteroids appears safe and rational method of reducing postoperative edema and pain in III molar removal, osteotomies, and major faciomaxillary surgical procedures.

(IV) Anticonvulsant drugs

Epilepsy belongs to a group of disorders involving recurrent attacks of involuntary experiences in terms of neurological functions. Each experience is called seizure. It is accompanied by convulsions. Anticonvulsant drugs used for controlling the seizures are CNS depressants without causing drowsiness. Although mechanisms of action are not definitely known, these agents prevent the spread of abnormal electric discharges from the brain.

Carbamazepine, one of the anticonvulsant drugs, is related to tricyclic antidepressants. Its anticonvulsant action involves limiting the seizures by reducing posttetanic potentness of synaptic transmission. It was incidentally found to reduce synaptic transmission within the trigeminal nucleus. This has led to the use of this anticonvulsant in trigeminal neuralgia as the drug of choice. In the elderly patients, dosage should be low to cut down the side effects of the drug. Later 200 mg may be given at a time every 2 to 3 days with an average of 600-1200 mg to gain good pain control. Drug should be taken 30 minutes before eating and double the dose at night. The drug effect is rapid. Side effects are most predominant at the initiation of therapy. The serious adverse effects are on hemopoietic, hepatic and renal systems. The most common symptoms in the elderly are dizziness, nausea, skin reactions and generalized weakness. Hematological effects are related to depression of bone marrow with anemia, leukopenia and thrombocytopenia. Hence, it is absolutely essential to monitor these patients with hematological and biochemical tests at monthly intervals.

It also possesses interaction with many drugs due to its ability to induce liver enzymes. Clinically, significant drug interactions are the following:

(1) It can cause increased metabolism of drugs and hence reduce the effects of anticoagulants, oral contraceptives, antibiotics (like erythromycin, doxycycline and isoniazid).

(2) Metabolism of carbamazepine is inhibited by drugs like INH and erythromycin and lead to toxic effects.

(3) Carbamazepine concentrations are decreased if phenytoin or phenobarbitone are administered concurrently so that incidence of the side effects are decreased.

Although trigeminal neuralgia drives the patient to commit suicide, it is essentially a nonfatal disease. Now, there are a wide variety of therapeutic measures (both medical and surgical) available. Hence, patients must be informed of all the therapeutic possibilities. However, when offering the treatment, careful consideration must be given to the possible side effects of each modality and its effect on the quality of life. The present trend is to advise the medical management until the patient becomes refractory to drugs or develops unacceptable side effects. The quality of life of the patient is markedly affected. Depression and anxiety are frequently associated with this clinical entity. Typically, sleep brings relief from pain. It must be remembered that the main aim of the medical treatment is to control pain until remission occurs. There is no evidence that this drug prevents future attacks to alter the disease process. It only provides symptomatic relief.

(V) Antidepressant drugs

Some patients with chronic pain who verbalize reactive depression may respond to judicious therapeutic use of this group of drugs. Hence, this is becoming popular for the treatment of uncontrollable chronic, non-specific pain.

Noradrenaline is released as a neural transmitter at the postganglionic sympathetic nerve fibres. Part of the released noradrenaline is inactivated. The antidepressant drugs do not exhibit any inherent analgesic properties. But it is observed that patients get minimum antidepressant effects from these tricyclic agents who obtain minimal analgesic effects. Since very serious side effects develop, it should be administered only by a properly trained clinician. The success in pain control probably depends on the success in controlling the depression. Withdrawal of tricyclic antidepressive agents prior to general anesthesia must be carefully undertaken since the effect of this drug usually persists from 15 to 20 days. If the drug is withdrawn within this period, relapse of the depression is likely.

(VI) Placebo

Considerable number of patients are quite responsive to various intangible aspects of therapy of pain control. Pain may be relieved but side effects may not be produced by a non active agent if the patient *believes* that particular drug is effective. This phenomenon is called *"placebo"* effect which is subjective like intensity of pain. It also varies from patient to patient. The effect is greater when the anxiety is more or pain is severe. Psychological interactions and doctor-patient relationship seem to have strong influence on this effect. Therefore, the likelihood of success entirely depends on how the patient is fully convinced about the efficacy of the treatment.

ANTIBIOTIC THERAPY

The oral cavity is inhabited by a number of microorganisms. They maintain a balanced microflora of the oral cavity. Paradoxically, if antibiotics are given, such a therapy may cause adverse reaction by disturbing the normal oral microflora. However, judicious antibiotic therapy forms a potent weapon to control infection of the orofacial region. Although antibiotics are useful to complement the host defense, they are sometimes responsible for associated morbidities like allergy, toxic effects of the drug apart from the development of resistant strains of microorganisms. A careful analysis will reveal that antibiotic therapy alone cannot eradicate infection if appropriate surgical therapy is not instituted.

Antibiotics are defined as substances produced by microorganisms that act in minute concentrations to kill other organisms or prevent them from multiplication without affecting the host. Their activities are highly selective, acting against the metabolism of the microorganisms.

Bacterostatic. Any antibiotic drug that stops the bacteria from dividing but by itself does not kill the bacteria. Examples are Erythromycin, sulfa group of drugs, Tetracycline.

Bactericidal. Any antibiotic drug that kills the bacteria. Examples are Penicillin, Cephalosporin, Metranidazole. In normal subjects with well-functioning immunodefense systems, it may not be essential, if it is bacteriostatic. The defense system itself can get rid of the bacteria. In cases where immune system is *not* functioning optimally, it is better that an appropriate antibiotic is used.

Bacteremia refers to the presence of bacteria in the bloodstream occurring in relation to any surgical/dental procedure, lasting for 30 to 45 minutes.

Septicemia refers to the presence of bacteria in the bloodstream causing the symptoms of infection.

General principles of antibiotic therapy

(1) Empirical antibiotic therapy has a limited

role in the prevention of the management of infections.

(2) If no response is forthcoming within 3 days of therapy, organisms must be identified so that the antibiotics can be chosen to act against susceptible organisms. No single antibiotic is effective against the pathogens. Once the causative organisms are isolated, it becomes critical to identify the appropriate antibiotic therapy.

(3) The most common organisms are streptococci, staphylococci and bacteroids.

(4) Culture of the organisms and antibiotic sensitivity test assume greater importance in patients with (a) compromised defenses like diabetes, (b) immunosuppressed patients, (c) those who are vulnerable to infections like subacute bacterial endocarditis, (d) patients on dialysis, (e) patients who are on chemotherapy for malignancy and (f) in geriatric patients.

(5) For the drug to be therapeutically effective, the antibiotics must be given proper dose at proper intervals through appropriate route so that blood concentration of the drug is maintained at the desired level.

(6) The drug which is least toxic, most economical and most effective must be chosen for the therapy.

(7) To avoid the development of resistant strains, the drug with least spectrum must be chosen.

(8) The patient must be warned about the possibility of the side effects and complications. If any such untoward reactions develop, the patient must discontinue the therapy forthwith.

(9) Caution must be exercised in using newer drugs. Preference must be given to use the known drug with proven effectiveness.

(10) Wherever possible, judicious methods to accentuate the efficacy of antibiotics must be utilized.

Indications

It may be *curative* or *prophylactic*. Curative treatment is the primary aim of antibiotic therapy in the following clinical situations:

(1) Infections which cannot be treated by surgery alone, (e.g. incision and drainage).
(2) As supplement to surgery in cases of affected general condition or in case of risk of space infections involving inaccessible areas like parapharyngeal spaces.
(3) Deep seated infections like osteomyelitis, cervicofacial actinomycosis.
(4) Infections which respond to antibiotic therapy alone or along with other modes of therapy.

Prophylactic therapy is mainly to prevent the onset of infections following any invasive procedure. Usually, it is started one hour prior to any procedure. Following are the main indications:

(1) Diabetic patients who are subjected to major surgery.
(2) Immunocompromised patients: e.g., patients on steroids and immuno-suppressive patients.
(3) Patients who have been subjected to radiotherapy of the head and neck region during the past one year.
(4) Prior to the surgical closure of oroantral fistula.
(5) Transplantations of tissues like bone and reimplantaion of teeth.
(6) Patients who undergo dental extraction in the presence of infection.
(7) As a prophylactic antibiotic therapy to prevent serious infections like subacute bacterial endocarditis in patients with valvular disease or replacement. Similarly, in patients with diabetes, renal problems, patients on cancer chemotherapy, cirrhosis of the liver and other medically compromised patients.
(8) Patients with complicated jaw fractures.
(9) Surgical interventions causing large bony cavities.
(10)Extensive soft tissue lesions including

lesions of the floor of the oral cavity.

(11)Prior to the insertion of dental implants.

(12)Patients with respiratory disorders.

In the following conditions, routine prophylactic antibiotic therapy has been used. But, it is now believed that, no useful purpose may be served by antibiotic therapy in these conditions.

(1) Dental extraction including transalveolar extraction.
(2) Well-defined fluctuating abscess.
(3) Uncomplicated fracture of the facial skeleton.
(4) Minor oral surgery procedures in patients without any systemic disorders.

However, it has not been possible to lay down any rigid rule regarding the antibiotic therapy. These are only general guidelines for the clinicians.

Mechanism of action. Usually antibiotic agents act at the following sites:

(1) *Cell.* Penicillin and cephalosporin interfere with the formation of peptidoglycan layer so that bacterial wall absorbs water and bursts.

(2) *Inhibition of protein synthesis,* e.g. tetracycline, chloramphenicol, erythromycin and aminoglycosides interfere with the build up of peptide chain on the ribosomes.

(3) *Disrupting the cytoplasmic membrane of the microorganisms,*e.g. polymyxin-B, amphotericin and nystatin.

(4) *Nucleic acid metabolism.* Rifampicin interfere with RNA and DNA metabolism.

(5) *Intermediary metabolism.* Sulfa group of drugs interfere with bacterial metabolism.

(6) If the drugs kill the organisms, they are called bactericidal. If they interfere with multiplication, they are called bacteriostatic. If the dose is inadequate, the therapy may promote bacterial resistance. Multidrug therapy may be advantageous if they have synergistic effects. Sometimes, they may have antagonism to one another. Rarely, they may induce hypersensitive reaction like allergy or anaphylaxis.

The objective of antibiotic therapy is to ultimately kill or to prevent multiplication of the pathogenic organisms with minimal toxicity to the host.

Diagnosis. Diagnosis of the condition, identification of the organisms and the choice of antibiotics effective against the organisms and testing the antibiotic sensitivity are important. As already pointed out, ideally an antibiotic is chosen after identifying the causative organisms and sensitivity. In case of serious infections, the choice depends on clinical grounds alone. If the infection fails to resolve in 48-72 hours, then therapy is changed to specific antibiotics. Very few infections are found to exhibit clear picture. The response is so reliable that very rarely sensitivity test is necessary, e.g. Vincent's infection responds quickly to metronidazole. Most often antibiotic therapy is empirical.

Dosage. The ultimate aim is to maintain sufficiently higher concentration of antibiotics in blood and tissues so that the drug is therapeutically effective. Duration depends on factors like precise nature of the infection and response to treatment.

Route of administration may be oral, intramuscular or intravenous. Therapy can even be started through parenteral route and maintained by oral route. If absorption in the gastrointestinal tract is effective, it should be started with an initial loading dose.

Combination of drugs. (a) Synergistic combination of drugs can be an effective form of therapy, e.g. sulfa drugs, penicillin and gentamycin (b) It may also prevent the development of resistant strains. For example, streptomycin, PAS and INH have been used in combination as antituberculous therapy, (c) To widen the antibiotic spectrum in mixed infections, (d) To reduce severity or incidence of adverse reactions by using low therapeutic dose of each drug.

Resistance to antibiotics. Microorganisms develop resistant strains either due to antibiotic tolerance or process of adaptation of mutation.

Some of the organisms may even become drug-dependent, e.g. staphylococcus. Drug resistance is known to be transferable from one organism to another. Cross-resistance between clinically related drugs are common. For example, organisms resistant to one tetracycline may become resistant to all the other members of the group of tetracyclines. Therefore, emergence of antibiotic resistant strains has become an inevitable consequence of the widespread and indiscriminate use of antibiotics. When an organism exhibits resistance to one antibiotic, it is wise to change over to a completely different type of antibiotic. This problem can be eliminated by avoiding the indiscriminate use of antibiotics. When necessary, adequate dose must be given for a sufficiently long period. In life-threatening infections, this problem can be resolved by instituting judicious multidrug therapy.

Drug interactions with antibiotics. Iron or calcium prevent absorption of tetracyclines by chelation. Careful analysis will reveal that the usefulness of antibiotics is limited and they are more often misused or abused. In practice, use of antibiotics must be restricted to prophylaxis. For example, to prevent subacute bacterial endocarditis. Surgical methods are always quick and effective. Hence, antibiotic therapy is useful to supplement rather than to replace surgical measures.

CLASSIFICATION OF ANTIBIOTICS

I. *Sulfonamides*

II. *Metronidazole*

III. *Penicillins*
  (1) Natural
    (a) Acid labile, e.g. benzyl Penicillin
    (b) Acid resistant, e.g. phenoxymethyl Penicillin
  (2) Semisynthetic
    (a) Ampicillin
    (b) Amoxicillin
    (c) Cloxacillin

IV. *Cephalosporins*
  (a) First generation
  (b) Second generation
  (c) Third generation

V. *Other antibiotics*
  (a) Tetracyclines
  (b) Erythromycin
  (c) Chloramphenicol
  (d) Newer antibiotics
  (e) Antifungal agents
  (f) Antiviral agents

VI. *Antibiotic for prophylaxis*
  (a) Against infective endocarditis.
  (b) Against wound infections in oral surgery

Sulfonamides

They act by interfering with bacterial synthesis of folic acid from para-amino-benzoic acid (PABA). Folic acid is necessary for the production of nucleic acid but microorganisms are not able to utilize preformed folic acid. Para-amino-benzoic acid chemically resembles sulfonamides. Hence, action of sulfonamides illustrates "competitive inhibition".

Sulfonamides exert bacteriostatic activity. But they have wide spectrum of activity against many gram-negative bacilli, gram-positive and gram-negative cocci, e.g. streptococci, pneumococci, gonococci, meningococci, gastrointestinal and urinary tract infections. This drug is absorbed well in the gastrointestinal tract. However, preparation for intramuscular and intravenous therapy are also available. It is excreted in urine in unchanged and conjugated form.

Toxic effects

(1) The risk of hypersensitive reactions and rash vary according to the compound used.
(2) Renal blockage due to crystalluria, low urinary output and acidic urine used to be one of the major problems. With the introduction of long-acting sulpha drugs

like sulfamethoxazole, the incidence has decreased.

(3) Some evidences for the development of Stevens-Johnson syndrome characterized by acute ulcerative stomatitis, bleeding and crusting of the lower lip and involvement of mucous membrane of the eyes.

(4) Local application of sulfonamide preparations can cause intractable contact dermatitis.

(5) Blood dyscrasias occasionally develop, e.g. depression of WBC formation.

Clinical applications

(1) Sulfamethoxazole is a highly potent sulfonamide used in combination with trimethoprim. Poorly soluble group is used for gastrointestinal disturbances, e.g. phthalyl sulfathiazole. Long acting sulfonamides need to be given once a day for a week. But they are more prone to cause adverse reactions.

(2) Sulfonamides are used as antimicrobial agents with a broad spectrum of activity.

(3) The use of sulfonamides declined markedly with the introduction of antibiotics. But with the introduction of cotrimoxazole, there has been a considerable revival in their use. Cotrimoxazole is a mixture of sulfamethoxazole with trimethoprim. Trimethoprim acts similar to the pathways of folic acid metabolism. The main side effect following prolonged therapy is the induction of folic acid deficiency and macrocytic anemia. They can occasionally cause bone marrow depression and sometimes fatal agranulocytosis.

Metronidazole

This is a synthetic antimicrobial marketed for the oral and intravenous routes. It is effective against obligate anaerobes and spirochetes. It is well absorbed when given through oral route and excreted in urine. It also appears in saliva. It has a low toxicity. Many patients complain of nausea due to bitter metallic taste. Its interactions with alcohol may cause sweating, flushing and palpitation. Therefore, patients must be warned that during metronidazole therapy, alcohol must be avoided.

This seems to be the drug of choice against gram negative microbia. Therefore, it can be effective in treating pericoronitis.

Penicillins

This was the first antibiotic to be discovered for use in clinical practice. The term 'penicillin" generally refers to benzyl penicillin (Penicillin G). It is effective against many gram-positive cocci and bacilli, gram-negative cocci with the exception of penicillinase producing staphylococci. The cell wall of gram-positive bacteria contains mucopeptide which is synthesized in a series of stages from acetylmuramic acid and other amino sugar molecules to form glycans. They are laid down as long strands, one layer over the other, united by cross linkages to form a single bag-shaped molecule. Penicillin is bactericidal by inhibiting the final cross-linking stage. Thus, failure of the biosynthesis of cell wall renders the bacteria vulnerable to osmotic damage. Penicillins attack the bacteria when they actively divide. Penicillin is not effective against gram-negative organisms. Since penicillin is not stable in acid medium, it is not reliable through oral route. If given through parenteral route, it is quickly absorbed reaching the maximum plasma concentration within 30 minutes and it is rapidly excreted. It has relatively narrow spectrum of activity.

Phenoxymethyl penicillin (Penicillin V) is an oral penicillin which resists destruction by gastric secretion. However, its activity is similar to penicillin G. It is reliably absorbed quickly from empty stomach. Its disadvantages are as follows:

(1) High serum level is not attained easily as benzyl penicillin.

(2) Like any other orally administered drug,

reliance has to be placed on the patients' cooperation to continue to take the drug.

(3) Vomiting may delay or prevent the rate of absorption.

(4) It is less active against streptococci and gram-negative organisms.

Both the preparations may initiate hypersensitive reactions in about 3-5% of the population. Mechanism of such an action is not certain. Probably, metabolites conjugate with the patient's proteins and thus act as haptens.

Clinically, in the absence of allergic reactions, it is the drug of choice for the dental infections. If it is not found to be effective within 2-3 days, some other antibiotics must be prescribed. In extremely severe oral infections, Penicillin G, 300-600 mg must be given every 6 hours. Otherwise, 2-3 ml of penicillin through intramuscular route can be given for 4-5 days. Sometimes, initially it can be given through intramuscular route and subsequently blood level can be maintained through oral route.

Skin test. Penicillin preparations have a bad reputation among the clinicians because of concern about the adverse reactions. It may not be feasible to carry out skin tests on all patients before administering penicillin. False positive tests will deny the advantages of penicillin to those who are not allergic while false negative results will fail to protect allergic patients. Therefore, in most of the developed countries, practices of "Test dose" has been abandoned since it does not give the reliable information that is designed to produce the test.

General guidelines

(1) The patient should be enquired about any previous adverse reactions to penicillin. If he gives history, alternative antibiotics must be administered.

(2) No harm in giving a test-dose injection but no useful purpose may be served. All patients must be advised to wait for 30 minutes after the administration.

(3) An emergency kit containing epinephrine, diphenhydramine and methyl prednisolone must be available readily if allergic reactions develop. Penicillin must not be administered without having these two emergency drugs.

(4) If reactions develop with fall in BP, 1 ml of 1:1000 aqueous solution of adrenaline should be given subcutaneously for adult patients. 0.1 ml for infants, 0.2 ml for 1-3 years of age, 0.3 ml to children over 3 years are advocated.

(5) Within 15 minutes, if the patient does not respond, injection adrenaline and steroid may be administered.

(6) Without any wastage of time, patient must be hospitalized to monitor.

Long-acting penicillin. "Procaine penicillin" is a stable salt. When injected through intramuscular route, it is released over the course of 24 hours. Hence, to avoid repeated injections at frequent intervals, this is used. But if a patient is allergic to penicillin the adverse reaction is more severe with procaine penicillin than any other form of penicillin.

Broad spectrum penicillin (e.g. Ampicillin). These are acid stable and effective against a wider range of gram-negative microorganisms in addition to those susceptible to Penicillin G. The range of activity is as wide as broad spectrum antibiotics like tetracyclines with the difference that ampicillin is bactericidal. But they are destroyed by penicillinase. Because of safety, broader spectrum and bactericidal effect, ampicillin is widely used in oral surgery practice.

Amoxicillin has identical spectrum of activity like ampicillin when given orally. The blood level of the drug is fairly high. Hence, it has become the drug of choice for prophylaxis against subacute bacterial endocarditis. Both these drugs carry the same range of toxicity like rashes, allergy or anaphylaxis as benzyl penicillin.

Cephalosporins

The chemical structure of cephalosporins resembles penicillin. The following are the main range of activities: (a) effective against penicillinase-producing staphylococci, (b) effective against gram negative bacilli. They are bactericidal in action. They are roughly classified into three generations based on their activity against gram-negative organisms.

First generation. They are active against Escherichia coli and other gram-negative organisms.

Second generation. They are active against a broader group of gram-negative organisms and increased activity against anaerobes. They are more effective against gram-positive organisms than the first generation.

Third generation. They are more active than first and second generation cephalosporins.

In oral surgery, first generation cephalosporins are more widely used. The toxicity is primarily related to allergy. Therefore, patients allergic to penicillin should not be given cephalosporins and hence, they are of very limited value in the management of orofacial infections. There is evidence that streptococcus viridans, resistant to penicillin, is also resistant to cephalosporins.

Aminoglycosides

General properties

(1) This group of drugs is poorly absorbed if administered orally. Hence, they must be administered by I.M. or I.V. route.

(2) Following injection, they are rapidly excreted through normal kidneys. In case of renal failure, the dose must be reduced accordingly.

(3) They are bactericidal and have broad antibacterial spectrum.

(4) Resistance to aminoglycosides can occur rapidly with a single mutation. Another mechanism is the metabolism of the agents by the bacterial membrane bound systems.

(5) Aminoglycosides are toxic to VIIIth cranial nerve causing auditory and vestibular disturbances.

(6) Nephrotoxicity. Kidney damage depends on the agent, age of the patient and blood level.

(7) Neuromuscular blockade. If aminoglycosides are given in combination with general anesthesia or skeletal muscle relaxants, they produce apnea, e.g. streptomycin.

It is synergistic to penicillin. Hence, streptopenicillin in injectable form are used for orofacial infections. Because of the high incidence of resistant strains, streptomycin must be carefully used.

Tetracyclines

This is a group of closely related antibiotics that provide a "broad spectrum" of activity. Hence, they are called broad spectrum antibiotics. Virtually, they are effective against many of the pathogens except fungi. They are bacteriostatic agents, which are incompletely absorbed through gastrointestinal tract. Tetracyclines combine with divalent metals like calcium or iron salts which interfere with the process of absorption. Addition of phosphates aid in absorption since calcium combines with phosphates instead of tetracyclines. Maximum concentration in blood is reached within 2 hours after oral administration and falls after 12 hours. Therefore, optimum plasma level can be maintained by the administration at six hourly intervals. They are localized in bone and teeth since they chelate with calcium. Tetracyclines act by interfering with protein synthesis. The following are some of the examples of this group:

Tetracycline hydrochloride (Achromycin)
Chlortetracycline hydrochloride (Aureomycin)
Oxytetracycline hydrochloride (Terramycin)
Demethylchlortetracycline hydrochloride (Ledermycin).

Undesirable effects

(1) Hypersensitive reaction, although it is very rare.

(2) Gastrointestinal disturbances include abdominal discomfort and nausea. Proteus and

pseudomonas strains may proliferate in the bowel causing diarrhea.

(3) Superinfection is common due to proliferation of candida albicans or staphylococci.

(4) The development of resistant strains to tetracycline occur. If an organism is resistant to one member of this group, it is resistant to all the other members of the group.

(5) Liver damage is seen with large doses of tetracyclines.

(6) Staining of teeth depends on the drug used. Chlortetracycline produces grey-brown discoloration while other tetracyclines produce yellow discoloration. In the mixed type, brownish-yellow discoloration is seen. The discoloration of teeth occurs only when these drugs are administered during the formative period of the fetus in pregnant women (first trimester).

(7) Tetracycline may produce marked depression of normal oral bacteria and produce altered microbial environment. Under such condition, overgrowth of candida albicans is of great concern to the oral surgeons.

Tetracyclines form useful alternatives to penicillin. They are marketed as capsules, tablets or injectables (250 mg). Capsules and tablets can be prescribed 6 hourly while injectables once a day. But this drug must not be used when bactericidal agent is required. Hence, this is contraindicated as a prophylactic agent prior to surgery.

Chloramphenicol

This is a broad spectrum antibiotic. It can be given through oral and parenteral route. Because of its toxicity, it is rarely used in oral surgery practice. It should be used only in severe infections that cannot be controlled with less toxic antibiotics. It is a potent inhibitor of bacterial protein synthesis with bacteriostatic action.

Erythromycin

Erythromycin, Oleandermycin and Spiramycin form a group. The activity is similar to penicillin. It is bactericidal in adequate concentration and acts by interfering with protein synthesis. In low concentration, it is bacteriostatic. It acts through oral route. Apart from hepatotoxic effect, this group is harmless. Erythromycin has the serious disadvantage of the development of resistance strains of staphylococci. This drug is not to be used in patients with depressed defenses.

Newer antibiotics

Carbenicillin and Ticarcillin are some of the recently introduced antibiotics, similar to penicillin, which are useful against pseudomonas and other troublesome gram-negative organisms in hospital infections. Newer aminoglycosides like gentamycin, Amikacin are also used in such hospital infections. Newer antitubercular drugs are rifampicin and ethambutol in the form of multidrug therapy along with streptomycin and isoniazid.

Antifungal agents

They fall broadly into two categories:

(1) Common superficial infections, e.g. ringworm and other dermatophytes.
(2) Systemic cases which are difficult to treat, e.g. candida albicans.

These two types differ widely in response to the antifungal agents.

Nystatin is effective against candida infections. It acts by linking itself to the cell membrane of the fungus, causing a change in its permeability with loss of potassium ions. This drug is almost insoluble and toxic. Hence, it is to be used topically. It has a bitter and unpleasant flavor. Candida does not become resistant to nystatin. Hence, it is used locally for all mucocutaneous candidosis.

Amphotericin-B is similar to nystatin in its chemical structure and mode of action. But it is absorbed in the GI tract to some extent. Intravenous injection may result in nausea, vomiting and fever. Irreversible renal damage is an inevitable complication.

Antiviral agents

Viruses have no enzyme systems. Hence, they colonize the host cells to utilize the nucleic acid metabolism. All the antiviral agents are synthetic in nature and their effectiveness is restricted. Idoxuridine resembles thymidine in structure. Hence, it acts as a thiamine antagonist. It is active against DNA tissues, e.g. herpes group. Amantadine is an antiviral agent, active against influenza A-interferons, form a group of substances with antiviral activity. They are species-specific and not virus-specific. Therefore, human interferons are active only in human beings. Recently, they have been found to inhibit multiplication of cells. Initial results are promising.

Prophylactic antibiotic therapy

Administration of antimicrobial agents to prevent surgically induced infection as a result of bacteremia in an otherwise healthy individual is considered to be of proved efficacy and safety. An antibiotic prophylaxis regimen must follow certain principles.

(1) The benefits of such therapy must outweigh the risks of antibiotics-induced complications including the emergence of drug-resistant microorganisms.

(2) The administered antibiotics must be present in the circulating blood in optimum concentration so that it is available in the target tissues prior to multiplication and dissemination of the microorganisms. A booster dose of the antibiotics may be necessary.

(3) The choice of the appropriate antibiotics should be based on the causative organisms and it must be continued so long as contamination persists.

The potential harm includes the increased risk of toxicities like drug-induced allergy, development of resistant strains and cross infection.

Oral surgical indications

1. Prevention of postoperative surgical infections following dental extractions, surgical endodontics and periodontics.
2. Prevention of infective endocarditis which may carry a mortality rate of 10-50%.

The rationale of antibiotic prophylaxis in the prevention of infections should relate to pathophysiology, clinical course, predisposing factors, microbial causation, association of dentally induced bacteremia, safety and efficacy of the proposed prophylactic antibiotic therapy, recommended regimen and patient benefit-risk ratio. Analysis of endocarditis serves as a model for prophylactic antibiotic therapy. The invasive dental procedures which induce bacteremia include dental extraction, periodontal surgery, endodontics etc. These dentist-induced bacteremias are usually of low-grade intensity. The extent of bacteremia is proportional to the degree of trauma, concentration of microorganisms in the area and the degree of inflammation present. Therefore, good oral health is particularly important in patients at high risk of endocarditis or its sequelae. Hence, parenteral antibiotics are recommended for dental patients with cardiac valve prosthesis. In addition, oral antiseptic mouth wash may aid in the reduction of bacteremia.

There is no absolute consensus on patients-at-risk. Dental patients with suppressed granulocyte counts may be at risk for bacteremia-induced infections. Acute rheumatic fever is a multisystem disorder, characterized by nonsuppurative inflammatory lesions of the heart, joints, central nervous systems and subcutaneous tissues. Patients undergoing hemodialysis and those who have indwelling catheter have a 5% risk. There is evidence that antibiotic prophylaxis is effective in preventing infections following clean surgery where the risk of infections is marginal but the consequences are grave. The oral cavity contains many major microbial pathogens. Therefore, "the routine use of antibiotics after oral surgical procedures amounts to attempting to prevent the infection of an unknown tissue with a drug of unknown efficacy at an undermined dosage which may not have occurred anyway." In fact, all of them constitute violations of the principles of antibiotic prophylaxis and hence misguided.

Risk-benefit rates

One of the most prevalent myths regarding antibiotic prophylaxis is that it does not harm. In some, prophylactic antibiotics has reached the highest level of efficacy. To its critics, it has rarely been proved to be effective and hence possess scientific justification. The truth seems to lie between these two extremes.

Antibiotic prophylaxis against wound infections

Oral surgery needs to be carefully evaluated since prevention of wound infection is one of the major goals of every oral surgeon. The principles of prevention of bacterial infection need to be reviewed periodically with better understanding of the pathology of wound infection and the management. The principles of prophylaxis are as follows:

Principle I. The surgical procedure should not have a significant risk of infection.

Class I procedures are called *clean surgery* in which there is no break in surgical aseptic techniques. Such clean surgery has an infection rate of 20% approximately, e.g. orthognathic surgery.

Class II procedures are called *clean contaminated surgery* in which no significant bacterial contamination results. Intraoral surgery is considered under this group. The expected infection rate is 10-15%.

Class III procedures are called *contaminated surgery*. Fresh traumatic cases are considered under this group. The anticipated infection rate is nearly 20-30%.

In Class IV procedures, there are established clinical infections, e.g. osteomyelitis, infected cysts and maxillary sinus and trauma cases of more than 8 hours duration. The infection rate is nearly 50%. It has been found that by the use of good surgical techniques, the infection rate can be reduced to 10% in class I cases. In prophylactic antibiotics, the incidence of the infection rate can be reduced approximately to 1% in class II cases and to less than 10% in class III cases.

If the operative procedures last longer than 2 hours or if it involves the insertion of major foreign bodies like implants, the infection rate increases. Even if the degree of contamination is less as in class I surgery, patients who have severe host defense problems will require appropriate prophylactic antibiotic therapy. In clinical practice, three types of patients have increased susceptibility to infection.

(1) Those who have poorly controlled metabolic diseases like diabetes, severe alcoholic cirrhosis and malnutrition syndrome.
(2) Those who have diseases that may interfere with the host defenses.
(3) Those who are on immunosuppressive drugs that may interfere with the host defenses like steroids and chemotherapy for malignancy.

Appropriate decision should be taken regarding the prophylaxis based on these clinical states.

Principle II. Appropriate antibiotics is to be selected for the surgical procedure. Vast majority of postoperative infections are caused by endogenous bacteria. The most likely contaminating organisms following oral surgery are streptococci, anaerobic gram-positive cocci and aerobic gram-negative rods. If the surgery were to be done extraorally, the most likely organisms causing infection are staphylococci from the skin.

The second factor to be considered is the least toxic, available antibiotic. The drug chosen for the purpose must be bactericidal. Thus, the drug of choice for transoral procedures is penicillin since it is effective against the oral bacterial spectrum. It is relatively non-toxic and bactericidal. For the transcutaneous extraoral procedures, first generation cephalosporin is the drug of choice, which is active against staphylococci.

Principle III. The antibiotic level in blood and target tissues must be fairly high. The plasma level must be high enough so as to allow diffusion of the antibiotics into the tissues contaminated by the microorganisms. To achieve this optimum level, the antibiotic must be given double the dose of the therapeutic level.

Principle IV. The administration of the appropriate dose of the appropriate antibiotics is equally important. As a general guideline, it must be understood that maximum effectiveness occurs when the antibiotic is already in the tissue and when bacteria reaches the tissue. Administration of antibiotics, after bacteremia develops, does not serve any useful purpose. High plasma levels must be maintained in prolonged surgical operations. As a rule, dosage interval must be one half of the usual therapeutic level.

Principle V. As far as possible, the shortest effective antibiotic exposure must be the objective. For example, in the case of short surgical procedures, a single dose of antibiotics given preoperatively is sufficient to prevent any wound infection. In the case of procedures of longer duration, intraoperative doses can be given as necessary with a final dose in the recovery room. The most important point in short-term usage is that any additional administration of antibiotics does not reduce the infection rate.

Complications

The effectiveness of high-dose antibiotic prophylaxis is an established fact. This type of prophylaxis is associated with total absence of any side effects and complications since antibiotics with less toxicity like penicillin or cephalosporins are used for shorter duration. Hence, shorter duration of antibiotic prophylaxis does not provide adequate time for the complications to arise. Perhaps, one of the factors which is likely to cause concern is the possibility of the emergence and growth of resistant strains. This is possible only when selective pressure for overgrowth of resistant bacteria begins after the susceptible organisms of the host are killed. This takes place approximately after 3 days of antibiotic therapy. Thus, short term therapy for a day is not likely to have any influence on the emergence and growth of resistant strains.

Applications

(1) The infection rate following routine dento-alveolar surgery appears to be very low. Therefore, in the normal healthy individual, most of these procedures do not require antibiotic prophylaxis to prevent wound infection. Even if needed, only a bactericidal antibiotics must be prescribed for a short duration. However, the patients' whose host defenses are in a compromised state, must be provided short-term antibiotic prophylaxis if the surgery cannot be deferred. Patients, whose metabolic disorder is under control, do not need antibiotic coverage. But if the patient is "brittle" with wide fluctuations in glucose level, prophylaxis is mandatory.

(2) Intraoral orthognathic, preprosthetic and tumor surgery, combined with extraoral procedures clearly fall under Class II (clean-contaminated surgery). The expected incidence of infection rate is in the range of 10-20%. The use of short-term preoperative antibiotic prophylaxis is necessary in most of these cases.

(3) Maxillofacial trauma: To prevent infection at the fracture site, antibiotic prophylaxis is necessary. It has been estimated that nearly 50% of these patients develop infection. Administration of antibiotics will reduce the infection rate to even 10%.

Conclusion

It is significant to note that prevention of wound infection in oral surgery under varied circumstances can be effectively achieved with appropriate antibiotic prophylaxis. In some procedures, infection rate is found to be unexpectedly high. The patients with compromised defenses are predisposed to wound infection.

To achieve the maximum benefit,

(a) The antibiotics must be administered before the onset of bacteremia.
(b) A high plasma level has to be maintained during surgery.
(c) The antibiotic therapy is to be stopped on completion of the procedure. It is also clear that a significant portion of infection control depends on the surgical skill in terms of the application of the basic principles of surgery. Antibiotics is not a substitute for surgery but an effective adjunct if it is used judiciously.

DRUGS AND MEDICALLY COMPROMISED PATIENTS

DIABETES

Defective control of carbohydrate metabolism is the main feature in diabetes. These patients are at risk of vascular disorders involving kidneys, extremities, heart and nervous system affecting cardio-respiratory reflexes. That is why it is safer to evaluate preoperatively all the obese patients above the age of 40 years to detect the existence of the diabetic state and if so, whether it is under control. If the patient gives history of diabetes, the practitioner must ascertain the diabetic state. In the initial stages, diabetic state can be controlled with diet alone. If it is not effective, oral hypoglycemic agents are useful, e.g. sulfonylureas. Their effectiveness depends on the ability to stimulate the secretion of endogenous insulin from beta cells. Drugs which may interact with these drugs and increase the risk of hypoglycemia are alcohol, barbiturates, salicylates and phenylbutazone.

The main antidiabetic sulfonylureas are tolbutamide and chlorpropamide. Glucagon is produced by alpha cells of pancreas and promotes fuel mobilization. During starvation, glucagon secretion increases and insulin secretion decreases. The only clinical use for glucagon is in the treatment of hypoglycemia. Dietary control continues to be the cornerstone of all antidiabetic agents or on replacement therapy with insulin. Onset and duration of action of different preparations of insulin are given in table 21.1. Insulin is usually administered by subcutaneous injection.

Patient may develop coma

(a) If the usual dose of insulin is taken without the meals,
(b) Due to unintentional insulin overdosage or
(c) Unaccustomed or unexpected exercise or stress.

During early reactions like sweating, nausea, weakness and tachycardia, the patient must be made to take sugar, soluble carbohydrates or fruit juice. If unconscious, it must be differentiated from syncope. Once it is confirmed that it is not syncope, glucose must be administered intravenously. To avoid damage to the vessel wall and thrombosis, injection of 5-10 ml of saline is given after the I.V. injection of glucose. If vein is not easily available, glucagon can be administered intramuscularly or subcutaneously. It mobilizes liver glycogen, thereby

Table 21.1 Onset and duration of action of insulin

	Types of insulin	*Onset of action*	*Duration of action*
1.	*Quick action* e.g., insulin plain	1 hour	10 hours
2.	*Intermediate acting* e.g., insulin zinc suspension (Lente insulin)	2 hours	24 hours
3.	*Long acting* e.g., protamine zinc insulin suspension	7 hours	36 hours

plasma level of glucose is raised. Patients who suffer from pain and hence unable to eat, predispose to the risk of hypoglycemia. Infection increases the insulin requirement. They also require vigorous antibiotic therapy.

In diabetic patients, a few important considerations are essential when considering to perform surgery under general anesthesia.

(1) Stress, due to anesthesia and surgery, is responsible for varying demand of insulin.

(2) Diabetic patients are at potential risk for cardiovascular problems.

(3) In case of short general anesthesia, insulin can be deferred and given after the patient comes out of anesthesia.

(4) As a rule, the patient is hospitalized 24 hours prior to anesthesia. Morning is the ideal time for surgery. Three hourly fasting and postprandial blood sugar level estimations are done.

(5) If the patient exhibits evidence of hypoglycemia, then 5% dextrose is given intravenously. Intraoperatively, all the insulin dependent diabetes are administered glucose intravenously. Insulin is given, based on the requirement. Postoperatively, it is absolutely essential to avoid hypoglycemia.

(6) Minor surgery under local anesthesia does not require any change in the patient's insulin or oral antidiabetic regime. It is desirable to confirm that the diabetic patient had sufficient food with adequate insulin preoperatively and postoperatively.

HYPERTENSION

Hypotensive drugs

Hypertension is one of the major risk factors of the cardiovascular diseases. Fortunately, early detection and its management with appropriate therapy reduces the possibility of damage to the vital organs and also to extend the life of the patient.

The hypertensive state can be divided into three degrees.

I. *Mild*. If diastolic is between 90 and 100 mm Hg.
II. *Moderate*. If diastolic is between 100 and 120 mm Hg.
III. *Severe*. If diastolic is above 130 mm Hg.

The hypertensive disease is divided into three categories based on the progression of the condition.

(1) Majority of the patients are diagnosed as primary or essential hypertension. The cause is not known although excessive sodium intake, genetic predisposition and anxiety are thought to be the causative factors.
(2) In secondary hypertension, patients are known to be associated with adrenal medullary tumor. In women, estrogen as a component of contraceptives may be the causative factor.
(3) In malignant hypertension, BP is very high with evidence of renal and retinal damage. Some believe that this is a severe form of essential hypertension.

Management of hypertension. Drug therapy aims at the important factors influencing BP: (a) peripheral resistance and (b) cardiac output since the maintenance BP depends on both these factors (Flowchart 21.1). It is found that the sympathetic nervous system activates renin-angiotensin mechanism. The non pharmacological measures include (a) reduction in the intake of sodium, alcohol and smoking, (b) weight reduction through dietary control and (c) planned exercise. But the therapeutic management of hypertension involves "stepped up care" approach.

Step I. Hypotensive therapy starts with minimal dose of beta adrenergic blocking agents and/or thiazide diuretics. Depending on the need, dosage of these drugs are increased.

Step II. Depending on the response, angiotensin converting enzyme inhibitors may be substituted as per

Flowchart 21.1 Factors influencing BP

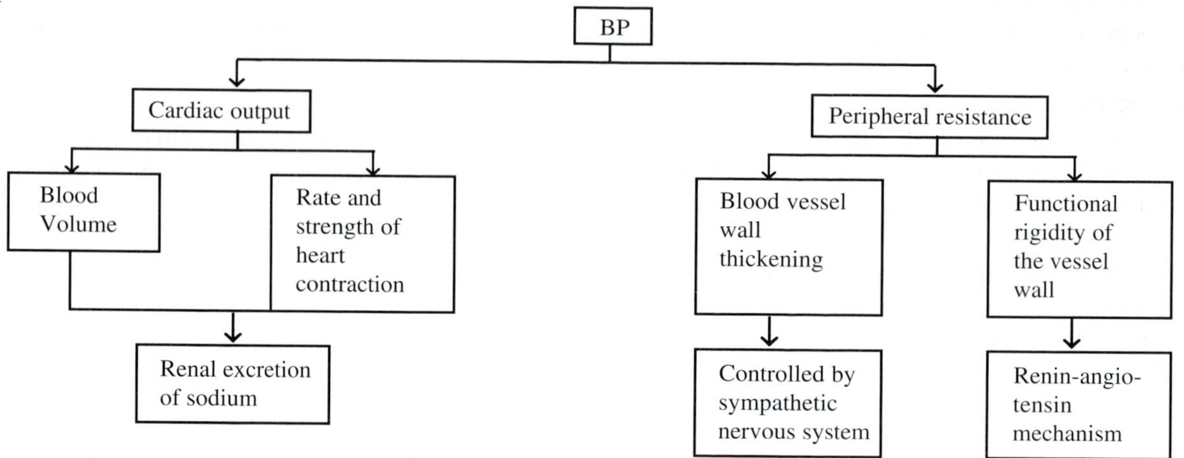

the requirement.

Step III. If BP is not under control, vasodilator may be added. Calcium channel blocking agents have been tried in steps II and III.

Step IV. If BP is not controlled, guanethidine is added. Reserpine, the principal alkaloid of rauwolfia, depletes norepinephrine by inhibiting the storage uptake mechanism in the adrenergic nerve terminal. It is seldom used as a single therapeutic hypotensive agent. Methyldopa (Aldomet) is a centrally acting antihypertensive agent. It is found to be most effective when it is combined with a diuretic. It stimulates alpha adrenergic receptors in the central nervous system which is associated with reduced sympathetic activity. This leads to decreased peripheral resistance. Many more newer forms of drug therapy are likely to be advocated in the near future. They are aimed at the etiology rather than providing symptomatic relief.

Therefore, a variety of drugs are being prescribed by the physicians to control hypertension as a combination therapy. It is safer to continue the drugs even if general anesthesia is contemplated. Withdrawal may result in rebound hypertension. Hence, it is safer to hospitalize the patients with uncontrolled hypertension. The use of local anesthetics in normal quantities is advocated. Hypertension is one of the causes of intraoperative and postoperative hemorrhage.

Hence, the clinician who encounters hypertensive patients in oral surgery practice will face the challenge of continued education and updating of knowledge on hypotensive drug therapy.

ORAL CONTRACEPTIVES

They usually contain progastrin with or without estrogen. One of the side effects is the possibility of thromboembolism. Risk is directly proportional to the estrogen content. These patients predispose to deep vein thrombosis and pulmonary embolism if the patients are confined to bed. Therefore, patients who are to undergo any elective in-patient surgery must discontinue the oral contraceptives 4-

8 days preoperatively. After surgery, the patient must be advised any alternative method of contraception during the next menstrual cycle. Drug that may interfere with the effectiveness of oral contraceptives are: (a) antibiotics like ampicillin, (b) hypnotics like barbiturates, (c) anticonvulsive drugs like carbamazepine. If the patient is on estrogen, excessive bleeding is likely. It is important that patients who are on oral contraceptives must be mobilized early postoperatively. Serious consideration may be required for the use of low-dose heparin as a prophylaxis against thromboembolism.

VITAMINS

They are organic compounds with low molecular weight which are essential in traces for the maintenance of normal cellular metabolism. They are broadly classified into two categories depending on the solubility.

I. **Water soluble vitamins**

(a) Primarily release energy from carbohydrates and fats B_1-thiamine, B_2-riboflavin, B_3-pyridoxine.

(b) Primarily catalyze the formation of RBCs, e.g. folic acid and B_{12}-cyanocobalamin.

(c) Not required in human nutrition, e.g. choline, inositol as members of B-complex. Vitamin C plays a role in accelerating hydroxylation reactions in biosynthetic pathways.

II. **Fat soluble vitamins.** Vitamin A, D, E, and K.

Vitamin A (retinol) is available in the form of capsules with 5000 to 50,000 units per capsule. It is useful in dermatological lesions.

Vitamin B complex is advocated in cases of angular cheilitis, stomatitis, dermatitis and glossitis in the form of capsules or solution.

Vitamin B_1 (thiamine) is useful in peripheral neuritis, muscular weakness, edema, burning tongue and loss of taste. It is available as 500 mg tablets and injectables in the form of aqueous solution of 50-100 mg/ml.

Vitamin B_2 (riboflavin) is prescribed in angular stomatitis glossitis and for the alcoholics.

Vitamin B_6 (pyridoxine) supplements must be routinely taken by women who use oral contraceptives. Available as 500 mg tablets and as injectable with 50-100 mg/ml.

Vitamin B_{12} (cyanocobalamin) is useful to treat pernicious anemia, glossitis, stomatitis and diminution of taste. This is available in the form of injectable isotonic saline solution with 30 mg/ml. It is not adequately absorbed in GI tract. Vitamin B_1, B_6, and B_{12} combinations are available as injectable preparations.

Vitamin C (ascorbic acid) is prescribed in case of defective wound healing, bone formation and bleeding from the gums due to the alteration in the integrity of capillary walls. It is available in the form of tablets containing 25 mg to 500 mg. Injection is also available containing 50 to 500 mg/ml of solution.

Vitamin D is prescribed in cases of rickets (in children) and osteomalacia (in adults). It is available with or without Vitamin A in the form of capsules.

Vitamin E (tocopherol) is used in cases of sterility and habitual abortion. It is available in the form of capsules containing 30-1000 international units of Vitamin E.

Vitamin K is essential for the synthesis of prothrombin and clotting factors VII, IX and X in liver. Prothrombin is the precursor of thrombin. Hence, deficiency of Vitamin K is called hypoprothrombinemia resulting in bleeding diathesis. Vitamin K is available as 5 mg tablets and emulsion of 2-10 mg/ml as injectable preparations.

ANTICOAGULANTS

Anticoagulant therapy reduces the incidence of intravascular clotting and prevents life-threatening emergencies. Hence, they are prescribed for deep vein thrombosis, patients with poorly-controlled fibrillation and patients with prosthetic valve. If the dosage is too large, hemorrhage occurs. If the dosage is too small, possibility of embolism occurs. If any patient on anticoagulant needs oral surgery, the physician responsible for the patient's care must be consulted to find out the possibility of adjusting the therapy since sudden stoppage may result in the rise of factor VIII above normal level. It is better to consult a competent hematologist before carrying out any oral surgery procedure in such patients. Intramuscular injections are contraindicated in patients receiving heparin.

SPECIAL CONSIDERATIONS

Drugs during pregnancy and lactation

Oral surgeon is sometimes confronted with the dilemma of prescribing drugs to pregnant or lactating women. This requires the clinician's understanding of the interaction between drugs and pregnancy to avoid indiscriminate use with undesirable consequences. At the same time, over-cautious timidity on the part of the doctor will deny the pregnant mother the benefit of the appropriate drug. Real need for any drug in such patients during pregnancy must be assessed. If needed, she should not be denied adequate treatment.

Fate of the drug during pregnancy. Response of drugs slightly differ because of certain physiological changes.

(a) *Absorption of the drug*. The high circulating progesterone slows gastric emptying and gut motility. Nausea, vomiting and fear may result in poor drug absorption.

(b) *Distribution*. There is an increase of total body water up to 8 litres. Nearly 30% increase of plasma volume leads to decrease in plasma albumin as a result of hemodilution. Therefore, volume of distribution of the drugs with low lipid solubility and high plasma protein binding decreases.

(c) *Metabolism*. Drug metabolizing hepatic enzymes are induced during pregnancy due to high level of progesterone leading to rapid metabolic degradation of highly soluble drugs.

(d) *Excretion*. Renal plasma flow increases by 100% and glomerular filtration rate by 70%. Hence, drugs like ampicillin, gentamycin and cephalexin are eliminated by the kidneys more rapidly.

Hence, dosage of ampicillin needs to be doubled during pregnancy. However, metronidazole does not require any alteration in the dose. Placenta acts as an intravenous portal for entry of drugs into the fetus. As pregnancy progresses, placenta increases in size and hence transplacental barrier becomes progressively thinner. Impaired conjugation of salicylates and chloramphenicol in the neonate can cause severe toxicity. Because of the low renal plasma flow and more acidic urine, drugs like aminoglycosides, penicillin and sulfa drugs are cleared slowly by the neonate. Hence, repeated administration to the mother can cause neonatal toxicity. In general, one must be cautious to prescribe any medication during first trimester of pregnancy to avoid birth defects.

In normal pregnancy, the following drugs are contraindicated:

(a) *Vaccination and immunizations*. They must be carefully monitored. Tetanus toxoid and cholera vaccine are safe.

(b) *Analgesics*. Aspirin is safe. But it is better to avoid it in women who are predisposed to premature labor and hemorrhage. Paracetamol is a safe alternative.

(c) *Antiemetics*. Pyridoxine alone or in combination with an antiemetic can be prescribed.

(d) *Diuretics*. They must be avoided as they reduce plasma volume and can cause intrauterine growth retardation.

(e) *Sedatives*. Diazepam, barbiturates and

phenothiazines can be safely prescribed.

(f) *Antibiotics*. If tetracyclines are given during second or third trimester, enamel hypoplasia and discoloration develop. Sulfonamides, metronidazole and aminoglycosides like gentamycin, streptomycin, kanamycin and neomycin should be used with caution. Penicillin, cephalosporins and erythromycin are safe antibiotics during pregnancy. Erythromycin estolate must be avoided because of its higher toxicity. Aminoglycosides are ototoxic to the fetus. Cotrimoxazole may be avoided during the first trimester because of trimethoprim content and during the third trimester because of its sulfonamide content.

(g) *Antihypertensives*. They can be used without any harm to the fetus.

(h) *Other drugs*. Cytotoxic drugs, oral anticoagulants and radioactive drugs are contraindicated. Anticonvulsants, oral hypoglycemic and corticosteroids must be prescribed with caution.

(i) *In lactating mothers*. Antiepileptic drugs, chloramphenicol and iodine are contraindicated.

The safety of metronidazole, sulfonamides, tetracyclines and reserpine are yet to be established. Antibiotics like ampicillin, cephalosporins, erythromycin, gentamycin, kanamycin, penicillin, streptomycin and analgesics like paracetamol and salicylates can be safely prescribed.

Antiallergic agents

The treatment of acute allergic reactions like anaphylaxis is by physiological antagonisms rather than specific antihistamine administration. Hence, epinephrine is the drug of choice. To treat bronchial asthma and pulmonary edema, aminophylline is useful due to its bronchodilator activity. Steroids are useful to suppress any inflammatory reactions. A sound pharmacological approach to treat hypersensitive and allergic reactions would be a selective inhibition of histamine release.

Antihistamines are those compounds which antagonize histamine-induced contraction of smooth muscles and reduction of anaphylactic responses. At present antihistamines are subdivided as H_1 and H_2 receptor blocking agents (antagonists). H_1 antihistamines produce sedation with or without dizziness, blurred vision, fatigue and gastrointestinal disturbances. They act by H_2-antihistamine action and by actions independent or blockade of histamine receptors. H_2 receptor antagonists are used for the suppression of gastric acid secretions.

Allergy is a loosely used term to denote the conditions where immune response becomes harmful to the patient.

Allergic reactions

These reactions, whether acute or chronic, are grouped under following four categories:

Type I (anaphylactic), e.g. anaphylaxis, urticaria, asthma. The specific antibody is cell bound to mast cells. Antigen triggers the release of substances producing vasodilatation, contraction of bronchial muscles and increased capillary permeability (Flowchart 21.2).

Type II (cytotoxic), e.g. blood transfusion reactions. Antibody reacts with antigen bound to the cell surface and the cells are damaged.

Type III (immune complex), e.g. serum sickness. Antigen-antibody reaction under certain conditions and fix the compliments, involving small blood vessels.

Type IV (cell-mediated, delayed hypersensitivity), e.g. skin reactions. Montou test, contact dermatitis and rejection of homografts.

Sensitized lymphocytes react with antigens, liberating cytotoxic substances. Release of histamine produces acute inflammatory response due to allergic reaction. Histamine is an important chemical mediator in allergy. It is in an inactive, cell bound form but becomes active when released in response to antigen-antibody reaction. The effect of histamine is counteracted by many ways. Antihistamines refer to a group of agents which block H_1 histamine receptors. They are administered through oral route. The effect lasts for many hours. Antihistamines are essentially receptor-blockers and hence compete with histamine for the receptor-sites as preventive agents. They are also useful for their sedative, antiemetic, antitussive and atropine-like effects.

Adrenaline and other related drugs are used in allergy which act as the mediator level. Adrenaline and isoprenaline act as physiological antagonists. Hence, adrenaline is useful in allergic emergencies like asthma, angioedema and anaphylaxis. It is useful by its bronchial relaxation, vasoconstriction, decreased capillary permeability and reduction of mucosal edema. It acts immediately but the effect lasts for 30-45 minutes. It is to be given intramuscularly. Accidental intravascular injection may cause dangerous cardiac arrhythmias, terminating in ventricular fibrillation.

Corticosteroids do not inhibit antigen-antibody reaction. It protects the target cells from the effects of the mediators released during the reactions. Capillary permeability is decreased and cell membrane is stabilized. Consequently, edema is reduced. It is found to be effective in type II reactions. In heavy doses, they are used for depressing cell mediated immune responses by acting against T-type lymphocytes. These actions contribute to their immunosuppressive action.

Levamisole, an antihelminthic agent, has been found to have some immunostimulant actions. Hence, it has been tried in the treatment of aphthous ulcers and in the treatment of rheumatoid arthritis. The toxic effects include agranulocytosis, disturbances of central nervous system and gastrointestinal tract.

Drug allergy. The most common sources of drug allergy are penicillin, sulfonamides, aspirin and few other drugs with allergic potential.

In cases of drug allergy,

(i) Further medications are to be stopped,
(ii) For skin lesions, like urticaria or vesicle formation, oral antihistamine, chlorpheniramine maleate (4 mg tablets) can be prescribed 2 or 3 times a day.
(iii) For orolabial, conjunctival and urethral inflammatory rashes, high doses of corticosteroids may be necessary, e.g. prednisone 20 mg thrice a day and gradually taper the dose after 7 days.
(iv) For angioneurotic edema, parenteral hydrocortisone and maintenance.
(v) In case of anaphylaxis, adrenaline or hydrocortisone through intramuscular route and oxygen may be administered.

Flowchart 21.2

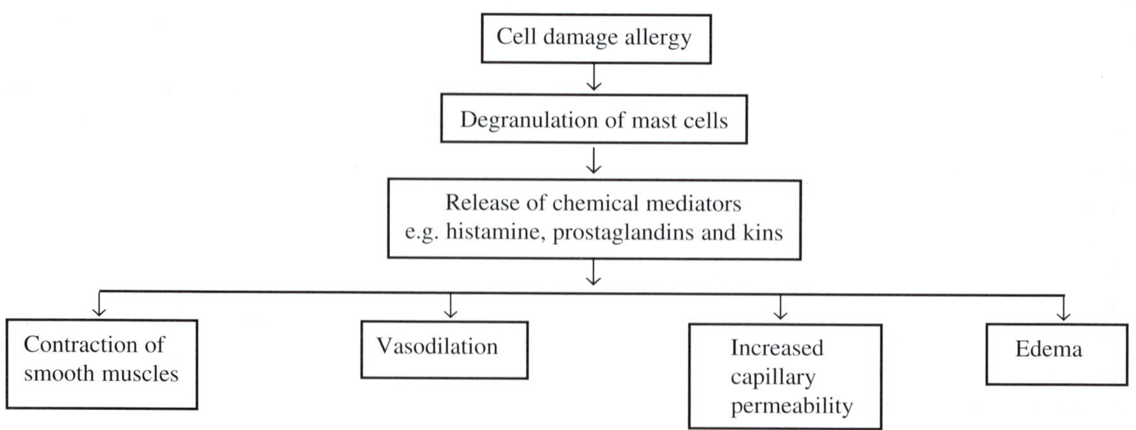

Chemotherapy of malignancy

These drugs are used clinically to destroy or to suppress the multiplication and spread of neoplastic cells to the other parts of the body at the levels of treatment of malignancy. For example, it is used to reduce the size of the neoplasms prior to irradiation or surgery. In the recent past, the philosophy of aggressively treating the neoplastic growth with these agents is receiving greater attention. Inspite of the fact that this approach promises to be more effective, the side effect is the discouraging factor which tends to be carefully managed. Efficacy is primarily based on their ability to interfere with the metabolism and the reproductive cycle of the tumor cells.

The cycle of the tumor cell consists of four distinct phases:

(1) Pre-DNA synthesis phase (postmitotic) cell is in the resting stage.
(2) Period of DNA synthesis.
(3) Post DNA synthesis phase (premitotic).
(4) Period of mitosis.

The antineoplastic agents may be "cycle dependent" or "cycle independent" indicating the level of their effectiveness. In general, antitumor drugs are grouped into four types:

(a) Alkylating agents.
(b) Antimetabolites.
(c) Miscellaneous.
(d) Hormones.

(a) **Alkylating agents.** They bind themselves firmly to both the strands of DNA in the cell nucleus in all the phases of the cell cycle and prevent their separation. Hence, cell division is prevented. This group is effective in lymphoma, chronic leukemia, Hodgkin's disease, breast and ovary carcinomas. The examples of such drugs are cyclophosphamide, melphalan and chlorambucil. Due to their action on the bone marrow, granulocytopenia, thrombocytopenia and anemia develop. They are also immunosuppressive agents.

(b) **Antimetabolites** block the synthesis of nucleic acid during the period of DNA synthesis. Hence nuclei cannot divide and cytoplasms cannot grow. Therefore, cell division is prevented, e.g. methotrexate (antifolate antimetabolite).

(c) **Miscellaneous group.** Actinomycin D blocks the protein synthesis and cell growth during metaphase. The other examples are Bleomycin and Mutamycin, Vinlatine and Vincristine, derived from vinca rosea plant alkaloids. Because of the low bone marrow toxicity, they are frequently used in combination therapy.

(d) **Hormones.** Adrenocorticosteroids are sex hormones found effective in certain specific neoplasms. For example, steroids are effective in leukemia. Estrogen can delay the extension of prostate carcinomas. Stilbestrol, glucocorticosteroid in very high doses are lymphocytotoxic and can also potentiate the action of other immunosuppressive drugs. They are very effective in acute lymphatic leukemia and Hodgkin's disease.

Complications

During antineoplastic therapy, there is a lack of selectivity between tumor cells and normal cells. In the process, even normal cells are also destroyed. The following are some of the principal adverse effects:

(i) *Bone marrow suppression.* It results in leukopenia thrombocytopenia, agranulocytosis and anemia depending on the dose of the drug and condition of the bone marrow. Hence, the patient is susceptible to infection causing oral ulcerations. Frequent mouth irrigation with antibiotic antifungal preparations like tetracycline with amphotericin B is found to be helpful.
(ii) *Immunosuppression* - cell mediated immunity is greatly impaired.
(iii) *Gastrointestinal disturbances* - like anorexia, nausea, vomiting and diarrhea with sloughing of gastrointestinal mucosa.
(iv) *Hepatotoxicity* - more common with methotrexate.

(v) *Neurotoxic effects* - like peripheral neuropathy and convulsion.
(vi) *Renal tubular impairment* - caused by rapid cell destruction.
(vii) *Cutaneous reactions* - may range from mild erythema to exfoliative dermatitis and alopecia.
(viii) *Inhibition of spermatogenesis and oogenesis.*
(ix) *Xerostomia.*

Diet and drugs

Route of administration forms one of the important considerations of any clinician while prescribing drugs. Perhaps, oral route is the simplest, frequently used and a convenient way to introduce a drug into the human system. It is well suited for self-medication. The large absorbing area of the intestine is the main advantage of the oral route. But the disadvantages are the delayed onset of action of the drug when compared with the parenteral route. Only one-third of the drug taken is absorbed into the system.

While prescribing any drug through oral route, the clinician must be taken into consideration, many factors to ensure maximum efficacy of the drug that is administered. The following are some of them:

(1) Presence or absence of food in the stomach.
(2) Emptying of the gastric contents.
(3) Pathology of GIT.
(4) Effect of gastric acidity.
(5) Hepatic-portal circulation.
(6) The nature of the drug.

Most of the patients enquire the clinician as to whether the drug has to be taken before or after the meals. From therapeutic point of view, administration of any drug through the oral route must be considered with reference to the meals in terms of efficacy of the drug, presence of pathology of GIT, alteration in the gastric acidity and emptying of the gastric contents. All of them play major roles in making the level of concentration of the drug in blood unpredictable through oral route when compared to parenteral administration. Every drug enters the hepaticportal circulation but some are destroyed in liver. Hence, such drugs are not effective through the oral route.

Sometimes, food can interact with certain medicines and can produce undesirable effects.

(a) A substance called tyramine in cheese and chicken liver can interact with monoamine oxidase and may lead to dangerously high blood pressure resulting in severe headache, cerebral hemorrhage and even death. Therefore, such patients must avoid wines, curd, bananas, beef, coffee, chocolates and cold beverages.
(b) Alcohol adversely interacts with antihistamines, antibiotics, antihypertensive drugs, anticoagulants and sedatives.
(c) Milk and milk products contain calcium. It interferes with absorption of tetracyclines.
(d) Patients on anticoagulants should not consume food rich in Vitamin K like liver and green leafy vegetables.
(e) Thyroid medications are inhibited by soyabeans, turnips and cabbage.
(f) Patients with barbiturates, tetracyclines, adrenal corticosteroids, oral contraceptives and aspirin must always be supplemented with Vitamin C.
(g) Anticonvulsant drugs can deplete folic acid and Vitamin D.
(h) Long-term therapy of sulfonamides and broad spectrum antibiotics can reduce bacterial synthesis of Vitamin K in the intestines. Malabsorption of Vitamin D is prevalent in the elderly patients who use liquid paraffin as laxatives. As little as 20 ml of liquid paraffin twice a day can interfere with absorption of Vitamin D and K.
(i) Chronic use of antacids can lead to phosphate depletion which may weaken the muscles. In severe form, it can cause Vitamin D deficiency.

(j) Iron taken along with meat, citrus fruits or juices result in greater absorption, but when taken with tea, cereals and milk products, absorption of iron is reduced.

Food influences the quantity and rate of absorption of the drug from GI tract by affecting the blood flow and gastric emptying. Some drugs can cause gastric irritation and may cause nausea and vomiting. Food that delays gastric emptying delays the absorption of the orally administered drug. Entry of low pH or high fat solutes into the upper part of the small intestine can delay gastric emptying. Hot meals and solutions rich in fat and carbohydrates slow gastric emptying. Retarded gastric emptying may also reduce the amount of drug absorbed because of the degradation of the drug in the acidic contents of the stomach. Absorption of drugs like aspirin and some types of penicillin are delayed in the presence of food. Drugs like griseofulvin, lithium citrate used for mental depression, analgesics like propoxyphene, antihypertensive drugs like propranolol undergo increased absorption. It has also been shown that liquid glucose meal decrease the blood flow while protein rich meal increases the flow.

Although aspirin is an extremely safe drug, it can cause GIT upset. It can be avoided by taking aspirin with food or at least with full glass of milk or water. Ingestion of liquid antacid can decrease the gastric irritation. If aspirin is taken on empty stomach, it can produce dyspepsia (heartburn) nausea, vomiting or even gastrointestinal bleeding. Blood loss produced by aspirin is exacerbated by ingestion of alcohol. Likewise, ibuprofen must be taken with full glass of water. It is still preferable if taken with food.

The following are some of the examples:

(a) Penicillin V tablet is to be taken one hour before meals.
(b) Erythromycin tablets, tetracycline capsules and cephalosporin capsules are to be taken 1 hour before meals.
(c) Benadryl elixir be diluted and used for rinsing the mouth 2 minutes before each meal in case of painful oral ulcerations.
(d) Applications of triamcinolone over the oral ulcerations after each meal.
(e) For aphthous ulceration, topical steroids are to be applied after each meal.
(f) Antiinflammatory drugs like oxyphenbutazone must be taken with some food. It should not be taken on empty stomach.

Therefore, as a rule, if the food delays absorption of drugs, taking the drug at least one hour before meals will minimize this effect. If the food enhances the drug absorption, drug is taken with meals.

EMERGENCY DRUGS (Table 21.2)

The following are the important criteria to be taken into account when selecting appropriate emergency drugs:

(1) Drugs which are to be considered essential for the first line management of medical emergencies, that is, drugs which will act as an adjunct to basic life support and other life saving measures within the first 15 to 20 minutes of an emergency.
(2) Drugs which can be used by a dental practitioner at the dental clinic set up.

Management of emergencies depends on the early diagnosis of the problem. Essentially, it is based on vital signs like respiration and circulation. Proper positioning of the patient, maintenance of patent airway and adequate administration of oxygen are mandatory. Drugs are only ancillary to these measures. The ultimate goal in any resuscitative measures is the maintenance of adequate tissue oxygenation. Brain is unable to survive for more than 4 minutes under anaerobic conditions. Even though organs like heart and kidneys are capable of metabolic adjustment through anaerobic glycolysis, accumulation of toxic products results in irreversible

Table 21.2 Emergency drugs

	Drugs	*Formulations*	*Route of administration*	*Indication*
(1)	Oxygen	Cylinders	Inhalation	All emergencies
(2)	Adrenaline	1 mg in 1 ml (1:1000) solution	Intramuscular	Anaphylaxis
(3)	Hydrocortisone Sodium succinate	100 mg powder plus 2 ml distilled water	Intramuscular	Anaphylaxis and adrenal crisis
(4)	Glucose	Powder	Oral	Diabetic hypoglycemia (conscious)
(5)	Aspirin	300 mg dispersible tablets	Oral	Myocardial Infarction
(6)	Chlorpheniramine maleate	10 mg in 1 ml solution	Intramuscular	Anaphylaxis
(7)	Glucagon	1 mg powder plus 1 ml sterile water	Intramuscular	Diabetic hypoglycemia (unconscious)
(8)	Solbutamol inhaler	0.1 mg per dose	Inhalation	Asthma
(9)	Glyceryl trinitrate	0.5 mg tablet or 0.4 mg per dose spray	Sublingual	Angina
(10)	Midazolam	10 mg in 2 ml solution	Intramuscular	Status epilepticus

condition unless they are corrected sufficiently early. The time of therapeutic support depends on the type of emergency.

(1) **Adrenaline (epinephrine)** is required for treating anaphylaxis, cardiac arrest and shock although its efficacy is questionable in shock. In such conditions, administration of adrenaline may interfere with venous return and tissue perfusion. There is a possibility of precipitation of ventricular fibrillation in the ischemic and irritable myocardium. In case of cardiac arrest, metabolic acidosis reaches a critical level. The build up of lactic acid from hypoxic tissues require compensatory measures. I.V. sodium carbonate is useful as adjunctive therapy. However, adrenaline in grave emergencies including anaphylaxis has proved to be a drug of choice.

(2) **Aromatic spiritus ammonia.** It is useful in cases of syncope. After positioning the patient with elevation of legs, inhalation of spiritus ammonia is helpful. It stimulates trigeminal nerve endings, resulting in reflex stimulation of vasomotor and medullary respiratory centres.

(3) **Nitroglycerin (glyceryl trinitrate).** It is useful to relieve the anginal pain. It is believed to dilate the coronary artery so that pain due to myocardial ischemia is relieved. This becomes more important in patients who are on drugs that tend to produce orthostatic hypotension, e.g. reserpine, methyldopa as hypotensive drugs. Since the shelf life is only 6 months, periodically, expiry date of the drug must be monitored. 0.6 mg tablet held under the tongue with the patient in a semiprone or sitting position provides relief from pain within 2-3 minutes. In addition, elimination of stressful situations, reassurance and administration of oxygen are equally important under such emergency situations. Failure to respond indicates that it is a case of myocardial infarction.

(4) **Diphenhydramine** (Benadryl). After the administration of any drug , if the patient develops allergic reaction like urticaria, pruritis with or without respiratory distress, this is useful. Since antihistamines compete with histamine for tissue receptor site, immediate relief with antihistamines may not be possible. This drug is indicated in the

treatment of extrapyramidal reactions like spasm of neck muscles, restlessness, trismus and Parkinson-like movement following phenothiazine group of drugs like chlorpromazine.

(5) **Diazepam.** It is a popular anticonvulsant drug. It is relatively safe if given intramuscularly or intravenously.

(6) **5% Dextrose solution.** Most of the drugs in emergency situations can be conveniently given through intravenous route. Fluid replacement is equally important in emergency situations. Hence, 5% glucose solution must be readily available.

(7) **Methylprednisolone sodium succinate.** It is an important drug in the management of anaphylaxis, acute adrenocortical insufficiency and cardiac arrest. Dose: 125 mg I.V. This is the drug of choice in patients who are on long-term steroid therapy and collapse in the dental chair.

Hospital Oral Surgery

GENERAL CONSIDERATIONS

The hospital has a responsibility to the community to provide comprehensive oral care for their patients. In this direction, the level of oral care varies from the ward consultation to emergency care and elective oral surgery. Usually oral surgeons are able to understand the hospital protocol and feel "at home" at the hospital environment than any other oral health professional. A general dental practitioner can also extend the hospital training so that scope of the extended service makes one's own experience most rewarding. Out of many oral surgery procedures, a few situations may demand the need to perform oral surgery in the hospital. The following are some of those situations:

- (a) Some medically compromised patients may require careful evaluation and monitoring of health status during and after surgery in the hospital.
- (b) Patient may need general anesthesia
  - (i) because the surgery is a major procedure and
  - (ii) in case of uncooperative patients of extremes of age.
- (c) Due to the time factor, patients who prefer to undergo surgery in one appointment which otherwise may require many appointments, e.g. multiple extractions.
- (d) Procedures which demand strict asepsis or which may not be possible in the dental office, e.g. transplants and implants.
- (e) If the patient's postsurgical complications need hospitalization, e.g. hemorrhage, shock, etc.
- (f) If the patient is hospitalized for some other purpose, may need oral surgery.

Under these circumstances, it is obligatory on the part of the oral surgeon, who wishes to practise "hospital oral surgery", to be familiar with hospital routine, protocol, clinical privileges and responsibilities associated with in-patient service. General guidelines for hospital oral surgery practice is provided here. Although hospital protocol and rules may vary from hospital to hospital, basic guidelines remain constant everywhere.

ADMISSION INTO THE HOSPITAL

At least 24 hours prior to any elective surgery, the patient must be admitted to enable the anesthetist and the physician to evaluate the patient for fitness to undergo surgery. The following are some of the routine investigations to be carried out:

(1) Blood investigations
   (a) RBC count and Hb%
   (b) WBC - total and differential counts
   (c) Platelet count
   (d) Bleeding and coagulation time
   (e) Urine analysis for sugar and albumin
   (f) Blood sugar level, if necessary
   (g) Any other specific investigations depending on the patient's need.
(2) Chest posteroanterior radiograph.
(3) If the patient is over 40 years, ECG must be taken.

At the time of admission, the following data must be provided:

(1) Name, age, sex and permanent address.
(2) Brief personal, family history and details of clinical examination.
(3) Reasons for admission and provisional diagnosis.
(4) Anticipated duration of stay in the hospital.
(5) Details of previous hospitalization, if any.
(6) Request for any further investigation to be ordered, if necessary.

On admission, anesthetist will examine the patient. Once the patient is declared fit for surgery by the anesthetist,

(1) The patient must be advised mild sedation to ensure comfortable night sleep prior to surgery to allay the fear and anxiety. The clinician's order primarily serves as the medium of communications with the staff of the hospital.
(2) Oral feed is normally withheld at least 6 hours prior to general anesthesia. This is to avoid postoperative vomiting and foreign body aspiration into the respiratory tract.
(3) Oral prophylaxis prior to oral surgery is preferable.
(4) Close shave of the face must be advised in male patients.
(5) Details of premedications are best left to the direction of the anesthetist.
(6) Details of medications as instructed by the family physician must be provided in the medically compromised patients.
(7) Indications regarding the requirements of transfusions must be considered.
(8) Advance intimations are required by the hospital if consultations with specialists are required.
(9) Surgeon must ensure that patient's signature has been obtained in the consent form.

The following additional information must be provided:

(a) Brief outline of the surgical procedure.
(b) Anticipated duration of surgery and blood loss.
(c) Positioning of the patient.
(d) Necessity for intermaxillary immobilization.
(e) Provision of nasogastric tube postoperatively.
(f) Drugs that are likely to be injected during anesthesia.

After the admission, it is the duty of the hospital staff to ensure that the case sheet is complete in all aspects.

To set up a drip

Prior to taking the patient into the operation theatre, it is always better to set up a drip and keep it in position. This is useful for the following purposes:

(1) Premedication.
(2) Fluid maintenance.
(3) During emergency, ready I.V. route is available, which otherwise will be difficult to gain access into the vein.
(4) Postoperative fluid maintenance and delivery of drugs.

Almost any visible or palpable vein can be used for peripheral cannulation, but certain sites are preferred. The reasons are - ease of access and patients' comfort. The common sites are forearm and hand. Tourniquet is applied to obstruct the venous return while it continues to fill from the arterial circulation. The pressure applied by the tourniquet should therefore be less than arterial pressure. Continued presence of the radial pulse after the application of tourniquet is a simple test. Repeated tapping of the vein or exercising the site repeatedly produces enlargement of the veins.

After the preparation of the skin, the needle is used to gain access into the vein. There are three types of cannulae: (a) Winged steel needles, e.g., butterfly, (b) Plain plastic cannulae and (c) Ported cannulae e.g., venflon. They are available in a wide range of sizes. Winged steel needles are used during the induction of anesthesia.

Having identified the vein and skin is prepared, limb is held steady with one hand, which also pulls the skin taut over the vein. For a short distance, cannula is advanced through the skin away from the vein and a second discreet action advances the needle tip into the vein. "Flash back" of blood into the needle hub indicates venepuncture. Now complete cannula and needle should be advanced along the long axis of the vein for 1 mm. Counterpuncture must be avoided. After releasing the tourniquet, pressure with a finger is applied on the vein above the point of insertion of the needle to avoid any loss of blood. Cannula is anchored firmly with adhesive tape. Specialized dressings are available for Venflon cannulae.

The minimum flow rate needed to maintain cannula patency is difficult to estimate although 3 ml per hour is sufficient. Stopping the infusion allows blood to track back up the cannula which may eventually clot. Lowering the bag of fluid when transporting the patient with drips encourages this reflex of blood. Therefore it is advisable to close the roller clamp during the transport of the patient.

OPERATING ROOM PROCEDURES

The oral surgeon must be familiar with the operation theatre dress regulations, scrub techniques and other protocol. Usually, access into the operating room is restricted to persons with change over to theatre dresses, footwear, cap and mask. Nails should be clipped properly. The operating room is characterized by certain features which differ from the dental clinic.

(a) **Topographic location.** It is usually located in an area of the hospital with controlled access and limited entry.

(b) **Additional provisions.** Adequate space is provided outside the operating room for anesthesia office, sterilization area, non-sterile dress-changing room, scrub area and sterile instruments and linen storage area.

(c) **Bacterial isolation.** Every effort is made to ensure that bacterial invasion is prevented from outside by preventing the entry of outside clothing and footwear. Similarly, adequate provision is made for the safe disposal of the soiled instruments and linen.

(d) **Centralization of personnel.** The expertise of the trained personnel in the operating room is available to the surgeon to promote great deal of efficiency, skill and cooperation.

(e) **Centralization of equipment and instruments.** The operation theatre functions as an integrated unit. Its main objection is to provide a suitable atmosphere for safe surgery. The available equipment and instruments are at the disposal of the operating team. Every member must be familiar with the usage of equipment and instruments. Otherwise, inefficient or careless handling will put the other operating teams into avoidable inconvenience. Therefore, a thorough knowledge of the operation theatre environment is absolutely essential.

The oral surgeon must also be familiar with the operating room personnel and their specific duties.

(a) **Anesthesiologist.** They have very important roles to play in the maintenance of anesthesia, controlling medical problems of the patient and monitoring the fluid balance during the patient's stay in the operation theatre, the maintenance of anesthetic record and supervision of immediate pre and postoperative phase.

(b) **Surgical nurse.** She is an important member of the surgical team to assist the oral surgeon. She is mainly responsible to sterilize and to lay the instrument tray required for the surgery. Conventionally, another surgeon assists the surgeon. But in the absence of such an assisting surgeon, the surgical nurses assume the role of the assistants.

(c) **Circulating nurse.** She mainly plays an intermediary role between the surgical team and the rest of the operating personnel. She helps to set up power equipment, suction apparatus, etc. and assists the anesthetist since she is free to move around the operation theatre.

(d) **Nursing assistants.** They help the surgical nurse in performing her duties to prepare the operating suite. They also assist during scrubbing of the members of the surgical team. They are semiskilled and non-technical personnel. They play an important role in shifting the patient into the operation theatre preoperatively and back into the ward postoperatively.

Scrubbing technique

This is done in the scrubbing room situated at a convenient place adjoining the operating suite. Usually, all the members of the surgical team who handle the surgical field must wear cap and mask before scrubbing. The scrubbing should be done for at least 10 minutes in the following manner:

(a) Both the hands and arms above the elbow level must be washed with soap and water for one or two minutes. This forms part of *gross cleaning*.

(b) After washing both the hands with running water, liquid detergent soap is applied up to the elbow level and scrubbed with sponge brush. The scrubbing must start from the finger nails, fingers, hands and then the arms for 6-7 minutes.

(c) The arms up to the elbow level are rinsed in running water. Care is taken to keep the hands at a higher level than elbows so that rinsed water drains towards the elbows.

(d) After rinsing, antiseptic scrubbing solution is applied over the scrubbed area and washed towards both the elbows with sterile water.

(e) Both the hands are raised above the elbow level and kept in the same position for a minute so that the water drains out completely. This position is not altered until gloves are worn.

Application of gown and gloves

After scrubbing is completed, circulation nurse helps the members of the surgical team to wear the gown. She will also tie the gown at the back. In some places, surgeon has to unfold the gown and must wear without the help of the nurse. Then, he must learn to wear the gloves in the proper way. In some theatres, the nurse holds the gloves in such a way that the surgeon inserts the hands directly into the gloves. Otherwise, he must wear the gloves one by one. From now on, one must strictly enforce self-discipline regarding the operation theatre asepsis techniques.

Preparation of the operating site and draping

Before draping, positioning of the patient is an important procedure. For most of the oral surgical procedures, a sandbag is placed below the shoulder so that neck and submandibular region are extended.

In order to keep the head at the desired position, a ring is kept at the back of the head. It is firmly supported by a suitable rest to prevent the head from rotating sidewise.

As already described under "sterilization", the surgical field must be properly cleaned with antiseptics and draped so that it will be isolated from rest of the region. Prior to draping, the area must be scrubbed with antiseptic solution thoroughly. With a wet gauze, the area is wiped and cleaned. Now, the patient is ready for draping.

For oral surgery, it is preferable to keep two towels one over the other and placed below by lifting the head. One towel is spread and the upper towel is used to drape the head, exposing only the orofacial region. Towels are fixed in position with towel clips. Chest and rest of the body are covered with a sheet spread.

Thus, the entire body is covered in such a way that the orofacial surgical field alone is exposed for surgery. The surgeon must ensure that,

(1) The operating area alone is isolated.
(2) Endotracheal tube is placed through the opposite nostril.
(3) Throat pack is securely placed. Its functions are as follows:
   (a) Protection of the airway.
   (b) Prevention of aspiration of foreign body.
   (c) To keep the endotracheal tube in position without shifting to any one side.
   (d) To prevent escape of anesthetic gas from the lungs.
   (e) If any other fields are involved in the surgical procedure, arrangement is done accordingly for draping those areas also.
   (f) The oral cavity cannot be completely disinfected like skin surface. However, every effort must be directed to lower the bacterial count significantly and to reduce the incidence of bacteria.
   (g) Special care is taken to protect the patient's eyes with petrolatum.
   (h) After ensuring that draped area is isolated from the nondraped area of the body, the surgeon must ensure that,
      (i) The patient is positioned in the centre of the table.
      (ii) Arms are not left unsupported.
      (iii) Legs are not crossed.
      (iv) All monitoring devices are properly secured. As usual, if the draping is done by the first assistant, then it is more important that the surgeon should satisfy before commencing the surgery.

Care and use of surgical instruments

The surgical instruments represent a major and expensive investment of every operation theatre. Their life expectancy is greatly reduced when they are subjected to improper handling, inadequate maintenance or when abused. As the surgical science is dynamic, so is the complexity of surgical instruments. Each instrument is designed for a specific purpose. Therefore, the surgeon must take reasonable precautions to protect the quality of the instruments.

In general, these instruments can be divided into six basic categories:

(1) *Cutting instruments,* e.g. scissors, scalpels, bone cutting instruments.
(2) *Clamping instruments,* e.g. hemostats, tissue clamps, bone holding forceps.
(3) *Grasping or holding instruments,* e.g. forceps.
(4) *Instruments for keeping the surgical field clear,* e.g. retractors.
(5) *Special category.* Special instruments for specific requirements require special handling, e.g. grafting knife.

Unfortunately, scissors are most frequently abused by the surgical team. For example, tissue scissors meant to cut tissues must not be used for cutting stainless steel wires. Fine scissors are meant for delicate dissection and hence not to be used for cutting thick bandages, stainless steel wire, etc. The hemostats are meant for clamping the vessels and not for using them as towel clips, needle holder or for holding the sponge and suction tube. Such abuses result in improper alignment. Every instrument should be inspected before and after every surgery for any defect and improper functioning. The instruments put in a haphazard heap can cause extensive damage. All the hinged instruments like forceps and clamps must be checked for their alignment of jaws, stiffness and whether ratchets close and hold firmly. Cutting instruments must be properly sharpened before sterilization. The surgeon should never carelessly drop any instruments on the floor. With these rigorous demands of surgery, it is of greatest importance that surgical instruments should receive the highest form of cleaning, maintenance and sterilization. With proper care and handling, the patient is less prone to trauma and risk of infection. The surgical procedure will then be as smooth and quick as possible.

Care of eyes during surgery

Corneal abrasion is the most common eye injury during surgery. Because of the proximity of the orbital region to the maxillofacial region, the patient may experience increased risk of ophthalmic injuries. Ocular injury may occur after the induction of general anesthesia due to loss of pain perception or absence of corneal reflex and inadequate closure of the eyelids. Inadvertant instillation of antibiotics and skin preparation solutions into the eyes may result in corneal injury. Therefore, adequate eye protection is mandatory soon after induction of general anesthesia. They include (a) manual closure of eyelids, (b) taping the eyelids after the application of eye ointment and (c) in extensive surgery of the region, tarsorrhaphy sutures may be necessary. The occurrence of corneal abrasion is identified only after the completion of anesthesia. Such patients complain of specific ocular symptoms like eye irritation, pain, lacrimation, photophobia, a sense of the presence of a foreign body, etc. Most of the uncomplicated abrasions heal within a day or two. Corneal abrasion may lead to inflammation of the uveal tract. Topical antibiotic application will help. Topical anesthetics should be avoided since they are toxic to corneal epithelium and hence believed to retard healing. Topical corticosteroids may enhance the severity of infections if it is used without antibiotic component.

Postoperative care

It is the anesthetist's responsibility to ensure that the patient's recovery from anesthesia is as quick and safe as possible. However, the patient's management during the first 24 hours in some cases may be handled by the staff of the intensive care unit or recovery ward. The surgeon must realize that postoperative care of the patient involves two phases: (a) systemic care and (b) local care of the surgical field. Improper management may lead to life-threatening emergencies. Management of postoperative complications is different from negligence. For example, wherever intermaxillary fixation is involved, wire cutter must be provided at the bedside. Failure to do so may lead to respiratory emergencies in certain circumstances. Postoperatively, *temperature-pulse-BP-respiration chart* is maintained at regular intervals.

Drug therapy and diet

Drug therapy and diet also need equal attention depending on the needs of the patient. Usually, inadequate attention is given to control post-operative infection, pain and sedation. Overdosage is as undesirable as underdosage. The surgeon should never ignore the complaints of patients, however trivial they might appear to be. Clear instructions are mandatory regarding the dietary requirements of the patient.

(1) Consistency: liquid or semi solid diet.

(2) Nature of the diet - whether rich in fat, protein, carbohydrates or vitamins.
(3) Timing, frequency and mode of feeding.
(4) Details of intravenous infusions and medications in relation to diet.
(5) The progress report must be recorded including:
   (a) subjective and objective assessment and
   (b) plan for further management.

Nasogastric feeding

Following most of the intraoral procedures, the maxillofacial surgeons prefer to feed the patient without soiling the oral cavity, at least during the first 2 to 3 days postoperatively. The person who inserts the nasogastric tube must be well trained and must have clear understanding of the anatomy. One must also be aware of the possible sites where problems may be encountered while inserting the tube. It is advisable to use a thin Ryle's tube. The use of free flowing liquid diet reduces the chances of the risk of aspiration pneumonia and contamination.

Procedure

(1) The patient should be explained the entire procedure. He is instructed to swallow, breathe through the mouth and to control the cough reflex.
(2) The patient is placed in a reclined or sitting position with the neck flexed slightly. Nostril is examined to determine the optimal patency. It is confirmed by making the patient breath through one nostril with the other nostril occluded temporarily.
(3) Length of the feeding tube to be inserted is estimated by measuring the distance from the xiphoid process to the nose and nose to the ear lobe.
(4) The feeding tube is then lubricated with jelly containing a mild local anesthetic agent like Lidocaine hydrochloride 5% jelly. If the patient is cooperative, then he should be asked to swallow water to facilitate easy passage of the tube.
(5) After confirming that there is no coiling of the tube in the mouth, the tube is passed beyond the nasopharynx. Now, the patient is asked to swallow as the tube is advanced.
(6) If the patient coughs, the tube is withdrawn from the nasopharynx and passage is reattempted.
(7) Once the tube reaches the stomach, the patient is turned to the right side.
(8) Verification of the distal tip of the tube is done as follows:
   (a) Gastrointestinal contents are aspirated with 20 cc syringe.
   (b) If there is no aspiration, 5 to 10 cc of air is pushed through the syringe and epigastric region is auscultated for any bubbling sound.
   (c) Alternatively, the outer end of the tube is placed into a bowl of water to check for bubbling. There should not be any bubbling.
   (d) If the position cannot be confirmed, radiographic confirmation is mandatory. Without confirmation, tube feeding should not be attempted.
(9) The tube is fixed by a tape secured to the bridge of the nose.
(10)For the safety of the patient, head should be elevated during feeding and for one hour thereafter to prevent regurgitation and possible aspiration.
(11)After every feed, the feeding tube must be rinsed with 30 ml of plain sterile water to maintain patency of the tube.

Management of postoperative urinary retention

Urinary retention is a troublesome condition that may be encountered following any surgical procedure under general anesthesia. A brief account is presented about anatomy, physiology, etiology and management of this problem.

Anatomy. Main components of the bladder are the body and bladder neck. Body is the main collecting area and the neck known as posterior urethra connects urethra. Ureters empty into a smooth area of the posterior urethra called trigone. In the area of the bladder neck, continuation of the involuntary muscular layer of the bladder forms the internal sphincter of the bladder. Where the urethra passes through the urogenital diaphragm, a smooth muscle ring forms the external sphincter of the bladder.

Micturition cycle involves an involuntary reflex with central voluntary overriding control. As urine empties into the bladder, intravesicular pressure increases slowly until nearly 200 ml of urine is collected. Pressure then begins to increase rapidly. Micturition reflex is initiated by stretch receptors within the bladder wall. This reflex results in contraction until bladder is completely empty.

Urinary retention following maxillofacial surgery is likely due to interplay of multiple factors like reduced activity, sedation, anesthetic agents, fluid overload, perioperative medications, pain and such factors.

(a) During the early postoperative period, due to sedation, awareness about the bladder fullness may be depressed.
(b) Similarly, drugs play an important role in urinary retention in non-urinogenital surgery. Anticholinergic effects of drugs like atropine, diazepam, antihistamines may cause inhibition of the neuroeffector junction of the bladder muscle thereby decreasing the strength of bladder contraction and disturbing the bladder function. Narcotic medications, beta-adrenergic agents and other antihypertensive agents and antispasmodic drugs are associated with urinary retention secondary to the increase of sphincter tone in the bladder.
(c) Perioperative fluid management plays a significant role in urinary retention. Fluid restriction decreases the rate of bladder filling. The patient therefore gains additional time to metabolize the drugs and increase physical activity, thereby regains bladder function before overdistension occurs. On the other hand, drugs with diuretic effects including caffeine will increase bladder overdistension during the early postoperative period. Therefore, it is postulated that restriction of fluid and avoidance of diuretic substances postoperatively decrease the urinary retention.

Management. Usually, awareness of bladder fullness starts at a volume of 100 ml but cortical regulation normally suppresses the desire to micturate. Unexplained tachycardia or hypertension in a sedated or comatose patient may indicate the possibility of over distended bladder. In such patients, dribbling small amounts of urine at frequent intervals are misinterpreted as return of the bladder function but it only indicates over distension of the bladder.

(a) Providing privacy or helping the patient to the toilet or bathroom is a natural environment for urination.
(b) Use of heat to relax urinary sphincters may be helpful. This is in the form of warm compresses to the perineum.This will prompt urination.
(c) If the patient does not urinate for 8 to 12 hours, catheterization will be helpful. Depending on the need, continuous catheterization for 24 to 72 hours is advocated. The patient should be monitored for urinary tract infection since it may carry the risk of bacteriuria. Postoperative Foley's catheter-related urinary tract infections increase the hospital stay by 2 to 3 days.
(d) If such non-invasive measures are not helpful, urological consultation will be necessary.

DISCHARGE OF THE PATIENT FROM THE HOSPITAL

This is the responsibility of the surgeon in charge of the patient. Hence, planning must be done well ahead about the discharge. If needed, necessary arrangements must be made for transporting the patient by the ambulance. At the time of discharge, the patient or the relatives must be provided with a discharge summary with the following data:

(1) Name with reference number, if any.
(2) Date of admission, operation and discharge.
(3) Diagnosis and medications.
(4) Postdischarge instructions for follow-up care.
(5) Physiotherapy, if any.
(6) Date of the appointment for review. The surgeon must always remember that the surgery is not complete until the patient stops complaining postoperatively.

Role of the "extended day care"

Surgical day care is defined as care of a patient who is admitted for investigation or for treatment on a planned non-resident basis during the night. This excludes minor operative procedures that are carried out in out patient or casualty departments. The provision of day surgery is further described as "being useful" for those operations which require a relatively short general anesthesia and which do not carry the risk of postoperative complications that require management in hospital. The routine use of modern inhalational anesthetic agents and short-acting intravenous induction agents render many operative procedures in maxillofacial surgery amenable to day care anesthesia. The physical status of ASA I and II satisfies the admission requirements for day care. Some of these patients are taken up for "extended day care service." This is the facility for the patients who require overnight admission for postoperative pain control or for observation when anesthetic time exceeds 45 to 60 minutes and without any escort to return back home or the housing conditions which render them unsuitable for same day discharge. In other words, no patient is discharged without being assessed by the anesthetist. In the recent past, there have been an increased number of admissions for this facility. The clinician must be judicious in taking decision to utilize this facility.

CHAPTER 23 Transplantation of Tissues

GENERAL CONSIDERATIONS

Tissues of the orofacial region which are damaged or lost due to trauma, disease or surgery must be replaced to restore the anatomy, function and esthetics. While doing so, many factors must be taken into consideration since the outcome - success or failure - depends on them. They can be categorized under the following groups:

(a) Nature of the graft
(b) Surgical technique
(c) Graft host response.

Nature of the graft

Organs or tissues from a living person can include blood, bone, bone marrow, portion of liver, tooth bud, kidney, pancreas, eyes, skin, fascia, heart valves, tendons, cartilage, veins, arteries and even ear oscicles. In the field of oral surgery, skin, tooth bud and bone have been extensively used for transplantation purposes. Wherever any difficulty is anticipated, materials like metallic alloys, plastics and silastics have been used. The advantages of such materials are obvious. The widely used acrylic is a standing example to replace the lost teeth. Attempts have been made to utilize tooth grafts with varying success. There seems to be a wide scope for improving the possibility of tooth banks like blood banks. In the recent past, there has been renewed interests on dental implants. Attempts have been widespread on the transplantation of biological grafts. It has now become an accepted therapeutic consideration. Many problems are encountered depending on the type of the transplants. That is why, sometimes we make use of artificial prosthesis. (Fig. 23.1).

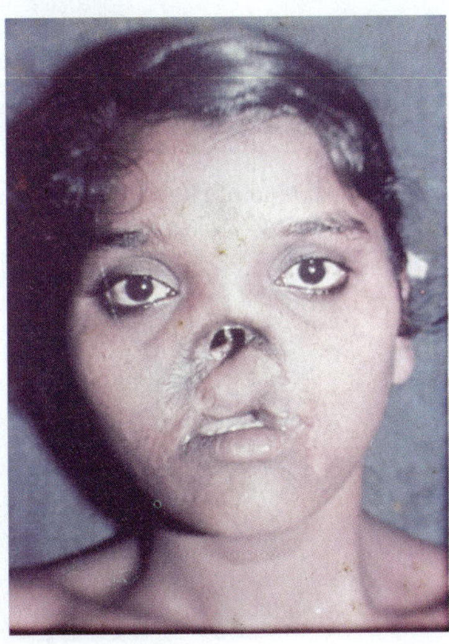

Fig. 23.1 (a) Loss of nose due to cancrum oris.

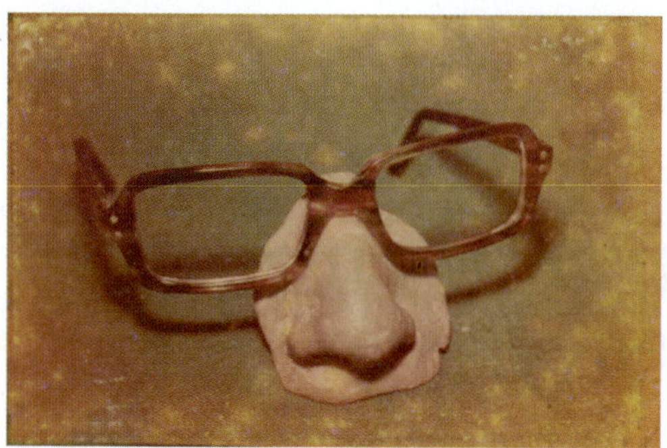

Fig. 23.1 (b) Nasal prosthesis attached to the spectacle frame.

Types of the graft

(1) **Autograft** denotes that the graft has been derived from the same person from one anatomical site to another, e.g., bone graft, skin graft, tooth bud, tube pedicle. (Fig. 23.2) soft-tissue flaps (Fig. 23.6).

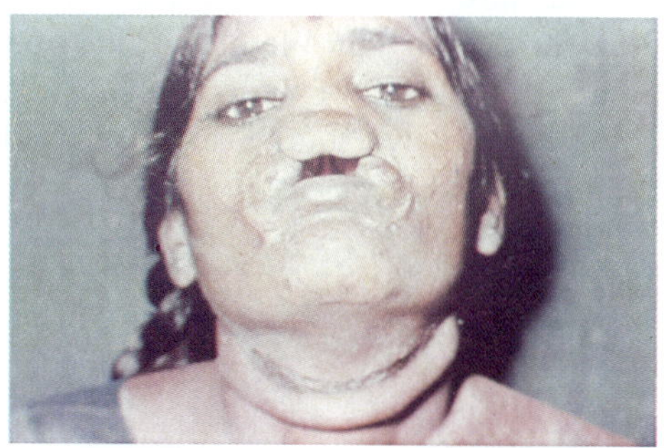

Fig. 23.2 (a) Reconstruction of the upper lip by tube pedicle from the neck region.

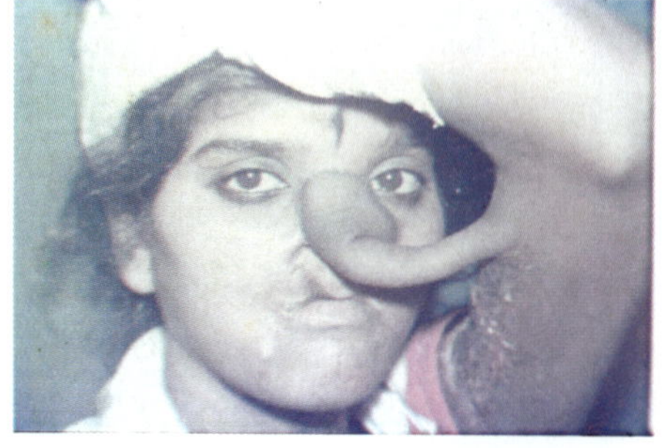

Fig. 23.2 (b) In the second stage, tube pedicle is transported to the nasal region by attaching it with forearm.

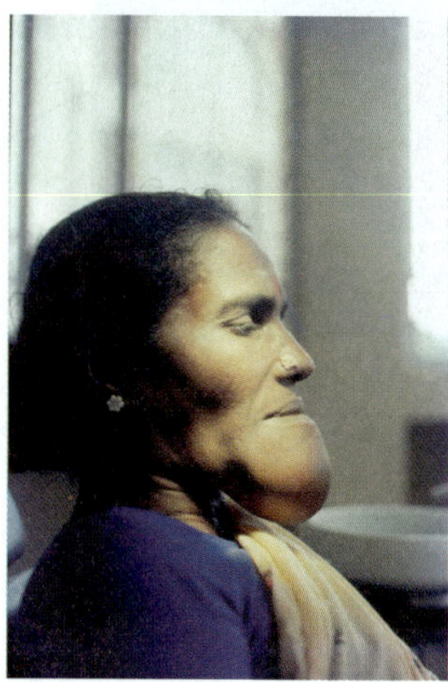

Fig. 23.3 (a) A huge ameloblastoma of the mandible.

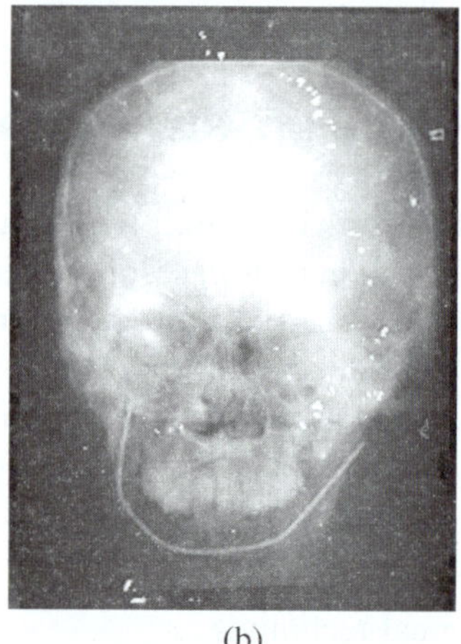

(b)

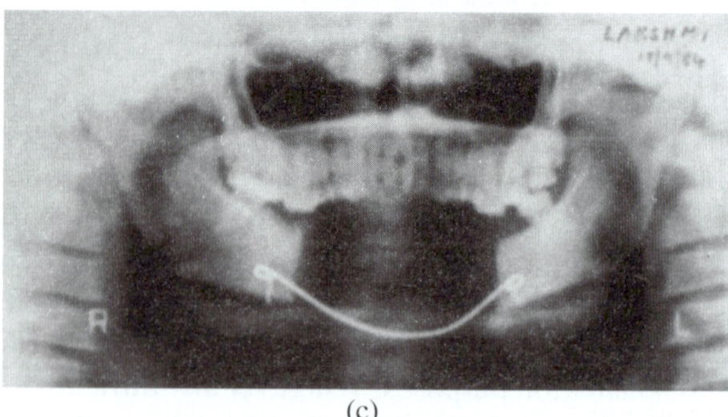

(c)

Fig. 23.3 (b) & (c) X-ray shows K-wire used for stabilizing the mobile bone fragments with K-wire. Later it becomes unstable.

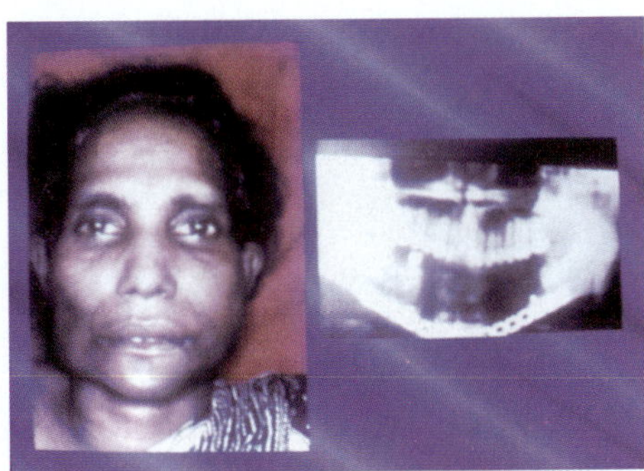

Fig. 23.3 (d) Postoperative appearance after plate fixation to bridge the gap.

(2) **Homograft** denotes that the graft has been derived from another person of the same species, differing in genetic disposition, e.g., blood transfusion.
(3) **Isograft** denotes that the graft has been derived from a person of the same species and genetic disposition.
(4) **Heterograft** denotes that the graft has been derived from another species of different genetic disposition.
(5) **Allograft** denotes the non-biological materials like plastics, metallic alloys, silastics etc. e.g., titanium implant as root analog.

The logistics of its (i) availability, (ii) storage facility, (iii) ethical and economic considerations, (iv) feasibility under the available conditions, (v) supporting mechanisms, (vi) success rate under normal circumstances, (vii) acceptability of the patients and (viii) the availability of alternate forms of therapy are some of the important factors to be taken into considerations for the choice of the transplant material. In routine clinical practice, reasonable success is encountered with regard to autografts. Barring the surgical techniques, major problems in the failure of transplantation are graft-tissue reactions in the form of immune response due to the genetic predisposition and the consequent rejection phenomenon.

The area from where the graft is obtained is called *donor area* and the area where the graft is placed is called *recipient area*.

Because of the complexity of the process of transplantation, it should be undertaken only by a trained oral surgeon. However, general principles involved in transplants and implants are discussed here. Since skin and bone are the common transplants used in the field of oral surgery, general account of the autogenous bone grafting and skin grafting is provided with a brief note on the rejecting phenomenon of the homografts. Regarding the dental implants, a broad outline is provided so that the practitioner's interest is stimulated for further training in this field of clinical oral surgery practice. (Chapter 24).

BONE GRAFTING

Autografts and processed homografts have been used extensively in oral surgery. However, one should carefully evaluate the capacity and limitation of such bone grafts procedures under varied conditions and circumstances.

Indications

(1) To fill the defective bony cavities following the enucleation of large cysts of the jaws where the bony cavities are unable to heal by regeneration, autogenous and inorganic bone grafts are used. Similarly, alveolor bone grafting in alveolor clefts is also widely practiced.
(2) To obtain an absolute increase in the height of the alveolar ridge as a preprosthetic procedure.
(3) To treat non-united fractures, the bone ends are freshened. In the process, the consequent bony deficiency is made good by placing the bone graft so that it will restore the continuity of bone and will hasten the bony union.
(4) In cases of neoplasms, elimination of the

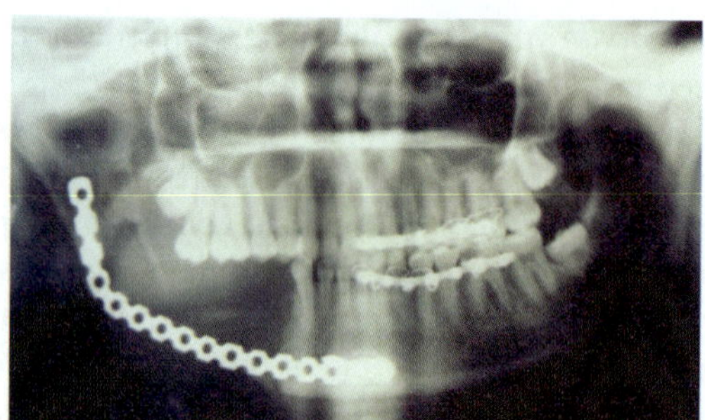

Fig. 23.4 (a) Reconstruction plate in position after hemimandibulectomy.

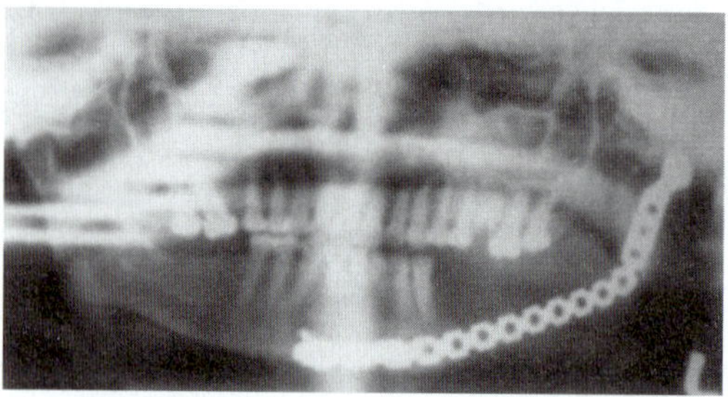

Fig. 23.4 (b) Metallic joint replacement.

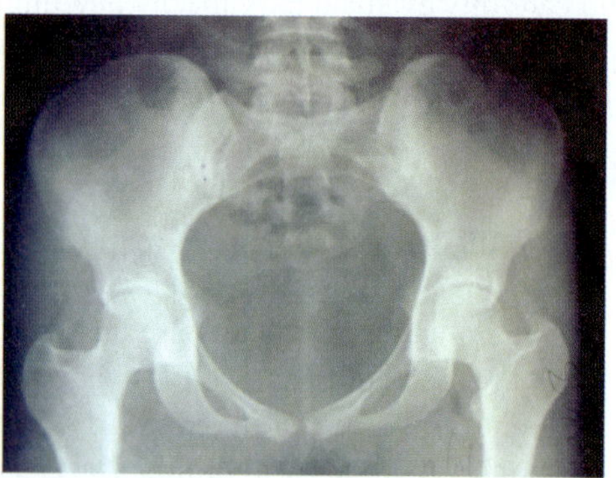

Fig. 23.4 (c) Iliac crest as the donor area for bone graft.

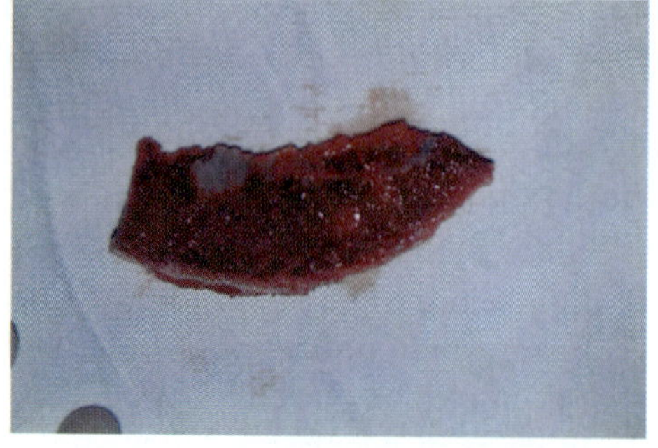

Fig. 23.4 (d) Free bone graft from iliac crest.

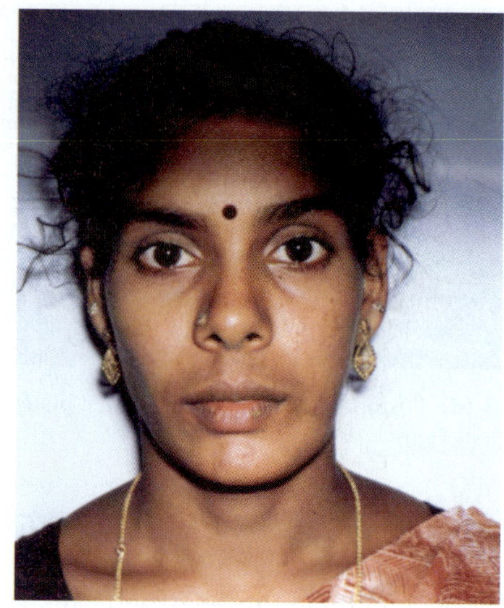

Fig. 23.4 (e) Left mandible reconstructed with iliac crest bone graft –postoperative appearance.

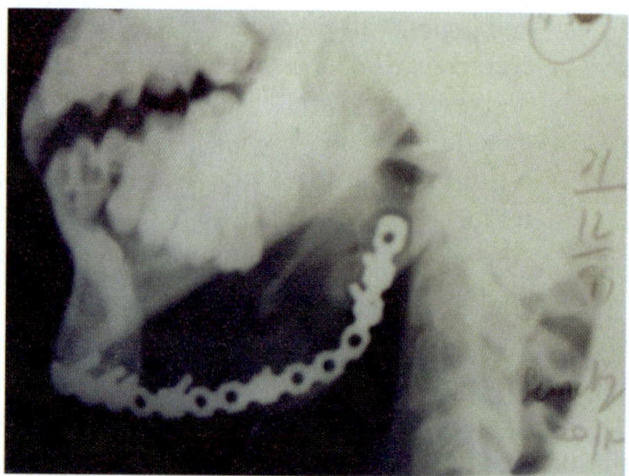

Fig. 23.4 (f) Lateral oblique view mandible demonstrating plate fixed between body and condyle of the mandible.

pathology results in a defect. Bone graft is utilized to replace the excised segments of bone thereby restoring the continuity of the jaw bone. (Fig. 23.4)

(5) In osteotomies, to correct the jaw deformities e.g. hypoplasia, the interfragmentary gap can be bridged by the bone graft.

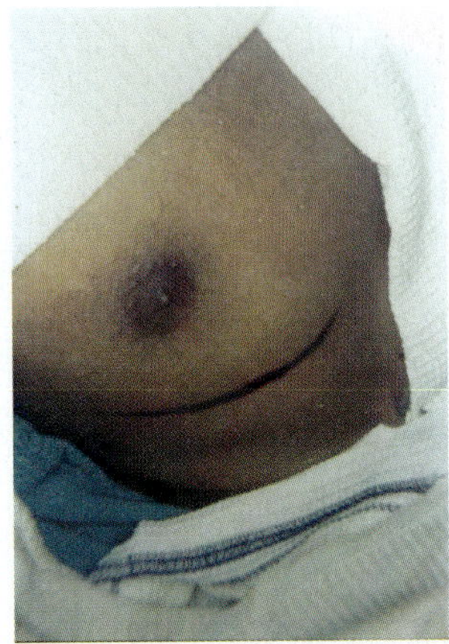

Fig. 23.5 (a) Surface marking for submammary incision for a rib graft.

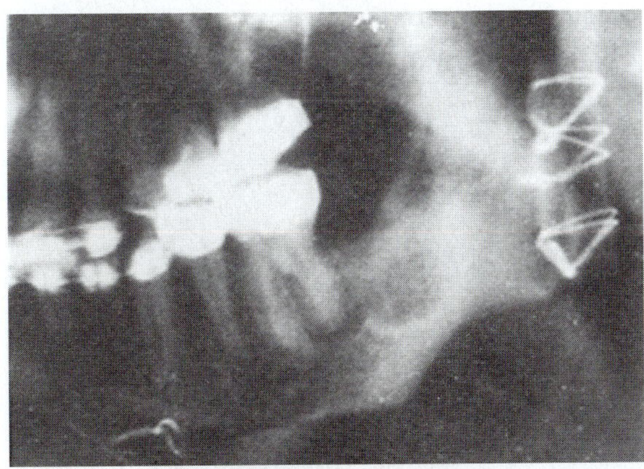

Fig. 23.5 (b) Rib graft fixed with wires to treat ankylosis of T.M. joint.

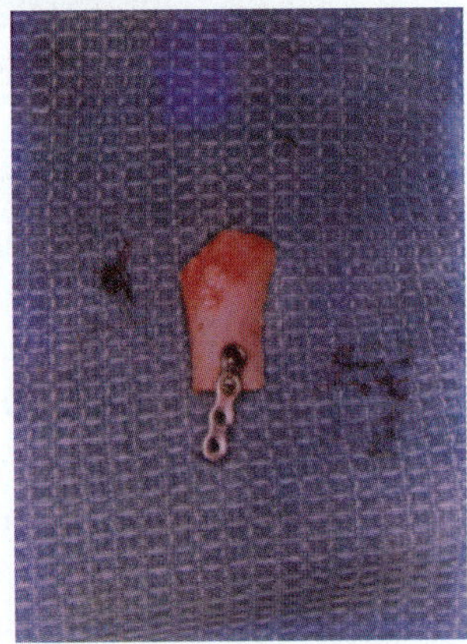

Fig. 23.5 (c) Free sternoclavicular head graft fixed with 4 holed plate.

(6) In reconstructive surgery of the facial bony deformities, the bone grafts can be used as onlay grafts to recontour the bone. Another example is reconstruction of the floor of the orbit in blow-out fractures.

(7) In case of ankylosis of the temporomandibular joint, surgery is performed to release the ankylosis and the joint can be reconstructed by providing a costochondral graft to serve as a condyle. (Fig. 23.5 a, b, c)

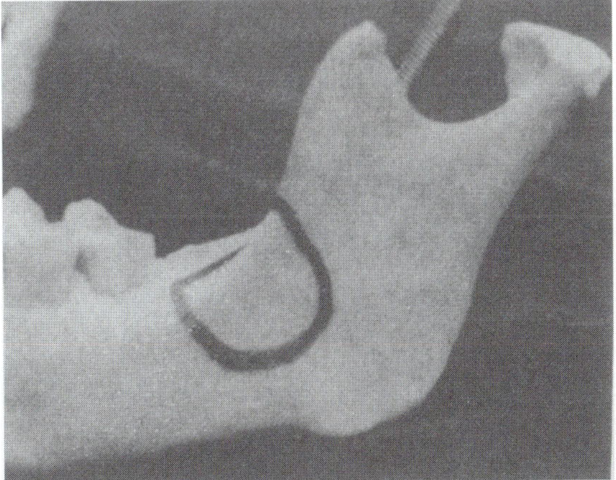

Fig. 23.6 Donor area for bone grafting in fractured floor of the orbit.

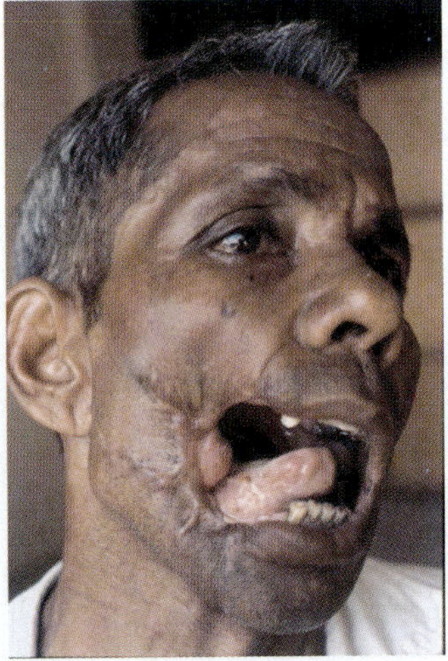

Fig. 23.7 (a) Defect of the left cheek after excision of a growth.

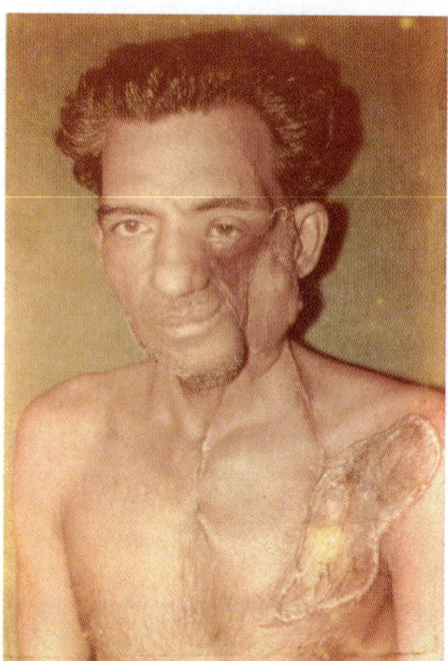

Fig. 23.7 (b) Reconstruction of full thickness cheek defect with deltopectoral flap (front view).

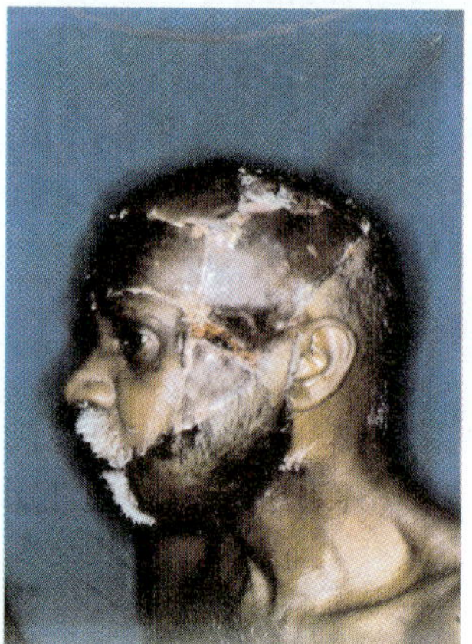

Fig. 23.7 (c) Reconstruction of full thickness cheek with temporal flap (side view).

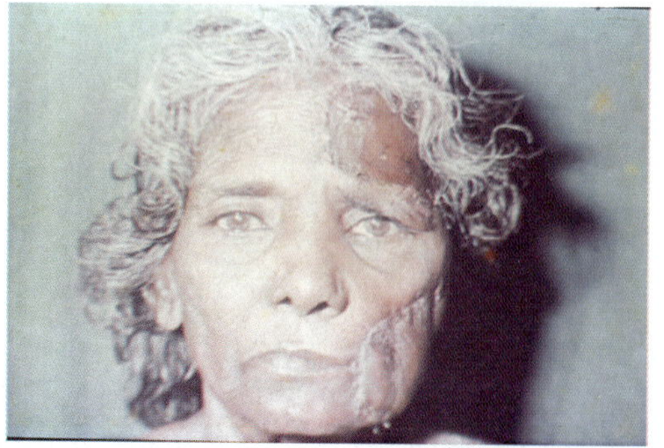

Fig. 23.7 (d) Reconstruction of full thickness cheek defect with forehead flap for mucosa and deltopectoral flap for skin.

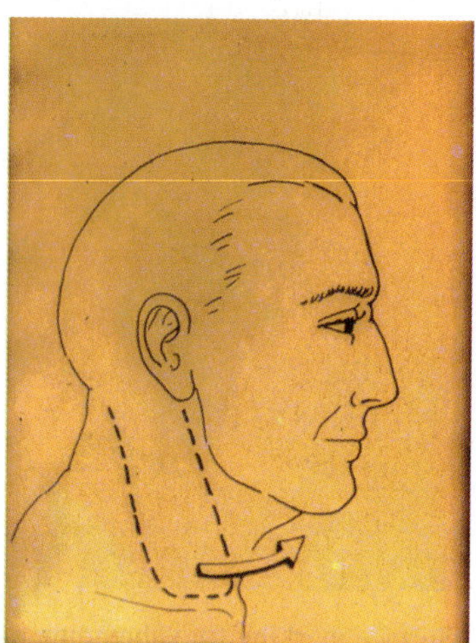

Fig. 23.7 (e) Diagram showing sternomastoid myocutaneous flap for face reconstruction.

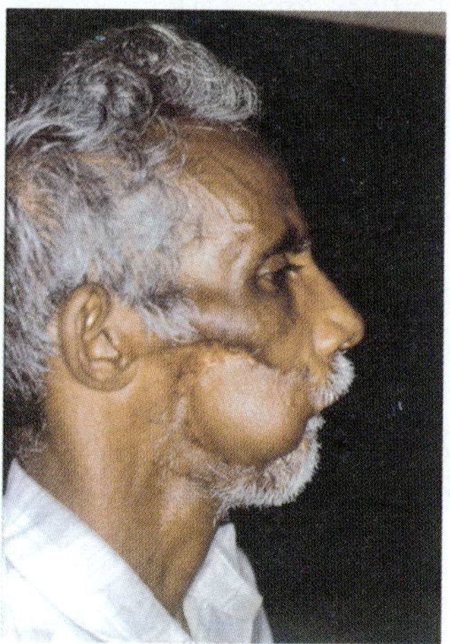

Fig. 23.7 (f) Full thickness reconstruction (side view).

In many children and adolescent patients, it has been noticed that resected bone has exhibited remarkable range of regeneration of bone, wherever periosteum has been retained.

Donor sites

Iliac crest, rib, calvarium and tibia have been the sites from where grafts of bone have been utilized frequently. The choice of the donor area is left to the individual surgeon depending on many variable factors.

Critical zones in the success of bone grafting

(a) Choice of the graft
(b) Infection
(c) Recipient site
(d) Contact between the graft and recipient bone ends.

(a) Choice of the graft

(i) *Fate of the autograft.* The grafted bone does not survive for a long time. It is an established fact that the vast majority of the bone cells present in the transplanted bone die in course of time. The granulation tissue invades the cancellous space of the graft. The osteoclastic resorption of the graft is followed by new bone deposition on the graft trabeculae. Hence, the role of the bone graft is "scaffolding". Relatively, a few superficial osteoblasts of the autograft may survive, resulting in the inductive change. It is attributed to the chemical substance present in the graft, known as "osteogenic". It has been observed that the granulation invades the cancellous bone more easily than the cortical bone. Attempts have also been made to deep freeze or to boil the resected jaw bone and the bone is replaced in the original site. However, the success has been relatively low.

(ii) *Fate of the homograft.* The invasion of the graft by the granulation is very similar to autografts. But due to the immune response of the homograft, there is no evidence of survival of any donor cells. The calcified matrix exhibits inductive influence resulting in osteogenesis. Since homograft does not require a second surgery on the same patient, it is advantageous. Hence, when a thoracic surgeon performs thoracotomy or nephrectomy, the resected ribs can be stored and used as homografts-particularly in preprosthetic surgery for ridge reconstruction.

(iii) *Anorganic bone.* It is prepared by treating with certain chemicals appropriately. Similarly, kiel bone is from bovine bone treated with hydrogen peroxide. After defattening, it is sterilized and freeze-dried for storage. Unfortunately, all these materials are of limited use. During the initial phase, all these inert graft materials are invaded by the granulation tissue. But subsequent reactions like osteogenesis are same. Sometimes, they are infiltrated by inflammatory cells like plasma cells, macrophages and lymphocytes. Unlike autografts, the ultimate success of these grafts is unpredictable. Hence, their use is restricted in the field of oral surgery.

(b) Infection

If the infection sets in the bone graft, its behavior is very similar to infected fractured bone. If the graft is infected before or during vascularization, it will become a sequestrum. Hence, every precaution must be taken during the bone grafting procedure to prevent the onset of infection. In other words, greater aseptic precautions are necessary while inserting the bone grafts. Wound infection must be prevented, particularly if intraoral procedure is involved in the grafting. Strict aseptic precautions, thorough irrigation of the wound and instillation of appropriate antibiotics are some of the measures to be adapted to prevent the onset of infection. The failure of the graft is directly proportional to the infection.

(c) Recipient site

Since the graft must be infiltrated by the granulation tissue, the bed of the recipient site must have optimum vascularity and hence adequate nourishment of the graft. If the vascularity is strangulated, it will lead to the failure of the bone graft.

(d) Contact between the graft and the recipient bone

When the graft material is trimmed and prepared for the grafting procedure, care should be taken to prepare the bone ends which come in contact with the graft. Broad and close surface contact between the bone ends and graft will ensure success. An appropriate fixation is provided so that the *graft host bone interface* provides optimum environment conducive for the success of the graft. Otherwise, it will behave very similarly to the fractured bone ends which are not adequately fixed and immobilized. Consequently, the loss of contact of the graft with bone ends or the mobile interface leads to failure of the graft. Therefore, lack of movement and degree of contact are the two important factors with reference to the success of the graft.

Precautions related to graft material

When the graft is removed from the donor site, care must be taken to ensure that the technique of removal must be least traumatic. For example, if the rotatory instruments like bur is used, the operator must avoid thermal necrosis of the bone. This can be done by regulating and lowering the speed of the revolution of the bur. Simultaneously, copious irrigation of an appropriate coolant is necessary to reduce the heat produced during bone cutting. At the same time, irrigation promotes mechanical cleansing of the bone. During the preparations of the graft, the graft must not be allowed to dry. Constantly, the graft must be in contact with normal saline.

Rejection phenomenon in homografts

To study this phenomenon, skin graft is more suitable since the progress of the graft is obvious and the tissue reaction is more sensitive to rejection process. For example, for the first few days, the graft remains viable, but only to be rejected after 10 days. If the graft is repeated from the same donor, subsequent graft is rejected rapidly with an obvious lack of vascularization. Thus, the features of the rejection phenomenon could be summarized in the following sequence:

(i) Initial healthy state during the first week indicates the acquired state of the host. It is responsible for the destruction of tissues.

(ii) This is viewed to be the demonstration of memory wherein it appears to be better equipped for the rejection. Therefore, this phenomenon is specific in that, the subsequent grafts exhibit accelerated rejection, depending on the genetic disposition.

Based on these findings, if any homografts exhibit rejection phenomenon, agents which are known (a) for their antimitotic activities, (b) to inhibit growth and cell regeneration and (c) to inhibit immune response have been used. However, these agents must be used with great care to avoid the associated complications. Hence, wherever any homograft is used, all these factors must be taken into consideration.

TOOTH TRANSPLANTATION

The organ transplantation has undergone revolutionary changes with tissue banking procedures, better understanding of the immunological concepts, development of histocompatibility tests and sophisticated surgical techniques. For example, there has been renewed interests in the recent past for the transplantation of kidney homografts. Unfortunately, corresponding progress on tooth banking has not been popularized. Perhaps, its failure to elicit the obvious immune responses may be due to many factors. The following are some of the observations:

(a) Chronic inflammatory infiltration of cells involve the pulpal tissue around the dental transplant.

(b) But pulp fails to function as a dentin-forming agent and hence the transplant is unable to assist in the completion of root formation.

(c) On the contrary, fibrous encapsulation and root absorption results in the replacement by bone.

(d) The immune response can be identified into two phases. The early phase concerns with the reaction of the soft-tissue component of the transplant. The later weak phase is related to the less antigenic hard tissue components of the transplant.

Many attempts to preserve the tooth buds by freezing techniques or tissue culturing have not been found to be successful. In some cases, clinical acceptance without immediate rejection has also been recorded. Necrosis of pulpal tissue invariably occurs. If pulpless teeth are transplanted, the initial apparent success is followed by ankylosis and progressive root absorption. Hence, autogenous tooth transplantation seems to be the only method which is clinically successful to a reasonable extent. A standing example is the transplantation of the developing third molar tooth bud to replace the first molar in younger age group of patients. Hence, a general account of this procedure is described here.

Technique

(a) **Proper case selection.** This is a critical factor. Apart from general consideration for fitness to undergo surgery, the assessment of adequate mesiodistal width of the host implant site, satisfactory oral health status, absence of acute periodontal and periapical inflammatory states and tooth transplant of optimal root development are some of the very important factors to be considered to ensure the success of the transplantation.

(b) **Removal of first molar.** Under inferior dental block anesthesia, a suitable mucoperiosteal flap is raised to expose the first molar region. The extraction of the first molar is done with least trauma.

(c) **Preparation of the recipient site.** The recipient site is surgically prepared by adequately removing interradicular septum and alveolar crest with Rongeur's forceps or bur to produce proper size to receive the transplant. The alveolar socket is irrigated and packed with sterile gauze to secure hemostasis.

(d) **Removal of the graft.** The tooth bud is exposed at the donor site. Some surgeons advocate the removal of the tooth bud along with the surrounding dental follicle. But there is no controversy about the importance of avoiding damage to the soft tissue of the root sac. Similarly, once the graft is removed from the donor site, it must be washed in normal saline solution before placing it in the recipient site.

(e) **Placement of the graft in the recipient site.** The tooth bud is placed in the recipient site below the occlusal level. The graft is stabilized with soft stainless steel ligature wire crossed over the occlusal surface of the graft in the form of figure of eight extending between second premolar and second molar teeth. Periodontal pack is placed around the graft and the wire ligature. Some prefer the use of prefabricated acrylic splint for stabilization. The mucoperiosteal flap is sutured and the wound is closed in the usual way.

(f) **Postoperative follow-up.** During the immediate postoperative period, healing is usually uneventful. Subsequently, the radiological follow-up reveals the failure of complete root formation. In fact, it is not uncommon to notice root resorption. It is directly proportional to the damage of the periodontal and other soft tissues during the surgical procedure. In practice, it has been found that the presence of periodontal ligament around the roots of the transplant inhibits root resorption. The autotransplantation of fully developed tooth is invariably followed by root resorption within a period of 5 years.

If a tooth is extracted or accidentally removed, placement of the tooth back into the socket is called *reimplantation*. The sequence of the events are the same as that of autograft. If the tooth is endodontically treated, the process of root resorption is hastened. Thus, it is found that ample scope exists for more investigations in the transplantation of teeth.

Introduction to Dental Implantology

GENERAL CONSIDERATIONS

Tooth loss, as a consequence of dental disease, is mutilating and therefore provides a strong incentive to the patient to seek appropriate dental care to preserve or to restore normal speech, masticatory function and socially acceptable appearance. Extraction of the tooth relieves pain but the dental surgeon is unable to prevent or control the mutilation like changes in the hard and soft tissues of the orofacial region and distortion of the facial morphology. The specialties of oral surgery and prosthodontics can justifiably boast of an ancient heritage in that a variety of treatment options have been made available to treat the edentulousness. For example, complete edentulousness is conventionally managed by complete denture therapy. But if any patient does not adapt to wearing complete dentures, the dental surgeon has to look for a viable alternative for such maladaptive situations. For a very long period, the concept of dental implantology did not enjoy a favorable reputation until the placement of a tooth root analogue in the jaw bones through *"osseointegration"* became a reality. The present day dental surgeons can now offer all the edentulous patients two options - *tissue-supported complete dentures or implant-supported prosthesis.* Ideally, the clinical decision should reflect the dentist's knowledge of the selected treatment efficacy and effectiveness as well as the patient's understanding of the risks and cost-effectiveness. Most of the patients prefer complete denture option because it is an economical, non-invasive procedure. On the other hand, implant-supported prosthesis combines the best of both options without either method's restrictions. Functional and esthetic requirements are better achieved and maintained by this option. Unless the patient and the clinician are motivated, there may be an inherent fear that the conventional complete denture service may be replaced by an implant-supported prosthesis. The logical decision must be to look at implants as one of the viable alternatives rather than a replacement to the conventional options.

Predicament of edentulousness

Partial or complete edentulousness may lead to drastic alterations in the stomatognathic system through excessive resorption of alveolar ridges. The dynamic activity of the oral tissues is related to the masticatory load. Usually, patients provided with dentures develop compromised denture stability, inflammation and denture sore. This is more common in mandible and they are responsible for the patient to discontinue to wear the dentures. Consequent to reduced efficacy in oral function, the need to overcome these major denture difficulties make the patient seek a suitable remedy. Hence, one of the challenges in oral surgery is to provide solution to this problem. Preprosthetic surgery has been developed to enlarge the denture bearing area in the form of

(a) ridge preservation procedures,
(b) corrective or recontouring procedures,
(c) ridge extension procedures and
(d) reconstruction methods.

If these procedures do not offer long-term solutions, then the accessory aids like (a) creation of undercuts and (b) onlay denture have been tried. In spite of all these measures, some patients find it extremely dificult to wear the dentures successfully. This indicates that we are dealing with both quantitative and qualitative compromise in load-bearing potential. Sometimes, mucosa demonstrates little tolerence or adaptability to wear the denture. The residual alveolar bone appears to be vulnerable to masticatory load. It responds by an ongoing and irreversible reduction in alveolar bone, resulting in an atrophic mandible. With aging, many elderly patients who wear complete dentures experience difficulty in adapting to their prostheses. In such clinical situations, dental surgeon looks for a viable alternative to provide stable mechanical support to the dental prosthesis. This was how dental implantology established its importance in clinical practice. Even though dental implants have been used for many decades, they have not been enjoying favorable reputation due to many inherent problems. Therefore, sustained interest on dental implants was absent among the dental practitioners. Everytime implant was introduced with bouts of enthusiasm only to recede from the clinical scene. This situation has dramatically changed with better understanding of the following :

(a) biomaterials,
(b) their relative biocompatibility,
(c) nature of the implant- tissue interface,
(d) factors responsible for the long-term success and
(e) philosophy of implant therapy.

With improved acceptance of dental implants, they are even considered as the nearest equivalent replacement to natural teeth. Basic understanding of the principles and philosophy of dental implantology and proper patient selection seem to be the crucial factors in the successful implantology practice. Many dental implant systems have emerged, backed by good scientific research and clinical trials. In the present day clinical practice, implantology certainly offers a reasonable option for the satisfactory management of all stages of edentulousness. Since these procedures are *technique-sensitive*, practitioner should not practice this branch of clinical dentistry without appropriate training. Since success depends on so many variable factors, there is no substitute for meticulous attention to all these aspects. If they are carried out properly, success is predictable. Failure to do so will result in higher failure rate and avoidable complications. Hence, it is the intention to introduce the technology and basic principles of dental implantology, leaving the specific techniques to the respective practitioners to practise depending on ones own knowledge of the implant systems, skill and scope of practice. The essence of dental implantology practice is that it offers the possibility of inserting the prosthesis into the jaws which would be regarded as part of human stomatognathic system and is expected to behave similar to the natural teeth.

Definitions

The following are some of the commonly used terms in the field of implantology:

ENDOSSEOUS IMPLANT:
A device inserted into the bone to support the prosthesis. In case of dental implants, it refers to the *"root" analogue* of the tooth.

OSSEOINTEGRATION:
A direct structural and functional connection between the living bone and the surface of the load-bearing implant.

IMPLANT ABUTMENT:
The component attached to the implant that supports the prosthesis (interface between the implant and the prosthesis).

Transmucosal abutment passes through the mucosa overlying the implant.

ABUTMENT SCREW:
A screw used to connect the abutment to the implant.

SINGLE STAGE IMPLANT:
An implant that is left exposed to the oral cavity following its surgical insertion. It is also called *non-submerged implant.*

TWO STAGE IMPLANT:
An implant that is left buried under the mucosa during the initial surgical placement and subsequently exposed during a second procedure after a few months. It is also called *submerged implant*.

IMPLANT SYSTEM - CLASSIFICATION

Implants have been classified based on various criteria. The following are some of them:

I. *Depending on the implant-tissue interface,* implants can be classified as:

   (a) Direct *bone-implant* interface, e.g. endosseous implants (*osseo-integration*). (Fig. 24.1)
   (b) Indirect interface, e.g. blade and subperiosteal implants.

Note: Formerly, attempts were made to reproduce the biological tooth attachment, but such fibrous attachment has to give way for the concept of osseointegration.

II. According to various *criteria involving the design, implantation, tissue implant response and the location,* implants are classified as:

   (a) Submucous,
   (b) Supra/subperiosteal,
   (c) Subperiosteal,
   (d) Endosseous,
   (e) Transosseous and
   (f) Endodontic.

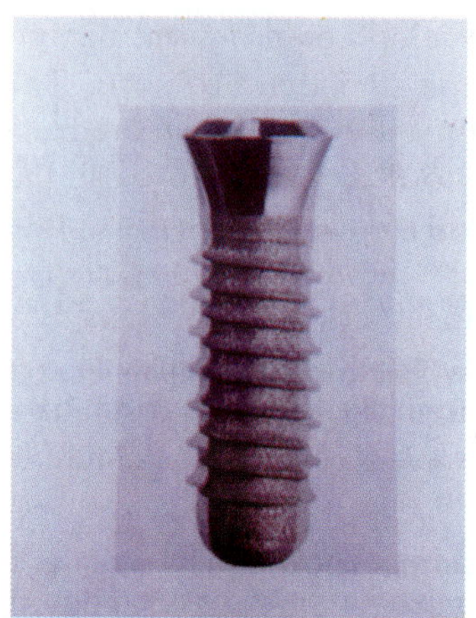

Fig. 24.1 I.T.I. dental implant.

III. Based on *function,* implants can also be classified as:

   (a) Retentive implants and
   (b) Supportive implants.

Retentive type has the sole purpose of providing additional retention for the prosthesis, e.g. mucosal inserts and magnetic implants. The entire functional load is transmitted through the mucous membrane.

The *supportive type* provides support to the prosthesis. At the same time, mucous membrane and teeth are relieved from the functional load. They may be interosseous or extraosseous (subperiosteal).

IV. Depending on the *implant material*, they can be classified to signify its biocompatibility as:
   (a) Metallic implants,
   (b) Polymer implants,
   (c) Ceramic implants, and
   (d) Vitreous carbon implants.

BIOLOGICAL CONSIDERATIONS

I. Biocompatibility of the implants.
II. Stable implant-tissue interface.
III. Acceptable load transfer.

I. Biocompatibility

"thou shalt not violate biocompatibility"

Many alloys with variable properties have been experimented. For any material to be biologically acceptable, it must be biocompatible. It should also have a surface bioactivity to resist any mechanism involved in the rejection phenomenon. Steel, chrome-cobalt-molybdenum alloy and titanium have been found to be corrosion-resistant. But titanium continues to be the material of choice. Hydroxyapatite has been tried extensively but found to fail over the long term which is controlled by many factors. Because of the initial success followed by increasing failure, Branemark prophesed that titanium will be the implant material. The fact that titanium can answer an immune system attack by turning it down makes it unique.

II. Stable implant-tissue interface

However as the implant material is biocompatible, it evokes some tissue response. In turn, implant material also undergoes some changes in due course of time. Such an implant-tissue interface depends on:

(a) Type of implant material, design, shape and surface of the implant

One of the fundamental engineering principles is that the screw offers greater fixation stability than a plug or nail design. Moreover a screw can be placed very precisely and can easily be removed if needed. It has been found that a threaded implant provides a good interface between bone and the implant. Mechanical retention of the screw design makes it possible to withstand the masticatory load efficiently. When compared to the plain surface, the thread provides greater surface area with bone bed. It also minimizes shear stress between the fixture and bone, thereby enhancing the chances for the successful tissue integration. The very fact that so many types of implants are commercially available with claims and counterclaims, it only indicates that the choice of any implant is based on so many variable factors. A delicate balance has to be established and maintained constantly between these variable factors. Ultimately, it is the adaptation and stability of the functional implant in relation to the tissues alone ensure success.

(b) Soft tissue interface

The dental sulcus epithelium differs from the gingival epithelium in appearance and function. It is more permeable to fluids, cells and immunoglobulins. At the base of the sulcus is the epithelial attachment which forms the first line of defense. The junctional epithelium is a very specialized structure, characteristic to dental apparatus. At its junctional epithelium-tooth interface, basement lamina is seen with ultramicroscopic hemidesmosomes. They are made up of a pair of these plates found one in each of the two adjoining epithelial cells. They represent the intercellular adhesion and contact. Hemidesmosome is found wherever an epithelial cell meets other type of cell like connective tissues or against the tooth surface. Such an unique arrangement is responsible for inert materials like tooth or biomaterials to penetrate the oral epithelium and at the same time the integrity of the outer epithelial covering is maintained. The nature of this interface material is PAS (Periodic Acid Scihffs positive) indicating that it is a mucopolysaccharide cement substance. A similar tissue implant interface is required for a healthy implant to function in the oral cavity. But in practice, histochemically, an oracin positive layer has been found at the interface between the junctional epithelium and the surface of the implant material. It has also been found that an increase in cervicular fluid volume around the implants indicates the existence of inflamed tissue at the periimplant region. The collagen fibers at the junctional region extend from the crestal alveolar bone to the epithelium interfacing with the implant. In other words, they are seen at right angles to the surface of the implant, an arrangement consistent with the direction of tensile strength. Thus, it has been shown that the integrity of the interface is the critical factor for the long-term success of the implant. The tight cuff of the fibrous connective tissue fibers parallel to the implant surface support the epithelial seal and forms as effective barrier to periimplant pocket formation and bone loss. Maintenance of gingival health around the osseo-integrated implant is found to be relatively easy. But in the subperiosteal implants, extensive pocket formation is a severe problem.

(c) Implant bed

"Thou shalt address the status of the implant bed"

The status of the implant bed involves consideration of the local physiological factors with the superimposed factors relating to the health of the individual. Local osteogenic and remodelling capacity of the bone determines as to whether osseointegration will take place or not. Bone quantity and quality predisposes to different success rates of the implants in different zones of the jaws. For example, symphysis of the mandible is the most predictable zone while posterior maxilla is the dubious zone. Number of medically compromised conditions are to be considered with respect to the fixture success and failure. In general, patients with altered inflammatory response or compromised healing states should be considered with caution. In case of patients treated with chemotherapy and immunosuppressive drugs and who are on long-term antiinflammatory and immunosuppressive medications may present unpredictable response. Increased failure rates have been reported in case of patients with tobacco smoking. Erosive Lichen planus can give rise to long-term soft tissue management problems around the abutments.

(d) Atraumatic surgery

"Thou shalt utilise atraumatic surgical technique"

A high degree of respect for the living tissue with an emphasis on minimal trauma is mandatory during the preparation of the implant bed. Even though osseointegration is triggered by the invasive nature of implant surgery, it will be possible only when narrow limits, which prevent permanent tissue damage, are not crossed. This is applicable to surgical, postoperative healing and remodelling phases. Prognostic predictability could be a reality if only, a scientifically developed protocol is developed. Although internally cooled drill is advocated, caution is required because excessive flushing action may prove to be counter productive. Excessive removal of local osteogenic cells may interfere with bone healing. Similarly, violation of the established protocol is the use of airmotors in implant surgery due to the possibility of embolus formation from the surgical site.

III. Acceptable load transfer

"Thou shalt formulate optimal loading conditions"

The *"support: load"* ratio indicates the quantum of support by the bone to the implant when compared to the actual load placed on it. If the implant is in the form of a small screw with nonporous surface, the surface "area : load" ratio is low. Hence, with direct bone interface, such an implant can function for an extended period. The "crown : root" ratio becomes critical. If occlusal load can be translated over a large surface area, by increasing the surface, surface roughness and porosity, long-term function is possible. The nature and degree of force distribution at the implant interface determines the long-term stability and success of the implant. The load and force distribution depend on many factors:

(1) Difference in elastic modulus between the host tissue and the implant.
(2) Size, surface and the overall design of the implant.
(3) Prosthesis and occlusion.

The implant design must provide adequate surface area for the mechanical force transfer. The direct osseointegrated interface seems to have superior pattern of load transfer. A number of factors must be taken into consideration while planning the prosthetic loading of the implants. It is better to follow the basic biomechanical principles in the selection, placement and angulations of the fixtures. That means, prosthesis geometry and fixture placement are closely interrelated in the matter of determining the ultimate prosthetic load on the biomechanical interface.

Long-term studies have revealed that negative bone loss occurs around the fixtures. This increase in the marginal bone height is of great clinical significance although the mechanism is not clear. On the contrary, bone loss around the fixtures have been observed in overload situations. This is accentuated by bad oral hygiene and plaque accumulation.

Thus, the treatment protocols have been based on the supposition that tooth root biology and periimplant biology are analogous. The science of osseointegration is well established. Number of biological and technical factors are known to influence prognostic predictability. The clinical procedures that are not documented by long-term prospective trial should not be practiced by the clinicians.

Teeth and implants

Clinicians require an understanding of the nature of osseointegration and the important differences between dental implants and natural teeth.

(a) *Gingiva versus periimplant soft tissues:* Healthy gingival margin is located on enamel. It is scalloped and forms a shallow sulcus at the teeth surface. The periodontal fibres are inserted into the root cementum between the alveolar crest and cementoenamel junction. Therefore, they are dependent upon the presence of natural teeth.

In the case of implants, a transmucosal element protrudes through the overlying mucosa which heals and adapts around the implant without a cementum attachment. The collagen fibres within the periimplant mucosa run parallel to the abutment with no insertion into the abutment surface.

(b) *Junctional epithelium:* This is attached to enamel by hemidesmosomal contacts and a basal lamina-like structure formed by the epithelial cells. The biological attachment mechanism is considered to be mediated through a cell adhesion mechanism. This will also form on root surface cementum, dentine and on titanium of the implants.

(c) *Biological width:* In teeth, zone of attached connective tissue seperates the underlying alveolar bone from the apical termination of the junctional epithelium. This zone is around 2 mm wide. In case of implants, it is according to the design of the implant.

(d) *Periodontal ligament versus osseo-integration:* Periodontal ligament is a complex structure, 0.1 to 0.2 mm in width providing support to the teeth in a viscoelastic manner. The collagen fibres are embedded as Sharpey's fibres in the root cementum and alveolar bone. It has a proprioceptive sensitive mechanism.

The precise nature of osseointegration at the molecular level is not fully understood. There is a very close adaptation of the bone to the implant surface. The narrow gap between the implant surface and bone is occupied by an intervening collagen rich zone adjacent to the bone and a more amorphous zone adjacent to the implant surface. This implant-bone interface is considered as a dynamic process in which bone turnover occurs. This is more akin to ankylosis, where absence of mobility and no intervening fibrous tissue capsule is the sign of successful osseointegration.

EVALUATION OF THE PROSPECTIVE IMPLANT PATIENT

In most of the patients, complete or partial dentures provide the cost effective and predictable restorations to manage the edentulous problems. For any reason, if these patients are not found to be satisfied, the patient must be carefully evaluated to find out the reason for the dissatisfaction and psychosocial problems. The existence of any of the following traits in these patients need to be identified:

(i) Structural deficiency (anatomical),
(ii) Functional deficiency (physiological) and
(iii) Psychosocial disturbances
 (a) Emotionally intolerant person.
 (b) One who wants perfection.

Prior to the placement of implants, the assessment of patients include

(a) Medical and dental history,
(b) Clinical examination and
(c) Radiographic examination.

Periapical and panoramic radiographs provide adequate informations with reference to the volume and quality of bone and the location of anatomic limiting factors. CT Scan provides useful information for the placement of implants.

Structural deficiencies that may interfere with denture retention include atrophic ridge, abnormal tongue position, inadequate and shallow vestibule, unfavorable ridge form or abnormal jaws relationship. Due to functional or physiological deficiencies like low threshold of pain or hypersensitive gag reflex, even a well-fitting denture becomes unsatisfactory. Emotionally intolerant or perfection seeking patients may not be willing to wear the conventional dentures. Such patients express the desire to have implant dentures with the hope that it will be like a natural dentition.

Patient selection

(1) The practitioner must ensure that the provision of implants will provide better prosthodontic service.
(2) If so, one has to verify the availability of sufficient bone to accommodate the implant.
(3) The general condition including the status of oral health need to be evaluated.
(4) Ridge should have sufficient thickness of alveolar bone at the site where implant is to be inserted.
(5) Vertically, the height of the alveolar ridge must be at least 10 mm between the crest of the alveolus and the mandibular canal. In maxilla, it is between the alveolar crest and the nasal or sinus floor.
(6) In buccolingual direction, alveolar ridge should have a minimum of 6 mm width to accommodate any type of implant with a safety margin of 1 mm on either side of the implant.
(7) Mesiodistally, minimum of 5 mm of alveolar bone is present for single tooth implants with 1 mm of safety margin on either side.
(8) In mandibular molar region, bony contour below the mylohyoid line must be evaluated. In case of extensive undercuts, the implant can perforate the lingual cortex.
(9) Study models are necessary to determine the ideal position of the implants and to critically evaluate the occlusion.
(10) Radiographic evaluation is very important in treatment planning.

Indications

In general, they could be classified as relative and absolute indications. Complete edentulousness could be considered as absolute indication - especially, if the complete removable denture is unsatisfactory, implant therapy seems to be the only alternative solution. But in other conditions as mentioned below, implants are to be considered as one of the viable alternatives. Hence the following could be considered as relative indications.

(1) Replacement for one edentulous jaw opposing dentulous jaw. (Fig. 24.2b, c, d)
(2) Multiple teeth replacement. (Fig. 24.3a, b)
(3) Single tooth replacement. (Fig. 24.4a, b, c, d)
(4) Multiple teeth replacement with free end edentulous area.

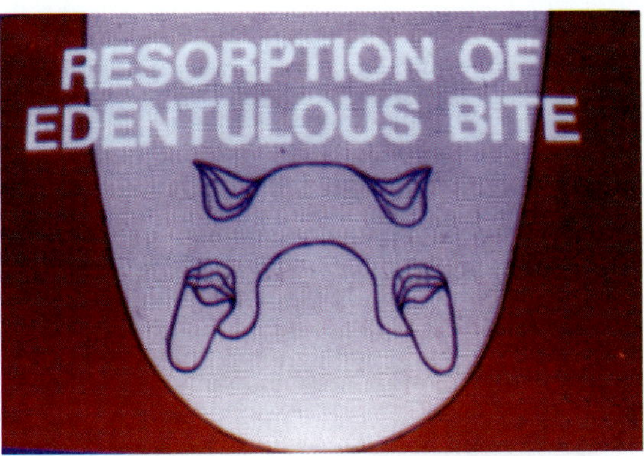

Fig. 24.2 (a) Pattern of bone resorption in the edentulous jaws.

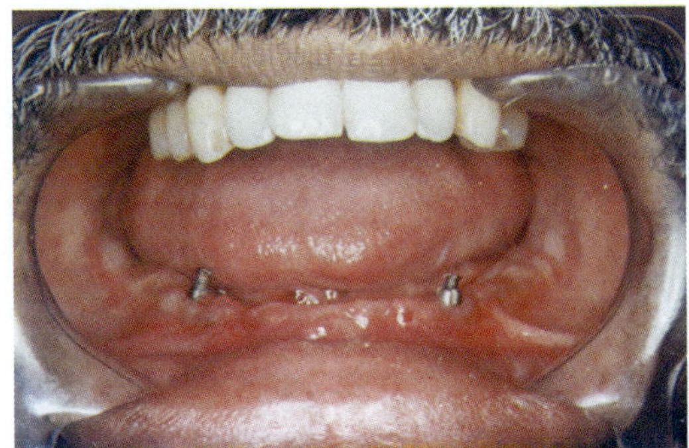

Fig. 24.2 (b) Two implants in the mandible for placing a lower complete denture with natural maxillary teeth.

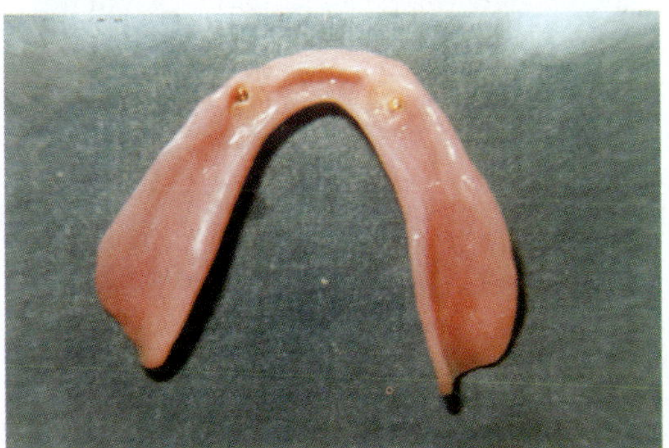

Fig. 24.2 (c) Lower denture impression surface showing the female component for accommodating the implants head.

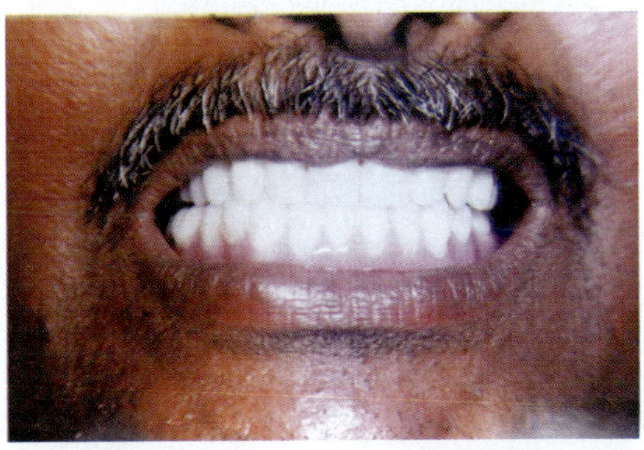

Fig. 24.2 (d) Lower denture in position against maxillary natural teeth.

(5) Replacement for both the edentulous jaws.
(6) Preventive implantation to retard the ridge resorption following dental extraction.

Contraindications

(1) Patients should be carefully selected since unmotivated patients are not good candidates for dental implants.
(2) Systemic contraindications for surgery.
(3) Presence of pathology within the bone.
(4) Patients with unrealistic expectations.
(5) Patients with bad oral hygiene and habits like smoking, chewing etc.
(6) Anatomic limitations like inferior dental canal.

(Note: maxillary sinus is no more a contraindication since sinus lift procedure is performed to overcome this limitation).

Preventive implantation

It has been observed that wherever submerged roots are retained, they incidentally prevent ridge resorption and thereby the volume of alveolar ridge is maintained. Therefore, it seems to be a logical approach to substitute these submerged roots with biologically compatible root substitutes. Although it has not been possible to construct artificial periodontium, attempts have been directed to induce the root implants chemically to react with alveolar bone to produce ankylosis type of bonding. Metallic

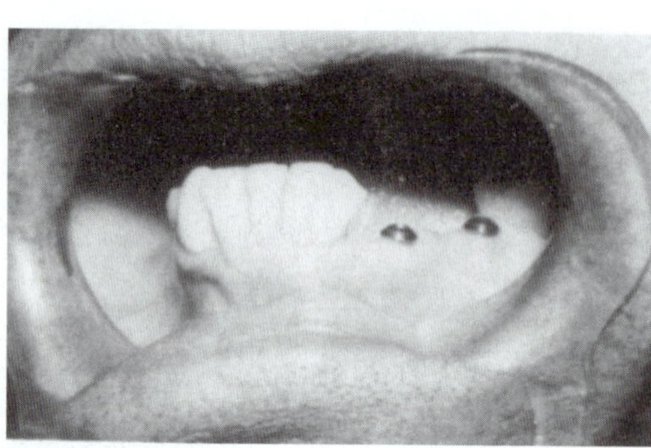

(a)

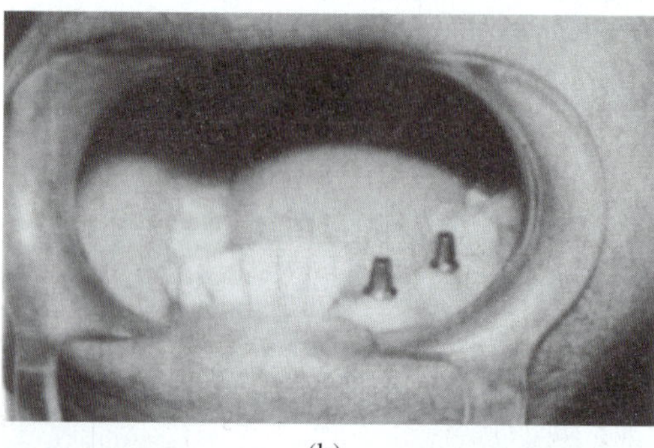

(b)

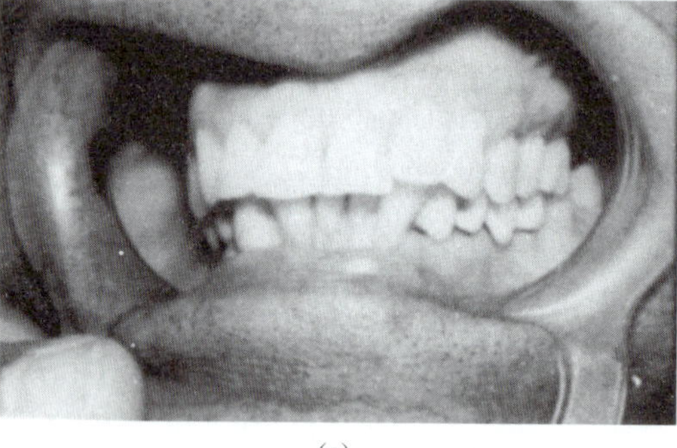

(c)

Fig. 24.3 (a) & (b) Mandibular left posterior edentulous ridge with two implants in position, (c) Implant supported prosthesis in position.

and plastic implants are not suitable for this purpose. Hence, hydroxyapatite implants have been the natural choice. After extraction, buccal and lingual plates collapse towards each other during the healing phase producing a narrower ridge. The root implants are intended to prevent such a collapse by acting as space maintainers. The volume of the ridge could

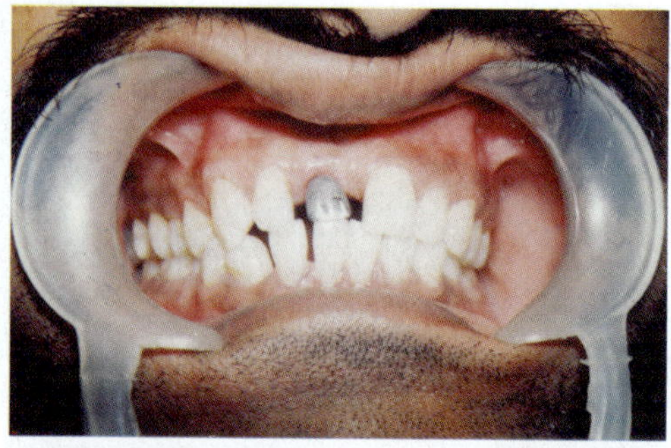

Fig. 24.4 (a) Non vital maxillary right central incisor tooth.

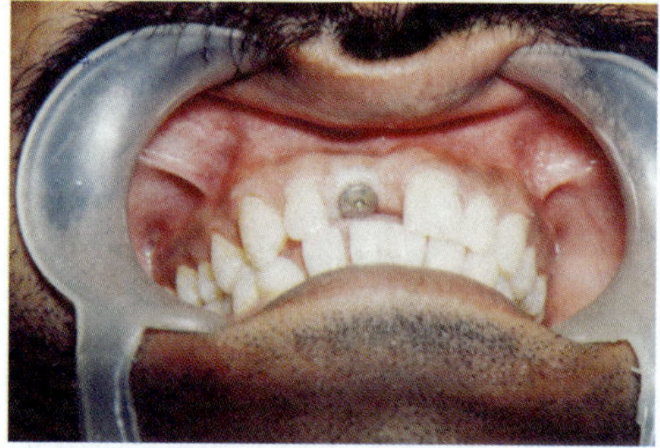

Fig. 24.4 (b) After non vital tooth extraction site healed up implant insertion with healing cap in position.

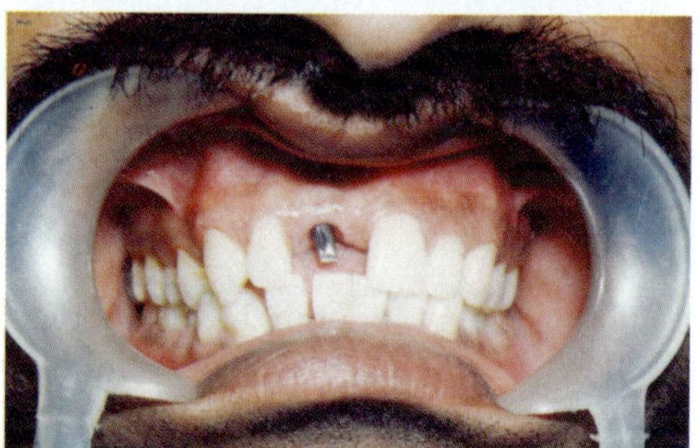

Fig. 24.4 (c) Abutment in position.

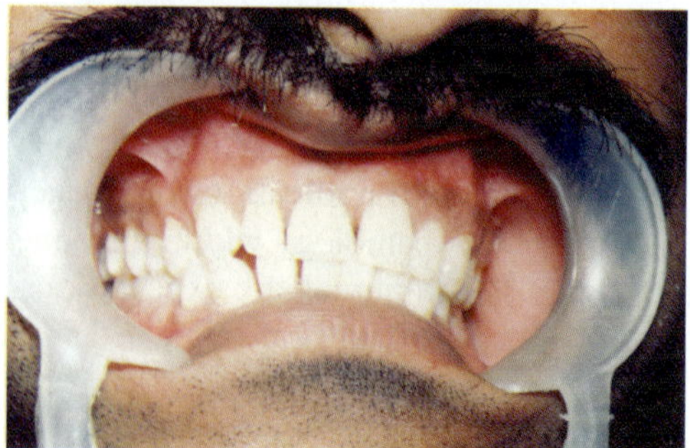

Fig. 24.4 (d) Porcelain restoration in place.

also be preserved in a horizontal direction so that there is no alteration in the vestibular curvature of the ridge at the site of extraction.

Criteria for implant success

Commercially, so many types of dental implants have been introduced. The practitioner is at a loss to select the type of implant which ensures clinical success. It has been observed that the successful outcome of any implant procedure depends on the interrelationship of various components.

(1) Biocompatibility of the implant material.
(2) Nature of the implant tissue interface.
(3) Status of the implant bed in the context of quality of bone and absence of infection.
(4) Surgical technique.
(5) Undisturbed healing phase.
(6) Prosthetic design and long-term loading phase.

The following criteria have been suggested for its success:

(a) Individual implant should be relatively immobile or mobility is less than 1 mm in any direction, when tested clinically.
(b) Radiograph criteria: The ideal bone level is judged against a specific landmark on the implant, like implant-abutment junction. A progressive change in the bone loss (peri-implant radiolucency) is a worrying sign of implant failure. For example, vertical bone loss is less than 0.2 mm annually following the implant's first year of service. Anything more than this must be viewed as peri-implant disease.
(c) The individual implant's performance is characterized by the absence of irreversible features like infection, neuropathies, paresthesia, or violation of anatomical structures like mandibular canal, nasal passage or maxillary sinus.
(d) In view of these considerations, for any type of implant to be considered successful, the success rate of 85% at the end of five-year's observation period and 80% at the end of ten years' period are the criteria for the success.
(e) Implants placed in the mandible[anterior to mental foramen] usually enjoy a higher success rate.

Osseointegration is essentially a histological term but only partially a clinical and radiological one. The clinical evidence of mobility and radiographic bone response should be judged after a substantial period of implant service. Conventional gingival and periodontal indices are not included in this criteria. It is impossible to separate the quality of the implant anchorage from its subsequent loaded assignment. Therefore, it is presumed that the same surgical skill that ensured biomechanical anchorage is matched by the prosthodontic skill that maintains it. Either or both can compromise the implant system. Therefore, for any implant system, both should be a common denominator and both are evenly balanced.

Implant design has a greater influence on the primary stability and subsequent function. Following are some of the main design parameters:

(a) *Implant length:* In general, most commonly employed implants vary between 8 and 15 mm. This is because, the range corresponds to respective normal root lengths.
(b) *Implant diameter:* Mostly, the implants used are approximately 4 mm in diameter. To ensure adequate strength, it must be at least 3.25 mm in diameter. The implants with larger diameter can be placed if only, bone width is correspondingly large.
(c) *Implant shape:* To maximize the potential area for osseointegration and to provide primary stability, implants have been designed in many shapes. Screw shaped implants offer higher degree of stability.
(d) *Surface characteristics:* Degree of surface roughness, plasma spray etc have been tried to achieve success. But, optimum surface morphology is yet to be defined.

Loading conditions: It is important that the implant is not loaded during the early healing.

TYPES OF IMPLANTS

(i) Subperiosteal implants

(a) The metal framework is constructed by different materials like vitallium with titanium coated surface etc. They have the longest period of clinical trial. These implants are not anchored inside the bone. As the name indicates, it is shaped to "ride" on the residual bony ridge. Hence, they are not osseointegrated. Prior to the introduction of osseointegration, these implants alone were more often tried in edentulous mandible.

(b) During primary surgery, bony surface is exposed after raising the mucoperiosteal flap. After the impression is taken, the flap is sutured. Then the metal framework is fabricated. Only during secondary stage, implant is fixed. Then, the prosthetic super structure is attached to the implant.

(c) Complications like inflammation, post-insertion altered sensation, swelling, pain and progressive bone resorption have been reported. If due to some reason, implant is removed, prosthodontic treatment will be further complicated.

(d) Clinical results. Success rate after 7 years period has been discouraging. Significant loss of implants with passage of time has been mainly responsible for the clinicians to look for more predictable implants.

(ii) Vitreous carbon implants

These implants have a core of stainless steel covered by 99.99% carbon. They were used as single free-standing units or splinted with adjoining teeth. During insertion, low speed instrumentation with copious irrigation of saline is advocated. After insertion, soft tissue is closed to allow undisturbed healing, at least for a minimum period of 4-5 months. Complications like osteomyelitis and paresthesia with substantial bone loss have been reported. Success rate of 0-65% at the end of 5 years period has been reported. Hence, results have been discouraging.

(iii) Blade implants

Originally these implants were introduced by Linkow. This was widely used for some time. Many materials like vitreous carbon, titanium alloy and aluminum oxide were being used. They are usually recommended for single tooth replacements and also for edentulous jaws. The surgical insertion has been a single stage. Success rate of 50-55% at the end of 5 years period has been claimed. In spite of many modifications over the past 30-40 years, all have proved to be inadequate to justify its widespread usage.

(iv) Osseointegrated titanium implants (Fig. 24.1)

These implants are screw shaped, made from commercially pure titanium. The surface is unique and machine produced implants are anchored in bone without the intervening fibrous tissue.

No other implant has been so thoroughly investigated as this implant. They have been successful in the edentulous jaws although it has also been used in partially edentulous jaws and proved to be one of the viable alternatives to the conventional prosthesis. Most of these implants are inserted in the mandible, anterior to the mental foramen.

Surgical technique: Under (local/general) appropriate anesthesia, suitable mucoperiosteal flap is raised and the prospective implant site is exposed. The implants are inserted with a graded series of drills and controlled surgical techniques. Soft tissue is sutured. Only after 3-6 months, abutments are attached and the implants are connected to a prosthesis. No serious complications are reported. Success rate of over 80% after 5-12 years follow-up have been reported. Higher success rate in mandibular implants has been due to the bone quantity and quality in the anterior part of the mandible. The longest follow-up has been over 20 years with good success rate.

Surgical considerations and shortcomings of host sites

Implant therapy is based on surgical and prosthetic procedures. The outcome is dependent on how these two parts are performed. The treatment goals of surgical procedure are (a) to create the anchorage unit, (b) to establish increased retention for the prosthetic devices. They depend on the following factors:

(a) Preoperative examination and assessment of the patient.
(b) Treatment planning
(c) Clinical procedures.

Soft tissues around the osseointegrated implants

The biological considerations in implant dentistry have focused on bone-implant interface. The long-term stability depends on the anchorage in bone. Teeth have periodontium and remain structurally continuous with these tissues, while the implants are placed into an osseous receptor site. The surrounding tissues are expected to adapt to the inserted post, allowing them to function as tooth substitutes. The gingiva-like tissue is present around the transmucosal implant or the abutment. This consists of a dense, collagenous lamina propria, covered by squamous, keratinizing oral epithelium. Main difference from the natural dentition is the manner in which periimplant connective tissue interface with the implant tissues.

MANAGEMENT OF IMPLANT DISEASE

As already discussed, the success rate of the implants indicates the probable period after which they are lost due to mobility. All the etiological factors related to tissue pathology with the exception of physical, chemical or structural failures can be considered under the following heads:

(1) Adverse systemic conditions.
(2) Overloading of the prosthesis on the implants and the consequent bone loss.
(3) Inadequate motivation of the patient and the consequent poor oral hygiene.

Bad oral hygiene may contribute to the implant use failure under the following situations:

(a) Inadequate motivation of the patient.
(b) Improperly designed implant.
(c) Selection of the implant with low success rate.
(d) Unsatisfactory surface of the implant.
(e) Improper insertion of the implant.
(f) Prosthesis improperly executed.
(g) Unsatisfactory home care.
(h) Inadequate follow-up by the dental surgeon.

Poor oral hygiene by itself can result in early loss of the implants. Unfortunately, some of these patients lack the requisite psychomotor skills needed for the satisfactory oral hygiene measures.

The clinicians who practise implant dentistry require an understanding of the nature of osseointegration and fundamental differences between dental implants and natural dentition.

(a) Gingiva and periimplant soft tissues (Fig. 24.5 (a))

In healthy adult, gingival margin is located on enamel. The gingival margin is scalloped and forms a shallow sulcus. Between the teeth, it forms a complex structure called interdental papilla. A complex group of gingival connective tissue fibres form well defined bundles - interdental fibres, dentogingival fibres, circular fibres and alveolar crest fibres. Since many of these fibres are inserted into the root cementum between the alveolar crest and cementoenamel junction, they depend on the presence of natural teeth.

In case of implants, a transmucosal element protrudes through the overlying mucosa which adapts around the implant. The collagen fibres within the periimplant mucosa run parallel to the abutment with no insertion into the abutment surface. The papilla around the single implant may be supported by collagen fibres attached to the adjacent natural tooth. But in case of implants without any neighboring natural teeth, formation of soft tissue papilla is less predictable.

(b) Junctional epithelium

In natural healthy teeth, it is attached to enamel by hemidesmosomal contacts and a basal lamina-like structure formed by the epithelial cells. Normal junctional epithelium can be regenerated from the adjacent oral mucosa following excision/damage. It is therefore well equipped to deal with the problems of any breach in the integrity of the junctional epithelium - both around natural teeth and implants.

(c) Biological width

In case of teeth, the concept of biological width is well established. Zone of attached connective tissue seperates the underlying alveolar bone from the apical termination of the junctional epithelium. The length of the junctional epithelium is about 1.5 mm and the connective tissue zone is about 2 mm wide. This may vary in various implant systems. Periodontal probing of natural teeth forms an important part of any dental examination.

The probe penetrates the junctional epithelium to some degree while examining and this penetration increases in the presence of inflammation. It stops usually about 2 mm from the bone. In implants, probing depth is generally deeper than around the natural teeth. Hence, clinicians are adviced to rely on radiographic assessment of bone levels rather than probing. Perhaps digital pressure on the externa aspect of the periimplant soft-tissue will reveal the signs of inflammation like bleeding or suppuration.

(d) Periodontal ligament and osseointegration

Periodontal ligament is a complex structure of 0.1 to 0.2 mm width, which provide support to the natural teeth. The Sharpey's fibres are embedded in the root cementum and alveolar bone. Blood supply and connective tissue ground substance provide the other key elements of the supporting mechanism. It has a delicate proprioceptive mechanism by which even minute changes in the masticatory load on the tooth can be detected. Forces transmitted through the periodontal apparatus can lead to remodelling and tooth movement as seen in orthodontic movement of teeth.

On the contrary, the precise nature of osseointegration at the molecular level is not yet defined. At the low power microscopic level, the bone is very closely adapted to the implant. However, at a higher magnification, a small gap can be identified, occupied by the intervening collagen rich zone near the bone and an amorphous zone near the implant surface. Therefore it is stated that, osseointegration is not an absolute phenomenon. It only represents the proportion of the total implant surface that is in contact with bone. It is similar to ankylosis where absence of mobility and the absence of intervening fibrous tissue is the indication of successful osseointegration.

(e) Periimplantitis and periodontitis (Fig. 24.5b, c, d, e, f, g)

The microorganisms responsible for both the conditions seem to be the same. The destruction of the supporting tissues of teeth and implants have many similarities.

Periimplantitis affects the entire circumference of the implant resulting in a "gutter" like bone loss filled with inflammatory tissue. But, teeth affected by periodontitis have irregular loss of supporting tissues, confining to proximal surfaces leading to infrabony defects. It is described in the literature that, in both the clinical entities, the destructive inflammatory lesions have stages in which the disease process is rapid, called "burst phenomenon". It is followed by periods of relative dormancy.

Implants have been used to treat edentulousness for many decades but they did not enjoy favorable reputation. With advances in biotechnology and clear understanding of the fundamental differences between teeth and implants, the situation has changed

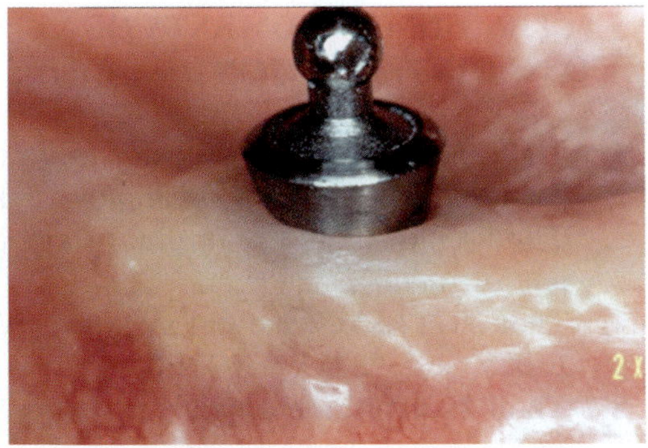

Fig. 24.5 (a) Periimplant soft tissues.

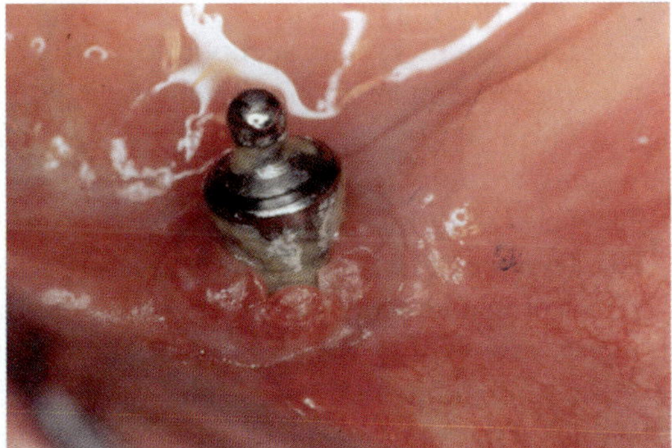

Fig. 24.5 (b) Periimplantitis.

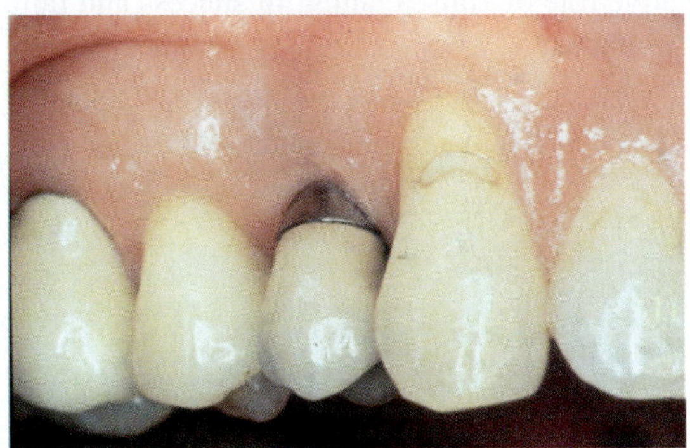

Fig. 24.5 (c) Gingival recession.

dramatically.

Thus it is to be noted that, now oral implantology certainly can be considered as one of the viable alternatives in the management of all the stages of edentulousness. But careful patient selection is

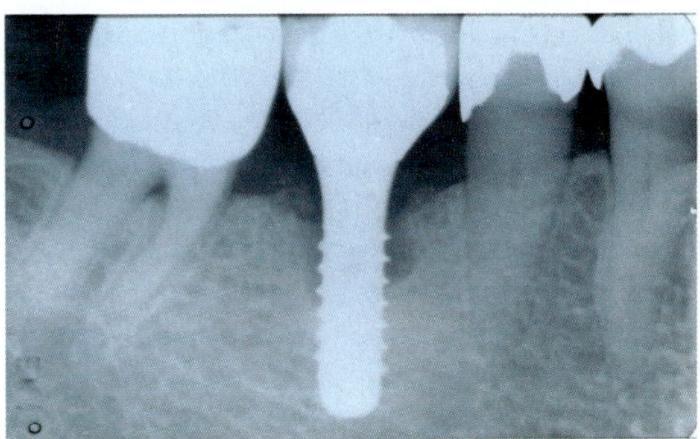

Fig. 24.5 (d) Radiograph showing periimplant bone resorption.

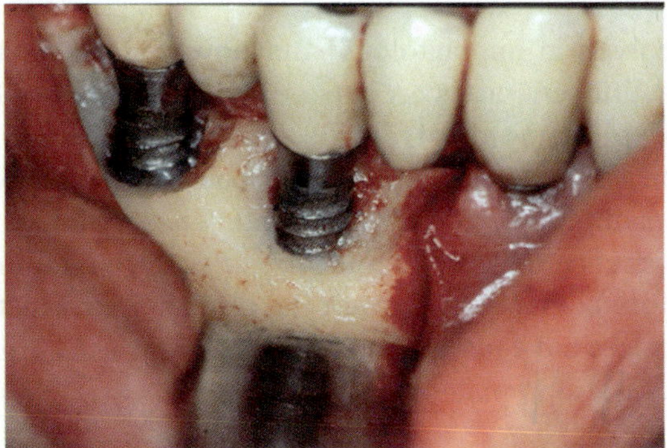

Fig. 24.5 (e) Clinical photograph demonstrating severe boneloss around the implants.

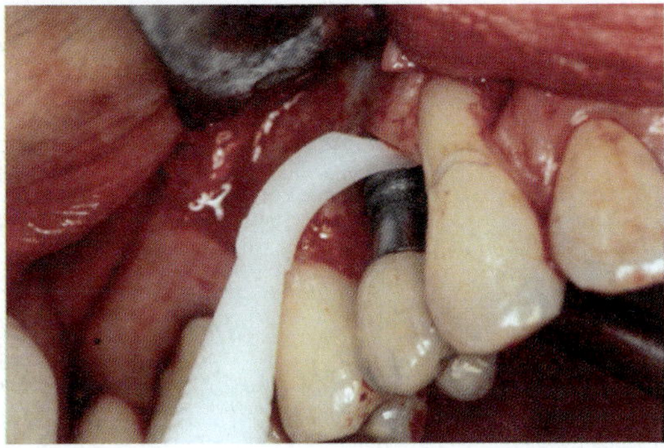

Fig. 24.5 (f) Photograph showing flap procedure and emettage.

needed to ensure success. In the recent past, there has been an explosion of interest and knowledge of oral implantology. Formerly, only specialists were

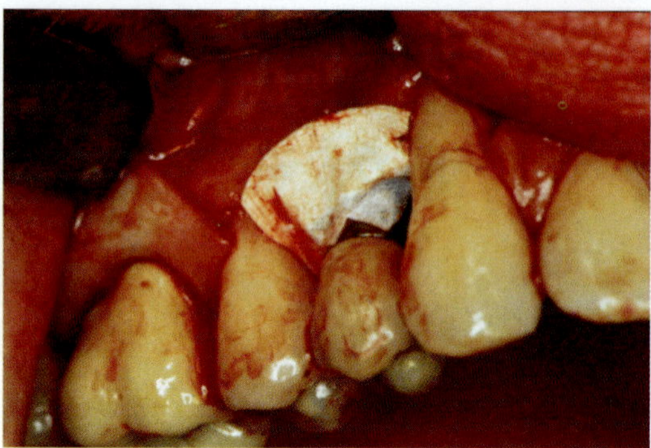

Fig. 24.5 (g) Periodontal pack in position after emettage.

involved in implantology. But now general dental practitioners, after a course of training, undertake the placement of implants. The scope has considerably widened. Hence, basic principles on implantology has been provided. Those who wish to practice oral implantology must undergo training before attempting to insert the implants. Prosthetic services are equally important as a team work for a successful implantology practice.

TEN COMMANDMENTS OF OSSEOINTEGRATION (*Henry P.*)

1. Thou shalt not violate *biocompatibility*.
2. Thou shalt not compromise *implant design*.
3. Thou shalt respect implant *surface microstructure*.
4. Thou shalt address the status of the *implant bed*.
5. Thou shalt utilize *atraumatic surgical techniques*.
6. Thou shalt formulate *optimal loading conditions*.
7. Thou shalt create acceptable *soft tissue interface* and esthetic harmony.
8. Thou shalt monitor and *maintain all restorations*.
9. Thou shalt love thy neighbor as thyself.
10. Thou shalt not bear false witness.

The "commandments" summarize the important statements concerning the implantology practice. The 9th commandment stresses the importance of the health of the neighboring dentition. The tenth statement stresses the importance of realizing the relative role of "false claims" of success and failure of implants.

Ethics and Medicolegal Considerations

Principles of ethics are the aspirational goals of the profession. They provide guidance and offer justification for the code of professional conduct. They are not imposed by any legislation. They are voluntarily accepted by the members of the profession to maintain high standard of practice. According to the American Dental Association, the following are the five fundamental principles that form the foundation of the code of ethics:

(a) Patient autonomy (self-governance),
(b) Nonmalfeasance (do no harm),
(c) Beneficence (do good),
(d) Justice (fairness),
(e) Veracity (truthfulness).

The Federation Dentaire Internationale (FDI) has formulated International Principles of Ethics for the Dental Profession. The essence of these principles could be summarized as the obligation of the dental surgeon to work constantly for the progress of the speciality by service to the *patient, community* and the *profession*. In the triad, (triangle), even if one component fails, the triangle becomes unstable.

Patient

The main duty of the dental surgeon is to safeguard the oral health of the patients irrespective of caste, creed, religion, sex or nationality. The professional secrecy is mandatory.

Community

Dentist should promote all accepted measures to improve the oral and general health of the population. The dentist must assume the responsible role in the life of the community.

Profession

The dentist should maintain the integrity, honor and morality of the profession. One must also maintain the professional knowledge and skill by updating through periodic continuing education. Dental surgeon should not criticize the services of another professional colleague and that too in the presence of the patient.

GENERAL CONSIDERATIONS

During clinical practice, one may encounter certain situations that may be unavoidable in spite of exercising reasonable skill and care. Occasionally, the practitioner may have to face an embarrassing situation due to the lack of appreciation and awareness of professional code of ethics. But there can be no two opinions that all efforts should be directed to reduce the potential legal liabilities of the dental practitioner. This involves (a) proper documentation, (b) communication between the patient and the practitioner, (c) informed consent and (d) ability to minimize or manage the complications by the practitioner.

Note : Please refer chap. 28 regarding the advantages and importance of computerization to promote documentation and communication between the practitioner and the patient.

Negligence can be defined as a failure to exercise reasonable skill and care ordinarily possessed and demonstrated by the members of the profession practicing under similar circumstances.

Malpractice is defined as negligent acts of a member of any profession while discharging duty in one's professional capacity.

Any patient can initiate the legal proceeding against the practitioner to recover compensation on the grounds of negligence. But a few factors are required to be established for the legal suit to be successful.

(1) *Duty of care:* Once the patient is accepted for treatment, the practitioner is obliged to provide a reasonable and acceptable standard of professional care under prevailing circumstances.
(2) *Breach of care:* The very act of acceptance of a patient for treatment is a form of "implied contract" between the patient and the clinician. Failure to provide a reasonable and acceptable standard of care constitutes breach of contract.
(3) *Cause of the injury:* This is one of the most crucial factors for any legal proceedings to be successful. It is absolutely essential to realise that the failure to provide reasonable and standard care expected from any professional has been the cause of injury and the damage has occurred as a result of such negligence.
(4) *Injury:* Demonstration of such a damage as an unfavorable outcome of treatment is equally important. In other words, even gross negligence and carelessness, which have not lead to any harm, will not provide a ground for the patient to claim damages. Hence, the principle "no injury - no liability" seems to be most appropriate.

A brief account of various relevant terms is provided here for the proper understanding of the medicolegal considerations as related to oral surgery practice.

DOCUMENTATION

Documentation of all the relevant records related to the treatment provided to the patient may not necessarily be a legal requirement. But good record keeping should be considered as a safe practice. It also forms an integral part of reasonable skill and care. The maintenance of accurate and concise records of all the treatment provided to any patient constitutes one of the important factors in self protection against any possible legal considerations. All troublesome patients must be considered as potential litigants and even the so-called *emergency patient* is not an exception. Mere production of a comprehensive record is sufficient to protect oneself against the initiation of a legal action. Hence, all the relevant records are the property of the practitioner concerned. It is also desirable to retain all the relevant records for a reasonable period of time after the completion of treatment.

COMMUNICATION

One of the methods of improving the *patient-doctor relationship* is effective communication with the patient by providing information considered as relevant. Usually well informed patients understand the specific problems better. Such patients are usually more realistic in their expectations and about the outcome of the treatment. Hence, it is reasonable to develop and provide standardized information packages on specific procedures in a simple layman's language about the nature of the problem, suggested treatment, alternative plans, probable and possible complications and the duration of surgery.

CONSENT FOR TREATMENT

In legal terms, any form of treatment including examination of a patient without the consent constitutes assault. For the consent to be valid, it should be in the form of an *informed consent*. It may be implied, oral or written. In the absence of any written consent, it is always preferable or even advantageous to carry out the treatment in the presence of a third party. In case of minor children, the guardian's consent alone is legally valid. A standard basic consent form is provided. While there is no need to emphasize the importance of the informed consent, one must also realize that emergencies need not wait for the consent.

In addition to fulfilling the required legal obligations, there are several benefits of informed consent which are self-explanatory. The process of informed consent could be considered in three phases:

(1) Discussion with the patient and the patient's guardian,
(2) Written consent from the patient or patient's guardian and
(3) Documentation of the patient's records.

The following are some of the specific situations where informed consent may not be necessary:

(a) The patient may request that he/she need not be informed about the details of the procedure because of the fear complex.
(b) In case of emergencies, treatment precedes the consent. However, it becomes mandatory for all the elective procedures, particularly when performed under general anesthesia.

The following situations will illustrate the above statements:

Case I - Examination of the patient. A child was brought from a school in an emergency situation with a history of fall in the school playground. The child was found to be noncooperative. The dental surgeon hurriedly examined and certified that there is no cause for worry. The patient was discharged after the first aid measures. The child apparently returned to normal life but only to return to the same dental surgeon with his parents after 6 months with the complaint that the child has restricted mouth opening. To rule out the possibility of ankylosis of the temporomandibular joint, the patient was referred to an oral surgeon, who confirmed the diagnosis of ankylosis of the temporomandibular joint, possibly due to intraarticular injury. Under such circumstances, knowledgeable parents took up the matter seriously and accuse the dental surgeon of negligence. The possibilities are as follows:

(1) The dental surgeon failed to diagnose the temporomandibular joint injury soon after the accident.
(2) Failed to take reasonable decisions on the basis of investigations like radiographic examinations of the jaws, etc.
(3) If the practitioner was not competent enough, the clinician ought to have referred the child for an expert opinion, even in the first instance.
(4) Failed to advise the child for periodic reviews to look for the sequelae of joint injury.

This case amply forewarns the practitioner that no risk is involved in carrying out the first aid measures in an emergency situation. But such patients should be referred for expert opinion unless he/she is competent to undertake such professional responsibilities. Failure to recognize this fact will make the practitioner vulnerable to legal implications at a later date.

Case II - Inhalation of a tooth during extraction. An apprehensive patient attended a dental clinic for dental extraction. Under inferior dental nerve block anesthesia, when the dental surgeon applied the extraction forceps, the patient moved the head out of fear. During the process, the doctor lost control of the patient. The tooth suddenly disappeared from the surgical field and the socket looked empty. Search into the oral cavity failed to locate the displaced tooth. The patient was referred to an ENT surgeon. Bronchoscopic examination also did not help the surgeon to identify the displaced tooth. However, radiographic examination revealed its presence in the bronchus. Hence, the patient had to be operated for the removal of the foreign body.

Under such circumstances, the dental surgeon is liable to be charged with negligence on any of the following accounts:

(1) The dental surgeon failed to produce satisfactory anesthesia.
(2) Failed to use the appropriate instrument to grasp the tooth securely during extraction.
(3) Failed to take reasonable precautions against slipping of the tooth into the throat.
(4) Failed to locate the tooth in the mouth within a reasonable period before being aspirated into the respiratory system.

Discussion

In **Case I**, the parents of the child are right in expecting the dental surgeon to advice them properly. If the dental surgeon did not feel competent, the child ought to have been referred to the specialist for an expert opinion after rendering first aid treatment. Secondly, radiographs should have been taken as a record of the patient's documents to state that, clinically and radiologically, there was no evidence of any joint or bony injury. Lastly, any child with history of injury to the jaws is a case of potential hemarthrosis. Hence, such children should be periodically followed up for a reasonable period. With such reasonable precautions, if the child develops ankylosis, then, it cannot be called negligence.

Note: Children with history of injury require careful handling with a reasonable period of follow up.

Regarding **Case II**, it is evident that the accident had occurred. Dental surgeon has taken all the necessary remedial steps to retrieve the foreign body. If (a) the doctor has anesthetized the patient adequately, (b) the doctor extracted the tooth with appropriate instruments adopting correct techniques and (c) if the doctor had taken due precautions by bending the patient forwards to prevent the tooth to move into the throat, no case of negligence can be made out. If so, this accident should have occurred because of some action of the patient, which could be termed as "contributory negligence". Probably, this accident could have occurred since the apprehensive patient grabbed the surgeon's hand while the surgery was in progress which distracted the dental surgeon from performing his duty properly.

Warning: Dental surgeon must take all precautions to avoid such accidents, especially when dealing with apprehensive patients and children.

Res ipsa loquitur is a legal term which means "the thing that spoke for itself". That means the very nature of the incident is sufficient to prove the guilty which is obvious. A simple example to illustrate a case of the obvious mistake of extracting a wrong tooth.

Case III. A lady got a mandibular third molar removed under general anesthesia. The surgery and the postoperative wound healing was uneventful. But the patient developed thermal burn at the angle of the mouth and the mucous membrane of the lower lip due to overheating of the handpiece. Later, the patient became very sensitive to the burn scar and had to undergo plastic surgery. Psychiatric evaluation revealed that the young female patient was suffering from depression, social anxiety and fear complex.

Such complications can also occur due to the chemicals or hot instruments which are insufficiently cooled before use or inadvertent injection of an incorrect solution for providing local anesthesia. Similarly, such common problems arising out of local anesthesia are breakage of the needle, nerve injuries, postoperative complications and discomforts, hematoma, ecchymosis and allergy/ anaphylaxis. The dental surgeon is expected to take due precaution to avoid any such complications. If they occur, it is self explanatory.

Complications could be grouped as avoidable and unavoidable. Even with due precaution, the occurrence of unavoidable accidents cannot be prevented. But there is no excuse if preventable accidents occur. Under such circumstances, one has to keep in mind the "emergencies and complications in oral surgery" so that negligence could be totally avoided. If it occurs, it speaks for itself.

CHAPTER 26

Essentials of Laboratory Investigations

GENERAL CONSIDERATIONS

A dental surgeon may have to order for a few laboratory diagnostic investigations to evaluate the patient for fitness to undergo the treatment or to diagnose the systemic status of the patient. Hence, it is mandatory for the dental surgeon to be aware of the scope and usefulness of some of the common diagnostic investigations. Practitioner should have adequate knowledge about the normal range of physiological variations and to interpret the laboratory reports in relation to the systemic disorders which are responsible for the abnormal values of the investigations. The concise knowledge of these facts will also be useful to formulate appropriate differential diagnosis. The following are the routine laboratory investigations with the normal range of values within the physiological limits. Failure to realize this aspect may lead to errors in the systemic evaluation of the patients and the diagnosis.

Normal values

1. *RBC count:* 4.5 -5 million/cu.mm
2. *Hemoglobin:* 12-16 gm/100 ml of blood
3. *WBC*

   Total count: 6,000-8,000/ml

   Differential count

   Polymorphs: 65-75%
   Lymphocytes: 25-35%
   Monocytes: 4-8%
   Eosinophils: 0.5-4%
   Basophils: 0-1%
4. *Erythrocyte sedimentation rate* (ESR)

   Males: 0-1mm/hour
   Females: 1-15 mm/hour
5. *Platelet count:* 150,000-400,000/ml
6. *Bleeding time:* Ivy's method 1-9 minutes
   Duke's method 1-4 minutes
7. *Coagulation time:* 3-10 minutes (Lee and White Method) 1-5 minutes (capillary tube method)
8. *Blood volume:* 3000-7000 ml
9. *Prothrombin time:* 11-16 seconds
10. *Capillary fragility test:* 10-15 petechiae/sq.inch (Hess test)
11. *Blood chemistry*

    Blood calcium: 8.5-10.5 mg/100 ml
    Blood cholesterol: 120-140 mg/100 ml
    Serum alkaline phosphatase: 2-4.5 Bodansky units

Acid phosphatase	0-5.2 Bodansky units
Blood urea:	10-20 mg/100 ml

12. *Urinalysis*

pH:	4.8-7.8
Specific gravity:	1.01-1.04

INVESTIGATIONS

HEMATOLOGY

(a) Red blood cell count

(a) Size - Normocytic, microcytic and macrocytic.

(b) Decrease in RBC count is suggestive of several disorders but by itself is not a reliable indicator.

The following disorders can cause a decrease in RBC count:

(i) Hemolytic anemias,
(ii) Hemorrhage,
(iii) Hypersplenism,
(iv) Lead poisoning,
(v) Burns and
(vi) Uremia and liver disorders.

(c) Shape - Normally it is round. Abnormal shapes may be oval, fragmented or crenated cells.

(d) Hemoglobin concentration - Normochromic or hypochromic.

(e) Immature cells - Polychromatic cells, nucleated red cells etc.

Increase in RBC count is called polycythemia found in persons at high altitudes of 3000 meters and above the sea level.

(b) Hemoglobin

Decrease in hemoglobin can be observed in certain anemias. It can also occur due to hemolytic microorganisms, severe hemorrhage, certain poisons and snake venoms.

Increase in hemoglobin level can occur due to physiological response to increased oxygen consumption and demand as seen in athletes, chronic cigarette smokers and persons living in high altitudes.

(c) WBC total count

Overall increase in WBC count is called leucocytosis. This is possible in acute infections, hemolysis of RBC, tissue necrosis and intoxication. Examples of localized acute infections are pneumonia, abscess and tonsillitis. Septicemia and rheumatic fever are examples of acute systemic infections. Examples of intoxication are:

(a) Metabolic disorders like uremia and acidosis,

(b) Poisoning by venoms, drugs and other chemicals.

Tissue necrosis like acute myocardial infarction, burns, necrosis of tumors and bacterial necrosis may also be responsible for leucocytosis. It is also seen in physiological conditions like exercise, emotional stress and menstruation.

Leucopenia denotes overall decrease in WBCs. This may be due to certain drugs, chemicals, shock, cachexia, renal injury and certain infections like miliary tuberculosis, infectious mononucleosis, hepatitis, influenza, measles and malarial fever. Some of the drugs which may be responsible are sulphonamides, antibiotics, analgesics, bone marrow depressants and antithyroid drugs. Leucopenia is possible in pernicious anemia, aplastic anemia, hypersplenism, ionizing radiation, anaphylactic shock and cachexia.

(d) WBC differential count

This helps the clinician to arrive at the differential diagnosis, depending on the variation of the specific type of white blood corpuscles.

Increase in neutrophils is found in (a) pyogenic bacterial infections and inflammations, (b) tissue destruction like trauma, abscess, infarction or burns, (c) metabolic states like diabetic acidosis, uremia, (d) steroid therapy, (e) subsequent to acute hemorrhage, (f) malignancy, and (g) collagen disorders.

Neutropenia - Hepatitis, deficiency in the maturation factor (e.g. pernicious factor, cytotoxic drugs, miliary tuberculosis).

Eosinophilia is the increase in the number of eosinophils. It may be due to parasitic infection, acute allergic reactions, chronic dermatological disorders, hemopoietic diseases like pernicious anemia, leukemia, Hodgkin's disease, ulcerative colitis after irradiation and following splenectomy.

Basophil increase in viral infections, chronic infections, autoimmune diseases, Vitamin B_{12} or folic acid deficiency, lymphatic leukemia, thyrotoxicosis, mumps, infectious mononucleosis and infective hepatitis.

Monocytosis. Bacterial infections like tuberculosis, subacute bacterial endocarditis, typhoid, infectious mononucleosis, monocytic leukemia, collagen disorders.

(e) Erythrocyte sedimentation rate (ESR)

This denotes velocity of sedimentation of RBC per unit of time and is expressed in terms of tuberculosis mm/hour. An increase in ESR can be noticed in chronic and long standing conditions like chronic infections where tissue necrosis is present. Extreme elevation is seen in tuberculosis, malignant lymphomas, myelomas, collagen disorders like rheumatoid arthritis and renal disorders. ESR is useful to detect occult disease or to follow the course of conditions like tuberculosis and rheumatic disease. It is also useful to confirm the diagnosis of (a) myocardial infarction as opposed to angina pectoris and (b) rheumatoid arthritis as opposed to osteoarthritis.

(f) Platelet count

It is increased in

(a) disseminated, advanced or inoperable cases of malignancy,
(b) chronic myelogenous leukemia,
(c) collagen disorders, e.g. rheumatoid arthritis,
(d) iron deficiency anemia.

It is decreased in thrombocytopenic purpura.

(g) Bleeding time

It is prolonged in

(a) thrombocytopenia,
(b) von Willebrand's disease,
(c) increased capillary fragility and
(d) coagulation defects.

(h) Coagulation time

It is prolonged in severe deficiency of any known plasma clotting factors including hemophilia.

(i) Prothrombin time

It is prolonged by the defect in

Factor I (fibrinogen),
Factor II (prothrombin),
Factor V (labile factor),
Factor VII (stable factor) and
Factor X (Stuart-Prower factor).

Prothrombin time is prolonged in

(a) Inadequate Vitamin K,
(b) Poor fat absorption, e.g. obstructive jaundice, chronic diarrhea,
(c) Severe liver damage and Vitamin K deficiency, e.g. hepatitis, cirrhosis, poisoning and obstructive jaundice and
(d) Patients on coumarin type of drug, administered for anticoagulant therapy.

This is very useful for the long-term control of oral anticoagulant therapy. This test is a measure of the length of time, as to when a fibrin clot is formed. It is most useful to demonstrate the defects in stage III of blood coagulation. Prothrombin time is not affected in stage I and II and hence not sensitive to factors VIII, IX, XI and XII.

(j) Capillary fragility test (Hess test)

This is also known as Tourniquet test. It is a rough test for platelet and vascular function. This test is positive in:

(a) Thrombocytopenic purpura, and
(b) Scurvy.

BLOOD CHEMISTRY

(a) Blood calcium

Serum calcium is increased in

(a) hyperparathyroidism,
(b) hematologic malignancies,
(c) excess of Vitamin D intake,
(d) metastatic carcinomas,
(e) acute osteoporosis,
(f) hyperthyroidism and
(g) myxedema.

Serum calcium is decreased in

(a) hypothyroidism - surgical or idiopathic,
(b) malabsorption of calcium and Vitamin D,
(c) nephrotic syndrome,
(d) cachexia,
(e) chronic renal disease with uremia,
(f) bone disorders like osteomalacia, rickets,
(g) starvation and
(h) late pregnancy.

(b) Blood serum cholesterol

It is increased in

(a) biliary obstruction, e.g. stone, carcinoma of the duct,
(b) hypothyroidism,
(c) nephrosis due to chronic nephritis, amyloidosis, systemic lupus erythematosis and
(d) pancreatic disorders like diabetes and chronic pancreatitis.

It is decreased in

(a) severe liver cell damage due to chemicals or drugs,
(b) hyperthyroidism,
(c) malnutrition, e.g. starvation, terminal stage of malignancy, uremia,
(d) hemolytic anemia,
(e) hypochromic anemia and
(f) ACTH and cortisone therapy.

(c) Blood glucose

It is increased in

(a) diabetes mellitus,
(b) Cushing's syndrome (with insulin-resistant diabetes),
(c) increased circulating adrenaline, e.g. stress like emotion, burns, shock and anesthesia.
(d) pancreatitis - acute and chronic and
(e) ACTH administration.

It is decreased in

(a) pancreatic disorders like islet cell tumor and pancreatitis,
(b) hepatic disease, e.g. hepatitis, poisoning, cirrhosis, primary or metastatic hepatic tumors,
(c) endocrine disorders, hypopituitarism, hypothyroidism and early diabetes mellitus,
(d) functional disturbances like post gastrectomy, autonomic nervous system disorders and
(e) miscellaneous, e.g. exogenous insulin, oral hypoglycemic medications, malnutrition and hypothalamic lesions.

(d) Serum alkaline phosphatase

It is increased in

(a) increased deposition of calcium in bone, e.g. hyperparathyroidism, Paget's disease, healing of fractures, osteoblastic bone tumors like osteosarcoma and metastatic carcinomas, osteogenic imperfecta, osteomalacia, rickets, late pregnancy and in growing children.
(b) liver disorders, e.g. any obstruction to the biliary system like stone, carcinoma, swellings of liver - metastatic tumor,

abscess, cyst, amyloidosis, leukemia, hepatitis, adverse reactions to drugs, e.g. chlorpropamide.

(c) hyperthyroidism.
(d) I-V injection of albumin and
(e) patients with myocardial or pulmonary infarction.

It is decreased in

(a) excess Vitamin D intake,
(b) scurvy,
(c) hypothyroidism,
(d) pernicious anemia and
(e) malnutrition.

(e) Serum acid phosphatase

It is increased in

(a) carcinoma prostrate,
(b) operative trauma to prostate,
(c) excessive destruction of platelets, e.g. idiopathic thrombocytopenic purpura,
(d) thromboembolism,
(e) hemolytic crisis,
(f) diseases of bone and liver and
(g) disorders of reticuloendothelial system with bone or liver involvement.

Decrease is not clinically significant.

URINALYSIS

This can be useful when correlated with other clinical signs and laboratory studies. It is said that "the urine reflects not only physiologic system of extracellular fluid but also intrarenal and many extrarenal conditions which may become manifest in the urine." It establishes the values and characteristics related to the following:

1. Volume,
2. Color,
3. Specific gravity,
4. pH,
5. Glucose and protein (albumin),
6. Ketonuria,
7. Bile and
8. Microscopic examination of urinary sediments.

(a) Volume

Average daily urine output is between 1200-1500 ml. Polyuria is excess excretion of urine greater than 2000 ml/day. Oliguria can result in conditions like severe dehydration, vomiting, fever and other modes of fluid loss from the body. Disorders in renal circulation, congestive cardiac failure, hypotension and hemorrhagic state like surgery.

Polyuria results following excessive fluid intake, use of diuretics, diabetes (mellitus and insipidus).

(b) Color and appearance

The following are said to be abnormal

(a) Pale green color - diabetes,
(b) Red - hematuria,
(c) Brownish - bile, blood in urine,
(d) Dark brown or black - extensive melanotic melanoma and
(e) Dark orange - bile or Pyridium in urinary tract.

(c) Specific gravity

This is an useful parameter for measuring renal tubular function. This may not be significant in routine urine analysis due to changes over the course of the day.

Moderate increase may be due to

(a) protein casts (possibly renal disease),
(b) hyaline casts (possible glomerulonephritis, benign essential hypertension and pyelonephritis),
(c) granular casts (possibly autoimmune renal disorder),
(d) dehydration (concentration of urine),
(e) glycosuria and
(f) albuminuria, hematuria.

(d) pH

pH determination is of little value. Increased acidity may be an attempt by the kidneys to compensate for the metabolic acidosis. Metabolic alkalosis and urine standing at room temperature becomes more alkaline.

(e) Glycosuria

Glucose is absent in the normal urine. If blood glucose level is above 120 mg/100ml, kidneys are unable to filter adequately. Thus, excess is passed in urine. The causes are:

(a) diabetes mellitus,
(b) Cushing's syndrome,
(c) infection,
(d) exogenous steroid therapy,
(e) pancreatitis,
(f) increased intracranial pressure,
(g) renal glucosuria without hyperglycemia,
(h) glycosuria of pregnancy,
(i) pheochromocytoma (adrenal tumors) and
(j) emotional stress.

(f) Proteinuria

The presence of negligible amount of protein in the urine is within normal limits. Albumin tends to be the dominant type of protein found in proteinuria. This is found in:

(a) normal physiologic response to severe muscle exertion and pregnancy,
(b) pyrexia,
(c) cardiac failure (with venous congestion),
(d) shock and anemia,
(e) renal disorders and
(f) Bence-Jones proteinuria found in 60-85% of patients with multiple myeloma.

(g) Ketonuria

The presence of ketone bodies (acetone) in the urine of diabetic patient indicates lack of insulin for glucose metabolism. Instead of glucose, the body is metabolizing fat for energy. This is the sign of ketoacidosis and coma.

In non-diabetic patients, ketonuria can occur due to starvation. The process of fat metabolism is responsible for this condition. Serum glucose levels will be low.

(h) Bile

This is not abnormal constituent of urine. Its presence indicates hepatic obstruction, e.g. hepatitis and biliary duct obstruction.

(i) Urinary sediments (microscopic examination)

This is carried out on centrifuged urinary sediment. Normally, urine contains very few cellular elements like RBC, WBC and casts. Their conspicuous presence indicates the following respectively.

RBC. Gross urinary bleeding due to calculi, tumor, acute glomerulonephritis, bleeding disorders, bladder and prostatic disorders. In female patients, bleeding from external genitalia may be responsible for the presence of RBC in urine. Hence, collection of urine from the midstream is recommended.

WBC. May originate from any part of the urinary tract and hence may indicate the possibility of urinary tract disorders.

CASTS. They are protein conglomerations, outlining the shape of the tubules in which casts were formed. They may be of two types - cellular and hyaline. Cellular casts are always significant of some abnormal process. However, their presence must be correlated with other clinical features. The presence of hyaline casts is of less significance.

BONE MARROW ASPIRATION

It may be useful in

1. metastatic tumor,
2. infections, e.g. tuberculosis,
3. granulomas e.g. Hodgkin's disease, sarcoidosis,

4. hematologic diseases, e.g. aplastic anemias, multiple myeloma, myeloid leukemia, agranulocytosis, megaloblastic anemias, hemorrhage, iron deficiency anemia and pernicious anemia and
5. uremia.

CHAPTER 27 Decision Making in Oral Surgery

GENERAL CONSIDERATIONS

Decision making is undoubtedly one of the most important responsibilities of any health professional. Since traditionally many modalities are available, clinicians used to make the decision by using various combinations of one's own past knowledge, subjective perception of the experience and the practiced traditions of the region. In the past, the process of making decisions in such clinical situations was being considered as a natural and inherent part of the practitioner's skill. It was left entirely to the individual to acquire such a skill through one's own experience. This aspect was rarely taught by the teacher to the student. In the recent past, many scientific approaches including computer applications to decision making have been developed in all the academic spheres. In health sciences, decision analysis provides useful information and methods to assist the profession to face the impact of rapid development of science and technology. This is applied to problems related to maintenance of records, diagnosis, clinical judgement and the patient management. It is unfortunate that dentistry has lagged behind in the development and application of such a decision methodology.

Decision making is defined as *"a structured approach to guide a person or a group to workable solutions of a problem to make plans and to evaluate the data."*

Since the modern clinician is overloaded with so much of data, one should realize that the available clinical information by itself cannot establish the diagnosis. It becomes the duty of the health professional to determine the accuracy of the various diagnostic tests and aids. Each clinical finding allows the probable outcome of various diagnostic alternatives to be reviewed. Depending on other findings, diagnostic implications of various tests vary from patient to patient. Therefore, every test must be evaluated to determine its sensitivity and specificity. The term *sensitivity* refers to the proportion of individuals with a clinical entity who test positively for a specific disease, e.g. cultures may be *"true positive"* to the specific causative organism in such patients. On the contrary some may not suffer from the disease but yet the test may be positive. This is called *"false positive"*. Likewise, the term specificity refers to the proportion of individuals who do not have the disease and hence test is negative. This is called *"true negative"*. Even if the test is negative in an individual who suffers from the disease, it is called *"false negative"*. Therefore, *"true positive"* and *"true negative"* results are of value, but *"false positive"* and *"false negative"* results are of doubtful value. Once, sensitivity and specificity of a test are known, it is possible to formulate the possibility statements about the presence of the disease in any patient.

(1) **Design of the decision tree.** The analysis involves the identification of all the available choices, potential outcome of each choice and structuring a model of the decision process. It is helpful to identify various strategies for the management and to analyze the likelihood of the outcome of the surgery that is adopted. This also helps to evaluate the feasibility, utility and relative worth of various procedures so that the practitioner is able to come to a logical conclusion.

(2) **Sensitivity analysis.** It allows the practitioner to assess the potential impact of changing specific criteria for the decision analysis. The rationale is to consider the consequence of different choices.

(3) **Utilities assessment.** It is helpful to measure the relative versus apparent value of an outcome. Recently, clinical decisions analysis has developed better methods to permit patient's attitudes and values to be incorporated into utility measures.

(4) **Interpretation of the analysis.** If the difference in the expected utility between diagnostic or therapeutic options is small and hence clinically insignificant, it is termed as *"close call"*. Development of understanding in close call helps to define the kind of data needed for the decision analysis and decision making process.

(5) **Automation.** Clinical applications of decision analysis were limited by the time factor involved in calculations. Now, programs are readily available to analyze the decision process which reduces the burden of manual calculations and sensitivity analysis. Such programs are always designed to be flexible and user friendly. Such examples include software on orthognathic surgery, cleft lip and palate etc.

Thus, it is quite evident that the successful outcome of the clinical practice rests with proper decision making. The consistency depends on the nature of diagnostic data. Some may even question the quality and accuracy of the unaided clinical judgement. The present day practitioner is faced with the dilemma as to whether to make an objective decision or to make decision on subjective data alone. In practice, judgement and decision making shall not depend entirely on subjective evaluation or through the automation process alone. However, a word of caution is essential to ensure that automation is one of the aids in diagnosis and decision making but it is not to replace clinical evaluation of the patients. The clinician must also realize that one is bound to face the impact of changes in epidemiology shifting demographic findings and rapid advancement of technology in the practice. (Please refer to chapter 28 for further details).

Application in clinical practice

Decision studies have been reported on diagnosis, treatment planning and disease prediction. The studies included those which applied formal decision making methods to (a) problems of diagnosis, (b) decision making methods, (c) techniques applicable to treatment planning, (d) choice of treatment and (e) the implications of decision analysis for predicting the incidence of the disease. Computer-assisted decision-making is relatively new in oral surgery practice. It is built on the informations collected during the previous decades. The step beyond applying computers is to apply them to treatment planning. The purpose of formal analysis is to enhance understanding and description of a problem and also to aid the decision maker in being comprehensive to search for a preferred course of action. The utilities analysis will benefit by the application of decision methods. Although computers cannot replace the skill and knowledge of outstanding clinicians, there is no doubt that they will become an integral part of oral surgery practice in the years to come.

To illustrate, the decision tree is drawn on hemorrhage as a model. The oral surgery trainee is adviced to work out the decision trees on the following aspect depending on the personal surgical capability, available facilities and scope of oral surgery concerning diagnosis and treatment planning.

1. Dentoalveolar injuries,
2. Unerupted teeth,
3. Periapical lesions,
4. Craniofacial pain,
5. Orthognathic problems,
6. Radiolucent lesions in the jaws,
7. Unconscious patient,
8. Preprosthetic surgery,
9. Ulcers of the oral cavity,
10. Radioopaque lesions of the jaws and
11. Inability to open the mouth.

Recent Innovations and Changing Concepts

In the new millennium, when we examine the recent past, we can identify a number of unprecedented discoveries in the health sciences. The field of oral and maxillofacial surgery has been very dynamic. The oral surgeons have been quick to apply many of the newer techniques of other specialties successfully. Adapting a new technique does not mean discarding the existing technique. It only means, that the new technique is to be considered as one of the viable alternative treatment options. Their efficacy will be known only after extensive clinical trials. The following are some of them, worthy of serious considerations.

1. Cyanoacrylates in wound closure

They were first introduced in 1949. In 1960s, they were introduced experimentally as wound adhesives. Special surgical team forseferace was sent to Vietnam, trained and equipped to use cyanocrylate adhesives. A spray over the wounds was found to arrest bleeding. The possibilities were immediately seized by the medical community of Europe and Far East. Today, the adhesive property of **n-Butyl 2-Cyanoacrylate** is found useful in a variety of clinical applications. It is biocompatible and has the ability to hold tightly the living tissues. Thus, it helps to keep the wound edges closely bound together, thereby allowing primary wound healing. The process of polymerization is completed within a minute or so. It is possible to achieve barely visible and cosmetically faultless skin and mucosa closure resulting in minimal scarring. The active ingredient exerts a powerful hemostatic effect. Since it is self-sterilized and has bacteriostatic effect, it helps to prevent superadded infection of the wounds.

It is commercially available in India with the brand name - **Nectacryl.** They are derivatives of acrylic acid in its monomer form. It polymerizes quickly as it comes in contact with water or body moisture. The contents of the ampoule is meant for external use only and not to be injected. The manufactures have advocated a few *Do's* and *Don'ts.*

(a) The ampoule is supplied with 0.25 ml, 0.50 ml and 1.0 ml of blue colored fluid. It is for single use only. The residual material must be discarded. Therefore, depending on the use, the packing is to be chosen.
(b) It should be applied over the approximated edges of the wound and not inside the wound.
(c) The sealed area should not be washed with water at least for four days.
(d) It should not be used to close the infected

wounds.

(e) Correction of the wound edges cannot be done once the adhesive has dried.

(f) It is supplied in liquid form. Therefore, the condition can be assessed before opening the adhesive ampoule. Even if it is viscous, it must be discarded.

(g) It should be stored below 15°C but not to be stored in the freezer.

(h) It is relatively safe since it is better tolerated. No toxic reactions have been observed.

However, due to improper applications, side effects of local nature have been observed. Very occasionally, allergic reactions have been observed.

2. T.M. joint arthroscopy

This is a minimally invasive surgical procedure, used to visualize, diagnose and manage the problems of the temporomandibular joint. The surgeon makes a small preauricular incision to insert a pencil-sized instrument which contains a small lens and a fibre optics lighting system to illuminate and magnify the intraarticular structures. By attaching the arthroscope to a miniature telecamera, it displays the image of the joint on the television screen.

The diagnosis of the temporomandibular joint disorders is difficult for a variety of reasons.

(a) Joint position below the skull base complicates clinical and radiographic examinations.

(b) The close relationship between the insertion of the jaw muscles and joint structures complicates the distinction between the clinical features, caused by muscular hyperactivity due to the organic joint disease.

This procedure involves direct visual inspection of the internal structures of the joint. It forms an important adjunct to other techniques like tomography, arthrography and MRI. The risk of complications is extremely low and diagnostic accuracy is high.

Indications

(a) *Disc derangement* with intermittent locking called *closed lock* is an indication. Arthroscopy reveals the typical changes in texture and vascularity of the posterior disc attachment.

(b) *Osteoarthrosis:* In different imaging techniques, it is difficult to detect the various stages of the disease process. But, arthroscopy reveals the different stages of the disease and provides the possibility for biopsy. It is also possible for the simultaneous irrigation of the joint cavity to remove the debris and other inflammatory products called *lavage*.

(c) *Posttraumatic problems:* Fracture of the condylar neck is associated with damage of the soft tissues. In these cases, arthroscopy is useful to assess the intraarticular damage.

Contraindications

It includes infections of the T.M. joint and extreme impairment of the joint mobility.

How to perform?

(a) Prior to arthroscopy, radiographic examination must be done to reveal the joint position, thickness of the roof of the glenoid fossa and translation capacity of the disc-condyle complex.

(b) Under local anesthesia, the joint puncture is performed in the safe area between the temporal vessels posteriorly and the superior branches of the facial nerve anteriorly.

(c) The lateral contour of the glenoid fossa is palpated and the puncture points are selected. A guideline from the posterior midpoint on tragus to the lateral canthus is drawn and puncture points are located below the line and 10 to 20 mm anteriorly along that line.

(d) Mouth is kept open to create enlargement of the posterior joint space.

(e) Small vertical incision is made through which, puncture is performed in a medial and slightly anterosuperior direction. Slight resistance is encountered before the lateral capsule is perforated.

(f) Sharp trocar is then exchanged with blunt one and the sheath is further introduced into the joint. Video camera is attached and the entrance is confirmed through the telescope.

(g) Second portal is then created approximately 10 mm anterior and 5 mm inferior to the arthroscopic sheath outflow.

(h) Arthroscopic examination is performed with 30 degrees wide angled telescope. It covers the major part of the superior compartment of the joint. Posterior half of the inferior joint compartment can also be covered after redirection.

(i) Joint cavity is thoroughly irrigated to remove small blood clots. Cannula is then removed and the incision is closed and dressing is applied. Patient is placed on a soft diet for a few days.

Arthroscopic surgery

This is difficult to perform unless one gains experience in diagnostic arthroscopy and open joint surgery followed by training through well-designed hands-on courses. Second portal is necessary for the insertion of the surgical instruments.

Indications include biopsy, lavage, lysis of adhesions and smoothening procedures. The quantum of surgery and recovery time depends on the complexity of the problem. Occasionally, during the surgery, surgeon may discover that the disease or injury cannot be treated adequately through arthroscopy alone. In such instances, open surgery of the joint alone will be helpful. Possible complications are infection, phlebitis, excessive edema, bleeding, damage to the nerve and breakage of instruments. Inspite of the problems and complexity of the procedures, the following distinct advantages are the positive aspects:

(a) Less invasive procedures than open surgery of the joint.

(b) Can be performed as an outpatient procedure.

More and more usage of this procedure alone will provide the clue regarding the viability, when compared to the other established and conventional procedures.

3. Endoscopic surgery of the maxillary sinus (Fig 28.1)

Profound knowledge of the anatomy of the lateral nasal wall in the area of the middle meatus is essential to understand the etiology and pathophysiology of sinusitis. Infundibulum is the "bottleneck" of the entire drainage and ventilation of the paranasal sinuses. The vicious circle is initiated by an infundibulum blockage. Interruption of ventilation and drainage caused by ostial obstruction leads to stagnation of the secretary product and damage to the ancillary function of the respiratory epithelium with consequent inflammation. The inflamed mucosa in turn contributes to the ostial obstruction, thus closing the circle. The anterior ethmoid bone is the key factor since infundibulum is assigned to it. The infection begins at this stage.

Diagnosis of this condition has progressed enormously due to the development of rigid and flexible endoscopes. The endoscopes permit excellent internal vision in the middle meatus so that even the small polyps which block infundibulum can be

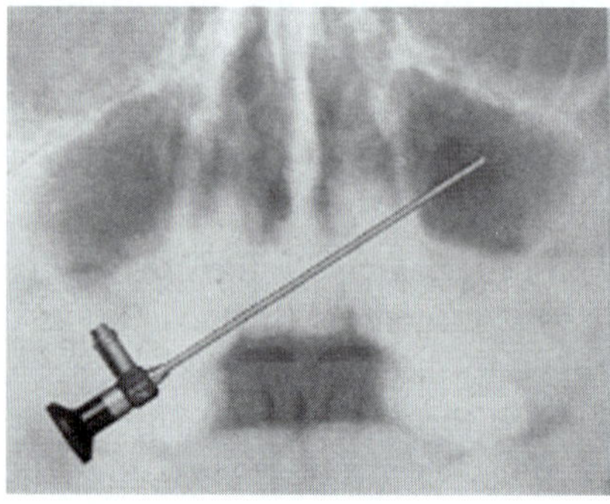

Fig. 28.1 Endoscopy of maxillary sinus.

recognized. Scopy of the interior of the maxillary sinuses provides information about the condition of the mucosa and the ostium of the maxillary sinus.

The most important additional method of examination is computed tomography, which has practically replaced the conventional radiographic diagnosis. In the coronary projection, infundibulum and anterior ethmoid cells are clearly visualized.

Based on this knowledge, it is now established that the aim of the treatment is to restore ventilation and drainage of the blocked paranasal sinuses by a procedure called infundibulotomy.

From the widened infundibulum, all the other paranasal sinuses can be operated and treated surgically.

4. Advances in dental anesthesia

It is an established fact that patients develop fear-phobia due to the painful needle prick. Even though efforts are taken to make the needle entry through the mucosa least painful, the very sight of the needle is enough to induce the fear. Therefore, a "needle-free injector" has been introduced. A forceful jet is introduced into the tissues at selected sites to achieve anesthesia. (Fig. 28.2)

The various sites for this technique are as follows:

(a) *Mandibular foramen:* Two injections are necessary. Inject anterior to the foramen where the needle is usually first inserted. Then inject the jet in close proximity to the foramen.

(b) *Mental foramen:* Inject directly over the mental foramen area.

(c) *Lingual region of the mandible:* Inject the interradicular area towards the bony underlying structures.

(d) *Nasopalatine foramen:* Make two injections, one on each side of the incisive papilla.

(e) For other areas of the maxilla, repeat the injection procedure just like anesthesia with needle injection.

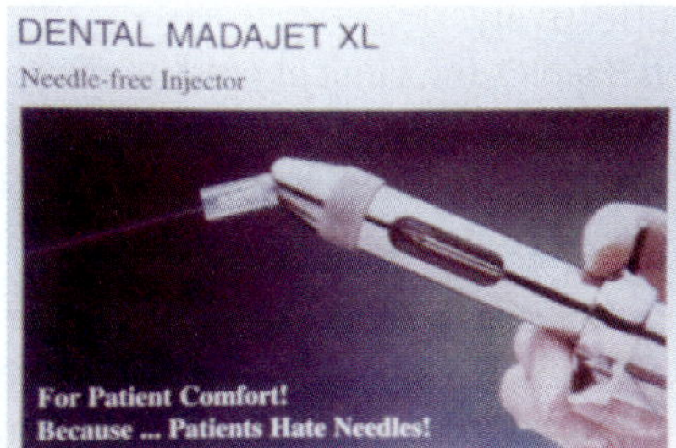

Fig. 28.2 Dental Madajet: Needle free injector.

Advantages

(a) Fear and trauma associated with traditional needle injections are eliminated.

(b) Prevents cross infection since needle prick is avoided.

(c) Anesthesia is instant and effective.

(d) Can be used in all age groups of patients.

5. Antioxidants in oral and maxillofacial surgery practice

Oxidative stress

Oxygen, the most critical nutrient for life, is the main source of free radicals. The free radicals are highly reactive oxygen fragments that are created by normal chemical processes in the cells. During the cellular respiration that creates energy, some oxygen molecules are converted into "free radicals" when one of the electrons in the molecules is lost. The only way it can replace the missing electron is to take it from another molecule. Then, that healthy cell will be damaged leading to a number of diseases including tumor. Such increased production of free radicals in the body is known as *oxidative stress*.

The free radicals are inherently unstable containing "extra" energy. In order to reduce their energy load, free radicals react with certain cells of the body and interfere with the cell's ability to function normally. If free radicals are left undestroyed, they would enter into oxidative reactions with vital cellular components containing lipids, proteins, nucleic acid and carbohydrate.

Human body which has to endure the constant production of free radicals also has natural protection from their harmful oxidizing effects - *antioxidants*. The body makes a series of antioxidant enzymes that can neutralize these free radicals. Oxidants, the byproducts of human metabolism, are believed to deliver damaging blows to the cells's DNA. Repair enzymes cut out much of the damage most of the times. If the attack of the oxidants on cells outpace the ability of the enzymes to remove the lesions, the cumulative damage is believed to be a major factor in the development of many lesions, particularly age-related lesions like joint problems and cardiovascular disease.

The scientists have pointed out that the disease prevention potential of the antoxidant properties are found in certain nutrients like Vitamin A, C and E, beta carotine and minerals. In other words, free radicals (highly reactive species that have the potential to oxidize biological molecules including proteins, lipids and DNA) are capable of creating imbalance between the "oxidative stress" and "antioxidative defence" resulting in many diseases like inflamma-tory conditions of the joints, neurological disorders, diabetes, cancer and cardiovascular diseases. Any advanced antioxidant provides full therapeutic concentration of all known micronutrient vitamins and all known antioxidant minerals like copper, manganese, zinc and selenium.

It is now an established fact that the anti-oxidant shields against cardiovascular disease - particularly-retardation of atherogenic process, maintenance of optimal blood pressure and reduction of the risk of non-fatal heart attacks. In cases of potential cancer-risk persons, it reduces the cancer risk for smokers and 13% risk reduction in cancer deaths. It also shields against neurological diseases by enhancing the recovery of the injured cells and in Parkinson's disease. It is also believed to play a role of "wonder bodyguard" in health and disease conditions in cases of diabetic nephropathy and diabetic retinopathy, cataract, rheumatoid arthritis, inflammatory bowel disease and a host of degenerative diseases. There are many preparations available in the market. Recommended dose is one or two capsules a day as a prophylactic or therapeutic dose.

6. Evidence-based clinical practice

We live in an age of information, innovation and change. The decision making in clinical practice based on good quality evidence should lead to more effective and efficient treatment. The use of techniques or treatments based on the views of authority, rather than evidence, may lead to the wrong treatment being performed. Evidence-based clinical practice is a process that restructures the way in which we think about clinical problems. It is an approach to clinical problem solving that has evolved from self-directed and problem-based approach to the learning rather than the traditional didactic form. This is the process of making decisions based on known evidence. The first stage is to identify the clinical problem. Following this, evidence to help solve the problems must be located. Having identified a clinical problem, there are four basic routes to find good evidence. They include:

(a) To enquire other professionals.
(b) To refer a standard textbook.
(c) To find out a relevant reference article.
(d) To utilize bibliographical database like Medline etc.

The advantages of evidence-based clinical practice are:

(a) It improves the effective use of research evidence in clinical practice.
(b) It uses the available resources more effectively.
(c) It enables the clinical practitioner to monitor and develop the clinical performance.
(d) It relies on evidence rather than authority for clinical decision making.

To use this approach, there is an urgent need for the development of new skills to identify the clinical problems, literature search and critical appraisal.

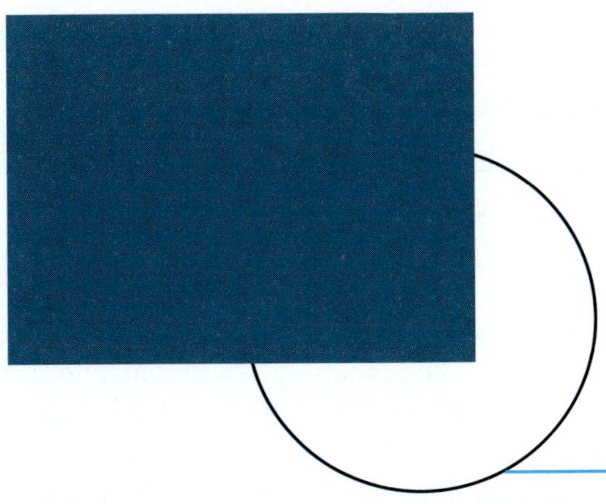

Appendices

Appendix I. DENTOALVEOLAR INJURIES
[Protocol for management]

1. Uncomplicated, crown fracture involving only enamel	(a) In clean fractures, crown fragment can be reattached using dentine-bonding agent. (b) With acid-etch technique, reconstruct the crown with composite resin.
2. If dentine is involved	Seal the dentine tubules and restore it with composite resin.
3. Pulp exposure	(a) Pulp capping if pulp horn is involved. (b) Pulpotomy and then restore the crown. (c) Pulp extirpation and RCT filling.
4. If epithelial attachment is involved	(a) Removal of loose crown fragment and supragingival restoration after rough edges along the fracture surface below the gingiva is smoothened. (b) Removal of the crown fragment, supplemented by gingivectomy, osteotomy and subsequent restoration with postcrown. (c) Removal of crown fragment, with surgical/orthodontic extrusion of the root.
5. Root fracture	(a) Reposition of the tooth fragment and splinting until hard tissue callus is formed. (b) In severely extruded root fracture, under local anesthesia, root fragment is guided to its place. Coronal fragment is endodontically treated and root canal is sealed.
6. Concussion and subluxation	Split the tooth and release the occlusal interference by selective grinding of the opposing tooth.
7. Extrusion and lateral luxation	Reposition and splinting.
8. Intrusion	(a) If the tooth is with immature root formation, spontaneous eruption is expected. (b) In other cases, orthodontic extrusion.
9. Avulsion	Replantation with or without RCT.
10. Alveolar process is also fractured	Repositioning and splinting. Check for occlusal interference
11. If primary teeth are injured	Assess the damage, and periodically monitor

Appendix II. DECISION MAKING IN POSTOPERATIVE BLEEDING

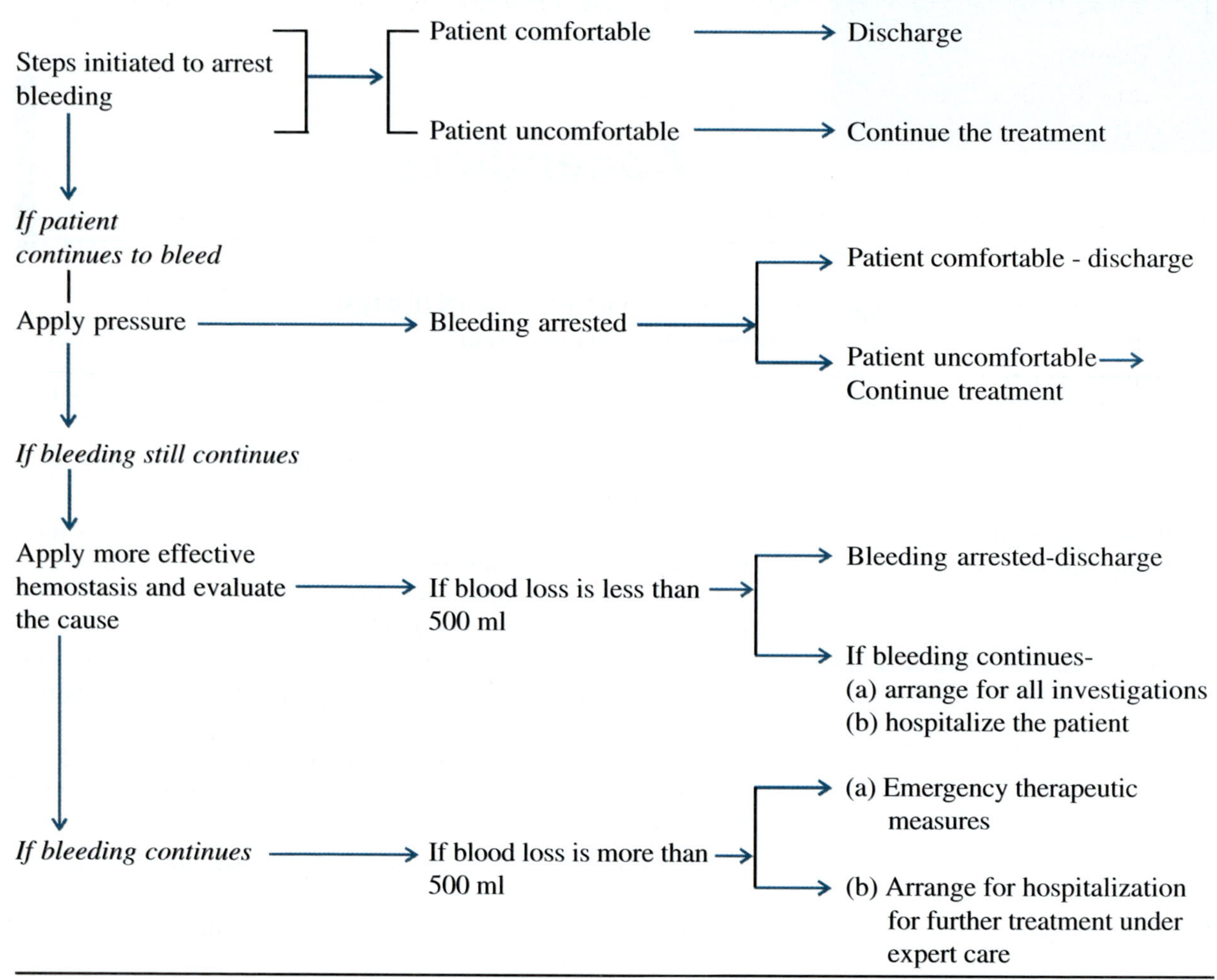

Appendix III. GENERAL PRINCIPLES OF CANCER THERAPY

1. In stage II, III and IV of oral cancers, survival rate is low with single modality of treatment.

   Reason:

   (a) Persistant recurrence at the primary site.

   (b) Regional nodes involvement.

   Hence, initial therapeutic measures must be vigorous.

2. Surgery (in well differentiated lesions) and radiotherapy (in undifferentiated lesions) are the primary modes of treatment.

3. Combined modality therapy (surgery and radiation) offers significantly higher survival rate.

4. Timing of combined modality therapy is of great importance. Hence careful planning is essential on the following factors

   (a) Margins and extent of the lesion.

   (b) Regional lymph nodes involvement.

5. Maintain proper records of the lesion including:

   (a) Accurate description.

   (b) Diagram or photograph outlining the lesion.

6. Surgery is more effective for radiation failures rather than radiation for surgical failures.

Guidelines for Oral Cancer Therapy

Staging	*At the primary site*	*Management of regional lymph nodes*
Stage I - $T_2 N_0$	Surgery or radiation	Periodical review
Stage II - $T_2 N_0$	Surgery and radiation (chemotherapy optional)	Radiotherapy-pre or postsurgical or either surgery or radiation
Stage III - T_3N_0 $T_1 N_1$ $T_2 N_1$ $T_3 N_1$	Pre or postsurgical radiation with chemotherapy	Pre or postsurgical radiation
Stage IV - T_1 T_2 or T_3 with N_2 N_3 and M_1	-do-	-do

Appendix IV. COMMON DRUG INTERACTIONS IN ORAL SURGICAL PRACTICE

Drug	Interacting drug	Drug interaction
1. Antihistamines	CNS depressants	Increased drowsiness and sedation.
2. Salicylates	1. Anticoagulants (dicoumarin)	1. Increased risk of bleeding.
	2. Antacids	2. Premature release of aspirin. Therefore, interval of 1-2 hours is advocated.
	3. Corticosteroids	3. Increase risk of gastrointestinal bleeding.
	4. Methotrexate	4. Increased risk of methotrexate toxicity.
	5. Oral hypoglycemics	5. Potentiates the hypoglycemic drugs effect.
	6. Phenytoin	6. Increased effect of antiepileptics.
3. Atropine	Alcohol	Impaired motor performance and increased drowsiness.
4. Carbamazepine	1. Alcohol	1. Depressed CNS.
	2. Barbiturates, doxycycline, oral hypo glycemics and steroids	2. Retarded effect of the drug.
	3. Erythromycin	3. Increased carbamazepine isoniazid plasma level resulting in sedation.
5. Corticosteroids	1. Antidiabetic drugs	1. Corticosteroids may exacerbate diabetic state by the hypoglycemic action.
	2. Antihypertensives	2. Antagonism due to fluid retention.
	3. Oral contraceptives	3. Increased antiinflammatory response to topical steroids.
6. Cotrimoxazole	1. Diuretics	1. Increased risk of thrombocytopenia in the elderly.
	2. Anticoagulants, antlepileptic and oral hypoglycemics	2. Potentiated action of these agents.

7. Diazepam	CNS depressants	Intensified sedative effects.
8. Doxycycline	1. Penicillins 2. Barbiturates and antiepileptics	1. Reduced effect of penicillin. 2. Possibility of reduced plasma concentration of doxycycline.
9. Metronidazole	1. Alcohol 2. Antiepileptics 3. Anticoagulants 4. Barbiturates	1. Antagonism, therefore alcohol must be avoided. 2. Increased risk of toxicity of phenytoin. 3. Potentiated anticoagulant effect. 4. Reduced plasma level of metronidazole.
10. Penicillins	Oral contraceptives	Increased bleeding, possibly with contraceptive failure.
11. Tetracyclines	1. Oral contraceptives 2. Oral hypoglycemic agents 3. Methotrexate	1. Increased bleeding due to contraceptive failure. 2. Increased hypoglycemic effect. 3. Increased methotrexate toxicity.

Appendix V. INABILITY TO OPEN THE MOUTH

I. **Trismus** (indicates muscle spasm)

Type	*Etiology*
1. Odontogenic	- Infective (a) Periodontitis. (b) Pericoronitis. (c) Space infections. (d) Parotitis. - Myofascial pain dysfunction syndrome due to (a) eruption of teeth and (b) traumatic occlusion.
2. Traumatic	- Fractured teeth and jaws.
3. Neoplastic	- Tumors eroding the muscles of mastication.
4. Neurotoxic	- Tetanus.
5. Psychogenic	- Hysteria.
6. Pharmacological	- Phenothiazine group of drugs.

II. **Pseudoankylosis** (indicates mechanical interference)

1. Traumatic	- Depressed fracture of the zygomatic arch resulting in the mechanical obstruction to the coronoid process.
2. Hyperplastic	1. Hyperplasia of the coronoid process. 2. Relative hyperplasia of the coronoid due to the short ramus or condylar deformity.
3. Neoplastic	- Neoplasms of the coronoid process.
4. Miscellaneous	1. Myositis ossificans. 2. Submucous fibrosis.

III. **False Ankylosis** (indicates the extracapsular causes)

1. Infective	- Periarticular suppurations.
2. Traumatic	1. Periarticular fibrosis. 2. Dislocation of longer duration.
3. Neoplastic	- Neoplasm of the periarticular tissues (capsule).
4. Miscellaneous	- Periarticular fibrosis following irradiation.

IV. **True Ankylosis** (Indicates the intraarticular causes)

1. Infective	1. Regional spread of infection from middle ear (otitis media) and osteomyelitis of the mandible. 2. Hematogenous spread
2. Traumatic	1. Intracapsular fracture resulting in hemarthrosis. 2. Penetrating wounds into the joint. 3. Birth injury during forceps delivery.
3. Systemic	1. Juvenile arthritis 2. Rheumatoid arthritis 3. Ankylosing spondylitis
4. Neoplastic	- Primary or metastatic tumors of the condyle

Appendix VI. SURGICAL ACCESS TO THE T.M. JOINT

1. Preauricular.
2. Supraauricular.
3. Postauricular.
4. Endaural.
5. Horizontal-along the zygomatic arch.
6. Submandibular.
7. Intraoral.
8. Transcranial.

Appendix VII. PREPROSTHETIC SURGERY

Classification of Alveolar Ridges

Class I	The height of the alveolar ridge is adequate but the width is inadequate. It may also exhibit significant undercut areas.
Class II	Ridge is deficient in height and width, e.g. knife-ridge.
Class III	Ridge is resorbed upto the level of the basal bone.
Class IV	Ridge resorption into the basal bone resulting in concave ridge. It is severe enough that it may even predispose to pathological fracture.

Treatment

1. Patients with class I and II ridges can be treated by any one of the preprosthetic corrective surgery like vestibuloplasty or alveoloplasty.
2. Patients with class III and IV ridges usually require augmentation or reconstructive preprosthetic surgery.

Appendix VIII. COMPARISON OF IMPORTANT NEURALGIAS

Factor	*Vth nerve*	*VIIth nerve*	*IXth nerve*	*Postherpetic*
1. Terminology	Trigeminal	Ramsay-Hunt syndrome	Glossopharyngeal	Postherpetic
2. Incidence	Common	Very rare	Rare	Uncommon
3. Onset of pain	4th decade	3-5th decade	4th decade	6th decade
4. Site involved	Unilateral, one or more branches are involved	External auditory canal and auricle	Unilateral around the base of the tongue, tonsil and soft palate	Confined to 5th dermatome
5. Duration of pain	Seconds to minutes	Seconds to minutes	Seconds to minutes	Chronic
6. Character of pain	Severe stabbing or burning	Severe stabbing	Less severe boring or burning	Burning with hyperesthesia
7. Effect on the trigger zone	Tactile stimulation precipitates the attack	No effect	Swallowing or touching provokes the attack	No effect
8. Other features	Paroxysmal attack	Associated with tinnitus and vertigo, cardiac syncope	Associated with hypotension, bradycardia	Herpes zoster outbreak precedes this condition
9. Medication to relieve the pain	Carbamazepine	Carbamazepine	Carbamazepine	Antiinflammatory drugs and analgesics
10. Other methods of treatment	Alcohol injection, peripheral neurectomy, microsurgery	Neurosurgery	Neurosurgery	Nerve blocks

Appendix IX. PATHOGENESIS OF PERICORONITIS

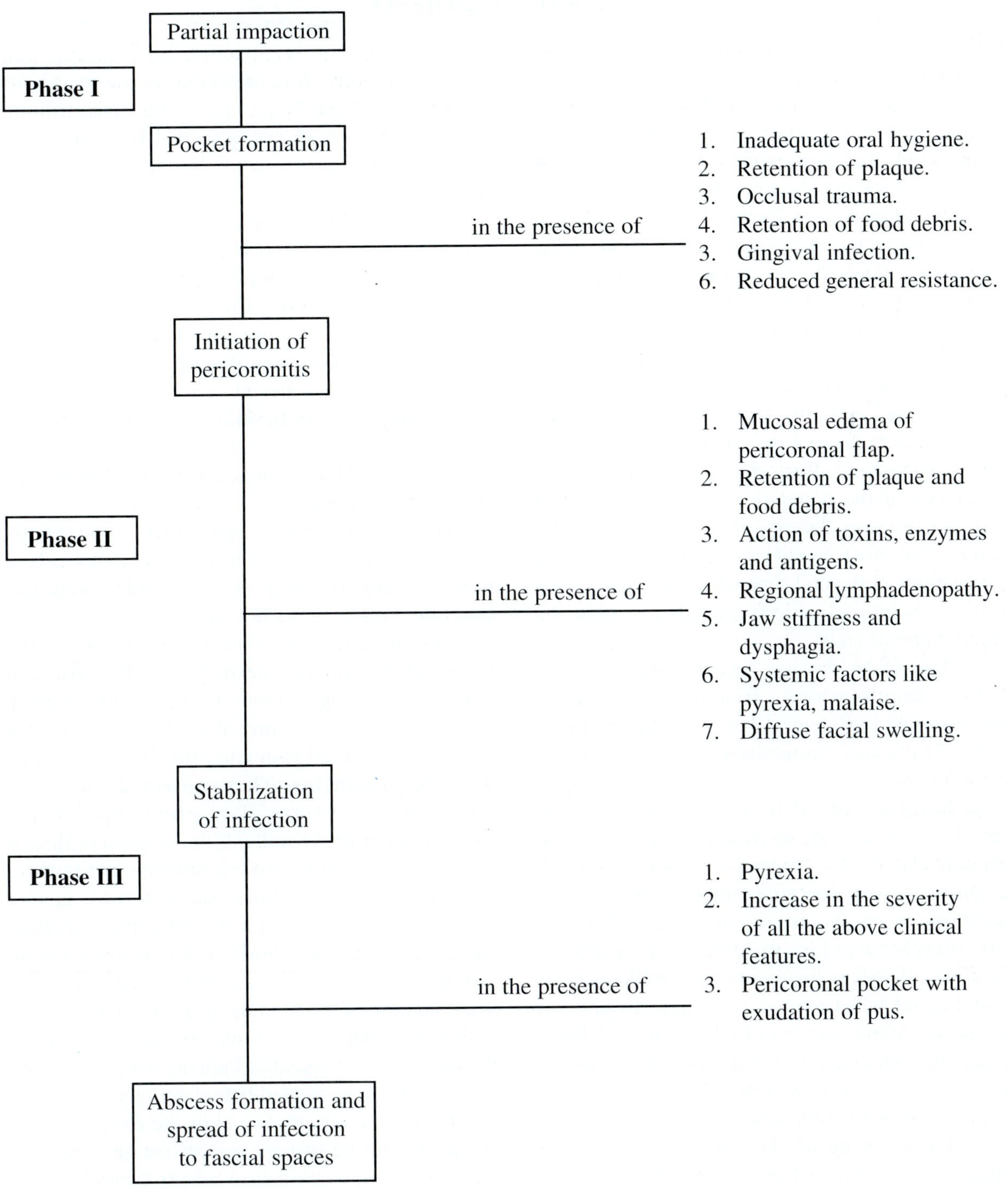

Appendix X. PREVENTION OF COMPLICATIONS ASSOCIATED WITH GENERAL ANESTHESIA

Development of general anesthesia in oral surgery was hampered mainly because, maintenance of anesthesia and airway become difficult due to the location of the oral cavity at the entrance of the airway. In this direction, endotracheal anesthesia has contributed safety to anesthetic procedures. Secondly, advancement includes the utilization of combination of anesthetic agents like short acting barbiturates, diazepam as a minor tranquilizer and halothane as the inhalation anesthetic agent. However, sometimes it may lead to complications during (a) induction (b) maintenance, (c) recovery and (d) postoperative phase. The general anesthetic techniques and complications and the role of the oral surgeons to prevent the complications must be clearly understood. With the increase in the life expectancy of the population, more and more of aged patients over the age of 50 years attend the clinics for oral surgery. Hence, it is the responsibility of the oral surgeon to take precautions to avoid the complications and also to plan the surgery appropriately.

1. **Age.** Older the age, higher is the incidence of the complications. Hence, preoperative evaluation of the general health status assumes greater significance, particularly in patients over the age of 40 years.

2. **Surgical risk.** Patients over the age of 60 years and those who are medically compromised are generally classified as "high-risk" group. Hence, all the efforts must be directed to improve the systemic conditions except in case of emergencies. Patients with cardiovascular problems, respiratory conditions, diabetes, liver and renal problems must be stabilized before subjecting them to general anesthesia. Administration of inhalation anesthesia in patients with respiratory infections may result in increased secretion which might disturb the ventilation or may predispose to pneumonia.

3. **Anesthetic agents.** Halothane produces more complications during induction or maintenance, e.g. tachycardia, supraventricular arrhythmias and muscular rigidity. It is preferable to use the agents with minimal inhibitary action on myocardium, particularly in high risk patients. It is safer and therefore mandatory to use monitoring devices during anesthesia.

4. **Surgical procedure.** Resection of malignant turnouts form the high levels of surgical stress, particularly when performed in aged patients. In temporomandibular joint ankylosis, trismus complicates the induction of anesthesia and maintenance of airway during anesthesia until mouth opening is achieved.

5. **Stage of anesthesia.** Complications must be considered under the following phases: (a) Induction, (b) Maintenance, (c) Recovery phase, (d) Postoperative phase.

During induction. Anesthetist exposes the laryngeal opening gently to pass the endotracheal tube smoothly. Bleeding, secretion and trismus may interfere with the induction process.

During the maintenance phase. It is the responsibility of the anesthetist to diagnose and manage the complications. However, the surgeon must be able to recognize them by observing the monitor so that surgeon can effectively cooperate with the anesthetist. They are supraventricular arrhythmias, ventricular premature beats, tachycardia or bradycardia. If the surgeon infiltrates the surgical fields with solutions containing adrenaline for hemostasis, surgeon must ensure before starting surgery that no arrhythmias develop. Hence it is better to wait for a few minutes before commencing surgery. Excessive secretion or accumulation of blood in the pharynx may interfere with airway. Hence, care must be taken to aspirate the collections frequently. Patients with respiratory infection must be treated before surgery.

If there is any need to shift the patient's head frequently during surgery, anesthetist must be forewarned so that endotracheal tube is securely fixed.

Alteration in body temperature, muscular rigidity and phlebitis are the possible complications postoperatively.

During the recovery phase, vomiting soon after the removal of the endotracheal tube may result in asphyxia or aspiration pneumonia. To prevent these complications, it is safer to aspirate the stomach contents through nasogastric tube preoperatively. Bleeding inside the oropharynx also must be closely monitored. Dyspnea, hypertension and delay in regaining consciousness are the other problems. Sometimes, infants may develop subglottic edema soon after the removal of the endotracheal tube. Such infantile subglottic edema may lead to obstruction of the airway. If it develops, corticosteroids must be administered and the patient must be monitored carefully. If there is severe airway obstruction, reintubation may be required.

During the postoperative phase, if complications related to airway like dyspnea, arrhythmias, hypertension and hyperthermia develop, the condition must be diagnosed so that appropriate treatment can be instituted promptly.

Frequently, one may encounter complications, if the patient is not properly evaluated or not hospitalized. Just because the surgery is of short duration, the dental surgeon must not perform oral surgery under general anesthesia as an outpatient procedure. However minor it may be, unless the patient is hospitalized and properly evaluated, surgery should not be undertaken under general anesthesia. If the patient recovers quickly and does not develop any of these anesthetic complications, then the patient can be discharged. After all, success in day-care anesthesia depends on the proper selection of patients.

Set-up of the operation theatre for oral surgery. Since most of the cases are *"clean-contaminated"* in the field of oral surgery, prophylactic antibiotic coverage and premedication are given before the commencement of surgery. The patient is brought inside the operation theatre, with I.V. dripset in position so that intravenous route is readily available for the administration of drugs. It has become a standard procedure to place all the leads of monitoring devices, securely fixed, before anesthetizing the patients.

Anesthesia. Once the anesthetist is satisfied that adequate level of anesthesia is maintained, the endotracheal tube and the connecting ducts are properly fixed and positioned, usually between the first and the second assistant. The connections to the anesthetic equipment are placed at a fairly safe distance. The patient's contralateral arm is kept abducted at right angles to the body away from the surgical field. This will provide ready access to the anesthetist for the intravenous route and the monitoring devices. Even though anesthetist will be stationed away from the patient, he/she be located in the vicinity of the outstretched left arm of the patient. At the time of draping, anesthetist should be available, to help the surgeon and at the same time to ensure that anesthetic and monitoring connections are undisturbed. If the electrocautery machine, suction and drilling equipment are to be used, they must be placed behind and between the surgeon and the staff nurse. The connections must be securely placed separately after ensuring that they are in working condition. The foot controls must be within the easy access of the surgeon or to one of the assistants. It is better to keep two waste disposal buckets, one on either side of the patient. A polythene bag can be kept in the open position inside the bucket, so that once surgery is over, bag along with the contents can be transported without spilling them during transit.

Position of the members of the surgical team. For the right handed operation procedures, the surgeon stands on the right side of the head and neck, with first assistant standing opposite to the surgeon and the second assistant at the head end of the patient on the left side of the surgeon. The staff nurse will be on the right side of the surgeon and the patient. Since abdomen should not bear the weight of equipment and instruments, a Mayo's table is adjusted above the abdomen so that, the necessary instruments for immediate use could be arranged here. However, the main instruments' trolley must be on the right side of the nurse with all the instruments etc. arranged properly on the trolley.

Position and draping. Patient is positioned on the operation table in such a way that neck is extended. To facilitate this position, a sand bag may be placed under the shoulder to raise the shoulder level. Otherwise, head end of the operation table is lowered. Since it is in 2 sections, head-board drops atleast 35° so as to provide adequate neck extension. When the patient is placed on the operating table, proper care is taken to ensure that the arms are not left unsupported. If the arm is allowed to hang out of the operation table, the pressure at the elbow level may result in ulnar palsy. A cap should be placed to conceal the hair.

Head end of the patient can be draped by placing two towels together below the head. One towel is left covering the head end of the table, while the other towel is used to drape around the patient's head leaving the surgical field uncovered. Then a sheet is used to cover the rest of the body of the patient. The draped linens are securely fixed with towel clips leaving only the surgical fields open. After instilling eye drops, the eyelids are secured with adhesive tape so that cornea is prevented from any injury or getting dried up. Some surgeons like to cover the eyelids with wet-gauge pad to protect the eyes. The surgical field is finally scrubbed with antiseptics. Now the patient is ready for the surgical procedure.

Appendix XI. MASSETER HYPERTROPHY

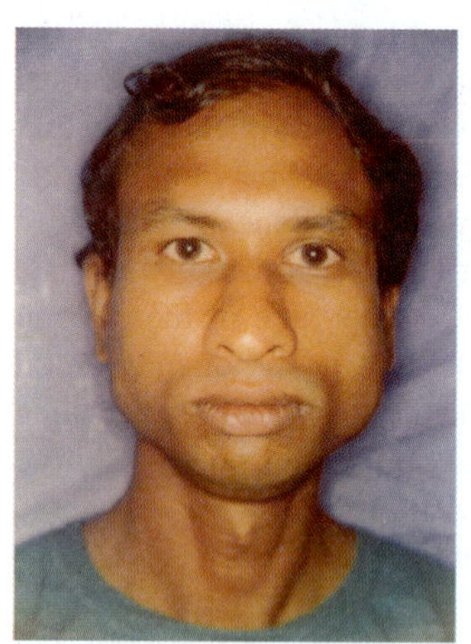

(a) Preoperative.

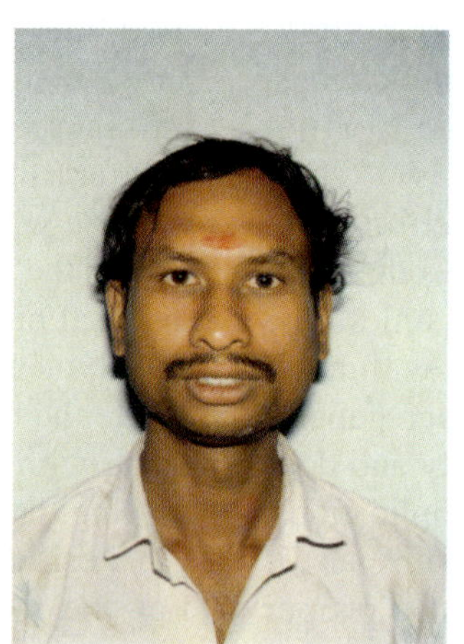

(b) Postoperative.

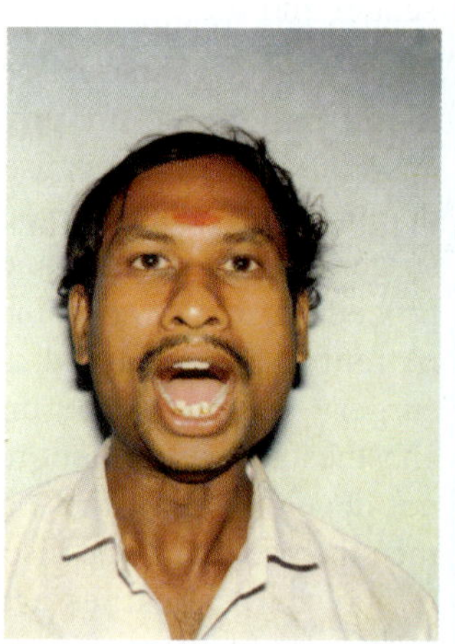

(c) Patient demonstrating functionally undisturbed masseter.

Fig. XI.1 (a), (b), (c)

Appendix XII. COMPUTERS IN ORAL AND MAXILLOFACIAL SURGERY PRACTICE

The use of computers has become an integral part of the clinicians. Computer link allows the maxillofacial surgeon to access the wealth of informations and resources of the internet. The aim is to introduce the technology and to act as a guide to introduce the subject for further exploration.

Electronic mail (E-mail)

This refers to the transmission of text based messages between networked computers. Its advantages over the conventional mail (usually referred to as snail-mail) are speed and cost. The e-mail can be received at its destination anywhere in the world within seconds. In terms of expenditure, there is no need to go to the post office either to buy stamps and envelops or to send it. The e-mail is sent via the modem (of the computer) connected to the telephone system.

E-mail consists of details of e-mail i.d of the sender and the receiver(s), subject and the contents of the e-mail. It also contains the date and time of sending and receiving the mail. The biggest advantage is the access of the sender and receiver to the e-mail system by using the respective secret code called *password*, irrespective of their location anywhere in the world. It is also possible to develop and maintain an electronic address book from the incoming mails. One can create one's own personalized mailboxes and store important mails under different files. This system ensures secrecy among the persons who have access to the secret code (password). If a surgeon wants to receive mails regularly from various sources, they must include their e-mail i.d into the mailing list of those sources. Photographs, videos, sound files, illustrations and database can also be sent or downloaded through e-mail.

There is a standard format for an e-mail address. (e-mail i.d). It has the following format:

Username @ user's location. e.g., *drbeeess@hotmail.com.*

In other words, my e-mail address can be broken down into different parts. I have condensed my name - DR.B.Srinivasan (DR.B.S) as the user's name: dr(DR), bee(B) and ess(S). @ represents - "at". hotmail.com is my user's location, referring to my internet access provider. It is left to the choice of the user to develop i.d.

The world wide web

The word internet refers to a set of computers linked together across the world through physical or wireless links using standard protocols so as to communicate with each other. The individuals usually pay a nominal charge to an internet access provider. Once connected to the "net", the user has an unlimited access to electronic messages.

World Wide Web (www) is the world's largest store of easily accessible information. The interlinked documents are grouped in the web page. It can be retrieved through the specific *world wide web* (www). Therefore, www and internet are actually two different things with www as a subsect of the internet. Anyone with the right software and access can also publish informations on the web.

Net "surfing" involves tracing a path from one computer to another. More can be learnt on this aspect only by one's own experience. The net is truly interactive. URL (*uniform resource locator*) is the standard form of address that one has to type into the browser, to indicate from where the informations are to be retrieved.

www is different from more traditional sources of information like books, journals and other library information resources. For example, web pages can be linked by "hyperlinks". Hence it is easy to jump over from one page to another. Since related documents are linked, it is easy to find more informations almost effortlessly. It is also possible to update the informations. The web has tools called "search engines" which will enable us to search for all the available informations through the use of the keyword. One has to remember that the content of the www constantly changes.

Cyber oral and maxillofacial surgery - A few examples are provided here.

http://www.atmeda.org. - American telemedicine association.

http://www.laserdentistry.org - Academy of laser dentistry.

http://www.aads.edu - Association of dental schools in U.S

http://www.nidr.nih.gov — useful link to many medical and dental sites.

http:// www.dental site.com - excellent source of oral health related knowledge.

http://www.ada.org — American Dental Association.

http://implanet.com — Implant Dentistry.

http://www.osseous.org — Academy of Osseointegration.

http://aaomfs.org — Academy of American oral and maxillofacial surgeons.

http//www.dentalgate.com — search engine for dental purposes.

http://www.medsite.com - a premier medical search engine.

Electronic access to the web-based MEDLINE searches

MEDLINE is a biographic database of the National Library of Medicine that contains bibliographic citations and abstracts from over 400 biomedical journals published nationally and internationally. Therefore, MEDLINE is a tool with a potential to instantly allow us to critically review and evaluate the scientific literature, enrich our knowledge and ultimately uplift our level of care of the patients.

To illustrate the usefulness of internet, a few examples of multimedia images are furnished below.

Under the title "Evaluation of maxillofacial neoplasms using computer graphics from three-dimensional (3D) spiral CT images", the website of Virtual Dental Centre, Martindale's Health Sciences, hosted by the University of Iowa College of Medicine has provided many multimedia images. Some of them have been downloaded and displayed here (Figs XII. 1 – 4).

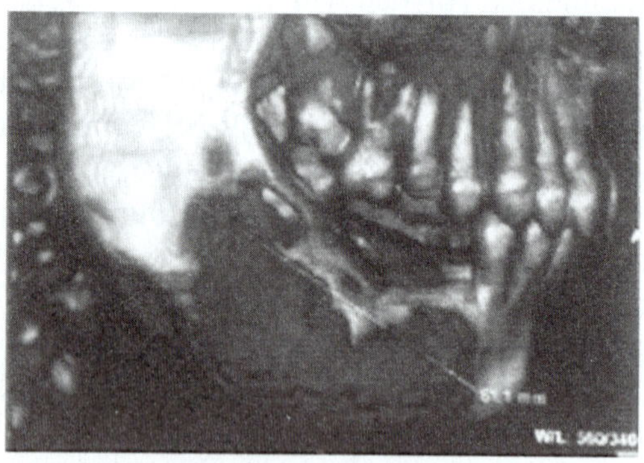

Fig. XII.1 (a)

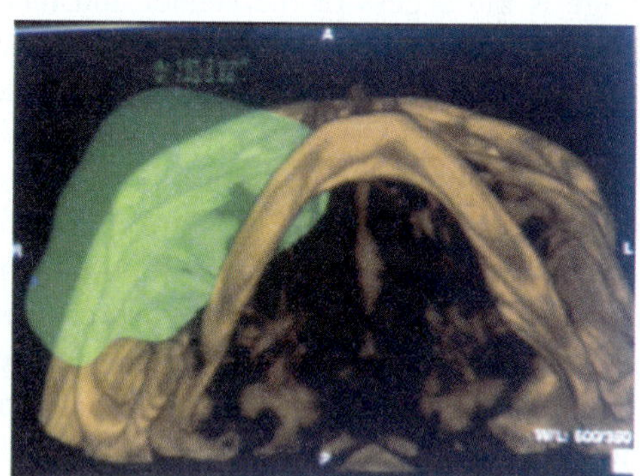

Fig. XII.1 (b)

Fig. XII.1 (a) & (b) 3-D CT scan of the mandible showing the extension of the tumor.

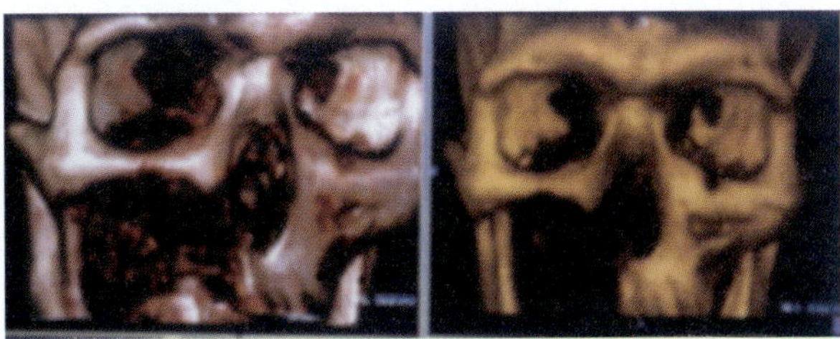

Fig. XII.2 3-D CT scan showing the anticipated postoperative view of the midface, if surgery is performed to remove the tumor of maxilla.

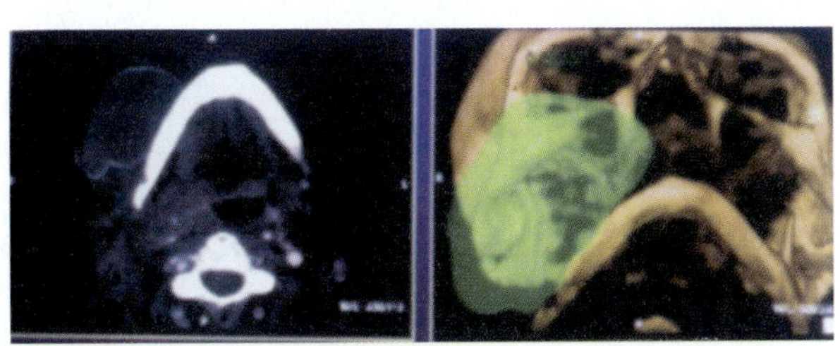

Fig. XII.3 (a)

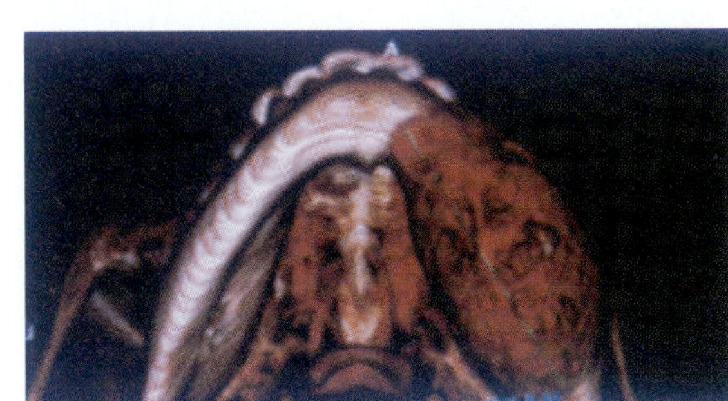

Fig. XII.3 (b)

Fig. XII.3 (a) & (b) 3-D CT scan showing the extension of the tumor of maxilla.

Fig. XII.4 (b)

Fig. XII.4 (a)

Fig. XII.4 (c)

Fig. XII.4 (d)

Fig. XII.4 (a), (b), (c), (d) What a coincidence ?

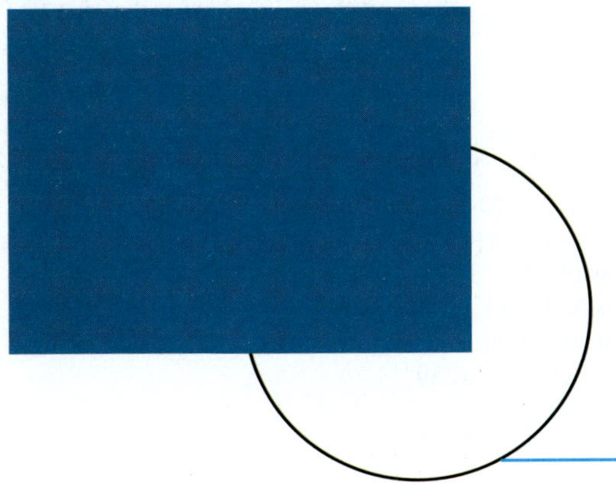

Index